RECONSTRUCTING GENDER

RECONSTRUCTING GENDER
A Multicultural Anthology

Third Edition

Estelle Disch
University of Massachusetts Boston

Boston Burr Ridge, IL Dubuque, IA Madison, WI New York
San Francisco St. Louis Bangkok Bogotá Caracas Kuala Lumpur
Lisbon London Madrid Mexico City Milan Montreal New Delhi
Santiago Seoul Singapore Sydney Taipei Toronto

McGraw-Hill Higher Education

A Division of The ***McGraw-Hill*** *Companies*

RECONSTRUCTING GENDER: A MULTICULTURAL ANTHOLOGY

Published by McGraw-Hill, a business unit of The McGraw-Hill Companies, Inc., 1221 Avenue of the Americas, New York, NY, 10020.

This book is printed on acid-free paper.

1 2 3 4 5 6 7 8 9 0 FGR/FGR 0 9 8 7 6 5 4 3 2

ISBN 0-7674-2771-8

Publisher: *Phillip A. Butcher*
Sponsoring editor: *Sally Constable/Sherith Pankratz*
Developmental editor: *Jill Gordon*
Senior marketing manager: *Daniel M. Loch*
Project manager: *Christina Thornton-Villagomez*
Production supervisor: *Susanne Riedell*
Senior designer/cover design: *Jenny El-Shamy*
Supplement producer: *Kate Boyland*
Cover image: Conversaciones, *Luz Inez Mercier/Praxis International Art*
Typeface: *10/12 Book Antiqua*
Compositor: *ElectraGraphics, Inc.*
Printer: *Quebecor World Fairfield Inc.*

Library of Congress Cataloging-in-Publication Data

Reconstructing gender: a multicultural anthology / [edited by] Estelle Disch—3rd ed.
p. cm.
Includes bibliographical references and index.
ISBN 0-7674-2771-8 (soft cover : alk. paper)
1. Sex role. 2. Masculinity. 3. Femininity. 4. Women—Psychology. 5. Socialization. I. Disch, Estelle.

HQ1075.R43 2003
305.3—dc21 2002021278

www.mhhe.com

Contents

Preface

A few years ago, in my undergraduate Sociology of Gender course,[1] I asked the class to sit in small groups and identify gender-related problems that each student was currently facing and that were not too personal to discuss in the class. I then asked the students to assess to what extent their problems were personal troubles, that is, specific to themselves as individuals, or public issues, reflective of wider issues in the social order and experienced by many people.[2] When the groups reported back, two men responded, "We were raised never to hit girls, and now with the women's movement, we want to know whether or not that's OK." Their question was serious, and the class exploded. Many women in the room became very upset and started yelling at the two men. (I later learned that at least a third of the women in the room had been raped.) I was caught off guard and realized that the course was not designed to effectively address the various issues embedded in the men's question. I did not have nearly enough material on men's socialization and behavior. I was particularly concerned about providing students with enough information to help them begin to make sense of the high rates of men's violence toward women and toward each other.

In my search for better materials about men's socialization, I found a growing literature in men's studies to accompany the already huge literature in women's studies and the sociology of gender. But my favorite articles were scattered in a wide range of sources. Although some excellent anthologies were available about and by women and men separately,[3] no one volume available at that time and appropriate for use in a social science course gave substantial attention to both genders. Although the choice of texts has grown considerably since 1996, I have chosen to revise this one twice in order to keep it current. Thus, this book is designed to meet the needs of faculty who want to teach about both women and men from a multicultural perspective but who want to use one anthology instead of two. I define *multicultural* broadly to include the perspectives and experiences of a wide range of people within the context of power and inequality.

The creation of this book has been made possible by the explosion of work by and about people of color, people of various ethnicities, gay men, lesbians, bisexuals, transgendered people, people with disabilities, and working-class people. Most of the readings included here are ones that colleagues and I have used in classrooms with success. By success, I mean that many students have become engaged with the material in various ways: becoming excited or angered by the ideas expressed, talking with friends and family about the material, making sense of their own experience in relation to the authors' experiences, feeling excited to learn more about a particular issue, or becoming politically involved in response to what they are learning. I teach in a way that encourages interaction among students,[4] and I am particularly committed to using articles that stimulate discussion. I welcome readers' feedback about what works in classrooms and what doesn't.

This book also emerges, in part, from questions and concerns that I've experienced in my own life, especially my own experience growing up in a sexist, racist, anti-Semitic, white, economically privileged, Protestant family. With three older brothers and a sports-oriented father who was a physician, I often felt like I was immersed in a male club. This club demanded rigid gender expectations of my brothers. My least-athletic brother was brutally teased and called a sissy because of his lack of athletic ability, his pain while watching my father and my other brothers shoot ducks, his interest in music, his ability to cry, and his chubby body. I watched my father rage when my aunt bought that particular brother a pink shirt. My survival strategy in this system was to attempt to fit into the male club. By about age seven I had learned to shoot frogs with a .22 rifle, to clean fish, to brace myself against the pain I felt watching a duck thrash in the water after being shot, to enjoy watching baseball games (or to pretend that I did), and to be otherwise tough and strong.

I also learned about racist and anti-Semitic attitudes in my family. I can remember my grandmother expressing disapproval that my best friend was Jewish and my father telling me an anti-Semitic "joke" that I repeated to my best friend, who didn't find it funny. Unfortunately, we had no skills at age 10 or so to discuss what was wrong with the "joke." And I can remember my father complaining about the presence of Black baseball players, actors, and newscasters on TV—"That man's got a white man's job." Luckily, my mother provided a contrast to my father's views. She did not participate in his racist and anti-Semitic discussions, spoke freely about her poverty-stricken origins, and left me with the opportunity to question his values.

I am impressed to this day at the contradictions embedded in what my father expected of boys and men. On the one hand, he seemed at his happiest in the all-male hunting and fishing cultures in which he spent as much free time as he could. When these men went hunting, they slept in close quarters, spent days together in tiny gunning boats or hiding in duck blinds, cooked elaborate meals at the end of the day, and kept house—all with no women present. (I begged to go on these trips but was barred.) On the other hand, his homophobia was always there, levying disrespect at any boy or man who might be "too feminine," who might acknowledge his love for a man, or who might choose to make a life with men doing much of what my father, his friends, and my brothers did on hunting trips.

Another personal interest that informs my selections for this anthology is my knowledge about male violence and sexual abuse toward boys, girls, women, and men. I continue to be baffled at our inability to effectively prevent that abuse. I am not so much shocked by the facts (I have accepted them after years of awareness), but by the entrenched system of violence and domination that teaches new generations of people, especially men, how to be violent and oppressive. For 12 years, I worked with survivors of sexual abuse committed by health care and mental health care providers and clergy, and have been struck by the fact that the vast majority of offenders—against both men and women—are men.[5] Although offenses of this type are brutally damaging when perpetrated by members of either gender, the overwhelming imbalance toward male perpetrators has led me to wonder what has caused so many of them to be so exploitative or violent. I am reminded of a very disturbing photo essay of men who had attended a residential religious school in which male clergy physically and sexually abused many of the boys.[6] One of the men shown tells of the abuse he suffered as a child and reports that when he learned that his younger brother was about to be put in the same school, he killed his brother to save him from the abuse. It appears that the only way he had learned to resolve brutal situations was to be brutal himself.

I am also informed here by 25 years of working collectively with others: 10 years working with white, almost exclusively heterosexual women and men in alternative mental health centers; 10 years in a feminist therapy collective where a group of white heterosexual women and lesbians learned to work closely together; and in working groups at the University of Massachusetts Boston, where faculty, students, and staff built a multicultural, broad-based coalition to win the passage of a diversity requirement for undergraduate students.[7] I have learned that diverse women and men can work together using decision-making processes in which conflict is discussed, compromises are negotiated, and leadership and rewards are shared. If people are committed to communicating and working together and working on their prejudices, then differences of gender, race, culture, class, sexual orientation, disability, and age can be addressed and dealt with in order to accomplish common goals.

I am also concerned in this anthology with the entrenchment of privilege. I have observed how much time and attention it has taken me to unravel my own prejudices and become aware of my privileges, and I wonder how we will ever construct a humane social order when it is so difficult for those with privilege to see how caught we are in its cushioned web. Even with an education that communicated democratic values, a mother who worked full time and talked extensively about growing up poor, an older brother who mentored me into liberal/radical views, and a feminist movement and support system that has especially supported my anti-racist and multicultural activism, I still find it difficult to stay fully conscious of some of the oppressive attitudes I have learned. Although I have analyzed enough of my socialization to feel fully capable of working on my attitudes and to apologize for any lingering insensitivities, I believe that I will be working on this for the rest of my life. I hope the readings that follow will help those with more privilege become clear about what that means for them, that those with less privilege will find inspiration for empowerment, and that both groups will find ways to work toward a more egalitarian social order—one in which all people will have an opportunity to work with others in shared ways, in which real community can evolve from positions of equal respect, and in which all people enjoy basic human rights free of poverty, violence, preventable illness, and discrimination.

I have chosen to include increasingly more material on international issues with each revision of this book, always centering on issues with a direct connection to the United States. The events of September 11, 2001, led me to include several essays aimed at helping readers understand some of the issues surrounding those events.

Many people have helped with this book. Serina Beauparlant, my former editor at Mayfield Publishing, approached this project with enthusiasm and support throughout its birth and development and saw the book through two editions. My editors at McGraw-Hill—Sally Constable and Jill Gordon—energetically embraced the third edition and moved the project to completion. Becky Thompson convinced me that I should do the book in the first place and provided ongoing support, feedback, and creative suggestions as it evolved. Our ongoing discussions about racism and teaching over the years have contributed to my thinking in many ways. Prerevision and postrevision reviewers were helpful as I grappled with major changes in the book following September 11. They are Kristine DeWelde, University of Colorado; Heather Dillaway, Michigan State University; Carol Miller, University of Wisconsin-La Crosse; Jodi Brodsky, College of New Jersey; Connie Chan, University of Massachusetts–Boston, Eleanor Hubbard, University of Colorado, and Naomi Pinion, Northern Arizona University.

Other friends, family, colleagues, and students provided direct or indirect suggestions for readings, sources, or other intellectual support for this edition, including Larry Blum, Deborah Brome, Elly Bulkin, Connie Chan, Robert Disch, Linda Dittmar, Cynthia Enloe, Gerry Garrett, Lisa Gonsalves, Susan Gore, Jean Hardisty, Kathleen Kelley, Esther Kingston-Mann, Madhulika Khandelwal, Winston Langley, Siamak Movahedi, Gautam Premnath, Jim Ptacek, Russell Schutt, Tim Sieber, Raul Ybarra, and Vivian Zamel. The production staff at McGraw-Hill—Christina Thornton-Villagomez, Project Manager—kept the project moving smoothly and on schedule. My compañera and intellectual colleague Rita Arditti talked with me extensively about all three editions of the book as they evolved, helped me to clarify my thoughts, suggested new articles and references, and lent me numerous books from her library on feminist and multicultural studies. Finally, thanks go to my best teachers—the terrific students at the University of Massachusetts Boston, who frequently challenge and always engage me.

Supplements

Instructor's Manual/Test Bank

Kristine DeWelde, University of Colorado has prepared the Instructor's Manual/Test Bank. For each reading and part introduction, there are multiple choice, true/false, and short answer/essay questions. There are also questions for classroom discussion, journal reading, and take home exams.

Race/Class/Gender/Sexuality SuperSite

This companion website provides information about the book, including an overview, summaries of key features and what's new in the third edition, information about the authors, and Practice Test Questions.

Non-text-specific content on this site includes an annotated list of Web links to useful sites; a list of professional resources (e.g., professional journals); links to websites offering Census 2000 information; a glossary; flashcards; and a comprehensive list (annotated and listed by category) of films and videos in the areas of race, class, gender, ethnicity, and sexuality.

Visit the SuperSite by going to www.mhhe.com/raceclassgender.

NOTES

1. This was a course at the University of Massachusetts Boston, a public urban university with about 12,000 students, all of whom commute.
2. The class had read an excerpt from C. Wright Mills, *The Sociological Imagination* (New York: Oxford University Press, 1959), in which Mills discusses personal troubles and public issues.
3. Anthologies regarding women (or primarily women) include Margaret L. Andersen and Patricia Hill Collins, eds., *Race, Class, and Gender: An Anthology,* 3rd ed. (Belmont, CA: Wadsworth Publishing Company, 1998); Myra Marx Ferree, Judith Lorber, and Beth B. Hess, *Revisioning Gender* (Thousand Oaks, CA: Sage, 1999); Jo Freeman, ed., *Women: A Feminist Perspective,* 5th ed. (Mountain View, CA: Mayfield, 1995); Mary M. Gergen and Sara N. Davis, eds., *Toward a New Psychology of Gender* (New York: Routledge, 1997); Gwyn Kirk and Margo Okazawa-Rey, *Women's Lives: Multicultural Perspectives* (Mountain View, CA: Mayfield, 1998); Laurel Richardson, Verta Taylor, and Nancy Whittier, eds., *Feminist Frontiers IV* (New York: McGraw-Hill, 1997).

   Anthologies regarding men (or primarily men) include Franklin Abbott, ed., *Boyhood, Growing Up Male: A Multicultural Anthology* (Freedom, CA: The Crossing Press, 1993); Harry Brod, ed., *The Making of Masculinities: The New Men's Studies* (Boston: Allen & Unwin, 1987); Michael S. Kimmel and Michael A. Messner, eds., *Men's Lives,* 4th ed. (Boston: Allyn & Bacon, 1998); Ronald F. Levant, and William S. Pollack, eds., *A New Psychology of Men* (New York: Basic Books, 1995); Christopher McLean, Maggie Carey, and Cheryl White, eds., *Men's Ways of Being* (Boulder, CO: Westview Press, 1996).

   A recent anthology designed for composition courses that does foreground gender and that includes material about both women and men is Karin Bergstrom Costello, ed., *Gendered Voices: Readings from the American Experience* (New York: Harcourt Brace, 1996). Since the publication of the first edition of this book, Maxine Baca Zinn, Pierette Hondagneu-Sotelo, and Michael A. Messner have edited *Through the Prism of Difference: Readings on Sex and Gender* (Boston: Allyn and Bacon, 1997).
4. This teaching method is described in Estelle Disch, "Encouraging Participation in the Classroom," in Sara Davis et al., eds., *Coming Into Her Own: Educational Success for Girls and Women* (Jossey-Bass, 1999); Becky Thompson and Estelle Disch, "Feminist,

Anti-Racist, Anti-Oppression Teaching: Two White Women's Experience," *Radical Teacher* 41 (Spring 1992), pp. 4–10.

5. In a study of survivors of sexual professional abuse, in which I am the principal investigator, 88 percent of the women and 94 percent of the men were abused by men.
6. Photo essay by E. Jan Mundy, "Wounded Boys, Courageous Men," displayed at the Linkup Conference, Chicago, September 1–4, 1995.
7. I have documented this work in an essay entitled, "The Politics of Curricular Change: Establishing a Diversity Requirement at the University of Massachusetts at Boston," in Becky W. Thompson and Sangeeta Tyagi, eds., *Beyond a Dream Deferred: Multicultural Education and the Politics of Excellence* (Minneapolis: University of Minnesota Press, 1993), pp. 195–213.

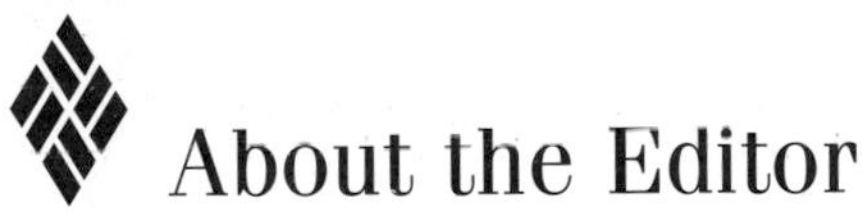

About the Editor

Estelle Disch is professor of sociology at the University of Massachusetts Boston where she has been active in curricular transformation, general education reform, and faculty development. She has written extensively on pedagogical issues in diverse classrooms. Her research focuses on the effects of sexual abuse by professionals and on assessing learning in university courses. She has served as a consultant and trainer related to creating more open and accepting campus climates and has run many workshops for professionals related to maintaining appropriate professional boundaries.

About the Contributors

Randy Albelda is a professor of economics at the University of Massachusetts Boston. She writes and teaches about women in the U.S. economy.

Paula Gunn Allen is professor of English at UCLA. She was awarded the Native American Prize for Literature in 1990. That same year her anthology of short stories, *Spider Woman's Granddaughters,* was awarded the American Book Award, sponsored by the Before Columbus Foundation, and the Susan Koppleman Award. A major Native American poet, writer, and scholar, she has published seven volumes of poetry, a novel, a collection of essays, and two anthologies. Her prose and poetry appear widely in anthologies, journals, and scholarly publications.

Robert L. Allen is a teacher, writer, and community activist who is deeply interested in men's issues. Since 1986 he has worked with the Oakland Men's Project, a community education organization that conducts workshops dealing with male violence, sexism, racism, and homophobia. At the University of California at Berkeley, he teaches African American and Ethnic Studies and a new course called "Men of Color." Senior Editor of *The Black Scholar* journal, Allen is also coeditor of a recent book titled *Brotherman: The Odyssey of Black Men in America.* He is the father of a son, Casey.

Rina Amiri is a specialist in Southwest Asian affairs and Afghan politics at the Fletcher School of Law and Diplomacy at Tufts University. She is also a senior associate at the Women and Public Policy Program at Harvard University's John F. Kennedy School of Government. The views expressed in this article are Ms. Amiri's and do not reflect the views of her institutional affiliations.

Ruth Atkin is a middle-class, Ashkenazi Jewish feminist activist born in the Midwest. She has been involved in progressive Jewish publishing since 1979 and is a founding and current editor of *Gesher's* successor, *Bridges: A Journal for Jewish Feminists and Our Friends.* On weekdays Ruth works as a medical social worker in an outpatient clinic serving veterans.

Tommi Avicolli has adopted his mother's maiden name and is now using the name Tommi Avicolli Mecca. He is a working-class, Southern Italian American, queer writer, activist, and performer living in San Francisco. He has recently written and performed *Il Disgraziato* (The Shameful One), a play about coming out gay.

Evelyn L. Barbee is a Black feminist nurse anthropologist who was educated at Teachers College, Columbia University and at the University of Washington. Her writings are published in anthropology and nursing journals. Her current research interests are cultural strategies used by women of color to deal with dysphoria, and violence against women of color. She is currently at the School of Nursing at Boston College.

Barry A. Bass, Ph.D. received his B.A. in Psychology from Rutgers University and his Ph.D. in Clinical Psychology from the University of Tennessee. Dr. Bass, who has an independent practice specializing in the treatment of individuals and couples with relationship and sexual concerns, is also the director of the Graduate Program in Clinical Psychology at Towson University in Baltimore, Maryland.

Harry Brod is assistant professor in the Philosophy Department at the University of Delaware. He is editor of *The Making of Masculinities: The New Men's Studies, A Mensch Among Men: Explorations in Jewish Masculinity,* and most recently (with Michael Kaufman) *Theorizing Masculinities.* He is author of *Hegel's Philosophy of Politics.* He is a spokesperson for the National Organization for Men Against Sexism. Born in Berlin as a child of temporary (i.e., died prematurely) Holocaust survivors, he grew up in New York City and currently lives in Philadelphia with his family.

Joan Jacobs Brumberg is a historian at Cornell University and author of "The Body Project: An Intimate History of American Girls."

Charlotte Bunch is currently a professor with the Bloustein School of Planning and Public Policy at Rutgers University, and serves on the Boards of the Ms. Foundation for Women, and the Women's Division of Human Rights Watch. Professor Bunch has been an activist, author and organizer in the women's and civil rights movements for over three decades. She has edited seven anthologies, and coauthored the recently published *Demanding Accountability: The Global Campaign and Vienna Tribunal for Women's Human Rights.*

Dr. Rafael Campo teaches and practices internal medicine at Harvard Medical School and Beth Israel Deaconess Medical Center in Boston. He is the award-winning author of several books, including "The Poetry of Healing" (W. W. Norton, 1997) and the collection of poems "Diva" (Duke University Press, 1999). The "Unidos para la Vida" summit was held one year ago, sponsored by the Harvard AIDS Institute. None of the prominent Latinos mentioned in this article attended.

Connie S. Chan was born in Hong Kong, grew up in Hawaii, and now lives in Boston, Massachusetts. Bilingual and bicultural in her upbringing, she has experienced the world from a multicultural perspective. She is Professor of Human Services and Codirector of the Institute for Asian American Studies at the University of Massachusetts Boston. Her research and publications focus on the intersection of gender, culture, and sexuality issues in Asian American women. She continues to work within Asian American communities to provide access to culturally appropriate health services.

Joan C. Chrisler is a professor of psychology at Connecticut College. She earned her doctorate in experimental psychology at Yeshiva University while working nights as a waitress and serving as a shop steward in the hotel and restaurant workers union. Dr. Chrisler has published extensively on the psychology of women and women's health issues, and is particularly known for her work on weight and eating behavior and on psychosocial aspects of the menstrual cycle. She is coeditor of four books: *Arming Athena: Career Strategies of Women in Academe, Lectures on the Psychology of Women, Variations on a Theme: Diversity and the Psychology of Women,* and *New Directions in Feminist Psychology.*

Judith Ortiz Cofer grew up in Puerto Rico and New Jersey. She is the author of *The Line of the Sun,* a novel; *Silent Dancing,* a collection of essays and poetry; *Terms of Survival* and *Reaching for the Mainland,* two books of poetry; and *The Latin Deli: Prose* and *Poetry.* Her work has appeared in *Glamour, The Georgia Review, Kenyon Review,* and other journals. She has been anthologized in *The Best American Essays, The Norton Book of Women's Lives, The Pushcart Prize,* and the *O. Henry Prize Stories.* She has received fellowships from the National Endowment for the Arts and the Witter Bynner Foundation for Poetry. She is an associate professor of English and creative writing at the University of Georgia. Her most recent book is a collection of short stories, *An Island Like You: Stories of the Barrio* (Orchard Books, 1995).

Patricia Hill Collins is the Charles Taft Professor of Sociology in the Department of African-American Studies at the University of Cincinnati. She is also the author of *Fighting Words: Black Women and the Search for Justice.* Her first edition of *Black Feminist Thought* won the Association for Women in Psychology's Distinguished Publication Award, the Society for the Study of Social Problems' C. Wright Mills Award, and the Association of Black Women Historians' Letitia Woods Brown Memorial Book Prize.

Martha Coventry, when asked by a photographer what culture she came from that would clitoridectomize its daughters, laughed and answered, "WASP culture." A middle-aged midwestern mother of two daughters, Coventry writes and speaks about intersexuality in order to change a world that treats different bodies as wrong bodies.

Ann Crittenden is the author of *Killing the Sacred Cows: Bold Ideas for a New Economy.* A former reporter for The *New York Times* and a Pulitzer Prize nominee, she has also been a reporter for *Fortune,* a financial writer for *Newsweek,* a visiting lecturer at M.I.T. and Yale, and an economics commentator for CBS News. Her articles have appeared in *The Nation, Foreign Affairs, McCall's,* and *Working Woman,* among others. She lives with her husband and son in Washington, DC.

Linnea Due is a writer and managing editor of *Express,* an alternative weekly in Berkeley, California, where she lives. She is the author of three novels, *High and Outside, Give Me Time,* and *Life Savings,* and she was the coeditor of the anthology *Dagger: On Butch Women.* In 1992, her series on gay and lesbian teenagers won an award as one of the top six underreported stories of the year from Media Alliance/Project Censored.

Cynthia Enloe grew up on Long Island during the 1940s and 1950s. She went to public high school and to the then-all-women's Connecticut College and received her Ph.D. in Political Science at the University of California, Berkeley. She is currently a professor of government and women's studies at Clark University in Massachusetts. Her research and teaching has taken her to Malaysia, Guyana, and Great Britain to live. Among her most recent books are *Bananas, Beaches and Bases: Making Feminist Sense of International Politics,* and *The Morning After: Sexual Politics at the End of the Cold War.* Her newest book is *Maneuvers: The International Politics of Militarizing Women's Lives.*

Martín Espada has published his fifth book of poems, *Imagine the Angels of Bread* (W. W. Norton), which won an American Book Award and was a finalist for the National Book Critics' Circle Award. A former tenant lawyer, Espada currently teaches in the English Department at the University of Massachusetts, Amherst.

Ann Arnett Ferguson is assistant professor of African American Studies and Women's Studies, Smith College.

Michelle Fine is professor of social psychology and women's studies at the Graduate Center, CUNY. She is coauthor, with Jane Balin and Lani Guinier, of *Becoming Gentlemen: Women, Law School, and Institutional Change* (Boston: Beacon, 1997), and, with Lois Weis, of *The Unknown City: Lives of Poor and Working-Class Young Adults* (Boston: Beacon, 1998), and coeditor with Lois Weis, of *Beyond Silenced Voices: Class, Race, and Gender in United States Schools* (Albany: SUNY Press, 1993), and coeditor, with Linda Powell, Lois Weis, and Mun Wong, of *Off White: Readings on Race, Power, and Society* (New York: Routledge, 1997).

Anne Finger is a writer of fiction and nonfiction whose work grapples most often with issues of disability and gender. She has published three books: a novel, *Bone Truth* (Coffee House Press); an autobiographical essay, *Past Due: A Story of Disability, Pregnancy, and Birth* (Seal Press); and a short story collection, *Basic Skills.*

Ben Fong-Torres is a journalist in the San Francisco Bay area. His most recent book is *The Rice Room: Growing Up Chinese-American.*

Kathleen Gerson is professor of sociology at New York University and the author of several books, including *No Man's Land: Men's Changing Commitments to Family and Work* (Basic Books, 1993) and *Hard Choices: How Women Decide about Work, Career, and Motherhood* (University of California Press,

1985). She is at work on a study of how new generations of young women and men are responding to the transformation in family life and gender relationships that has been a hallmark of growing up in late-twentieth-century America. She lives with her spouse, John Mollenkopf, and their daughter, Emily, in New York City.

Jan Goodwin is the author of *Caught in the Crossfire* (1987) about Afghanistan and *Price of Honor: Muslim Women Lift the Veil of Silence on the Islamic World* (1995).

Stan Gray worked as an assembler at Westinghouse in Hamilton, Ontario, Canada, from 1973 to 1984, where he was the union health and safety representative and the shop steward. From 1984 to 1990, he was the director of a province-wide health and safety clinic sponsored by a number of unions. The clinic diagnosed industrial diseases and organized workers around job hazards such as asbetos, PCBs, and sexual harassment. Stan is currently living in Hamilton and works as an independent advocate for workers and unions on issues of health and safety, human rights, and worker's compensation.

Theresa Halsey (Standing Rock Sioux) is a long-time community activist, mostly focusing on educational issues. She is currently director of the Title V American Indian Education Program with the Boulder Valley (Colorado) School District.

Christy Haubegger, a Mexican-American native of Houston, attended the University of Texas at Austin and received a B.A. in philosophy. She attended Stanford Law School and was president of her class. Frustrated with the lack of positive media portrayal of Latinas in the United States, she put her law degree under her bed to pursue the entrepreneurial venture of creating a magazine for women like herself. *Essence* magazine and Alegre Enterprises, of which Haubegger is the chief executive officer, formed a new joint venture, Latina Publications, to publish *Latina* magazine, the first bilingual lifestyle magazine for Latinas in the United States.

bell hooks (nee Gloria Watkins) is Distinguished Professor of English at City College in New York. Although hooks is mainly known as a feminist thinker, her writings cover a broad range of topics on gender, race, teaching and the significance of media for contemporary culture. She is the author of many books, the most recent of which is *Communion: The Search for Female Love.*

Nan D. Hunter is associate professor of law at Brooklyn Law School. She is a former lawyer for the American Civil Liberties Union, where she was a founding director of Projects on Lesbian and Gay Rights and AIDS. She is coeditor of *AIDS Agenda: Emerging Issues in Civil Rights* and coauthor of *The Rights of Lesbians and Gay Men* and *Sexuality, Gender and the Law.*

Jacquelyn Jackson is a women's health advocate in Washington.

M. Annette Jaimes has changed her name to Mariana Jaimes-Guerrero. She is an enrolled Juañeno/Yaqui and has been a writer and researcher for Women of All Red Nations (WARN), supporter of the Indigenous Women's Network, and a board member of the American Indian Anti-Defamation Council. A former instructor with the Center for Studies of Ethnicity and Race in America at the University of Colorado, she was instrumental in developing the American Indian Studies Program on that campus. In addition to her many published articles on indigenous people, she is editor of and contributor to *The State of Native North America* (South End Press), which was awarded a Gustavus Myers International Human Rights Award, and is author of *Native Womanism: Blueprint for a Global Revolution* (South End Press). Jaimes-Guerrero recently established the Center for Indigenous Global Studies.

Robert W. Jensen joined the University of Texas faculty in 1992 after completing his Ph.D. in the School of Journalism and Mass Communication at the University of Minnesota. He teaches graduate and undergraduate courses in media law and ethics, qualitative methods and critical theory, and writing and editing. He has nine years of professional journalism experience. In his research on media law/ethics/politics, Jensen draws on feminist theory, lesbian/gay studies, critical legal studies, and cultural studies. Much of his research has focused on pornography and the radical feminist critique of sexuality. He is coeditor with David S. Allen of *Freeing the First Amendment: Critical Perspectives on Freedom of Expression* (New York University Press, 1995), and coauthor with Gail Dines and Ann Russo of *Pornography: The Production and Consumption of Inequality* (Routledge, 1998). He grew up lower middle class in North Dakota and is of white Northern European family background.

Melanie Kaye/Kantrowitz was born in 1945 in Brooklyn, New York, and has worked in social change movements since the sixties. A graduate of the City College of New York, she earned her Ph.D. in Comparative Literature at the University of California at Berkeley. A writer, activist, and teacher, she lives in New York City, where she is director of Jews for Racial and Economic Justice. She is author of *My Jewish Face & Other Stories,* coeditor of *The Tribe of Dina: A Jewish Woman's Anthology,* and former editor and publisher of *Sinister Wisdom,* a lesbian/feminist journal.

Danny Kaplan is an occupational psychologist and is conducting research for a Ph.D. at Ben-Gurion University, Beer Sheva, Israel. He is the author of *David, Yonatan, ve-chayalim achersim: Al zehut, gavriyet, ve-miniyut be-yechidot kraviyot betzahal* (David, Jonathan and other soldiers: Identity, masculinity and sexuality in combat units in the Israeli Army), Tel Aviv: Ha-Kibbutz Ha-Meuchad, 1999. His main research interests focus on men's friendships and cultural narratives.

Michael S. Kimmel is professor of Sociology at SUNY at Stony Brook. His books include *Changing Men* (1987), *Men Confront Pornography* (1990), *Men in the United States* (1992), *Manhood in America* (1996), and *The Politics of Manhood* (1996). He is the editor of Masculinities, a scholarly journal, and National Spokesperson for the National Organization for Men Against Sexism (NOMAS).

Leonard Kriegel, author of the novel *Quitting Time* and of the collection of essays *Falling,* is a professor of English and director of the Center for Worker Education at the City University of New York.

Terry A. Kupers, M.D., a professor in the Graduate School of Psychology at The Wright Institute in Berkeley, California, practices psychiatry in Oakland. The author of *Public Therapy: The Practice of Psychotherapy in the Public Mental Health Clinic* (1981), and *Ending Therapy: The Meaning of Termination* (1988), he is married and has three young adult sons.

Marilyn Little earned a Ph.D. at the University of Minnesota and is currently at the Centre for Ecology and Spirituality in Ontario, Canada. A medical geographer by specialization, her research is primarily concerned with the political ecology of malnutrition. A recent publication is "Charity versus Justice: The New World Order and the Old Problem of World Hunger," in *Eliminating Hunger in Africa* (eds. Newman and Griffith).

Judith Lorber taught for twenty-five years at Brooklyn College and the Graduate School, CUNY, and was the first coordinator of the GC Women's Studies Certificate Program, as well as the founding editor of *Gender & Society.* She also raised a son as a single parent and wrote and edited books on gender.

Audre Lorde, who passed away in 1992, grew up in the West Indian community of Harlem in the 1930s, the daughter of immigrants from Grenada. She attended Hunter College (later becoming professor of English there), ventured to the American expatriate community in Mexico, and participated in the Greenwich Village scene of the early 1950s. She is a major figure in the lesbian and feminist movements. Among her works are *Sister Outsider, Zami: A New Spelling of My Name, Uses of the Erotic, Chosen Poems Old and New, The Black Unicorn,* and *From a Land Where Other People Live.*

Barbara Macdonald was an Anglo-European lesbian feminist theorist and lecturer who died at age 86 in June 2000. *Look Me in the Eye: Old Women, Aging, and Ageism* (Spinsters Ink, 1983) has recently appeared in an expanded edition (2001).

Manning Marable is a professor of history and director of the Institute for Research in African-American Studies at Columbia University, New York City. An African American scholar/activist, he is a cofounder of the Black Radical Congress. Professor Marable's political and intellectual work makes important connections between race, gender, and class oppression.

Nathan McCall grew up in Portsmouth, Virginia. He studied journalism at Norfolk State University after serving three years in prison. He reported for the *Virginian Pilot-Ledger Star* and the *Atlanta Journal-Constitution* before moving to the *Washington Post* in 1989.

Peggy McIntosh, associate director of the Wellesley College Center for Research on Women, is founder and co-director of the United States S.E.E.D. Project on Inclusive Curriculum (Seeking Educational Equity and Diversity). She is best known for her work on curricular revision, privilege systems, and feelings of fraudulence.

Michael A. Messner spent most of his free time through high school shooting hoops and dreaming of becoming a professional athlete. Drawing on his experience as a "failed" athlete and as a youth league coach and referee, he later became a sport sociologist. He is now associate professor of sociology and gender studies at the University of California, and has written *Power at Play: Sports and the Problem of Masculinity* and other books and articles on gender and sport. His five-year-old son, Sasha, just started playing soccer, while his nine-year-old son, Miles, plays baseball and electric guitar (though not simultaneously).

Cherríe Moraga is a poet, essayist, editor, and playwright. She is author of *Loving in the War Years – Lo que nunca paso por sus labios,* a collection of essays and poetry. She coedited the groundbreaking anthology *This Bridge Called My Back: Writing by Radical Women of Color* and *Cuentos,* the first collection of stories by Latina feminists published in the United States. She has completed three full-length plays: *Giving Up the Ghost,* which premiered at Theatre Rhinoceros in 1989; *Shadow of a Man,* presented by Brava! for Women in the Arts and the Eureka Theatre in 1990; and *Heroes and Saints,* which was commissioned by the Los Angeles Theatre Center and produced by Brava! in 1992.

National Organization for Men Against Sexism www.nomas.org

Pat Parker, Black lesbian poet, feminist medical administrator, mother of two daughters, lover of women, softball devotee, and general progressive troublemaker, died of breast cancer on June 17, 1989, at the age of 45. Her 1978 work, *Movement in Black,* has recently been republished by Firebrand Books.

Rosalind P. Petchesky is Distinguished Professor of Political Science of Hunter College of the City University of New York and a MacArthur Fellow. Her more recent book *Negotiating Reproductive Rights: Women's Perspectives Across Countries and Cultures* (with Karen Judd) was published in 1998 by Zed Books, which will publish her forthcoming *Gender, Health and Human Rights: On a Collision Course with Global Capitalism* in 2002.

Julie Peteet is associate professor and chair of the Anthropology Department at the University of Louisville. She is the author of *Gender in Crisis, Women and the Palestinian Resistance Movement* (New York: Columbia University Press, 1991) and has published articles in *Signs, Cultural Anthropology, American Ethnologist,* and *Social Analysis.* She is currently completing a book on place and identity in Palestinian refugee camps. Her areas of research interest are violence and culture, displacement and identity, and gender.

Phil Petrie is a freelance writer in New Jersey.

William S. Pollack, Ph.D., a clinical psychologist, is the codirector of the Center for Men at McLean Hospital/Harvard Medical School, an assistant clinical professor of psychiatry at the Harvard Medical School, and a founding member and Fellow of the Society for the Psychological Study of Men and Masculinity of the American Psychological Association. He is coauthor of *In a Time of Fallen Heroes: The Re-Creation of Masculinity* and coeditor of *A New Psychology for Men.* He and his family live in Massachusetts.

Roberta Praeger is a long-time Cambridge, Massachusetts, activist who has worked on housing, welfare, and women's issues.

Barbara Reskin is a professor of sociology at Harvard University, having formerly taught at several Big Ten universities. She was drawn to sociology because it provides a framework for studying the factors that contribute to and reduce race and sex inequality. Her goal is to bring sociological knowledge on inequality to policymakers, and she has occasionally served as an expert witness in discrimination cases. Her research and teaching focus primarily on sex, race, and ethnic inequality at work. She brings personal experience to her research: before becoming a sociologist, she held a variety of jobs in the "real world."

Adrienne Rich, the daughter of a Jewish father and a non-Jewish mother, is a poet and nonfiction writer and an activist. She worked for eight years in New Jewish Agenda, a national organization for progressive Jews, and was a founding editor of *Bridges: A Journal for Jewish Feminists and Our Friends.* Her most recent books are *What Is Found There: Notebooks on Poetry and Politics* and *Dark Fields of the Republic: Poems 1991–1995.* She lives in California.

Lillian B. Rubin, as a girl growing up in an immigrant working-class family, experienced firsthand the injuries this society inflicts on those who are born outside the golden circle of gender and class privilege. Since receiving her doctorate in 1971, she has published nine books, all dealing with some aspect of gender and class.

Paula C. Rust, Ph.D., is assistant professor of sociology at Hamilton College in Clinton, New York, where she teaches LesBiGayTrans studies. She is author of *Bisexuality and the Challenge to Lesbian Politics: Sex, Loyalty, and Revolution.*

Don Sabo, Ph.D., is professor of sociology at D'Youville College in Buffalo, New York. His latest books include (with Michael Messner) *Sex, Violence & Power in Sport* (Crossing Press) and (with Dave Gordon) *Men's Health & Illness: Gender, Power, & the Body* (Sage Publishers). He coauthored the 1997 President's Council on Physical Fitness and Sport report *Physical Activity and Sport in the Lives of Girls.* He directed the nationwide Women's Sports Foundation study *Sport and Teen Pregnancy* (1998).

Elayne A. Saltzberg Daniels is a Psychology Fellow at the Yale University School of Medicine, where, among other activities, she works at the Yale Psychiatric Institute with women who have eating disorders. She earned her doctorate in clinical psychology at Rhode Island University and her master's degree at Connecticut College. She has recently completed a research project on the impact of breast cancer surgery on women's body image and sexual functioning, and she has published several articles on body image, eating disorders, and women's pursuit of beauty.

Marsha Saxton, Ph.D. teaches Disability Studies at the University of California, Berkeley, School of Public Health, and works as a researcher at the

World Institute on Disability in Oakland, California. She has special interests in women's issues, genetic technologies and personal assistance services. She has published many articles about disability rights, women's health, and genetic screening issues.

Ruth Sidel is professor of sociology at Hunter College. She has long been concerned about the well-being of women, children, and families in the United States and in other countries. Her most recent book is *Keeping Women and Children Last: America's War on the Poor* (Penguin).

Brent Staples is assistant metropolitan editor of the *New York Times.*

Sandra Steingraber, Ph.D., is currently on the faculty at Cornell University's Center for the Environment in Ithaca, New York. She is the author of *Living Downstream: An Ecologist Looks at Cancer and the Environment* and *Having Faith: An Ecologist's Journey to Motherhood.*

John Stoltenberg is the author of *Refusing to Be a Man: Essays on Sex and Justice* (Meridian, 1990), *The End of Manhood: A Book for Men of Conscience* (Plume, 1994), and *What Makes Pornography "Sexy"?* (Milkweed Editions, 1994). He is a frequent speaker and workshop leader, and he is executive editor of *On the Issues: The Progressive Woman's Quarterly.* He was born in Minneapolis in 1944 to working-class parents—his mother is German, and his father is Norwegian. He grew up queer, and he has lived with the writer Andrea Dworkin since 1974.

Gila Svirsky is a peace and human rights activist in Israel. She is a member of Women in Black and cofounder of the Coalition of Women for a Just Peace, which has engaged in a number of dramatic acts of resistance to end Israel's occupation of the Palestinian territories. She has been arrested several times in connection with acts of civil disobedience to protest the occupation and human rights violations.

Deborah Tannen, a professor of linguistics at Georgetown University, has published sixteen books, as well as essays, poems, and plays. She has appeared on such television and radio shows as *"Oprah," "Good Morning America," "20/20,"* and *"Larry King Live."* Born and bred in Brooklyn, New York, she is proud that her parents were born in Russia and Poland.

Desiree Taylor is a student at the University of Massachusetts-Boston completing an individualized major in gender, religion, and the arts. She is extremely lucky and has known far too many people just like herself who haven't been. She is an intern at *Sojourner* and lives in Jamaica Plain, Massachusetts.

Becky Thompson is the author of *A Hunger So Wide and So Deep: A Multiracial View of Women's Eating Problems* (1994), *A Promise and a Way of Life: White Anti-Racist Activism* (2001), and *Mothering Without a Compass: White Mother's Love, Black Son's Courage* (2000). She coedited, with Sangeeta Tyagi, *Names We Call Home: Autobiography on Racial Identity* (1996) and *Beyond a Dream De-*

ferred: Multicultural Education and the Politics of Excellence (1993). She is an associate professor of sociology at Simmons College where she teaches courses in African American studies, women's studies, and sociology.

Barrie Thorne, after becoming a mother in the early 1970s, began to ponder children's experiences of gender. She pursued this topic through fieldwork in elementary schools, culminating in the book *Gender Play* (1993) and subsequent research on childhood in two areas of California. She teaches sociology and women's studies at the University of California, Berkeley.

Bonnie Thornton Dill earned her Ph.D. at New York University after working for a number of years in anti-poverty and open-admissions programs in New York. She is currently Professor of Women's Studies at the University of Maryland, College Park, and was the founding director of the Center for Research on Women at Memphis State University. She has contributed articles to such journals as *Signs, Journal of Family History,* and *Feminist Studies* and is co-editor with Maxine Baca Zinn of the book *Women of Color in American Society* for Temple University Press. She is also conducting research on single mothers, race, and poverty in the rural South with a grant from the Aspen Institute and the Ford Foundation.

Chris Tilly, an economist at the University of Massachusetts at Lowell and an editor of *Dollars and Sense* magazine, does research on low-wage work. Both his wife (before he met her) and his daughter have spent time as single mothers on welfare. With Randy Albelda, he coauthored *Glass Ceilings and Bottomless Pits: Women's Work, Women's Poverty* (South End Press, 1997).

Susan R. Walen, Ph.D. received her Ph.D. from the University of Maryland, and did post-graduate training at the Albert Ellis Institute in NYC and the Center for Cognitive Therapy in Philadelphia. She taught for many years at Towson State University and at Johns Hopkins Hospital, Department of Psychiatry. Currently, Dr. Walen is in independent practice in Bethesda, Maryland.

Lois Weis is professor of sociology of education at the State University of New York, Buffalo. She is author of *Working Class without Work: High School Students in a De-Industrializing Economy* (New York: Routledge, 1990); coauthor, with Michelle Fine, of *The Unknown City: Lives of Poor and Working-Class Young Adults* (Boston: Beacon, 1998); and coeditor, with Michelle Fine, of *Beyond Silenced Voices: Class, Race, and Gender in United States Schools* (Albany: SUNY Press, 1993), with Maxine Seller, of *Beyond Black and White: New Faces and Voices in United States Schools* (Albany: SUNY Press, 1997), and, with Michelle Fine, Linda Powell, and Mun Wong, of *Off White: Readings on Race, Power and Society* (New York: Routledge, 1997).

Walter L. Williams is associate professor of anthropology and the study of women and men in society at the University of Southern California. He received his Ph.D. from the University of North Carolina and has taught at the University of Cincinnati and at UCLA. His books include *Black Americans and* *the Evangelization of Africa, Southwestern Indians Since the Removal Era, Indian Leadership,* and his study of the berdache, *The Spirit and the Flesh: Sexual Diversity in American Indian Culture.* In 1987–1988 he was a Fulbright Professor of American Studies at Gadjah Mada University in Indonesia. His most recent book is *Javanese Lives: Women and Men in Modern Indonesian Society.*

Kai Wright is a freelance writer based in Washington, D.C. More of his work is available at *www.kaiwright.com.* He can be contacted at wright_kai@hotmail.com.

Raul Ybarra, Ph.D. says about himself: Somehow I managed to receive my bachelors in Plant Science and masters in English Composition from California State University Fresno. I then graduated with my doctorate from the University of Illinois at Chicago, specializing in language, literacy and rhetoric. I am currently an assistant professor at the College of Public and Community Service at the University of Massachusetts Boston. This excerpt is from a much larger piece entitled *I Am A Man* in which I chronicle my struggles to get my formal education. I often come to school early on my teaching days at the University of Massachusetts Boston. I go to the Wits End Café, buy a cup of black coffee and sit alone trying to prepare mentally for the day's events. This is also the time when I most often think about home, about how I managed to end up 3,000 miles from home. I think about what I've done, what I have accomplished.

Helen Zia, the daughter of Chinese immigrants, grew up in the fifties when there were only 150,000 Chinese Americans in the entire country. An award-winning journalist, Zia has covered Asian American communities and social and political movements for more than twenty years. She lives in the San Francisco Bay Area.

Maxine Baca Zinn teaches in the Department of Sociology at Michigan State University. She has written widely in the area of family relations, Chicano studies, and gender studies, including (most recently) *Women of Color in U.S. Society* (with Bonnie Thornton Dill), *Diversity in Families* (with Stanley Eitzen, and *The Reshaping of America.*

General Introduction

. . . the system of patriarchy . . . seems to have nearly run its course – it no longer serves the needs of men or women and in its inextricable linkage to militarism, hierarchy, and racism it threatens the very existence of life on earth.

GERDA LERNER[1]

As a Black lesbian feminist comfortable with the many different ingredients of my identity, and a woman committed to racial and sexual freedom from oppression, I find I am constantly being encouraged to pluck out some one aspect of myself and present this as a meaningful whole, eclipsing or denying the other parts of self. But this is a destructive and fragmenting way to live.

AUDRE LORDE[2]

No one is simply a man or a woman. Each of us embodies intersecting statuses and identities, empowered and disempowered, including physical and demographic traits, chosen and unchosen. In any discussion of gender, serious students of the social order need to be prepared to ask, Which men? Which women? If students of gender studies choose to be conscious of the complexity of human life, much of the literature on human nature and gender needs to be read carefully, and any generalizations made with extreme caution. Sometimes findings about men are generalized to describe people in general. Sometimes data from racially mixed populations are combined and analyzed as a whole, leaving out the details and differences between groups. And sometimes when there are only small numbers of, say, women or people of color in a study, those respondents are excluded from analysis for lack of a large enough group. In any of these cases, the voices of the few are obscured by those of the many. Unless we focus on the few alongside the many, we not only lose the voices of the few, but we also lose any meaningful understanding of the relationship between the few and the many, particularly in terms of power, privilege, disempowerment, and empowerment. The readings in this book invite you to hear the perspectives of many women and men whose voices have been ignored, marginalized, or silenced in the past.

This collection of readings focuses on power, addressing the conditions under which the gender system intersects with other factors to create various kinds of power and powerlessness. The readings also address how people empower themselves, both personally and collectively. This book is grounded in several important intellectual perspectives that support the acquisition of inclusive knowledge as a prerequisite to empowerment. These perspectives are based on the assumption that we need to understand the complexity of human experience in order to develop effective strategies for humane, inclusive social change.

Gender in Historical Perspective—Using a Sociological Imagination

An important sociological knowledge seeker, C. Wright Mills, argued in 1959 that it is possible to understand human lives only if we can understand the connections between those lives and the social and historical contexts in which they are lived. He further argued that people need to understand the sources of their problems in order to fully understand why their lives are difficult. Thus, he encouraged people to distinguish between problems that affect only themselves and perhaps a few others from those problems experienced by large numbers of people and that have their cause in social structures beyond particular individuals or families. He referred to the former as "personal troubles" and to the latter as "public issues." He urged people to develop a "sociological imagination" so that they could place themselves in social context and identify how public issues affect them at the personal level, arguing that people need to know the source of their difficulties in order to make sense of their lives.[3] Understanding the source of one's difficulties opens the possibility of shifting the blame off of oneself and onto the social order, when appropriate. It also opens the possibility of working with others to change aspects of the social order that create difficulties for many individuals. Thus, our mental health and our effective resistance to social structures we find oppressive depend upon our possession of a sociological imagination.

The second wave of the feminist movement in the United States, which started in the mid-1960s, incorporated a sociological imagination when it adopted the phrase "the personal is political." Arguing that larger political realities were felt at the personal level, women were encouraged to look beyond themselves for the sources of their problems in order to feel less alone and less to blame for the difficulties they faced. Analysis of the real sources of problems allowed women both to understand their personal situations better and to devise individual and collective means of resistance. In many situations, women have used the link between the political and the personal to help each other understand sexism as it is played out in the political structure, the community, the workplace, schools, families, and bedrooms. In response to this awareness, women have established a national network of services for women, such as shelters for battered women, rape crisis centers, and health centers, and have worked for legal changes to help end discrimination on the basis of sex or gender.[4]

A sociological imagination is essential for helping us to understand both ongoing realities—such as gender discrimination—and events such as the attacks on the World Trade Center and the Pentagon on September 11, 2001. Without an understanding of the historical context, the latter might be comprehensible only in terms of individual psychopathology. A look at other factors, however, offers both plausible explanations and suggestions for how future attacks might be rendered less likely. The history of U.S. policy toward Saudi Arabia, the Gulf War, the Israeli-Palestinian conflict, religious fundamentalism, and recent history in Afghanistan all help to set the stage for making sense of the attacks and their gendered nature. People caught up in these events or their aftermaths are finding their personal lives deeply affected. Apart from the horrendous grief and turmoil in families who lost loved ones in the attacks, the personal implications are wide ranging. Consider, for example, the effects of the U.S. counterattack on the people of Afghanistan, most of whom had nothing to do with the conflict but were caught in the cross fire, often forced to flee for their lives. Consider women in Afghanistan, free of Taliban rule but now living under a government controlled by a regime that has its own record of violence. Consider U.S. soldiers mobilized for war, pulled out of school or careers and away from their loved ones in response to government mandates. Consider the partners of the men and women called to combat, worrying about their loved ones and coping at home without the support of their partners. Consider Arab American men, targeted now for racial profiling because men from Arab countries perpetrated the attacks on September 11. Consider innocent dark-skinned men from any cultural group, ordered off planes because they "look Arabic." Consider men detained under the new anti-terrorism legislation without the ordinary due process of law that U.S. citizens and residents have come to expect. Consider a U.S. citizen who criticizes the U.S. government's response to September 11 and finds his or her job threatened because of the criticism. Consider previously comfortable U.S. citizens, now afraid to fly or open their mail. Or consider the rise in Christian white supremacist hate group activity following September 11.

A sociological imagination helps us see that the personal problems that evolve from the events of September 11 are by no means personal troubles in Mills's use of that term. They are public issues, shared by many others, reflective of realities that go way beyond individual motivation or control, and that stretch, in fact, into the highly complex realms of international trade, foreign policy, and religious values; these problems cannot be addressed by individuals alone. Some of the readings in this book will attempt to put September 11 in perspective. A major goal of this book generally is to help readers explore many of the social realities and events that surround and explain individual experiences.

The material in this book was written primarily in the United States in the late twentieth and early twenty-first centuries, a period in which many gender-related trends and events were occurring. This period of history has seen growing scholarship and activism among women, especially women of color. This period of history also saw conflict among white women, including writings and activism by those who object to feminism and by those who critique what mainstream feminism has stood for.[5] This time in history also saw an increase in research and writing by pro-feminist men, especially those working for changes in men's usual roles.[6] During this period, other groups of men also became increasingly public about their various disenchantments with either their own roles or those of women. A men's rights movement emerged to protest the kinds of power its members perceived women to have. A Christian men's movement emerged calling for men to take back the power they had lost as women began to develop more public power. A "mythopoetic" men's movement began to hold men-only retreats at which primarily white, middle-class men attempted to contact their "essential masculinity." The Million Man March in 1995 provided an empowering experience for many Black men, highlighted some of the tensions and conflicts over men's roles and responsibilities in the Black community, and elicited a range of responses from Black women and men.[7]

Increased attention to the situations of boys emerged in the 1990s, matching to some extent the attention to girls that had been going on since the 1980s. Some authors attended to boys in general, looking at everyday violence and school failure, calling for more careful attention to boys' emotional and educational needs.[8] Others addressed the needs of boys in urban contexts, considering the impact of poverty and racism.[9] Others decried the lack of attention to boys in the context of criticizing the feminist-driven attention to girls.[10]

A series of school shootings, such as the one at Columbine High School in Littleton, Colorado, brought particular attention to the potential for violence of seemingly normal white, middle-class boys.[11] Sociologist Michael Kimmel, critical of the media discussion of "youth violence," emphasized that what had occurred was *male,* rather than *youth,* violence, encouraging a discussion of masculinity: "In a way, Eric Harris and Dylan Klebold weren't deviants, but over-conformists to norms of masculinity that prescribe violence as a solution. Like real men, they didn't just get mad, they got even."[12] Standard masculinity, all these authors argue, can be detrimental. Embedded in the attention to boys is a concern by some authors that expected standards of behavior do not fit boys and men and that we might, in fact, be attempting to impose on males the standards of expression of feeling, open communication, and "good behavior" that are more likely to be found in girls and women.[13] The lesson from this is that boys as well as girls need serious attention, within the various contexts in which they attempt to live satisfying lives.

The nineties also brought increased attention to men, particularly white men who have felt left out of major trends in the wider society. Some feel left out of the (now disappearing) economic boom; others feel alienated by the increase in attention to women; some feel troubled by the increasing diversification of U.S. society; and some feel troubled by all of these.[14]

Another growing trend that has garnered a lot of attention in the past few years is attention to same sex marriage and gay and lesbian families more generally. Here in the United States, Vermont became the first state to allow civil unions of same-sex couples in July 2000. In the Netherlands and in Germany, gay marriage is now legal. In May 1999, the Supreme Court of Canada ordered the province of Ontario to provide same-sex couples with the same rights and privileges as common-law heterosexual couples.[15] In France, same-sex couples may make a "Civil Pact of Solidarity" and receive some of the privileges of heterosexual marriage.[16] Lesbian and gay parents in the United States who want to co-adopt each other's children have recently received the support of the American Academy of Pediatrics, which recommended legalizing same-sex adoption, arguing that children ". . . deserve the security of two legally recognized parents."[17] In Florida, gay, civil rights, and children's advocacy groups, with the support of Rosie O'Donnell and the American Civil Liberties Union, are pressuring Governor Jeb Bush to lift a ban on gay and lesbian adoptions. The latter effort followed the planned removal of a 10-year-old boy who had been in foster care with a gay couple in Florida since birth. His foster fathers want to adopt him.[18] A recent court ruling in Delaware acknowledged the legitimacy of a lesbian couple when it ordered the non-birth mother to pay child support after the couple separated.[19]

Although there is substantial backlash to efforts to institute gay civil rights in the United States, public homophobia seems to be softening a bit both here and abroad. Even President George W. Bush and Secretary of State Colin Powell have been accused of being too pro-gay because of allowing gay men to serve the current administration in various ways.[20] Following the supreme court's support in June 2000 of the Boy Scouts policy of barring gays as scout leaders and members, objection to the policy began to grow not only in the ranks of scout members and leaders (with membership reportedly down 4.5 percent nationwide), but in the institutions in which scouts tend to recruit new members—in schools and other public settings, making recruitment more difficult. A Boston-area Boy Scout council voted to adopt a "don't ask, don't tell" policy so that gay leaders and members could remain members without technically breaching the national ban on gays.[21] The National Education Association recently adopted a plan to make schools more respectful, and hopefully safer for lesbian, gay, bisexual and transgendered students and school employees.[22] And in Japan, a youth center was found guilty of discrimination when it banned a gay youth group from using the center. The discrimination occurred in 1990, and the Tokyo High Court handed down its decision seven and a half years later.[23]

Another trend that characterizes this time in history is growing public awareness of transgender issues. Media and scholarly attention to this issue has grown substantially in the six years since I assembled the first edition of this book. The literature includes writings by scholars documenting third and fourth genders in Native American and other cultures[24] as well as writings by people interested in stretching gender boundaries and challenging the two-gender system as it is currently constructed in mainstream U.S. culture.[25] Leslie Feinberg, a central spokesperson for what she calls "Trans liberation," describes the participants in this movement:

> We are masculine females and feminine males, cross-dressers, transsexual men and women, intersexuals born on the anatomical sweep between female and male, gender blenders, many other sex and gender-variant people, and our significant others. All told, we expand understanding of how many ways there are to be a human being.[26]

The *Utne Reader* brought attention to this issue on a recent cover: "It's 2 AM. Do you know what sex you are? Does Anybody?" Even *Cosmopolitan* ran a story in November 1998 entitled "The man I married was really a woman."[27] The editors of *Utne Reader* summed up the issue this way:

> Queer theorists call gender a social construct, saying that when we engage in traditional behaviors and sexual practices, we are nothing but actors playing ancient, empty roles. Others suggest that gender is performance, a collection of masks we can take on and off at will. So are we witnessing the birth of thrilling new freedoms, or the disintegration of values and behaviors that bind us together? Will we encounter new opportunities for self-realization, or hopeless confusion? Whatever the answers, agreeing that our destinies aren't preordained will launch a search that will profoundly affect society, and will eventually engage us all. (p. 45)

In an unusual twist, a same-gendered couple in Texas was allowed to marry because one of them was transgendered and was genetically male.[28] How transgender issues will intersect with other issues of oppression is yet to be defined, although Leslie Feinberg, the primary spokesperson for the Trans movement, is deeply committed to seeing Trans liberation in the context of other social justice struggles and is herself actively engaged in social justice struggles for all oppressed people.

The writings in this book have also emerged in a virulent political era in which attacks on feminists, people of color, poor people, Jewish people, and gay men, lesbians, and transgendered people have been and continue to be common. The hate murders of James Byrd, Jr., a Black man in Texas, and Matthew Shepard, a gay man in Wyoming, are recent examples.[29] Reports of bias against Muslims are up since September 11, 2001, in a context laden with fear and hostility.[30] Issues of affirmative action remain on the table as universities struggle with how to legally address the need for a diverse student body. Assaults on people with disabilities, including sexual assaults on over 75 percent of mentally disabled women according to some studies, continue seemingly unchecked.[31] The supreme court struck a serious blow to the 1990 Americans with Disabilities Act in February 2001 by supporting a state's right to not provide reasonable accommodations in a case in Alabama in which a man with asthma was not assured a smoke-free environment and a woman with breast cancer was demoted.[32] Threats to Social Security, Medicare, Medicaid, and reproductive rights are real, along with cuts to welfare, education, and other social services. The costs of the U.S. response to September 11 are likely to serve as the rationale for cutting services even further.

Another recent trend that sets the stage for an analysis of gender is increased awareness of globalization. Major shifts in the world's economy that seem to favor industrialized nations over developing ones have provoked international protests against the World Trade Organization, the World Bank, the G-8 nations (the world's most economically powerful countries), and the International Monetary Fund. Growing awareness of structural adjustment policies that increasingly impoverish developing nations has provoked these protests, such as those in Seattle, Montreal, and Genoa, as people (many of them young) attempt to right the wrongs they see occurring. As U.S. corporations establish factories overseas in order to take advantage of inexpensive labor, women have begun to organize for better wages and working conditions (see Enloe, Part VIII). Understanding of the workings of Mexican border factories (*maquiladoras*) where the products of U.S. corporations are assembled or built, primarily by women, has provoked outrage due to the poor working conditions and sweatshop wages. And sweatshop conditions within the United States persist, in part because workers are afraid that corporations will move the factories to other countries if they fight too hard for better wages or working conditions.[33]

These changes are occurring in a context in which it appears to some observers that many people in the United States are increasingly less likely to engage with each other in mutually supportive ways, leading to what sociologist Robert Putnam calls a decline in "social capital," which in turn seems to lead to less safety, declining health, and less civic engagement.[34] Writers and activists, however, continue to describe the complexity of gender issues and to engage in progressive social change. Young feminists have established magazines to address girls' and young women's needs. *Teen Voices, New Moon* (for girls 8 to 14), *Bitch, Bust,* and *Fabula* join an array of books by "third wave" feminists.[35] Membership on the Third Wave Foundation stood at about 5,000 members in 2000.[36] How all this activism will evolve is unpredictable, but I am heartened by this clarity of thought and continuing struggle for justice in an era of hate crimes, backlash, and economic conservatism. People committed to democracy and pluralism will especially need the knowledge that inclusive scholarship provides, both now and in the future, as people formerly silenced make themselves heard and suffer the anger and violence of those who would prefer them to be invisible or at least silent. For example, as the U.S. population became more multicultural and less white, white supremacist and militia activity increased. As gay, lesbian, bisexual, and transgendered people have increasingly refused to be labeled and closeted, more resistance to freedom of sexual and affectional expression has been mounted. Continued resistance to the same-sex marriage movement in spite of small gains provides a powerful example. And as the wealth in the United States has been moving increasingly into the hands of a small proportion of very rich people, poor women and children, especially those on welfare (or removed from welfare because of time limits imposed by the new Temporary Aid to Needy Families program), continue to suffer. Even though the cost of the now-defunct AFDC (Aid to Families with Dependent Children) constituted less than 1 percent of the federal budget, welfare under the Clinton presidency was treated as if it were a major cause of the national deficit, and few voices are calling for a more family-friendly policy.[37]

Dissident Voices

Hearing from a wide range of men and women across many disciplines is crucial to an effective understanding of what is going on about gender. Sociology; women's studies; men's studies; African American studies; multicultural studies; gay, lesbian, bisexual, transgender, and queer studies; disability studies; studies of aging; and American studies have welcomed the voices and experiences of previously silenced people into scholarly discourse. The expansion of work by people in these fields has provided a rich, exciting base of new information that continues to grow. This book includes research, essays, and autobiographical material from this literature.[38]

By including men's studies in this book, I do not mean to imply that the situations of men are equivalent to those of women. Although women are almost all oppressed in one way or another by some men and by patriarchal structures, the reverse is not true. Thus, while men might suffer from detrimental aspects of male socialization such as participation in war, premature death, increased exposure to violence, and higher rates of suicide, it is generally not women who control the outcome of men's lives. Male-dominated institutions and individual powerful men control both women and less-empowered men. And powerful men reap great benefits from our male-dominant structure even if they do tend to die younger than women and suffer other difficulties related to being male.

Many of the writers in men's studies are dissatisfied with male-dominated society, having personally experienced the painful aspects of male socialization. This perspective puts these writers in a good position to analyze masculinities from within. Their voices are dissident within the ranks of powerful men, and many would not be particularly welcome in boardrooms, locker rooms, or faculty meetings. They are outsiders as they critique the bastions of hegemonic masculinity—the dominant, white, heterosexual, patriarchal, privileged masculinity that still controls many aspects of people's lives. Hegemonic masculinity, which promotes the tough, take-charge, don't-feel image of men, frequently dominates the socialization process in spite of increasing efforts to develop other masculinities and femininities.[39] The writers referred to earlier who are concerned with the fate of boys are particularly attuned to the damage that hegemonic masculinity can do.

An examination of masculinity in male-dominated society is a crucial aspect of both women's studies and men's studies, especially if we try to understand how to work toward a social order in which there is less violence. A look at the literature on men violently abused as children, for example, suggests that about a third of them grow up to violently abuse others.[40] An understanding of adult male abusers leads us to examine how children are socialized and helps us to understand the process by which many baby boys grow into violent or controlling men. Another perspective suggests that circumstances at any point in life can contribute to violent responses, lending support to the sociological perspective that propensity to violence is socialized rather than inherent. For example, the Israeli-Palestinian conflict seems to have produced a substantial number of fighters and potential suicide bombers among young Palestinian men who grew up in the midst of political violence.[41] Many of the men included in this book critique the gender system and are committed to working to end a social system that teaches men to be violent and that leaves boys and men frequently victimized and revictimized by other violent men.

It is useful here to mention some potential conflicts between women's studies and men's studies. One basic question concerns the extent to which men can effectively criticize a system in which they have experienced various amounts of privilege. Another question is the issue of crossover—can men effectively study women or women effectively study men?[42] The study of women by men raises the larger question of whether it is possible for someone from a more-empowered group to study, effectively understand, and analyze the experiences of people from a less-empowered group. Certainly there is a long history of "scholarship" by men distorting or ignoring the lives of women and by white people distorting or ignoring the lives of people of color. A third area of conflict is the use of the term "feminist" when applied to men. Both sides of this question have passionate proponents, including those who claim that the term "feminist man" is an inherent contradiction and others who claim that it isn't.[43] Finally, limited resources in academia are an issue. The development of gender studies and men's studies poses a potential threat to women's studies on some campuses, just as multicultural studies can pose a threat to Black studies in some situations. These threats include both possible cutbacks in resources and the potential of these programs being placed in a larger structure controlled by someone from another discipline. Harry Brod addresses some of these issues in relation to men's studies in Part VII and concludes that men's studies are necessary but that resources for the development of this relatively new field should not come from women's studies.

Intersecting Identities

Another recent effort at truth seeking is the attention now paid to the complex combination of identities held by each individual.[44] The readings included here address the concerns of Patricia Hill Collins, Audre Lorde, Gloria Anzaldúa,

James Baldwin, W. E. B. Du Bois, Suzanne Pharr, and others who ask us to acknowledge such complexities. Sociologist W. E. B. Du Bois, writing in 1903, called for awareness of what he named the "double-consciousness" of African Americans—the awareness that they can't simply be Americans, working toward whatever goals they might have; rather, they are simultaneously forced to deal with racism, seeing themselves through the eyes of hateful others. Thus, Du Bois says, African American men and women can never experience themselves as simply men or women because they are constantly hated or pitied.[45]

The importance of acknowledging multiple aspects of identity is also powerfully stated by Patricia Hill Collins, who addresses the complex combination of oppression and privilege held by each individual. She argues that individuals can simultaneously be members of both privileged and oppressed groups, citing the example of white women who are "penalized by their gender but privileged by their race."[46] Collins also argues that there is a matrix of domination, compelling us to look at the intersecting aspects of oppression in individuals and groups. She names race, class, and gender as the three axes of oppression that typically characterize Black women's experiences, and she lists other axes of oppression as well that may or may not affect particular individuals such as sexual orientation, religion, and age. Collins further argues that people experience domination at several levels, including personal biography, group-community interaction, and social institutions.[47] The readings in this volume have been chosen to reflect experience in and analysis of oppression, privilege, or both at all three levels, as well as reflecting people's empowerment struggles at these various levels.

Naming and Owning Privilege

This book is also grounded in the tradition of scholars and activists who struggle to bring privilege into focus.[48] In her well-known essay on white privilege, women's studies scholar Peggy McIntosh names her professional white privilege and heterosexual privilege and discusses how difficult it was to hold onto her awareness of her privileges as she worked on the essay; ideas about how she was privileged kept slipping away unless she wrote them down.[49] Sociologist Michael S. Kimmel tells about his difficulty in naming and owning his race and gender. Before attending a seminar on feminist theory in which race and gender were discussed, when he looked in the mirror, Kimmel saw ". . . a human being . . . universally generalizable . . . the generic person." As a middle-class, white man, he had difficulty identifying how gender and race had affected his experience.[50] Anti-violence and anti-racist activist Paul Kivel, in a recent guide for white people who want to work for racial justice, provides a "white benefits checklist" that addresses the intersections of class and race. He also provides a checklist of the "costs of racism for white people."[51]

Similar to the matrix of domination argued for by Patricia Hill Collins, we might also conceive of a matrix of privilege. Assuming that most people and groups possess some degree of privilege, however limited, we can frequently examine oppression and privilege together. We can identify where privilege lies and analyze how it smoothes the way for those who possess it and simultaneously makes life more difficult for those who don't. The issue here, however, is not simply to identify privilege. Rather, as the late writer Audre Lorde said, we should make it available for wider use. Thus, a white person who opposes racism might use his or her contacts with groups of white people as opportunities to educate them about racism. A man who opposes sexism might use his contacts with other men to educate them about sexism.

Privilege is a difficult concept for many of those who have it because it is frequently unnamed in wider U.S. society. In a social order whose mainstream values include individual achievement and competition, many people with privilege are supported to assume that they deserve the "luck" or "normalcy" they experience, whereas those who lack privilege are encouraged to blame themselves.[52] Thus, an able-bodied person might experience the ability to walk up a flight of stairs as simply a normal thing to do, rather than seeing the expectation that all people walk as part of a system that treats stair climbing as normal and thus fails to build ramps for those on wheels. A white person might assume that white is "normal," might feel lucky to be white, and fail to see that the alleged superiority of whiteness is a piece of a racist system that keeps people of color from moving freely in the social order. A person born wealthy is likely to be taught that he or she deserves the wealth, rather than to be taught how wealth is related to poverty in U.S. society. Although people with less privilege are usually astute analysts of how privilege works, those who enjoy it are frequently less conscious of its impact.[53] Thus, a challenge for progressive people with privilege, especially for those with substantial privilege, is to become aware of the nuances of privilege and to learn how to use it in ways that raise consciousness about oppression and promote fairness.

Another possibility for those with privilege is to identify some of the liabilities that accompany privilege and to use that awareness to work toward changing the system. For example, many white professional men lead highly stressful, dissatisfying lives, with restricted access to their feelings and a limited capacity for intimacy. Writer Mark Gerzon, a white professional man, convincingly criticizes the roles and role models available to men like himself and calls for new roles to replace them. After describing what he believes are archetypal roles for men, he asks men to reject these roles in exchange for more democratic and humane ones. Instead of frontiersmen, he wants men to be healers—of both people and the earth; instead of breadwinners, men should be companions; instead of soldiers, mediators; instead of experts, colleagues; and instead of lords, nurturers. Gerzon's work emerged from his dissatisfaction with being male in spite of his race and class privilege.[54]

A denial of privilege can greatly limit our understanding of how our worlds work and how losing that privilege might affect us. White people who are not conscious of their white privilege, or who simply accept the system around them without question, spend their lives in what I think of as powerful denial—knowing at some unconscious level that they do not deserve and did not earn the skin-color privilege they enjoy, yet pretending at some level that they deserve it. Many temporarily able-bodied people are thrown into deep shock when they become disabled because they have structured their lives in ways that avoided people with disabilities and that allowed them to pretend that disability would never affect them. They therefore have no framework in which to combine personhood and disability and have suddenly become something that they have previously despised. I have heard many of my students, especially male students, say that they'd rather be dead than physically disabled.

The Reconstruction of Knowledge

Based on the kinds of truth telling identified thus far—the importance of a sociological imagination and the need to hear marginalized voices, acknowledge intersecting identities, and name privilege—numerous scholars have called for the reconstruction of knowledge.[55] Philosopher Elizabeth Minnich, for example, argues convincingly that four basic errors in knowledge need to be corrected as we move toward more inclusive knowing.[56] The first error is overgeneralization based on information gathered from small sectors of the population throughout history—primarily empowered male writers and the people they chose to acknowledge in their writing. Philosopher Harry Brod argues assertively that the study of men as men, in all the nuances of their experiences with masculinity, is crucial to the study of human beings. He asserts that to generalize from male experience to human experience not only distorts what human experience is, but also distorts what is specifically male.[57] Historian Gerda Lerner calls for a restructuring of thought and for an analysis that acknowledges that half the people in the world are women. She argues that all generalizations about human beings need to acknowledge this fact.[58] The selections in this book should help readers challenge inaccurate generalizations about men and women and develop new, more limited generalizations.

A second error in knowledge identified by Elizabeth Minnich is circular reasoning, which justifies traditional knowledge based on the standards embedded in that knowledge. In sociology, for example, for many years certain topics were not studied at all, particularly women's experiences. Students, especially women students, who couldn't relate to the material presented were seen as inadequate. Ultimately, women sociologists began studying gender, and the field of sociology was forced to become more inclusive. Joyce Ladner, for example, in *Tomorrow's Tomorrow,* not only studied Black adolescent girls but refused to accept the standard sociological definition of their lives as "deviant." Rather, she identified some of the ways in which her respondents found empowerment in an economically limited, racist context.[59] Ladner studied and redefined a population that usually had no direct voice in the sociological literature.

The third knowledge error identified by Minnich is our attachment to mystified concepts. When we let go of these concepts, new questions and new avenues for research emerge. Masculinity and femininity are two mystified concepts that are frequently used but seldom accurately defined in everyday discourse. Yet as we examine the literature in women's studies and men's studies, for example, we find that many men and women do not conform to the dominant Anglo ideals of femininity and masculinity. Many men, for instance, do not fit the strong, tough, take-charge mode; do not enjoy fighting; and would like more freedom to express their feelings. And, in fact, many men do express themselves openly.[60] Martín Espada (Part I), Tommi Avicolli (Part II), Phil Petrie (Part IV), and Don Sabo (Part V) all provide examples of men breaking ranks with the masculine norms presented in mainstream U.S. culture. Many women also do not fit the stereotypical visions of women presented in mainstream culture, especially in the media. Christy Haubegger (Part III), Martha Coventry (Part III), bell hooks (Part VII), and Melanie Kaye/Kantrowitz (Part IX), among others, provide examples of women who refuse narrow and limited ideas about gender.

Gender itself is a mystified concept for the many people who see it as biologically determined. Recent scholars in gender studies argue convincingly, however, that there is nothing necessary or predictable about gender. In fact, it is becoming more commonly known that human bodies do not come in just two sexes but rather fall along a continuum between female and male.[61] Gender, then, rather than being dictated by body types, is socially determined, or "constructed" in various contexts. Sociologist Judith Lorber, in her recent book *Paradoxes of Gender,* encourages us to "challenge the validity, permanence, and necessity of gender."[62]

Heterosexuality is another mystified concept related to masculinity and femininity that has proven hard to even question. So "normal" is heterosexuality that it is difficult to imagine a world without this expectation.[63] The "sissy" and "lezzie" insults levied at boys and girls who do not conform to heterosexist expectations have a lot to teach us about how charged and compelling the heterosexual mandate is. In spite of the fashion trend toward androgynous clothing in the mainstream media, individuals who choose to express themselves through androgynous presentations risk ridicule and ostracism in many circles. Some of the ridicule stems from standards of masculinity and femininity; some of it relates more directly to homophobia.[64] Those who love someone of the same sex know at deeply painful levels the costs of breaking with the heterosexual ideal. This ideal is also tightly bound up with the requirement to match gender with sex. For example, an ironic twist of fate occurred in a tragic atrocity; the man who massacred thirteen women in Montreal because they were studying engineering spared one of the women present because he perceived her to be a man.[65]

Many new questions emerge if we examine the heterosexual ideal: What would life be like without the insults and labels aimed at boys who are gentle, at girls who are athletes, at women who study engineering, or at men who study nursing? What explains the discomfort of the majority of us who want or need people to fit into gender categories? How does this affect the lives of girls, boys, men, and women who express love for someone of the same sex or live their lives in the gender to which they have not been assigned? How does it affect the social order when bisexual women and men who could choose to relate sexually/affectionally to members of the opposite gender choose to do so with the same gender instead? We cannot begin to address these questions without careful attention to the heterosexual ideal and its accompanying homophobia. I often ask myself how gender roles might look without homophobia. Would there even be gender roles as we know them? (Michael Kimmel addresses this issue in more detail in Part II.)

Finally, the fourth knowledge error identified by Minnich is our inability, without new knowledge systems, to discard or correct prior ones. If, however, we can embrace new models of knowledge, we can discard or adapt the old ones. Sociologist Charles Lemert's edited volume, *Social Theory: The Multicultural and Classic Readings,* provides an excellent example of this. By expanding the definition of who is considered a social theorist, Lemert allows new voices to enter sociological discourse and invites readers to consider a wide range of contemporary thinkers not usually included in texts on sociological theory.[66] Ronald Takaki's *A Different Mirror: A History of Multicultural America* provides another very good example of a new knowledge system. Takaki focuses on the lives of ordinary people, including those in various racial and ethnic groups, rather than on the lives of politicians and other famous people. He examines class and gender within the groups he studies.[67]

Empowerment—Challenging the Patriarchal System

The need for inclusive knowledge has broad implications for empowerment at the interpersonal, community, and policy levels. Without inclusive knowledge, we cannot develop comprehensive empowerment strategies or inclusive social policy. Without seeing the complexity of human experience and the complexity of human oppression, we cannot begin to address the real needs of human beings caught in systematically oppressive social structures. Marilyn Frye makes this point effectively and graphically with the metaphor of the bird cage in her essay "Oppression."[68] She argues that when someone is caged, or oppressed, it is crucial to examine all the bars of the cage to get a full understanding of the inability to escape; close, myopic examination of just one bar will not give a full understanding of why the person is trapped. For example, if we look at gender discrimination on the job, we might wonder why women can't just overcome the prejudice and discrimination they experience and get on with their lives, even if they make less money, are passed over for promotion, and can support their families only marginally. But if we simultaneously look at other factors, such as sexual harassment within the workplace, racism, fatphobia, heterosexism, ableism, and violence against women and children, we will come to a clearer understanding of how certain people and groups are caught in a web that they often can't escape; barriers, the bars of the cage, are erected everywhere they turn.

Another metaphor I find useful in making sense of oppression and privilege in order to frame social change is the idea of being tied down. If a person is tied by one oppression rope, say, sexual harassment, it's likely that she or he has some movement, is able to see how the knots are tied, and may be able to maneuver to untie the knots, slide under the rope, or move in and out of the rope at different times, depending on the context. If a rope is light, she or he might even break it. But if someone is tied by several ropes, such that she or he cannot move enough to clearly see the sizes and quality of the ropes or the configurations of the knots, there is little possibility for escape. If we imagine that each oppression is a different rope and that the power of oppressions might vary, creating light ropes and heavy ones, a person could be tied down by an almost infinite combination of ropes of different sizes and strengths. And occasionally there will be people tied by no ropes at all at various moments, such as wealthy, white, Anglo-Saxon, Protestant, heterosexual, married (to emotionally stable women), able-bodied, muscular, normal-weight, physically attractive, tall (but not too tall) men in their middle years who are in good health and have not been in psychotherapy or addiction treatment.

The presence or absence of ropes is a public, not a private, matter. The vast majority of people do not tie themselves down; they are born with limitations due to the structure of the socioeconomic system in which they are situated. German social theorist Max Weber called this system of possibilities "life chances," referring to the array of opportunities, however limited or plentiful, with which a person is born.[69] Although we live in an alleged democracy that offers the potential for upward mobility for anyone, the probability of that happening is severely limited, especially for those born under multiple ropes. Equal access to wealth and other privileges is not structurally guaranteed, even for white, able-bodied men; and many white people in the middle class are currently experiencing downward mobility.[70]

There is no systematic training for untying or breaking the ropes of oppression. Those held by fewer ropes are usually not encouraged to share their privilege by helping others to escape their ropes. Those tied down often learn survival, resilience, resistance, and liberation skills from their families, cultures, and communities but are offered little systematic support from the wider social order. Instead, those tied by many ropes are likely to attend poor schools in which race, class, gender, disability, and sexual orientation interact to produce high rates of failure or marginal functioning.

The oppressive social structure surrounding many people sets in place some probabilities for success or failure. It is important to acknowledge, however, how groups and individuals blocked from success in the privileged, wealthy centers of power find ways to empower themselves, solve problems, and survive against very difficult odds. They do, at times, escape from multiple ropes. For example, some people from highly dysfunctional families have grown up to establish healthy relationships for themselves. The strength and resilience found in poor communities, especially in communities of color, also portray empowerment within otherwise very trying circumstances.[71] Many of the readings in this book report on resilience and personal agency in response to various oppressions.

A look at the web of ropes that surrounds us or the structure of the cages we are in can help us understand how our lives are limited and how to develop institutional, community, and individual strategies for empowerment. An understanding of multiple oppressions helps us see how people can resist oppression at both individual and collective levels and helps us understand why people don't usually escape from multiple ropes. This understanding is especially important in a patriarchal social order in which virtually every woman is tied down by some variety of gender oppression.

Patriarchy, defined in various ways by various theorists, has as its core male control of women. The pervasiveness of the effects of gender oppression and gender socialization has led sociologist Judith Lorber to call gender a social institution (see Part II of this book). Feminist historian Gerda Lerner names an array of ways in which women are socialized, indoctrinated, and coerced into cooperation with patriarchal systems. For example, women are prevented from fully participating in such empowering activities as education (including learning women's history), politics, and the use of economic resources. Lerner names several dynamics particular to women that make this cooperation with patriarchy especially difficult to resist or subvert. First, she argues, women have internalized the idea of their own inferiority. Second, historically, wives and daughters have lived under male domain where they exchange submission for protection and unpaid labor for economic maintenance. Third, women with substantial class privilege have a more difficult time seeing themselves as deprived and subordinated, thus making it especially hard for women of different classes to work together. Fourth, women are separated by their differences in sexual expression and sexual activities.[72] When we add race, age, and ability differences to these class and sexual divisions, the likelihood of women uniting against patriarchy becomes even less probable.

In spite of these extremely powerful structures that conspire to limit the roles and options of both genders and render those who are multiply oppressed close to powerless at times, there is a long history of resistance to patriarchy.[73] Although a unified revolt against patriarchy will probably not occur in the forseeable future, people are fighting back in various ways and struggling to change the systems that support inequality. Many of the writers in this book have struggled for empowerment of one sort or another and provide hopeful exceptions to this often-oppressive picture. The pages that follow contain examples of people finding their voices, telling unpopular truths, taking charge of their own needs, offering concrete advice for improving the lives of women and men, and organizing for change. Don Sabo, for example, critiques male sports culture (Part V); Christy Haubegger embraces her round body (Part III); Stan Gray fights to include women as equals in his factory (Part VIII); and Robert Allen works to prevent male violence (Part XI).

I define power broadly to include a range of personal and collective actions. At a personal level, empowerment includes the ability to name and assert one's identity in all its complexity, including the naming of one's privilege and oppression. Related to this is the refusal to accept someone else's definition of who one is. Possessing a sociological imagination is another form of personal power; this allows us to know where we fit historically in the world, to know what our options are likely to be, and to know how to determine whether our pain stems from a personal trouble or from a public issue felt at the personal level. A sociological imagination contributes to the ability to challenge dominant ideas and to develop a healthy skepticism about how the world works. Based on informed analyses of what is wrong with the social order, people can use the power of knowledge to determine what kinds of social changes to work toward. Finally, people can empower themselves by taking political action, both individually and collectively.

Empowerment develops in stages. The first stage is awareness that something is not right. In order to conceptualize what's wrong, people need inclusive knowledge to develop a case for what feminist writer Elizabeth Janeway calls "disbelief," a piece of which is the refusal to accept the definition of oneself that is put forward by those with more power.[74] Janeway argues that in order to mistrust or disbelieve the messages of those in power, validation from others is necessary. Speaking of women, she argues, "the frightening experience of doubting society's directives and then doubting one's right to doubt them is still very recent."[75] Thus, if one's mistrust of the system is not solid, the presence of other disbelievers is likely to strengthen one's position. The role of Black churches in validating this mistrust has been well documented; congregants name how the racist power structure perpetuates itself, and they support each other to work to lessen its onslaught.[76] Women's consciousness-raising groups have also served this purpose.[77] The civil rights movement served to do this for its members in the 1960s as organizations like the National Association for the Advancement of Colored People and the Student Nonviolent Coordinating Committee supported their members to define the system of racism as unacceptable and to fight against it as they registered voters, engaged in sit-ins and boycotts, and integrated formerly white establishments and institutions in the face of virulent opposition.

Once people are convinced that something is wrong or unfair in their lives, they can consider taking steps toward making it right at several levels. At the individual level, people can practice personal acts of passive resistance, direct confrontation, or other actions such as telling the truth about how they really feel; challenging someone who said something hurtful or insulting; leaving an abusive relationship; insisting on not always being in a particular role in a relationship; avoiding contact with people whose attitudes are disrespectful, including refusing to frequent certain places; and making a public statement. On a collective level, people can resist oppressive arrangements by joining forces. This might happen in small or large ways, including movements for social change in communities, institutions, legislative bodies, other governmental structures, and international forums. All of these levels of resistance to oppressive structures and relationships are necessary if we are to create, in Gerda Lerner's words, ". . . a world free of dominance and hierarchy, a world that is truly human."[78]

This book begins with a section entitled Social Contexts of Gender, in which the authors explore gender expression in various racial and ethnic contexts. The intersections of identity and oppression are obvious here. This section closes with a theoretical essay that sets a framework for many of the essays in this book: "Theorizing Difference from Multiracial Feminism" by Maxine Baca Zinn and Bonnie Thornton Dill. Part II, Gender Socialization, presents two theoretical pieces related to the social construction of gender and explores aspects of childhood and adult socialization. Part III, Embodiment, examines the pressures to look "typically" female or male, which in many cases means white, muscular, slim, and young. Eating disorders and intersex issues are addressed here as well.

Parts IV, V, and VI deal with interpersonal relationships. Part IV, Communication, examines a wide range of communication challenges between men and women, across racial and cultural differences. Part V, Sexuality, looks at various aspects of sexuality, the challenge of nonexploitative heterosexual relationships, sexuality issues for people with disabilities, and the intersection of race and culture with sexual orientation among bisexual people. An essay on sexuality in Muslim contexts is included as well. Part VI, Families, explores the division of labor within the household, structural barriers to men's involvement in their children's lives, various kinds of families, and how gender affects people's lives within families. It also includes an essay on close men's friendships in other cultures. Part VII, Education, and Part VIII, Paid Work and Unemployment, examine issues that get in the way of equal opportunity in both realms. Part IX, Violence, focuses on two general issues. First, several authors address some of the causes and effects of September 11. Then several other authors look at violence in the United States. Part X, Health and Illness, documents ways that gender appears to affect health, including cultural contexts of health difficulties. Part XI, A World That Is Truly Human, concludes the book with some perspectives on human rights and social change with implications for empowerment and/or policy changes at the individual, community, and global levels.

NOTES

1. Gerda Lerner, *The Creation of Patriarchy* (New York: Oxford, 1986), pp. 228–29.
2. Audre Lorde, "Age, Race, Class, and Sex: Women Defining Difference," in *Sister Outsider* (Freedom, CA: Crossing Press, 1984), p. 120.

3. C. Wright Mills, *The Sociological Imagination* (New York: Oxford University Press, 1959).
4. For a review of legal changes and challenges ahead, see Jo Freeman, "The Revolution for Women in Law and Public Policy," in Jo Freeman, ed., *Woman: A Feminist Perspective,* 5th ed. (Mountain View, CA: Mayfield, 1995), pp. 365–404.
5. For objections to feminism, see writings by Beverly LaHaye (Concerned Women for America) and Phyllis Schlafly; for critiques of mainstream feminism, see Camille Paglia, *Sexual Personae: Art and Decadence from Nefertiti to Emily Dickinson* (London: Penguin, 1990); Christina Sommers, *Who Stole Feminism?* (New York: Simon & Schuster, 1994); Katie Roiphe, *The Morning After: Sex, Fear, and Feminism* (London: H. Hamilton, 1994).
6. For a summary of the development of the contemporary women's movement, including a review of women's activism from the nineteenth century to the present, see Margaret Andersen, *Thinking about Women: Sociological Perspectives on Sex and Gender,* 3rd ed. (New York: Macmillan, 1993), pp. 277–85. For a representative look at the scholarship of pro-feminist men, see Michael S. Kimmel and Michael A. Messner, eds., *Men's Lives,* 4th ed. (Boston: Allyn & Bacon, 1998).
7. For an overview of public masculinity movements and politics see Michael A. Messner, *Politics of Masculinities: Men in Movements* (Thousand Oaks, CA: Sage, 1998). For a critique of the mythopoetic men's movement, see Michael S. Kimmel and Michael Kaufman, "The New Men's Movement: Retreat and Regression with America's Weekend Warriors," *Feminist Issues* (fall 1993), pp. 3–21. For a look inside Promise Keepers, one of the large evangelical men's organizations, from the perspective of a feminist woman observer, see Donna Minkowitz, "In the Name of the Father" *Ms.* (November/December 1995), pp. 64–71. For a discussion of the Million Man March and the O. J. Simpson case, see Henry Louis Gates, Jr., "Thirteen Ways of Looking at a Black Man," *The New Yorker* (October 23, 1995), p. 56ff. For a presentation of various men's movement positions not represented in this book, see Robert Bly, *Iron John* (New York: Random House, 1990); Stephen B. Boyd, *The Men We Long to Be: Beyond Domination to a New Christian Understanding of Manhood* (New York: HarperCollins, 1995); Warren Farrell, *The Myth of Male Power: Why Men Are the Disposable Sex* (New York: Berkeley Books, 1993); Sam Keen, *Fire in the Belly: On Being a Man* (New York: Bantam, 1991); Keith Thompson, ed., *To Be a Man: In Search of the Deep Masculine* (New York: Putnam, 1991).
8. William Pollock. *Real Boys: Rescuing Our Sons from the Myths of Boyhood* (New York: Random House, 1998); Daniel Kindlon and Michael Thompson, *Raising Cain: Protecting the Emotional Life of Boys* (New York: Ballantine Books, 1999, 2000).
9. Geoffrey Canada. *Reaching Up for Manhood: Transforming the Lives of Boys in America* (Boston: Beacon Press, 1998); Ann Arnett Ferguson, *Bad Boys: Public Schools and the Making of Black Masculinity* (Ann Arbor; University of Michigan Press, 2000); James Garbarino, *Lost Boys: Why Our Sons Turn Violent and How We Can Save Them* (New York: Free Press, 1999, 2000).
10. Christina Hoff Sommers, *The War Against Boys: How Misguided Feminism Is Harming Our Young Men.* (New York: Simon & Schuster, 2000).
11. James Garbarino, "Some Kids Are Orchids," *Time* 154, no. 25 (1999), p. 51.
12. Michael S. Kimmel, *The Gendered Society.* (New York: Oxford University Press, 2000).
13. Kimmel, *The Gendered Society;* William Pollock, *Real Boys.*
14. Susan Faludi, *Stiffed: The Betrayal of Modern Man* (New York: Harper Collins, 1999); Michelle Fine, Lois Weis, Judi Addelston, and Julia Marusza, "(In)Secure

Times: Constructing White Working-Class Masculinities in the Late 20th Century, in Theodore F. Cohen, ed., *Men and Masculinity: A Text Reader* (Belmont, CA: Wadsworth, pp. 422–435 (2001); Sally Robinson, *Marked Men: White Masculinity in Crisis.* New York: Columbia University Press, 2000).

15. Ginger Otis, "Score One for Same-Sex Couples," *Ms.* 10, no. 1 (December 1999/January 2000), p. 22.
16. Natacha Henry, "Voulez-vous Pacser avec moi?" *Ms.*, 10, no. 2 (February/March 2000), p. 32.
17. American Academy of Pediatrics Press Release [no author], "AAP Supports Adoption by Same-Sex Parents" (Feb. 4, 2002. www.aap.org/advocacy/releases/febsamesex.htm).
18. Dana Kennedy, "Groups Fight Florida's Ban on Gay Adoptions," The New York Times on the Web, March 15, 2002. www.nytimes.com/2002/03/15/nati . . ./15ADOP.html?todaysheadlines=&pagewanted=prin
19. Randall Chase, "Estranged Lesbian Partner Is Told to Pay Child Support," *The Boston Globe,* March 18, 2002, p. A3.
20. Barbara Summerhawk, Cheiron McMahill, and Darren McDonald, trans. eds., *Queer Japan: Personal Stories of Japanese Lesbians, Gays, Bisexuals and Transsexuals* (Norwich, VT: New Victoria Publishers, 1998).
21. See, for example, "Jobs and Money: A Small Step Forward for Same-Sex Couples," *The Guardian* (London). (April 7, 2001), p. 7; Ben White, "Conservatives Rip Bush as Soft on Gays" *The Boston Globe,* 260, no. 93 (2001), p. B2.
22. Catherine Holahan, "Mass. Scout Unit Allows Gay Leaders," *The Boston Globe,* 260 no. 32, (Wednesday August 1, 2001), pp. A1, A15; Claudia Kolker, "Scouts Divided: A Fixture Under Seige," *The Boston Globe* (November 26, 2000), p. A25.
23. National Education Association [news release, no author], NEA Board Adopts Plan to Make Schools Safer" February 8, 2002. www.nea.org/nr/nr020208.html
24. Sabine Lang, *Men as Women, Women as Men: Changing Gender in Native American Cultures* (Austin, TX: University of Texas Press, 1998); Stephen O. Murray and Will Roscoe, *Boy-Wives and Female Husbands: Studies in African Homosexualities* (New York: St. Martin's Press, 1998); Will Roscoe, *Changing Ones: Third and Fourth Genders in Native North America* (New York: St. Martin's Press, 1998).
25. Phyllis Burke, *Gender Shock* (New York: Anchor/Doubleday, 1996); Cheryl Chase, "Hermaphrodites with Attitude: Mapping the Emergence of Intersex Political Activism," *GLQ* 4, no. 2 (1998), pp. 189–211; Martha Coventry, "The Tyranny of the Esthetic: Surgery's Most Intimate Violation," *On the Issues,* VII, no. 3 (Summer 1998), pp. 16ff [reprinted in Part V of this book]; Leslie Feinberg, *Transgender Warriors: Making History from Joan of Arc to Ru Paul* (Boston: Beacon Press, 1996); Leslie Feinberg, *Trans Liberation: Beyond Pink or Blue* (Boston: Beacon Press, 1998).
26. Feinberg, *Trans Liberation,* p. 5
27. *UTNE Reader* (September–October 1998); "The Man I Married Was Really A Woman," as told to James Oliver Cury, *Cosmopolitan* (November 1998), pp. 176ff.
28. Michelle Koidin, "Transsexual Union Sanctioned: Chromosomes Key as Couple is Granted Texas Marriage License." *The Boston Globe* (September 7, 2000), p. A18.
29. For ongoing lists of bias-related murders, assaults, arson attacks, bombings, threats, cross burnings, harassment, intimidation, and vandalism, see *Klanwatch Intelligence Report,* published by the Southern Poverty Law Center, Montgomery, AL. For reports on right-wing political activity in general, see *The Public Eye,* published by Political Research Associates, Somerville, MA. For examples of anti-abortion violence, see *Ms.* (May/June 1995). See also Patricia Wong Hall and Victor M Hwang, *Anti-Asian Violence in North America.* (Lanham, MD: Rowman

& Littlefield, 2001); Helen Zia, *Asian American Dreams: The Emergence of an American People.* (New York: Farrar, Straus and Giroux, 2000).

30. Diane E. Lewis. "Workplace Bias Claims Jump After Sept. 11," *The Boston Globe,* 260, no. 145 (November 22, 2001), p. B1.
31. David Crary, "Assaults on Disabled People Called Epidemic, 'Invisible,'" *The Boston Globe,* (Tuesday, December 26, 2000), pp. A20, A21.
32. Derrick Z. Jackson, "High Court Makes a Case for Discrimination," *The Boston Globe,* (Wednesday, February 28, 2001), p. A19.
33. Altha J. Cravy, *Women and Work in Mexico's Maquiladoras* (Lanham, MD: Rowman & Littlefield Publishers, Inc., 1998); Miriam Ching Yoon Louie, *Sweatshop Warriors: Immigrant Women Workers Take on the Global Factory* (Cambridge, MA: South End Press, 2001); Crista Wichterich, *The Globalized Woman: Reports from a Future of Inequality* (New York: Zed Books, 2000).
34. Robert D. Putnam, *Bowling Alone: The Collapse and Revival of American Community* (New York: Simon & Schuster, 2000).
35. Jennifer Baumgardner and Amy Richards, *Manifesta: Young Women, Feminism, and the Future* (New York: Farrar, Straus and Giroux, 2000); Barbara Findlen, ed., *Listen Up: Voices from the Next Feminist Generation* (Seattle: Seal Press, 2001), Rebecca Walker, ed., *To Be Real: Telling the Truth and Changing the Face of Feminism* (New York: Anchor Books, 1995); Uphira Edut, ed., *Body Outlaws: Young Women Write about Body Image and Identity* (Seattle, WA: Seal Press, 1998 and 2000).
36. Anastasia Higginbotham, "Alive and Kicking," *The Women's Review of Books,* XVIII, no. 1 (October 2000), pp. 1ff.
37. Randy Albelda and Chris Tilly, "It's a Family Affair: Women, Poverty, and Welfare" in Diane Dujon and Ann Withorn, eds., *For Crying Out Loud: Women's Poverty in the United States* (Boston: South End Press, 1996), p. 79. (Reprinted in Part VIII of this book.)
38. For anthologies with substantial attention to race, class, and gender, see Endnotes 3 and 4 in the Preface to this book. For a look at some of the voluminous literature available, consider some of the following. For an extensive bibliography on the sociology of women and women's studies, see Margaret L. Andersen, *Thinking about Women* (Boston: Allyn and Bacon, 2000), pp. 353–87. For an extensive bibliography on the sociology of gender, with references to other disciplines as well, see Claire M. Renzetti and Daniel J. Curran, *Women, Men, and Society* (Boston: Allyn & Bacon, 1995), pp. 525-85. For books and journal articles related to African American men, see Don Belton, ed., *Speak My Name: Black Men on Masculinity and the American Dream* (Boston: Beacon Press, 1995); Richard G. Majors and Jacob U. Gordon, eds., *The American Black Male: His Present Status and His Future* (Chicago: Nelson-Hall Publishers, 1994); and Herb Boyd and Robert L. Allen, eds., *Brotherman: The Odyssey of Black Men in America – An Anthology* (New York: Ballantine, 1995). For references to gay, lesbian, bisexual, and queer studies, see Henry Abelove, Michele Aina Barale, and David M. Halperin, eds., *The Lesbian and Gay Studies Reader* (New York: Routledge, 1993); Christie Balka and Andy Rose, eds., *Twice Blessed: On Being Lesbian or Gay and Jewish* (Boston: Beacon Press, 1989); Monica Dorenkamp and Richard Henke, *Negotiating Lesbian and Gay Subjects* (New York: Routledge, 1995); Thomas Geller, ed., *Bisexuality: A Reader and Sourcebook* (Ojai, CA: Times Change Press, 1990); Karla Jay, ed., *Dyke Life: A Celebration of the Lesbian Experience* (New York: Basic Books, 1995); Kobena Mercer, *Welcome to the Jungle: New Positions in Black Cultural Studies* (New York: Routledge, 1994); Michael Warner, ed., *Fear of a Queer Planet* (Minneapolis: University of Minnesota Press, 1993). For information on gender, aging, and other intersections, see especially Eleanor Palo Stoller and Rose Campbell Gibson, eds., *Worlds of Difference: Inequality in the Aging Experience*

(Thousand Oaks, CA: Pine Forge, 1994); and James S. Jackson, Linda M. Chatters, and Robert Joseph Taylor, eds., *Aging in Black America* (Newbury Park, CA: Sage, 1993). For recent writing about Jewish women and men, see Aviva Cantor, *Jewish Women/Jewish Men: The Legacy of Patriarchy in Jewish Life* (San Francisco: Harper-SanFrancisco, 1995); Lynn Davidman and Shelly Tenenbaum, eds. *Feminist Perspectives on Jewish Studies* (New Haven: Yale University Press, 1994); T. M. Rudavsky, *Gender and Judaism: The Transformation of Tradition* (New York: New York University Press, 1995); Rachel Josefowitz Siegel and Ellen Cole, eds., *Celebrating the Lives of Jewish Women: Patterns in a Feminist Sampler* (New York: The Harrington Park Press, 1997). A recent anthology of writings by people with disabilities is Kenny Fries, ed., *Staring Back: The Disability Experience from the Inside Out* (New York: Plume, 1997).

39. For a discussion of hegemonic masculinity, see R. W. Connell, *Gender and Power* (Palo Alto: Stanford University Press, 1987) and Sharon R. Bird, "Welcome to the Men's Club: Homosociality and the Maintenance of Hegemonic Masculinity," *Gender & Society* 10, no. 2 (April 1996), pp. 120–32.

40. Bella English. "Looking Horror in the Eye," *The Boston Globe,* 259 (July 27, 2000), p. F1. For related work see Paul Miller and David Lisak, "Associations between Childhood Abuse and Personality Disorder Symptoms in College Males," *Journal of Interpersonal Violence,* 14, no. 6 (1999), p. 642(1); for a look at men and women who do not repeat destructive patterns from their families, see Steven J. Wolin and Sybil Wolin, *The Resilient Self: How Survivors of Troubled Families Rise above Adversity* (New York: Villard Books, 1994).

41. Julie Peteet, "Male Gender Rituals of Resistance in the Palestinian Intifada," in Mai Ghoussoub and Emma Sinclair-Webb, eds., *Imagined Masculinities: Male Identity and Culture in the Modern Middle East* (London: Saqi books, 2000), pp. 103–26; Nasra Hassan, "An Arsenal of Believers: Talking to the 'Human Bombs,'" *The New Yorker* (November 19, 2001), pp. 36–41.

42. For examples of recent crossover research, see Todd W. Crosset, *Outsiders in the Clubhouse: The World of Women's Professional Golf* (Albany: State University of New York Press, 1995); the late Elliot Liebow, *Tell Them Who I Am: The Lives of Homeless Women* (New York: Penguin, 1993); Lillian Rubin, *Families on the Fault Line* (New York: Harper, 1994); Kathleen Gerson, *No Man's Land: Men's Changing Commitments to Family and Work* (New York: Basic Books, 1993); and Christine L. Williams, *Still a Man's World: Men Who Do "Women's Work"* (Berkeley: University of California Press, 1995); Ronald Takaki, *A Different Mirror: A History of Multicultural America* (Boston: Little, Brown, 1993).

43. See Renate Duelli Klein, "The 'Men-Problem' in Women's Studies: The Expert, the Ignoramus and the Poor Dear," *Women's Studies International Forum 6,* no. 4 (1983), pp. 413–21; Michael Awkward, "A Black Man's Place(s) in Black Feminist Criticism," in Marcellus Blount and George P. Cunningham, eds., *Representing Black Men* (New York: Routledge, 1996), pp. 3–26.

44. Gloria Anzaldúa, *Borderlands/La Frontera: The New Mestiza* (San Francisco: Spinsters/Aunt Lute, 1987); Gloria Anzaldúa, ed., *Making Face, Making Soul/Haciendo Caras: Creative and Critical Perspectives by Women of Color* (San Francisco: Aunt Lute, 1987); Patricia Hill Collins, *Black Feminist Thought: Knowledge, Consciousness, and the Politics of Empowerment* (New York: Routledge, 1990); Patricia Hill Collins, *Fighting Words: Black Women and the Search for Justice* (Minneapolis: University of Minnesota Press, 1998); Audre Lorde, *Sister Outsider* (Freedom, CA: Crossing Press, 1984); Audre Lorde, *A Burst of Light* (Ithaca, NY: Firebrand Books, 1988); Cherrie Moraga and Gloria Anzaldúa, eds., *This Bridge Called My Back: Writings by Radical Women of Color* (Watertown, MA: Persephone Press, 1981); Rebecca Walker, ed., *To Be Real:*

Telling the Truth and Changing the Face of Feminism (New York: Anchor Books, 1995). See also W. E. B. Du Bois, *The Souls of Black Folk* (New York: Penguin, 1989).

45. Du Bois, *Souls,* p. 5.
46. Collins, *Black Feminist Thought,* p. 225.
47. Collins, *Black Feminist Thought,* p. 227.
48. See for example Elly Bulkin, Minnie Bruce-Pratt, and Barbara Smith, *Yours in Struggle: Three Perspectives on Anti-Semitism and Racism* (Ithaca, NY: Firebrand Books, 1984); Judith Katz, *White Awareness: Handbook for Anti-Racist Trainings* (Norman, OK: Oklahoma University Press, 1978); Jane Lazarre, *Beyond the Whiteness of Whiteness: Memoir of a White Mother of Black Sons* (Durham, NC: Duke University Press, 1996); Peggy McIntosh, "White Privilege and Male Privilege: A Personal Account of Coming to See Correspondences through Work in Women's Studies," in Margaret L. Andersen and Patricia Hill Collins, *Race, Class, and Gender, An Anthology* (Belmont, CA: Wadsworth, 1995), pp. 76–87; Ruth Frankenberg, *White Women, Race Matters: The Social Construction of Whiteness* (Minneapolis: University of Minnesota Press, 1993).
49. McIntosh, "White Privilege."
50. Michael S. Kimmel, "Invisible Masculinity," *Society* 30, no. 6 (September/October 1993), pp. 29–30.
51. Paul Kivel, *Uprooting Racism: How White People Can Work for Racial Justice* (Philadelphia: New Society Publishers, 1996), pp. 30–32 and 37–39.
52. For a critique of competition, see Alfie Kohn, *No Contest: The Case Against Competition* (Boston: Houghton Mifflin, 1986).
53. In the 1970s, I had difficulty teaching the concept of social class to students at an elite private college, whereas the working class and poor students I taught at a nearby public college grasped this concept with ease. For a discussion of people with less power as astute observers of those with more power, see Jean Baker Miller, *Toward a New Psychology of Women* (Boston: Beacon Press, 1977).
54. Mark Gerzon, *A Choice of Heroes: The Changing Face of American Manhood* (Boston: Houghton Mifflin, 1992), pp. 235–62.
55. Harry Brod, ed., *The Making of Masculinities: The New Men's Studies* (Boston: Allen & Unwin, 1987); Patricia Hill Collins, *Black Feminist Thought: Knowledge, Consciousness, and the Politics of Empowerment* (New York: Routledge, 1990); Patricia Hill Collins, *Fighting Words: Black Women and the Search for Social Justice* (Minneapolis, MN: University of Minnesota Press, 1998); Sandra Harding, *The Science Question in Feminism* (Ithaca, NY: Cornell University Press, 1986); bell hooks, *Feminist Theory from Margin to Center* (Boston: South End Press, 1984); Evelyn Fox Keller, *Reflections on Gender and Science* (New Haven, CT: Yale University Press, 1985); Kimmel and Messner, *Men's Lives;* Lerner, *The Creation of Patriarchy;* Elizabeth Kamarck Minnich, *Transforming Knowledge* (Philadelphia, PA: Temple University Press, 1990); Joseph H. Pleck and Jack Sawyer, eds., *Men and Masculinity* (Englewood Cliffs, NJ: Prentice Hall, 1974); Ronald Takaki, *A Different Mirror: A History of Multicultural America* (Boston: Little, Brown, 1993).
56. Minnich, *Transforming Knowledge,* pp. 185–87.
57. Harry Brod, "Scholarly Studies of Men: The New Field is an Essential Complement to Women's Studies," *The Chronicle of Higher Education* (March 1990). Reprinted in Karin Bergstrom Costello, ed., *Gendered Voices: Readings from the American Experience* (New York: Harcourt Brace, 1996), pp. 333–36.
58. Lerner, *The Creation of Patriarchy,* p. 220.
59. For some early work on gender by women sociologists, see Jessie Bernard, *Women, Wives, Mothers: Values and Options* (Chicago: Aldine, 1975); Joyce Ladner,

Tomorrow's Tomorrow (Garden City, NY: Doubleday, 1995); Marcia Millman and Rosabeth Moss Kanter, eds., *Another Voice* (Garden City, NY: Doubleday, 1975); Alice Rossi, ed., *Essays on Sex Equality* (Chicago: University of Chicago Press, 1970); Alice Rossi, ed., *The Feminist Papers* (New York: Columbia University Press, 1973); Anne Oakley, *The Sociology of Housework* (London: Mertin Robertson, 1974).

60. For a discussion of research on this issue, see Joseph H. Pleck, "The Gender Role Strain Paradigm: An Update" in Ronald F. Levant and William S. Pollack, eds., *A New Psychology of Men* (New York: Basic Books, 1995), pp. 11–32.
61. Anne Fausto-Sterling, "The Five Sexes: Why Male and Female Are Not Enough," in Karen E. Rosenblum and Toni-Michelle C. Travis, eds., *The Meaning of Difference: American Constructions of Race, Sex and Gender, Social Class, and Sexual Orientation* (New York: McGraw-Hill, 1996), pp. 68–73.
62. Judith Lorber, *Paradoxes of Gender* (New Haven: Yale University Press, 1994), p. 5.
63. Suzanne Pharr, *Homophobia: A Weapon of Sexism* (Chardon Press, Inverness, CA 1988); Adrienne Rich, "Compulsory Heterosexuality and Lesbian Existence," *Signs* 5 (Summer 1980) pp. 631–60.
64. Jennifer Reid Maxcy Myhre talks about reactions she receives as a woman with a crew cut: "'Daddy, is that a boy or a girl?' I hear the six-year-old girl whisper the question as I pass by. I smile at her; she articulates aloud what the adults around her are thinking. Her question does not offend me in the way that the 'What are you, some kinda monk?' from the burly man in the fast food restaurant, or the 'Hey, is that a fag?' shouted at me from behind as I walk hand-in-hand with a man down the street, offends me." "One Bad Hair Day Too Many or the Hairstory of an Androgynous Young Feminist," in Barbara Findlen, ed., *Listen Up: Voices from the Next Feminist Generation* (Seattle, WA: Seal Press, 1995), p. 132.

    I am reminded also of a talk I heard by the former director of a lobbying group for women's issues in Massachusetts. She reported that it was highly unacceptable for women to wear slacks in the Massachusetts State House if they expected to have any influence. She herself had decided to make the concession of wearing skirts and dresses in order to be more effective in her work.
65. Minnie Bruce Pratt, *S/HE* (Ithaca, NY: Firebrand Books, 1995), p. 186.
66. Charles Lemert, *Social Theory: The Multicultural and Classic Readings* (Boulder, CO: Westview Press, 1993). Lemert includes Audre Lorde, Gloria Anzaldúa, Cornell West, and Virginia Woolf, among many others.
67. Takaki, *A Different Mirror: A History of Multicultural America* (Boston: Little, Brown, 1993).
68. Marilyn Frye, "Oppression," in *The Politics of Reality: Essays in Feminist Theory* (Freedom, CA: The Crossing Press, 1983), pp. 1–16.
69. Max Weber, "Class, Status, Party," in S. M. Miller, ed., *Max Weber: Selections from His Work* (New York: Crowell, 1963), p. 43.
70. See Katherine S. Newman, *Falling from Grace: The Experience of Downward Mobility in the American Middle Class* (New York: Free Press, 1988) and *Declining Fortunes: The Withering of the American Dream* (New York: Basic Books, 1993).
71. For discussions of individual survival after painful childhoods, see Linda T. Sanford, *Strong at the Broken Places: Overcoming the Trauma of Childhood Abuse* (New York: Random House, 1990) and Stephen J. Wolin and Sybil Wolin, *The Resilient Self: How Survivors of Troubled Families Rise above Adversity* (New York: Villard Books, 1994).

    For a review of past and current literature on strategies for coping with poverty and racism, as well as some new qualitative data documenting creative responses to poverty among single African American women on AFDC, see Robin L. Jarrett, "Living Poor: Family Life among Single Parent, African-American Women," in *Social Problems* 41, no. 1 (February 1994), pp. 30–49.

72. Lerner, *The Creation of Patriarchy,* pp. 217–19.
73. Sandra Morgen and Ann Bookman, "Rethinking Women and Politics: An Introductory Essay," in Ann Bookman and Sandra Morgen, eds., *Women and the Politics of Empowerment* (Philadelphia: Temple University Press, 1988), p. 4.
74. Elizabeth Janeway, *Powers of the Weak* (New York: Knopf, 1980), p. 167.
75. Janeway, *Powers of the Weak,* p. 168.
76. James Blackwell, *The Black Community: Diversity and Unity* (New York: HarperCollins, 1991).
77. Hester Eisenstein, *Contemporary Feminist Thought* (Boston: G. K. Hall, 1983) cited in Andersen, *Thinking about Women;* Michael Gurian, *The Good Son: Shaping the Moral Development of Our Boys and Young Men* (New York: Jeremy Tarcher/Putnam, 1999, 2000); Kindlon and Thompson, *Raising Cain: Protecting the Emotional Life of Boys* (New York: Ballantine Books, 1999, 2000). Garbarino, *Lost Boys.*
78. Lerner, *The Creation of Patriarchy,* p. 229.

PART I
Social Contexts of Gender

Someday, my son will be called a spic for the first time; this is as much a part of the Puerto Rican experience as the music he gleefully dances to. I hope he will tell me. I hope that I can help him handle the glowing toxic waste of his rage. I hope that I can explain clearly why there are those waiting for him to explode, to confirm their stereotypes of the hot-blooded, bad-tempered Latino male.

MARTÍN ESPADA[1]

Once we acknowledge that all women are affected by the racial order of society, then it becomes clear that the insights of multiracial feminism provide an analytical framework, not solely for understanding the experiences of women of color but for understanding all women, and men, as well.

MAXINE BACA ZINN AND BONNIE THORNTON DILL[2]

The gender system is socially constructed. Political, educational, occupational, and religious institutions, along with the family, create and enforce expectations for how women and men should behave in all known societies. Although the gender rules vary from one cultural setting to another, all settings have such rules, and most of these rules are rooted in patriarchy—the control or dominance of women by men, and the control of less-empowered men by men with more power. Within these institutions, people are systematically socialized to become women or men via complex processes of learning and are frequently bombarded with gender rules from many sources simultaneously.

Although individuals can break or stretch the rules without changing the structures surrounding human lives, individual change will not have much impact on the structures. For example, many individual women in the United States are committed to holding jobs requiring high levels of responsibility and competence but are blocked from promotion for such reasons as sexism, racism, ageism, and homophobia. Men who want to be involved in their children's lives often find it difficult. For some, the need to hold more than one job in order to make ends meet severely limits their time at home. For those with more economic privilege, work demands often require long, inflexible hours at the office. Men who are unemployed and might have more time to spend with their children frequently find their inability to provide economic support to their families humiliating and thus stay away. And men who do find the time to get involved are often met with disbelief and disapproval from health care and educational systems accustomed to dealing only with mothers. Thus, even when individuals are motivated to stretch the boundaries of gender, social structures often impede them.

How we express our maleness or femaleness varies widely from one social context to another. Sociologists, anthropologists, biologists, and others argue convincingly that it is not reproductive biology alone that determines how a person develops. Rather, there is an interaction between one's genetic, biological makeup, usually referred to as *sex*, and the expectations for male and female behavior in the social contexts in which a person lives, usually referred to as *gender*.[3] In an interesting example of nonconformity, David Beuchner, a famous concert pianist, decided to change his gender and become Sara Beuchner. As Sara, she had a much more difficult time finding work; booking agents, and university hiring committees were unprepared and unaccepting of the gender switch, even though her skills at the piano remained unchanged.

Expectations for what constitutes femininity and masculinity along with the options available to different women and men are deeply affected by sexism, poverty, racism, homophobia, heterosexism, and other cultural constraints and expectations. Thus, in order to understand people's identities and opportunities, we need to understand the privilege or oppression that they experience, the historical times and the circumstances in which they are currently living, and the possibilities for empowerment that they encounter or create.

This part of the book includes seven essays that address the experiences of people from various groups: African American (Manning Marable), Asian American (Helen Zia), Latino (Martín Espada), Native American (Paula Gunn Allen), Jewish (Ruth Atkin and Adrienne Rich), transgendered (Kai Wright), and white heterosexual (Peggy McIntosh). The seventh essay in this section provides a conceptual framework that helps us understand the complexities of how race and gender intersect (Maxine Baca Zinn and Bonnie Thornton Dill). Though discrimination or hatred based on race or culture or gender or sexual orientation is described in all of these essays, it is experienced somewhat differently by members of each group. And the historical contexts, including such issues as broken treaties, immigration history, and attitudes and prejudices, vary enough to create different kinds of men and women in each of these groups. Zinn and Dill encourage us to let go of notions about imagined common experiences of "all women" or "all men" and to acknowledge the infinite diversity that we will encounter when we take a closer look not only at various groups but at individuals within those groups.

The authors in Part I identify intersecting oppressions in various combinations and encourage us to think in more complex ways about how people become who they are. They help us to look at what ties people down and what provides unearned privilege. These writers ask for a humane world in which economic and social injustice would not exist.

NOTES

1. Martín Espada, "The Puerto Rican Dummy and the Merciful Son" in Ray González, ed., *Muy Macho: Latino Men Confront Their Manhood* (New York: Doubleday/Anchor, 1996), p. 79.

2. Maxine Baca Zinn and Bonnie Thornton Dill, "Theorizing Difference from Multiracial Feminism," *Feminist Studies 22,* no. 2 (Summer, 1996), pp. 321–31.
3. For more about this issue, see Margaret Andersen, *Thinking about Women: Sociological Perspectives on Sex and Gender,* 3rd ed. (New York: Macmillan, 1993), chapter 2, pp. 21–51; Marion Lowe and Ruth Hubbard, eds., *Woman's Nature* (New York: Pergamon Press, 1983); Anne Fausto-Sterling, *Myths of Gender* (New York: Basic Books, 1985); Ruth Hubbard, M. S. Henifin, and B. Fried, eds., *Women Look at Biology Looking at Women* (Cambridge, MA: Schenckman, 1979).

1

TOWARD BLACK AMERICAN EMPOWERMENT

MANNING MARABLE

A spectre is haunting Black America—the seductive illusion that equality between the races has been achieved, and that the activism characteristic of the previous generation's freedom struggles is no longer relevant to contemporary realities. In collective chorus, the media, the leadership of both capitalist political parties, the corporate establishment, conservative social critics and public policy experts, and even marginal elements of the Black middle class, tell the majority of African-Americans that the factors which generated the social protest for equality in the 1950s and 1960s no longer exist.

The role of race has supposedly "declined in significance" within the economy and political order. And as we survey the current social climate, this argument seems to gain a degree of credibility. The number of Black elected officials exceeds 6,600; many Black entrepreneurs have achieved substantial gains within the capitalist economic system in the late 1980s; thousands of Black managers and administrators appear to be moving forward within the hierarchies of the private and public sector. And the crowning "accomplishment," the November, 1989, election of Douglas Wilder as Virginia's first Black governor, has been promoted across the nation as the beginning of the transcendence of "racial politics."

Wilder Model

The strategy of Jesse Jackson in both 1984 and 1988, which challenged the Democratic Party by mobilizing people of color and many whites around an advanced, progressive agenda for social justice, is dismissed as anachronistic and even "reverse racism." As in the Wilder model, racial advancement is projected as obtainable only if the Negro learns a new political and cultural discourse of the white mainstream. Protest is therefore passe. All the

---

Manning Marable, "Toward Black American Empowerment" (1995). Reprinted with the permission of the author.

legislative remedies which were required to guarantee racial equality, the spectre dictates, have already been passed.

It is never an easy matter to combat an illusion. There have been sufficient gains for African-Americans, particularly within the electoral system and for sectors of the Black petty bourgeoisie in the 1980s, that elements of the spectre seem true. But the true test of any social thesis is the amount of reality it explains, or obscures. And from the vantage point of the inner-cities and homeless shelters, from the unemployment lines and closed factories, a different reality behind the spectre emerges. We find that racism has not declined in significance, if racism is defined correctly as the systemic exploitation of Blacks' labor power and the domination and subordination of our cultural, political, educational and social rights as human beings. Racial inequality continues albeit within the false discourse of equality. Those who benefit materially from institutional racism now use the term "racist" to denounce Black critics who call for the enforcement of affirmative action and equal opportunity legislation.

Behind the rhetoric of equality exists two crises, which present fundamental challenges to African-Americans throughout the decade of the 1990s. There is an "internal crisis"—that is, a crisis within the African-American family, neighborhood, community, cultural and social institutions, and within interpersonal relations, especially between Black males. Part of this crisis was generated, ironically, by the "paradox of desegregation." With the end of Jim Crow segregation, the Black middle class was able to escape the confines of the ghetto. Black attorneys who previously had only Black clients could now move into more lucrative white law firms. Black educators and administrators were hired at predominantly white colleges; Black physicians were hired at white hospitals; Black architects, engineers, and other professionals went into white firms. This usually meant the geographical and cultural schism of elements of Black middle class from the working class and low income African-American population, which was still largely confined to the ghetto.

As Black middle class professionals retreated to the suburbs, they often withdrew their skills, financial resources, and professional contacts from the bulk of the African-American community. There were of course many exceptions, Black women and men who understood the cultural obligation they owed to their community. But as a rule, by the late 1980s, such examples became more infrequent, especially among younger Blacks who had no personal memories or experiences in the freedom struggles of two decades past.

The internal crisis is directly related to an external, institutional crisis, a one-sided, race/class warfare which is being waged against the African-American community. The external crisis is represented as the conjuncture of a variety of factors, including the deterioration of skilled and higher paying jobs within the ghetto, and the decline in the economic infrastructure; the decline in the public sector's support for public housing, health care, education and related social services for low-to-moderate income people; the demise of the enforcement of affirmative action, equal opportunity laws and related civil rights legislation; the increased racial conservatism of both major political parties and the ideological and programmatic collapse of traditional liberalism; and most importantly, the conscious decision by the corporate and public sector managerial elite to "regulate" the Black population through increasingly coercive means.

Violence

The major characteristic of the internal crisis is the steady acceleration and proliferation of *violence,* in a variety of manifestations. The most disruptive and devastating type of violence is violent crime, which includes homicide, forcible rape, robbery, and aggravated assault. According to the *Sourcebook of Criminal Justice Statistics* for 1981, the total number of Americans arrested was nearly 9.5 million. Blacks comprise only 12.5 percent of the total U.S. population, but represented 2.3 million arrests, or about *one-fourth of all arrests.* Black arrests for homicide and non-negligent manslaughter were 8,693, or about 48 percent of all murders committed in the U.S. For robbery, which is defined by law as the use of force or violence to obtain personal property, the number of Black arrests was 74,275, representing 57 percent of all robbery arrests. For aggravated assault, the number of African-Americans arrested was 94,624, about 29 percent of all arrests in this category. For motor vehicle theft, the number of Blacks arrested and charged was 38,905, about 27 percent of all auto theft crimes. Overall, for all violent and property crimes charged, Blacks totaled almost 700,000 arrests in the year 1979, representing nearly one-third of all such crimes.

One of the most controversial of all violent crimes is the charge of forcible rape. Rape is controversial because of the history of the criminal charge being used against Black men by the white racist legal structure. Thousands of Black men have been executed, lynched, and castrated for the imaginary offense of rape. Yet rape or forcible sexual violence is not imaginary when African-American women and young girls are victimized. In 1979, there were 29,068 arrests for forcible rape. Black men comprised 13,870 arrests, or 48 percent of the total. Within cities, where three-fourths of all rapes are committed, Blacks total 54 percent of all persons arrested for rape.

The chief victims of rape are not white women, but Black women. The U.S. Department of Justice's 1979 study of the crime of forcible rape established that overall most Black women are nearly *twice* as likely to be rape victims than are white women. The research illustrated that in one year, about 67 out of 100,000 white women would be rape victims; but the rate for Black and other nonwhite women was 115 per 100,000. In the age group 20 to 34 years, the dangers for Black women increase dramatically. For white women of age 20 to 34, 139 out of 100,000 are rape victims annually. For Black women the same age, the rate is 292 per 100,000. For attempted rape, white women are assaulted at the rate of 196 per 100,000; Black women are attacked sexually at a rate of 355 per 100,000 annually.

There is also a direct correlation between rape victimization and income. In general, poor women are generally the objects of sexual assault; middle class women are rarely raped or assaulted, and wealthy women almost never experience sexual assault. The statistics are clear on this point. White women who live in families earning under $7,500 annually have a 500 percent greater likelihood of being raped than white women who come from households with more than $15,000 income. The gap is even more extreme for African-American women. For Black middle class families, the rate of rape is 22 per 100,000. For welfare and low income families earning below $7,500 annually, the rate for rape is 127 per 100,000. For attempted rape, low income Black women are victimized at a rate of 237 per 100,000 annually.

Intraracial Phenomenon

Rape is almost always intraracial, not interracial. Nine out of ten times, a white rapist's victim is a white female. Ninety percent of all Black women who are raped have been assaulted by a Black male. Sexual violence within the African-American community, therefore, is not something "exported" by whites. It is essentially the brutality committed by Black men against our mothers, wives, sisters, and daughters. It is the worst type of violence, using the gift of sexuality in a bestial and animalistic way, to create terror and fear among Black women.

The type of violence which most directly affects Black men is homicide. Nearly half of all murders committed in any given year are Black men who murder other Black men. But that's only part of the problem. We must recognize, first, that the homicide rate among African-Americans is growing. Back in 1960, the homicide rate for Black men in the U.S. was 37 per 100,000. By 1979, the Black homicide rate was 65 per 100,000, compared to the white male homicide rate of 10 per 100,000. In other words, a typical Black male has a *six to seven times* greater likelihood of being a murder victim than a white male.

The chief victims of homicide in our community are young African-American males. Murder is the fourth leading cause of death for all Black men, and the leading cause of death for Black males of age 20 to 29 years. Today in the U.S., a typical white female's statistical chances of becoming a murder victim are one in 606. For white men, the odds narrow to one chance in 186. For Black women, the odds are one in 124. But for Black men, the chances are one in twenty-nine. For young Black men living in cities who are between age 20 to 29, the odds of becoming a murder victim are *less than one in twenty.* Black young men in American cities today are primary targets for destruction—not only from drugs and police brutality, but from each other.

Social Costs

The epidemic of violence in the Black community raises several related questions. What is the social impact of violence within our neighborhoods? What is the effect of violence upon our children? And most importantly, how do we develop a strategy to reverse the proliferation of Black-against-Black crime and violence?

Violence occurs so frequently in the cities that for many people, it has become almost a "normal" factor. We have become accustomed to burglar alarms and security locks to safeguard our personal property and homes. More than one in three families keeps a gun in their homes. We might try to avoid driving through neighborhoods where crack houses are located. We are trying to avoid the problem, but we're not taking steps to solve it. We need to keep in mind that in most of the violent crime cases, the assailant and the victim live in the same neighborhood, or are members of the same household. Half of all violent deaths are between husbands and wives. Many others include parents killing their children, or children killing parents, or neighbors killing each other. There are hundreds of murders among Blacks for the most trivial reasons—everything from fighting over parking spaces to arguing over five dollars.

Black men are murdering each other in part because of the deterioration of jobs and economic opportunity in our communities. For Black young men, the real unemployment rate exceeds 50 percent in most cities. Overall jobless rates for Black men with less than a high school diploma exceed 15 percent. High unemployment, crowded housing, and poor health care all contribute to an environment of social chaos and disruption, which create destructive values and behaviors.

The most tragic victims of violence are Black children. Black children between the ages of one and four have death rates from homicide which are four times higher than for white children the same age. According to the Children's Defense Fund, Black children are arrested at almost seven times the rates for white children for the most serious violent crimes and are arrested at more than twice the white rates for serious property crimes. More than half of the arrests for African-American teenagers are for serious property crimes or violent crimes. For instance, the arrest rate for Black youth aged 11 to 17 for forcible rape is six times higher than for whites. In terms of rates of victimization, non-white females are almost 40 percent more likely than white females to be raped, robbed, or victims of other violent crimes.

Identity

How do we understand the acts of violence committed by and against our children? We must begin by focusing on the cultural concept of identity. What is identity? It's an awareness of self in the context of one's environment.

Identity is based on the connections between the individual and his or her immediate family and community. We don't exist in isolation of each other. We develop a sense of who we are, of who we wish to become, by interacting with parents, friends, teachers, ministers, co-workers, and others.

Our identity is collective, in that it is formed through the inputs of thousands of different people over many years. If the people relate to an individual in a negative manner, an antisocial or deviant personality will be the result. If children are told repeatedly by teachers or parents that they are stupid, the children will usually do poorly in school, regardless of their natural abilities. If children are told that they are chronic liars and untrustworthy, they will eventually begin to lie and steal. If they are physically beaten by their parents frequently and unjustly, they will learn to resort to physical violence against others. People are not born hateful or violent. There's no genetic or biological explanation for Black-against-Black crime. Violence is *learned* behavior.

Violence between people of color is also directly linked to the educational system. If the curriculum of our public schools does not present the heritage, culture, and history of African-Americans, if it ignores or downgrades our vital contributions to a more democratic society, our children are robbed of their heritage. They acquire a distorted perspective about themselves and their communities. If they believe that African-American people have never achieved greatness, in the sciences, art, music, economics, and the law, how can they excel or achieve for themselves? Despite the many reforms accomplished to create a more culturally pluralistic environment for learning, most of our public schools are in the business of "miseducation" for people of color. Our children are frequently "cultural casualties" in the ideological warfare against Black people.

The dynamics of violence within the African-American community create such chaos and destructiveness, that they provide a justification for the public and private sectors' retreat from civil rights initiatives. The argument of the dominant white elites proceeds thus: "Blacks must bear the responsibility for their own poverty, crime, illiteracy, and oppression. Affirmative action is consequently harmful to Blacks' interests, since it rewards incompetence and advances individuals not on the basis of merit but race alone. Blacks should stop looking to the government to resolve their problems, and take greater initiatives within the private enterprise system to assist themselves. Through private initiatives, moral guidance and sexual abstinence, the status of the Negro will improve gradually without social dissent and disruption."

Sources of Crisis

We need to recognize that, fundamentally, there would be no internal crisis among African-Americans if the political economy and social institutions were designed to create the conditions for genuine democracy and human equality. The external crisis of the capitalist political economy is responsible for the internal crisis. All of the private initiatives, and all of the meager self-help efforts mounted at the neighborhood level, and the doubling of the number of Black entrepreneurs and enterprises, would not in any significant manner reverse the destructive trends which have been unleashed against our people. Institutional racism and class exploitation since 1619 have always been, and remain, the root causes of Black oppression.

Violence also takes the form of the proliferation of illegal drugs within the African-American community. The political economy of crack cocaine creates many more living victims than those who are killed by the drug. Crack is part of the new urban slavery, a method of disrupting lives and "regulating" the masses of our young people who otherwise would be demanding jobs, adequate health care, better schools, and control of their own communities. It is hardly accidental that this insidious cancer has been unleashed within the very poorest urban neighborhoods, and that the police concentrate on petty street dealers rather than those who actually control and profit from the drug traffic. It is impossible to believe that thousands and thousands of pounds of illegal drugs can be transported throughout the country, in airplanes, trucks, and automobiles, to hundreds of central distribution centers with thousands of employees and under the so-called surveillance of thousands of law enforcement officers, unless crack represented at a systemic level a form of social control.

Suicide Rates

The epidemic of violence, in combination with the presence of drugs, has directly contributed to another type of violence—the growth of African-American suicide rates, especially among the young. From 1950 to 1974, the suicide rate of African-American males soared from 6.8 per 100,000 to 11.4 per 100,000. In the same years, the Black female suicide rate rose from 1.6 per 100,000 to 3.5 per 100,000. A 1982 study by Robert Davis noted that nearly one-half of all suicides among Blacks now occur among people between age 20 to 34 years. Within this group, Black males who kill themselves account for 36 percent of the total number of suicides. Davis also observes that within the narrow age range of 25 to 29, the suicide rate among Black males is higher than that for white males in the same age group. For Black men and women who live in urban areas, the suicide rate is twice that for whites of the same age group who live in cities.

These facts must be understood against the background of social history of African-Americans. Traditionally, suicide was almost unknown within the Black community during slavery and the Jim Crow period. Blacks found ways to cope with stress and the constant disappointments of life, from singing the blues to mobilizing their sisters and brothers to fight against forms of oppression. Frantz Fanon's psychiatric insight, that struggle and resistance for the oppressed is therapeutic, is confirmed by the heritage of the Black liberation movement. But when people lose the will to resist oppression, when they no longer can determine their friends or enemies, they lack the ability to develop the mental and spiritual determination to overcome obstacles. Suicide, once an irrational or irrelevant act, becomes both rational and logical within the context of cultural and social alienation.

Death Penalty

The American legal system in the 1980s and 1990s also contributed to the violence within our communities in several ways. The patterns of institutional racism became far more sophisticated, as former President Reagan pursued a policy of appointing conservative, racist, elitist males to the federal district courts and the U.S. circuit courts of appeals. By 1989 Reagan had appointed over 425 federal judges, more than half of the 744 total judgeships. Increasingly, the criminal justice system was employed as a system of social control, for the millions of unemployed and underemployed African-Americans. The essential element of coercion within the justice system, within a racial context, is of course the utilization of the death penalty.

According to one statistical study by David C. Baldus based on over two thousand murder cases in Georgia during the 1970s, people accused of killing whites were about eleven times more likely to be given the death penalty than those who murdered Blacks. Over half of the defendants in white-victim crimes would not have been ordered to be executed if their victims had been African-Americans. Research on the death penalty in Florida during the 1970s illustrates that Florida Blacks who are accused and convicted of murdering whites are five times more likely to be given the death penalty than whites who murder other whites.

As of 30 June 1989, the nation's entire prison population reached 673,565 inmates, more than double the figure of 1980. At the current rate, just to keep pace with the increased penal population, authorities have to add eighteen hundred new prison beds *each week*. At the current rate, the African-American prisoner population by the year 2000 will exceed 600,000, or about one in sixty African-American men, women, and children.

Social Control

Under the conditions of race/class domination, prisons are the principal means for group social control, in order to regulate the labor position of millions of Black workers. Our free market system cannot create full employment for all; and the public sector is unwilling to devote sufficient resources to launch an economic reconstruction of the central cities, which in turn would greatly reduce the drug trade. Consequently, prisons become absolutely necessary for keeping hundreds of thousands of potentially rebellious, dissatisfied and alienated African-American youth off the streets.

Between 1973 and 1986, the average real earnings for young African-American males under 25 years fell by 50 percent. In the same period, the percentage of Black males aged 18 to 29 in the labor force who were able to secure full-time, year-round employment fell from only 44 percent to a meager 35 percent.

Is it accidental that these young Black men, who are crassly denied meaningful employment opportunities, are also pushed into the prison system, and subsequently into permanent positions of economic marginality and social irrelevancy? Within capitalism, a job has never been defined as a human right; but for millions of young, poor Black men and women, they appear to have a "right" to a prison cell or a place at the front on the unemployment line.

Strategy

The struggle against violence requires a break from the strategic analysis of the desegregation period of the 1960s. Our challenge is not to become part of the system, but to transform it, not only for ourselves, but for everyone. We must struggle against an acceptance of the discourse and perceptions of the dominant white political criminal justice and economic elites, in regards to Black-on-Black violence. If we focus solely on the need to construct more prisons and mandatory sentences for certain crimes, the crisis will continue to exist in our cities and elsewhere. People who have a sense of mastery and control in their lives do not violate their neighbors or steal their property.

An effective strategy for empowerment in the 1990s must begin with the recognition that the American electoral political system was never designed to uproot the fundamental causes of Black oppression. Most of the greatest advances in Black political activism did not occur at the ballot box, but in the streets, in the factories, and through collective group awareness and mobilization. Our greatest leaders in this century—Du Bois, Tubman, Garvey, Malcom, Martin, and many more—were not elected officials or governmental bureaucrats. Yet because of the electoral focus of most of the current crop of middle class Black elites, we now tend to think of power as an electoral process. But there is also power when oppressed people acquire a sense of cultural integrity and an appreciation of their political heritage of resistance. There is power when we mobilize our collective resources in the media, educational institutions, housing, health care, and economic development to address issues. There is power when African-American people and other oppressed constituencies mobilize a march or street demonstration, when we use a boycott or picket line to realize our immediate objectives.

A strategy for African-American empowerment means that Black politicians must be held more closely accountable to the interests of Black people.

Power implies the ability to reward and to punish friends and enemies alike. Can Blacks continue to afford to conduct voter registration and education campaigns, and then do nothing to check the voting behavior of our elected officials? Accountability must be measured objectively according to a list of policy priorities, and not determined by political rhetoric at election time. One method to consider could be the creation of "people power" assemblies, popular, local conventions open to the general Black public. Politicians of both major parties would be evaluated and ranked according to their legislative or executive records, and their responses on specific policy questions. Neither the Democratic nor the Republican party can be expected to provide this level of direct accountability.

Forward Path

We are losing the battle for the hearts and minds of millions of young African-Americans, who have no personal memory of the struggles waged to dismantle the system of Jim Crow segregation. They have no personal experience on the picket lines, in street demonstrations, and in the development of community-based organizations which reinforce and strengthen Black families, Black religious, civic, and social institutions. The path forward is to create a new generation of Black leaders who recognize that the effort to achieve social justice and human equality is unfinished, and that the status of Black people in America could easily deteriorate to a new type of repressive environment comparable to legal segregation in the pre–civil rights South. We must identify and cultivate the leadership abilities of young people who display a potential and interest in progressive social change.

We need to recognize that power in American society is exercised by hierarchies and classes, not by individuals. Part of the price for the individualism and blatant materialism within certain elements of the Black upper-middle class since the 1970s has been their alienation from the dilemmas confronting the Black working class, the poor and unemployed. Class elitism of any type, for a segment of the oppressed community, contributes to disintegration of solidarity and a sense of common values, goals and objectives. To end the dynamic of violence, we need to recognize that freedom is not rooted within individualism, in isolation from the majority. No single Black woman or man in America will ever transcend the impact of racism and class exploitation unless all of us, and especially the most oppressed among us, also gain a fundamental level of cultural awareness, collective respect, material security, and educational advancement. This requires a new vision of the struggle for power, a collective commitment to the difficult yet challenging project of remaking humanity and our social environment, rooted in a vision beyond self-hatred, chemical-dependency, and fratricidal violence. This must be at the heart of our strategy for cultural resistance and empowerment for the 1990s and beyond.

2

FROM NOTHING, A CONSCIOUSNESS

HELEN ZIA

Despite my deference to traditional Chinese behavior, the day finally came when I had to disobey my father. I had received several offers of full scholarships to attend college. Like the Chinese who lined up for the imperial civil service examinations in hopes of a new life, I viewed college as my means of escape from the narrow life of making flower shop baby novelties in our dull New Jersey town.

Though my father was proud of my educational achievement, he didn't want me to leave for college. He had already stated his desire for me to attend the closest school to home. When the time came for him to sign the college registration forms, he refused. "The proper place for an unmarried daughter is at home with her parents," he insisted. He wanted to keep me out of trouble until I found a husband to do the overseeing.

I could see the doors to my future slamming shut. At age seventeen, I had never knowingly disobeyed my father. I policed myself, turning down dates, invitations to parties, and even educational opportunities away from home, because I thought Dad would disapprove. I was caught between two conflicting Asian ideals. The Three Obediences* demanded subservience from females, but the primacy of education taught me to seek advancement through study. My American side told me to heed my own call.

Somehow I mustered the courage to shout, "No! I'm going to college." I don't know who was more surprised by my outburst, my father or me. He said nothing more about the subject, and I continued my preparations to leave. I also finally learned that the world wouldn't end if I challenged authority, a lesson I would take with me to college.

My father was right on one account—I intended to look for trouble in the campus political and social movements that appeared on the news each night. The call for civil rights was all around me, beginning in my own high school. Women's liberation offered an alternative to the Three Obediences. Then there was the war in Vietnam, involving yet another Asian enemy. My

*[The daughter obeys the father, the wife obeys the husband, and, eventually, the widow obeys the son.]

father was against the war because he saw U.S. involvement in Southeast Asia as a continuation of American domination over the people of Asia. At the dinner table my father lectured us about the immorality of the war; the next day I'd go to school and sit through government propaganda films and civics teachers condemning the Communist scourge and extolling the importance of the war effort to democracy.

For an Asian American kid, the worst part about the Vietnam War was watching the carnage on the news every night, with people who looked like my mom and dad machine-gunned from U.S. helicopters, scorched by American-made napalm, executed at point-blank range, igniting themselves with gasoline in protest, being massacred in their homes and ridiculed on TV shows. It seemed that we had killed the entire population of Vietnam many times over for all the dead who were reported in the body counts each night.

The constant barrage aimed at stirring up patriotic zeal against the Vietnamese enemy took its toll on Asian Americans, in the same way that the previous hostilities with Japan, China, and North Korea had. Many kids in my school had relatives fighting—and dying—in Vietnam. One classmate could barely look at me because I reminded her of the war that killed her older brother. Encountering her in gym class was awkward and sad. At the dry cleaner's and the doughnut shop where I worked in the summers, plenty of GIs would stop in, and some would have to comment. "They're everywhere, aren't they? "a soldier customer said to his buddy as I handed him his laundered and starched fatigues. I had become the local personification of a war nearly ten thousand miles away. Since I looked like the enemy, I must be the enemy.

At the same time, there was no place for me in the debates over national issues like the war or racial equality. People like me were absent from everything that was considered to be "American"—from TV, movies, newspapers, history, and everyday discussions that took place in the school yard. It was hard to feel American when I wasn't treated like one. Yet I didn't feel Asian, either: I couldn't speak Chinese and I hardly knew Chinatown, let alone China. The void left me with many questions.

In the spring of my senior year in high school, the small group of Asian American undergraduates at Princeton University invited me to an orientation meeting. My incoming first-year class had the largest number of Asian Americans ever—sixteen men and four women, nearly as many as the three upper classes combined. I was excited to be part of this tiny but growing Asian student body, coming to Princeton on a full scholarship, part of the wave that drove the university to open its doors to women for the first time in more than two hundred years. In the decades before my arrival, Princeton and the other Ivy League schools accepted only a few Asian students a year, most likely from Asia, not American-born Asians. Though I graduated from high school at the top of my class, I knew that I never would have been admitted to Princeton were it not for the civil rights movement. I was eager to find this movement, as soon as I could escape the watchful eyes of my parents.

The day of my orientation program happened to coincide with a massive student protest and strike at Princeton. The common areas were a sea of young people with placards, banners, and peace signs. Some were locked in earnest debate; others were simply playing Frisbee in the sun. Excited to have found my element, I headed to the Little Hall dormitory to meet the Asian American students.

When I and the handful of other visiting high school seniors knocked on the door that afternoon, we were shocked to find that our hosts were still asleep. About a half-dozen or so Asian American undergraduates were sprawled in various parts of the dorm suite. Strewn around them were beer cans, liquor bottles, ashtrays full of cigarette butts, and other paraphernalia. I was glad that my non-smoking, teetotaler parents had not come along, or I might never have made it to college after all. Our student mentors had been up all night, protesting, partying, debating the role that Asian American students should play in the Third World liberation movement and antiwar student strikes. They regaled us with tales of their lives as Asian American student protesters. I was on the road to discovering my own identity as an Asian American.

I wasn't alone in my quest. The Asian American baby boomers were all approaching college age. For the first time in American history, we were being admitted into colleges and universities in visible numbers as racial barriers began to come down. Some students were from immigrant families like mine, while others were multi-generation Americans.

The foreign-born Chinese students called us American-born types "jook sings," or "hollow bamboo"—Chinese on the outside, but empty inside. The kids from Hawaii were so much more secure in both their Asianness and their Americanness, having grown up in an Asian American majority; they called Japanese Americans from the mainland "katonks"—empty coconuts. The Chinatown kids seemed streetwise and hip, while students from places such as Phoenix, Buffalo, and Columbus were more like me, having grown up without seeing many faces like our own. Some Asian Americans I met called for Yellow Power, in the same spirit as Black Power advocates; others were so assimilated that they were called "bananas."

For the first time in my life, I heard about the internment of 120,000 Japanese Americans from third-generation—Sansei—Japanese American students. The experience of being incarcerated for presumed disloyalty was so painful that many of their parents refused to discuss it with them. I heard about Chinese "paper sons" who were "adopted" by Chinese men living in the United States after all immigration records were destroyed in the San Francisco earthquake of 1906. And about the Filipino "manongs"—old uncles—who worked the farms of California and the West, moving from harvest to harvest. We taught ourselves much of this information, using dog-eared mimeographed course syllabi gathered from Asian American courses in California and elsewhere like a new Holy Grail.

I began to make the connections between past history and my own life, understanding, for example, how the effort to deport my father in the early 1950s was linked to Chinese Americans of the 1800s. When the Immigration and Naturalization Service debated whether to permit my underemployed father to stay in the United States, the fact that he was the sole breadwinner for two infant U.S. citizens by birth swayed their decision. Henry and I were Americans thanks to an 1898 Supreme Court decision in response to a lawsuit by Wong Kim Ark.

I imagined people with Asian faces taking part in American life in a way that I had never before dreamed possible. A new generation of Asian Americans was injecting itself into national debates on civil rights, equality for women, poverty, workplace and labor issues, South African apartheid—we didn't limit the breadth of our vision. Just like the other baby boomers of all races in that 1960s and 1970s era, we knew we were making history. The excitement of that historical sweep added an element of grandeur to our activities; we weren't afraid to think big.

In the spring of 1971, a joint committee of the black, Latino, and Asian American students decided it was time to make the university address the racial inequities on campus. Princeton had very few students of color then, about a hundred in an undergraduate student body of nearly four thousand. We agreed that life at Princeton for students of color was akin to being stuck in a vast snowdrift, and it was time to thaw the university out. Our small numbers didn't deter us.

The leadership wanted to make a bold, definitive statement, so they decided that our loose grouping of minority students—Third World students—should seize and occupy Firestone Library and call for a massive rally at the University Chapel. We would denounce racism at Princeton and the racist war in Vietnam. We would demand an end to the war, as well as the creation of programs, courses, and a center for Third World students. To a first-year student from a sheltered Confucian home in New Jersey, this was the big time.

Princeton in 1971 was almost entirely male, having admitted its first women undergraduates in 1969. I was one of the half-dozen Asian American women students on campus, and the only one involved in this grandiose plan. Until then I assisted the guys by taking on useful "female" chores like learning to run a mimeograph machine. But this ambitious library plan caught us shorthanded, and somehow I was assigned the task of handling security for the takeover.

Firestone Library is bigger than most castles—and built like one. In my one previous attempt at security, I had installed a padlock on my bedroom door so my brothers wouldn't trash my room; that failed when they screwed the latch off the door. But I took my job very seriously and ran through all of Firestone, getting a good aerobic workout. Our little band of Third World men and a few women entered Firestone one afternoon and refused to come out. We secured the building and declared it occupied. I missed the main action, if there was any, because I was so busy running around and checking all the doors and windows.

The next day, we marched out of Firestone and declared victory before a huge rally at the chapel. My brush with student activism changed my life.

Not just because of my successful tenure as security czar, during which I protected our sit-in from Princeton's wild squirrels, but because of the rally that followed. In the days leading up to our library takeover, it was somehow decided that several Asian Americans should speak about the racism of the Vietnam War. This was an important moment, because, as relative political newcomers, we would often defer to the more numerous black and Latino students. But we had a lot to say about racism and the war, and our Asian faces would make a powerful statement. It was also decided that an Asian woman should be among the speakers.

This idea posed a certain logistical problem, since there were so few Asian American female undergraduates. None of us would do it. I had never spoken to a group larger than my fifth-grade class, and the very idea made my stomach churn. Yet the thought that no one would talk about women of Vietnam and the war seemed terribly wrong. In the course of my patrol runs through Firestone the night before the rally, I decided that someone had to do it, even if it had to be me.

During our triumphant march out of the library and into the crowded chapel, packed with a thousand or more people, I fought nausea and panic. I had never met a Vietnamese woman, and what did I know about war? But my mother's stories rescued me: stories of the war that she had witnessed from her childhood spent fleeing Japanese soldiers, of the terrible brutality, of rape, torture, mutilation, and murder, and of the tremendous will to survive. I managed to walk through the long chapel without stumbling, and to speak of my mother's experiences and the inhumanity of this war.

After the rally, an undergraduate student from Vietnam thanked me. Marius Jansen, one of my professors and a distinguished scholar of Japanese history, gave me a puzzled look and told me I didn't sound like myself at all. His comment made me pause to think, for the first time, about the images I must project as an Asian American woman, and the images that might be projected back on me. Most of all, I was relieved and astonished that I, who a year earlier couldn't correct my teacher's pronunciation of my name, had spoken out loud. This Asian American movement was transforming me in a way such that I might transform others. Through it, I began to find my voice.

Finding my voice didn't always mean that my words were welcome, even among my Asian American pals. One day early in my second year, I was walking across campus with my classmate Alan, a street-smart Chinatown boy from California. We were headed to the newly established Third World Center—the prize from our student strike and occupation of the library. On the way, we argued over the relative importance of race and gender. "The revolution must fight racism first," Alan said to me. "Race is primary. Only after we eliminate racism can we fight sexism. Women will have to wait." It was like being at home with my brothers. I called Alan a male chauvinist; a pig, even.

Furious at such attitudes from our "revolutionary" Asian American brothers, the Asian American women at Princeton organized a seminar on

Asian American women. Our numbers had grown enough to establish the first course on this topic on the East Coast, perhaps in the country. We didn't ask the men *not* to participate, but they didn't anyway. In our own space, we explored the social, historical, and political context of our mothers' and grandmothers' lives in Asia, their journeys to America, their experiences in sweatshops, on plantations, at home. We discussed our lives as Asian American women. I began to understand the Confucian hierarchy that forced women and girls into perpetual subordination. We, on the other hand, vowed never to accept being less than equal to our brothers.

But our class on Asian American women didn't explore the silences that our newly created Asian American "family" imposed on us. We didn't talk about sexual harassment or date rape within our own community. The language and the concepts didn't quite exist yet. But the incidents did. My academic adviser, a distinguished Chinese professor, gave unsolicited advice—about sex—to his female students during their faculty consultations. When the professor added such tidbits to the discussion of my thesis, my newly discovered voice failed me. I had run headlong into the quandary common to women of color and others from beleaguered communities: if we air our dirty laundry, we bring shame on ourselves and our community. With the status of Asian Americans so fragile, why drag down one of the few respected Asian American professors? Years later, I learned that another female student, a European American, had filed a report with the university. The esteemed professor had been disgraced—but, at least, not by one of "his own."

Women's liberation didn't offer much help at the time. I felt alienated after my visits to the campus women's center. The women I met were more interested in personal consciousness raising than social consciousness raising. I wanted to do both, but their lives as white women were so removed from mine, which was entwined with my life as an Asian American. Yet this distance didn't prove that race was primary, either. Other experiences made that clear, such as the time I met Gus Hall, a perennial candidate for president, on the ticket of the American Communist Party. He was speaking at Princeton with his running mate, Herbert Aptheker. Some Third World students were invited to a small luncheon for them; Alan and I went as representatives of the newly formed Asian American Students Association. Throughout the entire reception and luncheon, Hall and Aptheker, who were both white, spoke primarily to the African American students, pointedly ignoring Alan and me. To these American Communists, Asian Americans had no political currency; in their eyes, we didn't exist, or perhaps they assumed from our Asian faces that we were predisposed to support China, a bitter foe of the Soviets. It was the first time I witnessed such a blatant race ploy by political "progressives," but it wouldn't be the last.

A whole generation of Asian Americans was getting an education about our identity. We couldn't wait to leave the safe confines of our campuses, to share our lessons and our pride in this newfound heritage. Many of us went into Asian American enclaves as community organizers, intent on making changes there. Our campus experiences made it abundantly clear that if Asian Americans were to take our rightful place in American society, we would have to scratch and dig and blast our way in, much as the railroad workers had through the Rockies one hundred years earlier.

Few in America, or even in our own communities, paid much attention to these young Asian Americans. Among the separate—and expanding—Asian immigrant groups, the vision of pan-Asian unity was not compelling; survival was their main focus.

Still, a dynamic process was set in motion: we were reclaiming our stake in a land and a history that excluded us, transforming a community that was still in the process of becoming. We were following our destinies as Asian Americans.

3

THE PUERTO RICAN DUMMY AND THE MERCIFUL SON

MARTÍN ESPADA

I have a four-year-old son named Clemente. He is not named for Roberto Clemente, the baseball player, as many people are quick to guess, but rather for a Puerto Rican poet. His name, in translation, means "merciful." Like the cheetah, he can reach speeds of up to sixty miles an hour. He is also, demographically speaking, a Latino male, a "macho" for the twenty-first century.

Two years ago, we were watching television together when a ventriloquist appeared with his dummy. The ventriloquist was Anglo; the dummy was a Latino male, Puerto Rican, in fact, like me, like my son. Complete with pencil mustache, greased hair, and jawbreaking Spanish accent, the dummy acted out an Anglo fantasy for an Anglo crowd that roared its approval. My son was transfixed; he did not recognize the character onscreen because he knows no one who fits that description, but he sensed my discomfort. Too late, I changed the channel. The next morning, my son watched Luis and María on *Sesame Street*, but this is inadequate compensation. *Sesame Street* is

---

the only barrio on television, the only neighborhood where Latino families live and work, but the comedians are everywhere, with that frat-boy sneer, and so are the crowds.

However, I cannot simply switch off the comedians, or explain them (how do you explain to a preschooler that a crowd of strangers is angrily laughing at the idea of *him?*). We live in western Massachusetts, not far from Springfield and Holyoke, hardscrabble small cities that, in the last generation, have witnessed a huge influx of Puerto Ricans, now constituting some of the poorest Puerto Rican communities in the country. The evening news from Springfield features what I call the "Puerto Rican minute." This is the one minute of the newscast where we see the faces of Puerto Rican men, the mug shot or the arraignment in court or witnesses pointing to the bloodstained sidewalk, while the newscaster solemnly intones the mantra of gangs, drugs, jail. The notion of spending the Puerto Rican minute on a teacher or a health care worker or an artist in the community never occurs to the television journalists who produce this programming.

The Latino male is the bogeyman of the Pioneer Valley, which includes the area where we live. Recently, there was a rumor circulating in the atmosphere that Latino gangs would be prowling the streets on Halloween, shooting anyone in costume. My wife, Katherine, reports that one Anglo gentleman at the local swimming pool took responsibility for warning everyone, a veritable Paul Revere in swim trunks wailing that "The Latinos are going to kill kids on Halloween!" Note how 1) Latino gangs became "Latinos" and 2) Latinos and "kids" became mutually exclusive categories. My wife wondered if this warning contemplated the Latino males in her life, if this racially paranoid imagination included visions of her professor husband and his toddling offspring as gunslingers in full macho swagger, hunting for "gringos" in Halloween costumes. The rumor, needless to say, was unfounded.

Then there is the national political climate. In 1995, we saw the spectacle of a politician, California Governor Pete Wilson, being seriously considered for the presidency on the strength of his support for Proposition 187, the most blatantly anti-Latino initiative in recent memory. There is no guarantee, as my son grows older, that this political pendulum will swing back to the left; if anything, the pendulum may well swing farther to the right. That means more fear and fury and bitter laughter.

Into this world enters Clemente, which raises certain questions: How do I think of my son as a Latino male? How do I teach him to disappoint and disorient the bigots everywhere around him, all of whom have bought tickets to see the macho pantomime? At the same time, how do I teach him to inoculate himself against the very real diseases of violence and sexism and homophobia infecting our community? How do I teach Clemente to be Clemente?

My son's identity as a Puerto Rican male has already been reinforced by a number of experiences I did not have at so early an age. At age four, he has already spent time in Puerto Rico, whereas I did not visit the island until I was ten years old. From the time he was a few months old, he has witnessed his Puerto Rican father engaged in the decidedly nonstereotypical business of giving poetry readings. We savor new Spanish words together the same way we devour mangoes together, knowing the same tartness and succulence.

And yet, that same identity will be shaped by negative as well as positive experiences. The ventriloquist and his Puerto Rican dummy offered Clemente a glimpse of his inevitable future: not only bigotry, but his growing awareness of that bigotry, his realization that some people have contempt for him because he is Puerto Rican. Here his sense of maleness will come into play, because he must learn to deal with his own rage, his inability to extinguish the source of his torment.

My father has good reason for rage. A brown-skinned man, he learned rage when he was arrested in Biloxi, Mississippi, in 1950, and spent a week in jail for refusing to go to the back of the bus. He learned rage when he was denied a college education and instead struggled for years working for an electrical contractor, hating his work and yearning for so much more. He learned rage as the political triumphs of the 1960s he helped to achieve were attacked from without and betrayed from within. My father externalized his rage. He raged at his enemies and he raged at us. A tremendous ethical and cultural influence for us nonetheless, he must have considered himself a failure by the male career-obsessed standards of the decade into which I was born: the 1950s.

By adolescence, I had learned to internalize my rage. I learned to do this, not so much in response to my father, but more in response to my own growing awareness of bigotry. Having left my Brooklyn birthplace for the town of Valley Stream, Long Island, I was dubbed a spic in an endless torrent of taunting, bullying, and brawling. To defend myself against a few people would have been feasible; to defend myself against dozens and dozens of people deeply in love with their own racism was a practical impossibility. So I told no one, no parent or counselor or teacher or friend, about the constant racial hostility. Instead, I punched a lamp, not once but twice, and watched the blood ooze between my knuckles as if somehow I could leech the poison from my body. My evolving manhood was defined by how well I could take punishment, and paradoxically I punished myself for not being man enough to end my own humiliation. Later in life, I would emulate my father and rage openly. Rarely, however, was the real enemy within earshot, or even visible.

Someday, my son will be called a spic for the first time; this is as much a part of the Puerto Rican experience as the music he gleefully dances to. I hope he will tell me. I hope that I can help him handle the glowing toxic waste of his rage. I hope that I can explain clearly why there are those waiting for him to explode, to confirm their stereotypes of the hot-blooded, bad-tempered Latino male who has, without provocation, injured the Anglo innocents. His anger—and that anger must come—has to be controlled, directed, creatively channeled, articulated—but not all-consuming, neither destructive nor self-destructive. I keep it between the covers of the books I write.

The anger will continue to manifest itself as he matures and discovers the utter resourcefulness of bigotry, the ability of racism to change shape and survive all attempts to snuff it out. "Spic" is a crude expression of certain sentiments that become subtle and sophisticated and insidious at other levels. Speaking of crudity, I am reminded of a group organized by white ethnics in New York during the 1960s under the acronym of SPONGE: The Society for the Prevention of the Niggers Getting Everything. When affirmative action is criticized today by Anglo politicians and pundits with exquisite diction and erudite vocabulary, that is still SPONGE. When and if my son is admitted to school or obtains a job by way of affirmative action, and is resented for it by his colleagues, that will be SPONGE, too.

Violence is the first cousin to rage. If learning to confront rage is an important element of developing Latino manhood, then the question of violence must be addressed with equal urgency. Violence is terribly seductive; all of us, especially males, are trained to gaze upon violence until it becomes beautiful. Beautiful violence is not only the way to victory for armies and football teams; this becomes the solution to everyday problems as well. For many characters on the movie or television screen, problems are solved by *shooting* them. This is certainly the most emphatic way to win an argument.

Katherine and I try to minimize the seductiveness of violence for Clemente. No guns, no soldiers, and so on. But his dinosaurs still eat each other with great relish. His trains still crash, to their delight. He is experimenting with power and control, with action and reaction, which brings him to an imitation of violence. Needless to say, there is a vast difference between stegosaurus and Desert Storm.

Again, all I can do is call upon my own experience as an example. I not only found violence seductive; at some point, I found myself enjoying it. I remember one brawl in Valley Stream when I snatched a chain away from an assailant, knocked him down, and needlessly lashed the chain across his knees as he lay sobbing in the street. That I was now the assailant with the chain did not occur to me.

I also remember the day I stopped enjoying the act of fistfighting. I was working as a bouncer in a bar, and found myself struggling with a man who was so drunk that he appeared numb to the blows bouncing off his cranium. Suddenly, I heard my fist echo: *thok.* I was sickened by the sound. Later, I learned that I had broken my right ring finger with that punch, but all I could recall was the headache I must have caused him. I never had a fistfight again. Parenthetically, that job ended another romance: the one with alcohol. Too much of my job consisted of ministering to people who had passed out at the bar, finding their hats and coats, calling a cab, dragging them in their stupor down the stairs. Years later, I channeled those instincts cultivated as a bouncer into my work as a legal services lawyer, representing Latino tenants, finding landlords who forgot to heat buildings in winter or exterminate rats to be more deserving targets of my wrath. Eventually, I even left the law.

Will I urge my son to be a pacifist, thereby gutting one of the foundations of traditional manhood, the pleasure taken in violence and the power derived from it? That is an ideal state. I hope that he lives a life that permits him pacifism. I hope that the world around him evolves in such a way that pacifism is a viable choice. Still, I would not deny him the option of physical self-defense. I would not deny him, on philosophical grounds, the right to resistance in any form that resistance must take to be effective. Nor would I have him deny that right to others, with the luxury of distance. Too many people in this world still need a revolution.

When he is old enough, Clemente and I will talk about matters of justification, which must be carefully and narrowly defined. He must understand that abstractions like "respect" and "honor" are not reasons to fight in the street, and abstractions like "patriotism" and "country" are not reasons to fight on the battlefield. He must understand that violence against women is not acceptable, a message which will have to be somehow repeated every time another movie trailer blazes the art of misogyny across his subconscious mind. Rather than sloganizing, however, the best way I can communicate that message is by the way I treat his mother. How else will he know that jealousy is not love, that a lover is not property?

Knowing Katherine introduced me to a new awareness of many things: compassion and intimacy, domestic violence and recovery. Her history of savage physical abuse as a child—in a Connecticut farming community—compelled me to consider what it means to heal another human being, or to help that human being heal herself. What small gestures begin to restore humanity?

WHEN THE LEATHER IS A WHIP

At night,
with my wife
sitting on the bed,
I turn from her
to unbuckle
my belt
so she won't see
her father
unbuckling
his belt

Clemente was born on December 28, 1991. This was a difficult birth. Katherine's coccyx, or tailbone, broken in childhood, would break again during delivery. Yet only with the birth could we move from gesture to fulfillment, from generous moments to real giving. The extraordinary healing that took place was not only physical but emotional and spiritual as well. After years of constant pain, her coccyx bone set properly, as if a living metaphor for the new opportunity represented by the birth of this child.

WHITE BIRCH

Two decades ago rye whiskey
scaled your father's throat,
stinking from the mouth
as he stamped his shoe
in the groove between your hips,
dizzy flailing cartwheel down the stairs.

The tail of your spine split,
became a scraping hook.
For twenty years a fire raced
across the boughs of your bones,
his drunken mouth a movie
flashing with every stabbed gesture.

Now the white room of birth is throbbing:
the numbers palpitating red on the screen of machinery
tentacled to your arm; the oxygen mask wedged
in a wheeze on your face; the numbing medication
injected through the spine.
The boy was snagged on that spiraling bone.

Medical fingers prodded your raw pink center
while you stared at a horizon of water
no one else could see, creatures leaping silver
with tails that slashed the air
like your agonized tongue.

You were born in the river valley,
hard green checkerboard of farms,
a town of white birches
and a churchyard from the workhorse time,
weathered headstones naming women
drained of blood with infants coiled inside
the caging hips, hymns swaying
as if lanterns over the mounded earth.

Then the white birch of your bones,
resilient and yielding, yielded again,
root snapped as the boy spilled out of you
into hands burst open by beckoning
and voices pouring praise like water,
two beings tangled in exhaustion,
blood-painted, but full of breath.
After a generation of burning

the hook unfurled in your body,
the crack in the bone dissolved:
One day you stood, expected again
the branch of nerves
fanning across your back to flame,
and felt only the grace of birches.

Obviously, my wife and son had changed me, had even changed my poetry. This might be the first Puerto Rican poem swaying with white birch trees instead of coconut palms. On the other hand, Katherine and I immediately set about making this a Puerto Rican baby. I danced him to sleep with blaring salsa. Katherine painted *coquís*—tiny Puerto Rican frogs—on his pajamas. We spoon-fed him rice and beans. He met his great-grandmother in Puerto Rico.

The behavior we collectively refer to as "macho" has deep historical roots, but the trigger is often a profound insecurity, a sense of being threatened. Clemente will be as secure as possible, and that security will stem in large part from self-knowledge. He will know the meaning of his name.

Clemente Solo Vélez was a great Puerto Rican poet, a fighter for the independence of Puerto Rico who spent years in a prison as a result. He was also our good friend. The two Clementes met once, when the elder Clemente was eighty-seven years old and the younger Clemente was nine months. Fittingly, it was Columbus Day, 1992, the five-hundredth anniversary of the conquest. We passed the day with a man who devoted his life and his art to battling the very colonialism personified by Columbus. The two Clementes traced the topography of one another's faces. Even from his sickbed, the elder Clemente was gentle and generous. We took photographs, signed books. Clemente Solo Vélez died the following spring, and eventually my family and I visited the grave in the mountains of Puerto Rico. We found the grave unmarked but for a stick with a number and letter, so we bought a gravestone and gave the poet his name back. My son still asks to see the framed photograph of the two Clementes, still asks about the man with the long white hair who gave him *his* name. This will be family legend, family ritual, the origins of the name explained in greater and greater detail as the years pass, a source of knowledge and power as meaningful as the Book of Genesis.

Thankfully, Clemente also has a literal meaning: "merciful." Every time my son asks about his name, an opportunity presents itself to teach the power of mercy, the power of compassion. When Clemente, in later years, consciously acts out these qualities, he does so knowing that he is doing what his very name expects of him. His name gives him the beginnings of a moral code, a goal to which he can aspire. "Merciful": Not the first word scrawled on the mental blackboard next to the phrase "Puerto Rican male." Yet how appropriate, given that, for Katherine and me, the act of mercy has become an expression of gratitude for Clemente's existence.

BECAUSE CLEMENTE MEANS MERCIFUL

—for Clemente Gilbert-Espada
February 1992

At three AM, we watched
the emergency room doctor
press a thumb against your cheekbone
to bleach your eye with light.
The spinal fluid was clear, drained
from the hole in your back,
but the X ray film
grew a stain on the lung,
explained the seizing cough,
the wailing heat of fever:
pneumonia at the age
of six weeks, a bedside vigil.
Your mother slept beside you,
the stitches of birth still burning.
When I asked, "Will he be OK?"
no one would answer: "Yes."
I closed my eyes and dreamed
my father dead, naked on a steel table
as I turned away. In the dream,
when I looked again,
my father had become my son.

So the hospital kept us: the oxygen mask,
a frayed wire taped to your toe
for reading the blood,
the medication forgotten from shift to shift,
a doctor bickering with radiology over the film,
the bald girl with a cancerous rib removed,
the pediatrician who never called, the yawning intern,
the hospital roommate's father
from Guatemala, ignored by the doctors
as if he had picked their morning coffee,
the checkmarks and initials at five AM,
the pages of forms flipping like a deck of cards,
recordkeeping for the records office,
the lawyers and the morgue.

One day, while the laundry
in the basement hissed white sheets,
and sheets of paper documented dwindling breath,
you spat mucus, gulped air, and lived.
We listened to the bassoon of your lungs,
the cadenza of the next century, resonate.

The Guatemalan father
did not need a stethoscope to hear
the breathing, and he grinned.
I grinned too, and because Clemente
means merciful, stood beside the Guatemalteco,
repeating in Spanish everything
that was not said to him.

I know someday you'll stand beside
the Guatemalan fathers,
speak in the tongue
of all the shunned faces,
breathe in a music
we have never heard, and live
by the meaning of your name.

Inevitably, we try to envision the next century. Will there be a men's movement in twenty years, when my son is an adult? Will it someday alienate and exclude Clemente, the way it has alienated and excluded me? The counterculture can be as exclusive and elitist as the mainstream; to be kept out of both is a supreme frustration. I sincerely do not expect the men's movement to address its own racism. The self-congratulatory tone of that movement drowns out any significant self-criticism. I only wish that the men's movement wouldn't be so *proud* of its own ignorance. The blatant expropriation of Native American symbols and rituals by certain factions of the movement leaves me with a twitch in my face. What should Puerto Rican men do in response to this colonizing definition of maleness, particularly considering the presence of our indigenous Tanío blood?

I remember watching one such men's movement ritual, on public television, I believe, and becoming infuriated because the drummer couldn't keep a beat. I imagined myself cloistered in a tent with some Anglo accountant from the suburbs of New Jersey, stripped to the waist and whacking a drum with no regard for rhythm, the difference being that I could hear Mongo Santamaría in my head, and he couldn't. I am torn between hoping that the men's movement reforms itself by the time my son reaches adulthood, or that it disappears altogether, its language going the way of Esperanto.

Another habit of language that I hope is extinct by the time Clemente reaches adulthood is the Anglo use of the term "macho." Before this term came into use to define sexism and violence, no particular ethnic or racial group was implicated by language itself. "Macho," as employed by Anglos, is a Spanish word that particularly seems to identify Latino male behavior as the very standard of sexism and violence. This connection, made by Anglos both intuitively and explicitly, then justifies a host of repressive measures against Latino males, as our presence on the honor roll of many a jail and prison will attest. In nearby Holyoke, police officers routinely round up Puerto Rican men drinking beer on the stoop, ostensibly for violating that city's "open container" ordinance, but also as a means of controlling the perceived threat of macho volatility on the street. Sometimes, of course, that perception turns deadly. I remember, at age fifteen, hearing about a friend of my father's, Martín "Tito" Pérez, who was "suicided" in a New York City jail cell. A grand jury determined that it is possible for a man to hang himself with his hands cuffed behind him.

While Latino male behavior is, indeed, all too often sexist and violent, Latino males in this country are in fact no worse in that regard than their Anglo counterparts. Arguably, European and European-American males have set the world standard for violence in the twentieth century, from the Holocaust to Hiroshima to Vietnam.

Yet, any assertiveness on the part of Latino males, especially any form of resistance to Anglo authority, is labeled macho and instantly discredited. I can recall one occasion, working for an "alternative" radio station in Wisconsin, when I became involved in a protest over the station's refusal to air a Spanish-language program for the local Chicano community. When a meeting was held to debate the issue, the protesters, myself included, became frustrated and staged a walkout. The meeting went on without us, and we later learned we were *defended,* ironically enough, by someone who saw us as acting macho. "It's their culture," this person explained apologetically to the gathered liberal intelligentsia. We got the program on the air.

I return, ultimately, to that ventriloquist and his Puerto Rican dummy, and I return, too, to the simple fact that my example as a father will have much to do with whether Clemente frustrates the worshippers of stereotype. To begin with, my very *presence*—as an attentive father and husband—contradicts the stereotype. However, too many times in my life, I have been that Puerto Rican dummy, with someone else's voice coming out of my mouth, someone else's hand in my back making me flail my arms. I have read aloud a script of cruelty or rage, and swung wildly at imagined or distant enemies. I have satisfied audiences who expected the macho brute, who were thrilled when my shouting verified all their anthropological theories about my species. I served the purposes of those who would see the Puerto Rican species self-destruct, become as rare as the parrots of our own rain forest.

But in recent years, I have betrayed my puppeteers and disappointed the crowd. When my new sister-in-law met me, she pouted that I did not look Puerto Rican. I was not as "scary" as she expected me to be; I did not roar or flail. When a teacher at a suburban school invited me to read there, and openly expressed the usual unspoken expectations, the following incident occurred, proving that sometimes a belly laugh is infinitely more revolutionary than the howl of outrage that would have left me pegged, yet again, as a snarling, stubborn macho.

MY NATIVE COSTUME

When you come to visit,
said a teacher
from the suburban school,

don't forget to wear
your native costume.

But I'm a lawyer,
I said.
My native costume
is a pinstriped suit.

You know, the teacher said,
a Puerto Rican costume.

Like a guayabera?
The shirt? I said.
But it's February.

The children want to see
a native costume,
the teacher said.

So I went
to the suburban school,
embroidered guayabera
short sleeved shirt
over a turtleneck,
and said, Look kids
cultural adaptation.

The Puerto Rican dummy brought his own poems to read today. *Claro que sí.* His son is always watching.

4

ANGRY WOMEN ARE BUILDING
Issues and Struggles Facing American Indian Women Today

PAULA GUNN ALLEN

The central issue that confronts American Indian women throughout the hemisphere is survival, *literal survival*, both on a cultural and biological level. According to the 1980 census, the population of American Indians is just over one million. This figure, which is disputed by some American Indians, is probably a fair estimate, and it carries certain implications.

Some researchers put our pre-contact population at more than 45 million, while others put it around 20 million. The U.S. government long put it at 450,000—a comforting if imaginary figure, though at one point it was put around 270,000. If our current population is around one million; if, as some researchers estimate, around 25 percent of Indian women and 10 percent of Indian men in the United States have been sterilized without informed consent; if our average life expectancy is, as the best informed research presently says, 55 years; if our infant mortality rate continues at well above national standards; if our average unemployment for all segments of our population—male, female, young, adult, and middle-aged—is between 60 and 90 percent; if the U.S. government continues its policy of termination, relocation, removal, and assimilation along with the destruction of wilderness, reservation land, and its resources, and severe curtailment of hunting, fishing, timber harvesting, and water-use rights—then existing tribes are facing the threat of extinction, which for several hundred tribal groups has already become fact in the past five hundred years.

In this nation of more than 200 million, the Indian people constitute less than one-half of one percent of the population. In a nation that offers refuge, sympathy, and billions of dollars in aid from federal and private sources in the form of food to the hungry, medicine to the sick, and comfort to the dying, the indigenous subject population goes hungry, homeless, impoverished, cut out of the American deal, new, old, and in between. Americans are daily made aware of the worldwide slaughter of native peoples such as the Cambodians, the Palestinians, the Armenians, the Jews—who constitute

---

only a few groups faced with genocide in this century. We are horrified by South African apartheid and the removal of millions of indigenous African black natives to what is there called "homelands"—but this is simply a replay of nineteenth-century U.S. government removal of American Indians to reservations. Nor do many even notice the parallel or fight South African apartheid by demanding an end to its counterpart within the border of the United States. The American Indian people are in a situation comparable to the imminent genocide in many parts of the world today. The plight of our people north and south of us is no better; to the south it is considerably worse. Consciously or unconsciously, deliberately as a matter of national policy, or accidentally as a matter of "fate," *every single government,* right, left, or centrist, in the western hemisphere is consciously or subconsciously dedicated to the extinction of those tribal people who live within its borders.

Within this geopolitical charnel house, American Indian women struggle on every front for the survival of our children, our people, our self-respect, our value systems, and our way of life. The past five hundred years testify to our skill at waging this struggle: for all the varied weapons of extinction pointed at our hands, we endure.

We survive war and conquest; we survive colonization, acculturation, assimilation; we survive beating, rape, starvation, mutilation, sterilization, abandonment, neglect, death of our children, our loved ones, destruction of our land, our homes, our past, and our future. We survive, and we do more than just survive. We bond, we care, we fight, we teach, we nurse, we bear, we feed, we earn, we laugh, we love, we hang in there, no matter what.

Of course, some, many of us, just give up. Many are alcoholics, many are addicts. Many abandon children, the old ones. Many commit suicide. Many become violent, go insane. Many go "white" and are never seen or heard from again. But enough hold on to their traditions and their ways so that even after almost five hundred brutal years, we endure. And we even write songs and poems, make paintings and drawings that say "We walk in beauty. Let us continue."

Currently our struggles are on two fronts: physical survival and cultural survival. For women this means fighting alcoholism and drug abuse (our own and that of our husbands, lovers, parents, children);[1] poverty; affluence—a destroyer of people who are not traditionally socialized to deal with large sums of money; rape, incest, battering by Indian men; assaults on fertility and other health matters by the Indian Health Service and the Public Health Service; high infant mortality due to substandard medical care, nutrition, and health information; poor educational opportunities or education that takes us away from our traditions, language, and communities; suicide, homicide, or similar expressions of self-hatred; lack of economic opportunities; substandard housing; sometimes violent and always virulent racist attitudes and behavior directed against us by an entertainment and education system that wants only one thing from Indians: our silence, our invisibility, and our collective death.

A headline in the *Navajo Times* in the fall of 1979 reported that rape was the number one crime on the Navajo reservation. In a professional mental health journal of the Indian Health Services, Phyllis Old Dog Cross reported that incest and rape are common among Indian women seeking services and that their incidence is increasing. "It is believed that at least 80 percent of the Native Women seen at the regional psychiatric service center (5 state area) have experienced some sort of sexual assault."[2] Among the forms of abuse being suffered by Native American women, Old Dog Cross cites a recent phenomenon, something called "training." This form of gang rape is "a punitive act of a group of males who band together and get even or take revenge on a selected woman."[3]

These and other cases of violence against women are powerful evidence that the status of women within the tribes has suffered grievous decline since contact, and the decline has increased in intensity in recent years. The amount of violence against women, alcoholism, and violence, abuse, and neglect by women against their children and their aged relatives have all increased. These social ills were virtually unheard of among most tribes fifty years ago, popular American opinion to the contrary. As Old Dog Cross remarks:

> Rapid, unstable and irrational change was required of the Indian people if they were to survive. Incredible loss of all that had meaning was the norm. Inhuman treatment, murder, death, and punishment was a typical experience for all the tribal groups and some didn't survive.
>
> The dominant society devoted its efforts to the attempt to change the Indian into a white-Indian. No inhuman pressure to effect this change was overlooked. These pressures included starvation, incarceration, and enforced education. Religious and healing customs were banished.
>
> In spite of the years of oppression, the Indian and the Indian spirit survived. Not, however, without adverse effect. One of the major effects was the loss of cultured values and the concomitant loss of personal identity. . . . The Indian was taught to be ashamed of being Indian and to emulate the non-Indian. In short, "white was right." For the Indian male, the only route to be successful, to be good, to be right, and to have an identity was to be as much like the white man as he could.[4]

Often it is said that the increase of violence against women is a result of various sociological facts such as oppression, racism, poverty, hopelessness, emasculation of men, and loss of male self-esteem as their own place within traditional society has been systematically destroyed by increasing urbanization, industrialization, and institutionalization, but seldom do we notice that for the past forty to fifty years, American popular media have depicted American Indian men as bloodthirsty savages devoted to treating women cruelly. While traditional Indian men seldom did any such thing—and in fact among most tribes abuse of women was simply unthinkable, as was abuse of children or the aged—the lie about "usual" male Indian behavior seems to have taken root and now bears its brutal and bitter fruit.

Image casting and image control constitute the central process that American Indian women must come to terms with, for on that control rests our sense of self, our claim to a past and to a future that we define and that we build. Images of Indians in media and education materials profoundly influence how we act, how we relate to the world and to each other, and how we value ourselves. They also determine to a large extent how our men act toward us, toward our children, and toward each other. The popular American media image of Indian people as savages with no conscience, no compassion, and no sense of the value of human life and human dignity was hardly true of the tribes—however true it was of the invaders. But as Adolf Hitler noted a little over fifty years ago, if you tell a lie big enough and often enough, it will be believed. Evidently, while Americans and people all over the world have been led into a deep and unquestioned belief that American Indians are cruel savages, a number of American Indian men have been equally deluded into internalizing that image and acting on it. Media images, literary images, and artistic images, particularly those embedded in popular culture, must be changed before Indian women will see much relief from the violence that destroys so many lives.

To survive culturally, American Indian women must often fight the United States government, the tribal governments, women and men of their tribe or their urban community who are virulently misogynist or who are threatened by attempts to change the images foisted on us over the centuries by whites. The colonizers' revisions of our lives, values, and histories have devastated us at the most critical level of all—that of our minds, our own sense of who we are.

Many women express strong opposition to those who would alter our life supports, steal our tribal lands, colonize our cultures and cultural expressions, and revise our very identities. We must strive to maintain tribal status; we must make certain that the tribes continue to be legally recognized entities, sovereign nations within the larger United States, and we must wage this struggle in many ways—political, educational, literary, artistic, individual, and communal. We are doing all we can: as mothers and grandmothers; as family members and tribal members; as professionals, workers, artists, shamans, leaders, chiefs, speakers, writers, and organizers, we daily demonstrate that we have no intention of disappearing, of being silent, or of quietly acquiescing in our extinction.

NOTES

1. It is likely, say some researchers, that fetal alcohol syndrome, which is serious among many Indian groups, will be so serious among the White Mountain Apache and the Pine Ridge Sioux that if present trends continue, by the year 2000

some people estimate that almost one-half of all children born on those reservations will in some way be affected by FAS. (Michael Dorris, Native American Studies, Dartmouth College, private conversation. Dorris has done extensive research into the syndrome as it affects native populations in the United States as well as in New Zealand.)

2. Phyllis Old Dog Cross, "Sexual Abuse, A New Threat to the Native American Woman: An Overview," *Listening Post: A Periodical of the Mental Health Programs of Indian Health Services,* vol. 6, no. 2 (April 1982) p. 18.
3. Old Dog Cross, p. 18.
4. Old Dog Cross, p. 20.

5

"J.A.P."-SLAPPING
The Politics of Scapegoating

RUTH ADKIN AND ADRIENNE RICH

Those who remember World War II may well recall the racist imagery and language levelled at Japanese people. The Japanese, formerly idealized as giving us exquisite art, magical paper toys, flower arranging, swiftly became the "Japs," to be "slapped" by American military force: yellow, toothy torturers with a genetic flair for cruelty, the dastardly bombers of Pearl Harbor: the people who would deserve the genocidal bombings of Hiroshima and Nagasaki. The word "Jap" held its own in the monosyllabic language of "kike," "wop," "spic," "chink," "bitch," "slut"—short, brutal sounds like the impact of a fist. "Slap That Jap" was a familiar wartime slogan.

These memories of the 1940s are part of the background some of us bring to the recent explosion of "Jewish-American Princess" stereotypes on Eastern college campuses. The Jewish feminist magazine *Lilith* first reported the phenomenon in its Fall 1987 issue (#17); since then, articles have appeared in the *New York Times* and the Jewish press. A column, "No Laughing Matter," by Suzanne Messing, appeared in the feminist paper *New Directions for Women.* On December 9, [1987], National Public Radio broadcast a segment on the spread of "J.A.P.-baiting," interviewing Evelyn Torton Beck, Professor of Women's Studies at the University of Maryland and editor of *Nice Jewish Girls: A Lesbian Anthology.*

Ruth Atkin and Adrienne Rich, "'J.A.P.'-Slapping: The Politics of Scapegoating" from *Gesher* (January 1988). Reprinted with the permission of the authors.

"J.A.P."-baiting has taken a range of forms: novels by post–World War II American Jewish writers such as Herman Wouk's *Marjorie Morningstar;* the routines of Jewish comedians; negative stereotyping of middle-class Jewish women in greeting cards, jewelry, T-shirts, graffiti; and ritualized verbal assaults on Jewish women on college campuses. The Jewish woman is stereotyped as rich, spoiled, avidly materialistic, and solely out for herself. Most of the negative attributes are, of course, familiar anti-Jewish stereotypes: here they are pushed onto the Jewish woman. *Lilith* reported that at Syracuse University basketball games, the pep band would point at certain women who stood up and chant "JAP, JAP, JAP." On other campuses have appeared such graffiti as: "I tolerate JAPS for sex"; "All JAPS are sluts"; "Solution to the JAP question: when they go for their nose jobs, tie their tubes as well." (This last graffito is packed with implications: the "J.A.P." is trying to assimilate, to pass; Jewish women should be sterilized [as thousands were under Hitler]. It implies a knowledge of Nazi vocabulary and practice that belies the theory of "J.A.P."-baiting as ignorant fun and games.)

A different kind of hostility identifies the "J.A.P." not as a "slut" but as a "frigid" woman, unwilling to "put out" sexually. Messing quotes a greeting card (published by Noble Press, New York): "Why do JAPS close their eyes while having sex? So they can pretend they're shopping." National Public Radio reports a fun-fair booth: "Make Her Prove She's Not a JAP—Make Her Swallow."

"J.A.P." imagery has been acceptable in the Jewish community and continues to be. According to the Chicago *Jewish Sentinel,* the National Federation of Temple Sisterhoods adopted a resolution at their national convention this fall condemning "J.A.P." jokes and images, since what began as an object of sexist humor has now become a tool of the anti-Semite. The resolution called on member sisterhoods to discontinue the sale of "J.A.P. items" in their Judaica shops. But if the sisterhoods had challenged the stereotyping of Jewish women from the first, it might have stood less chance to become the tool of the anti-Semite, and within the Jewish community "JAP items" would not have received the endorsement of the National Federation. The issue is sometimes trivialized as a matter of humor ("we can laugh at ourselves"), or on the grounds that the negative stereotypes contain a "kernel of truth." We need to examine these responses.

The semiotics, or signifying power, of the "J.A.P." stereotype is complex. A clear feminist perception is needed to decipher the scapegoating of the **women** within a historically scapegoated group. Within the Jewish community, scapegoating and negative labelling of Jewish women may reflect tensions over gender roles and conflicts specific to the group. They also reveal how Jews participate in the sexism of the society at large.

"Kaleidoscopic" is Susan Schnur's term (in *Lilith*) for the "JAP theme." Rarely have two forms of social hatred—misogyny and anti-Semitism—been so explicitly joined: the "materialistic, pushy" Jew and the "princess," the selfish, privileged rich woman. Conflate these two identities and you have an easy target in a time when the presence of women on campuses is threatening to men, when jobs after college are at a premium, and any woman can be perceived by any man as a competitor for his future job. In fact, "J.A.P." is a conflation of three hated identities: Jew, woman, and those people who are seen, in a society of vast inequalities and injustice, as having "made it."

But to understand the "J.A.P."-baiting phenomenon fully we need an understanding of how the mechanisms of anti-Jewish thought operate. The "Jewish Mother" stereotype—of a too-assertive, domineering woman, devouring the lives of her children—a leftover of the community-building, survival orientation of immigrant culture, is followed by the "Jewish American Princess." The next generation of epithets directed at Jewish women reflects the assimilation of the daughters into American society. As with any stereotype, a complex social pattern is crudely and simplistically caricatured. Young Jewish women are scapegoated for the material "success" of their parents' (usually their fathers') earning power. Scapegoating young Jewish women fits into the historic cyclical pattern of Jewish oppression, whereby some Jews have been allowed a limited access to power (as tax-collectors, money-lenders, etc.), creating the illusion of Jews overall having power. Every period of toleration of Jews in host countries has been followed by periods of economic and social unrest when ruling interests have withdrawn "protection" and support of Jews, and have encouraged the general population to direct their resentments against Jews. This phase has been brutal in the extreme: Eastern European pogroms; the Nazi camps.

Increasing numbers of people in America today are without basic necessities and comforts. The current atmosphere of growing resentment of material success is fully justified. But its historic precedents, for Jews, are troubling. As the economic situation in the U.S. widens the gap between rich and poor, we need to be on the alert for expressions of anger and frustration which divert attention from the real sources of economic hardship—the prioritizing of death over life, of profit over the basic needs of people. This hardship is shared by many Jews, especially older Jewish women. It is not a coincidence that "J.A.P."-baiting is occurring on college campuses, perceived as places of privilege.

Jews have been perceived, and to a certain extent correctly, as a "successful" minority group in America. Writing in *Lilith,* Francine Klagsbrun asks: "Isn't it odd that the term JAP, referring to a spoiled, self-indulgent woman, should be so widely used at a time when women are working outside their homes in unprecedented numbers, struggling to balance their home lives and their work lives, to give as much of themselves as they can to everybody—their husbands, their kids, their bosses?" In the same issue, Susan Schnur notes that "the characterizations of JAPs and Yuppies are often identical." She sees the label of Yuppies as "neutral or even positive," but many a bitter, long-stored anti-Yuppie joke was heard when Wall Street crashed last October. And it is perhaps not coincidental that the acronym "JAP" fits so neatly into a growing anti-Asian racism that has accompanied the increased perception of Asians as a "successful" minority. Insofar as a fraternity house booth inviting passers-by to "Slap a JAP" echoes the "Slap That Jap: Buy War Bonds" posters of World War II, it legitimizes anti-Semitism, misogyny, and anti-Asian racism simultaneously.

As the U.S. economy wavers, as American national identity itself wavers, anti-Semitism is one time-honored escape from critical thinking and political responsibility. Young Jewish women on college campuses may have received little in their education to help them interpret this double assault—especially since the "JAP" label can be applied to non-Jews as well. Some older Jewish women, too, as articles in both *Lilith* and *New Directions for Women* indicate, have reacted by accepting stereotyping, by suggesting that "We should be able to laugh at ourselves." Both Jewish men and women tell "J.A.P." jokes. But, according to Messing, "No one refers to herself as a JAP." Francine Klagsbrun observes, "When we put down other Jewish women, that is a form of self-hatred."

And yes, we do need to laugh at ourselves. But our humor cannot—for our own health—be founded on self-hatred. When we delight in ourselves as women, delight in ourselves as Jews, we can laugh out of the fullness of recognizing ourselves as necessarily flawed and sometimes ridiculous human beings. Our humor need not come out of the arsenal of those who would deny us our humanity.

NOTE

1. Thanks to *Lilith: The Jewish Women's Magazine,* 250 W. 57th Street, New York, NY 10107; *New Directions for Women,* 108 Palisade Ave., Englewood, NJ 07631; the Chicago *Jewish Sentinel,* 323 S. Franklin St., Rm. 501, Chicago, IL 60606.

6

TO BE POOR AND TRANSGENDER

KAI WRIGHT

Sharmus has been a sex worker for about five years. She started after breaking up with a boyfriend who was supporting her while she was out of work. It was quick money, and, as with many of her transgender friends, she didn't believe there were many other jobs out there for her.

Kai Wright, "To Be Poor and Transgender" from *The Progressive,* 65(10). Reprinted with the permission of *The Progressive* magazine, 409 East Main Street, Madison, WI 53703.

"You have your good nights, and your bad nights," says Sharmus, thirty-five. "There are no fringe benefits. Summer time is the best time; the winter is hard," she explains, casually ticking off the pros and cons of being a prostitute. "It's just hard getting a job. Nobody really wants to hire you, and when they do hire you they give you a hard time."

Sex work was not in her plans back when she transitioned from male to female at age twenty-one. "Sometimes I regret it," she sighs. "My lifetime goal was to be a schoolteacher."

Her uncertainty is to be expected. Our culture depicts people whose discomfort with gender norms goes beyond being tomboys or feminine men as mere curiosity items for trash TV ("Your woman is really a man!" episodes of *Jerry Springer*). This collective ignorance leaves people like Sharmus without much guidance. Many go through puberty and into adulthood without meeting people like themselves. The resulting high rates of depression, drug use, violence, and suicidal thoughts are unsurprising.

"One of the greatest agonies one can experience is gender dysphoria," says transgender activist Jessica Xavier. "When your anatomy doesn't match who you are inside, it's the worst feeling in the world."

Sharmus and Xavier are part of a group whose existence challenges normative gender. They include drag performers, heterosexual cross-dressers, and people from all walks of life who live permanently in a gender other than that assigned at birth. They range from individuals who have had thousands of dollars worth of reconstructive surgery to people who simply style themselves in a way that feels comfortable.

Around the nation, a growing cadre of activists is working to build bridges between all of these populations and to encourage the formation of an umbrella community called "transgender." What the members of this latest American identity group share is a far more practical understanding of gender politics than that of the ethereal, academic world to which it is often relegated. From employment to health services, transgender folks, particularly those in low-income environments, face enormous barriers when navigating even the most basic aspects of life—all because of their gender transgressions.

"We continue to be one of the most stigmatized populations on the planet," says Xavier, the former director of a national coalition of transgender political groups called It's Time!—America. Xavier recently cajoled the local health department into financing a survey of around 250 transgender people in D.C. Forty percent of respondents had not finished high school, and another 40 percent were unemployed. Almost half had no health insurance and reported not seeing a physician regularly. A quarter reported being HIV-positive, and another 35 percent reported having seriously considered suicide.

Xavier's was the latest in a series of such studies done in cities where relatively emboldened trans activists have pushed local officials to begin considering public policy solutions to their health care concerns. Across the board, they have found largely the same thing: higher rates of just about every indicator of social and economic distress. "And all because of the stigma," Xavier concludes.

One problem that stands out, Xavier and others say, is the need for accessible counseling and medical supervision for those who are in the process of gender transitioning. Most medical professionals require certain steps, outlined in a set of protocols dubbed the "Benjamin Standards of Care." First, a therapist must diagnose you with "Gender Identity Disorder," which the American Psychiatric Association established in 1979. In adults, the diagnosis essentially confirms that your "gender dysphoria" is profound enough that the drastic step of making physiological alterations to God's plan is an acceptable treatment.

The diagnosis clears you for reconstructive surgery and hormone therapy. Hormone use for gender transitioning is strictly off-label, but select doctors will nevertheless prescribe a particular hormone and simply file paperwork for one of its approved usages. While there is disagreement within the trans community about how this process should be altered, most unite around frustration with the gatekeeping nature of it all—the notion that one must first ask permission, then be declared insane, before being allowed to violate our gender rules.

For Angela (a pseudonym), this means choosing between the career she's spent ten years building and her recent decision to live as a male. Angela, twenty-eight, gained security clearance while serving in the Marines. Despite having climbed to officer rank, she fled the forces when it became clear they were going to throw her out for being a lesbian.

As a civilian, her clearance allowed her to land a well-paying job at an aerospace engineering firm. The position has afforded her partner of four years a comfortable life, and even occasionally helps support her partner's budding acting career. But all of that will be jeopardized once a gender-identity-disorder diagnosis is placed in Angela's medical records. Technically, it's a mental health problem, and that would likely prompt the revocation of her clearance when it next comes up for review. So Angela and her partner are again searching for new ways she can use her skills.

Middle class professionals like Angela have options. The barriers to a legal and safe gender transition are surmountable, if profound. But for people like Sharmus, the whole discussion is absurd.

Sharmus has never had "body work" done, but she's taken some hormones in the past. In her world, spending thousands of dollars on therapy, surgery, and hormone treatments is impossible, but a hyper-feminine appearance is still highly valued—not only for personal aesthetics, but also for professional development. So a thriving black market has developed. In D.C., for $200 to $300, you can have silicone injected into your chest to create breasts. Thirty bucks will get you around 100 hormone pills, though injections are usually cheaper.

"When I was taking the hormone shots, my girlfriend was shooting me," Sharmus explains. "You get a knot in the breasts first, then your skin gets soft. After about two months, my breasts started forming."

With hormones, often someone who has taken them before supplies and mentors a curious friend. Similar arrangements develop with silicone, but just as often there's a dealer in town who also injects clients. The silicone is not encased, as it would be with an implant, but rather injected with large syringes directly into varying body parts. In some cases, the materials injected are not even silicone, but substitutes made from more readily available things such as dishwashing liquid or floor wax. Similarly, some men wanting estrogen will simply take birth-control pills. Testosterone is harder to improvise, but even the real thing can irreparably damage internal organs when taken improperly. All of this can result in fatalities.

"I have known several people that passed," Sharmus sighs. She steers clear of silicone and stopped taking unsupervised hormones. A couple of years ago, she started working with an organization called Helping Individual Prostitutes Survive, or HIPS. She conducts outreach for HIPS, offering information on how to protect against HIV and other sexually transmitted diseases, and encouraging colleagues to leave the silicone alone.

Omar Reyes, whose drag persona is former Miss Gay America, works for La Clinica del Pueblo, a D.C. clinic serving the city's ballooning Latino community. Reyes uses his male birth name and male pronouns but considers himself transgender because of his drag work and his discomfort with male gender "norms." In his monthly transgender support group and in conversations with other *dragas* he meets at his weekly show, Reyes harps on the *malas noticias* about silicone. But he recognizes why it's attractive: It's cheap, and it's fast.

"They put silicone in their face and their bodies and, in just a very short period, they can look like a woman," he says. This is particularly important for drag performers and sex workers, whose income may depend on how exaggeratedly feminine they look. "We have to deal with the fact that they want to look like a woman, and this is the short-term way to do it."

Reyes and Xavier want to see someone in D.C. start a low-cost clinic devoted to counseling and treatment for people who are transitioning. Gay health centers in Boston, Los Angeles, New York City, San Francisco, and Seattle all have such clinics already and are developing their own sets of protocols for how the process should work. Earlier this year, San Francisco became the first jurisdiction in the United States to include sex reassignment surgery and related treatments in its health plan for civil servants. This is the kind of thing Xavier says we need to see more of.

But even if the services were there, getting people into them would take work. Most transgender people tell horrifying stories of the treatment they have experienced in health care settings. In one of the most high-profile cases nationally, a trans woman named Tyra Hunter died in 1995 when D.C. paramedics refused to treat her wounds from a car accident. After removing her clothes at the scene of the accident and discovering her male genitals, a paramedic allegedly ceased treating Hunter and began shouting taunts. She died at the hospital later. Following a lengthy court battle, Hunter's family won a suit against the city.

There are many less prominent examples. From the hospital nurse who gawks when helping a trans woman into her dressing gown to the gynecologist who responds with disbelief when a trans man comes in for a checkup, the small indignities act as perhaps the greatest barriers to health care.

"They feel like when you go for services, people are going to give attitude," Reyes says. "Therefore, you find that they don't even think about going for help when they really need it."

Tanika Walker, who goes by Lucky, is your standard eighteen-year-old hard ass: short-sighted, stubborn-headed, determined to be the toughest guy in the room. Born and raised in rough-and-tumble southeast Washington, D.C., Lucky has a mop of dreadlocks, light mustache, tattoos, and brands—including the name of a deceased sibling spelled out in cigarette burns. These all send one message: I'm the wrong dude to mess with.

Like Angela, Lucky is in the process of transitioning genders to become a young man. It's an emotional journey she began when she was fourteen years old. Along the way, she's been yanked out of school and tossed out of her home. She's also been involved in a lot of disastrous relationships, marred by violence, often her own.

"I know that I'm homosexual, that I'm a lesbian," Lucky says, groping to explain her feelings. "But at the same time, it's like, I look so much like a boy. I act so much like a boy. I want to be a boy."

So far, however, Lucky's transition is primarily stylistic. She still uses her birth name and answers to female pronouns, but she describes her gender as "not anything." She uses only the men's bathroom because she's had too many fights with women who thought she was a Peeping Tom in the ladies' room. And she'd much rather her friends call her "dawg" than "girlfriend." Among African American lesbians, Lucky fits into a category of women often dubbed "doms," short for dominant.

"I never had chests," Lucky brags. "Never. Around the time you're supposed to start getting chests, I didn't get any. So I was like, am I made to be like this? I was the little girl all of the other little girls couldn't play with 'cause I was too boyish."

The dyke jokes started early, sometime in middle school. She settled on a violent response to the taunting just as early. Her fighting became routine enough that by her sophomore year the school suggested counseling for her "identity crisis." She balked and, instead, came out to her mom, who promptly threw her out of the house. "I was like, how am I having an identity crisis? I know what I am," Lucky remembers. "My mom said I had to go."

Lucky enrolled herself in the Job Corps and by the time she was seventeen had her GED. She came back to D.C., moved in with her godsister, and began dating a thirty-two-year-old woman.

But the relationship quickly turned violent, and the godsister put Lucky out as well. She turned to one of her brothers and started dating someone her own age. But it was a stormy relationship, and Lucky battered her partner. After one of their more brutal fights, the young woman called the police and Lucky wound up in jail for a month for aggravated assault. That was this April. In May, she started dating another young woman, and she believes this relationship will work out. She's also started hanging out at the Sexual Minority Youth Assistance League (SMYAL).

One urgent lesson she's trying to learn is that violence isn't her only option when conflict arises. But she dismisses the severity of her problem. "I would be, like, 'Go away and leave me alone,' " she says, describing how the fights started. "And she would just keep hitting me in the arm or something. But it didn't really affect me; it would just be real irritating. She used to do stupid stuff like that to aggravate me. So I just hit her. And when I hit her, I blacked her eye out or something."

She sums up her life in a gigantic understatement, saying, "It's just some things I've been through that a normal eighteen-year-old female wouldn't have been through."

Twenty-year-old Vassar College senior Kiana Moore began transitioning at seventeen. She is articulate and engaging, has never been in trouble, and is studying to become a clinical psychologist. As the only transgender person on her campus, she comes out to the entire first-year class every term during one of the school's diversity programs. She spent this summer interning at SMYAL, counseling Lucky and fifteen to twenty other mainly black transgender youth. What these young folks need, she says, are more role models.

"I am here at SMYAL working as an intern, but where else can you go around this country and see a trans intern? Where can you see a trans person who's in college?" Moore asks. "And so you don't really have anyone to connect to or know about. So if they are at high risk [for social problems], that's why. Because there's nothing there for them at all."

Moore has what Xavier calls "passing privilege." She's a beautiful and confident black woman most people would never assume is transgender. That's something usually achieved only by those with significant resources.

And once trans people have found they can pass—usually middle class whites living in the suburbs—they don't want to ruin it by becoming an activist or a role model.

"You lose something if you help, because then you put yourself in the spotlight. And if you are a pretty, passable female, you don't want to do that," Moore explains. "We don't want to be advocates, because then we're Kiana the transsexual instead of Kiana the new neighbor."

And thus the activists trying to build a transgender community and social movement face much the same battle gay activists confronted for years: Those with the resources to help have too much to lose.

But Moore sees promise in the youth she spent the summer with. "Every time I talk to them I always give them a big hug before, during, and after the session, because that's the only way I can say I'm here and I think you're stronger than me," she says. "They deal with their problems, and they come in here, and they smile, every day. And they take care of each other."

7

WHITE PRIVILEGE AND MALE PRIVILEGE
A Personal Account of Coming to See Correspondences through Work in Women's Studies

PEGGY McINTOSH

Through work to bring materials and perspectives from Women's Studies into the rest of the curriculum, I have often noticed men's unwillingness to grant that they are overprivileged in the curriculum, even though they may grant that women are disadvantaged. Denials that amount to taboos surround the subject of advantages that men gain from women's disadvantages. These denials protect male privilege from being fully recognized, acknowledged, lessened, or ended.

Thinking through unacknowledged male privilege as a phenomenon with a life of its own, I realized that since hierarchies in our society are interlocking, there was most likely a phenomenon of white privilege that was similarly denied and protected, but alive and real in its effects. As a white person, I realized I had been taught about racism as something that puts others at a disadvantage, but had been taught not to see one of its corollary aspects, white privilege, which puts me at an advantage.

I think whites are carefully taught not to recognize white privilege, as males are taught not to recognize male privilege. So I have begun in an untutored way to ask what it is like to have white privilege. This paper is a partial record of my personal observations and not a scholarly analysis. It is based on my daily experiences within my particular circumstances.

I have come to see white privilege as an invisible package of unearned assets that I can count on cashing in each day, but about which I was "meant" to remain oblivious. White privilege is like an invisible weightless knapsack of special provisions, assurances, tools, maps, guides, codebooks, passports, visas, clothes, compass, emergency gear, and blank checks.

Since I have had trouble facing white privilege, and describing its results in my life, I saw parallels here with men's reluctance to acknowledge male privilege. Only rarely will a man go beyond acknowledging that women are

---

disadvantaged to acknowledging that men have unearned advantage, or that unearned privilege has not been good for men's development as human beings, or for society's development, or that privilege systems might ever be challenged and *changed.*

I will review here several types or layers of denial that I see at work protecting, and preventing awareness about, entrenched male privilege. Then I will draw parallels, from my own experience, with the denials that veil the facts of white privilege. Finally, I will list forty-six ordinary and daily ways in which I experience having white privilege, by contrast with my African American colleagues in the same building. This list is not intended to be generalizable. Others can make their own lists from within their own life circumstances.

Writing this paper has been difficult, despite warm receptions for the talks on which it is based.[1] For describing white privilege makes one newly accountable. As we in Women's Studies work reveal male privilege and ask men to give up some of their power, so one who writes about having white privilege must ask, "Having described it, what will I do to lessen or end it?"

The denial of men's overprivileged state takes many forms in discussions of curriculum change work. Some claim that men must be central in the curriculum because they have done most of what is important or distinctive in life or in civilization. Some recognize sexism in the curriculum but deny that it makes male students seem unduly important in life. Others agree that certain *individual* thinkers are male oriented but deny that there is any *systemic* tendency in disciplinary frameworks or epistemology to overempower men as a group. Those men who do grant that male privilege takes institutionalized and embedded forms are still likely to deny that male hegemony has opened doors for them personally. Virtually all men deny that male overreward alone can explain men's centrality in all the inner sanctums of our most powerful institutions. Moreover, those few who will acknowledge that male privilege systems have overempowered them usually end up doubting that we could dismantle these privilege systems. They may say they will work to improve women's status, in the society or in the university, but they can't or won't support the idea of lessening men's. In curricular terms, this is the point at which they say that they regret they cannot use any of the interesting new scholarship on women because the syllabus is full. When the talk turns to giving men less cultural room, even the most thoughtful and fair-minded of the men I know will tend to reflect, or fall back on, conservative assumptions about the inevitability of present gender relations and distributions of power, calling on precedent or sociobiology and psychobiology to demonstrate that male domination is natural and follows inevitably from evolutionary pressures. Others resort to arguments from "experience" or religion or social responsibility or wishing and dreaming.

After I realized, through faculty development work in Women's Studies, the extent to which men work from a base of unacknowledged privilege, I understood that much of their oppressiveness was unconscious. Then I remembered the frequent charges from women of color that white women whom they encounter are oppressive. I began to understand why we are justly seen as oppressive, even when we don't see ourselves that way. At the very least, obliviousness of one's privileged state can make a person or group irritating to be with. I began to count the ways in which I enjoy unearned skin privilege and have been conditioned into oblivion about its existence, unable to see that it put me "ahead" in any way, or put my people ahead, overrewarding us and yet also paradoxically damaging us, or that it could or should be changed.

My schooling gave me no training in seeing myself as an oppressor, as an unfairly advantaged person, or as a participant in a damaged culture. I was taught to see myself as an individual whose moral state depended on her individual moral will. At school, we were not taught about slavery in any depth; we were not taught to see slaveholders as damaged people. Slaves were seen as the only group at risk of being dehumanized. My schooling followed the pattern which Elizabeth Minnich has pointed out: whites are taught to think of their lives as morally neutral, normative, and average, and also ideal, so that when we work to benefit others, this is seen as work that will allow "them" to be more like "us." I think many of us know how obnoxious this attitude can be in men.

After frustration with men who would not recognize male privilege, I decided to try to work on myself at least by identifying some of the daily effects of white privilege in my life. It is crude work, at this stage, but I will give here a list of special circumstances and conditions I experience that I did not earn but that I have been made to feel are mine by birth, by citizenship, and by virtue of being a conscientious law-abiding "normal" person of goodwill. I have chosen those conditions that I think in my case *attach somewhat more to skin-color privilege* than to class, religion, ethnic status, or geographical location, though these other privileging factors are intricately intertwined. As far as I can see, my Afro-American co-workers, friends, and acquaintances with whom I come into daily or frequent contact in this particular time, place, and line of work cannot count on most of these conditions.

1. I can, if I wish, arrange to be in the company of people of my race most of the time.
2. I can avoid spending time with people whom I was trained to mistrust and who have learned to mistrust my kind or more.
3. If I should need to move, I can be pretty sure of renting or purchasing housing in an area which I can afford and in which I would want to live.
4. I can be reasonably sure that my neighbors in such a location will be neutral or pleasant to me.
5. I can go shopping alone most of the time, fairly well assured that I will not be followed or harassed by store detectives.
6. I can turn on the television or open to the front page of the paper and see people of my race widely and positively represented.
7. When I am told about our national heritage or about "civilization," I am shown that people of my color made it what it is.

8. I can be sure that my children will be given curricular materials that testify to the existence of their race.
9. If I want to, I can be pretty sure of finding a publisher for this piece on white privilege.
10. I can be fairly sure of having my voice heard in a group in which I am the only member of my race.
11. I can be casual about whether or not to listen to another woman's voice in a group in which she is the only member of her race.
12. I can go into a book shop and count on finding the writing of my race represented, into a supermarket and find the staple foods that fit with my cultural traditions, into a hairdresser's shop and find someone who can deal with my hair.
13. Whether I use checks, credit cards, or cash, I can count on my skin color not to work against the appearance that I am financially reliable.
14. I could arrange to protect our young children most of the time from people who might not like them.
15. I did not have to educate our children to be aware of systemic racism for their own daily physical protection.
16. I can be pretty sure that my children's teachers and employers will tolerate them if they fit school and workplace norms; my chief worries about them do not concern others' attitudes toward their race.
17. I can talk with my mouth full and not have people put this down to my color.
18. I can swear, or dress in secondhand clothes, or not answer letters, without having people attribute these choices to the bad morals, the poverty, or the illiteracy of my race.
19. I can speak in public to a powerful male group without putting my race on trial.
20. I can do well in a challenging situation without being called a credit to my race.
21. I am never asked to speak for all the people of my racial group.
22. I can remain oblivious to the language and customs of persons of color who constitute the world's majority without feeling in my culture any penalty for such oblivion.
23. I can criticize our government and talk about how much I fear its policies and behavior without being seen as a cultural outsider.
24. I can be reasonably sure that if I ask to talk to "the person in charge," I will be facing a person of my race.
25. If a traffic cop pulls me over or if the IRS audits my tax return, I can be sure I haven't been singled out because of my race.
26. I can easily buy posters, postcards, picture books, greeting cards, dolls, toys, and children's magazines featuring people of my race.
27. I can go home from most meetings of organizations I belong to feeling somewhat tied in, rather than isolated, out of place, outnumbered, unheard, held at a distance, or feared.

28. I can be pretty sure that an argument with a colleague of another race is more likely to jeopardize her chances for advancement than to jeopardize mine.
29. I can be fairly sure that if I argue for the promotion of a person of another race, or a program centering on race, this is not likely to cost me heavily within my present setting, even if my colleagues disagree with me.
30. If I declare there is a racial issue at hand, or there isn't a racial issue at hand, my race will lend me more credibility for either position than a person of color will have.
31. I can choose to ignore developments in minority writing and minority activist programs, or disparage them, or learn from them, but in any case, I can find ways to be more or less protected from negative consequences of any of these choices.
32. My culture gives me little fear about ignoring the perspectives and powers of people of other races.
33. I am not made acutely aware that my shape, bearing, or body odor will be taken as a reflection on my race.
34. I can worry about racism without being seen as self-interested or self-seeking.
35. I can take a job with an affirmative action employer without having my co-workers on the job suspect that I got it because of my race.
36. If my day, week, or year is going badly, I need not ask of each negative episode or situation whether it has racial overtones.
37. I can be pretty sure of finding people who would be willing to talk with me and advise me about my next steps, professionally.
38. I can think over many options, social, political, imaginative, or professional, without asking whether a person of my race would be accepted or allowed to do what I want to do.
39. I can be late to a meeting without having the lateness reflect on my race.
40. I can choose public accommodation without fearing that people of my race cannot get in or will be mistreated in the places I have chosen.
41. I can be sure that if I need legal or medical help, my race will not work against me.
42. I can arrange my activities so that I will never have to experience feelings of rejection owing to my race.
43. If I have low credibility as a leader, I can be sure that my race is not the problem.
44. I can easily find academic courses and institutions that give attention only to people of my race.
45. I can expect figurative language and imagery in all of the arts to testify to experiences of my race.
46. I can choose blemish cover or bandages in "flesh" color and have them more or less match my skin.

I repeatedly forgot each of the realizations on this list until I wrote it down. For me, white privilege has turned out to be an elusive and fugitive subject. The pressure to avoid it is great, for in facing it I must give up the myth of meritocracy. If these things are true, this is not such a free country; one's life is not what one makes it; many doors open for certain people through no virtues of their own. These perceptions mean also that my moral condition is not what I had been led to believe. The appearance of being a good citizen rather than a troublemaker comes in large part from having all sorts of doors open automatically because of my color.

A further paralysis of nerve comes from literary silence protecting privilege. My clearest memories of finding such analysis are in Lillian Smith's unparalleled *Killers of the Dream* and Margaret Andersen's review of Karen and Mamie Fields' *Lemon Swamp*. Smith, for example, wrote about walking toward black children on the street and knowing they would step into the gutter; Andersen contrasted the pleasure that she, as a white child, took on summer driving trips to the south with Karen Fields' memories of driving in a closed car stocked with all necessities lest, in stopping, her black family should suffer "insult, or worse." Adrienne Rich also recognizes and writes about daily experiences of privilege, but in my observation, white women's writing in this area is far more often on systemic racism than on our daily lives as light-skinned women.[2]

In unpacking this invisible knapsack of white privilege, I have listed conditions of daily experience that I once took for granted, as neutral, normal, and universally available to everybody, just as I once thought of a male-focused curriculum as the neutral or accurate account that can speak for all. Nor did I think of any of these perquisites as bad for the holder. I now think that we need a more finely differentiated taxonomy of privilege, for some of these varieties are only what one would want for everyone in a just society, and others give license to be ignorant, oblivious, arrogant, and destructive. Before proposing some more finely tuned categorization, I will make some observations about the general effects of these conditions on my life and expectations.

In this potpourri of examples, some privileges make me feel at home in the world. Others allow me to escape penalties or dangers that others suffer. Through some, I escape fear, anxiety, insult, injury, or a sense of not being welcome, not being real. Some keep me from having to hide, to be in disguise, to feel sick or crazy, to negotiate each transaction from the position of being an outsider or, within my group, a person who is suspected of having too close links with a dominant culture. Most keep me from having to be angry.

I see a pattern running through the matrix of white privilege, a pattern of assumptions that were passed on to me as a white person. There was one main piece of cultural turf; it was my own turf, and I was among those who could control the turf. I could measure up to the cultural standards and take advantage of the many options I saw around me to make what the culture would call a success of my life. *My skin color was an asset for any move I was educated to want to make.* I could think of myself as "belonging" in major ways and of making social systems work for me. I could freely disparage, fear, neglect, or be oblivious to anything outside of the dominant cultural forms. Being of the main culture, I could also criticize it fairly freely. My life was reflected back to me frequently enough so that I felt, with regard to my race, if not to my sex, like one of the real people.

Whether through the curriculum or in the newspaper, the television, the economic system, or the general look of people in the streets, I received daily signals and indications that my people counted and that others *either didn't exist or must be trying, not very successfully, to be like people of my race.* I was given cultural permission not to hear voices of people of other races or a tepid cultural tolerance for hearing or acting on such voices. I was also raised not to suffer seriously from anything that darker-skinned people might say about my group, "protected," though perhaps I should more accurately say *prohibited,* through the habits of my economic class and social group, from living in racially mixed groups or being reflective about interactions between people of differing races.

In proportion as my racial group was being made confident, comfortable, and oblivious, other groups were likely being made unconfident, uncomfortable, and alienated. Whiteness protected me from many kinds of hostility, distress, and violence, which I was being subtly trained to visit in turn upon people of color.

For this reason, the word "privilege" now seems to me misleading. Its connotations are too positive to fit the conditions and behaviors which "privilege systems" produce. We usually think of privilege as being a favored state, whether earned, or conferred by birth or luck. School graduates are reminded they are privileged and urged to use their (enviable) assets well. The word "privilege" carries the connotation of being something everyone must want. Yet some of the conditions I have described here work to systemically overempower certain groups. Such privilege simply *confers dominance,* gives permission to control, because of one's race or sex. The kind of privilege that gives license to some people to be, at best, thoughtless and, at worst, murderous should not continue to be referred to as a desirable attribute. Such "privilege" may be widely desired without being in any way beneficial to the whole society.

Moreover, though "privilege" may confer power, it does not confer moral strength. Those who do not depend on conferred dominance have traits and qualities that may never develop in those who do. Just as Women's Studies courses indicate that women survive their political circumstances to lead lives that hold the human race together, so "underprivileged" people of color who are the world's majority have survived their oppression and lived survivors' lives from which the white global minority can and must learn. In some groups, those dominated have actually become strong through *not* having all of these unearned advantages, and this gives them a great deal to teach the others. Members of so-called privileged groups can seem foolish, ridiculous, infantile, or dangerous by contrast.

I want, then, to distinguish between earned strength and unearned power conferred systemically. Power from unearned privilege can look like strength when it is, in fact, permission to escape or to dominate. But not all of the privileges on my list are inevitably damaging. Some, like the expectation that neighbors will be decent to you, or that your race will not count against you in court, should be the norm in a just society and should be considered as the entitlement of everyone. Others, like the privilege not to listen to less powerful people, distort the humanity of the holders as well as the ignored groups. Still others, like finding one's staple foods everywhere, may be a function of being a member of a numerical majority in the population. Others have to do with not having to labor under pervasive negative stereotyping and mythology.

We might at least start by distinguishing between positive advantages that we can work to spread, to the point where they are not advantages at all but simply part of the normal civic and social fabric, and negative types of advantage that unless rejected will always reinforce our present hierarchies. For example, the positive "privilege" of belonging, the feeling that one belongs within the human circle, as Native Americans say, fosters development and should not be seen as privilege for a few. It is, let us say, an entitlement that none of us should have to earn; ideally it is an *unearned entitlement.* At present, since only a few have it, it is an *unearned advantage* for them. The negative "privilege" that gave me cultural permission not to take darker-skinned Others seriously can be seen as arbitrarily conferred dominance and should not be desirable for anyone. This paper results from a process of coming to see that some of the power that I originally saw as attendant on being a human being in the United States consisted in *unearned advantage* and *conferred dominance,* as well as other kinds of special circumstance not universally taken for granted.

In writing this paper I have also realized that white identity and status (as well as class identity and status) give me considerable power to choose whether to broach this subject and its trouble. I can pretty well decide whether to disappear and avoid and not listen and escape the dislike I may engender in other people through this essay, or interrupt, answer, interpret, preach, correct, criticize, and control to some extent what goes on in reaction to it. Being white, I am given considerable power to escape many kinds of danger or penalty as well as to choose which risks I want to take.

There is an analogy here, once again, with Women's Studies. Our male colleagues do not have a great deal to lose in supporting Women's Studies, but they do not have a great deal to lose if they oppose it either. They simply have the power to decide whether to commit themselves to more equitable distributions of power. They will probably feel few penalties whatever choice they make; they do not seem, in any obvious short-term sense, the ones at risk, though they and we are all at risk because of the behaviors that have been rewarded in them.

Through Women's Studies work I have met very few men who are truly distressed about systemic, unearned male advantage and conferred dominance. And so one question for me and others like me is whether we will be like them, or whether we will get truly distressed, even outraged, about unearned race advantage and conferred dominance and if so, what we will do to lessen them. In any case, we need to do more work in identifying how they actually affect our daily lives. We need more down-to-earth writing by people about these taboo subjects. We need more understanding of the ways in which white "privilege" damages white people, for these are not the same ways in which it damages the victimized. Skewed white psyches are an inseparable part of the picture, though I do not want to confuse the kinds of damage done to the holders of special assets and to those who suffer the deficits. Many, perhaps most, of our white students in the United States think that racism doesn't affect them because they are not people of color; they do not see "whiteness" as a racial identity. Many men likewise think that Women's Studies does not bear on their own existences because they are not female; they do not see themselves as having gendered identities. Insisting on the universal "effects" of "privilege" systems, then, becomes one of our chief tasks, and being more explicit about the *particular* effects in particular contexts is another. Men need to join us in this work.

In addition, since race and sex are not the only advantaging systems at work, we need to similarly examine the daily experience of having age advantage, or ethnic advantage, or physical ability, or advantage related to nationality, religion, or sexual orientation. Professor Marnie Evans suggested to me that in many ways the list I made also applies directly to heterosexual privilege. This is a still more taboo subject than race privilege: the daily ways in which heterosexual privilege makes some persons comfortable or powerful, providing supports, assets, approvals, and rewards to those who live or expect to live in heterosexual pairs. Unpacking that content is still more difficult, owing to the deeper imbeddedness of heterosexual advantage and dominance and stricter taboos surrounding these.

But to start such an analysis I would put this observation from my own experience: the fact that I live under the same roof with a man triggers all kinds of societal assumptions about my worth, politics, life, and values and triggers a host of unearned advantages and powers. After recasting many elements from the original list I would add further observations like these:

1. My children do not have to answer questions about why I live with my partner (my husband).
2. I have no difficulty finding neighborhoods where people approve of our household.
3. Our children are given texts and classes that implicitly support our kind of family unit and do not turn them against my choice of domestic partnership.

4. I can travel alone or with my husband without expecting embarrassment or hostility in those who deal with us.
5. Most people I meet will see my marital arrangements as an asset to my life or as a favorable comment on my likability, my competence, or my mental health.
6. I can talk about the social events of a weekend without fearing most listeners' reactions.
7. I will feel welcomed and "normal" in the usual walks of public life, institutional and social.
8. In many contexts, I am seen as "all right" in daily work on women because I do not live chiefly with women.

Difficulties and dangers surrounding the task of finding parallels are many. Since racism, sexism, and heterosexism are not the same, the advantages associated with them should not be seen as the same. In addition, it is hard to isolate aspects of unearned advantage that derive chiefly from social class, economic class, race, religion, region, sex, or ethnic identity. The oppressions are both distinct and interlocking, as the Combahee River Collective statement of 1977 continues to remind us eloquently.[3]

One factor seems clear about all of the interlocking oppressions. They take both active forms that we can see and embedded forms that members of the dominant group are taught not to see. In my class and place, I did not see myself as racist because I was taught to recognize racism only in individual acts of meanness by members of my group, never in invisible systems conferring racial dominance on my group from birth. Likewise, we are taught to think that sexism or heterosexism is carried on only through intentional, individual acts of discrimination, meanness, or cruelty, rather than in invisible systems conferring unsought dominance on certain groups. Disapproving of the systems won't be enough to change them. I was taught to think that racism could end if white individuals changed their attitudes; many men think sexism can be ended by individual changes in daily behavior toward women. But a man's sex provides advantage for him whether or not he approves of the way in which dominance has been conferred on his group. A "white" skin in the United States opens many doors for whites whether or not we approve of the way dominance has been conferred on us. Individual acts can palliate, but cannot end, these problems. To redesign social systems, we need first to acknowledge their colossal unseen dimensions. The silences and denials surrounding privilege are the key political tool here. They keep the thinking about equality or equity incomplete, protecting unearned advantage and conferred dominance by making these taboo subjects. Most talk by whites about equal opportunity seems to me now to be about equal opportunity to try to get into a position of dominance while denying that *systems* of dominance exist.

Obliviousness about white advantage, like obliviousness about male advantage, is kept strongly inculturated in the United States so as to maintain the myth of meritocracy, the myth that democratic choice is equally available to all. Keeping most people unaware that freedom of confident action is there for just a small number of people props up those in power and serves to keep power in the hands of the same groups that have most of it already. Though systemic change takes many decades, there are pressing questions for me and I imagine for some others like me if we raise our daily consciousness on the perquisites of being light-skinned. What will we do with such knowledge? As we know from watching men, it is an open question whether we will choose to use unearned advantage to weaken invisible privilege systems and whether we will use any of our arbitrarily awarded power to try to reconstruct power systems on a broader base.

NOTES

1. This paper was presented at the Virginia Women's Studies Association conference in Richmond in April, 1986, and the American Education Research Association conference in Boston in October, 1986, and discussed with two groups of participants in the Dodge seminars for Secondary School Teachers in New York and Boston in the spring of 1987.
2. Andersen, Margaret, "Race and the Social Science Curriculum: A Teaching and Learning Discussion." *Radical Teacher,* November, 1984, pp. 17–20. Smith, Lillian, *Killers of the Dream,* New York: W. W. Norton, 1949.
3. "A Black Feminist Statement," The Combahee River Collective, pp. 13–22 in G. Hull, P. Scott, B. Smith, Eds., *All Women Are White, All the Blacks Are Men, But Some of Us Are Brave: Black Women's Studies,* Old Westbury, NY: The Feminist Press, 1982.

8

THEORIZING DIFFERENCE FROM MULTIRACIAL FEMINISM

MAXINE BACA ZINN AND BONNIE THORNTON DILL

Women of color have long challenged the hegemony of feminisms constructed primarily around the lives of white middle-class women. Since the late 1960s, U.S. women of color have taken issue with unitary theories of gender. Our critiques grew out of the widespread concern about the exclusion of women of color from feminist scholarship and the misinterpretation of our experiences,[1] and ultimately "out of the very discourses, denying, permitting, and producing difference."[2] Speaking simultaneously from "within and against" *both* women's liberation *and* antiracist movements, we have insisted on the need to challenge systems of domination,[3] not merely as gendered subjects but as women whose lives are affected by our location in multiple hierarchies.

Recently, and largely in response to these challenges, work that links gender to other forms of domination is increasing. In this article, we examine this connection further as well as the ways in which difference and diversity infuse contemporary feminist studies. Our analysis draws on a conceptual framework that we refer to as "multiracial feminism."[4] This perspective is an attempt to go beyond a mere recognition of diversity and difference among women to examine structures of domination, specifically the importance of race in understanding the social construction of gender. Despite the varied concerns and multiple intellectual stances which characterize the feminisms of women of color, they share an emphasis on race as a primary force situating genders differently. It is the centrality of race, of institutionalized racism, and of struggles against racial oppression that link the various feminist perspectives within this framework. Together, they demonstrate that racial meanings offer new theoretical directions for feminist thought.

Maxine Baca Zinn and Bonnie Thornton, "Theorizing Difference from Multiracial Feminism" from *Feminist Studies 22*, No. 2 (Summer 1996): 321–331. Reprinted with the permission of the publisher, Feminist Studies, Inc.

Tensions in Contemporary Difference Feminism

Objections to the false universalism embedded in the concept "woman" emerged within other discourses as well as those of women of color.[5] Lesbian feminists and postmodern feminists put forth their own versions of what Susan Bordo has called "gender skepticism."[6]

Many thinkers within mainstream feminism have responded to these critiques with efforts to contextualize gender. The search for women's "universal" or "essential" characteristics is being abandoned. By examining gender in the context of other social divisions and perspectives, difference has gradually become important—even problematizing the universal categories of "women" and "men." Sandra Harding expresses the shift best in her claim that "there are no gender relations *per se,* but only gender relations as constructed by and between classes, races, and cultures."[7]

Many feminists now contend that difference occupies center stage as *the* project of women studies today.[8] According to one scholar, "difference has replaced equality as the central concern of feminist theory."[9] Many have welcomed the change, hailing it as a major revitalizing force in U.S. feminist theory.[10] But if *some* priorities within mainstream feminist thought have been refocused by attention to difference, there remains an "uneasy alliance"[11] between women of color and other feminists.

If difference has helped revitalize academic feminisms, it has also "upset the apple cart" and introduced new conflicts into feminist studies.[12] For example, in a recent and widely discussed essay, Jane Rowland Martin argues that the current preoccupation with difference is leading feminism into dangerous traps. She fears that in giving privileged status to a predetermined set of analytic categories (race, ethnicity, and class), "we affirm the existence of nothing but difference." She asks, "How do we know that for us, difference does not turn on being fat, or religious, or in an abusive relationship?"[13]

We, too, see pitfalls in some strands of the difference project. However, our perspectives take their bearings from social relations. Race and class differences are crucial, we argue, not as individual characteristics (such as being fat) but insofar as they are primary organizing principles of a society which locates and positions groups within that society's opportunity structures.

Despite the much-heralded diversity trend within feminist studies, difference is often reduced to mere pluralism: a "live and let live" approach where principles of relativism generate a long list of diversities which begin with gender, class, and race and continue through a range of social structures as well as personal characteristics.[14] Another disturbing pattern, which bell hooks refers to as "the commodification of difference," is the representation of diversity as a form of exotica, "a spice, seasoning that livens up the dull dish that is mainstream white culture."[15] The major limitation of these approaches is the failure to attend to the power relations that accompany difference. Moreover, these approaches ignore the inequalities that cause some characteristics to be seen as "normal" while others are seen as "different" and thus, deviant.

Maria C. Lugones expresses irritation at those feminists who see only the *problem* of difference without recognizing *difference.*[16] Increasingly, we find that difference *is* recognized. But this in no way means that difference occupies a "privileged" theoretical status. Instead of using difference to rethink the category of women, difference is often a euphemism for women who differ from the traditional norm. Even in purporting to accept difference, feminist pluralism often creates a social reality that reverts to universalizing women:

> So much feminist scholarship assumes that when we cut through all of the diversity among women created by differences of racial classification, ethnicity, social class, and sexual orientation, a "universal truth" concerning women and gender lies buried beneath. But if we can face the scary possibility that no such certainty exists and that persisting in such a search will always distort or omit someone's experiences, with what do we replace this old way of thinking? Gender differences and gender politics begin to look very different if there is no essential woman at the core.[17]

What Is Multiracial Feminism?

A new set of feminist theories has emerged from the challenges put forth by women of color. Multiracial feminism is an evolving body of theory and practice informed by wide-ranging intellectual traditions. This framework does not offer a singular or unified feminism but a body of knowledge situating women and men in multiple systems of domination. U.S. multiracial feminism encompasses several emergent perspectives developed primarily by women of color: African Americans, Latinas, Asian Americans, and Native Americans, women whose analyses are shaped by their unique perspectives as "outsiders within"—marginal intellectuals whose social locations provide them with a particular perspective on self and society.[18] Although U.S. women of color represent many races and ethnic backgrounds—with different histories and cultures—our feminisms cohere in their treatment of race as basic social division, a structure of power, a focus of political struggle, and hence a fundamental force in shaping women's and men's lives.

This evolving intellectual and political perspective uses several controversial terms. While we adopt the label "multiracial," other terms have been used to describe this broad framework. For example, Chela Sandoval refers to "U.S. Third World feminisms,"[19] while other scholars refer to "indigenous feminisms." In their theory text-reader, Alison M. Jagger and Paula S. Rothenberg adopt the label "multicultural feminism."[20]

We use "multiracial" rather than "multicultural" as a way of underscoring race as a power system that interacts with other structured inequalities to shape genders. Within the U.S. context, race, and the system of meanings and ideologies which accompany it, is a fundamental organizing principle of social relationships.[21] Race affects all women and men, although in different ways. Even cultural and group differences among women are produced through interaction within a racially stratified social order. Therefore, although we do not discount the importance of culture, we caution that cultural analytic frameworks that ignore race tend to view women's differences as the product of group-specific values and practices that often result in the marginalization of cultural groups which are then perceived as exotic expressions of a normative center. Our focus on race stresses the social construction of differently situated social groups and their varying degrees of advantage and power. Additionally, this emphasis on race takes on increasing political importance in an era where discourse about race is governed by color-evasive language[22] and a preference for individual rather than group remedies for social inequalities. Our analyses insist upon the primary and pervasive nature of race in contemporary U.S. society while at the same time acknowledging how race both shapes and is shaped by a variety of other social relations.

In the social sciences, multiracial feminism grew out of socialist feminist thinking. Theories about how political economic forces shape women's lives were influential as we began to uncover the social causes of racial ethnic women's subordination. But socialist feminism's concept of capitalist patriarchy, with its focus on women's unpaid (reproductive) labor in the home, failed to address racial differences in the organization of reproductive labor. As feminists of color have argued, "reproductive labor has divided along racial as well as gender lines, and the specific characteristics have varied regionally and changed over time as capitalism has reorganized."[23] Despite the limitations of socialist feminism, this body of literature has been especially useful in pursuing questions about the interconnections among systems of domination.[24]

Race and ethnic studies was the other major social scientific source of multiracial feminism. It provided a basis for comparative analyses of groups that are socially and legally subordinated and remain culturally distinct within U.S. society. This includes the systematic discrimination of socially constructed racial groups and their distinctive cultural arrangements. Historically, the categories of African American, Latino, Asian American, and Native American were constructed as both racially and culturally distinct. Each group has a distinctive culture, shares a common heritage, and has developed a common identity within a larger society that subordinates them.[25]

We recognize, of course, certain problems inherent in an uncritical use of the multiracial label. First, the perspective can be hampered by a biracial model in which only African Americans and whites are seen as racial categories and all other groups are viewed through the prism of cultural differences. Latinos and Asians have always occupied distinctive places within the racial hierarchy, and current shifts in the composition of the U.S. population are racializing these groups anew.[26]

A second problem lies in treating multiracial feminism as a single analytical framework, and its principal architects, women of color, as an undifferentiated category. The concepts "multiracial feminism," "racial ethnic women," and "women of color" "homogenize quite different experiences and can falsely universalize experiences across race, ethnicity, sexual orientation, and age."[27] The feminisms created by women of color exhibit a plurality of intellectual and political positions. We speak in many voices, with inconsistencies that are born of our different social locations. Multiracial feminism embodies this plurality and richness. Our intent is not to falsely universalize women of color. Nor do we wish to promote a new racial essentialism in place of the old gender essentialism. Instead, we use these concepts to examine the structures and experiences produced by intersecting forms of race and gender.

It is also essential to acknowledge that race is a shifting and contested category whose meanings construct definitions of all aspects of social life.[28] In the United States it helped define citizenship by excluding everyone who was not a white, male property owner. It defined labor as slave or free, coolie or contract, and family as available only to those men whose marriages were recognized or whose wives could immigrate with them. Additionally, racial meanings are contested both within groups and between them.[29]

Although definitions of race are at once historically and geographically specific, they are also transnational, encompassing diasporic groups and crossing traditional geographic boundaries. Thus, while U.S. multiracial feminism calls attention to the fundamental importance of race, it must also locate the meaning of race within specific national traditions.

The Distinguishing Features of Multiracial Feminism

By attending to these problems, multiracial feminism offers a set of analytic premises for thinking about and theorizing gender. The following themes distinguish this branch of feminist inquiry.

First, multiracial feminism asserts that gender is constructed by a range of interlocking inequalities, what Patricia Hill Collins calls a "matrix of domination."[30] The idea of a matrix is that several fundamental systems work with and through each other. People experience race, class, gender, and sexuality differently depending upon their social location in the structures of race, class, gender, and sexuality. For example, people of the same race will experience race differently depending upon their location in the class structure as working class, professional managerial class, or unemployed; in the gender structure as female or male; and in structures of sexuality as heterosexual, homosexual, or bisexual.

Multiracial feminism also examines the simultaneity of systems in shaping women's experience and identity. Race, class, gender, and sexuality are not reducible to individual attributes to be measured and assessed for their separate contribution in explaining given social outcomes, an approach that Elizabeth Spelman calls "popbead metaphysics," where a woman's identity consists of the sum of parts neatly divisible from one another.[31] The matrix of domination seeks to account for the multiple ways that women experience themselves as gendered, raced, classed, and sexualized.

Second, multiracial feminism emphasizes the intersectional nature of hierarchies at all levels of social life. Class, race, gender, and sexuality are components of both social structure and social interaction. Women and men are differently embedded in locations created by these cross-cutting hierarchies. As a result, women and men throughout the social order experience different forms of privilege and subordination, depending on their race, class, gender, and sexuality. In other words, intersecting forms of domination produce *both* oppression *and* opportunity. At the same time that structures of race, class, and gender create disadvantages for women of color, they provide unacknowledged benefits for those who are at the top of these hierarchies—whites, members of the upper classes, and males. Therefore, multiracial feminism applies not only to racial ethnic women but also to women and men of all races, classes, and genders.

Third, multiracial feminism highlights the relational nature of dominance and subordination. Power is the cornerstone of women's differences.[32] This means that women's differences are *connected* in systematic ways.[33] Race is a vital element in the pattern of relations among minority and white women. As Linda Gordon argues, the very meanings of being a white woman in the United States have been affected by the existence of subordinated women of color: "They intersect in conflict and in occasional cooperation, but always in mutual influence."[34]

Fourth, multiracial feminism explores the interplay of social structure and women's agency. Within the constraints of race, class, and gender oppression, women create viable lives for themselves, their families, and their communities. Women of color have resisted and often undermined the forces of power that control them. From acts of quiet dignity and steadfast determination to involvement in revolt and rebellion, women struggle to shape their own lives. Racial oppression has been a common focus of the "dynamic of oppositional agency" of women of color. As Chandra Talpade Mohanty points out, it is the nature and organization of women's opposition which mediates and differentiates the impact of structures of domination.[35]

Fifth, multiracial feminism encompasses wide-ranging methodological approaches, and like other branches of feminist thought, relies on varied theoretical tools as well. Ruth Frankenberg and Lata Mani identify three guiding principles of inclusive feminist inquiry: "building complex analyses, avoiding erasure, specifying location."[36] In the last decade, the opening up of academic feminism has focused attention on the social location in the production of knowledge. Most basically, research by and about marginalized women has destabilized what used to be considered as universal categories of gender. Marginalized locations are well suited for grasping social relations that remained obscure from more privileged vantage points. Lived experience, in other words, creates alternative ways of understanding the social world and the experience of different groups of women within it. Racially informed standpoint epistemologies have provided new topics, fresh questions, and new understandings of women and men. Women of color have, as Norma Alarçon argues, asserted ourselves as subjects, using our voices to challenge dominant conceptions of truth.[37]

Sixth, multiracial feminism brings together understandings drawn from the lived experiences of diverse and continuously changing groups of women. Among Asian Americans, Native Americans, Latinas, and Blacks are many different national cultural and ethnic groups. Each one is engaged in the process of testing, refining, and reshaping these broader categories in its own image. Such internal differences heighten awareness of and sensitivity of both commonalities and differences, serving as a constant reminder of the importance of comparative study and maintaining a creative tension between diversity and universalization.

Difference and Transformation

Efforts to make women's studies less partial and less distorted have produced important changes in academic feminism. Inclusive thinking has provided a way to build multiplicity and difference into our analyses. This has led to the discovery that race matters for everyone. White women, too, must be reconceptualized as a category that is multiply defined by race, class, and other differences. As Ruth Frankenberg demonstrates in a study of whiteness among contemporary women, all kinds of social relations, even those that appear neutral, are, in fact, racialized. Frankenberg further complicates the very notion of a unified white identity by introducing issues of Jewish identity.[38] Therefore, the lives of women of color cannot be seen as a *variation* on a more general model of white American womanhood. The model of womanhood that feminist social science once held as "universal" is also a product of race and class.

When we analyze the power relations constituting all social arrangements and shaping women's lives in distinctive ways, we can begin to grapple with core feminist issues about how genders are socially constructed and constructed differently. Women's difference is built into our study of gender. Yet this perspective is quite far removed from the atheoretical pluralism implied in much contemporary thinking about gender.

Multiracial feminism, in our view, focuses not just on differences but also on the way in which differences and domination intersect and are historically and socially constituted. It challenges feminist scholars to go beyond the mere recognition and inclusion of difference to reshape the basic concepts and theories of our disciplines. By attending to women's social location based on race, class, and gender, multiracial feminism seeks to clarify the structural sources of diversity. Ultimately, multiracial feminism forces us to see privilege and subordination as interrelated and to pose such questions as: How do the existences and experiences of all people—men and women, different racial-ethnic groups, and different classes—shape the experiences of each other? How are those relationships defined and reinforced through social institutions that are the primary sites for negotiating power within society? How do these differences contribute to the construction of both individual and group identity? Once we acknowledge that all women are affected by the racial order of society, then it becomes clear that the insights of multiracial feminism provide an analytical framework, not solely for understanding the experiences of women of color but for understanding all women, and men, as well.

NOTES

1. Maxine Baca Zinn, Lynn Weber Cannon, Elizabeth Higginbotham, and Bonnie Thornton Dill, "The Costs of Exclusionary Practices in Women's Studies," *Signs* 11 (winter 1986): 290–303.
2. Chela Sandoval, "U.S. Third World Feminism: The Theory and Method of Oppositional Consciousness in the Postmodern World," *Genders* (spring 1991): 1–24.
3. Ruth Frankenberg and Lata Mani, "Cross Currents, Crosstalk: Race, 'Postcoloniality,' and the Politics of Location," *Cultural Studies* 7 (May 1993): 292–310.
4. We use the term "multiracial feminism" to convey the multiplicity of racial groups and feminist perspectives.
5. A growing body of work on difference in feminist thought now exists. Although we cannot cite all the current work, the following are representative: Michèle Barrett, "The Concept of Difference," *Feminist Review* 26 (July 1987): 29–42; Christina Crosby, "Dealing with Difference," in *Feminists Theorize the Political,* ed. Judith Butler and Joan W. Scott (New York: Routledge, 1992), 130–43; Elizabeth Fox-Genovese, "Difference, Diversity, and Divisions in an Agenda for the Women's Movement," in *Color, Class, and Country: Experiences of Gender,* ed. Gay Young and Bette J. Dickerson (London: Zed Books, 1994), 232–48; Nancy A. Hewitt, "Compounding Differences," *Feminist Studies* 18 (summer 1992): 313–26; Maria C. Lugones, "On the Logic of Feminist Pluralism," in *Feminist Ethics,* ed. Claudia Card (Lawrence: University of Kansas Press, 1991), 35–44; Rita S. Gallin and Anne Ferguson, "The Plurality of Feminism: Rethinking 'Difference,'" in *The Woman and International Development Annual* (Boulder: Westview Press, 1993), 3: 1–16; and Linda Gordon, "On Difference," *Genders* 10 (spring 1991): 91–111.
6. Susan Bordo, "Feminism, Postmodernism, and Gender Skepticism," in *Feminism/Postmodernism,* ed. Linda J. Nicholson (London: Routledge, 1990), 133–56.
7. Sandra G. Harding, *Whose Science? Whose Knowledge? Thinking from Women's Lives* (Ithaca: Cornell University Press, 1991), 179.
8. Crosby, 131.
9. Fox-Genovese, 232.

10. Faye Ginsberg and Anna Lowenhaupt Tsing, Introduction to *Uncertain Terms: Negotiating Gender in American Culture,* ed. Faye Ginsburg and Anna Lowenhaupt Tsing (Boston: Beacon Press, 1990), 3.
11. Sandoval, 2.
12. Sandra Morgan, "Making Connections: Socialist-Feminist Challenges to Marxist Scholarship," in *Women and a New Academy: Gender and Cultural Contexts,* ed. Jean F. O'Barr (Madison: University of Wisconsin Press, 1989), 149.
13. Jane Rowland Martin, "Methodological Essentialism, False Difference, and Other Dangerous Traps," *Signs* 19 (spring 1994): 647.
14. Barrett, 32.
15. bell hooks, *Black Looks: Race and Representation* (Boston: South End Press, 1992), 21.
16. Lugones, 35–44.
17. Patricia Hill Collins, Foreword to *Women of Color in U.S. Society,* ed. Maxine Baca Zinn and Bonnie Thornton Dill (Philadelphia: Temple University Press, 1994), xv.
18. Patricia Hill Collins, "Learning from the Outsider Within: The Sociological Significance of Black Feminist Thought," *Social Problems* 33 (December 1986): 514–32.
19. Sandoval, 1.
20. Alison M. Jagger and Paula S. Rothenberg, *Feminist Frameworks: Alternative Theoretical Accounts of the Relations between Women and Men,* 3d ed. (New York: McGraw-Hill, 1993).
21. Michael Omi, and Howard Winant, *Racial Formation in the United States: From the 1960s to the 1980s,* 2d ed. (New York: Routledge, 1994).
22. Ruth Frankenberg, *The Social Construction of Whiteness: White Women, Race Matters* (Minneapolis: University of Minnesota Press, 1993).
23. Evelyn Nakano Glenn, "From Servitude to Service Work: Historical Continuities in the Racial Division of Paid Reproductive Labor," *Signs* 18 (autumn 1992): 3. See also Bonnie Thornton Dill, "Our Mothers' Grief: Racial-Ethnic Women and the Maintenance of Families," *Journal of Family History* 13, no. 4 (1988): 415–31.
24. Morgan, 146.
25. Maxine Baca Zinn and Bonnie Thornton Dill, "Difference and Domination," in *Women of Color in U.S. Society* (1994): 11–12.
26. See Omi and Winant, 53–76, for a discussion of racial formation.
27. Margaret L. Andersen and Patricia Hill Collins, *Race, Class, and Gender: An Anthology* (Belmont, Calif.: Wadsworth, 1992), xvi.
28. Omi and Winant.
29. Nazli Kibria, "Migration and Vietnamese American Women: Remaking Ethnicity," in *Women of Color in U.S. Society* (1994): 247–61.
30. Patricia Hill Collins, *Black Feminist Thought: Knowledge, Consciousness, and the Politics of Empowerment* (Boston: Unwin Hyman, 1990).
31. Elizabeth Spelman, *Inessential Women: Problems of Exclusion in Feminist Thought* (Boston: Beacon Press, 1988), 136.
32. Several discussions of difference make this point. See Baca Zinn and Dill, 10; Gordon, 106; and Lynn Weber, in the "Symposium on West and Fenstermaker's 'Doing Difference,'" *Gender & Society,* 9 (August 1995): 515–19.
33. Glenn, 10.
34. Gordon, 106.
35. Chandra Talpade Mohanty, "Cartographies of Struggle: Third World Women and the Politics of Feminism," in *Third World Women and the Politics of Feminism,* ed.

Chandra Talpade Mohanty, Ann Russo, and Lourdes Torres (Bloomington: Indiana University Press, 1991), 13.

36. Frankenberg and Mani, 306.
37. Norma Alarçon, "The Theoretical Subject(s) of *This Bridge Called My Back* and Anglo-American Feminism," in *Making Face, Making Soul, Haciendo Caras: Creative and Critical Perspectives by Women of Color,* ed. Gloria Anzaldúa (San Francisco: Aunt Lute, 1990), 356.
38. Frankenberg. See also Evelyn Torton Beck, "The Politics of Jewish Invisibility," *NWSA Journal* (fall 1988): 93–102.

PART II
Gender Socialization

Having been branded a sissy by neighborhood children because I preferred jump rope to baseball, and dolls to playing soldiers, I was often taunted with "hey sissy" or "hey faggot" or "yoo hoo honey" (in a mocking voice) when I left the house.

TOMMI AVICOLLI[1]

As a girl I was kept under strict surveillance, since virtue and modesty were, by cultural equation, the same as family honor. As a teenager I was instructed on how to behave as a proper señorita.

JUDITH ORTIZ COFER[2]

The gender system, embedded in other institutions, ensures its continuance through systematic socialization of children, adolescents, and adults. Even though there is substantial variation in how different cultural groups and families within the United States and throughout the world teach their children to be girls or boys, and even though men and women are more alike than they are different, the presence of gender training persists, and the larger institutional structures reinforce it. Sociologist Michael Messner, for example, in a telling account of white male socialization in childhood, describes the day he attended his first little league practice and was told by his father that he threw like a girl. A week later, after careful coaching by his father and intense fear of being thought a sissy, he had learned to throw like a man.[3] In a study of Black and white elementary school children, Jacqueline Jordan Irvine concluded that teachers systematically encouraged Black girls to act submissive, and that by upper elementary school, both Black and white girls are rendered relatively invisible in classrooms, receiving significantly less attention from teachers than boys of both races receive.[4]

From the time we are born until we die, gender socialization is a constant part of our lives. Although the genes that determine sex come in several combinations (not just two), and although the hormonal makeup and physical characteristics of human beings fall along a continuum defined as masculine at one end and feminine at the other, allowing for many combinations and permutations that define one's biological sex, the social contexts in which infants are assigned a gender do not allow for more than two categories in mainstream U.S. society. Based on examination of its genitalia, an infant will almost always be defined as female or male, whatever its chromosomal and hormonal makeup. Within this powerful system of gender assignment, women and men work to define their individual identities. Because gender is a socialized aspect of life rather than a purely genetic/biological one, and because it is largely "socially constructed" rather than instinctual, there is flexibility in how it is expressed.

In a distressing illustration of how girl and boy children are treated differently from very early in their lives, authors of a study of infants with abusive head trauma found that most of the infant victims were boys (60.3 percent). Both women and men tended to abuse boys more than girls in ways serious enough to inflict head injury via shaken baby syndrome or impact trauma. The majority of perpetrators were men in the infants' lives—most typically fathers, stepfathers, or the mother's partner. The authors of the study suggest that perhaps adults have different expectations of male and female infants. If the latter is the case, it could be that tolerance for crying in girl babies is higher than it is for boys. These authors and others call for better parenting training, especially focused on men and boys.[5] The resistance of parents to give dolls to boys seems to be one piece of the failure to teach boys to care for children. Given the fact that more women than ever before are involved in the paid work force, more men and boys are spending time with children, either because the parents are working split shifts (see Rubin, Part VI), or because men and boys are serving as babysitters more often.

A push toward gender equality in recent years has led to higher math scores and greater success in science among girls. It has also led to higher rates of smoking, drinking and drug use, according to a report sponsored by the National Council for Research on Women.[6]

The field of gender socialization is currently facing some redefinition related to the role of hormones and genitals in human development. Since 1972, many academics and medical professionals have been arguing that gender is primarily socialized, independent of genes and hormones—that infants are psychologically undifferentiated at birth. In short, they argue that any baby could be raised in either gender if the family and community gave the child consistent messages. This conclusion was based on a single case reported by psychologist John Money concerning a biological male whose penis was accidentally destroyed in a routine circumcision at 7 months of age. The parents, following the advice of Money and his medical team, decided to raise the child as a girl a year or so later and the child's testicles were surgically removed.[7] The early reports on this boy/girl's life claimed that "Joan" had made a successful adjustment as a girl. In 1997, however, psychologist Milton Diamond and psychiatrist Keith Sigmundson reported that Joan had rejected the sex reassignment treatments at age 14 and decided to live as a male. He is currently living life as a heterosexual man married to a woman. Adamantly rejecting the notion that gender must be based on genital appearance, size, and function, he stated "If that's all they think of me, that they gotta justify my worth by what I have between my legs, then I gotta be a complete loser."[8] Diamond and Sigmundson concluded that the early gender reassignment had been a mistake, and later the same year offered guidelines for how to address situations in which children had unusual or injured genitals.[9] Later journalist John Colapinto wrote a book about this case, describing in detail the experiences of David Reimer (his real name) and exposing what he believed were serious ethical breaches in Money's treatment of both Reimer and the readers of his publications.[10] This case suggests that the extent to which gender is hardwired to physical sex is still unclear and will require further study.

Sex reassignment seems most successful when chosen by the person him or herself. This has been made especially clear by members of the Intersex Society of North America who argue that forced sex and gender assignments that contradicted their bodily truths have been destructive. They recommend assigning a gender to an infant, avoiding any unnecessary surgery, and allowing the child to choose how to express itself once it is old enough to understand what version of intersexuality it has and how it might like to live within that particular bodily reality. An example from the Dominican Republic illustrates this point. Children in three villages inherited a syndrome that produced ambiguous genitalia at birth but that later became male genitalia at puberty. These children were raised as girls who knew that they might become boys at puberty. They received a third gender label, "male genitalia at twelve." Of eighteen children originally raised as girls, sixteen successfully assumed male genders after their penises developed.[11] At least one chose to remain female, even though her body had masculinized, because she enjoyed living as a girl/woman. The potential for resocialization is also clearly illustrated by adults who become transsexuals or transgendered, making a choice to resocialize themselves, to varying degrees, into the gender in which they were not raised. This resocialization process is often accompanied by a new sexual orientation as well.[12]

Research literature on adult development suggests that expressions of gender shift in various ways throughout the life cycle.[13] Men and women frequently grow more similar in midlife. Socialization patterns and expectations for male and female behavior also change over time, related to the historical context. For example, many women were needed in factories during World War II but were sent home when men, returning from the war, were given priority in hiring; these women were then encouraged to be housewives and mothers, forced to resocialize themselves to match prior expectations. Those who had to work, however, ended up with lower-paying jobs since the best jobs were given to men returning from the war.

Socialization as soldiers or fighters, increasingly obvious to people in the United States as we grapple with the aftermath of September 11, 2001, affects millions of young men (especially) worldwide. Recruitment of teenage men into national armies or resistance movements affects not only the young men themselves, but also their families and communities.[14] Turning people into fighters takes an intensive socialization process for which state armies are famous (see Kaplan this part). The effects of militarism on women as well are widespread and well documented (see Enloe, Part IX).[15]

This part of the book looks at selected aspects of gender socialization. A recurring theme in the study of gender socialization is the presence of homophobia overtly expressed against boys and girls who don't fit gender stereotypes and internalized by gay men, lesbians, bisexuals, and transgendered people as fear of ostracism or as self-hatred. The essays included here address the social construction of gender and gender inequality (Lorber), pressures for gender conformity (Avicolli, Due, and Kimmel), gender socialization in varied cultural/racial/class contexts in the United States (Messner, Collins, Cofer), and socialization as fighters in Israel and Palestine (Kaplan and Peteet).

These articles urge us to become more conscious of various aspects of gender socialization and to consider ways to change what limits people of both genders from being fully human in their own right. There are policy implications here regarding how we accept people who don't fit the norms of masculinity and femininity; regarding the negative effects of limited economic options for poor and working-class children; regarding the intersections of racism, homophobia, elitism, and sexism as they affect people's lives; and regarding the prevention of war and other kinds of violent conflict.

NOTES

1. Tommi Avicolli, "He Defies You Still: The Memoirs of a Sissy," in Paula S. Rothenberg, *Race, Class, and Gender in the United States: An Integrated Study,* 3rd ed. (New York: St. Martin's Press, 1995), p. 231.
2. Judith Ortiz Cofer, "The Myth of the Latin Woman: I Just Met a Girl Named Maria," in *The Latin Deli: Prose and Poetry.* (Athens, GA: University of Georgia Press, 1993).
3. Michael A. Messner, "Ah, Ya Throw Like a Girl!" in Michael A. Messner and Donald F. Sabo, eds., *Sex, Violence and Power in Sports: Rethinking Masculinity* (Freedom, CA: Crossing Press, 1994), pp. 28–32. Messner also reports that this way of throwing is so unnatural and injurious to the shoulder that few pitchers in childhood survive as pitchers into adulthood, having permanently injured their shoulders.
4. Jacqueline Jordan Irvine, "Teacher Communication Patterns as Related to the Race and Sex of the Student," *Journal of Educational Research* 78, no. 6 (1985), pp. 338–45; Jacqueline Jordan Irvine, "Teacher-Student Interactions: Effects of Student Race, Sex, and Grade Level," *Journal of Educational Psychology* 78, no. 1 (1986), pp. 14–21. Reported in Hilary M. Lips, "Gender-Role Socialization: Lessons in Femininity," in Jo Freeman, ed., *Women: A Feminist Perspective,* 5th ed. (Mountain View, CA: Mayfield, 1995), pp. 128–48.
5. Suzanne P. Starling, James R. Holden, and Carole Jenny, "Abusive Head Trauma: The Relationship of Perpetrators to Their Victims." *Pediatrics* 95, no. 2 (February 1995), pp. 259ff; Alisa Valdés-Rodríguez, "Shaken Baby Deaths Typically Involve Fathers: Young Males Need Infant-Care Training, Abuse Prevention Activists, Doctors Say," *The Boston Globe* (September 22, 1998), pp. B1, B8.
6. Lynn Phillips, *The Girls Report: What We Know & Need to Know about Growing Up Female.* (New York: National Council for Research on Women, 1998).
7. John Money and Anke A. Ehrhardt, *Man & Woman, Boy & Girl: The Differentiation and Dimorphism of Gender Identity from Conception to Maturity* (Baltimore: Johns Hopkins University Press, 1972).
8. Milton Diamond and H. Keith Sigmundson, "Sex Reassignment at Birth," *Archives of Pediatric and Adolescent Medicine,* 151, no. 3 (March, 1997), p. 301.

9. Milton Diamond and H. Keith Sigmundson, "Management of Intersexuality: Guidelines for Dealing with Persons with Ambiguous Genitalia," *Archives of Pediatric and Adolescent Medicine,* 151, no. 10 (October, 1997), pp. 1046–50.
10. John Colapinto, *As Nature Made Him: The Boy Who Was Raised as a Girl.* (New York: Harper Collins, 2000).
11. Anne Fausto-Sterling, *Myths of Gender* (New York: Basic Books, 1985), pp. 86–87.
12. For discussions of the experiences of transsexuals and gender benders, see the new *Journal of Gay, Lesbian, and Bisexual Identity.* Also see Paul Hewitt, *A Self-Made Man: The Diary of a Man Born in a Woman's Body* (London: Headline, 1995); Richard Ekins, *Blending Genders: Social Aspects of Cross-Dressing and Sex Changing* (New York: Routledge, 1995). For a critical look at solving gender confusion via transsexual surgery, see Janice Raymond, *The Transsexual Empire: The Making of the She-Male* (NY: Teachers College Press, 1994).
13. Margaret L. Andersen, *Thinking about Women: Sociological Perspectives on Sex and Gender,* 3rd ed. (New York: Macmillan, 1993), p. 44.
14. David Filipov, "Afghan Boys Take Up Rifles to Become Men," *Boston Sunday Globe* (October 28, 2001), p. A20.
15. Cynthia Enloe, *Maueuvers: The International Politics of Militarizing Women's Lives* (Berkeley, CA: University of California Press, 2000); Cynthia Enloe, *The Morning After: Sexual Politics at the End of the Cold War* (Berkeley, CA: University of California Press, 1993); Dafna N. Izraeli, "Paradoxes of Women's Service in the Israel Defense Forces," in Daniel Maman, Eyal Ben-Ari, and Zeev Rosenhek (eds.), *Military, State and Society in Israel* (New Brunswick, NJ: Transaction Publishers, 2001), pp. 203–38.

9

THE SOCIAL CONSTRUCTION OF GENDER

JUDITH LORBER

Talking about gender for most people is the equivalent of fish talking about water. Gender is so much the routine ground of everyday activities that questioning its taken-for-granted assumptions and presuppositions is like thinking about whether the sun will come up.[1] Gender is so pervasive that in our society we assume it is bred into our genes. Most people find it hard to believe that gender is constantly created and re-created out of human interaction, out of social life, and is the texture and order of that social life. Yet gender, like culture, is a human production that depends on everyone constantly "doing gender" (West and Zimmerman 1987).

And everyone "does gender" without thinking about it. Today, on the subway, I saw a well-dressed man with a year-old child in a stroller. Yesterday, on a bus, I saw a man with a tiny baby in a carrier on his chest. Seeing men taking care of small children in public is increasingly common—at least in New York City. But both men were quite obviously stared at—and smiled at, approvingly. Everyone was doing gender—the men who were changing the role of fathers and the other passengers, who were applauding them silently. But there was more gendering going on that probably fewer people noticed. The baby was wearing a white crocheted cap and white clothes. You couldn't tell if it was a boy or a girl. The child in the stroller was wearing a dark blue T-shirt and dark print pants. As they started to leave the train, the father put a Yankee baseball cap on the child's head. Ah, a boy, I thought. Then I noticed the gleam of tiny earrings in the child's ears, and as they got off, I saw the little flowered sneakers and lace-trimmed socks. Not a boy after all. Gender done.

Gender is such a familiar part of daily life that it usually takes a deliberate disruption of our expectations of how women and men are supposed to act to pay attention to how it is produced. Gender signs and signals are so ubiquitous that we usually fail to note them—unless they are missing or ambiguous. Then we are uncomfortable until we have successfully placed the other person in a gender status; otherwise, we feel socially dislocated. In our society, in addition to man and woman, the status can be *transvestite* (a person who dresses in opposite-gender clothes) and *transsexual* (a person who

---

has had sex-change surgery). Transvestites and transsexuals construct their gender status by dressing, speaking, walking, gesturing in the ways prescribed for women or men—whichever they want to be taken for—and so does any "normal" person.

For the individual, gender construction starts with assignment to a sex category on the basis of what the genitalia look like at birth.[2] Then babies are dressed or adorned in a way that displays the category because parents don't want to be constantly asked whether their baby is a girl or a boy. A sex category becomes a gender status through naming, dress, and the use of other gender markers. Once a child's gender is evident, others treat those in one gender differently from those in the other, and the children respond to the different treatment by feeling different and behaving differently. As soon as they can talk, they start to refer to themselves as members of their gender. Sex doesn't come into play again until puberty, but by that time, sexual feelings and desires and practices have been shaped by gendered norms and expectations. Adolescent boys and girls approach and avoid each other in an elaborately scripted and gendered mating dance. Parenting is gendered, with different expectations for mothers and for fathers, and people of different genders work at different kinds of jobs. The work adults do as mothers and fathers and as low-level workers and high-level bosses, shapes women's and men's life experiences, and these experiences produce different feelings, consciousness, relationships, skills—ways of being that we call feminine or masculine.[3] All of these processes constitute the social construction of gender.

Gendered roles change—today fathers are taking care of little children, girls and boys are wearing unisex clothing and getting the same education, women and men are working at the same jobs. Although many traditional social groups are quite strict about maintaining gender differences, in other social groups they seem to be blurring. Then why the one-year-old's earrings? Why is it still so important to mark a child as a girl or a boy, to make sure she is not taken for a boy or he for a girl? What would happen if they were? They would, quite literally, have changed places in their social world.

To explain why gendering is done from birth, constantly and by everyone, we have to look not only at the way individuals experience gender but at gender as a social institution. As a social institution, gender is one of the major ways that human beings organize their lives. Human society depends on a predictable division of labor, a designated allocation of scarce goods, assigned responsibility for children and others who cannot care for themselves, common values and their systematic transmission to new members, legitimate leadership, music, art, stories, games, and other symbolic productions. One way of choosing people for the different tasks of society is on the basis of their talents, motivations, and competence—their demonstrated achievements. The other way is on the basis of gender, race, ethnicity—ascribed membership in a category of people. Although societies vary in the extent to which they use one or the other of these ways of allocating people to work and to carry out other responsibilities, every society uses gender and age grades. Every society classifies people as "girl and boy children," "girls and boys ready to be married," and "fully adult women and men," constructs similarities among them and differences between them, and assigns them to different roles and responsibilities. Personality characteristics, feelings, motivations, and ambitions flow from these different life experiences so that the members of these different groups become different kinds of people. The process of gendering and its outcome are legitimated by religion, law, science, and the society's entire set of values.

Gender as Process, Stratification, and Structure

As a social institution, gender is a process of creating distinguishable social statuses for the assignment of rights and responsibilities. As part of a stratification system that ranks these statuses unequally, gender is a major building block in the social structures built on these unequal statuses.

As a *process,* gender creates the social differences that define "woman" and "man." In social interaction throughout their lives, individuals learn what is expected, see what is expected, act and react in expected ways, and thus simultaneously construct and maintain the gender order: "The very injunction to be given gender takes place through discursive routes: to be a good mother, to be a heterosexually desirable object, to be a fit worker, in sum, to signify a multiplicity of guarantees in response to a variety of different demands all at once" (J. Butler 1990, 145). Members of a social group neither make up gender as they go along nor exactly replicate in rote fashion what was done before. In almost every encounter, human beings produce gender, behaving in the ways they learned were appropriate for their gender status, or resisting or rebelling against these norms. Resistance and rebellion have altered gender norms, but so far they have rarely eroded the statuses.

Gendered patterns of interaction acquire additional layers of gendered sexuality, parenting, and work behaviors in childhood, adolescence, and adulthood. Gendered norms and expectations are enforced through informal sanctions of gender-inappropriate behavior by peers and by formal punishment or threat of punishment by those in authority should behavior deviate too far from socially imposed standards for women and men.

Everyday gendered interactions build gender into the family, the work process, and other organizations and institutions, which in turn reinforce gender expectations for individuals.[4] Because gender is a process, there is room not only for modification and variation by individuals and small groups but also for institutionalized change (J. W. Scott 1988, 7).

As part of a *stratification* system, gender ranks men above women of the same race and class. Women and men could be different but equal. In practice, the process of creating difference depends to a great extent on differential evaluation. As Nancy Jay (1981) says: "That which is defined, separated out, isolated from all else is A and pure. Not-A is necessarily impure, a random catchall, to which nothing is external except A and the principle of order that separates it from Not-A" (45). From the individual's point of view, whichever gender is A, the other is Not-A; gender boundaries tell the individual who is like him or her, and all the rest are unlike. From society's point of view, however, one gender is usually the touchstone, the normal, the dominant, and the other is different, deviant, and subordinate. In Western society, "man" is A, "wo-man" is Not-A. (Consider what a society would be like where woman was A and man Not-A.)

The further dichotomization by race and class constructs the gradations of a heterogeneous society's stratification scheme. Thus, in the United States, white is A, African American is Not-A; middle class is A, working class is Not-A, and "African-American women occupy a position whereby the inferior half of a series of these dichotomies converge" (P. H. Collins 1990, 70). The dominant categories are the hegemonic ideals, taken so for granted as the way things should be that white is not ordinarily thought of as a race, middle class as a class, or men as a gender. The characteristics of these categories define the Other as that which lacks the valuable qualities the dominants exhibit.

In a gender-stratified society, what men do is usually valued more highly than what women do because men do it, even when their activities are very similar or the same. In different regions of southern India, for example, harvesting rice is men's work, shared work, or women's work: "Wherever a task is done by women it is considered easy, and where it is done by [men] it is considered difficult" (Mencher 1988, 104). A gathering and hunting society's survival usually depends on the nuts, grubs, and small animals brought in by the women's foraging trips, but when the men's hunt is successful, it is the occasion for a celebration. Conversely, because they are the superior group, white men do not have to do the "dirty work," such as housework; the most inferior group does it, usually poor women of color (Palmer 1989).

Freudian psychoanalytic theory claims that boys must reject their mothers and deny the feminine in themselves in order to become men: "For boys the major goal is the achievement of personal masculine identification with their father and sense of secure masculine self, achieved through superego formation and disparagement of women" (Chodorow 1978, 165). Masculinity may be the outcome of boys' intrapsychic struggles to separate their identity from that of their mothers, but the proofs of masculinity are culturally shaped and usually ritualistic and symbolic (Gilmore 1990).

The Marxist feminist explanation for gender inequality is that by demeaning women's abilities and keeping them from learning valuable technological skills, bosses preserve them as a cheap and exploitable reserve army of labor. Unionized men who could easily be replaced by women collude in this process because it allows them to monopolize the better-paid, more interesting, and more autonomous jobs: "Two factors emerge as helping men maintain their separation from women and their control of technological occupations. One is the active gendering of jobs and people. The second is the continual creation of sub-divisions in the work processes, and levels in work hierarchies, into which men can move in order to keep their distance from women" (Cockburn 1985, 13).

Societies vary in the extent of the inequality in social status of their women and men members, but where there is inequality, the status "woman" (and its attendant behavior and role allocations) is usually held in lesser esteem than the status "man." Since gender is also intertwined with a society's other constructed statuses of differential evaluation—race, religion, occupation, class, country of origin, and so on—men and women members of the favored groups command more power, more prestige, and more property than the members of the disfavored groups. Within many social groups, however, men are advantaged over women. The more economic resources, such as education and job opportunities, are available to a group, the more they tend to be monopolized by men. In poorer groups that have few resources (such as working-class African Americans in the United States), women and men are more nearly equal, and the women may even outstrip the men in education and occupational status (Almquist 1987).

As a *structure,* gender divides work in the home and in economic production, legitimates those in authority, and organizes sexuality and emotional life (Connell 1987, 91–142). As primary parents, women significantly influence children's psychological development and emotional attachments, in the process reproducing gender. Emergent sexuality is shaped by heterosexual, homosexual, bisexual, and sadomasochistic patterns that are gendered—different for girls and boys, and for women and men—so that sexual statuses reflect gender statuses.

When gender is a major component of structured inequality, the devalued genders have less power, prestige, and economic rewards than the valued genders. In countries that discourage gender discrimination, many major roles are still gendered; women still do most of the domestic labor and child rearing, even while doing full-time paid work; women and men are segregated on the job and each does work considered "appropriate"; women's work is usually paid less than men's work. Men dominate the positions of authority and leadership in government, the military, and the law; cultural productions, religions, and sports reflect men's interests.

In societies that create the greatest gender difference, such as Saudi Arabia, women are kept out of sight behind walls or veils, have no civil rights, and often create a cultural and emotional world of their own (Bernard 1981). But even in societies with less rigid gender boundaries, women and men spend much of their time with people of their own gender because of the way work and family are organized. This spatial separation of women and men reinforces gendered differences, identity, and ways of thinking and behaving (Coser 1986).

Gender inequality—the devaluation of "women" and the social domination of "men"—has social functions and social history. It is not the result of sex, procreation, physiology, anatomy, hormones, or genetic predispositions. It is produced and maintained by identifiable social processes and built into the general social structure and individual identities deliberately and purposefully. The social order as we know it in Western societies is organized around racial, ethnic, class, and gender inequality. I contend, therefore, that the continuing purpose of gender as a modern social institution is to construct women as a group to be the subordinates of men as a group.

The Paradox of Human Nature

To say that sex, sexuality, and gender are all socially constructed is not to minimize their social power. These categorical imperatives govern our lives in the most profound and pervasive ways, through the social experiences and social practices of what Dorothy Smith calls the "everday/evernight world" (1990, 31–57). The paradox of human nature is that it is *always* a manifestation of cultural meanings, social relationships, and power politics; "not biology, but culture, becomes destiny" (J. Butler 1990, 8). Gendered people emerge not from physiology or sexual orientations but from the exigencies of the social order, mostly, from the need for a reliable division of the work of food production and the social (not physical) reproduction of new members. The moral imperatives of religion and cultural representations guard the boundary lines among genders and ensure that what is demanded, what is permitted, and what is tabooed for the people in each gender is well known and followed by most (C. Davies 1982). Political power, control of scarce resources, and, if necessary, violence uphold the gendered social order in the face of resistance and rebellion. Most people, however, voluntarily go along with their society's prescriptions for those of their gender status, because the norms and expectations get built into their sense of worth and identity as [the way we] think, the way we see and hear and speak, the way we fantasy, and the way we feel.

There is no core or bedrock in human nature below these endlessly looping processes of the social production of sex and gender, self and other, identity and psyche, each of which is a "complex cultural construction" (J. Butler 1990, 36). *For humans, the social is the natural.* Therefore, "in its feminist senses, gender cannot mean simply the cultural appropriation of biological sexual difference. Sexual difference is itself a fundamental—and scientifically contested—construction. Both 'sex' and 'gender' are woven of multiple, asymmetrical strands of difference, charged with multifaceted dramatic narratives of domination and struggle" (Haraway 1990, 140).

NOTES

1. Gender is, in Erving Goffman's words, an aspect of *Felicity's Condition:* "any arrangement which leads us to judge an individual's . . . acts not to be a manifestation of strangeness. Behind Felicity's Condition is our sense of what it is to be sane" (1983:27). Also see Bem 1993; Frye 1983, 17–40; Goffman 1977.

2. In cases of ambiguity in countries with modern medicine, surgery is usually performed to make the genitalia more clearly male or female.
3. See J. Butler 1990 for an analysis of how doing gender is gender identity.
4. On the "logic of practice," or how the experience of gender is embedded in the norms of everyday interaction and the structure of formal organizations, see Acker 1990; Bourdieu [1980] 1990; Connell 1987; Smith 1987.

REFERENCES

Acker, Joan. 1990. "Hierarchies, jobs, and bodies: A theory of gendered organizations," *Gender & Society* 4:139–58.

Almquist, Elizabeth M. 1987. "Labor market gendered inequality in minority groups," *Gender & Society* 1:400–14.

Bem, Sandara Lipsitz. 1993. *The Lenses of Gender: Transforming the Debate on Sexual Inequality.* New Haven: Yale University Press.

Bernard, Jessie. 1981. *The Female World.* New York: Free Press.

Bourdieu, Pierre. [1980] 1990. *The Logic of Practice.* Stanford, Calif.: Stanford University Press.

Butler, Judith. 1990. *Gender Trouble: Feminism and the Subversion of Identity.* New York and London: Routledge.

Chodorow, Nancy. 1978. *The Reproduction of Mothering.* Berkeley: University of California Press.

Cockburn, Cynthia. 1985. *Machinery of Dominance: Women, Men and Technical Know-how.* London: Pluto Press.

Collins, Patricia Hill. 1989. "The social construction of black feminist thought," *Signs* 14:745–73.

Connell, R. [Robert] W. 1987. *Gender and Power: Society, the Person, and Sexual Politics.* Stanford, Calif.: Stanford University Press.

Coser, Rose Laub. 1986. "Cognitive structure and the use of social space," *Sociological Forum* 1:1–26.

Davies, Christie. 1982. "Sexual taboos and social boundaries," *American Journal of Sociology* 87:1032–63.

Dwyer, Daisy, & Judith Bruce (eds.). 1988. *A Home Divided: Women and Income in the Third World.* Palo Alto, Calif.: Stanford University Press.

Frye, Marilyn. 1983. *The Politics of Reality: Essays in Feminist Theory.* Trumansburg, N.Y.: Crossing Press.

Gilmore, David D. 1990. *Manhood in the Making: Cultural Concepts of Masculinity.* New Haven: Yale University Press.

Goffman, Erving. 1977. "The arrangement between the sexes," *Theory and Society* 4:301–33.

Haraway, Donna. 1990. "Investment strategies for the evolving portfolio of primate females," in *Jacobus, Keller, and Shuttleworth.*

Jacobus, Mary, Evelyn Fox Keller, & Sally Shuttleworth (eds.). (1990). *Body/politics: Women and the Discourse of Science.* New York and London: Routledge.

Jay, Nancy. 1981. "Gender and dichotomy," *Feminist Studies* 7:38–56.

Mencher, Joan. 1988. "Women's work and poverty: Women's contribution to household maintenance in South India," In *Dwyer and Bruce.*

Palmer, Phyllis. 1989. *Domesticity and Dirt: Housewives and Domestic Servants in the United States, 1920–1945.* Philadelphia: Temple University Press.

Scott, Joan Wallach. 1988. *Gender and the Politics of History.* New York: Columbia University Press.

Smith, Dorothy. 1987. *The Everyday World as Problematic: A Feminist Sociology.* Toronto: University of Toronto Press.

__________. 1990. *The Conceptual Practices of Power: A Feminist Sociology of Knowledge.* Toronto: University of Toronto Press.
West, Candace, & Don Zimmerman. 1987. "Doing gender." *Gender & Society* 1:125–51.

10

MASCULINITY AS HOMOPHOBIA

Michael S. Kimmel

Even if we do not subscribe to Freudian psychoanalytic ideas, we can still observe how, in less sexualized terms, the father is the first man who evaluates the boy's masculine performance, the first pair of male eyes before whom he tries to prove himself. Those eyes will follow him for the rest of his life. Other men's eyes will join them—the eyes of role models such as teachers, coaches, bosses, or media heroes; the eyes of his peers, his friends, his workmates; and the eyes of millions of other men, living and dead, from whose constant scrutiny of his performance he will never be free. "The tradition of all the dead generations weighs like a nightmare on the brain of the living," was how Karl Marx put it over a century ago (1848/1964, p. 11). "The birthright of every American male is a chronic sense of personal inadequacy," is how two psychologists describe it today (Woolfolk & Richardson, 1978, p. 57).

That nightmare from which we never seem to awaken is that those other men will see that sense of inadequacy, they will see that in our own eyes we are not who we are pretending to be. What we call masculinity is often a hedge against being revealed as a fraud, an exaggerated set of activities that keep others from seeing through us, and a frenzied effort to keep at bay those fears within ourselves. Our real fear "is not fear of women but of being ashamed or humiliated in front of other men, or being dominated by stronger men" (Leverenz, 1986, p. 451).

This, then, is the great secret of American manhood: *We are afraid of other men.* Homophobia is a central organizing principle of our cultural definition of manhood. Homophobia is more than the irrational fear of gay men, more than the fear that we might be perceived as gay. "The word 'faggot' has nothing to do with homosexual experience or even with fears of homosexuals," writes David Leverenz (1986). "It comes out of the depths of manhood: a label of ultimate contempt for anyone who seems sissy, untough, uncool"

(p. 455). Homophobia is the fear that other men will unmask us, emasculate us, reveal to us and the world that we do not measure up, that we are not real men. We are afraid to let other men see that fear. Fear makes us ashamed, because the recognition of fear in ourselves is proof to ourselves that we are not as manly as we pretend, that we are, like the young man in a poem by Yeats, "one that ruffles in a manly pose for all his timid heart." Our fear is the fear of humiliation. We are ashamed to be afraid.

Shame leads to silence—the silences that keep other people believing that we actually approve of the things that are done to women, to minorities, to gays and lesbians in our culture. The frightened silence as we scurry past a woman being hassled by men on the street. That furtive silence when men make sexist or racist jokes in a bar. That clammy-handed silence when guys in the office make gay-bashing jokes. Our fears are the sources of our silences, and men's silence is what keeps the system running. This might help to explain why women often complain that their male friends or partners are often so understanding when they are alone and yet laugh at sexist jokes or even make those jokes themselves when they are out with a group.

The fear of being seen as a sissy dominates the cultural definitions of manhood. It starts so early. "Boys among boys are ashamed to be unmanly," wrote one educator in 1871 (cited in Rotundo, 1993, p. 264). I have a standing bet with a friend that I can walk onto any playground in America where 6-year-old boys are happily playing and by asking one question, I can provoke a fight. That question is simple: "Who's a sissy around here?" Once posed, the challenge is made. One of two things is likely to happen. One boy will accuse another of being a sissy, to which that boy will respond that he is not a sissy, that the first boy is. They may have to fight it out to see who's lying. Or a whole group of boys will surround one boy and all shout "He is! He is!" That boy will either burst into tears and run home crying, disgraced, or he will have to take on several boys at once, to prove that he's not a sissy. (And what will his father or older brothers tell him if he chooses to run home crying?) It will be some time before he regains any sense of self-respect.

Violence is often the single most evident marker of manhood. Rather it is the willingness to fight, the desire to fight. The origin of our expression that one has a chip on one's shoulder lies in the practice of an adolescent boy in the country or small town at the turn of the century, who would literally walk around with a chip of wood balanced on his shoulder—a signal of his readiness to fight with anyone who would take the initiative of knocking the chip off (see Gorer, 1964, p. 38; Mead, 1965).

As adolescents, we learn that our peers are a kind of gender police, constantly threatening to unmask us as feminine, as sissies. One of the favorite tricks when I was an adolescent was to ask a boy to look at his fingernails. If he held his palm toward his face and curled his fingers back to see them, he passed the test. He'd looked at his nails "like a man." But if he held the back of his hand away from his face, and looked at his fingernails with arm outstretched, he was immediately ridiculed as a sissy.

As young men we are constantly riding those gender boundaries, checking the fences we have constructed on the perimeter, making sure that nothing even remotely feminine might show through. The possibilities of being unmasked are everywhere. Even the most seemingly insignificant thing can pose a threat or activate that haunting terror. On the day the students in my course "Sociology of Men and Masculinities" were scheduled to discuss homophobia and male-male friendships, one student provided a touching illustration. Noting that it was a beautiful day, the first day of spring after a brutal northeast winter, he decided to wear shorts to class. "I had this really nice pair of new Madras shorts," he commented. "But then I thought to myself, these shorts have lavender and pink in them. Today's class topic is homophobia. Maybe today is not the best day to wear these shorts."

Our efforts to maintain a manly front cover everything we do. What we wear. How we talk. How we walk. What we eat. Every mannerism, every movement contains a coded gender language. Think, for example, of how you would answer the question: How do you "know" if a man is homosexual? When I ask this question in classes or workshops, respondents invariably provide a pretty standard list of stereotypically effeminate behaviors. He walks a certain way, talks a certain way, acts a certain way. He's very emotional; he shows his feelings. One woman commented that she "knows" a man is gay if he really cares about her; another said she knows he's gay if he shows no interest in her, if he leaves her alone.

Now alter the question and imagine what heterosexual men do to make sure no one could possibly get the "wrong idea" about them. Responses typically refer to the original stereotypes, this time as a set of negative rules about behavior. Never dress that way. Never talk or walk that way. Never show your feelings or get emotional. Always be prepared to demonstrate sexual interest in women that you meet, so it is impossible for any woman to get the wrong idea about you. In this sense, homophobia, the fear of being perceived as gay, as not a real man, keeps men exaggerating all the traditional rules of masculinity, including sexual predation with women. Homophobia and sexism go hand in hand.

The stakes of perceived sissydom are enormous—sometimes matters of life and death. We take enormous risks to prove our manhood, exposing ourselves disproportionately to health risks, workplace hazards, and stress-related illnesses. Men commit suicide three times as often as women. Psychiatrist Willard Gaylin (1992) explains that it is "invariably because of perceived social humiliation," most often tied to failure in business:

> Men become depressed because of loss of status and power in the world of men. It is not the loss of money, or the material advantages that money could buy, which produces the despair that leads to self-destruction. It is the "shame," the "humiliation," the sense of personal "failure."... A man despairs when he has ceased being a man among men. (p. 32)

In one survey, women and men were asked what they were most afraid of. Women responded that they were most afraid of being raped and murdered. Men responded that they were most afraid of being laughed at (Noble, 1992, pp. 105–106).

Power and Powerlessness in the Lives of Men

I have argued that homophobia, men's fear of other men, is the animating condition of the dominant definition of masculinity in America, that the reigning definition of masculinity is a defensive effort to prevent being emasculated. In our efforts to suppress or overcome those fears, the dominant culture exacts a tremendous price from those deemed less than fully manly: women, gay men, nonnative-born men, men of color. This perspective may help clarify a paradox in men's lives, a paradox in which men have virtually all the power and yet do not feel powerful (see Kaufman, 1993).

Manhood is equated with power—over women, over other men. Everywhere we look, we see the institutional expression of that power—in state and national legislatures, on the boards of directors of every major U.S. corporation or law firm, and in every school and hospital administration. Women have long understood this, and feminist women have spent the past three decades challenging both the public and the private expressions of men's power and acknowledging their fear of men. Feminism as a set of theories both explains women's fear of men and empowers women to confront it both publicly and privately. Feminist women have theorized that masculinity is about the drive for domination, the drive for power, for conquest.

This feminist definition of masculinity as the drive for power is theorized from women's point of view. It is how women experience masculinity. But it assumes a symmetry between the public and the private that does not conform to men's experiences. Feminists observe that women, as a group, do not hold power in our society. They also observe that individually, they, as women, do not feel powerful. They feel afraid, vulnerable. Their observation of the social reality and their individual experiences are therefore symmetrical. Feminism also observes that men, as a group, are in power. Thus, with the same symmetry, feminism has tended to assume that individually men must feel powerful.

This is why the feminist critique of masculinity often falls on deaf ears with men. When confronted with the analysis that men have all the power, many men react incredulously. "What do you mean, men have all the power?" they ask. "What are you talking about? My wife bosses me around. My kids boss me around. My boss bosses me around. I have no power at all! I'm completely powerless!"

Men's feelings are not the feelings of the powerful, but of those who see themselves as powerless. These are the feelings that come inevitably from the discontinuity between the social and the psychological, between the aggregate analysis that reveals how men are in power as a group and the psychological fact that they do not feel powerful as individuals. They are the feelings of men who were raised to believe themselves entitled to feel that power, but do not feel it. No wonder many men are frustrated and angry.

This may explain the recent popularity of those workshops and retreats designed to help men to claim their "inner" power, their "deep manhood," or their "warrior within." Authors such as Bly (1990), Moore and Gillette (1991, 1992, 1993a, 1993b), Farrell (1986, 1993), and Keen (1991) honor and respect men's feelings of powerlessness and acknowledge those feelings to be both true and real. "They gave white men the semblance of power," notes John Lee, one of the leaders of these retreats (quoted in Ferguson, 1992, p. 28). "We'll let you run the country, but in the meantime, stop feeling, stop talking, and continue swallowing your pain and your hurt." (We are not told who "they" are.)

Often the purveyors of the mythopoetic men's movement, that broad umbrella that encompasses all the groups helping men to retrieve this mythic deep manhood, use the image of the chauffeur to describe modern man's position. The chauffeur appears to have the power—he's wearing the uniform, he's in the driver's seat, and he knows where he's going. So, to the observer, the chauffeur looks as though he is in command. But to the chauffeur himself, they note, he is merely taking orders. He is not at all in charge.[1]

Despite the reality that everyone knows chauffeurs do not have the power, this image remains appealing to the men who hear it at these weekend workshops. But there is a missing piece to the image, a piece concealed by the framing of the image in terms of the individual man's experience. That missing piece is that the person who is giving the orders is also a man. Now we have a relationship *between* men—between men giving orders and other men taking those orders. The man who identifies with the chauffeur is entitled to be the man giving the orders, but he is not. ("They," it turns out, are other men.)

The dimension of power is now reinserted into men's experience not only as the product of individual experience but also as the product of relations with other men. In this sense, men's experience of powerlessness is *real*—the men actually feel it and certainly act on it—but it is not *true,* that is, it does not accurately describe their condition. In contrast to women's lives, men's lives are structured around relationships of power and men's differential access to power, as well as the differential access to that power of men as a group. Our imperfect analysis of our own situation leads us to believe that we men need more power, rather than leading us to support feminists' efforts to rearrange power relationships along more equitable lines.

Philosopher Hannah Arendt (1970) fully understood this contradictory experience of social and individual power:

> Power corresponds to the human ability not just to act but to act in concert. Power is never the property of an individual; it belongs to

> a group and remains in existence only so long as the group keeps together. When we say of somebody that he is "in power" we actually refer to his being empowered by a certain number of people to act in their name. The moment the group, from which the power originated to begin with . . . disappears, his "power" also vanishes. (p. 44)

Why, then, do American men feel so powerless? Part of the answer is because we've constructed the rules of manhood so that only the tiniest fraction of men come to believe that they are the biggest of wheels, the sturdiest of oaks, the most virulent repudiators of femininity, the most daring and aggressive. We've managed to disempower the overwhelming majority of American men by other means—such as discriminating on the basis of race, class, ethnicity, age, or sexual preference.

Masculinist retreats to retrieve deep, wounded masculinity are but one of the ways in which American men currently struggle with their fears and their shame. Unfortunately, at the very moment that they work to break down the isolation that governs men's lives, as they enable men to express those fears and that shame, they ignore the social power that men continue to exert over women and the privileges from which they (as the middle-aged, middle-class white men who largely make up these retreats) continue to benefit—regardless of their experiences as wounded victims of oppressive male socialization.

Others still rehearse the politics of exclusion, as if by clearing away the playing field of secure gender identity of any that we deem less than manly—women, gay men, nonnative-born men, men of color—middle-class, straight, white men can reground their sense of themselves without those haunting fears and that deep shame that they are unmanly and will be exposed by other men. This is the manhood of racism, of sexism, of homophobia. It is the manhood that is so chronically insecure that it trembles at the idea of lifting the ban on gays in the military, that is so threatened by women in the workplace that women become the targets of sexual harassment, that is so deeply frightened of equality that it must ensure that the playing field of male competition remains stacked against all newcomers to the game.

Exclusion and escape have been the dominant methods American men have used to keep their fears of humiliation at bay. The fear of emasculation by other men, of being humiliated, of being seen as a sissy, is the leitmotif in my reading of the history of American manhood. Masculinity has become a relentless test by which we prove to other men, to women, and ultimately to ourselves, that we have successfully mastered the part. The restlessness that men feel today is nothing new in American history; we have been anxious and restless for almost two centuries. Neither exclusion nor escape has ever brought us the relief we've sought, and there is no reason to think that either will solve our problems now. Peace of mind, relief from gender struggle, will come only from a politics of inclusion, not exclusion, from standing up for equality and justice, and not by running away.

NOTE

1. The image is from Warren Farrell, who spoke at a workshop I attended at the First International Men's Conference, Austin, Texas, October 1991.

REFERENCES

Arendt, H. (1970). *On revolution.* New York: Viking.

Bly, R. (1990). *Iron John: A book about men.* Reading, MA: Addison-Wesley.

Farrell, W. (1986). *Why men are the way they are.* New York: McGraw-Hill.

Farrell, W. (1993). *The myth of male power: Why men are the disposable sex.* New York: Simon & Schuster.

Ferguson, A. (1992, January). America's new men. *American Spectator,* 25 (1).

Gaylin, W. (1992). *The male ego.* New York: Viking.

Gorer, G. (1964). *The American people: A study in national character.* New York: Norton.

Kaufman, M. (1993). *Cracking the armour: Power and pain in the lives of men.* Toronto: Viking Canada.

Keen, S. (1991). *Fire in the belly.* New York: Bantam.

Leverenz, D. (1986, Fall). Manhood, humiliation and public life: Some stories. *Southwest Review,* 71.

Marx, K., & Engels, F. (1848/1964). The communist manifesto. In R. Tucker (Ed.), *The Marx-Engels reader.* New York: Norton.

Mead, M. (1965). *And keep your powder dry.* New York: William Morrow.

Moore, R., & Gillette, D. (1991). *King, warrior, magician lover.* New York: Harper Collins.

Moore, R., & Gillette, D. (1992). *The king within: Accessing the king in the male psyche.* New York: William Morrow.

Moore, R., & Gillette, D. (1993a). *The warrior within: Accessing the warrior in the male psyche.* New York: William Morrow.

Moore, R., & Gillette, D. (1993b). *The magician within: Accessing the magician in the male psyche.* New York: William Morrow.

Noble, V. (1992). A helping hand from the guys. In K. L. Hagan (Ed.), *Women respond to the men's movement.* San Francisco: HarperCollins.

Rotundo, E. A. (1993). *American manhood: Transformations in masculinity from the revolution to the modern era.* New York: Basic Books.

Woolfolk, R. L., & Richardson, F. (1978). *Sanity, stress and survival.* New York: Signet.

11

BOYHOOD, ORGANIZED SPORTS, AND THE CONSTRUCTION OF MASCULINITIES

MICHAEL A. MESSNER

The rapid expansion of feminist scholarship in the past two decades has led to fundamental reconceptualizations of the historical and contemporary meanings of organized sport. In the nineteenth and twentieth centuries, modernization and women's continued movement into public life created widespread "fears of social feminization," especially among middle-class men (Hantover, 1978; Kimmel, 1987). One result of these fears was the creation of organized sport as a homosocial sphere in which competition and (often violent) physicality was valued, while "the feminine" was devalued. As a result, organized sport has served to bolster a sagging ideology of male superiority, and has helped to reconstitute masculine hegemony (Bryson, 1987; Hall, 1988; Messner, 1988; Theberge, 1981).

The feminist critique has spawned a number of studies of the ways that women's sport has been marginalized and trivialized in the past (Greendorfer, 1977; Oglesby, 1978; Twin, 1978), in addition to illuminating the continued existence of structural and ideological barriers to gender equality within sport (Birrell, 1987). Only recently, however, have scholars begun to use feminist insights to examine men's experiences in sport (Kidd, 1987; Messner, 1987; Sabo, 1985). This article explores the relationship between the construction of masculine identity and boyhood participation in organized sports.

I view gender identity not as a "thing" that people "have," but rather as a *process of construction* that develops, comes into crisis, and changes as a person interacts with the social world. Through this perspective, it becomes possible to speak of "gendering" identities rather than "masculinity" or "femininity" as relatively fixed identities or statuses.

There is an agency in this construction; people are not passively shaped by their social environment. As recent feminist analyses of the

---

construction of feminine gender identity have pointed out, girls and women are implicated in the construction of their own identities and personalities, both in terms of the ways that they participate in their own subordination and the ways that they resist subordination (Benjamin, 1988; Haug, 1987). Yet this self-construction is not a fully conscious process. There are also deeply woven, unconscious motivations, fears, and anxieties at work here. So, too, in the construction of masculinity. Levinson (1978) has argued that masculine identity is neither fully "formed" by the social context, nor is it "caused" by some internal dynamic put into place during infancy. Instead, it is shaped and constructed through the interaction between the internal and the social. The internal gendering identity may set developmental "tasks," may create thresholds of anxiety and ambivalence, yet it is only through a concrete examination of people's interactions with others within social institutions that we can begin to understand both the similarities and differences in the construction of gender identities.

In this study I explore and interpret the meanings that males themselves attribute to their boyhood participation in organized sport. In what ways do males construct masculine identities within the institution of organized sports? In what ways do class and racial differences mediate this relationship and perhaps lead to the construction of different meanings, and perhaps different masculinities? And what are some of the problems and contradictions within these constructions of masculinity?

Description of Research

Between 1983 and 1985, I conducted interviews with 30 male former athletes. Most of the men I interviewed had played the (U.S.) "major sports"—football, basketball, baseball, track. At the time of the interview, each had been retired from playing organized sports for at least five years. Their ages ranged from 21 to 48, with the median 33; 14 were black, 14 were white, and 2 were Hispanic; 15 of the 16 black and Hispanic men had come from poor or working-class families, while the majority (9 of 14) of the white men had come from middle-class or professional families. All had at some time in their lives based their identities largely on their roles as athletes and could therefore be said to have had "athletic careers." Twelve had played organized sports through high school, 11 through college, and 7 had been professional athletes. Though the sample was not randomly selected, an effort was made to see that the sample had a range of difference in terms of race and social class backgrounds, and that there was some variety in terms of age, types of sports played, and levels of success in athletic careers. Without exception, each man contacted agreed to be interviewed.

The tape-recorded interviews were semi-structured and took from one and one-half to six hours, with most taking about three hours. I asked each man to talk about four broad eras in his life: (1) his earliest experiences with sports in boyhood, (2) his athletic career, (3) retirement or disengagement from the athletic career, and (4) life after the athletic career. In each era, I focused the interview on the meanings of "success and failure," and on the boy's/man's relationships with family, with other males, with women, and with his own body.

In collecting what amounted to life histories of these men, my overarching purpose was to use feminist theories of masculine gender identity to explore how masculinity develops and changes as boys and men interact within the socially constructed world of organized sports. In addition to using the data to move toward some generalizations about the relationship between "masculinity and sport," I was also concerned with sorting out some of the variations among boys, based on class and racial inequalities, that led them to relate differently to athletic careers. I divided my sample into two comparison groups. The first group was made up of 10 men from higher-status backgrounds, primarily white, middle-class, and professional families. The second group was made up of 20 men from lower-status backgrounds, primarily minority, poor, and working-class families.

Boyhood and the Promise of Sports

Zane Grey once said, "All boys love baseball. If they don't they're not real boys" (as cited in Kimmel, 1990). This is, of course, an ideological statement; in fact, some boys do *not* love baseball, or any other sports, for that matter. There are millions of males who at an early age are rejected by, become alienated from, or lose interest in organized sports. Yet all boys are, to a greater or lesser extent, judged according to their ability, or lack of ability, in competitive sports (Eitzen, 1975; Sabo, 1985). In this study I focus on those males who did become athletes—males who eventually poured thousands of hours into the development of specific physical skills. It is in boyhood that we can discover the roots of their commitment to athletic careers.

How did organized sports come to play such a central role in these boys' lives? When asked to recall how and why they initially got into playing sports, many of the men interviewed for this study seemed a bit puzzled: after all, playing sports was "just the thing to do." A 42-year-old black man who had played college basketball put it this way:

> It was just what you did. It's kind of like, you went to school, you played athletics, and if you didn't, there was something wrong with you. It was just like brushing your teeth: it's just what you did. It's part of your existence.

Spending one's time playing sports with other boys seemed as natural as the cycle of the seasons: baseball in the spring and summer, football in the fall, basketball in the winter—and then it was time to get out the old baseball glove and begin again. As a black 35-year-old former professional football star said:

> I'd say when I wasn't in school, 95% of the time was spent in the park playing. It was the only thing to do. It just came as natural.

And a black, 34-year-old professional basketball player explained his early experiences in sports:

> My principal and teacher said, "Now if you work at this you might be pretty damned good." So it was more or less a community thing—everybody in the community said, "Boy, if you work hard and keep your nose clean, you gonna be good." Cause it was natural instinct.

"It was natural instinct." "I was a natural." Several athletes used words such as these to explain their early attraction to sports. But certainly there is nothing "natural" about throwing a ball through a hoop, hitting a ball with a bat, or jumping over hurdles. A boy, for instance, may have amazingly dexterous inborn hand-eye coordination, but this does not predispose him to a career of hitting baseballs any more than it predisposes him to life as a brain surgeon. When one listens closely to what these men said about their early experiences in sports, it becomes clear that their adoption of the self-definition of "natural athlete" was the result of what Connell (1990) has called "a collective practice" that constructs masculinities. The boyhood development of masculine identity and status—truly problematic in a society that offers no official rite of passage into adulthood—results from a process of interaction with people and social institutions. Thus, in discussing early motivations in sports, men commonly talk of the importance of relationships with family members, peers, and the broader community.

Family Influences

Though most of the men in this study spoke of their mothers with love, respect, even reverence, their descriptions of their earliest experiences in sports are stories of an exclusively male world. The existence of older brothers or uncles who served as teachers and athletic role models—as well as sources of competition for attention and status within the family—was very common. An older brother, uncle, or even close friend of the family who was a successful athlete appears to have acted as a sort of standard of achievement against whom to measure oneself. A 34-year-old black man who had been a three-sport star in high school said:

> My uncles—my Uncle Harold went to the Detroit Tigers, played pro ball—all of 'em, everybody played sports, so I wanted to be better than anybody else. I knew that everybody in this town knew them—their names were something. I wanted my name to be just like theirs.

Similarly, a black 41-year-old former professional football player recalled:

> I was the younger of three brothers and everybody played sports, so consequently I was more or less forced into it. 'Cause one brother was always better than the next brother and then I came along and had to show them that I was just as good as them. My oldest brother was an all-city ballplayer, then my other brother comes along he's all-city and all-state, and then I have to come along.

For some, attempting to emulate or surpass the athletic accomplishments of older male family members created pressures that were difficult to deal with. A 33-year-old white man explained that he was a good athlete during boyhood, but the constant awareness that his two older brothers had been better made it difficult for him to feel good about himself, or to have fun in sports:

> I had this sort of reputation that I followed from the playgrounds through grade school, and through high school. I followed these guys who were all-conference and all-state.

Most of these men, however, saw their relationships with their athletic older brothers and uncles in a positive light; it was within these relationships that they gained experience and developed motivations that gave them a competitive "edge" within their same-aged peer group. As a 33-year-old black man describes his earliest athletic experiences:

> My brothers were role models. I wanted to prove—especially to my brothers—that I had heart, you know, that I was a man.

When asked, "What did it mean to you to be 'a man' at that age?" he replied:

> Well, it meant that I didn't want to be a so-called scaredy-cat. You want to hit a guy even though he's bigger than you to show that, you know, you've got this macho image. I remember that at that young an age, that feeling was exciting to me. And that carried over, and as I got older, I got better and I began to look around me and see, well hey! I'm competitive with these guys, even though I'm younger, you know? And then of course all the compliments come—and I began to notice a change, even in my parents—especially in my father—he was proud of that, and that was very important to me. He was extremely important . . . he showed me more affection, now that I think of it.

As this man's words suggest, if men talk of their older brothers and uncles mostly as role models, teachers, and "names" to emulate, their talk of their relationships with their fathers is more deeply layered and complex. Athletic skills and competition for status may often be learned from older brothers, but it is in boys' relationships with fathers that we find many of the keys to the emotional salience of sports in the development of masculine identity.

Relationships with Fathers

The fact that boys' introductions to organized sports are often made by fathers who might otherwise be absent or emotionally distant adds a powerful emotional charge to these early experiences (Osherson, 1986). Although playing organized sports eventually came to feel "natural" for all of the men interviewed in this study, many needed to be "exposed" to sports, or even gently "pushed" by their fathers to become involved in activities like Little League baseball. A white 33-year-old man explained:

> I still remember it like it was yesterday—Dad and I driving up in his truck, and I had my glove and my hat and all that—and I said, "Dad, I don't want to do it." He says, "What?" I says, "I don't want to do it." I was nervous. That I might fail. And he says, "Don't be silly. Lookit: There's Joey and Petey and all your friends out there." And so Dad says, "You're gonna do it, come on." And in my memory he's never said that about anything else; he just knew I needed a little kick in the pants and I'd do it. And once you're out there and you see all the other kids making errors and stuff, and you know you're better than those guys, you know: Maybe I *do* belong here. As it turned out, Little League was a good experience.

Some who were similarly "pushed" by their fathers were not so successful as the aforementioned man had been in Little League baseball, and thus the experience was not altogether a joyous affair. One 34-year-old white man, for instance, said he "inherited" his interest in sports from his father, who started playing catch with him at the age of four. Once he got into Little League, he felt pressured by his father, one of the coaches, who expected him to be the star of the team:

> I'd go 0-for-four sometimes, strike out three times in a Little League game, and I'd dread the ride home. I'd come home and he'd say, "Go in the bathroom and swing the bat in the mirror for an hour," to get my swing level. . . . It didn't help much, though, I'd go out and strike out three or four times again the next game too [laughs ironically].

When asked if he had been concerned with having his father's approval, he responded:

> Failure in his eyes? Yeah, I always thought that he wanted me to get some kind of [athletic] scholarship. I guess I was afraid of him when I was a kid. He didn't hit that much, but he had a rage about him—he'd rage, and that voice would just rattle you.

Similarly, a 24-year-old black man described his awe of his father's physical power and presence, and his sense of inadequacy in attempting to emulate him:

> My father had a voice that sounded like rolling thunder. Whether it was intentional on his part or not, I don't know, but my father gave me a sense, an image of him being the most powerful being on earth, and that no matter what I ever did I would never come close to him. . . . There were definite feelings of physical inadequacy that I couldn't work around.

It is interesting to note how these feelings of physical inadequacy relative to the father lived on as part of this young man's permanent internalized image. He eventually became a "feared" high school football player and broke school records in weight-lifting, yet

> As I grew older, my mother and friends told me that I had actually grown to be a larger man than my father. Even though in time I required larger clothes than he, which should have been a very concrete indication, neither my brother nor I could ever bring ourselves to say that I was bigger. We simply couldn't conceive of it.

Using sports activities as a means of identifying with and "living up to" the power and status of one's father was not always such a painful and difficult task for the men I interviewed. Most did not describe fathers who "pushed" them to become sports stars. The relationship between their athletic strivings and their identification with their fathers was more subtle. A 48-year-old black man, for instance, explained that he was not pushed into sports by his father, but was aware from an early age of the community status his father had gained through sports. He saw his own athletic accomplishments as a way to connect with and emulate his father:

> I wanted to play baseball because my father had been quite a good baseball player in the Negro leagues before baseball was integrated, and so he was kind of a model for me. I remember, quite young, going to a baseball game he was in—this was before the war and all—I remember being in the stands with my mother and seeing him on first base, and being aware of the crowd. . . . I was aware of people's confidence in him as a serious baseball player. I don't think my father ever said anything to me like "play sports." . . . [But] I knew he would like it if I did well. His admiration was important . . . he mattered.

Similarly, a 24-year-old white man described his father as a somewhat distant "role model" whose approval mattered:

> My father was more of an example . . . he definitely was very much in touch with and still had very fond memories of being an athlete and talked about it, bragged about it. . . . But he really didn't do that much to teach me skills, and he didn't always go to every game I played like some parents. But he approved and that was important, you know. That was important to get his approval.

> I always knew that playing sports was important to him, so I knew implicitly that it was good and there was definitely a value on it.

First experiences in sports might often come through relationships with brothers or older male relatives, and the early emotional salience of sports was often directly related to a boy's relationship with his father. The sense of commitment that these young boys eventually made to the development of athletic careers is best explained as a process of development of masculine gender identity and status in relation to same-sex peers.

Masculine Identity and Early Commitment to Sports

When many of the men in this study said that during childhood they played sports because "it's just what everybody did," they of course meant that is was just what *boys* did. They were introduced to organized sports by older brothers and fathers, and once involved, found themselves playing within an exclusively male world. Though the separate (and unequal) gendered worlds of boys and girls came to appear as "natural," they were in fact socially constructed. Thorne's observations of children's activities in schools indicated that rather than "naturally" constituting "separate gendered cultures," there is considerable interaction between boys and girls in classrooms and on playgrounds. When adults set up legitimate contact between boys and girls, Thorne observed, this usually results in "relaxed interactions." But when activities in the classroom or on the playground are presented to children as sex-segregated activities and gender is marked by teachers and other adults ("boys line up here, girls over there"), "gender boundaries are heightened, and mixed-sex interaction becomes an explicit arena of risk" (Thorne, 1986; 70). Thus sex-segregated activities such as organized sports as structured by adults, provide the context in which gendered identities and separate "gendered cultures" develop and come to appear natural. For the boys in this study, it became "natural" to equate masculinity with competition, physical strength, and skills. Girls simply did not (could not, it was believed) participate in these activities.

Yet it is not simply the separation of children, by adults, into separate activities that explains why many boys came to feel such strong connection with sports activities, while so few girls did. As I listened to men recall their earliest experiences in organized sports, I heard them talk of insecurity, loneliness, and especially a need to connect with other people as a primary motivation in their early sports strivings. As a 42-year-old white man stated, "The most important thing was just being out there with the rest of the guys—being friends." Another 32-year-old interviewee was born in Mexico and moved to the United States at a fairly young age. He never knew his father, and his mother died when he was only nine years old. Suddenly he felt rootless, and threw himself into sports. His initial motivations, however, do not appear to be based on a need to compete and win:

> Actually, what I think sports did for me is it brought me into kind of an instant family. By being on a Little League team, or even just playing with all kinds of different kids in the neighborhood, it brought what I really wanted, which was some kind of closeness. It was just being there, and being friends.

Clearly, what these boys needed and craved was that which was most problematic for them: connection and unity with other people. But why do these young males find *organized sports* such an attractive context in which to establish "a kind of closeness" with others? Comparative observations of young boys' and girls' game-playing behaviors yield important insights into this question. Piaget (1965) and Lever (1976) both observed that girls tend to have more "pragmatic" and "flexible" orientations to the rules of games; they are more prone to make exceptions and innovations in the middle of a game in order to make the game more "fair." Boys, on the other hand, tend to have a more firm, even [in]flexible orientation to the rules of a game; to them, the rules are what protects any fairness. This difference, according to Gilligan (1982), is based on the fact that early developmental experiences have yielded deeply rooted differences between males' and females' developmental tasks, needs, and moral reasoning. Girls, who tend to define themselves primarily through connection with others, experience highly competitive situations (whether in organized sports or in other hierarchical institutions) as threats to relationships, and thus to their identities. For boys, the development of gender identity involves the construction of positional identities, where a sense of self is solidified through separation from others (Chodorow, 1978). Yet feminist psychoanalytic theory has tended to oversimplify the internal lives of men (Lichterman, 1986). Males do appear to develop positional identities, yet despite their fears of intimacy, they also retain a human need for closeness and unity with others. This ambivalence toward intimate relationships is a major thread running through masculine development throughout the life course. Here we can conceptualize what Craib (1987) calls the "elective affinity" between personality and social structure: For the boy who both seeks and fears attachment with others, the rule-bound structure of organized sports can promise to be a safe place in which to seek nonintimate attachment with others within a context that maintains clear boundaries, distance, and separation.

Competitive Structures and Conditional Self-Worth

Young boys may initially find that sports give them the opportunity to experience "some kind of closeness" with others, but the structure of sports and athletic careers often undermines the possibility of boys learning to transcend their fears of intimacy, thus becoming able to develop truly close and intimate relationships with others (Kidd, 1990; Messner, 1987). The sports world is extremely hierarchical, and an incredible amount of importance is placed on winning, on "being number one." For instance, a few years ago I observed a basketball camp put on for boys by a professional basketball coach and his staff. The youngest boys, about eight years old (who could barely reach the basket with their shots) played a brief scrimmage. Afterwards, the coaches lined them up in a row in front of the older boys who were sitting in the grandstands. One by one, the coach would stand behind each boy, put his hand on the boy's head (much in the manner of a priestly benediction), and the older boys in the stands would applaud and cheer, louder or softer, depending on how well or poorly the young boy was judged to have performed. The two or three boys who were clearly the exceptional players looked confident that they would receive the praise they were due. Most of the boys, though, had expressions ranging from puzzlement to thinly disguised terror on their faces as they awaited the judgments of the older boys.

This kind of experience teaches boys that it is not "just being out there with the guys—being friends" that ensures the kind of attention and connection that they crave; it is being *better* than the other guys—*beating* them—that is the key to acceptance. Most of the boys in this study did have some early successes in sports, and thus their ambivalent need for connection with others was met, at least for a time. But the institution of sport tends to encourage the development of what Schafer (1975) has called "conditional self-worth" in boys. As boys become aware that acceptance by others is contingent upon being good—a "winner"—narrow definitions of success, based upon performance and winning, become increasingly important to them. A 33-year-old black man said that by the time he was in his early teens:

> It was expected of me to do well in all my contests—I mean by my coaches, my peers, and my family. So I in turn expected to do well, and if I didn't do well, then I'd be very disappointed.

The man from Mexico, discussed above, who said that he had sought "some kind of closeness" in his early sports experiences, began to notice in his early teens that if he played well, was a *winner,* he would get attention from others:

> It got to the point where I started realizing, noticing that people were always there for me, backing me all the time—sports got to be really fun because I always had some people there backing me. Finally my oldest brother started going to all my games, even though I had never really seen who he was [laughs]—after the game, you know, we never really saw each other, but he was at all my baseball games, and it seemed like we shared a kind of closeness there, but only in those situations. Off the field, when I wasn't in uniform, he was never around.

By high school, he said, he felt "up against the wall." Sports hadn't delivered what he had hoped it would, but he thought if he just tried harder, won one more championship trophy, he would get the attention he truly craved. Despite his efforts, this attention was not forthcoming. And, sadly, the pressures he had put on himself to excel in sports had taken most of the fun out of playing.

For many of the men in this study, throughout boyhood and into adolescence, this conscious striving for successful achievement became the primary means through which they sought connection with other people (Messner, 1987). But it is important to recognize that young males' internalized ambivalences about intimacy do not fully determine the contours and directions of their lives. Masculinity continues to develop through interaction with the social world—and because boys from different backgrounds are interacting with substantially different familial, educational, and other institutions, these differences will lead them to make different choices and define situations in different ways. Next, I examine the differences in the ways that boys from higher- and lower-status families and communities related to organized sports.

Status Differences and Commitments to Sports

In discussing early attractions to sports, the experiences of boys from higher- and lower-status backgrounds are quite similar. Both groups indicate the importance of fathers and older brothers in introducing them to sports. Both groups speak of the joys of receiving attention and acceptance among family and peers for early successes in sports. Note the similarities, for instance, in the following descriptions of boyhood athletic experiences of two men. First, a man born in a white middle-class family:

> I loved playing sports so much from a very early age because of early exposure. A lot of the sports came easy at an early age, and because they did, and because you were successful at something, I think that you're inclined to strive for that gratification. It's like, if you're good, you like it, because it's instant gratification. I'm doing something that I'm good at and I'm gonna keep doing it.

Second, a black man from a poor family:

> Fortunately I had some athletic ability, and, quite naturally, once you start doing good in whatever it is—I don't care if it's jacks—you show off what you do. That's your ability, that's your blessing, so you show it off as much as you can.

For boys from both groups, early exposure to sports, the discovery that they had some "ability," shortly followed by some sort of family, peer, and community recognition, all eventually led to the commitment of hundreds and thousands of hours of playing, practicing, and dreaming of future stardom. Despite these similarities, there are also some identifiable differences that begin to explain the tendency of males from lower-status backgrounds to develop higher levels of commitment to sports careers. The most clear-cut difference was that while men from higher-status backgrounds are likely to describe their earliest athletic experiences and motivations almost exclusively in terms of immediate family, men from lower-status backgrounds more commonly describe the importance of a broader community context. For instance, a 46-year-old man who grew up in a "poor working class" black family in a small town in Arkansas explained:

> In that community, at the age of third or fourth grade, if you're a male, they expect you to show some kind of inclination, some kind of skill in football or basketball. It was an expected thing, you know? My mom and my dad, they didn't push at all. It was the general environment.

A 48-year-old man describes sports activities as a survival strategy in his poor black community:

> Sports protected me from having to compete in gang stuff, or having to be good with my fists. If you were an athlete and got into the fist world, that was your business, and that was okay—but you didn't have to if you didn't want to. People would generally defer to you, give you your space away from trouble.

A 35-year-old man who grew up in "a poor black ghetto" described his boyhood relationship to sports similarly:

> Where I came from, either you were one of two things: you were in sports or you were out on the streets being a drug addict, or breaking into places. The guys who were in sports, we had it a little easier, because we were accepted by both groups. . . . So it worked out to my advantage, cause I didn't get into a lot of trouble—some trouble, but not a lot.

The fact that boys in lower-status communities faced these kinds of realities gave salience to their developing athletic identities. In contrast, sports were important to boys from higher-status backgrounds, yet the middle-class environment seemed more secure, less threatening, and offered far more options. By the time most of these boys got into junior high or high school, many had made conscious decisions to shift their attentions away from athletic careers to educational and (nonathletic) career goals. A 32-year-old white college athletic director told me that he had seen his chance to pursue a pro baseball career as "pissing in the wind," and instead focused on education. Similarly, a 33-year-old white dentist who was a three-sport star in high school, decided not to play sports in college, so he could focus on getting into dental school. As he put it,

> I think I kind of downgraded the stardom thing. I thought it was small potatoes. And sure, that's nice in high school and all that, but on a broad scale, I didn't think it amounted to all that much.

This statement offers an important key to understanding the construction of masculine identity within a middle-class context. The status that this boy got through sports had been *very* important to him, yet he could see that "on a broad scale," this sort of status was "small potatoes." This sort of early recognition is more than a result of the oft-noted middle-class tendency to raise "future-oriented" children (Rubin, 1976; Sennett and Cobb, 1973). Perhaps more important, it is that the *kinds* of future orientations developed by boys from higher-status backgrounds are consistent with the middle-class context. These men's descriptions of their boyhoods reveal that they grew up immersed in a wide range of institutional frameworks, of which organized sports was just one. And—importantly—they could see that the status of adult males around them was clearly linked to their positions within various professions, public institutions, and bureaucratic organizations. It was clear that access to this sort of institutional status came through educational achievement, not athletic prowess. A 32-year-old black man who grew up in a professional-class family recalled that he had idolized Wilt Chamberlain and dreamed of being a pro basketball player, yet his father discouraged his athletic strivings:

> He knew I liked the game. I *loved* the game. But basketball was not recommended; my dad would say, "That's a stereotyped image for black youth. . . . When your basketball is gone and finished, what are you gonna do? One day, you might get injured. What are you gonna look forward to?" He stressed education.

Similarly, a 32-year-old man who was raised in a white middle-class family had found in sports a key means of gaining acceptance and connection in his peer group. Yet he was simultaneously developing an image of himself as a "smart student," and becoming aware of a wide range of non-sports life options:

> My mother was constantly telling me how smart I was, how good I was, what a nice person I was, and giving me all sorts of positive strokes, and those positive strokes became a self-motivating kind of thing. I had this image of myself as smart, and I lived up to that image.

It is not that parents of boys in lower-status families did not also encourage their boys to work hard in school. Several reported that their parents "stressed books first, sports second." It's just that the broader social context—education, economy, and community—was more likely to *narrow* lower-status boys' perceptions of real-life options, while boys from higher-status backgrounds faced an expanding world of options. For instance, with a different socioeconomic background, one 35-year-old black man might have become a great musician instead of a star professional football running back. But he did not. When he was a child, he said, he was most interested in music:

> I wanted to be a drummer. But we couldn't afford drums. My dad couldn't go out and buy me a drum set or a guitar even—it was just one of those things; he was just trying to make ends meet.

But he *could* afford, as could so many in his socioeconomic condition, to spend countless hours at the local park, where he was told by the park supervisor

> that I was a natural—not only in gymnastics or baseball—whatever I did, I was a natural. He told me I shouldn't waste this talent, and so I immediately started watching the big guys then.

In retrospect, this man had potential to be a musician or any number of things, but his environment limited his options to sports, and he made the best of it. Even within sports, he, like most boys in the ghetto, was limited:

> We didn't have any tennis courts in the ghetto—we used to have a lot of tennis balls, but not racquets. I wonder today how good I might be in tennis if I had gotten a racquet in my hands at an early age.

It is within this limited structure of opportunity that many lower-status young boys found sports to be *the* place, rather than *a* place, within which to construct masculine identity, status, the relationships. A 36-year-old white man explained that his father left the family when he was very young and his mother faced a very difficult struggle to make ends meet. As his words suggest, the more limited a boy's options, and the more insecure his family situation, the more likely he is to make an early commitment to an athletic career:

> I used to ride my bicycle to Little League practice—if I'd waited for someone to pick me up and take me to the ball park I'd have never played. I'd get to the ball park and all the other kids would have their dad bring them to practice or games. But I'd park my bike to the side and when it was over I'd get on it and go home. Sports was the way for me to move everything to the side—family problems, just all the embarrassments—and think about one thing, and that was sports. . . . In the third grade, when the teacher went around the classroom and asked everybody, "What do you want to be when you grow up?" I said, "I want to be a major league baseball player," and everybody laughed their heads off.

This man eventually did enjoy a major league baseball career. Most boys from lower-status backgrounds who make similar early commitments to athletic careers are not so successful. As stated earlier, the career structure of organized sports is highly competitive and hierarchical. In fact, the chances of attaining professional status in sports are approximately 4:100,000 for a white man, 2:100,000 for a black man, and 3:1 million for a Hispanic man in the United States (Leonard and Reyman, 1988). Nevertheless, the immediate rewards (fun, status, attention), along with the constricted (nonsports) structure of opportunity, attract disproportionately large numbers of boys from lower-status backgrounds to athletic careers as their major means of constructing a masculine identity. These are the boys who later, as young men, had to struggle with "conditional self-worth," and, more often than not, occupational dead ends. Boys from higher-status backgrounds, on the other hand, bolstered their boyhood, adolescent, and early adult status through their athletic accomplishments. Their wide range of experiences and life changes led to an early shift away from sports careers as the major basis of identity (Messner, 1989).

Conclusion

The conception of the masculinity-sports relationship developed here begins to illustrate the idea of an "elective affinity" between social structure and personality. Organized sports is a "gendered institution"—an institution constructed by gender relations. As such, its structure and values (rules, formal organization, sex composition, etc.) reflect dominant conceptions of masculinity and femininity. Organized sports is also a "gendering institution"—an institution that helps to construct the current gender order. Part of this construction of gender is accomplished through the "masculinizing" of male bodies and minds.

Yet boys do not come to their first experiences in organized sports as "blank slates," but arrive with already "gendering" identities due to early developmental experiences and previous socialization. I have suggested here that an important thread running through the development of masculine identity is males' ambivalence toward intimate unity with others. Those boys who experience early athletic successes find in the structure of organized sport an affinity with this masculine ambivalence toward intimacy: The rule-bound, competitive, hierarchical world of sport offers boys an attractive means of establishing an emotionally distant (and thus "safe") connection with others. Yet as boys begin to define themselves as "athletes," they learn that in order to be accepted (to have connection) through sports, they must be winners. And in order to be winners, they must construct relationships with others (and with themselves) that are consistent with the competitive and hierarchical values and structure of the sports world. As a result, they often develop a "conditional self-worth" that leads them to construct more instrumental relationships with themselves and others. This ultimately exacerbates their difficulties in constructing intimate relationships with others. In effect, the interaction between the young male's preexisting internalized ambivalence toward intimacy with the competitive hierarchical institution of sport has resulted in the construction of a masculine personality that is characterized by instrumental rationality, goal orientation, and difficulties with intimate connection and expression (Messner, 1987).

This theoretical line of inquiry invites us not simply to examine how social institutions "socialize" boys, but also to explore the ways that boys' already-gendering identities interact with social institutions (which, like organized sport, are themselves the product of gender relations). This study has also suggested that it is not some singular "masculinity" that is being constructed through athletic careers. It may be correct, from a psychoanalytic perspective, to suggest that all males bring ambivalences toward intimacy to their interactions with the world, but "the world" is a very different place for males from different racial and socioeconomic backgrounds. Because males have substantially different interactions with the world, based on class, race, and other differences and inequalities, we might expect the construction of masculinity to take on different meanings for boys and men from differing backgrounds (Messner, 1989). Indeed, this study has suggested that boys from higher-status backgrounds face a much broader range of options than do their lower-status counterparts. As a result, athletic careers take on different meanings for these boys. Lower-status boys are likely to see athletic careers as *the* institutional context for the construction of their masculine status and identities, while higher-status males make an early shift away from athletic careers toward other institutions (usually education and nonsports careers). A key line of inquiry for future studies might begin by exploring this irony of sports careers: Despite the fact that "the athlete" is currently an example of an exemplary form of masculinity in public ideology, the vast majority of boys who become most committed to athletic careers are never well rewarded for their efforts. The fact that class and racial dynamics lead boys from higher-status backgrounds, unlike their lower-status counterparts, to move into nonsports careers illustrates how the construction of different kinds of masculinities is a key component of the overall construction of the gender order.

REFERENCES

Birrell, S. (1987) "The woman athlete's college experience: knowns and unknowns." *J. of Sport and Social Issues* 11:82–96.

Benjamin, J. (1988) *The Bonds of Love: Psychoanalysis, Feminism, and the Problem of Domination.* New York: Pantheon.

Bryson, L. (1987) "Sport and the maintenance of masculine hegemony." *Women's Studies International Forum* 10:349–360.

Chodorow, N. (1978) *The Reproduction of Mothering.* Berkeley: Univ. of California Press.

Connell, R. W. (1990) "An iron man: the body and some contradictions of hegemonic masculinity," in M. A. Messner and D. F. Sabo (eds.) *Sport, Men and the Gender Order: Critical Feminist Perspectives.* Champaign, IL: Human Kinetics.

Craib, I. (1987) "Masculinity and male dominance." *Soc. Rev.* 38:721–743.

Eitzen, D. S. (1975) "Athletics in the status system of male adolescents: a replication of Coleman's *The Adolescent Society.*" *Adolescence* 10:268–276.

Gilligan, C. (1982) *In a Different Voice: Psychological Theory and Women's Development.* Cambridge, MA: Harvard Univ. Press.

Greendorfer, S. L. (1977) "The role of socializing agents in female sport involvement." *Research Q.* 48:304–310.

Hall, M. A. (1988) "The discourse on gender and sport: from femininity to feminism." *Sociology of Sport J.* 5:330–340.

Hantover, J. (1978) "The boy scouts and the validation of masculinity." *J. of Social Issues* 34:184–195.

Haug, F. (1987) *Female Sexualization.* London: Verso.

Kidd, B. (1987) "Sports and masculinity," pp. 250–265 in M. Kaufman (ed.) *Beyond Patriarchy: Essays by Men on Pleasure, Power, and Change.* Toronto: Oxford Univ. Press.

Kidd, B. (1990) "The men's cultural centre: sports and the dynamic of women's oppression/men's repression," in M. A. Messner and D. F. Sabo (eds.) *Sport, Men and the Gender Order: Critical Feminist Perspectives.* Champaign, IL: Human Kinetics.

Kimmel, M. S. (1987) "Men's responses to feminism at the turn of the century." *Gender and Society* 1:261–283.

Kimmel, M. S. (1990) "Baseball and the reconstitution of American masculinity: 1880–1920," in M. A. Messner and D. F. Sabo (eds.) *Sport, Men and the Gender Order: Critical Feminist Perspectives.* Champaign, IL: Human Kinetics.

Leonard, W. M. II and J. M. Reyman (1988) "The odds of attaining professional athlete status: refining the computations." *Sociology of Sport J.* 5:162–169.

Lever, J. (1976) "Sex differences in the games children play." *Social Problems* 23:478–487.

Levinson, D. J. et al. (1978) *The Seasons of a Man's Life.* New York: Ballantine.

Lichterman, P. (1986) "Chodorow's psychoanalytic sociology: a project half-completed." *California Sociologist* 9:147–166.

Messner, M. (1987) "The meaning of success: the athletic experience and the development of male identity," pp. 193–210 in H. Brod (ed.) *The Making of Masculinities: The New Men's Studies.* Boston: Allen & Unwin.

Messner, M. (1988) "Sports and male domination: the female athlete as contested ideological terrain." *Sociology of Sport J.* 5:197–211.

Messner, M. (1989) "Masculinities and athletic careers." *Gender and Society* 3:71–88.

Oglesby, C. A. (ed.) (1978) *Women and Sport: From Myth to Reality.* Philadelphia: Lea & Farber.

Osherson, S. (1986) *Finding our Fathers: How a Man's Life is Shaped by His Relationship with His Father.* New York: Fawcett Columbine.

Piaget, J. H. (1965) *The Moral Judgment of the Child.* New York: Free Press.

Rubin, L. B. (1976) *Worlds of Pain: Life in the Working Class Family.* New York: Basic Books.

Sabo, D. (1985) "Sport, patriarchy and male identity: new questions about men and sport." *Arena Rev.* 9:2.

Schafer, W. E. (1975) "Sport and male sex role socialization." *Sport Sociology Bull.* 4:47–54.

Sennett, R. and J. Cobb (1973) *The Hidden Injuries of Class.* New York: Random House.

Theberge, N. (1981) "A critique of critiques: radical and feminist writings on sport." *Social Forces* 60:2.

Thorne, B. (1986) "Girls and boys together . . . but mostly apart: gender arrangements in elementary schools," pp. 167–184 in W. W. Hartup and Z. Rubin (eds.) *Relationships and Development.* Hillsdale, NJ: Lawrence Erlbaum.

Twin, S. L. (ed.) (1978) *Out of the Bleachers: Writings on Women and Sport.* Old Westbury, NY: Feminist Press.

12

COLOR, HAIR TEXTURE, AND STANDARDS OF BEAUTY

PATRICIA HILL COLLINS

Like everyone else, African-American women come to understand the workings of intersecting oppressions without obvious teaching or conscious learning. The controlling images of Black women are not simply grafted onto existing social institutions but are so pervasive that even though the images themselves change in the popular imagination, Black women's portrayal as the Other persists. Particular meanings, stereotypes, and myths can change, but the overall ideology of domination itself seems to be an enduring feature of intersecting oppressions (Omi and Winant 1994).

African-American women encounter this ideology through a range of unquestioned daily experiences. But when the contradictions between Black women's self-definitions and everyday treatment are heightened, controlling images become increasingly visible. Karen Russell, the daughter of basketball great Bill Russell, describes how racial stereotypes affect her:

> How am I supposed to react to well-meaning, good, liberal white people who say things like: "You know, Karen, I don't understand what all the fuss is about. You're one of my good friends, and I never think of you as black." Implicit in such a remark is, "I think of you as white," or perhaps just, "I don't think of your race at all." (Russell 1987, 22)

Ms. Russell was perceptive enough to see that remarks intended to compliment her actually insulted African-Americans. As the Others, U.S. Blacks are assigned all of the negative characteristics opposite and inferior to those reserved for Whites. By claiming that Ms. Russell is not really "black," her friends unintentionally validate this system of racial meanings and encourage her to internalize those images.

Although most Black women typically resist being objectified as the Other, these controlling images remain powerful influences on our relationships with Whites, Black men, other racial/ethnic groups, and one another.

Dealing with prevailing standards of beauty—particularly skin color, facial features, and hair texture—is one specific example of how controlling images derogate African-American women. A children's rhyme often sung in Black communities proclaims:

> Now, if you're white you're all right,
> If you're brown, stick around,
> But if you're black, Git back! Git back! Git back!

Prevailing standards of beauty claim that no matter how intelligent, educated, or "beautiful" a Black woman may be, those Black women whose features and skin color are most African must "git back." Within the binary thinking that underpins intersecting oppressions, blue-eyed, blond, thin White women could not be considered beautiful without the Other—Black women with African features of dark skin, broad noses, full lips, and kinky hair.

Race, gender, and sexuality converge on this issue of evaluating beauty. Black men's blackness penalizes them. But because they are not women, valuations of their self-worth do not depend as heavily on their physical attractiveness. In contrast, part of the objectification of all women lies in evaluating how they look. Within binary thinking, White and Black women as collectivities represent two opposing poles, with Latinas, Asian-American women, and Native American women jockeying for positions in between. Judging White women by their physical appearance and attractiveness to men objectifies them. But their White skin and straight hair simultaneously privilege them in a system that elevates whiteness over blackness. In contrast, African-American women experience the pain of never being able to live up to prevailing standards of beauty—standards used by White men, White women, Black men, and, most painfully, one another. Regardless of any individual woman's subjective reality, this is the system of ideas that she encounters. Because controlling images are hegemonic and taken for granted, they become virtually impossible to escape.

In her Preface to *Skin Deep: Women Writing on Color, Culture and Identity,* editor Elena Featherstone suggests that contrary to popular belief, "issues of race and color are *not* as simple as Black and white—or Red, Yellow, or Brown and white" (1994, vi). Featherstone is right, and volumes such as hers remain necessary. Yet at the same time, colorism in the U.S. context operates the way that it does because it is deeply embedded in a distinctly American form of racism grounded in Black/White oppositional differences. Other groups "of color" must negotiate the meanings attached to their "color." All must position themselves within a continually renegotiated color hierarchy where, because they define the top and the bottom, the meanings attached to Whiteness and Blackness change much less than we think. Linked in symbiotic relationship, White and Black gain meaning only in relation to one another. However well-meaning conversations among "women of color" concerning the meaning of color in the United States may be, such conversations require an analysis of how institutionalized racism produces color hierarchies among U.S. women. Without this attention to domination, such conversations can work to flatten bona fide differences in power among White women, Latinas, Asian-American women, Native women, and Black women. Even Featherstone recognizes the fact of Blackness, by pointing out, "color is the ultimate test of 'American-ness,' and black is the most un-American color of all" (1994, iii).

Since U.S. Black women have been most uniformly harmed by the colorism that is a by-product of U.S. racism, it is important to explore how prevailing standards of beauty affect U.S. Black women's treatment in everyday life. The long-standing attention of musicians, writers, and artists to this theme reveals African-American women's conflicted feelings concerning skin color, hair texture, and standards of beauty. In her autobiography, Maya Angelou records her painful realization that the only way she could become truly beautiful was to become white:

> Wouldn't they be surprised when one day I woke out of my black ugly dream, and my real hair, which was long and blond, would take the place of the kinky mass that Momma wouldn't let me straighten? . . . Then they would understand why I had never picked up a Southern accent, or spoke the common slang, and why I had to be forced to eat pigs' tails and snouts. Because I was really white and because a cruel fairy stepmother . . . had turned me into a too-big Negro girl, with nappy black hair. (Angelou, 1969, 2)

Gwendolyn Brooks also explores the meaning of skin color and hair texture for U.S. Black women. During Brooks's childhood, having African features was so universally denigrated that she writes, "when I was a child, it did not occur to me even once, that the black in which I was encased . . . would be considered, one day, beautiful" (Brooks 1972, 37). Early on, Brooks learned that a clear pecking order existed among African-Americans, one based on one's closeness to Whiteness. As a member of the "Lesser Blacks," those furthest from White, Brooks saw firsthand the difference in treatment of her group and that of the "Brights":

> One of the first "world" truths revealed to me when I at last became a member of SCHOOL was that, to be socially successful, a little girl must be Bright (of skin). It was better if your hair was curly, too—or at least Good Grade (Good Grade implied, usually, no involvement with the Hot Comb)—but Bright you marvelously *needed* to be. (1972, 37)

This division of African-Americans into two categories—the "Brights" and the "Lesser Blacks"—affects dark-skinned and light-skinned women differently. Darker women face being judged inferior and receiving the treatment afforded "too-big Negro girls with nappy hair." Institutions controlled by Whites clearly show a preference for lighter-skinned Blacks, discriminating against darker ones or against any African-Americans who appear to reject

White images of beauty. Sonia Sanchez reports, "Sisters tell me . . . that when they go out for jobs they straighten their hair because if they go in with their hair natural or braided, they probably won't get the job" (Tate 1983, 141).

Sometimes the pain most deeply felt is the pain that Black women inflict on one another. Marita Golden's mother told her not to play in the sun because "you gonna have to get a light husband anyway, for the sake of your children" (1983, 24). In *Color,* a short film exploring the impact of skin color on Black women's lives, the dark-skinned character's mother tries to get her to sit still for the hot comb, asking "don't you want your hair flowing like your friend Rebecca's?" We see the sadness of a young Black girl sitting in a kitchen, holding her ears so they won't get burned by the hot comb that will straighten her hair. Her mother cannot make her beautiful, only "presentable" for church. Marita Golden's description of a Black beauty salon depicts the internalized oppression that some African-American women feel about African features:

> Between customers, twirling in her chair, white-stockinged legs crossed, my beautician lamented to the hairdresser in the next stall, "I sure hope that Gloria Johnson don't come in here asking for me today. I swear 'fore God her hair is this long." She snapped her fingers to indicate the length. Contempt riding her words, she lit a cigarette and finished, "Barely enough to wash, let alone press and curl." (Golden 1983, 25)

African-American women who are members of the "Brights" fare little better, for they too receive special treatment because of their skin color and hair texture. Harriet Jacobs, an enslaved light-skinned woman, was sexually harassed because of her looks. Her straight hair and fair skin, her appearance as a dusky White woman, made her physically attractive to White men. But the fact that she was Black made her available to White men as no group of White women had been. In describing this situation, Jacobs notes, "if God has bestowed beauty upon her, it will prove her greatest curse. That which commands admiration in the white woman only hastens the degradation of the female slave" (Washington 1987, 17).

This different valuation and treatment of dark-skinned and light-skinned Black women influences the relationships among African-American women. Toni Morrison's (1970) novel *The Bluest Eye* explores this theme of the tension that can exist among Black women grappling with the meaning of prevailing standards of beauty. Frieda, a dark-skinned, "ordinary" Black girl, struggles with the meaning of these standards. She wonders why adults always got so upset when she rejected the White dolls they gave her and why light-skinned Maureen Peal, a child her own age whose two braids hung like "lynch-ropes down her back," got the love and attention of teachers, adults, and Black boys alike. Morrison explores Frieda's attempt not to blame Maureen for the benefits her light skin and long hair afforded her as part of Frieda's growing realization that the "Thing" to fear was not Maureen herself but the "Thing" that made Maureen beautiful.

Gwendolyn Brooks (1953) captures the anger and frustration experienced by dark-skinned women in dealing with the differential treatment they and their lighter-skinned sisters receive. In her novel *Maud Martha,* the dark-skinned heroine ponders actions she could take against a red-headed Black woman whom her husband found so attractive. "I could," considered Maud Martha, "go over there and scratch her upsweep down. I could spit on her back. I could scream. 'Listen,' I could scream, 'I'm making a baby for this man and I mean to do it in peace.'" (Washington 1987, 422). But Maud Martha rejects these actions, reasoning, "If the root was sour what business did she have up there hacking at a leaf?"

This "sour root" also creates issues in relationships between African-American women and men. Maud Martha explains:

> It's my color that makes him mad. I try to shut my eyes to that, but it's no good. What I am inside, what is really me, he likes okay. But he keeps looking at my color, which is like a wall. He has to jump over it in order to meet and touch what I've got for him. He has to jump away up high in order to see it. He gets awful tired of all that jumping. (Washington 1987, 421)

Her husband's attraction to light-skinned women hurt Maud Martha because his inability to "jump away up high" over the wall of color limited his ability to see her for who she truly was.

REFERENCES

Angelou, Maya. 1969. *I Know Why the Caged Bird Sings.* New York: Bantam.

Brooks, Gwendolyn. 1953. *Maud Martha.* Boston: Atlantic Press.

____. 1972. *Report from Part One: The Autobiography of Gwendolyn Brooks.* Detroit: Broadside Press.

Featherstone, Elena, ed. 1994. *Skin Deep: Women Writing on Color, Culture and Identity.* Freedom, CA: The Crossing Press.

Golden, Marita. 1983. *Migrations of the Heart.* New York: Ballantine.

Morrison, Toni. 1970. *The Bluest Eye.* New York: Pocket Books.

Omi, Michael, and Howard Winant. 1994. *Racial Formation in the United States: From the 1960s to the 1990s, Second Edition.* New York: Routledge.

Russell, Karen K. 1987. "Growing Up with Privilege and Prejudice." *New York Times Magazine,* June 14, 22–28.

Tate, Claudia, ed. 1983 *Black Women Writers at Work.* New York: Continuum Publishing.

Washington, Mary Helen, ed. 1987. *Invented Lives: Narratives of Black Women* 1860–1960. Garden City, NY: Anchor.

13

THE MYTH OF THE LATIN WOMAN
I Just Met a Girl Named María

JUDITH ORTIZ COFER

On a bus trip to London from Oxford University, where I was earning some graduate credits one summer, a young man, obviously fresh from a pub, spotted me and as if struck by inspiration went down on his knees in the aisle. With both hands over his heart he broke into an Irish tenor's rendition of "María" from *West Side Story.* My politely amused fellow passengers gave his lovely voice the round of gentle applause it deserved. Though I was not quite as amused, I managed my version of an English smile: no show of teeth, no extreme contortions of the facial muscles—I was at this time of my life practicing reserve and cool. Oh, that British control, how I coveted it. But María had followed me to London, reminding me of a prime fact of my life: you can leave the Island, master the English language, and travel as far as you can, but if you are a Latina, especially one like me who so obviously belongs to Rita Moreno's gene pool, the Island travels with you.

This is sometimes a very good thing—it may win you that extra minute of someone's attention. But with some people, the same things can make *you* an island—not so much a tropical paradise as an Alcatraz, a place nobody wants to visit. As a Puerto Rican girl growing up in the United States and wanting like most children to "belong," I resented the stereotype that my Hispanic appearance called forth from many people I met.

Our family lived in a large urban center in New Jersey during the sixties, where life was designed as a microcosm of my parents' casas on the island. We spoke in Spanish, we ate Puerto Rican food bought at the bodega, and we practiced strict Catholicism complete with Saturday confession and Sunday mass at a church where our parents were accommodated into a one-hour Spanish mass slot, performed by a Chinese priest trained as a missionary for Latin America.

As a girl I was kept under strict surveillance, since virtue and modesty were, by cultural equation, the same as family honor. As a teenager I was instructed on how to behave as a proper señorita. But it was a conflicting message girls got, since the Puerto Rican mothers also encouraged their daughters to look and act like women and to dress in clothes our Anglo friends and

---

their mothers found too "mature" for our age. It was, and is, cultural, yet I often felt humiliated when I appeared at an American friend's party wearing a dress more suitable to a semiformal than to a playroom birthday celebration. At Puerto Rican festivities, neither the music nor the colors we wore could be too loud. I still experience a vague sense of letdown when I'm invited to a "party" and it turns out to be a marathon conversation in hushed tones rather than a fiesta with salsa, laughter, and dancing—the kind of celebration I remember from my childhood.

I remember Career Day in our high school, when teachers told us to come dressed as if for a job interview. It quickly became obvious that to the barrio girls, "dressing up" sometimes meant wearing ornate jewelry and clothing that would be more appropriate (by mainstream standards) for the company Christmas party than as daily office attire. That morning I had agonized in front of my closet, trying to figure out what a "career girl" would wear because, essentially, except for Marlo Thomas on TV, I had no models on which to base my decision. I knew how to dress for school: at the Catholic school I attended we all wore uniforms; I knew how to dress for Sunday mass, and I knew what dresses to wear for parties at my relatives' homes. Though I do not recall the precise details of my Career Day outfit, it must have been a composite of the above choices. But I remember a comment my friend (an Italian-American) made in later years that coalesced my impressions of that day. She said that at the business school she was attending the Puerto Rican girls always stood out for wearing "everything at once." She meant, of course, too much jewelry, too many accessories. On that day at school, we were simply made the negative models by the nuns who were themselves not credible fashion experts to any of us. But it was painfully obvious to me that to the others, in their tailored skirts and silk blouses, we must have seemed "hopeless" and "vulgar." Though I now know that most adolescents feel out of step much of the time, I also know that for the Puerto Rican girls of my generation that sense was intensified. The way our teachers and classmates looked at us that day in school was just a taste of the culture clash that awaited us in the real world, where prospective employers and men on the street would often misinterpret our tight skirts and jingling bracelets as a come-on.

Mixed cultural signals have perpetuated certain stereotypes—for example, that of the Hispanic woman as the "Hot Tamale" or sexual firebrand. It is a one-dimensional view that the media have found easy to promote. In their special vocabulary, advertisers have designated "sizzling" and "smoldering" as the adjectives of choice for describing not only the foods but also the women of Latin America. From conversations in my house I recall hearing about the harassment that Puerto Rican women endured in factories where the "boss men" talked to them as if sexual innuendo was all they understood and, worse, often gave them the choice of submitting to advances or being fired.

It is custom, however, not chromosomes, that leads us to choose scarlet over pale pink. As young girls, we were influenced in our decisions about clothes and colors by the women—older sisters and mothers who had grown up on a tropical island where the natural environment was a riot of primary colors, where showing your skin was one way to keep cool as well as to look sexy. Most important of all, on the island, women perhaps felt freer to dress and move more provocatively, since, in most cases, they were protected by the traditions, mores, and laws of a Spanish/Catholic system of morality and machismo whose main rule was: *You may look at my sister, but if you touch her I will kill you.* The extended family and church structure could provide a young woman with a circle of safety in her small pueblo on the Island; if a man "wronged" a girl, everyone would close in to save her family honor.

This is what I have gleaned from my discussions as an adult with older Puerto Rican women. They have told me about dressing in their best party clothes on Saturday nights and going to the town's plaza to promenade with their girlfriends in front of the boys they liked. The males were thus given an opportunity to admire the women and to express their admiration in the form of piropos: erotically charged street poems they composed on the spot. I have been subjected to a few *piropos* while visiting the Island, and they can be outrageous, although custom dictates that they must never cross into obscenity. This ritual, as I understand it, also entails a show of studied indifference on the woman's part; if she is "decent," she must not acknowledge the man's impassioned words. So I do understand how things can be lost in translation. When a Puerto Rican girl dressed in her idea of what is attractive meets a man from the mainstream culture who has been trained to react to certain types of clothing as a sexual signal, a clash is likely to take place. The line I first heard based on this aspect of the myth happened when the boy who took me to my first formal dance leaned over to plant a sloppy overeager kiss painfully on my mouth, and when I didn't respond with sufficient passion said in a resentful tone: "I thought you Latin girls were supposed to mature early"—my first instance of being thought of as a fruit or vegetable—I was supposed to *ripen,* not just grow into womanhood like other girls.

It is surprising to some of my professional friends that some people, including those who should know better, still put others "in their place." Though rarer, these incidents are still commonplace in my life. It happened to me most recently during a stay at a very classy metropolitan hotel favored by young professional couples for their weddings. Late one evening after the theater, as I walked toward my room with my new colleague (a woman with whom I was coordinating an arts program), a middle-aged man in a tuxedo, a young girl in satin and lace on his arm, stepped directly into our path. With his champagne glass extended toward me, he exclaimed, "Evita!"

Our way blocked, my companion and I listened as the man half-recited, half-bellowed "Don't Cry for Me, Argentina." When he finished, the young girl said: "How about a round of applause for my daddy?" We complied, hoping this would bring the silly spectacle to a close. I was becoming aware that our little group was attracting the attention of the other guests. "Daddy" must have perceived this too, and he once more barred the way as we tried to walk past him. He began to shout-sing a ditty to the tune of "La Bamba"—except the lyrics were about a girl named María whose exploits all rhymed with her name and gonorrhea. The girl kept saying "Oh, Daddy" and looking at me with pleading eyes. She wanted me to laugh along with the others. My companion and I stood silently waiting for the man to end his offensive song. When he finished, I looked not at him but at his daughter. I advised her calmly never to ask her father what he had done in the army. Then I walked between them and to my room. My friend complimented me on my cool handling of the situation. I confessed to her that I really had wanted to push the jerk into the swimming pool. I knew that this same man—probably a corporate executive, well educated, even worldly by most standards—would not have been likely to regale a white woman with a dirty song in public. He would perhaps have checked his impulse by assuming that she could be somebody's wife or mother, or at least *somebody* who might take offense. But to him, I was just an Evita or a María: merely a character in his cartoon-populated universe.

Because of my education and my proficiency with the English language, I have acquired many mechanisms for dealing with the anger I experience. This was not true for my parents, nor is it true for the many Latin women working at menial jobs who must put up with stereotypes about our ethnic group such as: "They make good domestics." This is another facet of the myth of the Latin women in the United States. Its origin is simple to deduce. Work as domestics, waitressing, and factory jobs are all that's available to women with little English and few skills. The myth of the Hispanic menial has been sustained by the same media phenomenon that made "Mammy" from *Gone with the Wind* America's idea of the black woman for generations; María, the housemaid or counter girl, is now indelibly etched into the national psyche. The big and the little screens have presented us with the picture of the funny Hispanic maid, mispronouncing words and cooking up a spicy storm in a shiny California kitchen.

This media-engendered image of the Latina in the United States has been documented by feminist Hispanic scholars, who claim that such portrayals are partially responsible for the denial of opportunities for upward mobility among Latinas in the professions. I have a Chicana friend working on a Ph.D. in philosophy at a major university. She says her doctor still shakes his head in puzzled amazement at all the "big words" she uses. Since I do not wear my diplomas around my neck for all to see, I too have on occasion been sent to that "kitchen," where some think I obviously belong.

One such incident that has stayed with me, though I recognize it as a minor offense, happened on the day of my first public poetry reading. It took place in Miami in a boat-restaurant where we were having lunch before the event. I was nervous and excited as I walked in with my notebook in hand. An older woman motioned me to her table. Thinking (foolish me) that she wanted me to autograph a copy of my brand new slender volume of verse, I went over. She ordered a cup of coffee from me, assuming that I was the waitress. Easy enough to mistake my poems for menus, I suppose. I know that it wasn't an intentional act of cruelty, yet with all the good things that happened that day, I remember that scene most clearly, because it reminded me of what I had to overcome before anyone would take me seriously. In retrospect I understand that my anger gave my reading fire, that I have almost always taken doubts in my abilities as a challenge—and that the result is, most times, a feeling of satisfaction at having won a convert when I see the cold, appraising eyes warm to my words, the body language change, the smile that indicates that I have opened some avenue for communication. That day I read to that woman and her lowered eyes told me that she was embarrassed at her little faux pas, and when I willed her to look up to me, it was my victory, and she graciously allowed me to punish her with my full attention. We shook hands at the end of the reading, and I never saw her again. She has probably forgotten the whole thing but maybe not.

Yet I am one of the lucky ones. My parents made it possible for me to acquire a stronger footing in the mainstream culture by giving me the chance at an education. And books and art have saved me from the harsher forms of ethnic and racial prejudice that many of my Hispanic *compañeras* have had to endure. I travel a lot around the United States, reading from my books of poetry and my novel, and the reception I most often receive is one of positive interest by people who want to know more about my culture. There are, however, thousands of Latinas without the privilege of an education or the entrée into society that I have. For them life is a struggle against the misconceptions perpetuated by the myth of the Latina as whore, domestic, or criminal. We cannot change this by legislating the way people look at us. The transformation, as I see it, has to occur at a much more individual level. My personal goal in my public life is to try to replace the old pervasive stereotypes and myths about Latinas with a much more interesting set of realities. Every time I give a reading, I hope the stories I tell, the dreams and fears I examine in my work, can achieve some universal truth which will get my audience past the particulars of my skin color, my accent, or my clothes.

I once wrote a poem in which I called us Latinas "God's brown daughters." This poem is really a prayer of sorts, offered upward, but also, through the human-to-human channel of art, outward. It is a prayer for communication, and for respect. In it, Latin women pray "in Spanish to an Anglo God/with a Jewish heritage," and they are "fervently hoping/that if not omnipotent,/at least He be bilingual."

14

HE DEFIES YOU STILL
The Memoirs of a Sissy

TOMMI AVICOLLI

> You're just a faggot
> No history faces you this morning
> A faggot's dreams are scarlet
> Bad blood bled from words that scarred[1]

Scene One

A homeroom in a Catholic high school in South Philadelphia. The boy sits quietly in the first aisle, third desk, reading a book. He does not look up, not even for a moment. He is hoping no one will remember he is sitting there. He wishes he were invisible. The teacher is not yet in the classroom so the other boys are talking and laughing loudly.

Suddenly, a voice from beside him:

"Hey, you're a faggot, ain't you?"

The boy does not answer. He goes on reading his book, or rather pretending he is reading his book. It is impossible to actually read the book now.

"Hey, I'm talking to you!"

The boy still does not look up. He is so scared his heart is thumping madly; it feels like it is leaping out of his chest and into his throat. But he can't look up.

"Faggot, I'm talking to you!"

To look up is to meet the eyes of the tormentor.

Suddenly, a sharpened pencil point is thrust into the boy's arm. He jolts, shaking off the pencil, aware that there is blood seeping from the wound.

"What did you do that for?" he asks timidly.

"Cause I hate faggots," the other boy says, laughing. Some other boys begin to laugh, too. A symphony of laughter. The boy feels as if he's going to cry. But he must not cry. Must not cry. So he holds back the tears and tries to read the book again. He must read the book. Read the book.

When the teacher arrives a few minutes later, the class quiets down. The boy does not tell the teacher what has happened. He spits on the wound to clean it, dabbing it with a tissue until the bleeding stops. For weeks he fears some dreadful infection from the lead in the pencil point.

Tommi Avicolli, "He Defies You Still: The Memoirs of a Sissy" from *Radical Teacher,* 24 (1986). Reprinted with permission.

Scene Two

The boy is walking home from school. A group of boys (two, maybe three, he is not certain) grab him from behind, drag him into an alley and beat him up. When he gets home, he races up to his room, refusing dinner ("I don't feel well," he tells his mother through the locked door) and spends the night alone in the dark wishing he would die. . . .

These are not fictitious accounts—I *was* that boy. Having been branded a sissy by neighborhood children because I preferred jump rope to baseball and dolls to playing soldiers, I was often taunted with "hey sissy" or "hey faggot" or "yoo hoo honey" (in a mocking voice) when I left the house.

To avoid harassment, I spent many summers alone in my room. I went out on rainy days when the street was empty.

I came to like being alone. I didn't need anyone, I told myself over and over again. I was an island. Contact with others meant pain. Alone, I was protected. I began writing poems, then short stories. There was no reason to go outside anymore. I had a world of my own.

> In the schoolyard today
> they'll single you out
> Their laughter will leave your ears ringing
> like the church bells
> which once awed you. . . .[2]

School was one of the more painful experiences of my youth. The neighborhood bullies could be avoided. The taunts of the children living in those endless repetitive row houses could be evaded by staying in my room. But school was something I had to face day after day for some two hundred mornings a year.

I had few friends in school. I was a pariah. Some kids would talk to me, but few wanted to be known as my close friend. Afraid of labels. If I was a sissy, then he had to be a sissy, too. I was condemned to loneliness.

Fortunately, a new boy moved into our neighborhood and befriended me; he wasn't afraid of the labels. He protected me when the other guys threatened to beat me up. He walked me home from school; he broke through the terrible loneliness. We were in third or fourth grade at the time.

We spent a summer or two together. Then his parents sent him to camp and I was once again confined to my room.

Scene Three

High school lunchroom. The boy sits at a table near the back of the room. Without warning, his lunch bag is grabbed and tossed to another table. Someone opens it and confiscates a package of Tastykakes; another boy takes the sandwich. The empty bag is tossed back to the boy who stares at it, dumbfounded. He should be used to this; it has happened before.

Someone screams, "faggot," laughing. There is always laughter. It does not annoy him anymore.

There is no teacher nearby. There is never a teacher around. And what would he say if there were? Could he report the crime? He would be jumped after school if he did. Besides, it would be his word against theirs. Teachers never noticed anything. They never heard the taunts. Never heard the word, "faggot." They were the great deaf mutes, pillars of indifference; a sissy's pain was not relevant to history and geography and God made me to love honor and obey him, amen.

Scene Four

High school Religion class. Someone has a copy of *Playboy*. Father N. is not in the room yet; he's late, as usual. Someone taps the boy roughly on the shoulder. He turns. A finger points to the centerfold model, pink fleshy body, thin and sleek. Almost painted. Not real. The other asks, mocking voice, "Hey, does she turn you on? Look at those tits!"

The boy smiles, nodding meekly; turns away.

The other jabs him harder on the shoulder, "Hey, whatsamatter, don't you like girls?"

Laughter. Thousands of mouths; unbearable din of laughter. In the Arena: thumbs down. Don't spare the queer.

"Wanna suck my dick? Huh? That turn you on, faggot!"

The laughter seems to go on forever . . .

> Behind you, the sound of their laughter
> echoes a million times
> in a soundless place
> They watch you walk/sit/stand/breathe. . . .[3]

What did being a sissy really mean? It was a way of walking (from the hips rather than the shoulders); it was a way of talking (often with a lisp or in a high-pitched voice); it was a way of relating to others (gently, not wanting to fight, or hurt anyone's feelings). It was being intelligent ("an egghead" they called it sometimes); getting good grades. It means not being interested in sports, not playing football in the street after school; not discussing teams and scores and playoffs. And it involved not showing fervent interest in girls, not talking about scoring with tits or *Playboy* centerfolds. Not concealing naked women in your history book; or porno books in your locker.

On the other hand, anyone could be a "faggot." It was a catch-all. If you did something that didn't conform to what was the acceptable behavior of the group, then you risked being called a faggot. If you didn't get along with the "in" crowd, you were a faggot. It was the most commonly used put-down. It kept guys in line. They became angry when somebody called them a faggot. More fights started over someone calling someone else a faggot than anything else. The word had power. It toppled the male ego, shattered his delicate facade, violated the image he projected. He was tough. Without feeling. Faggot cut through all this. It made him vulnerable. Feminine. And feminine was the worst thing he could possibly be. Girls were fine for fucking, but no boy in his right mind wanted to be like them. A boy was the opposite of a girl. He was not feminine. He was not feeling. He was not weak.

Just look at the gym teacher who growled like a dog; or the priest with the black belt who threw kids against the wall in rage when they didn't know their Latin. They were men, they got respect.

But not the physics teacher who preached pacifism during lectures on the nature of atoms. Everybody knew what he was—and why he believed in the anti-war movement.

My parents only knew that the neighborhood kids called me names. They begged me to act more like the other boys. My brothers were ashamed of me. They never said it, but I knew. Just as I knew that my parents were embarrassed by my behavior.

At times, they tried to get me to act differently. Once my father lectured me on how to walk right. I'm still not clear on what that means. Not from the hips, I guess, don't "swish" like faggots do.

A nun in elementary school told my mother at Open House that there was "something wrong with me." I had draped my sweater over my shoulders like a girl, she said. I was a smart kid, but I should know better than to wear my sweater like a girl!

My mother stood there, mute. I wanted her to say something, to chastise the nun; to defend me. But how could she? This was a nun talking—representative of Jesus, protector of all that was good and decent.

An uncle once told me I should start "acting like a boy" instead of like a girl. Everybody seemed ashamed of me. And I guess I was ashamed of myself, too. It was hard not to be.

Scene Five

Priest: Do you like girls, Mark?

Mark: Uh-huh.

Priest: I mean *really* like them?

Mark: Yeah—they're okay.

Priest: There's a role they play in your salvation. Do you understand it, Mark?

Mark: Yeah.

Priest: You've got to like girls. Even if you should decide to enter the seminary, it's important to keep in mind God's plan for a man and a woman. . . .[4]

Catholicism of course condemned homosexuality. Effeminacy was tolerated as long as the effeminate person did not admit to being gay. Thus, priests could be effeminate because they weren't gay.

As a sissy, I could count on no support from the church. A male's sole purpose in life was to father children—souls for the church to save. The only hope a homosexual had of attaining salvation was by remaining totally celibate. Don't even think of touching another boy. To think of a sin was a sin. And to sin was to put a mark upon the soul. Sin—if it was a serious offense against God—led to hell. There was no way around it. If you sinned, you were doomed.

Realizing I was gay was not an easy task. Although I knew I was attracted to boys by the time I was about eleven, I didn't connect this attraction to homosexuality. I was not queer. Not I. I was merely appreciating a boy's good looks, his fine features, his proportions. It didn't seem to matter that I didn't appreciate a girl's looks in the same way. There was no twitching in my thighs when I gazed upon a beautiful girl. But I wasn't queer.

I resisted that label—queer—for the longest time. Even when everything pointed to it, I refused to see it. I was certainly not queer. Not I.

We sat through endless English classes, and history courses about the wars between men who were not allowed to love each other. No gay history was ever taught. No history faces you this morning. You're just a faggot. Homosexuals had never contributed to the human race. God destroyed the queers in Sodom and Gomorrah.

We learned about Michelangelo, Oscar Wilde, Gertrude Stein—but never that they were queer. They were not queer. Walt Whitman, the "father of American poetry," was not queer. No one was queer. I was alone, totally unique. One of a kind. Were there others like me somewhere? Another planet, perhaps?

In school, they never talked of the queers. They did not exist. The only hint we got of this other species was in religion class. And even then it was clouded in mystery—never spelled out. It was sin. Like masturbation. Like looking at *Playboy* and getting a hard-on. A sin.

Once a progressive priest in senior year religion class actually mentioned homosexuals—he said the word—but was into Erich Fromm, into homosexuals as pathetic and sick. Fixated at some early stage; penis, anal, whatever. Only heterosexuals passed on to the nirvana of sexual development.

No other images from the halls of the Catholic high school except those the other boys knew: swishy faggot sucking cock in an alley somewhere, grabbing asses in the bathroom. Never mentioning how much straight boys craved blow jobs, it was part of the secret.

It was all a secret. You were not supposed to talk about the queers. Whisper maybe. Laugh about them, yes. But don't be open, honest; don't try to understand. Don't cite their accomplishments. No history faces you this morning. You're just a faggot   faggot   no history   just a faggot

Epilogue

The boy marching down the Parkway. Hundreds of queers. Signs proclaiming gay pride. Speakers. Tables with literature from gay groups. A miracle, he is thinking. Tears are coming loose now. Someone hugs him.

> You could not control
> the sissy in me
> nor could you exorcise him
> nor electrocute him
> You declared him illegal illegitimate
> insane and immature
> But he defies you still.[5]

NOTES

1. From the poem "Faggot" by Tommi Avicolli, published in *GPU News*, Sept. 1979.
2. Ibid.
3. Ibid.
4. From the play *Judgment of the Roaches* by Tommi Avicolli, produced in Philadelphia at the Gay Community Center, the Painted Bride Arts Center and the University of Pennsylvania; aired over WXPN-FM, in four parts; and presented at the Lesbian/Gay Conference in Norfolk, VA, July, 1980.
5. From the poem "Sissy Poem," published in *Magic Doesn't Live Here Anymore* (Philadelphia: Spruce Street Press, 1976).

15

GROWING UP HIDDEN

LINNEA DUE

Growing up hidden—coming of age not only invisible but embattled in that invisibility—is hard to describe to someone who has not experienced it. A phrase like "a wolf in sheep's clothing" takes on special meaning to a gay kid—at least it did for me. Was I hiding because I was bad? Why didn't I feel bad if I was so bad I had to hide? What I should have asked—why do I have to hide?—was too obvious to require an answer, and yet it turned out to be the real question.

I don't remember ever not knowing who I was. For a while I revealed myself, saying I wanted to be strong ("Girls don't need to be strong"), that when I got married, my wife and I would have a wonderful house ("You won't have a wife, you'll have a husband"). By the time I went to summer camp, at age seven, I was already trying to tone myself down: people told me I was too raucous, too wild, and I had to drop that damn fool idea about getting married to a woman. I decided to shut up—not that I'd changed my mind, but it was easier than trying to explain myself to people who'd never met a girl like me.

In the closing days of camp, we were supposed to say who we were going steady with. No one was actually going with anybody—we were all too young—but I was still thrown into a quandary. If I were going to pledge my troth, it certainly would be to Stacy, with whom I'd been sneaking off all summer to plan our life together. Ken snagged me after dinner one night, just before campfire. "Look," he said bluntly, "you want to go with Stacy and I want to go with Roger. So what we'll do is tell everybody you're going with me and she's going with Rog."

God, what a mind! Such duplicity would never have occurred to me. It made me feel a little funny—wasn't it like lying?—but it wasn't a long stretch from the silence I'd been cultivating for a time anyway. As I became older, I edited myself more and more, especially after I realized that it wasn't that people hadn't known about girls like me, but that those girls were so horrible no one wanted to ever talk about them.

By then, I knew what I was called. I'd been risking my life balancing on my father's office chair, snatching books off the uppermost shelf as I rolled by. Richard von Krafft-Ebing's *Psychopathia Sexualis.* Havelock Ellis's *Sexual Inversion.* Freud. Erikson. I'd also been haunting the paperback rack at my neighborhood grocery, ripping off the romances of the '50s—*Beebo Brinker,* Ann Bannon, *Women on the Edge of Twilight.* Krafft-Ebing made me popular on the playground—I was the Susie Bright of Hilltop Elementary School—but my knowledge was a mixed blessing. I was glad to know people like me existed, but I also knew from my dad that a psychopath was the worst thing you could be. Finding my sexuality among those who fucked chickens or corpses made me feel—well, a little queer.

Still, I figured I was hiding successfully until the day my Girl Scout troop leader threw me out for being "too masculine." My world fell apart. I had believed censoring my thoughts was enough; I hadn't realized my manner and my body—the very way I moved—were betraying me daily. Something drastic had to be done.

Something was. I dropped out of the athletics I loved, wore nylons and makeup, carried my books in front of me, shortened my stride. I developed an imperious persona to go along with my new look and pretended an interest in boys (a breach of ethics I tried to mitigate by not letting them come too close). It was like learning a foreign language—and not coincidentally, I began drinking to blackouts.

From seventh through twelfth grades, I functioned as another person, someone I became in the morning and shed in the evening when, safely in my room, I could pore over my romances and daydream about kissing my own raven-haired beauty. It never occurred to me to look for her; my dreams ranked alongside my classmates' fantasies of becoming famous actresses or politicians. That I was labeling illusory the most important stuff of life—my identity and my relationships—didn't seem odd. Staying undercover was job number one.

My life as a spy reached a pinnacle of the absurd during my first year at Sarah Lawrence. I received a visit from several of my elementary school friends; they had traveled from Smith, from Brandeis, from Boston University, certain that I, the amateur sexologist, could set their minds at ease. They were worried, they explained haltingly, about those sailor/whore games we had played at slumber parties. Wasn't it weird for thirteen-year-old girls to practice kissing each other? Was I concerned that we had lesbian tendencies? Not at all, I replied heartily, and proceeded to regale them with a lot of assurances they wanted to hear. They went back to Massachusetts much relieved, and I lay on my bed and stared at the ceiling, wondering who was the bigger fool. Two years later, I didn't lie when the college president asked if I was a lesbian, though it meant leaving the school I loved; I would never lie again—not about that anyway.

16

THE MILITARY AS A SECOND BAR MITZVAH
Combat Service as Initiation to Zionist Masculinity

DANNY KAPLAN

Despite growing criticism of the military and of militarism more generally, the Israeli Defence Forces (IDF) still hold a central place in Israeli society today. Military service is a core aspect of this and is considered almost a prerequisite for entering adult life. A variety of studies conducted in recent years have demonstrated the military's predominant role as an agent of socialization into Israeli society in general (Azarya 1983;

Danny Kaplan, excerpt from "The Military as a Second Bar Mitzvah: Combat Service as Initiation to Zionist Masculinity" from *Imagined Masculinities: Male Identity in the Modern Middle East,* edited by Mai Ghoussoub and Emma Sinclair-Webb (London: Saqi Books, 2000), pp. 127–135. Reprinted with the permission of the publishers.

Lieblich 1989) and into hegemonic masculinity in particular (Lomsky-Feder 1992; Ben-Ari 1998; Kaplan 1999). This article explores combat culture and its underlying Zionist ideology as they powerfully shape the masculine identity of Israeli Jewish youth.

Although the IDF is the only conscript army with compulsory service for women, the military is based on a regime which intensifies gender distinctions (Izraeli 1997). Regular service begins at the age of eighteen. Men are recruited for three years whereas women are discharged after a year and nine months or less. Only men may participate in combat-related activity and are called up annually for varying periods of reserve duty throughout much of their adult life. Functioning as the all-Israeli "melting pot," the military attempts to mould all men in a uniform guise of masculinity. It does so through an organizational culture that encourages ideal assets of soldiery such as physical ability, endurance, self-control, professionalism, sociability, aggressiveness and heterosexuality. These traits tap on masculine performance by contrasting them with images of "otherness" such as femininity, homosexuality and the Arab enemy. For example, the curse "Go find yourself a red-headed Arab to shake your ass about" denotes a man who is submissive enough to be penetrated, and not just by another man, but by an Arab—the national enemy—and a red-headed one at that: the ultimate expression of biological otherness. These various images of the "other" are all related and serve to construct the hegemonic images of Israeli masculinity.

The IDF is also bound by underlying Zionist ideology. The Zionist revolution entailed not only the return of the Jewish people to their "old-new" homeland, but also an emancipation of the Jewish man. The image of the Jewish man was now to be rid of associations with its Diaspora version that spelled a dislocated, "sheep-like" passive-effeminate existence and replaced with images of physical strength, labouring, prowess, harshness and sexuality. Zionist masculinity was reconstructed as a masculinity of body, realized through territorial settlement and self-defence, accomplished through military power (Biale 1992; Boyarin 1997). Influenced by other European national movements, the Zionist project endorses what Mosse (1990) called the "myth of participation in war." This view crystallized with the 1948 generation of the "Sabra"[1]—the Israeli-born male youth (predominantly of Eastern and Central European origin) who fought for the establishment of the Israeli state. The Sabra represented everything that the old Jew lacked: youth, strength, health, physical labour and deep-rootedness (Rubinstein 1977). The Kibbutz agricultural settlements, inspired by socialist ideology, were a major force in the Zionist revolution and the Kibbutz-born youth, who participated in quasi military activity, came to embody the Sabra ethos (Almog 1997).

Following the founding of the IDF, the image of the Jewish warrior has been reinforced as a state institution. The IDF has become the dominant socialization agent. Military training attempts to remodel the new recruits coming from various sub-cultures of segmented Israeli society and to mould them through one common denominator—that of hegemonic Zionist masculinity.

Despite an official policy of universal conscription, in practice different arrangements prevail for different groups of citizens within Israeli society. Their positioning is determined by their relationship to masculinity, Judaism and Zionism. Women are excluded from most combat roles, the archetypal "manly" activity. Ultraorthodox Jews who hold non-Zionist views rarely serve and, if they do, are usually confined to religious service jobs. While most Muslims and Christians of the non-Zionist Arab minority are excluded from service altogether, men from the Druze, Circassian and some Bedouin communities, who are minorities within the Arab minority, are eligible for combat service, yet are channeled to specific posts (see Lomsky-Feder and Ben-Ari forthcoming). In contrast, *Mizrachi* men (originating from Middle Eastern and North African Jewish communities), men of national-religious affiliation, and some of the new immigrants (predominantly from Russia), being both men and fully Zionist, are closer in their starting position to the hegemonic Sabra and thus are gradually assuming a more central place in military ranks. All that it takes is an effective "melting pot" process to have them qualify for the hegemonic ideal.

Since active service of three years is an obligatory and self-evident stage for most Jewish-Israeli youths, it is the much smaller group of male soldiers who serve in combat units and risk their lives on a daily basis who attract adoration. These men, stationed in a variety of units, are trained to be fighters, and engage in operational duty on the borders, in south Lebanon and in the Palestinian territories. Combat roles are the archetype of the military organization: they are the organization's most important roles, claim the highest status, and define the meaning of military service both on a personal and collective level (Devilbiss 1994: 143). Through their very participation in combat duty, individuals act according to various values of the Zionist masculine ethos.

I shall demonstrate how present-day Israeli men establish their multifaceted identity using a case study of informants who hold a unique position in this culture—combat soldiers who have developed a homosexual identity. I will focus on the story of one soldier, Nir (pseudonym), born and raised in a Kibbutz, who served in an elite unit of the Giv'ati infantry brigade. Like most gay soldiers, Nir refrained from disclosing his sexual orientation in the military (see also Segal, Gade and Johnson 1993).[2] He acted as a full participant in combat culture, with no distinctive patterns of behaviour and with no overt conflict with his surroundings. In other words, unlike other minorities who serve in the Israeli army, his otherness within military culture remained invisible. Yet, having a strong internal notion of himself as different prior to joining the army—he regarded himself as bisexual at the time—his military experience became a voyage of self-exploration. By probing his own evolving identity as an invisible "other" vis-à-vis hegemonic military masculinity, his case serves to point out and elucidate underlying processes by which various aspects of cultural identity are negotiated by all men in the military.

My analysis will be based on the conceptualization of current Israeli mainstream society as a civil religion. This concept, elaborated by Liebman and Don-Yehiya, refers to a system of sacred symbols expressed through belief and practice which "integrate the society, legitimate the social order and mobilize the population in social effort while transmitting the central values and world-view that dominate the society" (Liebman and Don-Yehiya 1983: 24). Within this framework, the "religion of security" (a term coined by Arian, Talmud and Hermann 1988: 49) serves as a core unifying force of Israeli society. The pervasiveness of security issues has put the military in a position of sacredness. Aronoff (1989: 132) has made the explicit observation that service in the IDF is "the primary rite of passage that initiates one into full membership in the Zionist civil religion."

Using Nir as a case study, I shall demonstrate how the military, as an ongoing initiation rite based on sacred symbols, works on the *individual level*—how in Israel it mobilizes a young man and proceeds to transmit and simultaneously legitimize to him the central values of Israeli society. I will discuss, through Nir's narrative, various negotiations of male Zionist identity: negotiation of militarism, the enemy, left-right politics and religion, all combined within the initiation rite to masculinity.

Nir's Story

Nir, aged 20 at the time of the interview, wanted to join a combat unit from the very beginning. As he explained to me, the Kibbutz ideology strongly indoctrinates its youth to participate in combat service. Most of his older fellow men in the Kibbutz, as well as his father and brother, had served in combat units. He and his peers had been preoccupied with listening to stories about various prestigious units that had partaken in military warfare. In his high school class all but one male student had indeed made it to fighting units. Nir's own dream was to join the most prestigious reconnaissance unit, Sayeret Matkal, which is involved in secret operations behind enemy lines.[3] After failing at the second stage of the meticulous and arduous screening process, he was referred to the more conventional infantry unit of Giv'ati, where he passed yet another selective screening and was assigned to an elite unit in one of the Brigade's special companies. He underwent the four months of initial training and two additional months of advanced infantry training which together formed his basic training as a combat fighter. He was then assigned, together with his platoon members, to Giv'ati's operational duties in Israeli-controlled territories in the Gaza strip and later on the Lebanese border. In between stints of operational duty, his unit took part in exercises and large-scale drills.

Giv'ati, a relatively new brigade, has specialized in recent years in recruiting new immigrants from Russia as well as from national-religious circles. The latter have become known for their motivation, and their numbers in elite combat units are constantly increasing. In his own platoon, Nir was one of the few "secular" soldiers and the only one from a Kibbutz. Kibbutz men are more prone to enlist in the well-established and highly acclaimed Paratroopers brigade, a unit that is still identified with the founding principles of the IDF, and with the Sabra ethos. He remembered his puzzlement on first arriving in Giv'ati's boot camp: "I scratched my head and thought, 'What is this Giv'ati, what on earth am I doing here?' The human composition seemed to me very odd. Everybody was either religious or a new immigrant." From this point onwards Nir had to negotiate his position, his attitudes and his identity in relation to the surrounding environment. The striking feature of his narrative is a constant shift between partial criticism of some aspects of his military experience, especially that which opposes his initial belief and value system, and a rhetoric of full identification with his unit and its underlying military ideology. The result of this tension is a growing adherence to the one binding force of Israeli society—the religion of security.

Starting with the issue of military training and socialization, Nir recounts: "Let me tell you how your day starts in Giv'ati boot camp. Every morning when you wake up, the first thing you hear is the Giv'ati hymn, 'He who has dreamt Giv'ati,' ten times in a row, coming from huge loudspeakers. Every morning. You get a heart attack from that. As soon as you hear it you know your short sleep has ended and another day of drilling and harassment is coming your way." Yet, after this rather critical picture of military training as brainwashing, he immediately switches to a rhetoric that defends this method of drilling: "They try to look after the soldier's health. Nobody in our unit ever got injured from getting the run around. Okay, you crawl in the disgusting sand for an hour, you get yourself all covered in mud, it's physically difficult, but it's not dangerous."

Nir was assigned to a prestigious and highly sought-after weapon in the platoon—a heavy machine gun. It became a source of satisfaction to him: "I was especially keen on the firearm drills. I was like Rambo. I was in charge of a heavy machine gun. There is competition over some of the tasks and that's one of them. I loved the special role the heavy gun plays in ambush procedures. That's the real action of combat service." The size of the heavy machine gun requires physical ability and strength beyond that of other weapons (see also Sion 1997), and winning this prestigious position singled him out and reinforced his masculine image.

The process of becoming a combat fighter of the Giv'ati Brigade is marked by a final forced march of around 90 kilometres from the unit's base to the official Giv'ati memorial site. The march terminates with a ceremony where the soldiers take an oath to the military and get presented with the unit's purple beret. Nir recounts the ceremony as, "one of the most exhilarating experiences of my life . . . You feel like you finally made it, you got your own special beret, after all my pals in the Kibbutz were laughing at me for being in Giv'ati. It was a divine feeling . . . There were really important people at the ceremony, including the legendary chief commander who built up the unit. He is still a role model for Giv'ati soldiers, especially the religious ones. They got as excited as if they'd seen the Messiah in flesh and blood."

This last comment is again one of mixed feelings—a tremendous pride in his new unit combined with some criticism towards the adoration, bordering on sacred worship, of the chief commander. It also raises another important arena of negotiation in Nir's narrative—his position as secular and "leftist" compared with his religious- and conservative-inclined fellow platoon members. This issue arises in particular in relation to his unit's participation in policing Palestinian civilians in the Gaza strip.

Nir was first deployed in the territories during the unit's advanced training period. Asked how he felt serving there, he described the activity in professional military terms: "Operational duty in the territories is different. It's LOTAR [Israeli military acronym for anti-terrorism combat techniques]. It's combat in built-up area conditions." Yet, when I asked him in what way it was combat, he reflected in a more reserved way: "You can call it combat. In good conscience, I can't shoot a ten-year-old who is confronting me and throwing stones at me. I remember each and every stone that hit me . . . It's insulting. It's one thing if the religious guys get hit, but me with my leftist ideology—wanting to get the hell out of there and leave them to have their own state—why do I deserve to get stoned? Why do I have to be there and run after ten-year-old kids?"

Nir complained about the prolonged training period, recalling how he waited month after month eager to start the real action—that is, to participate in operational activity in Lebanon. He describes his first entry to a post in the Israeli-controlled area of south Lebanon. "We rode in a convoy, under the back-up of artillery shelling from behind us. Shells fell 200 meters away, it's very scary at first. You almost piss in your pants, sitting in the armoured personnel carrier and looking all around you. It's definitely frightening, but it's part of a routine you get used to, it's your job."

Later he started to participate in ambushes against Hizbollah guerrillas. His initial description of the first encounter with the enemy is technical and report-like in nature: "During that period we had one encounter, nothing serious. We were expecting them to come. There was no surprise factor. It was an ambush in a classic design. Each one took his place, I was with my machine gun in a cover position. When they arrived, the commander yells, 'Fire,' and that's it, it ended very quickly. I think our snipers took down the first two in a matter of seconds. A third one tried to hide under a rock and got a bullet in the leg. I don't know if it was my shots that killed them, but they were totally full of holes." Understanding that he had actually seen the bodies, I asked him about it, upon which he responded: "They were all torn apart. When you stop and think about it, he is a human being too. Was a human being a minute ago." Yet in practice, one didn't stop and think about it, but kept in mind only one thought: "You know that it's either you or them, so why not do it? At the minute we first spot them you don't stop to think at all. You shoot."

This description is typical of the way military logic works to accomplish its missions through a process of dehumanization. The enemy is depersonalized and objectified—as a target to be hit or as an obstacle to be dealt with. Focusing on the technical, machine-like operation is not devoid of strong emotions. Nir recalls his feelings during the act and reflects on the atmosphere in his platoon after the successful assignment: "Your heart starts beating strongly. I think it was one of the most thrilling experiences I ever had in my life. Everybody was in a state of ecstasy. When you think about it it's not so difficult, forty men against a few *mehablim* [guerrilla fighters; literally, saboteurs]. But the morale was high. People really got high on it—the fact that our guys got to do the job, and not another Brigade, that we actually killed *mehablim.*" Here is another aspect of military performance. Through inspiring pride in the unit, competition with other units, and focusing on the end result of the operation—the number of casualties to the enemy—the activity is perceived as if it were like winning a match. In addition, the feelings triggered in combat activity as a joint group endeavour evoke, in case of victory, a quasi-religious atmosphere of ecstasy which plays a major motivational role for the participating individual.

The importance of the military performance as a collective endeavour is especially noteworthy in Nir's case: not only in terms of his sexual identity but, perhaps more importantly, with his secular background he was somewhat of an outsider to the group. Coming to the issue of his place among religious soldiers, Nir explained:

> My home is especially anti-religious. For example, if I had told my mother, not that I am gay, but that I intend to become religious, she would have taken that much more severely. So there was a lot of alienation. I was prejudiced against religious people. It turns out that I was wrong about many things. In practice they are a bunch of great guys. We were very much united. On the Sabbath [the Jewish day of rest], I'd even attend Synagogue prayers with them at base. The "distance" between the commanders and the soldiers would tend to break as well, since the commanders are religious too and come to Synagogue to pray. I consider it a foreign custom, but it was nice. They have fun, they have this commitment to being happy on Friday nights. They stay up and sing till late. There is a problem as they come from various traditions—Ashkenazi, Mizrachi, and Hasidic [one of the ultraorthodox religious streams]—each one with its own songs. So the best thing was to stick with the Giv'ati songs. They would sing Giv'ati songs all the time!

Sion (1997) has demonstrated how the ceremony of breaking "distance" between soldiers and commanders serves to strengthen the new soldier's identification with the military. In the above example, the same process operates at a much deeper level, incorporated as it is within a ritual that has a strong emotional resonance. The traditional Jewish Sabbath singing ritual is animated by jovial group activity performed in a new, non-religious context. The ritual in turn is reinforced by the particular context of its performance in military life: the harsh discipline of basic training is suddenly broken and replaced by a friendly social atmosphere. Being able to integrate the men of various backgrounds under the Giv'ati songs bolsters the military as a unifying religion that all can identify with, regardless of their views towards Jewish tradition.

Another broad issue Nir addressed was homosexuality and masculinity. First, he explained why disclosing his gay identity to military officials was out of the question, for fear of being marked and possibly denied future promotion. Second, he told of his hesitation to disclose himself to friends in his unit: "There's no one to talk to. For religious people, homosexuality is the end of the road. Something which the Torah [Jewish Old Testament] condemns to death." He did, however, tell another secular guy who became his best friend and a source of support within the unit. What is more interesting is how his resolution to join combat service to begin with singled him out from among his existing group of gay friends. These friends, with their antipathy to military Zionism, represented for him another strain prevalent within Israeli society among secular-liberal urban circles: "If I am gay, it means that I am leftist, that I won't do combat service, all the typical things. I can't justify that . . . In the Kibbutz, it's in their blood, they educate for Zionism and combat service more than in the city. In the city nobody appreciates you for serving there, they see it as a waste of time."

To conclude, Nir needs constantly to manoeuvre his multi-faceted identity between various opposing positions within Israeli discourse. The only way he can make sense of his socialist Kibbutz upbringing on the one hand, of a national-religious inclined unit on the other, and of his new reference group of secular-liberal urban gay men, is to adhere to the one binding force available for him—his identification with the military. This identification immediately draws on the question of masculinity: "Perhaps someone who defines himself as gay to begin with would not go to combat service. Indeed I have. But I wasn't looking for my masculinity . . . I was like this before the army, I'll be the same after it. I won't adopt feminine behaviour just because I'm gay."

It is obvious that Nir's identification with militarism is embedded deeply in his Kibbutz upbringing and cannot be attributed solely to his conscript military service. Military-like activities are a hobby among his peer group, as Nir mentions: "In my Kibbutz there is a tradition that you gather unused bullets from your army drills and bring them back home, and on Saturday all the guys get together and go to the Kibbutz shooting range. Everyone tries out other people's weapons." Yet Nir's narrative demonstrates how the very expectation and eventual participation in the combat military ordeal gives this early indoctrination its meaning and fulfilment as a man. In order to negotiate between various aspects of his own unique identity, Nir relies on the imagined Zionist masculinity achieved by combat military service.

NOTES

1. The *sabra* is the name of a fruit imported into the region two hundred years ago. It also refers to a person who is rough and prickly on the outside, yet rich and tender inside (Almog, 1997: 15).
2. Since 1993 the Israeli military has had a non-discriminatory policy towards the enlistment of homosexuals and officially they may serve in any unit. For an elaborated discussion of homosexuals' experience in the IDF, see Kaplan (1999), and Kaplan and Ben-Ari (2000).
3. The two recent prime ministers in Israel—Binyamin Netanyahu and Ehud Barak—served in this very unit and eagerly mention the fact time and again.

REFERENCES

Almog, Oz 1997: *Ha-tzabar – dyokan* (The Sabra—a profile), Tel Aviv: Am Oved.

Arian, Asher, Talmud, Ilan, and Hermann, Tamar 1988: *National Security and Public Opinion in Israel,* Boulder, CO: Westview Press.

Aronoff, Myron J. 1989: *Israeli Visions and Divisions,* New Brunswick, N.J.: Transaction Books.

Azarya, Victor 1983: "Israeli armed forces," in M. Janowitz and S. D. Westbrood (eds.), *Civic Education in the Military,* vol. 2, pp. 99–127, California: Sage.

Ben-Ari, Eyal 1998: *Mastering Soldiers: Conflict, Emotions and the Enemy in an Israeli Military Unit,* Oxford: Berghahn Books.

Biale, David 1992: "Zionism as an erotic revolution," in: H. Eilberg-Schwartz (ed.), *People of the Body: Jews and Judaism from an Embodied Perspective,* pp. 281–308, New York: State University of New York Press.

Boyarin, Daniel 1997: "Masada or Yavneh? Gender and the arts of Jewish resistance," in Boyarin, D., and Boyarin, J. (eds.), *Jews and Other Differences: The New Jewish Cultural Studies,* pp. 306–29, Berkeley: University of California Press.

Devilbiss, M. C. 1994: "Best-kept secrets: A comparison of gays and women in the United States armed forces," in: W. J. Scott and S. C. Stanley (eds.), *Gays and Lesbians in the Military: Issues, Concerns and Contrasts,* pp. 135–48, New York: Aldone de Gruyter.

Izraeli, Dafna N. 1997: "Gendering military service in Israel Defence Forces," *Israel Social Science Research* 12 (1), 129–66.

Kaplan, Danny 1999: *David, yonatan, ve-chayalim acherim: Al zehut, gavriyut, veminiyut be-yechidot kraviyot be-tzahal* ("David, Jonathan and other soldiers: Identity, masculinity, and sexuality in combat units in the Israeli army"), Tel-Aviv: Ha-Kibbutz Ha-Meuchad (Hebrew).

Kaplan, Danny, and Ben-Ari, Eyal 2000: "Brothers and others in arms: Managing gay identity in combat units of the Israeli army," *Journal of Contemporary Ethnography,* 29 (4).

Lieblich, Amia 1989: *Transition to Adulthood during Military Service: The Israeli Case,* Albany: State University of New York Press.

Liebman, Charles S., and Don-Yehiya, Eliezer 1983: *Civil Religion in Israel: Traditional Judaism and Political Culture in the Jewish State,* Berkeley: University of California Press.

Lomsky-Feder, Edna 1992: "Youth in the shadow of war—war in the light of youth: Life stories of Israeli veterans," in: Wim Meeus et al. (eds.), *Adolescence, Careers and Culture,* pp. 393–408, The Hague: De Gruyter.

Lomsky-Feder, Edna and Ben-Ari, Eyal (forthcoming): "The 'people in uniform' to 'different uniforms for the people': Diversity, professionalism and minority groups in Israel," in: J. Soeters and J. Van Der Meulen (eds.), *Managing Diversity in the Armed Forces,* Purdue University Press.

Mosse, L. George 1990: *Fallen Soldiers: Reshaping the Memory of World Wars,* Oxford: Oxford University Press.

Rubinstein, Amnon 1977: *Le-hyot am chofshi* ("To be a free people"), Jerusalem: Schoken (in Hebrew).

Segal, David R., Gade, Paul A., and Johnson, Edgar M. 1993: "Homosexuals in Western armed forces," *Society* 31, (1), 37–42.

Sion, Liora 1997: *Dimuyey gavriyut etzel lochamim: Ha-sherut be-chativot chel raglim ketekes ma'avar me-na'arut le-bagrut* ("Images of manhood among combat soldiers: Military service in the Israeli infantry as a rite of initiation from youth to adulthood"), Shaine Working Papers, no. 3. Jerusalem: Hebrew University (in Hebrew).

17

MALE GENDER AND RITUALS OF RESISTANCE IN THE PALESTINIAN INTIFADA
A Cultural Politics of Violence

JULIE PETEET

At the time of writing this article,[1] around 40 percent (approximately 2,100,000) of Palestinians lived under Israeli rule, either in Israel proper (around 645,000), in the West Bank and East Jerusalem (around 938,000), or in the Gaza Strip (around 525,000).[2] From the beginning of the intifada in December 1987 through December 1990, an estimated 106,600 Palestinians were injured.[3] Beatings are not isolated in these statistics, so it is impossible to calculate with any certainty the numbers involved, though one would have been hard pressed to find a young male Palestinian under occupation who had not been beaten or who did not personally know someone who

Julie Peteet, "Becoming Men" from "Male Gender and Rituals of Resistance in the Palestine *Intifada:* A Cultural Politics of Violence" from *American Ethnologist* 21 (1) (1994). Reprinted with the permission of *American Ethnologist.*

had been.[4] This article examines the attainment and enactment of manhood and masculinity among Palestinian male youths in relation to these beatings and detention in the occupied West Bank. The beatings (and detention) are framed as rites of passage that became central in the construction of an adult, gendered (male) self with critical consequences for political consciousness and agency. . . .

Becoming Men

> One sign of things to come—amidst the jokes and nervous laughter there were signs of genuine excitement by some soldiers at the prospect of "teaching them not to raise their heads." [Israeli soldier in the occupied territories, quoted in Peretz 1990: 122])

I first had an inkling of the meaning of the beating and imprisonment as rites of passage when Hussein, 24 years old and resident in Jalazon refugee camp, remarked casually and with a hint of resignation that, on his first evening home from a nine-month stint in prison, a neighbour had come to ask his help in mediating a dispute he was involved in with another neighbour. Hussein pleaded fatigue and the crush of visitors to avoid assuming this mantle of community responsibility, a responsibility that carries with it substantial moral authority. To be a mediator is a position and task usually the preserve of well-respected, older men know for their sagacity and even temperament. Such men are thought to have attained *'aql* (reason or social common sense).[5]

Hussein did handle the matter the next day, talking to both parties, eventually hammering out a compromise solution. Like many young men of his generation and experience, he suddenly found himself faced with responsibility for managing community affairs, mainly such tasks as mediation in disputes and participating in popular tribunals to try suspected collaborators.[6]

During visits to Hussein's family, I began to notice the deference paid him by his father, an unusual state of affairs in Arab family relations where sons are usually deferential to their fathers. Much about hierarchy and submission can be read in seemingly mundane, everyday gestures. Seating patterns in Arab culture are spatial statements of hierarchy. Those who stand or sit closest to the door are usually subordinate, younger males, while those farthest from the door and centrally positioned are older, respected men who are able to command obedience. The spatial arrangement of visitors and family members when congregating at Hussein's home did not conform to the traditional pattern. Indeed Hussein often was centrally positioned with his father clearly on the periphery. During conversations where his father was present, along with other family members and friends, his father deferred to Hussein in speech, allowing his son to interrupt him. Hussein's father listened attentively as his son talked for lengthy periods of time before interjecting himself. In short, he gave Hussein the floor. When Hussein would describe his prolonged torture at the hands of the interrogators, his father was quiet, only occasionally to interject, "Prison is a school, a university" and "Prison is for men."

In observing resistance activities in camps, villages, and urban neighbourhoods, it was clear the older men played little, if any role. It was the preserve of the young (under 25 years of age), and as such they embodied the prestige and respect that come from, and yet give one access to, leadership positions. It did not take long to realize that Hussein was a member of the local underground leadership. He had spent 19 months in jail on charges of organizing local forms of escalation, such as stone throwing and barricade building. Chased and publicly beaten in the camp's alleyways before being thrown into a jeep, he was then taken to prison and subjected to 18 days of interrogation. Naked, deprived of food, water and sanitation facilities for the first three days, he was subjected to beatings with fists, pipes and rifle butts, which alternated with questioning over an 18-day period.

Once interrogation procedures are completed, prisoners join their fellow inmates in daily prison routine. Palestinian political prisoners are highly organized. Classes are conducted daily in a variety of subjects ranging from foreign languages to maths, science and history. Classes in political theory and practice are the high points in this educational project. For this reason, it is commonplace in contemporary Palestinian discourse to hear the comment, "Prison is a university." A leadership hierarchy emerges, and as young men are released they take up the leadership mantle of those who are newly detained. In this way, young men circulate between prison and leadership positions. This circulation of young men ensures a leadership in spite of the campaign of massive arrests and detention of young males.

Upon his release, Hussein returned home to several days of visitors—kin, friends and neighbours—and new responsibilities in the camp leadership. Within the prisons, recruitment to political organizations flourishes, and leaders of each political faction emerge to lead their followers. From the prison they can have some voice in the daily actions and policies of the intifada as they confer instructions and ideas on prisoners about to be released. Upon returning to their communities, young men like Hussein have acquired the stature to lead. They have withstood interrogation and not given away information or become collaborators. More importantly, however, they return "educated men." Hussein and other released detainees spoke of prison as a place where they learned not only academic subjects, but also about power and how to resist.

Another young man I became acquainted with in the West Bank was Ali. Ali's experience of bodily inflictions of violence began substantially before the intifada. Within a five-year period, he had been detained 17 times.

Politically inactive before he was taken away from home in the middle of the night during his last year of high school, the soldiers assured his frightened parents that they would just ask him a few questions and let him go. Handcuffed and blindfolded, he was placed on the floor of a jeep where he was repeatedly kicked and hit with rifle butts. He recalls that the jeep stopped and picked up someone else. Once they started beating the other fellow, and he screamed, Ali realized it was his friend Sami. Sami told him: "Don't cry or shout. Don't let them know it hurts." He told me:

> At first, of course, I was scared to death, and then once you're in that room and they slap your face and start hitting you—that's it, it goes away and you start being a different person. All of a sudden you have a power inside you—a power to resist—you want to resist. You can't help it; you feel very strong, you even want to challenge them, though basically I had nothing to tell them since I had done nothing.

After his release several days later, he returned home. Two weeks later, soldiers appeared again and detained him, this time for about two weeks. Upon his release, he decided to join the underground resistance movement and after several months was active in the local-level leadership. He now had stature in the community as a result of the beatings, arrests and interrogations. He was effective in mobilizing others to join in demonstrations, national celebrations, and the resistance movement on the university campus he later attended.

Physical violence can be construed by its recipients as a "bridge-burning" activity (Gerlach and Hines 1970). One often hears comments such as "I've nothing left to lose" and "I've already paid the price, I might as well be active." Palestinian males need not necessarily do violence to become political agents as Fanon (1969) argued for the Algerian revolution. As its recipients, they acquire masculine and revolutionary credentials. Marks on the body, though certainly unwanted, signal a resistant, masculine subjectivity and agency. The pervasiveness of beatings/detention, their organizational format, and their construal by recipients as entry into the world of masculinity make possible their casting as a rite of passage.

In his classic study of rites of passage, Van Gennep (1909/1961) identified three characteristic stages: separation, marginality, and aggregation. A logic of sequences is apparent in the transformative process of physical violence. In the initial phase, the individual is physically detached from the group. He is either taken from his home and family to the jeep and then the interrogation room, or he is detached from the crowd in public and held by soldiers or settlers who try to keep at a distance those who would intervene. The second, or liminal, stage is a state of marginality and ambiguity and is one fraught with dangers. The young novice exists outside of social time, space, and the categories of the life cycle. Social rules and norms are suspended. Interrogation, with its applications of physical violence, is such a liminal stage during which social hierarchies of age and class are diluted. Oppositions between normal social life and liminality (Turner 1977) can be applied to the one being beaten, especially those in custody who are frequently naked, in a state of humility and without rank or status, and who silently undergo pain and suffering. Imprisonment is also a liminal period because communitas is achieved and expressed in the emergence of new hierarchies that rest on an ability to withstand physical violation and pain, political affiliation and rank, and ability to lead in the prison community.

The final sequence, aggregation or the post-liminal re-entry into normal social life, is verified and enacted by the family and the community at large. The return home is marked by a fairly well-defined celebratory etiquette. Relatives, friends and neighbours visit for several weeks to show respect to the released detainee and his family. Special foods, usually more expensive meat dishes, are prepared by the women of the household both to strengthen the detainee's often poor health as well as to show appreciation and respect for his endurance. New clothes are bought to mark re-entry into the community. The respect shown by deferential gestures to the former prisoner or beaten youth all mark his re-entry into society with a new status of respect and manhood.

In emerging from the beating unbowed and remaining committed to resistance activities, young men exhibit generosity to the point of sacrifice that asserts and validates a masculine self. The infliction of pain reveals, in the most intimate and brutal way, the nature of occupation and strengthens them, they contend, to confront it.

Endowed with the qualities of adulthood, honour and manhood, emergence from the ordeal dovetails with access to power and authority. In a reversal of meaning, the beating empowers the self and informs an agency of resistance. Palestinians, as participants in and as audience to the public spectacle of beatings, have consciously and creatively taken a coherent set of signs and practices of domination and construed them to buttress an agency designed to overthrow political hierarchies.

NOTES

1. This article was completed in November 1992 and is here reprinted in an abbreviated form with small modifications by permission of the American Anthropological Association (not for further reproduction). It has been decided not to attempt to "update" the original article or to change tenses throughout to reflect the fact that, with the institution of the Palestinian Authority, there have been changes in the status of some Palestinians. The article first appeared in *American Ethnologist* 21: 1 February 1994, and research for it was carried out in the West Bank during 1990. Funding for a year of fieldwork was generously provided by the Fulbright Islamic Civilization Program. The Palestinian Academic Society for the Study of International Affairs (PASSIA) graciously provided institutional support and hospitality. I would like to extend my appreciation to Mary Hegland, Yvonne Jones

and William Young for comments on an earlier draft and to the four anonymous reviewers for *American Ethnologist* for their helpful comments and suggestions for revision.

2. See Hajjar and Beinin (1988). This is a primer designed to provide a very basic overview of twentieth-century Palestinian history and society.
3. This encompasses injuries sustained from live ammunition, which includes plastic bullets, rubber bullets, metal marbles and tear gas.
4. The Palestine Human Rights and Information Committee (PHRIC) cautions that the figure of 106,600 should probably be doubled, especially the beatings. They receive their information from hospitals and clinics, and many people do not seek medical care. Moreover, they do not receive figures on beating cases treated in emergency rooms, in local or private clinics, or by the medical communities. The figures from the Gaza Strip for the month of December 1990 indicate 273 reported beatings (66 were of women, 45 of children) (Palestine Human Rights and Information Campaign 1990).
5. For an extensive discussion of the concept of *'aql,* see Rosen (1984). *'Aql* has been described as the "faculty of understanding, rationality, judiciousness, prudence, and wisdom" (Altorki 1986: 51). Males begin to acquire *'aql* around the age of 20. While acquisition of this quality has no definable starting date, it does grow with marriage, and most men attain it fully "no earlier than 40, or mature adulthood, when men are perceived to have achieved sufficient capacity to deal with the complex problems of social existence" (Altorki 1986: 52). Milestones along this path to adulthood are circumcision, educational achievements, marriage, income earning, the birth of children, and the acquisition of wisdom that comes from knowledge of one's society and its customs. See Granqvist (1931, 1935, 1947), for a description of circumcisions and weddings in Mandate Palestine.
6. For discussion of Palestinian popular tribunals and popular justice committees during the intifada, see McDowell (1989) and Peretz (1990). A similar process of legal development occurred in Lebanon under the PLO (Peteet 1987).

REFERENCES

Altorki, Soraya 1986: *Women in Saudi Arabia: Ideology and Behavior among the Elite,* New York: Columbia University Press.

Fanon, Frantz 1969: *The Wretched of the Earth,* Harmondsworth: Penguin Books.

Feldman, Allen 1991: *Formations of Violence: The Narrative of the Body and Political Terror in Northern Ireland,* Chicago: University of Chicago Press.

Gerlach, Luther, and Hines, Virginia 1970: *People, Power and Change: Movements of Social Transformation,* Indianapolis: Bobbs-Merrill Educational Publications.

Granqvist, Hilma 1931 & 1935: *Marriage Conditions in a Palestinian Village,* 2 vols., Helsingfors, Finland: Societas Scientiarum Fennica.

Granqvist, Hilma 1947: *Birth and Childhood among the Arabs: Studies in a Muhammadan Village in Palestine,* Helsingfors, Finland: Soderstrom & Co.

Hajjar, Lisa, and Beinin, Joel 1988: "Palestine for Beginners," *Middle East Report* 154: 17–20.

McDowell, David 1989: *Palestine and Israel: The Uprising and Beyond,* Berkeley: University of California Press.

Palestine Human Rights and Information Campaign 1990: *Palestine Human Rights and Information Campaign* 3: 13, Human Rights Update.

Peretz, Don 1990: *Intifada: The Palestinian Uprising,* Boulder, CO: Westview Press. Peteet, Julie 1987: "Socio-political Integration and Conflict Resolution in a Palestinian Refugee Camp," *Journal of Palestine Studies* 16(2): 29–44.

Rosen, Lawrence 1984: *Bargaining for Reality: The Construction of Social Relations in a Muslim Community,* Chicago: University of Chicago Press.

Turner, Victor 1977: *The Ritual Process: Structure and Anti-Structure,* Ithaca, NY: Cornell University Press.

Van Gennep, Arnold 1909/1961: *The Rites of Passage,* Chicago: University of Chicago Press.

PART III
Embodiment

I didn't see myself as fat. I didn't see myself. I wasn't there. I get so sad about that because I missed so much.

"MARTHA"[1]

In time, I learned to smother the rage I felt at so often being taken for a criminal. Not to do so would surely have led to madness.

BRENT STAPLES[2]

One afternoon they all decided to go skinny dipping. . . . They hassled me until I finally stripped and jumped in the water. It was about the worst experience of my life. First off, the other guys had better bodies than I did. My stomach stuck out, . . . and I had no shoulders or chest, and of course, no biceps. . . . [Then] an ex-girlfriend of mine swam by with the man she was living with at the time and made a comment about how I won the "funniest-shape-of-the-day award."

"LARRY"[3]

Our relationships to our bodies and our decisions about how we present ourselves to the world are heavily influenced by the historical and cultural contexts in which we live. In U.S. society, these contexts are determined to a large extent by the media. A brief look at the history of clothing and fashion or at the history of women in sports, for example, shows changes in the ideal female body image over time. Laced corsets, once very popular, are now used by few women. Sports such as track and field, once considered unacceptable for women, are now acceptable for women athletes, although female athletes are much more easily accepted if they appear to be feminine. Current media images of young women support sexualized, thin, bodies with bare midriffs.[4] Many of the dominant messages about bodies are tied to images of gender, race, and class, mandating different expectations for various women and men.[5] For example, in a study of Asian American women and cosmetic surgery, Eugenia Kaw reports an increase in the number of people from racial and ethnic minority groups in the U.S. electing racially specific plastic surgery. Whereas white women tend to choose liposuction, breast augmentation, or reduction of wrinkles, Asian American women, for example, tend to choose eyelid surgery to make their eyes wider, and nasal surgery to make their noses more prominent. Kaw concludes that Asian American women do this in order to escape racial prejudice by looking more Anglo. She further concludes that Asian American women are heavily influenced by the "medicalization" of racial features; rather than seen as normal, their eyelids and noses are seen as something to be fixed by medical intervention.[6]

Physical appearance is often an obsession for people in U.S. society, especially for people privileged enough to have the time and money to attend to their bodies. The pressure to look "right" can be internalized as profound self-disapproval. It drives many people to spend long hours exercising and preening and many years dieting. Even for people who would be considered attractive within their own communities, the dominant culture's obsession with youth, muscles, whiteness, blondness, and thinness can undermine positive attitudes for many.[7] With rare exceptions, most of us will look seriously "wrong" at some point if we have the privilege of growing old. People whose bodies don't match dominant images of what is defined as normal suffer immense discrimination, especially on the basis of skin color, weight, looks, age, or disability.[8] In one study, low-income middle school African American girls suffered more from both depression and poor body image than did their male counterparts, although many of the boys, too were concerned about their weight.[9]

Boys and men seem to be increasingly concerned with their looks. Muscles are a big issue, leading to obsessive weight lifting and/or steroid use.[10] Gay men, adopting the pressure to please men that is pervasive in mainstream heterosexual culture, also suffer from body image dissatisfaction, topping the dissatisfaction list in some studies (followed by heterosexual women). Heterosexual men and lesbians seem to feel the most accepting of their bodies when these groups are compared.[11]

Plastic surgery grows in popularity, in spite of its high cost. A case in England illustrates the pressure on teenage girls to have "perfect" bodies. Intense debate ensued when parents gave their teenage daughter, Jenna Franklin, a gift of silicone breast implants for her sixteenth birthday. The parents run a plastic surgery clinic and were supportive of their daughter's decision to have implants (the news reports said that she had been wanting implants since age twelve). Critics worried that surgery on someone that young could cause psychological damage and be done for the wrong reasons, and even the surgeon that Franklin's parents chose refused to do the surgery until she was at least eighteen years old; he was apparently concerned about both psychological issues and doing surgery on immature breasts, so Franklin will have to wait.[12] The demand for inexpensive plastic surgery has apparently stimulated the growth of underground beauty treatments performed by unlicensed practitioners who typically inject liquid silicone into lips, faces, or breasts, frequently leaving a wide range of health problems in their wake.[13]

The pressure to maintain virginity until marriage provoked the development of hyman reconstruction surgery long ago, but the issue seems to be getting more attention lately. Women from cultures where virginity at marriage is particularly important can protect their "honor" by having the surgery done. A surgeon in Toronto reports that primarily Muslim women inquire about or have the surgery. In Brooklyn, NY, plastic surgery clinics advertise "reconstrucción del himen" for Latina women.[14]

The pressure toward perfect male and female bodies is perhaps most powerfully expressed in the treatment of infants born neither male nor female but intersex. In cases where medical teams cannot tell whether the infant is a boy or a girl, which is estimated to occur in about 1 in 1,500 births, the child is assigned to one sex or the other based on visual appearance of the genitals.[15] Then, typically, a series of surgical and hormonal treatments is done in order to bring the child's body into conformity with the assigned gender. The lack of tolerance for a body that does not conform with gender appears to be most profound in medical settings. There is resistance to this pressure, however, on various fronts. The Intersex Society of North America (ISNA) (http://www.isna.org) has begun to organize around this issue, arguing against surgical and hormonal intervention until the child is old enough to decide for her/himself. Occasionally parents have also resisted the pressure for sex reassignment, creating serious frustration for medical professionals at times.[16] And in some unusual cases, children are allowed to choose for themselves whether to change their bodies physically, though all are assigned a gender at birth.[17] Some professionals in the United States and Canada are supporting the recommendation of ISNA on the heels of the outrage expressed by many intersex people whose lives have been fraught with identity confusion, emotional pain, and lack of sexual sensation as a result of medical treatment and as a result of the lies that frequently surround these cases.[18]

The need to convert bodies might not be so intense if third-gender options existed in mainstream U.S. society. Males who live as females in many societies (called berdaches, hijiras, or xaniths, and common in many Native American tribes) have a specific role that allows for a break from what is expected.[19] Other societies have female men—women who behave as men in terms of work, marriage, parenting, and possession of the economic resources to purchase a wife.[20] Societies that have these options might be better equipped to deal with intersex people since there are already more than two genders.

Sports-oriented culture intensifies the pressure for a perfect body. Sports themselves are also a problem for many athletes, because sports are highly competitive, few participants are able to make a career of sports (see Messner, Part II), sports injuries occur frequently, sexism pervades sports, and sports support heterosexism and homophobia. Homophobia is ever-present; male athletes are pressured to nurture their homophobia as they express their athletic masculinity in homoerotic contexts, and female athletes are pressured to be feminine, lest they look too much like men and challenge the division of the world into male and female.[21] The intersex issue plays a role here too. Genetic testing is sometimes required of athletes to assure that there are not any men competing as women or vice versa. Occasionally (perhaps as often as 1 in 500 tested athletes), someone who has lived her life, say, as a woman is informed that she has a Y chromosome and is actually male and therefore disqualified. In one such case a woman with a Y chromosome was disqualified from competition because she was genetically male, but later gave birth to a child.[22]

Objectification pervades our understanding of gender. People are frequently seen not for who they are, but for what they represent to both themselves and observers. People may become beauty objects, sex objects, racial objects, athletic objects, unattractive objects, disabled objects, or simply objects to abuse. The media feed this process by providing distorted messages about how people should look, what makes people happy, and how people spend their time: middle-class, white housewives excited over laundry detergent or toothpaste, white men buying cars and selling life insurance, Black men with muscular bodies playing sports, and so on. Few women believe they have acceptable bodies, and the media nurture this insecurity and self-hatred, pounding away at the expectation of perfection, leading people to see themselves as imperfect objects. Even men are now seeking plastic surgery in increasing numbers to mask the effects of aging or to lengthen or enlarge their penises.[23]

According to a recent television documentary, of 40,000 female applicants to a modeling agency, only four were selected as acceptable.[24] Despite the impossibility of ever looking like a model for the vast majority of women, the media message is so powerful that many women wish they did. Many will have face-lifts, get breast implants, or go on extreme diets in quest of the perfect body, in spite of the health risks involved. According to a study by sociologists Diana Dull and Candace West, plastic surgery is a heavily gendered process. The plastic surgeons they interviewed readily supported plastic surgery to enhance a woman's appearance, but they did not support it to enhance a man's appearance.[25]

The National Institutes of Health recently lowered the point at which a person is defined as overweight, effectively affixing a stigmatizing label to an additional twenty-nine million people who were not defined as overweight before the change in definition. Many of these newly "overweight" people can expect to suffer weight discrimination, including lectures about weight from their doctors and increased difficulty getting health insurance.[26] Author and nurse Pat Lyons, director of Free at Last: The Women's Body Sovereignty Project, asks people to help diminish fat discrimination by doing such things as not commenting about weight, accepting bodies as they are, not telling "fat jokes," and supporting healthy lifestyles for people of all sizes.[27] Christy Haubegger (this part) represents some of what Lyons is fighting for in her love of her large body as it is.

The authors in this section address various aspects of embodiment, including women's pursuit of the perfect body (Elayne Saltzberg and Joan Chrisler); eating troubles among women of color and white women (Becky Thompson); the social cost of living in a Black male body (Brent Staples); the struggle for manhood in the face of disability (Leonard Kriegel); the experience of living with an aging body (Barbara Macdonald); embracing a round woman's body in a Latino context (Christy Haubegger); dealing with the impact of genital surgery among intersexuals (Martha Coventry); and the explorations of the impact on women of restrictive Muslim culture and restrictive Western culture (Joan Jacobs Brumberg and Jacqueline Jackson).

The authors in this chapter argue either directly or indirectly for a world in which people are seen for who they are as people, rather than as physical objects to be liked, ridiculed, abused, or ignored. I am reminded here of a day a few years ago when a person walked past my office. I couldn't tell whether the person was male or female, noticed only that the person was medium height, white, and solidly built with relatively short brown hair. I found myself thinking, "That person is in an interesting package." I have since then pondered the package image. In most circumstances, when given a package, our impulse is to open it to find out what's inside. In the case of bodies, however, the wrapping frequently has such an impact that we have no interest in opening the package—that is, finding out more about the person within it—simply because the person's packaging does not appeal to us for whatever reason. And, as a result of external responses, the person inside risks incorporating those responses into their personalities, frequently as internalized oppression. Many of the authors in this section would like to see a world in which the person inside was more important than the packaging, and in which the packaging would not become a cause for hatred, physical harm, or blocked access to opportunities.

NOTES

1. Quoted in Becky W. Thompson, "'A Way Outa No Way': Eating Problems among African-American, Latina and White Women," *Gender & Society* 6, no. 4 (December 1992), pp. 546–561.
2. Brent Staples, "Just Walk on By: A Black Man Ponders His Power to Alter Public Space," *Ms.* (September 1986), Vol. 15, pp. 54–55.
3. "Larry" interviewed by Barry Glassner. "Men and Muscles," in *Bodies: Why We Look the Way We Do (And How We Feel about It)* (New York: Putnam, 1988). Reprinted in *Men's Lives,* 3rd ed., quote, pp. 254–255; article, pp. 252–261.
4. Frontline (Public Broadcasting System), *The Merchants of Cool,* video aired January 31, 2002.
5. On the history of fashion and clothing, see Saltzberg and Chrisler, this chapter. For a discussion of clothing and identity, see Mary Ellen Roach-Higgins, Joanne B. Eichner, and Kim K. P. Johnson, eds., *Dress and Identity* (New York: Fairchild Publishers, 1995). For a history of women in sports, see Susan K. Cahn, *Coming on Strong: Gender and Sexuality in Twentieth-Century Women's Sport* (Cambridge, MA: Harvard University Press, 1994). For perspectives on the influence of the media on gender, see Gail Dines and Jean M. Humez, eds., *Gender, Race and Class in Media: A Text-Reader* (Thousand Oaks, CA: Sage, 1995).
6. Eugenia Kaw, "Medicalization of Racial Features: Asian-American Women and Cosmetic Surgery" in Rose Weitz, ed., *The Politics of Women's Bodies: Sexuality, Appearance, and Behavior* (New York: Oxford, 1998), pp. 167–183.
7. For an interesting discussion of the use of blue contact lenses by people with brown eyes, including women of color, see Susan Bordo, "'Material Girl'—The

Effacements of Postmodern Culture," in *Unbearable Weight: Feminism, Western Culture and the Body* (Berkeley, CA: University of California Press, 1993), pp. 245–249.

8. For discussions of the impact of looks, obesity, and various kinds of disabilities on employment and other aspects of life, see Susan E. Browne, Debra Connors, and Nanci Stern, eds., *With the Power of Each Breath* (Pittsburgh: Cleis Press, 1985); Lisa Schoenfielder and Barbara Wieser, eds., *Shadow on a Tightrope* (Iowa City: Aunt Lute, 1983); Irving Kenneth Zola, *Missing Pieces: A Chronicle of Living with a Disability* (Philadelphia: Temple University Press, 1982); Gwyneth Matthews, *Voices from the Shadows: Women with Disabilities Speak Out* (Toronto: Women's Educational Press, 1983); Lucy Grealy, *Autobiography of a Face* (Boston: Houghton Mifflin, 1994); Kennie Fries, ed., *Staring Back: The Disability Experience from the Inside Out* (New York: Plume, 1997).
9. Kathryn Grant, Aoife Lyons, Dana Landis, Mi Hyon Cho, Maddalena Scudiero, Linda Reynolds, Julie Murphy, and Heather Bryant, "Gender, Body Image, and Depressive Symptoms Among Low-Income African American Adolescents," *Journal of Social Issues* 55, no. 2 (1999), pp. 299–316.
10. Barbara Meltz, "Boys and Body Image," *The Boston Globe* (June 1, 2000), pp. F1ff; Alan M. Klein, "Life's Too Short to Die Small: Steroid Use Among Male Bodybuilders," in Donald F. Sabo and David Frederick Gordon, eds., *Men's Health and Illness: Gender, Power and the Body* (Thousand Oaks, CA: Sage, 1995), pp. 105–120.
11. Dawn Atkins, "Introduction: Looking Queer," in Dawn Atkins, ed., *Looking Queer: Body Image and Identity in Lesbian, Bisexual, Gay, and Transgender Communities* (New York: Haworth Press, 1998), pp. xxix–li.
12. Chris Holme, "'You've Got to Have Breasts to Be Successful. Every Other Person You See on TV Has Had Implants': Teenager Justifies Decision in Face of Outrage from Experts." *The Herald* (Glasgow) (January 5, 2001), p. 3.
13. Aime Parnes, "In Florida, Risky Shots at Being Beautiful," *The Boston Globe* (May 1, 2001), p. A1 ff.
14. Sylvana Paternostro, "Northern Ladies," in *In the Land of God and Man: A Latin Woman's Journey* (New York: Penguin Putnam, Inc., 1999), pp. 270–288; Susan Oh, "Just Like a Virgin? Surgeons Restore Hymens for Cultural Reasons and Tighten Vagina Walls for Better Sex," *Maclean's* 113, no. 24 (June 12, 2000), p. 44ff.
15. Phyllis Burke, *Gender Shock: Exploding the Myths of Male and Female.* (New York: Anchor, 1966); Cheryl Chase, "Hermaphrodites with Attitude: Mapping the Emergence of Intersex Political Activism," *GLQ* 4, no. 2 (1998); Alice Domurat Dreger, "'Ambiguous' Sex—Or Ambivalent Medicine? Ethical Issues in the Treatment of Intersexuality," *The Hastings Center Report* 28, no. 3 (May–June 1998), pp. 24–35. The estimate of number of cases is from Dreger.
16. Katherine Rossiter and Shonna Diehl, "Gender Reassignment in Children: Ethical Conflicts in Surrogate Decision-Making," *Pediatric Nursing* 24 no. 1 (January–February 1998), pp. 59–62.
17. Froukje M. E. Slijper, Stenvert L. S. Drop, Jan C. Molenaar, and Sabine M. P. F. de Muinck Keizer-Schrama, "Long-Term Psychological Evaluation of Intersex Children," *Archives of Sexual Behavior* 27 no. 2 (April–May 1998), p. 125(20) p. 6, internet version. William George Reiner, "Case Study: Sex Reassignment in a Teenage Girl," *Journal of the American Academy of Child and Adolescent Psychiatry* 35, no. 6 (June 1996), p. 799(5). The latter article describes an intersex Hmong child who was raised as a girl and decided she wanted to be a boy at age 14. Her doctors supported her decision and provided relevant medical treatment to help her body become more male.

18. Milton Diamond and H. Keith Sigmundson, "Management of Intersexuality: Guidelines for Dealing with Persons with Ambiguous Genitals," *Archives of Pediatric and Adolescent Medicine* 151, no. 10 (October 1997), pp. 1046–1050.
19. Gary Mihalik, "More Than Two: Anthropological Perspectives on Gender," *Journal of Lesbian and Gay Psychotherapy* 1, no. 1 (1989), pp. 105–118.
20. Judith Lorber, *Paradoxes of Gender* (New Haven: Yale University Press, 1994), pp. 17–18.
21. For research and critical analysis of gender and sports, see Greta Cohen, ed., *Women in Sports: Issues and Controversies* (Newbury Park, CA: Sage, 1993); Susan K. Cahn, *Coming on Strong* (Toronto: Free Press, 1994); Pat Griffin, *Strong Women, Deep Closets: Lesbians and Homophobia in Sport* (Champaign, IL: Human Kinetics, 1998); Michael A. Messner, *Power at Play: Sports and the Problem of Masculinity* (Boston: Beacon Press, 1992); Michael A. Messner and Donald F. Sabo, Sex, *Violence and Power in Sport: Rethinking Masculinity* (Freedom, CA: Crossing Press, 1994).
22. Phyllis Burke, *Gender Shock* (New York: Anchor/Doubleday, 1996), p. 229.
23. Dale Koppel, "About Face: The Focus on Appearance Is Becoming a Male Obsession," *Your Health, The Boston Globe* (April 23, 1995), pp. 10, 23, 26. An ad in *The Boston Globe* announced plastic surgery for "male enhancement" in May 1995.
24. *The Famine Within,* Public Broadcasting System (winter 1995).
25. Diana Dull and Candace West, "Accounting for Cosmetic Surgery: The Accomplishment of Gender," *Social Problems* 38, no. 1 (February 1991), pp. 54–70.
26. Pat Lyons, "The Great Weight Debate: Where Have All the Feminists Gone?" *The Network News* 23, no. 5 (September–October 1998), pp. 1ff.
27. Lyons, p. 5.

18

BEAUTY IS THE BEAST
Psychological Effects of the Pursuit of the Perfect Female Body

ELAYNE A. SALTZBERG AND JOAN C. CHRISLER

Ambrose Bierce (1958) once wrote, "To men a man is but a mind. Who cares what face he carries or what he wears? But woman's body is the woman." Despite the societal changes achieved since Bierce's time, his statement remains true. Since the height of the feminist movement in the early 1970s, women have spent more money than ever before on products and treatments designed to make them beautiful. Cosmetic sales have increased annually to reach $18 billion in 1987 (Ignoring the economy, 1989), sales of women's clothing averaged $103 billion per month in 1990 (personal communication, U.S. Bureau of Economic Analysis, 1992), dieting has become a $30-billion-per-year industry (Stoffel, 1989), and women spent $1.2 billion on cosmetic surgery in 1990 (personal communication, American Society of Plastic and Reconstructive Surgeons, 1992). The importance of beauty has apparently increased even as women are reaching for personal freedoms and economic rights undreamed of by our grandmothers. The emphasis on beauty may be a way to hold on to a feminine image while shedding feminine roles.

Attractiveness is prerequisite for femininity but not for masculinity (Freedman, 1986). The word *beauty* always refers to the female body. Attractive male bodies are described as "handsome," a word derived from "hand" that refers as much to action as appearance (Freedman, 1986). Qualities of achievement and strength accompany the term *handsome;* such attributes are rarely employed in the description of attractive women and certainly do not accompany the term *beauty,* which refers only to a decorative quality. Men are instrumental; women are ornamental.

Beauty is a most elusive commodity. Ideas of what is beautiful vary across cultures and change over time (Fallon, 1990). Beauty cannot be quantified or objectively measured; it is the result of the judgments of others. The concept is difficult to define, as it is equated with different, sometimes contradictory, ideas. When people are asked to define beauty, they tend to

---

Elayne A. Salzberg and Joan C. Chrisler, "Beauty Is the Beast: Psychological Effects of the Pursuit of the Perfect Female Body" from *Women: A Feminist Perspective,* edited by Jo Freeman. Reprinted with permission.

mention abstract, personal qualities rather than external, quantifiable ones (Freedman, 1986; Hatfield & Sprecher, 1986). The beholder's perceptions and cognitions influence the degree of attractiveness at least as much as do the qualities of the beheld.

Because beauty is an ideal, an absolute, such as truth and goodness, the pursuit of it does not require justification (Herman & Polivy, 1983). An ideal, by definition, can be met by only a minority of those who strive for it. If too many women are able to meet the beauty standards of a particular time and place, then those standards must change in order to maintain their extraordinary nature. The value of beauty standards depends on their being special and unusual and is one of the reasons why the ideal changes over time. When images of beauty change, female bodies are expected to change, too. Different aspects of the female body and varying images of each body part are modified to meet the constantly fluctuating ideal (Freedman, 1986). The ideal is always that which is most difficult to achieve and most unnatural in a given time period. Because these ideals are nearly impossible to achieve, failure and disappointment are inevitable (Freedman, 1988).

Although people have been decorating their bodies since prehistoric times, the Chinese may have been the first to develop the concept that the female body can and should be altered from its natural state. The practice of foot binding clearly illustrates the objectification of parts of the female body as well as the demands placed on women to conform to beauty ideals. The custom called for the binding of the feet of five-year-old girls so that as they grew, their toes became permanently twisted under their arches and actually shrank in size. The big toe remained untouched. The more tightly bound the feet, the more petite they became and the more attractive they were considered to be (Freedman, 1986; Hatfield & Sprecher, 1986; Lakoff & Scherr, 1984). The painful custom of foot binding finally ended in the twentieth century after women had endured over one thousand years of torture for beauty's sake (Brain, 1979).

In the sixteenth century, European women bound themselves into corsets of whalebone and hardened canvas. A piece of metal or wood ran down the front to flatten the breasts and abdomen. This garment made it impossible to bend at the waist and difficult to breathe. A farthingale, which was typically worn over the corset, held women's skirts out from their bodies. It consisted of bent wood held together with tapes and made such simple activities as sitting nearly impossible. Queen Catherine of France introduced waist binding with a tortuous invention consisting of iron bands that minimized the size of the waist to the ideal measurement of thirteen inches (Baker, 1984). In the seventeenth century, the waist was still laced, but breasts were once again stylish, and fashions were designed to enhance them. Ample breasts, hips, and buttocks became the beauty ideal, perhaps paralleling a generally warmer attitude toward family life (Rosenblatt & Stencel, 1982). A white pallor was also popular at that time, probably as an indication that the woman was so affluent that she did not need to work outdoors, where the sun might darken her skin. Ceruse, a white lead-based paint now known to be toxic, was used to accentuate the pallor.

Tight corsets came back into vogue in Europe and North America in the mid-nineteenth century, and many women were willing to run the risk of developing serious health problems in order to wear them. The tight lacing often led to pulmonary disease and internal organ damage. American women disregarded the advice of their physicians, who spoke against the use of corsets because of their potential to displace internal organs. Fainting, or "the vapors," was the result of wearing such tightly laced clothing that normal breathing became impossible. Even the clergy sermonized against corsets; miscarriages were known to result in pregnant women who insisted on lacing themselves up too tightly. In the late nineteenth century, the beauty ideal required a tiny waist and full hips and bustline. Paradoxically, women would go on diets to gain weight while, at the same time, trying to achieve a smaller waistline. Some women were reported to have had their lower ribs removed so that their waists could be more tightly laced (Brain, 1979).

In the twentieth century, the ideal female body has changed several times, and American women have struggled to change along with it. In the 1920s, the ideal had slender legs and hips, small breasts, and bobbed hair and was physically and socially active. Women removed the stuffing from their bodices and bound their breasts[1] to appear young and boyish. In the 1940s and 1950s, the ideal returned to the hourglass shape. Marilyn Monroe was considered the epitome of the voluptuous and fleshy yet naive and childlike ideal. In the 1960s, the ideal had a youthful, thin, lean body and long, straight hair. American women dieted relentlessly in an attempt to emulate the tall, thin, teenage model Twiggy, who personified the 1960s' beauty ideal. Even pregnant women were on diets in response to their doctors' orders not to gain more than twenty pounds, advice physicians later rejected as unsafe (Fallon, 1990). Menopausal women begged their physicians to prescribe hormone replacement therapy, which was rumored to prevent wrinkles and keep the body youthful, and were willing to run any health risk to preserve their appearance (Chrisler, Torrey, & Matthes, 1989). In the 1970s, a thin, tan, sensuous look was "in." The 1980s' beauty ideal remained slim but required a more muscular, toned, and physically fit body. In recent decades the beauty ideal has combined such opposite traits as erotic sophistication with naive innocence, delicate grace with muscular athleticism (Freedman, 1988), and thin bodies with large breasts. The pressure to cope with such conflicting demands and to keep up with the continual changes in the ideal female body is highly stressful (Freedman, 1988) and has resulted in a large majority of American women with negative body images (Dworkin & Kerr, 1987; Rosen, Saltzberg, & Srebnik, 1989). Women's insecurity about their looks has made it easy to convince them that small breasts are a "disease" requiring surgical intervention. The sophisticated woman of the 1990s who is willing to accept the significant health risks of breast implants in order to mold her body to fit the beauty ideal has not progressed far beyond her sisters who bound their feet and waists.

The value of beauty depends in part on the high costs of achieving it. Such costs may be physical, temporal, economic, or psychological. Physical costs include the pain of ancient beauty rituals such as foot binding, tattooing, and nose and ear piercing as well as more modern rituals such as wearing pointy-toed, high-heeled shoes, tight jeans, and sleeping with one's hair in curlers. Side effects of beauty rituals have often been disastrous for women's health. Tattooing and ear piercing with unsanitary instruments have led to serious, sometimes fatal, infections. Many women have been poisoned by toxic chemicals in cosmetics (e.g., ceruse, arsenic, benzene, and petroleum) and have died from the use of unsafe diet products such as rainbow pills and liquid protein (Schwartz, 1986). The beauty-related disorders anorexia nervosa and bulimia have multiple negative health effects, and side effects of plastic surgery include hemorrhages, scars, and nerve damage. Silicone implants have resulted in breast cancer, autoimmune disease, and the formation of thick scar tissue.

Physical costs of dieting include a constant feeling of hunger that leads to emotional changes, such as irritability; in cases of very low caloric intake, dieters can experience difficulty concentrating, confusion, and even reduced cognitive capacity. The only growing group of smokers in the United States are young women, many of whom report that they smoke to curb their appetites (Sorensen & Pechacek, 1987). High heels cause lower back pain and lead to a variety of podiatric disorders. Furthermore, fashion trends have increased women's vulnerability in a variety of ways; long hair and dangling earrings have gotten caught in machinery and entangled in clothing and led to injury. High heels and tight skirts prevent women from running from danger. The *New York Times* fashion reporter Bernardine Morris was alarmed to see in Pierre Cardin's 1988 summer fashion show tight wraps that prevented the models from moving their arms (Morris, 1988).

Attaining the beauty ideal requires a lot of money. Expensive cosmetics (e.g., makeup, moisturizers, and hair dyes and straighteners) are among the most popular and are thought to be the most effective, even though their ingredients cost the same (and sometimes are the same) as those in less expensive products (Lakoff & Scherr, 1984). Health spas have become fashionable again as vacation spots for the rich and famous, and everyone wants to wear expensive clothing with designer labels. Plastic surgery has become so accepted and so common that, although it's quite expensive, surgeons advertise their services on television. Surgery is currently performed that can reduce the size of lips, ear lobes, noses, buttocks, thighs, abdomens, and breasts; rebuild a face; remove wrinkles; and add "padding" to almost any body part. Not surprisingly, most plastic surgery patients are women (Hamburger, 1988).

Beauty rituals are time-consuming activities. Jokes about how long women take to get ready for a date are based on the additional tasks women do when getting dressed. It takes time to pluck eyebrows, shave legs, manicure nails, apply makeup, and arrange hair. Women's clothing is more complicated than men's, and many more accessories are used. Although all women know that the "transformation from female to feminine is artificial" (Chapkis, 1986, p. 5), we conspire to hide the amount of time and effort it takes, perhaps out of fear that other women don't need as much time as we do to appear beautiful. A lot of work goes into looking like a "natural" beauty, but that work is not acknowledged by popular culture, and the tools of the trade are kept out of view. Men's grooming rituals are fewer, take less time, and need not be hidden away. Scenes of men shaving have often been seen on television and in movies and have even been painted by Norman Rockwell. Wendy Chapkis (1986) challenges her readers to "imagine a similar cultural celebration of a woman plucking her eyebrows, shaving her armpits, or waxing her upper lip" (p. 6). Such a scene would be shocking and would remove the aura of mystery that surrounds beautiful women.

Psychological effects of the pursuit of the perfect female body include unhappiness, confusion, misery, and insecurity. Women often believe that if only they had perfect looks, their lives would be perfectly happy; they blame their unhappiness on their bodies. American women have the most negative body image of any culture studied by the Kinsey Institute (Faludi, 1991). Dissatisfaction with their bodies is very common among adolescent girls (Adams & Crossman, 1978; Clifford, 1971; Freedman, 1984), and older women believe that the only way to remain attractive is to prevent the development of any signs of aging. Obsessive concern about body shape and weight have become so common among American women of all ages that they now constitute the norm (Rodin, Silberstein, & Striegel-Moore, 1985). The majority of women in the United States are dieting at any given time. For them, being female means feeling fat and inadequate and living with chronic low self-esteem (Rodin et al., 1985). Ask any woman what she would like to change about her body and she'll answer immediately. Ask her what she likes about her body and she'll have difficulty responding.

Those women who do succeed in matching the ideal thinness expected by modern beauty standards usually do so by exercising frenetically and compulsively, implementing severely restrictive and nutritionally deficient diets, developing bizarre eating habits, and using continuous self-degradation and self-denial. Dieting has become a "cultural requirement" for women (Herman & Polivy, 1983) because the ideal female body has become progressively thinner at the same time that the average female body has become progressively heavier. This cultural requirement remains in place despite the fact that physiology works against weight loss to such an extent that 98 percent of diets fail (Chrisler, 1989; Fitzgerald, 1981). In fact, it is more likely for someone to fully recover from cancer than for an obese person to lose a significant amount of weight and maintain that loss for five years (Brownell, 1982). Yet a recent study (Davies & Furnham, 1986) found that young women rate borderline anorexic bodies as very attractive. Thus, even the thinnest women find it nearly impossible to meet and maintain the beauty ideal.

The social pressure for thinness can be directly linked to the increasing incidence of anorexia nervosa and bulimia among women (Brumberg, 1988; Caskey, 1986). There are presently at least one million Americans with anorexia nervosa, and 95 percent of them are women. Between sixty thousand and 150,000 of them will die as a result of their obsession (Schwartz, 1986). Although cases of anorexia nervosa have been reported in the medical literature for hundreds of years (Bell, 1985), it was considered to be a rare disorder until the 1970s. Today's anorexics are also thinner than they were in the past (Brumberg, 1988). It is estimated that at least seven million American women will experience symptoms of bulimia at some point in their lives (Hatfield & Sprecher, 1986). A recent study (Hall & Cohn, 1988) found that 25 to 33 percent of female first-year college students were using vomiting after meals as a method of weight control. An accurate estimate of the number of women who are caught in the binge-purge cycle is difficult because women with bulimia are generally secretive about their behavior and the physical signs of bulimia are not nearly as obvious as those of anorexia nervosa.

Exercise has become for many women another manifestation of their body dissatisfaction. Studies have found that most men who exercise regularly do so to build body mass and to increase cardiovascular fitness; most women who exercise do so to lose weight and to change the shape of their bodies in order to increase their attractiveness (Garner, Rockert, Olmstead, Johnson, & Coscina, 1985; Saltzberg, 1990). Exercise has lost its status as a pleasurable activity and become yet another way for women to manipulate their bodies, another vehicle for narcissistic self-torture. Reports of the number of women exercising compulsively are increasing and may become as widespread as compulsive calorie counting and the compulsive eating habits of anorexics and bulimics.

Beauty ideals are created and maintained by society's elite. Racism, class prejudice, and rejection of the disabled are clearly reflected (Chapkis, 1986) in current American beauty standards. For example, women from lower socioeconomic groups typically weigh more than women in higher socioeconomic groups (Moore, Stunkard, & Srole, 1962); they are thus excluded by popular agreement from being considered beautiful. The high costs of chic clothing, cosmetics, tanning salons, skin and hair treatments, weight loss programs, and plastic surgery prevent most American women from access to the tools necessary to approach the ideal. Furthermore, the beauty standard idealizes Caucasian features and devalues those of other races (Lewis, 1977; Miller, 1969). In recent years, Asian American and African American women have sought facial surgery in order to come closer to the beauty ideal (Faludi, 1991), and psychotherapists have noted increased reports from their black women clients of guilt, shame, anger, and resentment about skin color, hair texture, facial features, and body size and shape (Greene, 1992; Neal & Wilson, 1989; Okazawa-Rey, Robinson, & Ward, 1987). Obviously, women with visible disabilities will never be judged to have achieved "perfection." Whoopi Goldberg's routine about the black teenager who wrapped a towel around her head to pretend it was long, blonde hair and Alice Walker's (1990) essay about her psychological adjustment after the eye injury that resulted in the development of "hideous" scar tissue provide poignant examples of the pain women experience when they cannot meet beauty standards.

The inordinate emphasis on women's external selves makes it difficult for us to appreciate our own internal selves (Kano, 1985). The constant struggle to meet the beauty ideal leads to high stress and chronic anxiety. Failure to meet the beauty ideal leads to feelings of frustration, low self-worth, and inadequacy in women whose sense of self is based on their physical appearance. The intensity of the drive to increase attractiveness may also contribute to the high rate of depression among women.[2]

Insecurity is common even among beautiful women, and studies show that they are as likely as their plain sisters to be unhappy about their looks (Freedman, 1988). Beautiful women are all too aware of the fleeting nature of their beauty; the effects of aging must be constantly monitored, and these women worry that the beauty ideal they've tried so hard to match may change without warning. When such women lose their beauty due to illness or accidents, they often become depressed and are likely to have difficulty functioning in society and to believe that their entire identity has been threatened.

Given the high costs of striving to be beautiful, why do women attempt it? Attractiveness greatly affects first impressions and later interpersonal relationships. In a classic study titled "What Is Beautiful Is Good," psychologists Kenneth Dion, Ellen Berscheid, and Elaine Walster Hatfield (1972) asked college students to rate photographs of strangers on a variety of personal characteristics. Those who were judged to be attractive were also more likely to be rated intelligent, kind, happy, flexible, interesting, confident, sexy, assertive, strong, outgoing, friendly, poised, modest, candid, and successful than those judged unattractive. Teachers rate attractive children more highly on a variety of positive characteristics including IQ and sociability, and attractive babies are cuddled and kissed more often than unattractive babies (Berscheid & Walster, 1974). Attractive people receive more lenient punishment for social transgressions (Dion, 1972; Landy & Aronson, 1969), and attractive women are more often sought out in social situations (Walster, Aronson, Abrahams, & Rottman, 1966; Reis, Nezlek, & Wheeler, 1980).

Furthermore, because unattractive people are more harshly punished for social transgressions and are less often sought after as social partners, failure to work toward the beauty ideal can result in real consequences. Television newswoman Christine Craft made the news herself when she was fired for being too old and too unattractive. Street harassers put women "in their place" by commenting loudly on their beauty or lack of it. Beauty norms limit the opportunities of women who can't or won't meet them. Obese women, for example, have experienced discrimination in a number of instances including hiring and promotion (Larkin & Pines, 1979; Rothblum, Miller, & Gorbutt, 1988) and college admissions (Canning & Mayer, 1966). Obese people even have a harder time finding a place to live; Lambros Karris (1977) found that landlords are less likely to rent to obese people. Even physicians view their obese patients negatively (Maddox & Liederman, 1969).

There is considerable evidence that women's attractiveness is judged more harshly than men's. Christine Craft was fired, yet David Brinkley and Willard Scott continue to work on major television news shows; their abilities are not thought to be affected by age or attractiveness. Several studies (Adams & Huston, 1975; Berman, O'Nan, & Floyd, 1981; Deutsch, Zalenski, & Clark, 1986; Wernick & Manaster, 1984) that asked participants to rate the attractiveness of photographs of people of varying ages found that although attractiveness ratings of both men and women decline with age, the rate of decline for women was greater. In one study (Deutsch, Zalenski, & Clark, 1986), participants were asked to rate the photographs for femininity and masculinity as well as attractiveness. The researchers found that both the attractiveness and femininity ratings of the female photographs diminished with age; the masculinity ratings were unaffected by the age or attractiveness of the photographs. Women are acutely aware of the double standard of attractiveness. At all ages women are more concerned than men about weight and physical appearance and have lower appearance self-esteem; women who define themselves as feminine are the most concerned about their appearance and have the lowest self-esteem (Pliner, Chaiken, & Flett, 1990). In fact, women are so concerned about their body size that they typically overestimate it. Women who overestimate their size feel worse about themselves, whereas men's self-esteem is unrelated to their body size estimates (Thompson, 1986). In a review of research on the stigma of obesity, Esther Rothblum (1992) concluded that the dieting industry, combined with Western attitudes toward weight and attractiveness, causes more pain and problems for women than for men.

Thus, the emphasis on beauty has political as well as psychological consequences for women, as it results in oppression and disempowerment. It is important for women to examine the effects that the pursuit of the perfect female body has had on their lives, challenge their beliefs, and take a stand against continued enslavement to the elusive beauty ideal. Women would then be able to live life more freely and experience the world more genuinely. Each woman must decide for herself what beauty really is and the extent to which she is willing to go to look attractive. Only a more diverse view of beauty and a widespread rebellion against fashion extremes will save us from further physical and psychological tolls.

Imagine an American society where the quality and meaning of life for women are not dependent on the silence of bodily shame. Imagine a society where bodies are decorated for fun and to express creativity rather than for self-control and self-worth. Imagine what would happen if the world's women released and liberated all of the energy that had been absorbed in the beautification process. The result might be the positive, affirming, healthy version of a nuclear explosion!

NOTES

1. Bras were originally designed to hide breasts.
2. Statistics indicate that women are far more likely than men to be diagnosed as depressed. The ratio is at least 3:1 (Williams, 1985).

REFERENCES

Adams, Gerald R., & Crossman, Sharyn M. (1978). *Physical attractiveness: A cultural imperative.* New York: Libra.

Adams, Gerald R., & Huston, Ted L. (1975). Social perception of middle-aged persons varying in physical attractiveness. *Developmental Psychology, 11,* 657–58.

Baker, Nancy C. (1984). *The beauty trap: Exploring woman's greatest obsession.* New York: Franklin Watts.

Bell, Rudolph M. (1985). *Holy anorexia.* Chicago: University of Chicago Press.

Berman, Phyllis W., O'Nan, Barbara A., & Floyd, Wayne. (1981). The double standard of aging and the social situation: Judgments of attractiveness of the middle-aged woman. *Sex Roles,* 7, 87–96.

Berscheid, Ellen, & Walster, Elaine. (1974). Physical attractiveness. *Advances in Experimental Social Psychology,* 7, 158–215.

Bierce, Ambrose. (1958). *The devil's dictionary.* New York: Dover.

Brain, R. (1979). *The decorated body.* New York: Harper & Row.

Brownell, Kelly. (1982). Obesity: Understanding and treating a serious, prevalent, and refractory disorder. *Journal of Consulting and Clinical Psychology, 55,* 889–97.

Brumberg, Joan J. (1988). *Fasting girls.* Cambridge, MA: Harvard University Press.

Canning, H., & Mayer, J. (1966). Obesity: An influence on high school performance. *Journal of Clinical Nutrition, 20,* 352–54.

Caskey, Noelle. (1986). Interpreting anorexia nervosa. In Susan R. Suleiman (Ed.), *The female body in western culture* (pp. 175–89). Cambridge, MA: Harvard University Press.

Chapkis, Wendy. (1986). *Beauty secrets: Women and the politics of appearance.* Boston: South End Press.

Chrisler, Joan C. (1989). Should feminist therapists do weight loss counseling? *Women & Therapy, 8*(3), 31–37.

Chrisler, Joan C. , Torrey, Jane W., & Matthes, Michelle. (1989, June). *Brittle bones and sagging breasts, loss of femininity and loss of sanity: The media describe the menopause.* Paper presented at the meeting of the Society for Menstrual Cycle Research, Salt Lake City, UT.

Clifford, Edward. (1971). Body satisfaction in adolescence. *Perceptual and Motor Skills, 33,* 119–25.

Davies, Elizabeth, & Furnham, Adrian. (1986). The dieting and body shape concerns of adolescent females. *Child Psychology and Psychiatry, 27,* 417–28.

Deutsch, Francine M., Zalenski, Carla M., & Clark, Mary E. (1986). Is there a double standard of aging? *Journal of Applied Social Psychology, 16,* 771–85.

Dion, Kenneth K. (1972). Physical attractiveness and evaluation of children's transgressions. *Journal of Personality and Social Psychology, 24,* 207–13.

Dion, Kenneth, Berscheid, Ellen, & Walster [Hatfield], Elaine. (1972). What is beautiful is good. *Journal of Personality and Social Psychology, 24,* 285–90.

Dworkin, Sari H., & Kerr, Barbara A. (1987). Comparison of interventions for women experiencing body image problems. *Journal of Consulting and Clinical Psychology, 34,* 136–40.

Fallon, April. (1990). Culture in the mirror: Sociocultural determinants of body image. In Thomas Cash & Thomas Pruzinsky (Eds.), *Body images: Development, deviance, and change* (pp. 80–109). New York: Guilford Press.

Faludi, Susan. (1991). *Backlash: The undeclared war against American women.* New York: Crown Publishers.

Fitzgerald, Faith T. (1981). The problem of obesity. *Annual Review of Medicine, 32,* 221–31.

Freedman, Rita. (1984). Reflections on beauty as it relates to health in adolescent females. In Sharon Golub (Ed.), *Health care of the female adolescent* (pp. 29–45). New York: Haworth Press.

Freedman, Rita. (1986). *Beauty bound.* Lexington, MA: D. C. Heath.

Freedman, Rita. (1988). *Bodylove: Learning to like our looks—and ourselves.* New York: Harper & Row.

Garner, David M., Rockert, Wendy, Olmstead, Marion P., Johnson, C., & Coscina, D. V. (1985). Psychoeducational principles in the treatment of bulimia and anorexia nervosa. In David M. Garner & Paul E. Garfinkel (Eds.), *Handbook of psychotherapy for anorexia nervosa and bulimia* (pp. 513–62). New York: Guilford.

Greene, Beverly. (1992). Still here: A perspective on psychotherapy with African American women. In Joan C. Chrisler & Doris Howard (Eds.), *New directions in feminist psychology: Practice, theory, and research* (pp. 13–25). New York: Springer.

Hall, L., & Cohn, L. (1988). *Bulimia: A guide to recovery.* Carlsbad, CA: Gurze Books.

Hamburger, A. C. (1988, May). Beauty quest. *Psychology Today, 22,* 28–32.

Hatfield, Elaine, & Sprecher, Susan. (1986). *Mirror, mirror: The importance of looks in everyday life.* Albany: State University of New York Press.

Herman, Peter, & Polivy, Janet. (1983). *Breaking the diet habit.* New York: Basic Books.

Ignoring the economy, cosmetic firms look to growth. (1989, July 13). *Standard and Poor's Industry Surveys, 1,* 37–38.

Kano, Susan. (1985). *Making peace with food: A step-by-step guide to freedom from diet/weight conflict.* Danbury, CT: Amity.

Karris, Lambros. (1977). Prejudice against obese renters. *Journal of Social Psychology, 101,* 159–60.

Lakoff, Robin T., & Scherr, Raquel L. (1984). *Face value: The politics of beauty.* Boston: Routledge & Kegan Paul.

Landy, David, & Aronson, Elliot. (1969). The influence of the character of the criminal and his victim on the decisions of simulated jurors. *Journal of Experimental Social Psychology, 5,* 141–52.

Larkin, Judith, & Pines, Harvey. (1979). No fat person need apply. *Sociology of Work and Occupations, 6,* 312–27.

Lewis, Diane K. (1977). A response to inequality: Black women, racism, and sexism. *Signs, 3*(2), 339–61.

Maddox, G., & Liederman, V. (1969). Overweight as a social disability with medical implications. *Journal of Medical Education, 44,* 214–20.

Miller, E. (1969). Body image, physical beauty, and color among Jamaican adolescents. *Social and Economic Studies, 18*(1), 72–89.

Moore, M. E., Stunkard, Albert, & Srole, L. (1962). Obesity, social class, and mental illness. *Journal of the American Medical Association, 181,* 138–42.

Morris, Bernardine. (1988, July 26). Paris couture: Opulence lights a serious mood. *New York Times,* p. B8.

Neal, Angela, & Wilson, Midge. (1989). The role of skin color and features in the black community: Implications for black women and therapy. *Clinical Psychology Review, 9,* 323–33.

Okazawa-Rey, Margo, Robinson, Tracy, & Ward, Janie V. (1987). Black women and the politics of skin color and hair. *Women & Therapy, 6*(1/2), 89–102.

Pliner, Patricia, Chaiken, Shelly, & Flett, Gordon L. (1990). Gender differences in concern with body weight and physical appearance over the life span. *Personality and Social Psychology Bulletin, 16,* 263–73.

Reis, Harry T., Nezlek, John, & Wheeler, Ladd. (1980). Physical attractiveness in social interaction. *Journal of Personality and Social Psychology, 38,* 604–17.

Rodin, Judith, Silberstein, Lisa, & Striegel-Moore, Ruth. (1985). Women and weight: A normative discontent. In Theo B. Sonderegger (Ed.), *Nebraska symposium on motivation: Psychology and gender* (pp. 267–307). Lincoln: University of Nebraska Press.

Rosen, James C., Saltzberg, Elayne A., & Srebnik, Debra. (1989). Cognitive behavior therapy for negative body image. *Behavior Therapy, 20,* 393–404.

Rosenblatt, J., & Stencel, S. (1982). *Weight control: A natural obsession.* Washington, DC: Congressional Quarterly.

Rothblum, Esther D. (1992). The stigma of women's weight: Social and economic realities. *Feminism & Psychology, 2*(1), 61–73.

Rothblum, Esther D., Miller, Carol, & Gorbutt, Barbara. (1988). Stereotypes of obese female job applicants. *International Journal of Eating Disorders, 7,* 277–83.

Saltzberg, Elayne A. (1990). *Exercise participation and its correlates to body awareness and self-esteem.* Unpublished master's thesis, Connecticut College, New London, CT.

Schwartz, Hillel. (1986). *Never satisfied: A cultural history of diets, fantasies, and fat.* New York: Free Press.

Sorensen, Gloria, & Pechacek, Terry F. (1987). Attitudes toward smoking cessation among men and women. *Journal of Behavioral Medicine, 10,* 129–38.

Stoffel, Jennifer. (1989, November 26). What's new in weight control: A market mushrooms as motivations change. *New York Times,* p. C17.

Thompson, J. Kevin. (1986, April). Larger than life. *Psychology Today,* pp. 41–44.

Walker, Alice. (1990). Beauty: When the other dancer is the self. In Evelyn C. White (Ed.), *The black women's health book: Speaking for ourselves* (pp. 280–87). Seattle: Seal Press.

Walster, Elaine, Aronsen, Vera, Abrahams, Darcy, & Rottman, Leon. (1966). Importance of physical attractiveness in dating behavior. *Journal of Personality and Social Psychology, 4,* 508–16.

Wernick, Mark, & Manaster, Guy J. (1984). Age and the perception of age and attractiveness. *Gerontologist, 24,* 408–14.

Williams, Juanita H. (1985). *Psychology of women: Behavior in a biosocial context.* New York: Norton.

19

"A WAY OUTA NO WAY" Eating Problems among African-American, Latina, and White Women

BECKY W. THOMPSON

Bulimia, anorexia, binging, and extensive dieting are among the many health issues women have been confronting in the last 20 years. Until recently, however, there has been almost no research about eating problems among African-American, Latina, Asian-American, or Native American women; working-class women; or lesbians.[1] In fact, according to the normative epidemiological portrait, eating problems are largely a white, middle- and upper-class heterosexual phenomenon. Further, while feminist research has documented how eating problems are fueled by sexism, there has been almost no attention to how other systems of oppression may also be implicated in the development of eating problems.

In this article, I reevaluate the portrayal of eating problems as issues of appearance based in the "culture of thinness." I propose that eating problems begin as ways women cope with various traumas including sexual abuse, racism, classism, sexism, heterosexism, and poverty. Showing the interface between these traumas and the onset of eating problems explains why women may use eating to numb pain and cope with violations to their bodies. This theoretical shift also permits an understanding of the economic, political, social, educational, and cultural resources that women need to change their relationship to food and their bodies.

Existing Research on Eating Problems

There are three theoretical models used to explain the epidemiology, etiology, and treatment of eating problems. The biomedical model offers important scientific research about possible physiological causes of eating prob-

---

lems and the physiological dangers of purging and starvation (Copeland 1985; Spack 1985). However, this model adopts medical treatment strategies that may disempower and traumatize women (Garner 1985; Orbach 1985). In addition, this model ignores many social, historical, and cultural factors that influence women's eating patterns. The psychological model identifies eating problems as "multidimensional disorders" that are influenced by biological, psychological, and cultural factors (Garfinkel and Garner 1982). While useful in its exploration of effective therapeutic treatments, this model, like the biomedical one, tends to neglect women of color, lesbians, and working-class women.

The third model, offered by feminists, asserts that eating problems are gendered. This model explains why the vast majority of people with eating problems are women, how gender socialization and sexism may relate to eating problems, and how masculine models of psychological development have shaped theoretical interpretations. Feminists offer the culture of thinness model as a key reason why eating problems predominate among women. According to this model, thinness is a culturally, socially, and economically enforced requirement for female beauty. This imperative makes women vulnerable to cycles of dieting, weight loss, and subsequent weight gain, which may lead to anorexia and bulimia (Chernin 1981; Orbach 1978, 1985; Smead 1984).

Feminists have rescued eating problems from the realm of individual psychopathology by showing how the difficulties are rooted in systematic and pervasive attempts to control women's body sizes and appetites. However, researchers have yet to give significant attention to how race, class, and sexuality influence women's understanding of their bodies and appetites. The handful of epidemiological studies that include African-American women and Latinas casts doubt on the accuracy of the normative epidemiological portrait. The studies suggest that this portrait reflects which particular populations of women have been studied rather than actual prevalence (Andersen and Hay 1985; Gray, Ford, and Kelly 1987; Hsu 1987; Nevo 1985; Silber 1986).

More important, this research shows that bias in research has consequences for women of color. Tomas Silber (1986) asserts that many well-trained professionals have either misdiagnosed or delayed their diagnoses of eating problems among African-American and Latina women due to stereotypical thinking that these problems are restricted to white women. As a consequence, when African-American women or Latinas are diagnosed, their eating problems tend to be more severe due to extended processes of starvation prior to intervention. In her autobiographical account of her eating problems, Retha Powers (1989), an African-American woman, describes being told not to worry about her eating problems since "fat is more acceptable in the Black community" (p. 78). Stereotypical perceptions held by her peers and teachers of the "maternal Black woman" and the "persistent mammy-brickhouse Black woman image" (p. 134) made it difficult for Powers to find people who took her problems with food seriously.

Recent work by African-American women reveals that eating problems often relate to women's struggles against a "simultaneity of oppression" (Clarke 1982; Naylor 1985; White 1991). Byllye Avery (1990), the founder of the National Black Women's Health Project, links the origins of eating problems among African-American women to the daily stress of being undervalued and overburdened at home and at work. In Evelyn C. White's (1990) anthology, *The Black Woman's Health Book: Speaking for Ourselves,* Georgiana Arnold (1990) links her eating problems partly to racism and racial isolation during childhood.

Recent feminist research also identifies factors that are related to eating problems among lesbians (Brown 1987; Dworkin 1989; Iazzetto 1989; Schoenfielder and Wieser 1983). In her clinical work, Brown (1987) found that lesbians who have internalized a high degree of homophobia are more likely to accept negative attitudes about fat than are lesbians who have examined their internalized homophobia. Autobiographical accounts by lesbians have also indicated that secrecy about eating problems among lesbians partly reflects their fear of being associated with a stigmatized illness ("What's Important" 1988).

Attention to African-American women, Latinas, and lesbians paves the way for further research that explores the possible interface between facing multiple oppressions and the development of eating problems. In this way, this study is part of a larger feminist and sociological research agenda that seeks to understand how race, class, gender, nationality, and sexuality inform women's experiences and influence theory production.

Methodology

I conducted 18 life history interviews and administered lengthy questionnaires to explore eating problems among African-American, Latina, and white women. I employed a snowball sample, a method in which potential respondents often first learn about the study from people who have already participated. This method was well suited for the study since it enabled women to get information about me and the interview process from people they already knew. Typically, I had much contact with the respondents prior to the interview. This was particularly important given the secrecy associated with this topic (Russell 1986; Silberstein, Striegel-Moore, and Rodin 1987), the necessity of women of color and lesbians to be discriminating about how their lives are studied, and the fact that I was conducting across-race research.

To create analytical notes and conceptual categories from the data, I adopted Glaser and Strauss's (1967) technique of theoretical sampling, which directs the researcher to collect, analyze, and test hypotheses during the sampling process (rather than imposing theoretical categories onto the data). After completing each interview transcription, I gave a copy to each woman who wanted one. After reading their interviews, some of the women clarified or made additions to the interview text.

Demographics of the Women in the Study

The 18 women I interviewed included 5 African-American women, 5 Latinas, and 8 white women. Of these women, 12 are lesbian and 6 are heterosexual. Five women are Jewish, 8 are Catholic, and 5 are Protestant. Three women grew up outside of the United States. The women represented a range of class backgrounds (both in terms of origin and current class status) and ranged in age from 19 to 46 years old (with a median age of 33.5 years).

The majority of the women reported having had a combination of eating problems (at least two of the following: bulimia, compulsive eating, anorexia, and/or extensive dieting). In addition, the particular types of eating problems often changed during a woman's life span. (For example, a woman might have been bulimic during adolescence and anorexic as an adult.) Among the women, 28 percent had been bulimic, 17 percent had been bulimic and anorexic, and 5 percent had been anorexic. All of the women who had been anorexic or bulimic also had a history of compulsive eating and extensive dieting. Of the women, 50 percent were compulsive eaters and dieters (39 percent) or compulsive eaters (11 percent) but had not been bulimic or anorexic.

Two-thirds of the women have had eating problems for more than half of their lives, a finding that contradicts the stereotype of eating problems as transitory. The weight fluctuation among the women varied from 16 to 160 pounds, with an average fluctuation of 74 pounds. This drastic weight change illustrates the degree to which the women adjusted to major changes in body size at least once during their lives as they lost, gained, and lost weight again. The average age of onset was 11 years old, meaning that most of the women developed eating problems prior to puberty. Almost all of the women (88 percent) consider themselves as still having a problem with eating, although the majority believe they are well on the way to recovery.

The Interface of Trauma and Eating Problems

One of the most striking findings in this study was the range of traumas the women associated with the origins of their eating problems, including racism, sexual abuse, poverty, sexism, emotional or physical abuse, heterosexism, class injuries, and acculturation.[2] The particular constellation of eating problems among the women did not vary with race, class, sexuality, or nationality. Women from various race and class backgrounds attributed the origins of their eating problems to sexual abuse, sexism, and emotional and/or physical abuse. Among some of the African-American and Latina women, eating problems were also associated with poverty, racism, and class injuries. Heterosexism was a key factor in the onset of bulimia, compulsive eating, and extensive dieting among some of the lesbians. These oppressions are not the same nor are the injuries caused by them. And certainly, there are a variety of potentially harmful ways that women respond to oppression (such as using drugs, becoming a workaholic, or committing suicide). However, for all these women, eating was a way of coping with trauma.

Sexual Abuse

Sexual abuse was the most common trauma that the women related to the origins of their eating problems. Until recently, there has been virtually no research exploring the possible relationship between these two phenomena. Since the mid-1980s, however, researchers have begun identifying connections between the two, a task that is part of a larger feminist critique of traditional psychoanalytic symptomatology (DeSalvo 1989; Herman 1981; Masson 1984). Results of a number of incidence studies indicate that between one-third and two-thirds of women who have eating problems have been abused (Oppenheimer et al. 1985; Root and Fallon 1988). In addition, a growing number of therapists and researchers have offered interpretations of the meaning and impact of eating problems for survivors of sexual abuse (Bass and Davis 1988; Goldfarb 1987; Iazzetto 1989; Swink and Leveille 1986). Kearney-Cooke (1988) identifies dieting and binging as common ways in which women cope with frequent psychological consequences of sexual abuse (such as body image disturbances, distrust of people and one's own experiences, and confusion about one's feelings). Root and Fallon (1989) specify ways that victimized women cope with assaults by binging and purging: bulimia serves many functions, including anesthetizing the negative feelings associated with victimization. Iazzetto's innovative study (1989), based on in-depth interviews and art therapy sessions, examines how a woman's relationship to her body changes as a consequence of sexual abuse. Iazzetto discovered that the process of leaving the body (through progressive phases of numbing, dissociating, and denying) that often occurs during sexual abuse parallels the process of leaving the body made possible through binging.

Among the women I interviewed, 61 percent were survivors of sexual abuse (11 of the 18 women), most of whom made connections between sexual abuse and the beginning of their eating problems. Binging was the most common method of coping identified by the survivors. Binging helped women "numb out" or anesthetize their feelings. Eating sedated, alleviated anxiety, and combated loneliness. Food was something that they could trust and was accessible whenever they needed it. Antonia (a pseudonym) is an Italian-American woman who was first sexually abused by a male relative when she was four years old. Retrospectively, she knows that binging was a way she coped with the abuse. When the abuse began, and for many years subsequently, Antonia often woke up during the middle of the night with anxiety attacks or nightmares and would go straight to the kitchen cupboards to get food. Binging helped her block painful feelings because it put her back to sleep.

Like other women in the study who began binging when they were very young, Antonia was not always fully conscious as she binged. She described eating during the night as "sleep walking. It was mostly desperate—like I had to have it." Describing why she ate after waking up with nightmares, Antonia said, "What else do you do? If you don't have any coping mechanisms, you eat." She said that binging made her "disappear," which made her feel protected. Like Antonia, most of the women were sexually abused before puberty, four of them before they were five years old. Given their youth, food was the most accessible and socially acceptable drug available to them. Because all of the women endured the psychological consequences alone, it is logical that they coped with tactics they could do alone as well.

One reason Antonia binged (rather than dieted) to cope with sexual abuse is that she saw little reason to try to be the small size girls were supposed to be. Growing up as one of the only Italian Americans in what she described as a "very WASP town," Antonia felt that everything from her weight and size to having dark hair on her upper lip were physical characteristics she was supposed to hide. From a young age she knew she "never embodied the essence of the good girl. I don't like her. I have never acted like her. I can't be her. I sort of gave up." For Antonia, her body was the physical entity that signified her outsider status. When the sexual abuse occurred, Antonia felt she had lost her body. In her mind, the body she lived in after the abuse was not really hers. By the time Antonia was 11, her mother put her on diet pills. Antonia began to eat behind closed doors as she continued to cope with the psychological consequences of sexual abuse and feeling like a cultural outsider.

Extensive dieting and bulimia were also ways in which women responded to sexual abuse. Some women thought that the men had abused them because of their weight. They believed that if they were smaller, they might not have been abused. For example when Elsa, an Argentine woman, was sexually abused at the age of 11, she thought her chubby size was the reason the man was abusing her. Elsa said, "I had this notion that these old perverts liked these plump girls. You heard adults say this too. Sex and flesh being associated." Looking back on her childhood, Elsa believes she made fat the enemy partly due to the shame and guilt she felt about the incest. Her belief that fat was the source of her problems was also supported by her socialization. Raised by strict German governesses in an upper-class family, Elsa was taught that a woman's weight was a primary criterion for judging her worth. Her mother "was socially conscious of walking into places with a fat daughter and maybe people staring at her." Her father often referred to Elsa's body as "shot to hell." When asked to describe how she felt about her body when growing up, Elsa described being completely alienated from her body. She explained,

> Remember in school when they talk about the difference between body and soul? I always felt like my soul was skinny. My soul was free. My soul sort of flew. I was tied down by this big bag of rocks that was my body. I had to drag it around. It did pretty much what it wanted and I had a lot of trouble controlling it. It kept me from doing all the things that I dreamed of.

As is true for many women who have been abused, the split that Elsa described between her body and soul was an attempt to protect herself from the pain she believed her body caused her. In her mind, her fat body was what had "bashed in her dreams." Dieting became her solution, but, as is true for many women in the study, this strategy soon led to cycles of binging and weight fluctuation.

Ruthie, a Puerto Rican woman who was sexually abused from 12 until 16 years of age, described bulimia as a way she responded to sexual abuse. As a child, Ruthie liked her body. Like many Puerto Rican women of her generation, Ruthie's mother did not want skinny children, interpreting that as a sign that they were sick or being fed improperly. Despite her mother's attempts to make her gain weight, Ruthie remained thin through puberty. When a male relative began sexually abusing her, Ruthie's sense of her body changed dramatically. Although she weighed only 100 pounds, she began to feel fat and thought her size was causing the abuse. She had seen a movie on television about Romans who made themselves throw up and so she began doing it, in hopes that she could look like the "little kid" she was before the abuse began. Her symbolic attempt to protect herself by purging stands in stark contrast to the psychoanalytic explanation of eating problems as an "abnormal" repudiation of sexuality. In fact, her actions and those of many other survivors indicate a girl's logical attempt to protect herself (including her sexuality) by being a size and shape that does not seem as vulnerable to sexual assault.

These women's experiences suggest many reasons why women develop eating problems as a consequence of sexual abuse. Most of the survivors "forgot" the sexual abuse after its onset and were unable to retrieve the abuse memories until many years later. With these gaps in memory, frequently they did not know why they felt ashamed, fearful, or depressed. When sexual abuse memories resurfaced in dreams, they often woke feeling upset but could not remember what they had dreamed. These free-floating, unexplained feelings left the women feeling out of control and confused. Binging or focusing on maintaining a new diet were ways women distracted or appeased themselves, in turn, helping them regain a sense of control. As they grew older, they became more conscious of the consequences of these actions. Becoming angry at themselves for binging or promising themselves they would not purge again was a way to direct feelings of shame and self-hate that often accompanied the trauma.

Integral to this occurrence was a transference process in which the women displaced onto their bodies painful feelings and memories that actually derived from or were directed toward the persons who caused the abuse. Dieting became a method of trying to change the parts of their bodies they hated, a strategy that at least initially brought success as they lost weight. Purging was a way women tried to reject the body size they thought was responsible for the abuse. Throwing up in order to lose the weight they thought was making them vulnerable to the abuse was a way to try to find the body they had lost when the abuse began.

Poverty

Like sexual abuse, poverty is another injury that may make women vulnerable to eating problems. One woman I interviewed attributed her eating problems directly to the stress caused by poverty. Yolanda is a Black Cape Verdean mother who began eating compulsively when she was 27 years old. After leaving an abusive husband in her early 20s, Yolanda was forced to go on welfare. As a single mother with small children and few financial resources, she tried to support herself and her children on $539 a month. Yolanda began binging in the evenings after putting her children to bed. Eating was something she could do alone. It would calm her, help her deal with loneliness, and make her feel safe. Food was an accessible commodity that was cheap. She ate three boxes of macaroni and cheese when nothing else was available. As a single mother with little money, Yolanda felt as if her body was the only thing she had left. As she described it,

> I am here, [in my body] 'cause there is no where else for me to go, Where am I going to go? This is all I got . . . that probably contributes to putting on so much weight cause staying in your body, in your home, in yourself, you don't go out. You aren't around other people. . . . You hide and as long as you hide you don't have to face . . . nobody can see you eat. You are safe.

When she was eating, Yolanda felt a momentary reprieve from her worries. Binging not only became a logical solution because it was cheap and easy but also because she had grown up amid positive messages about eating. In her family, eating was a celebrated and joyful act. However, in adulthood, eating became a double-edged sword. While comforting her, binging also led to weight gain. During the three years Yolanda was on welfare, she gained seventy pounds.

Yolanda's story captures how poverty can be a precipitating factor in eating problems and highlights the value of understanding how class inequalities may shape women's eating problems. As a single mother, her financial constraints mirrored those of most female heads of households. The dual hazards of a race- and sex-stratified labor market further limited her options (Higginbotham 1986). In an article about Black women's health, Byllye Avery (1990) quotes a Black woman's explanation about why she eats compulsively. The woman told Avery,

> I work for General Electric making batteries, and, I know it's killing me. My old man is an alcoholic. My kid's got babies. Things are not well with me. And one thing I know I can do when I come home is cook me a pot of food and sit down in front of the TV and eat it. And you can't take that away from me until you're ready to give me something in its place. (p. 7)

Like Yolanda, this woman identifies eating compulsively as a quick, accessible, and immediately satisfying way of coping with the daily stress caused by conditions she could not control. Connections between poverty and eating problems also show the limits of portraying eating problems as maladies of upper-class adolescent women.

The fact that many women use food to anesthetize themselves, rather than other drugs (even when they gained access to alcohol, marijuana, and other illegal drugs), is partly a function of gender socialization and the competing demands that women face. One of the physiological consequences of binge eating is a numbed state similar to that experienced by drinking. Troubles and tensions are covered over as a consequence of the body's defensive response to massive food intake. When food is eaten in that way, it effectively works like a drug with immediate and predictable effects. Yolanda said she binged late at night rather than getting drunk because she could still get up in the morning, get her children ready for school, and be clearheaded for the college classes she attended. By binging, she avoided the hangover or sickness that results from alcohol or illegal drugs. In this way, food was her drug of choice since it was possible for her to eat while she continued to care for her children, drive, cook, and study. Binging is also less expensive than drinking, a factor that is especially significant for poor women. Another woman I interviewed said that when her compulsive eating was at its height, she ate breakfast after rising in the morning, stopped for a snack on her way to work, ate lunch at three different cafeterias, and snacked at her desk throughout the afternoon. Yet even when her eating had become constant, she was still able to remain employed. While her patterns of eating no doubt slowed her productivity, being drunk may have slowed her to a dead stop.

Heterosexism

The life history interviews also uncovered new connections between heterosexism and eating problems. One of the most important recent feminist contributions has been identifying compulsory heterosexuality as an institution which truncates opportunities for heterosexual and lesbian women (Rich 1986). All of the women interviewed for this study, both lesbian and heterosexual, were taught that heterosexuality was compulsory, although the versions of this enforcement were shaped by race and class. Expectations about heterosexuality were partly taught through messages that girls learned about eating and their bodies. In some homes, boys were given more food than girls, especially as teenagers, based on the rationale that girls need to be thin to attract boys. As the girls approached puberty, many were told to stop being athletic, begin wearing dresses, and watch their weight. For the women who weighed more than was considered acceptable, threats about their need to diet were laced with admonitions that being fat would ensure becoming an "old maid."

While compulsory heterosexuality influenced all of the women's emerging sense of their bodies and eating patterns, the women who linked heterosexism directly to the beginning of their eating problems were those who knew they were lesbians when very young and actively resisted heterosexual norms. One working-class Jewish woman, Martha, began compulsively eating when she was 11 years old, the same year she started getting clues of her lesbian identity. In junior high school, as many of her female peers began dating boys, Martha began fantasizing about girls, which made her feel utterly alone. Confused and ashamed about her fantasies, Martha came home every day from school and binged. Binging was a way she drugged herself so that being alone was tolerable. Describing binging, she said, "It was the only thing I knew. I was looking for a comfort." Like many women, Martha binged because it softened painful feelings. Binging sedated her, lessened her anxiety, and induced sleep.

Martha's story also reveals ways that trauma can influence women's experience of their bodies. Like many other women, Martha had no sense of herself as connected to her body. When I asked Martha whether she saw herself as fat when she was growing up she said, "I didn't see myself as fat. I didn't see myself. I wasn't there. I get so sad about that because I missed so much." In the literature on eating problems, *body image* is the term that is typically used to describe a woman's experience of her body. This term connotes the act of imagining one's physical appearance. Typically, women with eating problems are assumed to have difficulties with their body image. However, the term *body image* does not adequately capture the complexity and range of bodily responses to trauma experienced by the women. Exposure to trauma did much more than distort the women's visual image of themselves. These traumas often jeopardized their capacity to consider themselves as having bodies at all.

Given the limited connotations of the term *body image,* I use the term *body consciousness* as a more useful way to understand the range of bodily responses to trauma.[3] By body consciousness I mean the ability to reside comfortably in one's body (to see oneself as embodied) and to consider one's body as connected to oneself. The disruptions to their body consciousness that the women described included leaving their bodies, making a split between their body and mind, experiencing being "in" their bodies as painful, feeling unable to control what went in and out of their bodies, hiding in one part of their bodies, or simply not seeing themselves as having bodies. Binging, dieting, or purging were common ways women responded to disruptions to their body consciousness.

Racism and Class Injuries

For some of the Latinas and African-American women, racism coupled with the stress resulting from class mobility related to the onset of their eating problems. Joselyn, an African-American woman, remembered her white grandmother telling her she would never be as pretty as her cousins because they were lighter skinned. Her grandmother often humiliated Joselyn in front of others, as she made fun of Joselyn's body while she was naked and told her she was fat. As a young child, Joselyn began to think that although she could not change her skin color, she could at least try to be thin. When Joselyn was young, her grandmother was the only family member who objected to Joselyn's weight. However, her father also began encouraging his wife and daughter to be thin as the family's class standing began to change. When the family was working class, serving big meals, having chubby children, and keeping plenty of food in the house was a sign the family was doing well. But, as the family became mobile, Joselyn's father began insisting that Joselyn be thin. She remembered, "When my father's business began to bloom and my father was interacting more with white businessmen and seeing how they did business, suddenly thin became important. If you were a truly well-to-do family, then your family was slim and elegant."

As Joselyn's grandmother used Joselyn's body as territory for enforcing her own racism and prejudice about size, Joselyn's father used her body as the territory through which he channeled the demands he faced in the white-dominated business world. However, as Joselyn was pressured to diet, her father still served her large portions and bought treats for her and the neighborhood children. These contradictory messages made her feel confused about her body. As was true for many women in this study, Joselyn was told she was fat beginning when she was very young even though she was not overweight. And, like most of the women, Joselyn was put on diet pills and diets before even reaching puberty, beginning the cycles of dieting, compulsive eating, and bulimia.

The confusion about body size expectations that Joselyn associated with changes in class paralleled one Puerto Rican woman's association between her eating problems and the stress of assimilation as her family's class standing moved from poverty to working class. When Vera was very young, she was so thin that her mother took her to a doctor, who prescribed appetite stimulants. However, by the time Vera was eight years old, her mother began trying to shame Vera into dieting. Looking back on it, Vera attributed her mother's change of heart to competition among extended family members that centered on "being white, being successful, being middle class, . . . and it was always, 'Ay Bendito. She is so fat. What happened?'"

The fact that some of the African-American and Latina women associated the ambivalent messages about food and eating to their family's class mobility and/or the demands of assimilation while none of the eight white women expressed this (including those whose class was stable and changing) suggests that the added dimension of racism was connected to the imperative to be thin. In fact, the class expectations that their parents experienced exacerbated standards about weight that they inflicted on their daughters.

Eating Problems as Survival Strategies

Feminist Theoretical Shifts

My research permits a reevaluation of many assumptions about eating problems. First, this work challenges the theoretical reliance on the culture-of-thinness model. Although all of the women I interviewed were manipulated and hurt by this imperative at some point in their lives, it is not the primary source of their problems. Even in the instances in which a culture of thinness was a precipitating factor in anorexia, bulimia, or binging, this influence occurred in concert with other oppressions.

Attributing the etiology of eating problems primarily to a woman's striving to attain a certain beauty ideal is also problematic because it labels a common way that women cope with pain as essentially appearance-based disorders. One blatant example of sexism is the notion that women's foremost worry is about their appearance. By focusing on the emphasis on slenderness, the eating problems literature falls into the same trap of assuming that the problems reflect women's "obsession" with appearance. Some women were raised in families and communities in which thinness was not considered a criterion for beauty. Yet, they still developed eating problems. Other women were taught that women should be thin, but their eating problems were not primarily in reaction to this imperative. Their eating strategies began as logical solutions to problems rather than problems themselves as they tried to cope with a variety of traumas.

Establishing links between eating problems and a range of oppressions invites a rethinking of both the groups of women who have been excluded from research and those whose lives have been the basis of theory formation. The construction of bulimia and anorexia as appearance-based disorders is rooted in a notion of femininity in which white middle- and upper-class women are portrayed as frivolous, obsessed with their bodies, and overly accepting of narrow gender roles. This portrayal fuels women's tremendous shame and guilt about eating problems—as signs of self-centered vanity. This construction of white middle- and upper-class women is intimately linked to the portrayal of working-class white women and women of color as their opposite: as somehow exempt from accepting the dominant standards of beauty or as one step away from being hungry and therefore not susceptible to eating problems. Identifying that women may binge to cope with poverty contrasts the notion that eating problems are class bound. Attending to the intricacies of race, class, sexuality, and gender pushes us to rethink the demeaning construction of middle-class femininity and establishes bulimia and anorexia as serious responses to injustices.

Understanding the link between eating problems and trauma also suggests much about treatment and prevention. Ultimately, their prevention depends not simply on individual healing but also on changing the social conditions that underlie their etiology. As Bernice Johnson Reagon sings in Sweet Honey in the Rock's song "Oughta Be a Woman," "A way outa no way is too much to ask/too much of a task for any one woman" (Reagon 1980).[4] Making it possible for women to have healthy relationships with their bodies and eating is a comprehensive task. Beginning steps in this direction include ensuring that (1) girls can grow up without being sexually abused, (2) parents have adequate resources to raise their children, (3) children of color grow up free of racism, and (4) young lesbians have the chance to see their reflection in their teachers and community leaders. Ultimately, the prevention of eating problems depends on women's access to economic, cultural, racial, political, social, and sexual justice.

NOTES

Author's Note: The research for this study was partially supported by an American Association of University Women Fellowship in Women's Studies. An earlier version of this article was presented at the New England Women's Studies Association Meeting in 1990 in Kingston, Rhode Island. I am grateful to Margaret Andersen, Liz Bennett, Lynn Davidman, Mary Gilfus, Evelynn Hammonds, and two anonymous reviewers for their comprehensive and perceptive comments on earlier versions of this article. Reprint requests: Becky Wangsgaard Thompson, Dept. of Sociology, Simmons College, 300 The Fenway, Boston, MA 02115.

1. I use the term *eating problems* as an umbrella term for one or more of the following: anorexia, bulimia, extensive dieting, or binging. I avoid using the term *eating disorder* because it categorizes the problems as individual pathologies, which deflects attention away from the social inequalities underlying them (Brown 1985). However, by using the term *problem* I do not wish to imply blame. In fact, throughout, I argue that the eating strategies that women develop begin as logical solutions to problems, not problems themselves.
2. By trauma I mean a violating experience that has long-term emotional, physical, and/or spiritual consequences that may have immediate or delayed effects. One reason the term *trauma* is useful conceptually is its association with the diagnostic label Post Traumatic Stress Disorder (PTSD) (American Psychological Association 1987). PTSD is one of the few clinical diagnostic categories that recognizes social problems (such as war or the Holocaust) as responsible for the symptoms identified (Trimble 1985). This concept adapts well to the feminist assertion that a woman's symptoms cannot be understood as solely individual, considered outside of her social context, or prevented without significant changes in social conditions.
3. One reason the term *consciousness* is applicable is its intellectual history as an entity that is shaped by social context and social structures (Delphy 1984; Marx 1964). This link aptly applies to how the women described their bodies because their perceptions of themselves as embodied (or not embodied) directly relate to

their material conditions (living situations, financial resources, and access to social and political power).

4. Copyright © 1980. Used by permission of Songtalk Publishing.

REFERENCES

American Psychological Association. 1987. *Diagnostic and statistical manual of mental disorders.* 3rd ed. rev., Washington, DC: American Psychological Association.

Andersen, Arnold, and Andy Hay. 1985. Racial and socioeconomic influences in anorexia nervosa and bulimia. *International Journal of Eating Disorders* 4:479–87.

Arnold, Georgiana. 1990. Coming home: One Black woman's journey to health and fitness. In *The Black women's health book: Speaking for ourselves,* edited by Evelyn C. White. Seattle, WA: Seal Press.

Avery, Byllye Y. 1990. Breathing life into ourselves: The evolution of the National Black Women's Health Project. In *The Black women's health book: Speaking for ourselves,* edited by Evelyn C. White. Seattle, WA: Seal Press.

Bass, Ellen, and Laura Davis. 1988. *The courage to heal: A guide for women survivors of child sexual abuse.* New York: Harper & Row.

Brown, Laura S. 1985. Women, weight and power: Feminist theoretical and therapeutic issues. *Women and Therapy* 4:61–71.

———. 1987. Lesbians, weight and eating: New analyses and perspectives. In *Lesbian psychologies,* edited by the Boston Lesbian Psychologies Collective. Champaign: University of Illinois Press.

Chernin, Kim. 1981. *The obsession: Reflections on the tyranny of slenderness.* New York: Harper & Row.

Clarke, Cheryl. 1982. *Narratives.* New Brunswick, NJ: Sister Books.

Copeland, Paul M. 1985. Neuroendocrine aspects of eating disorders. In *Theory and treatment of anorexia nervosa and bulimia: Biomedical sociocultural and psychological perspectives,* edited by Steven Wiley Emmett. New York: Brunner/Mazel.

Delphy, Christine. 1984. *Close to home: A materialist analysis of women's oppression.* Amherst: University of Massachusetts Press.

DeSalvo, Louise. 1989. *Virginia Woolf: The impact of childhood sexual abuse on her life and work.* Boston, MA: Beacon.

Dworkin, Sari H. 1989. Not in man's image: Lesbians and the cultural oppression of body image. In *Loving boldly: Issues facing lesbians,* edited by Ester D. Rothblum and Ellen Cole. New York: Harrington Park Press.

Garfinkel, Paul E., and David M. Garner. 1982. *Anorexia nervosa: A multidimensional perspective.* New York: Brunner/Mazel.

Garner, David. 1985. Iatrogenesis in anorexia nervosa and bulimia nervosa. *International Journal of Eating Disorders* 4:701–26.

Glaser, Barney G., and Anselm L. Strauss. 1967. *The discovery of grounded theory: Strategies for qualitative research.* New York: Aldine DeGruyter.

Goldfarb, Lori. 1987. Sexual abuse antecedent to anorexia nervosa, bulimia and compulsive overeating: Three case reports. *International Journal of Eating Disorders* 6:675–80.

Gray, James, Kathryn Ford, and Lily M. Kelly. 1987. The prevalence of bulimia in a Black college population. *International Journal of Eating Disorders* 6:733–40.

Herman, Judith. 1981. *Father-daughter incest.* Cambridge, MA: Harvard University Press.

Higginbotham, Elizabeth. 1986. We were never on a pedestal: Women of color continue to struggle with poverty, racism and sexism. In *For crying out loud,* edited by Rochelle Lefkowitz and Ann Withorn. Boston, MA: Pilgrim Press.

Hsu, George. 1987. Are eating disorders becoming more common in Blacks? *International Journal of Eating Disorders* 6:113–24.

Iazzetto, Demetria. 1989. When the body is not an easy place to be: Women's sexual abuse and eating problems. Ph.D. diss., Union for Experimenting Colleges and Universities, Cincinnati, Ohio.

Kearney-Cooke, Ann. 1988. Group treatment of sexual abuse among women with eating disorders. *Women and Therapy* 7:5–21.

Marx, Karl. 1964. *The economic and philosophic manuscripts of 1844.* New York: International.

Masson, Jeffrey. 1984. *The assault on the truth: Freud's suppression of the seduction theory.* New York: Farrar, Strauss & Giroux.

Naylor, Gloria. 1985. *Linden Hills.* New York: Ticknor & Fields.

Nevo, Shoshana. 1985. Bulimic symptoms: Prevalence and ethnic differences among college women. *International Journal of Eating Disorders* 4:151–68.

Oppenheimer, R., K. Howells, R. L. Palmer, and D. A. Chaloner. 1985. Adverse sexual experience in childhood and clinical eating disorders: A preliminary description. *Journal of Psychiatric Research* 19:357–61.

Orbach, Susie. 1978. *Fat is a feminist issue.* New York: Paddington.

———. 1985. Accepting the symptom: A feminist psychoanalytic treatment of anorexia nervosa. In *Handbook of psychotherapy for anorexia nervosa and bulimia,* edited by David M. Garner and Paul E. Garfinkel. New York: Guilford.

Powers, Retha. 1989. Fat is a Black women's issue. *Essence,* Oct., 75, 78, 134, 136.

Reagon, Bernice Johnson. 1980. Oughta be a woman. On Sweet Honey in the Rock's album, *Good News.* Music by Bernice Johnson Reagon; lyrics by June Jordan. Washington, DC: Songtalk.

Rich, Adrienne. 1986. Compulsory heterosexuality and lesbian existence. In *Blood, bread and poetry.* New York: Norton.

Root, Maria P. P., and Patricia Fallon. 1988. The incidence of victimization experiences in a bulimic sample. *Journal of Interpersonal Violence* 3:161–73.

———. 1989. Treating the victimized bulimic: The functions of binge-purge behavior. *Journal of Interpersonal Violence* 4:90–100.

Russell, Diana E. 1986. *The secret trauma: Incest in the lives of girls and women.* New York: Basic Books.

Schoenfielder, Lisa, and Barbara Wieser, eds. 1983. *Shadow on a tightrope: Writings by women about fat liberation.* Iowa City, IA: Aunt Lute Book Co.

Silber, Tomas. 1986. Anorexia nervosa in Blacks and Hispanics. *International Journal of Eating Disorders* 5:121–28.

Silberstein, Lisa, Ruth Striegel-Moore, and Judith Rodin. 1987. Feeling fat: A woman's shame. In *The role of shame in symptom formation,* edited by Helen Block Lewis. Hillsdale, NJ: Lawrence Erlbaum.

Smead, Valerie. 1984. Eating behaviors which may lead to and perpetuate anorexia nervosa, bulimarexia, and bulimia. *Women and Therapy* 3:37–49.

Spack, Norman. 1985. Medical complications of anorexia nervosa and bulimia. In *Theory and treatment of anorexia nervosa and bulimia: Biomedical sociocultural and psychological perspectives,* edited by Steven Wiley Emmett. New York: Brunner/Mazel.

Swink, Kathy, and Antoinette E. Leveille. 1986. From victim to survivor: A new look at the issues and recovery process for adult incest survivors. *Women and Therapy* 5:119–43.

Trimble, Michael. 1985. Post-traumatic stress disorder: History of a concept. In *Trauma and its wake: The study and treatment of post-traumatic stress disorder,* edited by C. R. Figley. New York: Brunner/Mazel.

What's important is what you look like. 1988. *Gay Community News,* July, 24–30.

White, Evelyn C., ed. 1990. *The Black women's health book: Speaking for ourselves.* Seattle, WA: Seal Press.

———. 1991. Unhealthy appetites. *Essence,* Sept., 28, 30.

20

JUST WALK ON BY
A Black Man Ponders His Power to Alter Public Space

BRENT STAPLES

My first victim was a woman—white, well dressed, probably in her early twenties. I came upon her late one evening on a deserted street in Hyde Park, a relatively affluent neighborhood in an otherwise mean, impoverished section of Chicago. As I swung onto the avenue behind her, there seemed to be a discreet, uninflammatory distance between us. Not so. She cast back a worried glance. To her, the youngish black man—a broad six feet two inches with a beard and billowing hair, both hands shoved into the pockets of a bulky military jacket—seemed menacingly close. After a few more quick glimpses, she picked up her pace and was soon running in earnest. Within seconds she disappeared into a cross street.

That was more than a decade ago. I was 22 years old, a graduate student newly arrived at the University of Chicago. It was in the echo of that terrified woman's footfalls that I first began to know the unwieldy inheritance I'd come into—the ability to alter public space in ugly ways. It was clear that she thought herself the quarry of a mugger, a rapist, or worse. Suffering a bout of insomnia, however, I was stalking sleep, not defenseless wayfarers. As a softy who is scarcely able to take a knife to a raw chicken—let alone hold it to a person's throat—I was surprised, embarrassed, and dismayed all at once. Her flight made me feel like an accomplice in tyranny. It also made it clear that I was indistinguishable from the muggers who occasionally seeped into the area from the surrounding ghetto. That first encounter, and those that followed, signified that a vast, unnerving gulf lay between nighttime pedestrians—particularly women—and me. And I soon gathered that being perceived as dangerous is a hazard in itself. I only needed to turn a corner into a dicey situation, or crowd some frightened, armed person in a foyer somewhere, or make an errant move after being pulled over by a policeman. Where fear and weapons meet—and they often do in urban America—there is always the possibility of death.

In that first year, my first away from my hometown, I was to become thoroughly familiar with the language of fear. At dark, shadowy intersections in Chicago, I could cross in front of a car stopped at a traffic light and elicit

---

Brent Staples, "Just Walk on By: A Black Man Ponders His Power to Alter Public Space" from *Ms.* (September 1986). Reprinted with the permission of the author.

the *thunk, thunk, thunk, thunk* of the driver—black, white, male, female—hammering down the door locks. On less-traveled streets after dark, I grew accustomed to but never comfortable with people who crossed to the other side of the street rather than pass me. Then there were the standard unpleasantries with police, doormen, bouncers, cab drivers, and others whose business it is to screen out troublesome individuals *before* there is any nastiness.

I moved to New York nearly two years ago and I have remained an avid night walker. In central Manhattan, the near-constant crowd cover minimizes tense one-on-one street encounters. Elsewhere—visiting friends in SoHo, where sidewalks are narrow and tightly spaced buildings shut out the sky—things can get very taut indeed.

Black men have a firm place in New York mugging literature. Norman Podhoretz in his famed (or infamous) 1963 essay, "My Negro Problem—And Ours," recalls growing up in terror of black males; they "were tougher than we were, more ruthless," he writes—and as an adult on the Upper West Side of Manhattan, he continues, he cannot constrain his nervousness when he meets black men on certain streets. Similarly, a decade later, the essayist and novelist Edward Hoagland extols a New York where once "Negro bitterness bore down mainly on other Negroes." Where some see mere panhandlers, Hoagland sees "a mugger who is clearly screwing up his nerve to do more than just *ask* for money." But Hoagland has "the New Yorker's quick-hunch posture for broken-field maneuvering," and the bad guy swerves away.

I often witness that "hunch posture," from women after dark on the warrenlike streets of Brooklyn where I live. They seem to set their faces on neutral and, with their purse straps strung across their chests bandolier style, they forge ahead as though bracing themselves against being tackled. I understand, of course, that the danger they perceive is not a hallucination. Women are particularly vulnerable to street violence, and young black males are drastically overrepresented among the perpetrators of that violence. Yet these truths are no solace against the kind of alienation that comes of being ever the suspect, against being set apart, a fearsome entity with whom pedestrians avoid making eye contact.

It is not altogether clear to me how I reached the ripe old age of 22 without being conscious of the lethality nighttime pedestrians attributed to me. Perhaps it was because in Chester, Pennsylvania, the small, angry industrial town where I came of age in the 1960s, I was scarcely noticeable against a backdrop of gang warfare, street knifings, and murders. I grew up one of the good boys, had perhaps a half-dozen fist fights. In retrospect, my shyness of combat has clear sources.

Many things go into the making of a young thug. One of those things is the consummation of the male romance with the power to intimidate. An infant discovers that random flailings send the baby bottle flying out of the crib and crashing to the floor. Delighted, the joyful babe repeats those motions again and again, seeking to duplicate the feat. Just so, I recall the points at which some of my boyhood friends were finally seduced by the perception of themselves as tough guys. When a mark cowered and surrendered his money without resistance, myth and reality merged—and paid off. It is, after all, only manly to embrace the power to frighten and intimidate. We, as men, are not supposed to give an inch of our lane on the highway; we are to seize the fighter's edge in work and in play and even in love; we are to be valiant in the face of hostile forces.

Unfortunately, poor and powerless young men seem to take all this nonsense literally. As a boy, I saw countless tough guys locked away; I have since buried several, too. They were babies, really—a teenage cousin, a brother of 22, a childhood friend in his mid-twenties—all gone down in episodes of bravado played out in the streets. I came to doubt the virtues of intimidation early on. I chose, perhaps even unconsciously, to remain a shadow—timid, but a survivor.

The fearsomeness mistakenly attributed to me in public places often has a perilous flavor. The most frightening of these confusions occurred in the late 1970s and early 1980s when I worked as a journalist in Chicago. One day, rushing into the office of a magazine I was writing for with a deadline story in hand, I was mistaken for a burglar. The office manager called security and, with an ad hoc posse, pursued me through the labyrinthine halls, nearly to my editor's door. I had no way of proving who I was. I could only move briskly toward the company of someone who knew me.

Another time I was on assignment for a local paper and killing time before an interview. I entered a jewelry store on the city's affluent Near North Side. The proprietor excused herself and returned with an enormous red Doberman pinscher straining at the end of a leash. She stood, the dog extended toward me, silent to my questions, her eyes bulging nearly out of her head. I took a cursory look around, nodded, and bade her good night. Relatively speaking, however, I never fared as badly as another black male journalist. He went to nearby Waukegan, Illinois, a couple of summers ago to work on a story about a murderer who was born there. Mistaking the reporter for the killer, police hauled him from his car at gunpoint and but for his press credentials would have tried to book him. Such episodes are not uncommon. Black men trade tales like this all the time.

In "My Negro Problem—And Ours," Podhoretz writes that the hatred he feels for blacks makes itself known to him through a variety of avenues—one being his discomfort with that "special brand of paranoid touchiness" to which he says blacks are prone. No doubt he is speaking here of black men. In time, I learned to smother the rage I felt at so often being taken for a criminal. Not to do so would surely have led to madness—via that special "paranoid touchiness" that so annoyed Podhoretz at the time he wrote the essay.

I began to take precautions to make myself less threatening. I move about with care, particularly late in the evening. I give a wide berth to nervous people on the subway platforms during the wee hours, particularly when I have exchanged business clothes for jeans. If I happen to be entering a building behind some people who appear skittish, I may walk by, letting them clear the lobby before I return, so as not to seem to be following them.

I have been calm and extremely congenial on those rare occasions when I've been pulled over by the police.

And on late-evening constitutionals along streets less traveled by, I employ what has proved to be an excellent tension-reducing measure: I whistle melodies from Beethoven and Vivaldi and the more popular classical composers. Even steely New Yorkers hunching toward nighttime destinations seem to relax, and occasionally they even join in the tune. Virtually everybody seems to sense that a mugger wouldn't be warbling bright, sunny selections from Vivaldi's *Four Seasons.* It is my equivalent of the cowbell that hikers wear when they know they are in bear country.

21

TAKING IT

LEONARD KRIEGEL

In 1944, at the age of eleven, I had polio. I spent the next two years of my life in an orthopedic hospital, appropriately called a reconstruction home. By 1946, when I returned to my native Bronx, polio had reconstructed me to the point that I walked very haltingly on steel braces and crutches.

But polio also taught me that, if I were to survive, I would have to become a man—and become a man quickly. "Be a man!" my immigrant father urged, by which he meant "become an American." For, in 1946, this country had very specific expectations about how a man faced adversity. Endurance, courage, determination, stoicism—these might right the balance with fate.

"I couldn't take it, and I took it," says the wheelchair—doomed poolroom entrepreneur William Einhorn in Saul Bellow's *The Adventures of Augie March.* "And I *can't* take it, yet I do take it." In 1953, when I first read these words, I knew that Einhorn spoke for me—as he spoke for scores of other men who had confronted the legacy of a maiming disease by risking whatever they possessed of substance in a country that believed that such risks were a man's wagers against his fate.

How one faced adversity was, like most of American life, in part a question of gender. Simply put, a woman endured, but a man fought back. You were better off struggling against the effects of polio as a man than as a

---

woman, for polio was a disease that one confronted by being tough, aggressive, decisive, by assuming that all limitations could be overcome, beaten, conquered. In short, by being "a man." Even the vocabulary of rehabilitation was masculine. One "beat" polio by outmuscling the disease. At the age of eighteen, I felt that I was "a better man" than my friends because I had "overcome a handicap." And I had, in the process, showed that I could "take it." In the world of American men, to take it was a sign that you were among the elect—an assumption my "normal" friends shared. "You're lucky," my closest friend said to me during an intensely painful crisis in his own life. "You had polio." He meant it. We both believed it.

Obviously, I wasn't lucky. By nineteen, I was already beginning to understand—slowly, painfully, but inexorably—that disease is never "conquered" or "overcome." Still, I looked upon resistance to polio as the essence of my manhood. As an American, I was self-reliant. I could create my own possibilities from life. And so I walked mile after mile on braces and crutches. I did hundreds of push-ups every day to build my arms, chest, and shoulders. I lifted weights to the point that I would collapse, exhausted but strengthened, on the floor. And through it all, my desire to create a "normal" life for myself was transformed into a desire to become the man my disease had decreed I should be.

I took my heroes where I found them—a strange, disparate company of men: Hemingway, whom I would write of years later as "my nurse"; Peter Reiser, whom I dreamed of replacing in Ebbets Field's pastures and whose penchant for crashing into outfield walls fused in my mind with my own war against the virus; Franklin Delano Roosevelt, who had scornfully faced polio with aristocratic disdain and patrician distance (a historian acquaintance recently disabused me of that myth, a myth perpetrated, let me add, by almost all of Roosevelt's biographers); Henry Fonda and Gary Cooper, in whose resolute Anglo-Saxon faces Hollywood blended the simplicity, strength and courage a man needed if he was going to survive as a man; any number of boxers in whom heart, discipline and training combined to stave off defeats the boy's limitations made inevitable. These were the "manly" images I conjured up as I walked those miles of Bronx streets, as I did those relentless push-ups, as I moved up and down one subway staircase after another by turning each concrete step into a personal insult. And they were still the images when, fifteen years later, married, the father of two sons of my own, a Fulbright professor in the Netherlands, I would grab hold of vertical poles in a train in The Hague and swing my brace-bound body across the dead space between platform and carriage, filled with self-congratulatory vanity as amazement spread over the features of the Dutch conductor.

It is easy to dismiss such images as adolescent. Undoubtedly they were. But they helped remind me, time and time again, of how men handled their diseases and their pain. Of course, I realized even then that it was not the idea of manhood alone that had helped me fashion a life out of polio. I might write of Hemingway as "my nurse," but it was an immigrant Jewish mother—

already transformed into a cliché by scores of male Jewish writers—who serviced my crippled body's needs and who fed me love, patience and care even as I fed her the rhetoric of my rage.

But it was the need to prove myself an American man—tough, resilient, independent, able to take it—that pulled me through the war with the virus. I have, of course, been reminded again and again of the price extracted for such ideas about manhood. And I am willing to admit that my sons may be better off in a country in which "manhood" will mean little more than, say, the name for an after-shave lotion. It is forty years since my war with the virus began. At fifty-one, even an American man knows that mortality is the only legacy and defeat the only guarantee. At fifty-one, my legs still encased in braces and crutches still beneath my shoulders, my elbows are increasingly arthritic from all those streets walked and weights lifted and stairs climbed. At fifty-one, my shoulders burn with pain from all those push-ups done so relentlessly. And at fifty-one, pain merely bores—and hurts.

Still, I remain an American man. If I know where I'm going, I know, too, where I have been. Best of all, I know the price I have paid. A man endures his diseases until he recognizes in them his vanity. He can't take it, but he takes it. Once, I relished my ability to take it. Now I find myself wishing that taking it were easier. In such quiet surrenders do we American men call it quits with our diseases.

22

DO YOU REMEMBER ME?

BARBARA MACDONALD

I am less than five feet high and except that I may have shrunk a quarter of an inch or so in the past few years, I have viewed the world from this height for sixty-five years. I have taken up some space in the world; I weigh about a hundred and forty pounds and my body is what my mother used to call dumpy. My mother didn't like her body and so of course didn't like mine. My mother was not always rational and her judgment was further impaired because she was a recluse, but the "dumpy" was her word, and just as I have had to keep the body, somehow I have had to keep the word—thirty-eight-inch bust, no neck, no waistline, fat hips—that's dumpy.

My hair is grey, white at the temples, with only a little of the red cast of earlier years showing through. My face is wrinkled and deeply lined. Straight lines have formed on the upper lip as though I had spent many years with my mouth pursed. This has always puzzled me and I wonder what years those were and why I can't remember them. My face has deep lines that extend from each side of the nose down the face past the corners of my mouth. My forehead is wide and the lines across my forehead and between my eyes are there to testify that I was often puzzled and bewildered for long periods of time about what was taking place in my life. My cheekbones are high and become more noticeably so as my face is drawn further and further down. My chin is small for such a large head and below the chin the skin hangs in a loose vertical fold from my chin all the way down to my neck where it meets a horizontal scar. The surgeon who made the scar said that the joints of my neck were worn out from looking up so many years. For all kinds of reasons, I seldom look up to anyone or anything anymore.

My eyes are blue and my gaze is usually steady and direct. But I look away when I am struggling with some nameless shame, trying to disclaim parts of myself. My voice is low and my speech sometimes clipped and rapid if I am uncomfortable; otherwise I have a pleasant voice. I like the sound of it from in here where I am. When I was younger, some people, lovers mostly, enjoyed my singing, but I no longer have the same control of my voice and sing only occasionally now when I am alone.

My hands are large and the backs of my hands begin to show the brown spots of aging. Sometimes lately, holding my arms up reading in bed or lying with my arms clasped around my lover's neck, I see my own arms with the skin hanging loosely from my own forearm and cannot believe that the arm I see is really my own. It seems disconnected from me; it is someone else's, it is the arm of an old woman. It is the arm of such old women as I myself have seen, sitting on benches in the sun with their hands folded in their laps; old women I have turned away from. I wonder now, how and when these arms I see came to be my own—arms I cannot turn away from. . . .

The truth is I like growing old. Oh, it isn't that I don't feel at moments the sharp irrevocable knowledge that I have finally grown old. That is evident every time I stand in front of the bathroom mirror and brush my teeth. I may begin as I often do, wondering if those teeth that are so much a part of myself, teeth I've clenched in anger all my life, felt with my own tongue with a feeling of possession, as a cat licks her paw lovingly just because it is hers—wondering, will these teeth always be mine? Will they stay with me loyally and die with me, or will they desert me before the Time comes? But I grow dreamy brushing my teeth and find myself, unaware, planning as I always have when I brush my teeth—that single-handed crossing I plan to make. From East to West, a last stop in the Canaries and then the trade winds. What will be the best time of year? What boat? How much sail? I go over again the list of supplies, uninterrupted until some morning twinge in my left shoulder reminds me with uncompromising regret that I will never make that single-handed crossing—probably. That I have waited too long. That there is no turning back.

But I always say probably. Probably I'll never make that single-handed crossing. Probably, I've waited too long. Probably, I can't turn back now. But I leave room now, at sixty-five, for the unexpected. That was not always true of me. I used to feel I was in a kind of linear race with life and time. There were no probablies; it was a now or never time of my life. There were landmarks placed by other generations and I had to arrive on time or fail in the whole race. If I didn't pass—if the sixth grade went on to the seventh without me, I would be one year behind for the rest of my life. If I graduated from high school in 1928, I had to graduate from college in 1932. When I didn't graduate from college until 1951, it took me twenty years to realize the preceding twenty years weren't lost. But now I begin to see that I may get to have the whole thing and that no experience longed for is really going to be missed.

"I like growing old." I say it to myself with surprise. I had not thought that it could be like this. There are days of excitement when I feel almost a kind of high with the changes I feel taking place in my body, even though I know the inevitable course my body is taking will lead to debilitation and death. I say to myself frequently in wonder, "This is my body doing this thing." I cannot stop it, I don't even know what it is doing, I wouldn't know how to direct it; my own body is going through a process that only my body knows about. I never grew old before; never died before. I don't really know how it's done, I wouldn't know where to begin, and God knows, I certainly wouldn't know when to begin—for no time would be right. And then I realize, lesbian or straight, I belong to all the women who carried my cells for generations and my body remembers how for each generation this matter of ending is done.

Cynthia tells me now about being a young girl, watching and enjoying what her body was doing in preparation for her life. Seeing her breasts develop, watching the cleft disappear behind a cushion of dark pubic hair, discovering her own body making a bright red stain, feeling herself and seeing herself in the process of becoming.

When I was young, I watched this process with dread, seeing my breasts grow larger and larger and my hips widen. I was never able to say, "This is my body doing this wonderful unknown thing." I felt fear with every visible change, I felt more exposed, more vulnerable to attack. My swelling breasts, my widening hips, my growing pubic hair and finally the visible bleeding wound, all were acts of violence against my person, and could only bring me further acts of violence. I never knew in all the years of living in my woman's body that other women had found any pleasure in that early body experience, until Cynthia told me. But now, after a lifetime of living, my body has taken over again. I have this second chance to feel my body living out its own plan, to watch it daily change in the direction of its destiny. . . .

I wanted a different body when I was young. I have lived in this body for sixty-five years. "It is a good body, it is mine."

I wanted another mother and another beginning when I was young. I wanted a mother who liked herself, who liked her body and so would like mine. "My mother did not like herself and she did not like me; that is part of the definition of who she was and of who I am. She was my mother."

When I was fifty-two, my lover left me after fourteen years of living our lives together. I wanted her to return. I waited for many years and she did not come back. "I am the woman whose lover did not return."

I was lonely for years of my life and I wandered in search of a lover. "I am a person who loves again. I am a woman come home."

So often we think we know how an experience is going to end so we don't risk the pain of seeing it through to the end. We think we know the outcome so we think there is no need to experience it, as though to anticipate an ending were the same as living the ending out. We drop the old and take up the new—drop an idea and take up a new one—drop the middle-aged and old and start concentrating on the young, always thinking somehow it's going to turn out better with a new start. I have never had a child, but sometimes I see a young woman beginning to feel the urge to have a child at about the same time she feels some disappointment at how her own life is turning out. And soon the young mother feels further disappointment when her own mother withdraws her loving investment in her daughter to pour it into her grandchild. I see how all are devalued, the grandmother devalued by society, devalued by her own self, the daughter devalued by her mother, and the granddaughter, valued not for who she is but for who she may become, racing for the landmarks, as I once did.

We never really know the beginning or the middle, until we have lived out an ending and lived on beyond it.

Of course, this time, for me, I am not going to live beyond this ending. The strangeness of that idea comes to me at the most unexpected moments and always with surprise and shock; sometimes I am immobilized by it. Standing before the mirror in the morning, I feel that my scalp is tight. I see that the skin hangs beneath my jaw, beneath my arm; my breasts are pulled low against my body; loose skin hangs from my hips, and below my stomach a new horizontal crease is forming over which the skin will hang like the hem of a skirt turned under. A hem not to be "let down," as once my skirts were, because I was "shooting up," but a widening hem to "take up" on an old garment that has been stretched. Then I see that my body is being drawn into the earth—muscle, tendon, tissue and skin is being drawn down by the earth's pull back to the loam. She is pulling me back to herself; she is taking back what is hers.

Cynthia loves bulbs. She digs around in the earth every fall, looking for the rich loamy mold of decayed leaves and vegetation, and sometimes as she takes a sack of bone meal and works it into the damp earth, I think, "Why not mine? Why not?"

I think a lot about being drawn into the earth. I have the knowledge that one day I will fall and the earth will take back what is hers. I have no choice, yet I choose it. Maybe I won't buy that boat and that list of supplies; maybe I will. Maybe I will be able to write about my life; maybe I won't. But uncertainty will not always be there, for this is like no other experience I have ever had—I can count on it. I've never had anything before that I could really count on. My life has been filled with uncertainties, some were not of my making and many were: promises I made myself I did not keep, promises I made others I did not keep, hopes I could not fulfill, shame carried like a weight heavier by the years, at my failure, at my lack of clear purpose. But this time I can rely on myself, for life will keep her promise to me. I can trust her. She isn't going to confuse me with a multitude of other choices and beckon me down other roads with vague promises. She will give me finally only one choice, one road, one sense of possibility. And in exchange for the multitude of choices she no longer offers, she gives me, at last, certainty. Nor do I have to worry this time that I will fail myself, fail to pull it off. This time, for sure I am going to make that single-handed crossing.

23

I'M NOT FAT, I'M LATINA

CHRISTY HAUBEGGER

I recently read a newspaper article that reported that nearly 40 percent of Hispanic and African-American women are overweight. At least I'm in good company. Because according to even the most generous height and weight charts at the doctor's office, I'm a good 25 pounds overweight. And I'm still looking for the panty-hose chart that has me on it (according to Hanes, I don't exist). But I'm happy to report that in the Latino community, my community, I fit right in.

Latinas in this country live in two worlds. People who don't know us may think we're fat. At home, we're called *bien cuidadas* (well cared for).

I love to go dancing at Cesar's Latin Palace here in the Mission District of San Francisco. At this hot all-night salsa club, it's the curvier bodies like mine that turn heads. I'm the one on the dance floor all night while some of my thinner friends spend more time waiting along the walls. Come to think of it, I wouldn't trade my body for any of theirs.

Christy Haubegger, "I'm Not Fat, I'm Latina" from *Essence* (December 1994). Reprinted with the permission of the author.

But I didn't always feel this way. I remember being in high school and noticing that none of the magazines showed models in bathing suits with bodies like mine. Handsome movie heroes were never hoping to find a chubby damsel in distress. The fact that I had plenty of attention from Latino boys wasn't enough. Real self-esteem cannot come from male attention alone.

My turning point came a few years later. When I was in college, I made a trip to Mexico, and I brought back much more than sterling-silver bargains and colorful blankets.

I remember hiking through the awesome ruins of the Maya and the Aztecs, civilizations that created pyramids as large as the ones in Egypt. I loved walking through temple doorways whose clearance was only two inches above my head, and I realized that I must be a direct descendant of those ancient priestesses for whom those doorways had originally been built.

For the first time in my life, I was in a place where people like me were the beautiful ones. And I began to accept, and even like, the body that I have.

I know that medical experts say that Latinas are twice as likely as the rest of the population to be overweight. And yes, I know about the health problems that often accompany severe weight problems. But most of us are not in the danger zone; we're just bien cuidadas. Even the researchers who found that nearly 40 percent of us are overweight noted that there is a greater "cultural acceptance" of being overweight within Hispanic communities. But the article also commented on the cultural-acceptance factor as if it were something unfortunate, because it keeps Hispanic women from becoming healthier. I'm not so convinced that we're the ones with the problem.

If the medical experts were to try and get to the root of this so-called problem, they would probably find that it's part genetics, part enchiladas. Whether we're Cuban-American, Mexican-American, Puerto Rican or Dominican, food is a central part of Hispanic culture. While our food varies from fried plaintains to tamales, what doesn't change is its role in our lives. You feed people you care for, and so if you're well cared for, *bien cuidada*, you have been fed well.

I remember when I used to be envious of a Latina friend of mine who had always been on the skinny side. When I confided this to her a while ago, she laughed. It turns out that when she was growing up, she had always wanted to look more like me. She had trouble getting dates with Latinos in high school, the same boys that I dated. When she was little, the other kids in the neighborhood had even given her a cruel nickname: la seca, "the dry one." I'm glad I never had any of those problems.

Our community has always been accepting of us well-cared-for women. So why don't we feel beautiful? You only have to flip through a magazine or watch a movie to realize that beautiful for most of this country still means tall, blond and underfed. But now we know it's the magazines that are wrong. I, for one, am going to do what I can to make sure that *mis hijas,* my daughters, won't feel the way I did.

24

THE TYRANNY OF THE ESTHETIC
Surgery's Most Intimate Violation

MARTHA COVENTRY

Big clitorises aren't allowed in America. By big, I mean over three-eighths of an inch for newborns, about the size of a pencil eraser. Tiny penises, under one inch, aren't allowed either.[1] A big clitoris is considered too capable of becoming alarmingly erect, and a tiny penis is not quite capable enough. Such genitals are confounding to the strictly maintained and comforting social order in America today, which has everyone believing that bodies come in only two ways: perfectly female and perfectly male. But genitals are surprisingly ambiguous. At least one out of every 2,000 babies is born with genitals that don't elicit the automatic "It's a girl!" or "It's a boy!"[2] Many more have genitals that are perceived as "masculinized" or "feminized," although the child's sex is not in doubt.

The American Academy of Pediatrics recommends surgically altering these children between the ages of six weeks and 15 months to fashion their bodies into something closer to perfection.[3] Everyone can then breathe easier, except for the child, who may well spend the rest of her or his life trying to let the breath flow easy and full through the fear and shame created by such devastating surgery.

On a November night in 1958, I was playing in the bathtub in the cheery, country home of my childhood. I was six years old. My mother came in and sat on the edge of the tub, her kind face looking worried. I glanced up at her, wondering, "Time to get out so soon?" She told me that I had to go to the hospital the next day for an operation. I knew this was about something between my legs. My chest felt tight and there was a rushing sound in my ears. I begged not to go. Please. But my mother told me only that I must. Not a word was said about what was going to happen or why. The next day, it took the surgeon 30 minutes to make a U-shaped incision around my half-inch clitoris, remove it, and put it in a specimen dish to send to the lab. He then closed the wound and stitched the skin up over the stump.

Take no comfort in the fact that this took place 40 years ago. Today, most parents and doctors in this country are still unable to see that a child has a right to her or his own sexual body, even if that body is deemed "abnormal" by their standards. If a parent is uncomfortable, a doctor can be found who

---

Martha A. Coventry, "The Tyranny of the Esthetic: Surgery's Most Intimate Violation" from *On the Issues* (Summer 1998). Reprinted with the permission of the author.

will be willing to make irreversible changes in the child's body, in order to ease that discomfort. My gynecologist told me about a case in which he had been involved the year before: A woman brought her five-year-old daughter to his office in Minneapolis; the mother felt that the child's clitoris was too big. He examined the girl and assured the mother that her daughter would grow into her clitoris, which was no longer than the end of his little finger. The mother left. A few weeks later, he was called into an operating room to help another doctor who had run into trouble during a surgical procedure. On the table, he found the same little girl he had seen earlier. She was hemorrhaging from a clitorectomy attempted by the second doctor, from instructions he had read in a medical text. My physician stopped the bleeding, and managed to keep the girl's clitoris mostly intact.

It is not new in our culture to remove or alter the clitoris. Not so long ago, such surgery was commonly practiced to prevent masturbation and "unnatural sexual appetites." Although such justifications still lurk in the minds of parents and doctors ("Won't she become a lesbian?" is a concern of many mothers whose daughters have big clitorises), clitorectomies gained new status toward the end of the 1950s, as a "legitimate" way to make a child with atypical genitals feel and appear more normal. Surgical techniques learned during World War II led to advances in the field of cosmetic genital surgery; at about the same time, a new medical discipline—endocrinology, the study of the hormonal system—was established at Johns Hopkins University Medical School. A child's body could now be successfully altered by surgery and hormones to look just about any way you wanted it to look. And the controversial research into sex and gender roles by Johns Hopkins' John Money, Ph.D., led doctors to believe that by changing that body, you could make the child into a "normal" male or female, both physically and psychologically. Children could be made "right" if they were born "wrong." And American medicine, and our society at large, sees "imperfect" genitals as wrong.

That view is challenged by farsighted pediatric urologist Justine Schober, M.D., of Erie, Penn.: "Why should we say that, because this is a variation, that it is a wrong variation? If all their faculties work, their sexual sensitivities work, why should we presume that their body is wrong?"[4] But by seeing a child's body as wrong and by labeling such a child "intersexed," we turn a simple variation on a theme into a problem that can and should be fixed. And fixed it usually is, by surgery that sacrifices healthy erotic tissue for cosmetic reasons some five times a day in the U.S. The rules of the game are still the same as they were 40 years ago: Erase any sign of difference, tidy things up, and don't say another word.

After I had my clitorectomy, my innocent life became filled with fear and guilt. The secrecy surrounding my surgery began to undermine my entire sense of identity. I knew I had something between my legs cut off, and I could imagine only that it was a penis. Girls were Barbie-doll smooth, so there wasn't anything on a girl to cut off. Was I really a boy? Or perhaps the horrible thing I had somehow known about forever: hermaphrodite? The study of my father, a physician, was full of medical books, but I flipped through them quickly, drawn to the pictures of children with their eyes blacked out, knowing there was something we shared, yet terrified to find out what kind of freak I really was. Then, one night when I was 11 or 12, I found my parents, as they sat around the dining room table, looking at studio pictures of my sisters and me. My mother held up my photo and I heard her say the word "boy." My gut heaved. I was a boy. It was true. I blurted out, "What was that operation I had?" My father turned to me and said, "Don't be so self-examining." I never had the heart to tell this man who loved me so dearly that, by keeping the truth from me that night, by trying to protect me from my own wondering mind and wandering hands, he had sentenced me to a life of almost crippling fear in relation to my sexuality, even to a profound doubt of my right to be alive.

It would be 25 years before I could begin to start asking questions again. When I finally pressed my dying father as gently as I could for a reason why he and my mother wanted my clitoris removed, he said, "We didn't want you to be mistaken for a hermaphrodite." My father was a surgeon. No doctor had patronizingly spun to him tales of "improperly formed gonads," or lied to him about my medical condition, or told him I would become a lesbian if I had a big clitoris, or pretended that no other children like me existed. Just having a child with an abnormal body in Rochester, Minn., was bad enough for my parents. But doctors do lie—to parents and to children, in a gross insult to their intelligence and their right to the truth. Lying to children is a rule strictly adhered to, and enforced, by all but the most enlightened doctors. First, the surgery steals your body from you, then lies confirm that there is so little respect for you as a human being that you don't even deserve the truth.

X Marks the . . . .

Angela Moreno was a happy child growing up in the late seventies in Peoria, Ill. She was fairly sexually precocious with herself, and became very familiar with her clitoris: "I loved it, but had no name for it. I remember being amazed that there was a part of my body that was so intensely pleasurable. It felt wonderful under my hand. There was no fantasy, just pleasure—just me and my body." Life in the pleasure garden came to an abrupt end for Angela when, at age 12, her mother noticed her protruding clitoris while Angela was toweling off after a bath. After being examined by the family doctor, she was sent to an endocrinologist. The endocrinologist revealed to her parents that, instead of the two X chromosomes that characterize the female genotype, Angela had an X and a Y. She was "genetically male." She had the external genitalia of a female because the receptors for the "male" hormone testosterone did not function; that is, her body was unable to respond to the androgenizing or masculinizing hormones it produced. Her parents were assured that if surgeons removed Angela's internal testes, and shortened her clitoris, she would be a "very normal little girl," albeit one born without ovaries or a uterus. This was lie number one.

Just because your body may look "normal" is no guarantee that you will feel that way. The truth is that the very thing surgery claims to save us from—a sense of differentness and abnormality—it quite unequivocally creates.

Doctors then told Angela's parents that if she didn't have surgery she might kill herself when she found out that she was different from other girls. It had happened to another patient, the physicians said, and it could happen to Angela. Although such speculation is not a lie, it is also not the whole truth. In my talks with scores of people with atypical genitals, it is those who have been surgically altered as children and left alone with their trauma who most often become suicidal. The isolation from others who have experienced what we are going through, the loneliness, is what kills us. Angela's parents were justifiably frightened and agreed to the surgery.

The final lie was to Angela herself, with her distraught parents' complicity. She was told, at her physician's suggestion, that her nonexistent ovaries could become cancerous and that she would have to go into the hospital and have them removed.

In 1985, at a leading children's hospital in Chicago, doctors removed the testes from Angela's abdomen. The clitoris that had brought her so much joy was not merely shortened, it was all but destroyed. She woke up and discovered the extent of her deceit: "I put my hand down there and felt something like the crusty top of some horrible casserole, like dried caked blood where my clitoris was. I wondered why no one told me and I just figured it was the kind of thing decent people don't talk about."

Angela became depressed and severely bulimic. "I blamed my body. My body had betrayed me. Made me someone worthy of that kind of treatment. I just studied and puked." She was a straight-A student in high school, but otherwise, her adolescence was a nightmare. She avoided becoming close to other girls her age, afraid she would be asked questions about the menstrual period she knew she would never have. The uncomplicated sexuality she had reveled in before the clitorectomy was gone, and she was desolated by the loss of erotic sensation. In an attempt to find out the truth, she returned to her original endocrinologist, who told her that her gonads had not formed properly, and her clitoris had grown because of an abnormal level of hormones. She did not tell Angela about her XY status or her testes. Angela fell deeper into darkness, sensing that she had not been given the whole story. Finally, at 20, weakened by chronic and near-lethal bingeing and purging, and suicidal, she checked herself into a psychiatric unit.

After her release, she began seeing a therapist who finally hit on the connection between her bulimia and the control she lost over her body at the time of surgery. Angela knew she had to find out the mystery of her body in order to get well. By now she was 23 and could legally obtain her medical records, yet it took a year for her to find the courage to write for them. When she received them and read the truth about herself, she could begin at last to save her own life. "Although the doctors had claimed that knowing the truth would make me self-destructive, it was *not* knowing what had been done to me—and why—that made me want to die."

In my case, I have XX chromosomes, and my outsized clitoris was the only part of my body that was not like that of most other girls.

Do these facts make you want to differentiate me from Angela? To say, "Wait a minute. You were simply a girl born with a big clitoris, but Angela had a real pathological condition." But the doctors removed Angela's clitoris for exactly the same reason they removed mine—they thought it offensively large. Her chromosomes and her abdominal testes had no bearing on the decision.

If you rush to see Angela as fundamentally different from me, if you see her as a real intersexual and me as just a normal woman, you do two very damaging things: You may see it as justified to perform cosmetic surgery on her and not on me because she really is "abnormal," and you separate us from each other and deny our right to find solace and strength in the sameness of our experience.

The doctor who was kind enough to help me begin to explore my early surgery did just that to me. I found the Intersex Society of North America on my own several months after my initial visit with him, and told him later how healing it had been to find others who knew intimately what my life had been like.[5] He had known about ISNA all along, he said, but didn't pass the information on to me because I was not intersexed. I was a real woman. He had tried to save me from a pathologizing label, but ended up enforcing my isolation instead.

New and Improved?

When a baby is born today with genitals that are ambiguous, a team of surgeons, pediatric endocrinologists, and social workers scramble to relieve what is called a "psychosocial emergency." Tests are done and orifices explored to determine as nearly as possible the baby's "true sex." Then, in almost all cases, doctors perform surgery to make the child look more like a girl, because, they say, the surgery required is easier to perform than trying to make the child look like a boy.

The form this feminizing surgery most often takes is the dissection and removal of healthy clitoral tissue—a clitorectomy, also known as "clitoral recession," "clitoral reduction," and "clitoroplasty." Sensitive, erectile tissue is stripped away from the shaft of the clitoris, and the glans is tucked away so expertly that all you see is the cute little love button that is the idealized clitoris. But the pleasure is almost gone, or gone completely, for the owner of that dainty new clit. If orgasms are possible, and they aren't for many women subjected to clitoral surgery, the intensity is greatly diminished. One woman whose clitoris was "recessed" writes: "If orgasms before the recession were a deep purple, now they are a pale, watery pink."[6]

Doctors maintain that modern surgery retains more clitoral sensation than the older forms of surgery, but they base their assurance on nerve impulses measured by machines—supposedly accurate and unbiased information—and not the real experience of thousands and thousands of women in this country. This is because no long-term post-surgical studies have been done. I, who had the old-style surgery, have clitoral sensation and orgasmic function, while those subjected to more modern surgeries often have neither. How much do doctors truly care about a child's sexual future if they decimate the one organ in the body designed solely for pleasure?

In 1965, Annie Green, then three years old, took a car trip with her father from the small town in Idaho where she lived to Spokane, Wash. She sat in the back seat with her stuffed animal, unaware that she was on her way to the hospital. The next day doctors removed her inch-long clitoris. She was never given any explanation of her surgery. As she got older, her attempts to find pleasure in masturbation failed, and she began to suspect she was very different from other girls. Then, during a visit to her sister's house as a teenager, she found the book *Our Bodies, Ourselves:* "I studied the female anatomy and read about sex from that book. That was when I learned I didn't have a clitoris. I remember looking at the diagram, feeling myself, and reading what a clitoris was over and over. My God, I couldn't figure out why I didn't have one. I couldn't fathom anyone removing it if it was that important. I was stunned, and I held it all in. I was only 14. I became depressed. I was disgusted with my body, and I thought there was no hope that I would ever be loved by anyone. I became a little teenage alcoholic. I drank heavily every weekend. I really blew it because I had been a really good athlete and an honor student."

Clitoral surgery on children is brutal and illogical, and no matter what name you give it, it is a mutilation. When I use the word mutilation, I can hear doors slamming shut in the minds of doctors all over this country. John Gearhart, a pediatric urologist at Johns Hopkins, has said, "To compare genital mutilation of young girls in Africa to reconstructive surgery of a young baby is a giant, giant leap of misrepresentation."[7] But neither Dr. Gearhart, nor anyone else, has ever bothered to ask those of us subjected to clitoral surgery as children if being taken to the hospital without explanation, having your healthy genitals cut and scarred, then left alone with the results feels like mutilation or "reconstructive surgery." Gearhart's mistake is to judge surgery only by the surgeon's intent and not by the effect on the child. I spoke with a woman recently who is young enough to be my daughter. With great effort, she told me of her clitoral surgery as a child. She implored me, "Why do they have to cut so deep, Martha? Why do they do that?"

Of the notable feminist voices raised long and loud in outrage over traditional genital surgeries practiced in parts of Africa, which are now denounced as "female genital mutilation" (FGM), not a single woman has said a word about the equally mutilating practice of surgically destroying the healthy genitals of children in their own country. Like Gearhart, they shrink when we describe our surgeries as mutilation. But do they believe that African mothers, any more than American surgeons, cut their children out of malicious intent? Could their silence be because they don't know what is happening in American hospitals? It's possible, but the issue has received media coverage in the past year, and many of them have had the facts explained to them in person or in writing.

I could speculate that these women don't want to take on a foe as formidable and familiar as the medical profession, and that it is simpler to point fingers at more barbaric countries. They may not want to dilute their cause with the sticky subjects of sex and gender that surround the issue of ambiguous genitalia. Or perhaps they don't want to be aligned with children they can only see as freaks of nature. Even the liberal-thinking Joycelyn Elders, the former Surgeon General, refers to children who blur gender lines in a less-than-humane way. When Elders, a professor of pediatric endocrinology who continues to promote "reconstructive surgery" for girls with big clitorises, was asked about the wisdom of genital surgery on such children, she responded with, "Well, you just can't have an *it!*"[8]

Each woman has her own reasons for turning away from this issue. But I challenge them to pay attention to the fact that in hospitals just down the street in any big American city, five children a day are losing healthy, erotic parts of their bodies to satisfy a social demand for "normalcy." There is no federal ban to save them. The surgery is left out of the law against FGM because it is deemed "necessary to the health of the child on whom it is performed."[9] But as social psychologist Suzanne Kessler at the State University of New York at Purchase points out, "General ambiguity is corrected not because it is threatening to the infant's life, but because it is threatening to the infant's culture."[10]

Doctors and parents believe society will reject a child with atypical genitals, and the child is made to pay with her or his body for the shortcoming of our culture. What is happening in American hospitals to healthy children is just as mutilating to the bodies—no matter how exquisite the surgical craftsmanship—and violating to the souls of these children as FGM. And frequently, the surgical craftsmanship falls far short of exquisite.

The strict sexual agenda for bodies in America extends to little boys as well. To grow up to be a real man, a boy will have to be able to do two things—pee standing up and penetrate a vagina with his penis. If a little boy has to sit like a girl to urinate because his urethra exits somewhere along the shaft of his penis rather than the tip (a condition that can occur in as many as 8 out of 1,000),[11] he may be subjected to many disheartening surgeries over the course of his childhood to correct this "defect," and be left with a lifetime of chronic infections and emotional trauma. And if the baby is born with a "too-small" penis that doctors decide will never be big enough to "successfully" penetrate a woman, physicians will probably make him into a "girl" through surgery and hormone treatments, because, in the words of one surgeon, "It's easier to poke a hole than to build a pole."

In the 40 years since surgical intervention to "correct" genitals that are viewed as abnormal was first prescribed, treatment protocols have been rarely questioned. After all, it is much more comfortable for doctors to assume all is well than to start digging around to find out if it's really true. Until recently, all discussions of what is done to people's sexual bodies have been hidden safely away in the pages of medical texts, where real lives are only "interesting cases," and pictures of genitals are disembodied curiosities or teaching tools. Many doctors would like to keep things that way. For example, Dr. Kenneth Glassberg, a pediatric urologist associated with the American Academy of Pediatrics (AAP), insists that people who speak up and tell their stories are doing a disservice by "scaring patients away."[12]

In a blatant disregard for patient feedback not seen in any other medical field, the AAP still advocates early surgery and insists that the "management" of children with atypical genitals has improved over the past several decades. Their refusal to consider the reality of the lives of people who have been treated by this protocol can be likened to an astronomer gazing at Mars through his telescope while ignoring the real live Martian tugging at his sleeve. The messy truth of what happens to children treated with surgery and hormones is simply ignored by the AAP, as they stubbornly cling to a treatment paradigm that has never been anything but experimental.

Cosmetic genital surgery on children is out of control. As the practice has careened along unexamined for decades, illustrious careers and reputations have been made, consciences have been swallowed, and terrific damage has been done. For a doctor even to hesitate before operating takes tremendous effort and self-reflection. The need for babies to have genitals that look typical has been perceived as so unquestionable that surgeons travel all over the world to perform surgery on children free of charge as a "humanitarian gesture."

Dr. Justine Schober challenges her fellow surgeons to realize that "when you do [this kind of] surgery on someone, you are responsible for them for the rest of their lives."[13] In less than two hours in a sterile operating room, a child's personal and sexual destiny can be changed forever. The stakes are excruciatingly high for the sake of appearances. Angela's story, Annie's story, and my own tell only the smallest fraction of the terrible fallout from these surgeries. No one is naive enough to say that life in a body seen as abnormal is a ticket to bliss. But it is not the bodies of these children that are wrong, it is the way people see them. And if these children grow up and want to change their bodies one day, that will be their right. Nobody, but nobody, no matter how loving, no matter how well intentioned, should have the power to steal precious parts of a body from a child before she or he even gets started in life.

NOTES

1. Suzanne J. Kessler, "Meanings of Genital Variability," a paper presented as part of a plenary symposium titled "Genitals, Identity, and Gender." The Society for the Scientific Study of Sexuality, November 1995, San Francisco. Further reference: Barbara C. McGillivray, "The Newborn with Ambiguous Genitalia," *Seminars in Perinatology* 16, no. 6 (1992): 365–68.
2. Anne Fausto-Sterling (forthcoming). "How Dimorphic Are We?" *American Journal of Human Biology.*
3. News release from the American Academy of Pediatrics (American Academy of Pediatrics, 141 Northwest Point Blvd., Elk Grove, IL 60009-0927) distributed to the press on October 26, 1996.
4. Justine Schober, personal communication, March 1998.
5. Intersex Society of North America, PO Box 31791, San Francisco, CA, 415/575-3885 (email:info@isna.org, web:www.isna.org). ISNA is a peer-support and advocacy group operated by and for individuals born with anatomy or physiology that differs from cultural ideals of female and male.
6. Cheryl Chase, "Winged Labia:Deformity or Gift?" *Hermaphrodites with Attitude,* a publication of the Intersex Society of North America, 1, no. 1 (Winter 1994): 3–4.
7. Monika Bauerlein, "The Unkindest Cut," *Utne Reader* (September/October 1996): 16.
8. Joycelyn Elders, personal communication, September 1997.
9. Federal Prohibition of Female Genital Mutilation Act of 1995.
10. Suzanne J. Kessler, "The Medical Construction of Gender: Case Management of Intersexual Infants," *Signs: Journal of Women in Culture and Society* 16, no. 1 (1990): 3–26.
11. Justine Schober, personal communication, March 1998.
12. Geoffrey Cowley, "Gender Limbo," *Newsweek* (May 19, 1997): 64–66.
13. Justine Shober, personal communication, March 1998.

25

THE BURKA AND THE BIKINI

JOAN JACOBS BRUMBERG AND JACQUELYN JACKSON

The female body—covered in a burka or uncovered in a bikini—is a subtle subtext in the war against terrorism. The United States did not engage in this war to avenge women's rights in Afghanistan. How-

---

Joan Jacobs Brumberg and Jacquelyn Jackson, "The Burka and the Bikini" from *The Boston Globe* (November 29, 2001).

ever, our war against the Taliban, a regime that does not allow a woman to go to school, walk alone on a city street, or show her face in public, highlights the need to more fully understand the ways in which our own cultural "uncovering" of the female body impacts the lives of girls and women everywhere.

Taliban rule has dictated that women be fully covered whenever they enter the public realm, while a recent US television commercial for "Temptation Island 2" features near naked women. Although we seem to be winning the war against the Taliban, it is important to gain a better understanding of the Taliban's hatred of American culture and how women's behavior in our society is a particular locus of this hatred. The irony is that the images of sleek, bare women in our popular media that offend the Taliban also represent a major offensive against the health of American women and girls.

During the 20th century, American culture has dictated a nearly complete uncovering of the female form. In Victorian America, good works were a measure of female character, while today good looks reign supreme. From the hair removal products that hit the marketplace in the 1920s to today's diet control measures that seek to eliminate even healthy fat from the female form, American girls and women have been stripped bare by a sexually expressive culture whose beauty dictates have exerted a major toll on their physical and emotional health.

The unrealistic body images that we see and admire every day in the media are literally eating away at the female backbone of our nation. A cursory look at women's magazines, popular movies and television programs reveal a wide range of images modeling behaviors that directly assault the human skeleton. The ultra-thin woman pictured in a magazine sipping a martini or smoking a cigarette is a prime candidate for osteoporosis later in life.

In fact, many behaviors made attractive by the popular media, including eating disorders, teen smoking, drinking, and the depression and anxiety disorders that can occur when one does not measure up are taking a major toll on female health and well-being. The American Medical Association last year acknowledged a link between violent images on the screen and violent behavior among children. In a world where 8-year-olds are on diets, adult women spend $300 million a year to slice and laser their bodies and legal pornography is a $56 billion industry, it is time to note the dangers of unhealthy body images for girls and women.

Now that the Taliban's horrific treatment of women is common knowledge, dieting and working out to wear a string bikini might seem to be a patriotic act. The war on terrorism has certainly raised our awareness of the ways in which women's bodies are controlled by a repressive regime in a far away land, but what about the constraints on women's bodies here at home, right here in America?

In the name of good looks (and also corporate profits—the Westernized image of the perfect body is one of our most successful exports) contemporary American women continue to engage in behaviors that have created major public health concerns.

Although these problems may seem small in the face of the threat of anthrax and other forms of bioterrorism, there is still a need to better understand how American culture developed to the point that it now threatens the health of its bikini-clad daughters and their mothers.

Covered or uncovered, the homefront choice is not about morality but the physical and emotional health of future generations.

Whether it's the dark, sad eyes of a woman in purdah or the anxious darkly circled eyes of a girl with anorexia nervosa, the woman trapped inside needs to be liberated from cultural confines in whatever form they take. The burka and the bikini represent opposite ends of the political spectrum but each can exert a noose-like grip on the psyche and physical health of girls and women.

PART IV
Communication

The first thing you do is to forget that i'm Black.
Second, you must never forget that i'm Black.

PAT PARKER[1]

The whole goddam business of what you're calling intimacy bugs the hell out of me. I never know what you women mean when you talk about it. Karen complains that I don't talk to her, but it's not talk she wants, it's some other damn thing, only I don't know what the hell it is.

MAN INTERVIEWED BY LILLIAN RUBY[2]

American film has buttressed institutional teachings of mainstream America to invalidate all that is different, as well as to convince the "different" that they and their culture are invalid.

ELIZABETH HADLEY FREYDBERG[3]

Telling the truth about one's experience is one task of communicating with others. The other task, frequently more challenging than the first, is listening carefully, empathizing, and trying to understand other people without being defensive or interrupting. Most people have a sense of how difficult this can be. A growing literature, especially related to counseling and psychotherapy, focuses on basic communication skills, such as listening, and on multicultural communication skills, which include acknowledging how the various intersections of gender, race, class, ethnicity, disability, sexual orientation, and age affect communication. The task of becoming multiculturally competent takes time and effort, and it is necessary for all groups since most people are intimately familiar with only their own cultures.[4]

Communication patterns reflect power relationships. Those who have more power control what is communicated, including what gets media attention; they especially control the extent to which people with less power are listened to and seen for who they are without prejudice. In an examination of African American and Latina women in film, for example, Elizabeth Hadley Freydberg concludes that in spite of active protest from these two communities, the film industry continues to portray Latinas and African American women in stereotyped, insulting roles.

Theories of the limited images of women in the media examine, among other things, the absence of women in positions of power in the communications industries, as well as the capitalist system that sells products and avoids offending potential consumers with more realistic images.[5] If we add race, sexual orientation, class, disability, and age to what is missing in the centers of power, this absence of many underrepresented groups serves to eliminate accurate images of many groups of people in the media.[6]

The dream that the Internet might create a more level communication playing field, where demographic traits mattered less, has not become a reality. Access to the Internet is still tied to social class, race and ethnicity, and education, and women's roles in cyber-related activities and industries are not equal to those of men. High-level computer science jobs are male-dominated, and gender differences in interaction in chat rooms seems to parallel gender differences in other realms of communication. Women are responding to this by establishing technology programs and Internet resources for girls and women generally, for people with disabilities, for low-income people, and for people of color, in order to increase access and to develop web sites and e-mail lists and bulletins that are designed to be empowering.[7] Although feminist critiques of men's use of cyberspace to enhance their access to pornography, sex tours, and sex with children has incensed some feminists who had hoped for better things from the Internet,[8] feminists are finding ways to use this resource creatively.[9]

Literature from men's studies addresses the challenge of men's connections with each other, identifying various aspects of male-male communication that facilitate or impede close friendships. Sociologist Clyde Franklin,[10] for example, identified ways in which upward mobility interrupts Black men's friendships. Michael Messner, in a study of athletes, concluded that male athletes' "covert intimacy"—an intimacy based on doing things together rather than by intimate talk about personal issues—inhibits their ability to develop egalitarian relationships with either men or women.[11] Even when differences like race and class are not present and power between the people involved is relatively equal, difficulty sharing feelings, heavy competition for success, and fear of admitting dependency or vulnerability combine with homophobia to keep men apart in many circumstances in U.S. society[12] (see Kimmel, Part II).

Finally, communication is difficult because the array of prejudices we learn in childhood frequently follows us into adulthood, often unconsciously. As children, we learn attitudes in situations in which we have little or no control, and we frequently live in families in which communication is far from ideal.[13] Until schools and communities routinely work to help people appreciate diversity, acknowledge differences of power and privilege, listen to each other, and learn peaceful methods of dispute resolution, we are on our own as individuals to improve communication across differences.

The readings that follow address cross-sex and same-sex communication challenges between individuals and groups across differences of race and ethnicity in contexts of prejudice (Pat Parker, Phil Petrie, Nathan McCall, Annette Jaimes & Theresa Halsey). They also address communication between men and women in situations where other differences are not obvious (Deborah Tannen). The particular needs of boys are discussed as well (William Pollack).

NOTES

1. Pat Parker, "For the white person who wants to know how to be my friend" from *Movement in Black.* Reprinted in Gloria Anzaldúa, ed., *Making Face, Making Soul: Haciendo Caras* (San Francisco: Aunt Lute, 1990), p. 297.

2. Lillian B. Rubin, *Intimate Strangers: Men and Women Together* (New York: Harper & Row, 1983), p. 66.
3. Elizabeth Hadley Freydberg, "Sapphires, Spitfires, Sluts and Superbitches: Aframericans and Latinas in Contemporary American Film" in Kim Marie Vaz, ed., *Black Women in America* (Thousand Oaks, CA: Sage, 1995), p. 240.
4. See for example Joseph G. Ponterotto et al., eds. *Handbook of Multicultural Counseling* (Thousand Oaks: Sage, 1995); Larry A. Samovar and Richard E. Porter, eds., *Intercultural Communication: A Reader* (Belmont, CA: Wadsworth, 1991). For a report of how different ethnic groups in the United States see each other, including the stereotypes their members hold about each other, see "Taking America's Pulse: Summary Report of the National Conference Survey on Inter-Group Relations" (New York: The National Conference of Christians and Jews, 1994).
5. For a summary of these theoretical perspectives, see Margaret L. Andersen, *Thinking about Women: Sociological Perspectives on Sex and Gender,* 3rd ed. (New York: Macmillan, 1993), pp. 54–62.
6. For an examination of these issues see Gail Dines and Jean M. Humez, eds., *Gender, Race, and Class in Media: A Text-Reader* (Thousand Oaks, CA: Sage, 1995).
7. Joyce Slaton, "Mind the Gap: Three Women Working to Close the Digital Divide in Their Own Communities" *Ms.* (April–May 2001), pp. 42–44.
8. Donna Hughes, "The Internet and the Global Prostitution Industry," in Susan Hawthorne and Renate Klein, eds., *Cyberfeminism: Connectivity, Critique, and Creativity* (North Melbourne, Vic, Australia: Spinifex, 1999).
9. Susan Hawthorne and Renate Klein, eds., *Cyberfeminism: Connectivity, Critique, and Creativity.* (North Melbourne, Vic, Australia: Spinifex, 1999).
10. Clyde Franklin, "'Hey, Home—Yo, Bro': Friendship among Black Men" in Peter Nardi, ed., *Men's Friendships* (Thousand Oaks: Sage, 1992), pp. 201–214.
11. Michael A. Messner, "Like Family: Power, Intimacy, and Sexuality in Male Athletes' Friendships" in Peter Nardi, ed., *Men's Friendships* (Thousand Oaks: Sage, 1992), pp. 215–237.
12. Michael S. Kimmel and Michael A. Messner, eds., *Men's Lives,* 3rd ed. (Boston: Allyn & Bacon, 1995), p. 323; Gregory K. Lehne, "Homophobia among Men: Supporting and Defining the Male Role," in Kimmel and Messner, *Men's Lives,* pp. 325–336.
13. In my years as a teacher and psychotherapist, I have met only a small proportion of people who would like to continue using the communication patterns of the adults in the households in which they grew up; more frequently, they experienced successful communication with siblings—enjoying the relative equality of power that allowed for more open communication.

26

FOR THE WHITE PERSON WHO WANTS TO KNOW HOW TO BE MY FRIEND

PAT PARKER

The first thing you do is to forget that i'm black.
Second, you must never forget that i'm black.

You should be able to dig Aretha,
but don't play her every time i come over.
And if you decide to play Beethoven—don't tell me
his life story. They make us take music appreciation too.

Eat soul food if you like it, but don't expect me
to locate your restaurants
or cook it for you.

And if some Black person insults you,
mugs you, rapes your sister, rapes you,
rips your house or is just being an ass—
please, do not apologize to me
for wanting to do them bodily harm.
It makes me wonder if you're foolish.

And even if you really believe Blacks are better lovers than
Whites—don't tell me. I start thinking of charging stud fees.

In other words—if you really want to be my friend—*don't*
make a labor of it. I'm lazy. Remember.

27

INSIDE THE WORLD OF BOYS: BEHIND THE MASK OF MASCULINITY

WILLIAM POLLACK

I get a little down, Adam confessed, but I'm very good at hiding it. It's like I wear a mask. Even when the kids call me names or taunt me, I never show them how much it crushes me inside. I keep it all in.

The Boy Code: "Everything's Just Fine"

Adam is a fourteen-year-old boy whose mother sought me out after a workshop I was leading on the subject of boys and families. Adam, she told me, had been performing very well in school, but now she felt something was wrong.

Adam had shown such promise that he had been selected to join a special program for talented students, and the program was available only at a different—and more academically prestigious—school than the one Adam had attended. The new school was located in a well-to-do section of town, more affluent than Adam's own neighborhood. Adam's mother had been pleased when her son had qualified for the program and even more delighted that he would be given a scholarship to pay for it. And so Adam had set off on this new life.

At the time we talked, Mrs. Harrison's delight had turned to worry. Adam was not doing well at the new school. His grades were mediocre, and at midterm he had been given a warning that he might fail algebra. Yet Adam continued to insist, "I'm fine. Everything's just fine." He said this both at home and at school. Adam's mother was perplexed, as was the guidance counselor at his new school. "Adam seems cheerful and has no complaints," the counselor told her. "But something must be wrong." His mother tried to talk to Adam, hoping to find out what was troubling him and causing him to do so poorly in school. "But the more I questioned him about what was going on," she said, "the more he continued to deny any problems."

Adam was a quiet and rather shy boy, small for his age. In his bright blue eyes I detected an inner pain, a malaise whose cause I could not easily fathom.

I had seen a familiar look on the faces of a number of boys of different ages, including many boys in the "Listening to Boys' Voices" study. Adam looked wary, hurt, closed-in, self-protective. Most of all, he looked alone.

One day, his mother continued, Adam came home with a black eye. She asked him what had happened. "Just an accident," Adam had mumbled: He'd kept his eyes cast down, she remembered, as if he felt guilty or ashamed. His mother probed more deeply. She told him that she knew something was wrong, something upsetting was going on, and that—whatever it was—they could deal with it, they could face it together. Suddenly, Adam erupted in tears, and the story he had been holding inside came pouring out.

Adam was being picked on at school, heckled on the bus, goaded into fights in the schoolyard. "Hey, White Trash!" the other boys shouted at him. "You don't belong here with *us!*" taunted a twelfth-grade bully. "Why don't you go back to your own side of town!" The taunts often led to physical attacks, and Adam found himself having to fight back in order to defend himself. "But I never throw the first punch," Adam explained to his mother. "I don't show them they can hurt me. I don't want to embarrass myself in front of everybody."

I turned to Adam. "How do you feel about all this?" I asked. "How do you handle your feelings of anger and frustration?" His answer was, I'm glad to say, a refrain I hear often when I am able to connect to the inner lives of boys.

"I get a little down," Adam confessed, "but I'm very good at hiding it. It's like I wear a mask. Even when the kids call me names or taunt me, I never show them how much it crushes me inside. I keep it all in."

"What do you do with the sadness?" I asked.

"I tend to let it boil inside until I can't hold it any longer, and then it explodes. It's like I have a breakdown, screaming and yelling. But I only do it inside my own room at home, where nobody can hear. Where nobody will know about it." He paused a moment. "I think I got this from my dad, unfortunately."

Adam was doing what I find so many boys do: he was hiding behind a mask, and using it to hide his deepest thoughts and feelings—his real self—from everyone, even the people closest to him. This mask of masculinity enabled Adam to make a bold (if inaccurate) statement to the world: "I can handle it. Everything's fine. I am invincible."

Adam, like other boys, wore this mask as an invisible shield, a persona to show the outside world a feigned self-confidence and bravado, and to hide the shame he felt at his feelings of vulnerability, powerlessness, and isolation. He couldn't handle the school situation alone—very few boys or girls of fourteen could—and he didn't know how to ask for help, even from people he knew loved him. As a result, Adam was unhappy and was falling behind in his academic performance.

Many of the boys I see today are like Adam, living behind a mask of masculine bravado that hides the genuine self to conform to our society's expectations; they feel it is necessary to cut themselves off from any feelings that society teaches them are unacceptable for men and boys—fear, uncertainty, feelings of loneliness and need.

Many boys, like Adam, also think it's necessary that they handle their problems alone. A boy is not expected to reach out—to his family, his friends, his counselors, or coaches—for help, comfort, understanding, and support. And so he is simply not as close as he could be to the people who love him and yearn to give him the human connections of love, caring, and affection every person needs.

The problem for those of us who want to help is that, on the outside, the boy who is having problems may seem cheerful and resilient while keeping inside the feelings that don't fit the male model—being troubled, lonely, afraid, desperate. Boys learn to wear the mask so skillfully—in fact, they don't even know they're doing it—that it can be difficult to detect what is really going on when they are suffering at school, when their friendships are not working out, when they are being bullied, becoming depressed, even dangerously so, to the point of feeling suicidal. The problems below the surface become obvious only when boys go "over the edge" and get into trouble at school, start to fight with friends, take drugs or abuse alcohol, are diagnosed with clinical depression or attention deficit disorder, erupt into physical violence, or come home with a black eye, as Adam did. Adam's mother, for example, did not know from her son that anything was wrong until Adam came home with an eye swollen shut; all she knew was that he had those perplexingly poor grades.

The Gender Straitjacket

Many years ago, when I began my research into boys, I had assumed that since America was revising its ideas about girls and women, it must have also been reevaluating its traditional ideas about boys, men, and masculinity. But over the years my research findings have shown that as far as boys today are concerned, the old Boy Code—the outdated and constricting assumptions, models, and rules about boys that our society has used since the nineteenth century—is still operating in force. I have been surprised to find that even in the most progressive schools and the most politically correct communities in every part of the country and in families of all types, the Boy Code continues to affect the behavior of all of us—the boys themselves, their parents, their teachers, and society as a whole. None of us is immune—it is so ingrained. I have caught myself behaving in accordance with the code, despite my awareness of its falseness—denying sometimes that I'm emotionally in pain when in fact I am; insisting that everything is all right, when it is not.

The Boy Code puts boys and men into a gender straitjacket that constrains not only them but everyone else, reducing us all as human beings, and eventually making us strangers to ourselves and to one another—or, at least, not as strongly connected to one another as we long to be.

28

YOU JUST DON'T UNDERSTAND
Women and Men in Conversation

DEBORAH TANNEN

Intimacy is key in a world of connection where individuals negotiate complex networks of friendship, minimize differences, try to reach consensus, and avoid the appearance of superiority, which would highlight differences. In a world of status, *independence* is key, because a primary means of establishing status is to tell others what to do, and taking orders is a marker of low status. Though all humans need both intimacy and independence, women tend to focus on the first and men on the second. It is as if their lifeblood ran in different directions.

These differences can give women and men differing views of the same situation, as they did in the case of a couple I will call Linda and Josh. When Josh's old high-school chum called him at work and announced he'd be in town on business the following month, Josh invited him to stay for the weekend. That evening he informed Linda that they were going to have a houseguest, and that he and his chum would go out together the first night to shoot the breeze like old times. Linda was upset. She was going to be away on business the week before, and the Friday night when Josh would be out with his chum would be her first night home. But what upset her the most was that Josh had made these plans on his own and informed her of them, rather than discussing them with her before extending the invitation.

Linda would never make plans, for a weekend or an evening, without first checking with Josh. She can't understand why he doesn't show her the same courtesy and consideration that she shows him. But when she protests, Josh says, "I can't say to my friend, 'I have to ask my wife for permission'!"

To Josh, checking with his wife means seeking permission, which implies that he is not independent, not free to act on his own. It would make him feel like a child or an underling. To Linda, checking with

---

her husband has nothing to do with permission. She assumes that spouses discuss their plans with each other because their lives are intertwined, so the actions of one have consequences for the other. Not only does Linda not mind telling someone, "I have to check with Josh"; quite the contrary—she likes it. It makes her feel good to know and show that she is involved with someone, that her life is bound up with someone else's.

Linda and Josh both felt more upset by this incident, and others like it, than seemed warranted, because it cut to the core of their primary concerns. Linda was hurt because she sensed a failure of closeness in their relationship: He didn't care about her as much as she cared about him. And he was hurt because he felt she was trying to control him and limit his freedom.

A similar conflict exists between Louise and Howie, another couple, about spending money. Louise would never buy anything costing more than a hundred dollars without discussing it with Howie, but he goes out and buys whatever he wants and feels they can afford, like a table saw or a new power mower. Louise is disturbed, not because she disapproves of the purchases, but because she feels he is acting as if she were not in the picture.

Many women feel it is natural to consult with their partners at every turn, while many men automatically make more decisions without consulting their partners. This may reflect a broad difference in conceptions of decision making. Women expect decisions to be discussed first and made by consensus. They appreciate the discussion itself as evidence of involvement and communication. But many men feel oppressed by lengthy discussions about what they see as minor decisions, and they feel hemmed in if they can't just act without talking first. When women try to initiate a freewheeling discussion by asking, "What do you think?" men often think they are being asked to decide. . . .

Asymmetries: Women and Men Talking at Cross-Purposes

Eve had a lump removed from her breast. Shortly after the operation, talking to her sister, she said that she found it upsetting to have been cut into, and that looking at the stitches was distressing because they left a seam that had changed the contour of her breast. Her sister said, "I know. When I had my operation I felt the same way." Eve made the same observation to her friend Karen, who said, "I know. It's like your body has been violated." But when she told her husband, Mark, how she felt, he said, "You can have plastic surgery to cover up the scar and restore the shape of your breast."

Eve had been comforted by her sister and her friend, but she was not comforted by Mark's comment. Quite the contrary, it upset her more. Not only didn't she hear what she wanted, that he understood her feelings, but, far worse, she felt he was asking her to undergo more surgery just when she was telling him how much this operation had upset her. "I'm not having any more surgery!" she protested. "I'm sorry you don't like the way it looks." Mark was hurt and puzzled. "I don't care," he protested. "It doesn't bother me at all." She asked, "Then why are you telling me to have plastic surgery?" He answered, "Because you were saying *you* were upset about the way it looked."

Eve felt like a heel: Mark had been wonderfully supportive and concerned throughout her surgery. How could she snap at him because of what he said—"just words"—when what he had done was unassailable? And yet she had perceived in his words metamessages that cut to the core of their relationship. It was self-evident to him that his comment was a reaction to her complaint, but she heard it as an independent complaint of his. He thought he was reassuring her that she needn't feel bad about her scar because there was something she could *do* about it. She heard his suggestion that she do something about the scar as evidence that *he* was bothered by it. Furthermore, whereas she wanted reassurance that it was normal to feel bad in her situation, his telling her that the problem could easily be fixed implied she had no right to feel bad about it.

Eve wanted the gift of understanding, but Mark gave her the gift of advice. He was taking the role of problem solver, whereas she simply wanted confirmation for her feelings.

A similar misunderstanding arose between a husband and wife following a car accident in which she had been seriously injured. Because she hated being in the hospital, the wife asked to come home early. But once home, she suffered pain from having to move around more. Her husband said, "Why didn't you stay in the hospital where you would have been more comfortable?" This hurt her because it seemed to imply that he did not want her home. She didn't think of his suggestion that she should have stayed in the hospital as a response to her complaints about the pain she was suffering; she thought of it as an independent expression of his preference not to have her at home.

"They're My Troubles—Not Yours"

If women are often frustrated because men do not respond to their troubles by offering matching troubles, men are often frustrated because women do. Some men not only take no comfort in such a response; they take offense. For example, a woman told me that when her companion talks about a personal concern—for example, his feelings about growing older—she responds, "I know how you feel; I feel the same way." To her surprise and chagrin, he gets annoyed; he feels she is trying to take something away from him by denying the uniqueness of his experience.

A similar miscommunication was responsible for the following interchange, which began as a conversation and ended as an argument:

He: I'm really tired. I didn't sleep well last night.
She: I didn't sleep well either. I never do.
He: Why are you trying to belittle me?
She: I'm not! I'm just trying to show that I understand!

This woman was not only hurt by her husband's reaction; she was mystified by it. How could he think she was belittling him? By "belittle me," he meant "belittle my experience." He was filtering her attempts to establish connection through his concern with preserving independence and avoiding being put down.

"I'll Fix It for You"

Women and men are both often frustrated by the other's way of responding to their expression of troubles. And they are further hurt by the other's frustration. If women resent men's tendency to offer solutions to problems, men complain about women's refusal to take action to solve the problems they complain about. Since many men see themselves as problem solvers, a complaint or a trouble is a challenge to their ability to think of a solution, just as a woman presenting a broken bicycle or stalling car poses a challenge to their ingenuity in fixing it. But whereas many women appreciate help in fixing mechanical equipment, few are inclined to appreciate help in "fixing" emotional troubles. . . .

Trying to solve a problem or fix a trouble focuses on the message level of talk. But for most women who habitually report problems at work or in friendships, the message is not the main point of complaining. It's the metamessage that counts: Telling about a problem is a bid for an expression of understanding ("I know how you feel") or a similar complaint ("I felt the same way when something similar happened to me"). In other words, troubles talk is intended to reinforce rapport by sending the metamessage "We're the same; you're not alone." Women are frustrated when they not only don't get this reinforcement but, quite the opposite, feel distanced by the advice, which seems to send the metamessage "We're not the same. You have the problems; I have the solutions."

Furthermore, mutual understanding is symmetrical, and this symmetry contributes to a sense of community. But giving advice is asymmetrical. It frames the advice giver as more knowledgeable, more reasonable, more in control—in a word, one-up. And this contributes to the distancing effect. . . .

Matching Troubles

The very different way that women respond to the telling of troubles is dramatized in a short story, "New Haven," by Alice Mattison. Eleanor tells Patsy that she has fallen in love with a married man. Patsy responds by first displaying understanding and then offering a matching revelation about a similar experience:

> "Well," says Patsy. "I know how you feel."
> "You do?"
> "In a way, I do. Well, I should tell you. I've been sleeping with a married man for two years."

Patsy then tells Eleanor about her affair and how she feels about it. After they discuss Patsy's affair, however, Patsy says:

> "But you were telling me about this man and I cut you off. I'm sorry. See? I'm getting self-centered."
> "It's OK." But she is pleased again.

The conversation then returns to Eleanor's incipient affair. Thus Patsy responds first by confirming Eleanor's feelings and matching her experience, reinforcing their similarity, and then by encouraging Eleanor to tell more. Within the frame of Patsy's similar predicament, the potential asymmetry inherent in revealing personal problems is avoided, and the friendship is brought into balance.

What made Eleanor's conversation with Patsy so pleasing to Eleanor was that they shared a sense of how to talk about troubles, and this reinforced their friendship. Though Eleanor raised the matter of her affair, she did not elaborate on it until Patsy pressed her to do so. In another story by the same author, "The Knitting," a woman named Beth is staying with her sister in order to visit her sister's daughter Stephanie in a psychiatric hospital. While there, Beth receives a disturbing telephone call from her boyfriend, Alec. Having been thus reminded of her troubles, she wants to talk about them, but she refrains, because her sister doesn't ask. She feels required, instead, to focus on her sister's problem, the reason for her visit:

> She'd like to talk about her muted half-quarrels with Alec of the last weeks, but her sister does not ask about the phone call. Then Beth thinks they should talk about Stephanie.

The women in these stories are balancing a delicate system by which troubles talk is used to confirm their feelings and create a sense of community.

When women confront men's ways of talking to them, they judge them by the standards of women's conversational styles. Women show concern by following up someone else's statement of trouble by questioning her about it. When men change the subject, women think they are showing a lack of sympathy—a failure of intimacy. But the failure to ask probing questions could just as well be a way of respecting the other's need for independence. When Eleanor tells Patsy that she is in love with Peter, Patsy asks, "Are you sleeping with him?" This exploration of Eleanor's topic could well strike many men—and some women—as intrusive, though Eleanor takes it as a show of interest that nourishes their friendship.

Women tend to show understanding of another woman's feelings. When men try to reassure women by telling them that their situation is not so bleak, the women hear their feelings being belittled or discounted. Again, they encounter a failure of intimacy just when they were bidding to reinforce it. Trying to trigger a symmetrical communication, they end up in an asymmetrical one.

29

REAL MEN DON'T CRY . . . AND OTHER "UNCOOL" MYTHS

PHIL W. PETRIE

Things were not going well. Do they ever for young couples struggling to understand each other, raise a family, pay the mortgage and at least keep the Joneses in sight? I had wanted to comfort my pregnant wife, soothe her with words that would temper the harshness of our reality. The baby was due in two months and my employer had just informed me that I didn't have hospitalization coverage for childbirth. I was frustrated and wanted to scream, lay my head in my wife's lap and cry. I needed to be soothed as well as she. She wanted to talk about our predicament, needed to talk it out. So did I, but I couldn't. I felt that I had failed her. Guilt stood at my side. But how could she know any of that, since all I did was to turn on the stereo system—my electronic security blanket—and listen to Miles Davis. I was cool. Her words shot through the space of "All Blues." "You're a cold SOB," she hissed.

She's being emotional again, I thought, *Just like a woman.* I, on the other hand, was controlling the situation because I was cool—which in reality was only a few degrees away from being cold.

Phil W. Petrie, "Real Men Don't Cry . . . and Other 'Uncool' Myths" from *Essence* (November 1982). Reprinted with the permission of the author.

> Wasn't that what she really wanted from me as head of the household—control? Wasn't Freud correct when he proclaimed that our anatomy was our destiny (that is, our genitals determine our behavior)? In spite of her protestations that we had to talk, there was nothing in my upbringing that negated for me the power of coolness. I knew by the example of my elders that men controlled themselves and women did not.

In Mt. Olive, the Baptist church of my youth, it was expected that the "sisters" would "carry on" at church services. And they did. Moved by something that the preacher had said or by the mystery of a song, they would leap from their seats, run, scream, hurtle down the aisles. Transformed. Private feeling was suddenly public spectacle. Ushers came. White-gloved hands brushed away the tears. The men of the church, the elders, sat glued to their seats. I watched, instructed by this example of male control. I watched in silence but wished that I could know the electric transformation that moved those souls to dance.

"The larger culture creates expectations for males," says Dr. Walter Tardy, a psychiatrist in New York City. "In spite of the Women's Liberation Movement, men still live in a very macho culture and role play. Women tend to display their feelings more."

One of the roles men play is that of the rational being devoid of strong emotions. Profound feelings, it is thought, will interfere with the male task, whether that means making it at the nine-to-five or making it at war. Objective decisions must be made without distracting emotions, which women are thought to be prone to—even by some other women. For many persons, "being a man" is synonymous with being emotionless—cool.

One need not be told this. Like air, it seems to be a pervasive part of the male atmosphere. If one missed it at church (as I did not), one might pick it up at the barbershop or the playground—places where the elements of the culture are passed on without the benefit of critical examination.

> Didn't Wimpy Sheppard tell me at Tom Simon's Barbershop that only babies, women and sissies cried? A man, he said, ain't supposed to cry. That's why my father, at the death of his mother, slipped out to the backyard away from his family to sit among the chickens and wail. How could I explain to my wife—to myself—that I couldn't rest my head in her lap and weep? I had to protect my masculinity. Asking me to cry, to drop my cool, was asking me to redefine my life.

Says Margo Williams, a widow residing in San Diego, California, with her two children, "If you can't let down to your mate, friend or what have you, then you have to ask yourself what the relationship is all about—is it worth being involved with? For me, it's not about my man being strong and hard. I want him to be a human being—warm, sensitive and willing to share his life with me."

What if he balks? Williams is asked. "If the relationship is a serious one, I would urge him to let us try to work through the problems," she says. "I would want to establish a relationship wherein we could express to each other our needs and wants—even express our dislikes. We have to establish an honest relationship."

Dr. Tardy cautions that "there are degrees of honesty. Do you tell the truth all of the time, or is a white lie something appropriate? One can only be just so honest. The truth may set you free, but some truths should be withheld because they can hurt more than they help. But even if you don't tell it all, you must tell *something.* Communication is the key."

Therein lies the danger of being cool and playing roles. In doing this, one reveals a persona rather than a person, plays a part rather than being part of the relationship. Communication, by its root definition, means "sharing, making something common between people." It is this fear of sharing—giving up something—that drives some men into being noncommunicative except in the area of sex.

Robert Staples, a sociologist, states in his book *Black Masculinity* (Black Scholar Press) that when Black men "have been unable to achieve status in the workplace, they have exercised the privilege of their manliness and attempted to achieve it [power] in the bedroom. Feeling a constant need to affirm their masculinity, tenderness and compassion are eschewed as signs of weakness, which leaves them vulnerable to the ever-feared possibility of female domination."

It could be argued that in today's climate of women's liberation, all men are on the defensive because of the developing assertiveness of women. No doubt some men—if not many—use sex as a controlling force. "But," says Wilbur Suesberry, a pediatrician practicing in Compton, California, "I don't believe that sex is racially restrictive. Black sexuality is a myth started and supported by whites and perpetuated by Blacks. Men find it difficult to express their inner feelings but they must find a way to do it. If you have things pent up inside of you and they do not come out in a healthy way, then they exit in an unhealthy way. Sex as an outlet for your emotions is not good. To communicate you can't sulk or take to the bed, you must talk." Talk? Yes, talk is a more precise method of communicating than sex, intuition or an "understanding."

> "The birth is due in two months," she persisted. "What are we going to do?" Annoyed, not at her but at the apparent futility of the situation, I turned up the record player and went deeper into myself. Didn't she *understand* me well enough to know that I would do something? Hadn't I always? Couldn't she look at me and see that I was worried too? Didn't she *trust* me well enough to know that I would do something? All of those questions might have been eliminated with my telling her simply and directly what my feelings really were. How could she really know them unless

> she were a mind reader, just as I didn't know what she felt? Screaming and crying isn't quite the same thing as communicating effectively. I pulled her to me, caressed her.

Hugging and kissing are not substitutes for words, for language. Talking to each other allows us to bring order to the disruption and confusion engendered by silence. *Talk to me,* Little Willie John used to sing, *talk to me in your own sweet gentle way.*

This simple verbal act is made all the more difficult for men (and women, for that matter) if we don't know (or won't admit) what our feelings really are. We can't talk about things if we can't conceptualize them. Communication is more than mouthing words or rapping. I see it as defining an aspect of one's life by framing that aspect into words and then sharing it with someone. It is not only a problem for lovers; it also bedevils fathers and sons, mothers and daughters. It is problematic because it drives you within. The first act of communication is with your self—"the private self," Dr. Tardy calls it. This journey within involves both introspection and openness.

Yet what I face within myself—if indeed I face it—may never be completely shared with anyone. An insistence that I communicate *all* of my feelings is asking too much. We men are now being urged not only to redefine our roles and relationships with our mates and society but also to become vulnerable by revealing our private selves to another public, although it may be a public of only one. The degree to which I can do this—express *some* of my feelings—is determined by the self-awareness I have of myself and the trust I have for my spouse.

I closet my feelings out of self-protection and fear of the unknown. Women in their newfound drive for liberation have the example of men to direct them. It seems that all women are asking for are some of the prerogatives once claimed by men only. But what is to be the model for me? White men? I think not. Granted they are the movers and shakers within this society, but the madness of the world that they have created does not make them legitimate role models. Yet for many Black women the term *man* is synonymous with *white man.* I resent being asked to pattern myself after a man whose reality—full of avarice and destruction—is so antithetical to mine. I hold on to my cool.

For Black men, being cool is not just an attitude; it becomes a political stance, a metaphor for power. To give that up is, in effect, to render oneself powerless—to lose control. For Black men, who control so little, to lose this cool is to lose a weapon in their arsenal for survival. Do Black women know that?

> "Maybe you could call somebody [white?] who can help," she suggested, determined to get a word out of me. And if I can't find someone white to help us with my problems, I thought, then I can fold up and cry to you. Ugh. Is this what you ask of me: to imitate

> white men or act like women (that is, take control or cry)? What brave new world are you asking me to enter into by dropping my cool, discarding my role as leader, drowning my strength with tears? It is a scenario that no other group of men in history has ever played. Yet you ask me, the most politically weak person within the society, to lead the way to this new world. How can you ask me that, baby? And if I go, will you cast me aside as being weak? You scream about a man who is strong enough to cry, strong enough to admit weaknesses, and at the same time you want a "take-charge" person, a man who won't let anyone run over him. Caught between such confusion, I turn to the ball game, to the television, to the silence within myself. Love is withheld. Restrained. Tentative.

"I think that our generation is too tentative," says Lee Atkins, a publishing-company sales representative living in Chicago. "Those of us born in the 1940's and before were given too many caveats. Black men or boys were told not to do this and not to do that. Avoid the police. Stay out of trouble. All of this was done to protect us in an extremely racist and hostile society. In effect, we were being told: behave or you will be destroyed." That made us cautious and we are now paying the price for all that caution. As men we find that we are too careful, too private, not open and not willing to explore. We find it difficult to open up even to those we care about the most.

"Those kids born in the 1950's and 1960's," Atkins continues, "were born into a world where the expectations for the Black male were more positive. A whole set of new possibilities was suddenly available. Sexually, things were more permissive, and in the do-your-own-thing attitude of the 1960's and 1970's Black men were actually encouraged to be more unconventional, to open up."

This has led to young Black men who are more candid about their feelings, more carefree in their attitudes. "I would be surprised," says Dr. Tardy, "if these young adults weren't more open in their dealings with each other. The drawback may be that they don't want to establish the permanent relations that were expected in the past. I can imagine that many young women will say that the young men today aren't 'serious' or are too much into themselves. That's the legacy of hanging loose."

Whether we are young or old, one thing is certain: we men cannot expect to go through a lifetime in silence, repressing our feelings, denying our emotions, without being run down by frustrations, failed opportunities and unfulfilled promises. And why would we do this? Is it because of the protrusion dangling between our legs? Is it because we hold on to a fixed role in a changing world? Or is it because of our fear of losing an imagined power? Perhaps the answer is all of the above. If so, we must rush to get rid of these contrived ghosts. In the real world our women are calling to us. How long will they keep it up before they give up? Or as writer Amiri Baraka asks, "How long till the logic of our lives runs us down?"

She stood before me pleading, belly swollen with my seed. She wasn't asking for much, just that I talk to her. She was richly human and was demanding that I be nothing less, saying that I couldn't be a man until I showed that I was human—warm, tender, compassionate, feeling, and able to express that feeling. It was difficult, but with a guide so dedicated to my good health I began the journey from within to without that day. We found the money for the hospital. But more important, I found that I could talk to her about me, could share my life in trust with her. I write this as a souvenir of remembrance—a gift for her.

30

DANNY

NATHAN MCCALL

Sitting at my desk, working, I noticed a tall, lanky white dude walk into the newsroom and head toward my row. He was casually dressed: a silly-looking stingy-brimmed straw hat on his curly head, a lightweight mustard-colored zip-up jacket, paddy-boy slacks, and a pair of those shoes construction workers wear. No sport coat or tie. He was dressed so casual I assumed he'd come in for a story interview. Then he walked straight over to the aisle where I sat, plopped a notepad down on the empty desk behind me, and took a seat. I thought, *Just what I need. Another cracker near me.*

I stood up to go to the supply cabinet. Before I could leave, the new guy sprang from his seat, extended his hand, and said, "Hi. I'm Danny. Danny Baum." He was three inches from my face, smiling like there was something funny. I shook his hand. "I'm Nathan." And I walked away.

Later, I saw Danny walking across the newsroom. He had a goofy demeanor—long strides, arms swinging wild—like a northern Gomer Pyle or Mr. Green Jeans on *Captain Kangaroo.* A white woman reporter who sat near me leaned over to another white reporter, pointed at Danny, and whispered, "That's the new guy. Do you know what he did? He moved into a *black* neighborhood. Everybody's talking about it. *Somebody's* got to talk to him." Apparently unaware that I overheard, they burst out laughing, as if this new

---

guy—this crazy northerner—had done the stupidest thing in the world. I looked at them a minute and thought to myself, *Uh-huh. These are the same pseudo-liberal crackers who will get up in your face and swear they're not racist and they don't see color. Yet they thought it was hilarious that a white guy was so color-blind that he'd moved into a black neighborhood.* I decided that the next time a white person told me he didn't see color, I was gonna call him a liar to his face. Let him know that he can't insult my intelligence and get away with it.

After I finished going off on white people in my head, I turned my thoughts back to this Danny guy. What kind of a person *was* he to move into a black neighborhood? Was it a mistake on his part or did he do that intentionally?

Newsroom gossip held that he had come to the *Atlanta Journal-Constitution* from *The Wall Street Journal.* Normally, that's considered a step down professionally. *The Wall Street Journal* is, after all, one of the top newspapers in the country. When asked why he left the *Journal* to come to Atlanta, Danny had told someone, "The people at *The Wall Street Journal* were too stuffy and pretentious. I decided I'd get a real job with real people who would let me chase fire engines and write about it."

In the following weeks, I watched him closely to see what he was about. It didn't take long to see that there was something different about this cat. Other people in the newsroom, blacks and whites, recognized it, too. I found him to be different in a pleasant way. Whenever he said something to me, there was a straightforwardness, a childlike honesty, that I didn't get from most other white people. With him, I didn't feel the hesitancy I felt from other whites or the racial baggage getting in the way. And he'd ask me the damnedest things out of the blue. One day, he slid his swivel chair back near mine and asked, "Why aren't black reporters more aggressive around here, Nate?"

It was the kind of thing I knew a lot of whites around there wondered about but were afraid to ask for fear of sounding racist or for fear of revealing that they were, in fact, racist. But Danny didn't seem to care. I concluded it must have been because he was secure in his mind that he wasn't racist, and he had nothing to hide. He was simply curious. He didn't know, so he did what any intelligent person should have done: He asked rather than assume. I respected that about him and found that, in spite of myself, there was something about this dude I really liked.

Since we sat so close to each other, we began rapping a lot at our desks. I learned Danny had done his own examination of the white mainstream and reached some of the same conclusions as me: that it was totally fucked up, that they needed to scratch all the rules governing the macho corporate game and go back to drawing stickmen on cave walls because that's about how far they'd come in human development. By the time he came to the *Atlanta Journal-Constitution,* Danny had decided that he was no longer going to play the game by their silly rules. He didn't brownnose the bosses or try to join the white folks' privileged insiders' club in the newsroom. He didn't try to get in with all the *right* people to gain an edge. In fact, he held management in contempt and talked about them as much as I did.

When Hosea Williams led a march in Forsythe County to protest the racism and open hostility to blacks who moved there, Danny took part in the march, even though our bosses had ordered reporters to stay out of it for the sake of objectivity. When he did that, I concluded that this dude was *truly* wild.

One day, Danny slid his seat near mine and said, "Nate, how about coming over to my place for dinner this weekend?"

"Lemme see what I've got planned," I said, "and I'll get back to you on that." I didn't have anything planned. I said that to buy time to think about it. Thinking about it, even *considering* spending my free weekend time at a white person's house, was a major leap for me. Had it been anyone else I wouldn't have had to think about it at all. I'd have declined without blinking an eye. But I considered it with Danny and decided, *What the hell. I'll give it a try.* Besides, I wanted to see just where he lived and ask him why he had moved into a black neighborhood.

I went to Danny's place that weekend. He definitely lived in the 'hood. He'd rented a detached house in a working-class neighborhood in Hosea Williams's council district. Danny was dating another reporter at the paper, Meg Knox, who lived in Savannah and worked for the paper's bureau there, several hours from Atlanta. She seemed just as laid-back and cool as Danny. We ate, then went into his living room, sat down, talked, and drank beer. It was the most comfortable I'd ever felt around white people. I didn't feel like Danny and Meg were judging me by their standards all the time. They didn't try to pretend there were no differences between us, like everybody else I knew. They celebrated our differences, and we joked about contrasts in the way blacks and whites talked, cooked, dressed, danced, and did everything else.

At some point, Danny told me he'd moved into this black neighborhood because he could get the best deal for his money there. "I like this house. It has a porch and a yard. The neighbors are friendly. . . . Actually, I'm thinking about buying it."

We talked about our tastes in white music and black music. I told them how I'd learned about white music—about the time I stole those tapes out of some white person's car. Danny played a tape for me and explained why a particular white artist I'd asked about was currently so popular. The singer was Bruce Springsteen, and the tape was *Born in the U.S.A.*

We talked a lot about race. I guess it helped that Danny was Jewish. Danny told me that he'd had his share of brushes with racism, and it didn't sit well with him. He asked me about Louis Farrakhan, whom he said frightened Jews with his statement that Hitler was a great man. "Nate," he asked, "why does Farrakhan hate Jews?"

I said, "I don't agree with everything Farrakhan says, but I don't think he hates Jews. I think he's widely misunderstood and his comments are often taken out of context. He's simply pro-black. A lot of white people assume that if you're pro-black then you must be anti-white. . . . You have to listen closely to what Farrakhan says to understand where he's coming from."

He asked to borrow a tape of Farrakhan so that he could hear it for himself.

We talked about a lot of other things. I was surprised to learn that he had actually read books written by black people: James Baldwin, Richard Wright, Ralph Ellison. It amazed me that a white person would do that when it wasn't required of him. He seemed equally as surprised to learn that one of my favorite authors was the Jewish writer Chaim Potok.

I left Danny's place late that night surprised that time had passed so quickly and shocked that I had actually spent a weekend evening—voluntarily—with whites and had a grand time. In return, I invited Meg and Danny over to my place for dinner. They met Debbie and our small children. It was one of those evenings when the differences between Debbie and me seemed to vanish, a night when there were no arguments about in-laws and money problems. After we put the children to bed, the four of us sat on the front porch and laughed and talked for hours. It was the first time I'd had any white people over to my house.

After a while, I found that I looked forward to talking with Danny. We grew closer and, in jest, gave each other silly nicknames. I started calling him "Danny Boy," and he called me "Nate McMann." He'd walk into the newsroom, look at me, and say, "Nate McMann, how ya doin', bro." I'd say, "Fine, Danny Boy, just fine."

At some point during the two years he lived in Atlanta, somebody broke into Danny's house. I felt strange about that. On its face, it supported the stereotype of crime-ridden black neighborhoods. I wondered if it would conjure up racial stereotypes and send him running for cover, as it would many pretentious liberal whites I'd seen. But Danny treated it like any break-in. It didn't seem to matter to him whether the burglar was black or white. He stayed right in the neighborhood until he left Atlanta. More than anything else, that told me that this cat was for real.

When Danny found out that I had a bike, he suggested we get together and go riding one Saturday morning. I agreed, and we were on. He pulled up to my place the following Saturday driving an old green station wagon he'd bought from a colleague. We threw the bikes in and he drove deep into the country. We picked a turnoff spot, parked the car alongside the road, and unloaded the bikes. We rode for hours and talked about everything. I asked him tough questions about whites. He asked me tough questions about blacks. He'd offer his theory on a matter, then wait for my response. I respected his sincerity—so much so that I even confided in him that I'd been to prison. I hadn't told anyone else at the paper about my prison past, not even other blacks.

The country road was deserted, except for an occasional passing pickup truck. After a long period of silence, Danny came at me with another question. "You're pretty angry inside, aren't you, Nate McMann?"

"Naw, Danny Boy, I'm not angry. I'm fuckin' furious."

Danny frowned. "God, Nate, you think about race all the time. Give it a rest, man. It ain't healthy."

I told Danny I didn't have a choice in the matter. "You can sit around and intellectualize about race when you want to, and when you get tired of it you can set it aside and go surfing or hang gliding and forget about it. But I can't. Race affects every facet of my life, man. I can't get past race because white folks won't let me get past it. They remind me of it everywhere I go. Every time I step in an elevator and a white woman bunches up in the corner like she thinks I wanna rape her, I'm forced to think about it. Every time I walk into stores, the suspicious looks in white shopkeepers' eyes make me think about it. Every time I walk past whites sitting in their cars, I hear the door locks clicking and I think about it. I can't get away from it, man. I stay so mad all the time because I'm forced to spend so much time and energy reacting to race. I hate it. It wearies me. But there's no escape, man. No escape."

When I finished talking, I felt like I had preached a sermon. I didn't realize I had so much frustration bottled up until I let it out on Danny. At first, I wondered why I had told him so much of what was going on inside my head. Then I realized that despite all I'd said in the past about not caring what white folks thought, I cared a lot. In fact, I had spent my whole life reacting to what they thought. The notion that one of them cared, really cared, about what I thought moved me. Danny was the first white person I met whom I actually saw trying hard to understand. It meant a lot to me that he tried because he wanted to and not because he had to. By the same token, he helped me see the world through white eyes and helped me better understand the fear and ignorance behind prejudice.

I learned something else from Danny that hadn't been clear to me before. I learned how little even the most highly educated white folks really know about blacks. He was very well educated and yet he struggled to understand some of the most basic things about black life in America. He struggled because in school he hadn't been taught diddly about blacks. Even though he saw us every day and interacted with us, we were puzzles to him. That showed me that the education system in this country has failed white people more than it's failed anybody else. It has crippled them and limited their humanity. They're the ones who need to know the most about everybody because they're the ones running the country. They've been taught so little about anybody other than white people that they can't understand, even when they try.

During one of our bike rides, we stopped and sat down on the side of a grassy mound to take a break from the scorching sun. About a hundred yards behind us, there was a huge white house sitting on a large tract of land. We were sitting there, talking and tossing pebbles onto the street, when a white man crept up behind us. "Hi," he said.

We both said hello. I expected the man to tell us to get the hell off his grass. Instead, he said something that startled me. "You guys look hot. I've got a full-sized swimming pool in my backyard if you want to take a swim."

Initially, his words didn't register with me. In my mind, there was something wrong with that picture. After all, this *was* Deep South Georgia and we *were* in some country town. I'd come out there half expecting to encounter hillbillies with gun racks in the windows of their pickup trucks. Now this cat was inviting us—a black and a white—to take a dip in his swimming pool?

Danny looked at me and I said, "No thanks. We're about to leave."

The man was almost insistent. "Really, I don't mind. Help yourselves and cool off if you want."

"No, we've got to leave."

The man smiled warmly and said, "O.K. If you change your mind, feel free to come on over."

"Thanks."

We got up and rode off. Later, I reflected on what that might have been about. I think the white man was moved by the picture of a white guy and a black dude sitting on the side of the road, rapping. I could be wrong, but I think the sight of us warmed his heart and he wanted to take part in our interracial communion for reasons of his own. Danny and I never discussed it, but I never forgot it, because gestures like that were so rare in my experience.

Danny told me sometime in 1987 that he and Meg planned to go to Africa to travel and work as freelance writers for a while. Initially, I felt envious that he, a white guy, would get the chance to go to my homeland, which I'd never been to as an adult. I told him how I felt: "See, you white motherfuckas get to do everything in the world you wanna do."

He insisted, "Nate, there's nothing stopping you from doing what you want to do in life. You can go to Africa, too."

That started a running debate. "No, I can't, Danny. You don't understand. You white boys can take off from work anytime and hitchhike across the country or spend a coupla years hoboing in Europe. Then, when you get ready to resume your career, the white establishment will welcome you back with open arms. But if I tried to do some shit like that, Mr. Charlie's gonna wanna know where I been and why there's a gap on my résumé. He's gonna want me to give an account of any time that was not spent slaving for him."

I had no frame of reference for Danny's opinion. All I knew was that every black person I had ever met had lived life aware of the limitations imposed by race, and that those who had tried to do what they truly wanted were met with intense opposition. I felt it was easy for Danny to think there were no ceilings because he hadn't known any.

Danny didn't win me over on that issue before leaving Atlanta, but he dropped a piece of advice on me that changed my thinking about something else. He said, "Look, Nate McMann, you may not believe this, but there are several white people in the newsroom who are *really* good people. You should give them a chance before writing them off as racists. Get to know some of them. You might be pleasantly surprised."

Later, I thought about what he had said. I thought about those whites who had tried to be friendly and the semi-meaningful talks I'd had with some of them in the newsroom. Among them was a political reporter who seemed sincere and two editors I had grown to like. *Maybe,* I thought, *I should open up more and be receptive to the fact that there are some good whites in the world.*

Somehow, just thinking that thought made me feel better. I realized that I needed to know that there might be other white people like Danny and Meg, and that there was some reason for hope in this deeply disturbed nation of ours.

Danny and Meg just left for Africa. Of all the white people I know, they are among the very few I can call friends. It's sad, this gulf between blacks and whites. We're so afraid of each other. . . .

January 10, 1987

31

AMERICAN INDIAN WOMEN
At the Center of Indigenous Resistance in Contemporary North America

M. ANNETTE JAIMES WITH THERESA HALSEY

A people is not defeated until the hearts of its women are on the ground.

TRADITIONAL CHEYENNE SAYING

The United States has not shown me the terms of my Surrender.

MARIE LEGO, PIT RIVER NATION, 1970

The two brief quotations forming the epigraph of this chapter were selected to represent a constant pattern of reality within Native North American life from the earliest times. This is that women have always formed the backbone of indigenous nations on this continent. Contrary to those images of meekness, docility, and subordination to males with which we women typically have been portrayed by the dominant culture's books and movies, anthropology, and political ideologues of both rightist and leftist persuasions, it is women who have formed the very core of indigenous

---

M. Annette Jaimes with Theresa Halsey, "American Indian Women: At the Center of the Indigenous Resistance in Contemporary North America" from *The State of Native America: Genocide, Colonization, and Resistance,* edited by M. Annette Jaimes. Reprinted with the permission of the publisher, South End Press.

resistance to genocide and colonization since the first moment of conflict between Indians and invaders. In contemporary terms, this heritage has informed and guided generations of native women such as the elder Marie Lego, who provided crucial leadership to the Pit River Nation's land claims struggle in northern California during the 1970s.[1]

In Washington state, women such as Janet McCloud (Tulalip) and Ramona Bennett (Puyallup) had already assumed leading roles in the fishing rights struggles of the '60s, efforts which, probably more than any other phenomena, set in motion the "hard-line" Indian liberation movements of the modern day. These were not political organizing campaigns of the ballot and petition sort. Rather, they were, and continue to be, conflicts involving the disappearance of entire peoples. As Bennett has explained the nature of the fishing rights confrontations:

> At this time, our people were fighting to preserve their last treaty right—the right to fish. We lost our land base. There was no game in the area. . . . We're dependent not just economically but culturally on the right to fish. Fishing is part of our art forms and religion and diet, and the entire culture is based around it. And so when we talk about [Euroamerica's] ripping off the right to fish, we're talking about cultural genocide.[2]

The fish-ins . . . were initially pursued within a framework of "civil disobedience" and "principled nonviolence," which went nowhere other than to incur massive official and quasi-official violence in response. "They [the police] came right on the reservation with a force of three hundred people," Bennett recounts. "They gassed us, they clubbed people around, they laid $125,000 bail on us. At that time I was a member of the Puyallup Tribal Council, and I was spokesman for the camp [of local fishing rights activists]. And I told them what our policy was: that we were there to protect our Indian fishermen. And because I used a voice-gun, I'm being charged with inciting a riot. I'm faced with an eight year sentence."[3] It was an elder Nisqually woman who pushed the fishing rights movement in western Washington to adopt the policy of armed self-defense, which ultimately proved successful (the struggle in eastern Washington took a somewhat different course to the same position and results):

> Finally, one of the boys went down to the river to fish, and his mother went up on the bank. And she said: "This boy is nineteen years old and we've been fighting on this river for as many years as he's been alive. And no one is going to pound my son around, no one is going to arrest him. No one is going to touch my son or I'm going to shoot them. " And she had a rifle. . . . Then we had an armed camp in the city of Tacoma.[4]

The same sort of dynamic was involved in South Dakota during the early 1970s, when elder Oglala Lakota women such as Ellen Moves Camp and Gladys Bissonette assumed the leadership in establishing what was called the Oglala Sioux Civil Rights Organization (OSCRO) on the Pine Ridge Reservation. According to Bissonette, "Every time us women gathered to protest or demonstrate, they [federal authorities] always aimed machine guns at us women and children."[5] In response, she became a major advocate of armed self-defense at the reservation hamlet of Wounded Knee in 1973, remained within the defensive perimeter for the entire 71 days the U.S. government besieged the Indians inside, and became a primary negotiator for what was called the "Independent Oglala Nation."[6] Both women remained quite visible in the Oglala resistance to U.S. domination despite a virtual counterinsurgency war waged by the government on Pine Ridge during the three years following Wounded Knee.[7]

At Big Mountain, in the former "Navajo-Hopi Joint Use Area" in Arizona, where the federal government is even now attempting to forcibly relocate more than 10,000 traditional Diné (Navajos) in order to open the way for corporate exploitation of the rich coal reserves underlying their land, it is again elder women who have stood at the forefront of resistance, refusing to leave the homes of their ancestors. One of them, Pauline Whitesinger, was the first to physically confront government personnel attempting to fence off her land. Another, Katherine Smith, was the first to do so with a rifle.[8] Such women have constituted a literal physical barrier blocking consummation of the government's relocation/mining effort for more than a decade.[9] Many similar stories, all of them accruing from the past quarter-century, might be told in order to demonstrate the extent to which women have galvanized and centered contemporary native resistance.

The costs of such uncompromising (and uncompromised) activism have often been high. To quote Ada Deer, who, along with Lucille Chapman, became an essential spokesperson for the Menominee restoration movement in Wisconsin during the late 1960s and early '70s: "I wanted to get involved. People said I was too young, too naïve—you can't fight the system. I dropped out of law school. That was the price I had to pay to be involved."[10] Gladys Bissonette lost a son, Pedro, and a daughter, Jeanette, murdered by federal surrogates on Pine Ridge in the aftermath of Wounded Knee.[11] Other native women, such as American Indian Movement (AIM) members Tina Trudell and Anna Mae Pictou Aquash, have paid with their own and sometimes their children's lives for their prominent defiance of their colonizers.[12] Yet, it stands as a testament to the strength of American Indian women that such grim sacrifices have served, not to deter them from standing up for the rights of native people, but as an inspiration to do so. Mohawk activist and scholar Shirley Hill Witt recalls the burial of Aquash after her execution-style murder on Pine Ridge:

> Some women had driven from Pine Ridge the night before—a very dangerous act—"to do what needed to be done." Young women dug the grave. A ceremonial tipi was set up. . . . A woman seven

> months pregnant gathered sage and cedar to be burned in the tipi. Young AIM members were pallbearers: they laid her on pine boughs while spiritual leaders spoke the sacred words and performed the ancient duties. People brought presents for Anna Mae to take with her to the spirit world. They also brought presents for her two sisters to carry back to Nova Scotia with them to give to her orphaned daughters. . . . The executioners of Anna Mae did not snuff out a meddlesome woman. They exalted a Brave Hearted Woman for all time.[13]

The motivations of indigenous women in undertaking such risks are unequivocal. As Maria Sanchez, a leading member of the Northern Cheyenne resistance to corporate "development" of their reservation, puts it: "I am the mother of nine children. My concern is for their future, for their children, and for future generations. As a woman, I draw strength from the traditional spiritual people . . . from my nation. The oil and gas companies are building a huge gas chamber for the Northern Cheyennes."[14] Pauline Whitesinger has stated, "I think there is no way we can survive if we are moved to some other land away from ours. We are just going to waste away. People tell me to move, but I've got no place to go. I am not moving anywhere, that is certain."[15] Roberta Blackgoat, another leader of the Big Mountain resistance, concurs: "If this land dies, the people die with it. We are a nation. We will fight anyone who tries to push us off our land."[16] All across North America, the message from native women is the same.[17] The explicitly nationalist content of indigenous women's activism has been addressed by Lorelei DeCora Means, a Minneconjou Lakota AIM member and one of the founders of Women of All Red Nations (WARN):

> We are *American Indian* women, in that order. We are oppressed, first and foremost, as American Indians, as peoples colonized by the United States of America, *not* as women. As Indians, we can never forget that. Our survival, the survival of every one of us—man, woman and child—*as Indians* depends on it. Decolonization is the agenda, the whole agenda, and until it is accomplished, it is the *only* agenda that counts for American Indians. It will take every one of us—every single one of us—to get the job done. We haven't got the time, energy or resources for anything else while our lands are being destroyed and our children are dying of avoidable diseases and malnutrition. So we tend to view those who come to us wanting to form alliances on the basis of "new" and "different" or "broader" and "more important" issues to be a little less than friends, especially since most of them come from the Euroamerican population which benefits most directly from our ongoing colonization.[18]

As Janet McCloud sees it:

> Most of these "progressive" non-Indian ideas like "class struggle" would at the present time divert us into participating as "equals"

> in our own colonization. Or, like "women's liberation," would divide us among ourselves in such a way as to leave us colonized in the name of "gender equity." Some of us can't help but think maybe a lot of these "better ideas" offered by non-Indians claiming to be our "allies" are intended to accomplish exactly these sorts of diversion and disunity within our movement. So, let me toss out a different sort of "progression" to all you marxists and socialists and feminists out there. *You* join *us* in liberating *our* land and lives. Lose the privilege *you* acquire at *our* expense by occupying *our* land. Make *that* your first priority for as long as it takes to make it happen. *Then* we'll join you in fixing up whatever's left of the class and gender problems in your society, and our own, if need be. *But,* if you're not willing to do that, then don't presume to tell *us* how we should go about our liberation, what priorities and values we should have. Since you're standing on our land, we've got to view you as just another oppressor trying to hang on to what's ours. And that doesn't leave us a whole lot to talk about, now does it?[19]

The Road Ahead

Interestingly, women of other nonwhite sectors of the North American population have shared many native women's criticisms of the Euroamerican feminist phenomenon. African American women in particular have been outspoken in this regard. As Gloria Joseph argues:

> The White women's movement has had its own explicit forms of racism in the way it has given high priority to certain aspects of struggles and neglected others . . . because of the inherently racist assumptions and perspectives brought to bear in the first articulations by the White women's movement. . . . The Black movement scorns feminism partially on the basis of misinformation, and partially due to a valid perception of the White middle class nature of the movement. An additional reason is due to the myopic ways that white feminists have generalized their sexual-political analysis and have confirmed their racism in the forms their feminism has assumed.[20]

The "self-righteous indignation" and defensiveness that Joseph discerns as experienced by most Euroamerican feminists when confronted with such critiques is elsewhere explained by bell hooks as a response resting in the vested interest of those who feel it:

> Feminist emphasis on "common oppression" in the United States was less a strategy for politicization than an appropriation by conservative and liberal women of a radical political vocabulary

> that masked the extent to which they shaped the movement so that it addressed and promoted their class interests. . . . White women who dominate feminist discourse, who for the most part make and articulate feminist theory, have little or no understanding of white supremacy as a racial politic, of the psychological impact of class, of their [own] political status within a racist, sexist, capitalist state."[21]

"I was struck," hooks says in her book, *Ain't I a Woman,* "by the fact that the ideology of feminism, with its emphasis on transforming and changing the social structure of the U.S., in no way resembled the reality of American feminism. Largely because [white] feminists themselves, as they attempted to take feminism beyond the realm of radical rhetoric into the sphere of American life, revealed that they remained imprisoned in the very structures they hoped to change. Consequently, the sisterhood we all talked about has not become a reality."[22] It is time to "talk back" to white feminists, hooks argues, "spoiling their celebration, their 'sisterhood,' their 'togetherness.'"[23] This must be done because in adhering to feminism in its present form

> we learn to look to those empowered by the very systems of domination that wound and hurt us for some understanding of who we are that will be liberating and we never find that. It is necessary for [women of color] to do the work ourselves if we want to know more about our experience, if we want to see that experience from perspectives not shaped by domination.[24]

Asian American women, Chicanas, and Latinas have agreed in substantial part with such assessments.[25] Women of color in general tend not to favor the notion of a "politics" which would divide and weaken their communities by defining "male energy" as "the enemy." It is not for nothing that no community of color in North America has ever produced a counterpart to white feminism's SCUM (Society for Cutting Up Men). Women's liberation, in the view of most "minority" women in the United States and Canada, cannot occur in any context other than the wider liberation, from Euroamerican colonial domination, of the peoples of which women of color are a part. Our sense of priorities is therefore radically—and irrevocably—different from those espoused by the "mainstream" women's movement.

Within this alienation from feminism lies the potential for the sorts of alliances which may in the end prove most truly beneficial to American Indian people. By forging links to organizations composed of other women of color, founded not merely to fight gender oppression, but also to struggle against racial and cultural oppression, native women can prove instrumental in creating an alternative movement of women in North America, one which is mutually respectful of the rights, needs, cultural particularities, and historical divergences of each sector of its membership, and which is therefore free of the adherence to white supremacist hegemony previously marring feminist thinking and practice. Any such movement of women—including those

Euroamerican women who see its thrust as corresponding to their own values and interests as human beings—cannot help but be of crucial importance within the liberation struggles waged by peoples of color to dismantle the apparatus of Eurocentric power in every area of the continent. The greater the extent to which these struggles succeed, the closer the core agenda of Native North America—recovery of land and resources, reassertion of self-determining forms of government, and reconstitution of traditional social relations within our nations—will come to realization.

NOTES

1. For further information on Marie Lego and the context of her struggle, see Jaimes, M. Annette, "The Pit River Indian Land Claims Dispute in Northern California," *Journal of Ethnic Studies,* Vol. 4, No. 4, Winter 1987.
2. Quoted in Katz, Jane B., *I Am the Fire of Time: The Voices of Native American Women,* E. P. Dutton Publisher, New York 1977, p. 146.
3. Quoted in ibid., p. 147. Bennett was eventually acquitted after being shot, while seven months pregnant, and wounded by white vigilantes.
4. Ibid.
5. Quoted in ibid., p. 141.
6. The best account of the roles of Gladys Bissonette and Ellen Moves Camp during the siege may be found in Editors, *Voices from Wounded Knee, 1973, Akwesasne Notes,* Mohawk Nation via Rooseveltown, NY, 1974.
7. Churchill, Ward, and Tim Van der Wall. *The COINTELPRO Papers: Documents on the FBI's Secret Wars Against Dissent in the United States,* South End Press, Boston, 1990, pp. 231–302. Also see Matthiessen, Peter, *In the Spirit of Crazy Horse,* Viking Press, New York (2nd edition) 1991.
8. Kammer, Jerry, *The Second Long Walk: The Navajo-Hopi Land Dispute,* University of New Mexico Press, Albuquerque, 1980, pp. 1–2, 209.
9. For further information on Big Mountain, see Parlow, Anita, *Cry, Sacred Land: Big Mountain, USA,* Christic Institute, Washington. D.C., 1988.
10. Quoted in Katz. op. cit., p. 151. For further background on Ada Deer, see her autobiography (Deer, Ada, with R. E. Simon, Jr., *Speaking Out,* Children's Press, Chicago, 1970).
11. On the murders of Pedro and Jeanette Bissonette, see Churchill, Ward, and Jim Vander Wall, *Agents of Repression: The FBI's Secret Wars Against the Black Panther Party and the American Indian Movement,* South End Press, Boston, 1988, pp. 187, 200–3.
12. Concerning the murders of Tina Manning Trudell, her three children (Ricarda Star, age five; Sunshine Karma, three; and Eli Changing Sun, one), and her mother, Leah Hicks Manning, see ibid., pp. 361–4. On Aquash, see Brand, Johanna, *The Life and Death of Anna Mae Aquash,* James Lorimax Publishers, Toronto, 1978.
13. Hill Witt, Shirley, "The Brave-Hearted Women: The Struggle at Wounded Knee," *Akwesasne Notes,* Vol. 8, No. 2, 1976, p. 16.
14. Quoted in Katz, op. cit., pp. 145–6.
15. Quoted in Kammer, op. cit., p. 18.
16. From a talk delivered during International Women's Week, the University of Colorado at Boulder, April 1984 (tape on file).

17. Such sentiments are hardly unique to the United States. For articulation by Canadian Indian women, see Silman, Janet, *Enough Is Enough: Aboriginal Women Speak Out,* The Women's Press, Toronto, 1987.
18. From a talk delivered during International Women's Week, the University of Colorado at Boulder, April 1985 (tape on file).
19. From a talk delivered during International Women's Week, University of Colorado at Boulder, April 1984 (tape on file).
20. Joseph, Gloria I., and Jill Lewis, *Common Differences: Conflicts in Black and White Feminist Perspectives,* South End Press, Boston, 1981, pp. 4–6.
21. hooks, bell, *Feminist Theory: From Margin to Center,* South End Press, Boston, 1984, pp. 4–8.
22. hooks, bell, *Ain't I a Woman: Black Women and Feminism,* South End Press, Boston, 1981, p. 190.
23. hooks, bell, *Talking Back: Thinking Feminist, Thinking Black,* South End Press, Boston, 1989, p. 149.
24. Ibid., pp. 150–1.
25. For a sample of these perspectives, see Moraga, Cherríe, and Cloria Anzaldúa, eds., *This Bridge Called My Back: Writings by Radical Women of Color,* Kitchen Table Press, New York, 1983.

PART V
Sexuality

. . . all Black women are affected by the widespread controlling image that African-American women are sexually promiscuous, potential prostitutes.

PATRICIA HILL COLLINS[1]

Dating becomes a sport in itself, and "scoring," or having sex with little or no emotional involvement, is a mark of masculine achievement.

DON SABO[2]

The social construction of gender greatly affects how sexuality emerges in humans. Without the constraints put upon sexuality by gender, expressions of human sexuality would probably look very different than they currently do. In spite of these constraints, however, human sexuality encompasses a wide range of behaviors and identities. The expectation in mainstream U.S. society that feminine, heterosexual women and masculine, heterosexual men will have sex only with each other and by mutual agreement is challenged by many people who do not conform to the dominant norms. It is also challenged by the rates of abusive sexual exploitation perpetrated by the more powerful on the less powerful, most frequently by men against women and children.

The combinations and permutations of biological sex, gender, and sexual orientation are many. A person could be, for example, genetically and biologically female, actively heterosexual, and "masculine" in appearance or behavior (whatever masculine means in her social and cultural context). The American Psychiatric Association (APA) took on this issue when it reversed its designation of gay men and lesbians as mentally ill. Deciding that homosexuality was not, in itself, pathological, they did define as mentally ill those children who preferred to behave like people of the other gender. Reinforcing the assumption that sex and gender should match, gender identity disorder became the pathological label for feminine boys and masculine girls. Thus, Tommi Avicolli and Linnea Due (Part II) would probably have been labeled sick—Avicolli for his preference for jump rope and his manner of walking and Due for her too-masculine presentation and her wish to marry a woman. There is no suggestion by the APA that the boys who teased and ostracized Avicolli or the teachers who ignored them or the scout leader who rejected Due because of her "masculinity" might, in fact, be the sick ones. In part in response to this labeling, some gay men take on very masculine identities in adulthood, effectively distancing themselves from the "sissy" boys now considered pathological by the APA.[3] It is interesting to note that when high school football player Corey Johnson courageously came out as gay to his team, he was accepted and defended in an unusual example of community support; his masculinity seems to have bought him some privilege that Avicolli could not enjoy.[4]

When we acknowledge that one's genetic makeup is the only aspect of sexuality that is immutable, and that sexual behavior, sexual orientation, and gender do not necessarily line up in a predictable pattern, the options for the expression of gender and sexuality are many. Psychologist Carla Golden, in a study of undergraduates at an elite women's college in the Northeast, found that students' sexual identities did not necessarily match their sexual behavior. For example, some women who identified themselves as heterosexual were exclusively involved sexually with women; some who had never had a same-sex sexual experience nevertheless identified themselves as bisexual because they perceived in themselves the potential for same-sex attraction and sexual activity. Golden also interviewed women who identified themselves as "political lesbians" whose sexual behavior was exclusively heterosexual. Golden concludes that the congruence between sexual feelings, behavior, and identity is often lacking, and she urges people to acknowledge the complex expressions of sexuality and sexual identity that result.[5]

Apart from examining the complex ways in which people define and express their sexuality, passionate debates and interesting topics abound in the field of sexuality. The origins of sexual orientations have been the subject of much research, as scholars explore the extent to which genetic predispositions or cultural influences might cause people to become heterosexual, gay, lesbian, or bisexual, or to change sexual orientation.[6] Heated debate ensues about whether violent and degrading pornography should continue to be legal in the United States.[7] Others argue for or against butch-femme roles in lesbian and gay communities.[8] Still others debate the pros and cons of sadomasochistic sexual practices.[9] The debate about sex education in schools has created conflict in school districts in many parts of the United States (Should it exist? If so, with what content and starting at what age?).[10]

The emergence of Viagra has provoked interest in women's sexuality, as researchers explore whether it or a similar drug could increase women's sexual responses as well.[11] It has also provoked debate among pharmaceutical companies and feminist health advocates as the definition of "sexual dysfunction" is addressed. It is unclear to what extent women's sexual dysfunction even exists; whether, if it exists, it is similar to erectile dysfunction; and whether doctors and pharmaceutical companies are truly concerned about women's sexual well-being or simply concerned with profits. Feminist critics are worried that emphasis on sexual physiology and performance could obscure the complex psychosocial aspects of sexuality, and they question the alleged "equal opportunity" in the attempt to develop a female arousal drug.[12] The emergence of Viagra has also raised questions about insurance coverage of this male-specific, voluntary drug, especially in light of the fact that many health plans do not cover the costs of contraception.

Recently the reproductive technology that makes it possible for postmenopausal women to give birth has raised questions about the double standard related to women bearing children after their typical childbearing years. A sixty-three-year-old woman who gave birth in California was criticized for doing so, while men who become fathers at sixty-three are more likely to be cheered on.[13]

The sexual use and abuse of women and children is a major issue in the study of sexuality. Human beings' potential for healthy, nonexploitive, enjoyable sexual expression with others is heavily influenced by the level of decision-making power we have over our own bodily expressions and the kinds of caring (or lack thereof) that surrounds us as children.[14] The high rates of childhood sexual abuse (estimated at one in four girls, one in seven boys), followed by the rates of rape over a lifetime, suggest that sexual pleasure will be severely curtailed for a large proportion of the U.S. population. Boys seem to have an especially difficult time dealing with sexual abuse, in part because of homophobia. Many worry that they will be called gay if the perpetrator was male (and the perpetrator usually is male) or that they will be called unmanly if they didn't automatically enjoy forced sex with a woman, since many men and boys are socialized to accept and like heterosexual activity whatever the circumstance. If, in fact, children are gendered female by male perpetrators, a boy is apt to feel like a "girl" and have a difficult time admitting it.[15]

The widespread abuse of women in prostitution, trafficking in women, pornography, and interpersonal relationships leaves millions of women worldwide in a state of long-term sexual victimization. For that population, the choices related to sexual orientation and identity, freedom of sexual expression, and gender bending become largely irrelevant against a backdrop of the need to survive.[16] We have recently seen increased attention to "comfort women" who were forced into prostitution by the Japanese army during World War II, as these now-elderly women find their voices and tell the truth about what they experienced.[17] The use of prostitutes, including child prostitutes by the U.S. military abroad, has led to an effort to end soldiers' use of child prostitutes.[18] Publicity about international sex trafficking is bringing this issue to more readers in the United States, as illustrated by a recent report of female sex slaves from China in Chicago.[19]

HIV and AIDS have curtailed the sexual activity and, literally, the lives of a large segment of the world's population, leaving millions of people infected or dead. Young men ages 20–24 in the United States are currently at highest risk for sexually transmitted infections (STIs), tied, in part, to their commitment to the risk-taking aspects of masculinity.[20] An estimated one in four people in the United States will contract a sexually transmitted infection, some of which are without symptoms and can cause infertility and cancer.[21] AIDS and STI's have forced many people to communicate about sex in ways they didn't need to before, and they have stimulated changed sexual practices for a large proportion of the U.S. population, although some people are still in denial about the importance of condom use, even when they have access to condoms.[22] Even the Catholic Church is considering easing up on its policy against condom use, as the reality of the transmission of AIDS takes on a life of its own. A new perspective on condoms defines them as disease control rather then birth control, especially in developing countries with high rates of AIDS. It remains to be seen to what extent permission or recommendation for condom use will become church policy, especially in places where AIDS is not devastating the population.[23] Sylvana Paternostro, a journalist who grew up in Colombia, reports that AIDS in Latin America is often spread by heterosexually identified men who have unprotected sex with other men and infect their unsuspecting female partners; their lack of identification as gay and their consequent denial of the risks of same-sex unprotected sexual activity leave them at high risk both for the illness itself and to become agents of its transmission.[24]

All the above sexual issues are embedded in cultural, racial, and class contexts. Sociologist Patricia Hill Collins, for example, examined pornography, prostitution, and rape in the context of race, class, and gender oppression. She provides data about, and analysis of, the long-term sexual exploitation of African American women.[25]

In oppressed communities, there is sometimes pressure to not break rank with one's cultural group. Thus, sometimes women of color or women in small white ethnic communities are pressured not to address sexism within those communities. For similar reasons, gays, lesbians, and bisexuals sometimes feel pressured not to address homophobia. The larger mostly white movements that are fighting for gay/lesbian/transgender rights and women's rights have a history of racism that renders those movements uncomfortable, unsafe, or unacceptable for many people of color. Gays and lesbians of color, then, frequently deal with two communities that fail to acknowledge their whole selves: a gay /lesbian/bisexual/transgender community that fails to address racism and a racial/ethnic community that fails to address heterosexism.[26]

In an interesting and moving account of what it's like to be the only Black person in a group of white lesbians, writer Paula Ross reports,

> There is rarely a time when I can attend to my self as lesbian apart from my self as black, a diasporic offspring, one of the millions of Africa's daughters dispersed by imperialism, greed, and an overweening appetite for colonization. I stand around this campfire with fifteen other lesbians. We are all erotically and sexually connected to other women. My lover's butch and my femme identities are not questioned for an instant. But even here, I cannot forget about race. They can forget—perhaps at their own peril, but they do have the option.[27]

Homophobia thrives in many contexts. In a recent well-publicized trial in Egypt that was denounced by various human rights groups, twenty-three men were jailed for one to five years for homosexual activity.[28] The struggle for the right of same-sex couples to marry continues in most states in the United States. This issue was brought painfully home to the partners of people killed in the attacks on September 11, 2001; surviving partners in states without same-sex civil union options were often not defined as next of kin by government funding agencies. The U.S. military is still refusing to allow openly gay or lesbian people to serve.

In response to the homophobic atmosphere that exists in most places, many gays and lesbians wish they were straight. The ex-gay movement in the United States has attempted to assist with conversions to heterosexuality, with mixed success. Recently, some active spokespersons for the ex-gay movement have resumed their lives as gays, creating an ex-ex-gay movement.[29]

This part of this book addresses sexuality from a range of perspectives, including questioning whether sexuality needs to be linked to gender (John Stoltenberg); looking at the athlete's approach to sexuality (Don Sabo); exploring some of men's and women's experiences with pornography (Robert Jensen); considering some of the issues involved with female sexual satisfaction (Barry Bass and Susan Walen); issues of reproductive rights and sexuality for women with disabilities (Marsha Saxton); and the difficulties faced by bisexual people from various racial and ethnic groups (Paula Rust).

The authors in this part would like to see a world that is free of sexual exploitation and in which people are free to be sexual in any nonexploitative ways they choose. They also make clear how difficult it would be to achieve this ideal.

NOTES

1. Patricia Hill Collins, "The Sexual Politics of Black Womanhood," in *Black Feminist Thought* (New York: Routledge, 1991), p. 174.
2. Don Sabo, "The Myth of the Sexual Athlete," in Michael A. Messner and Donald F. Sabo, *Sex, Violence & Power in Sports* (Freedom, CA: Crossing Press, 1994), p. 38.
3. For an interesting discussion of the process by which the American Psychiatric Association removed homosexuality from the pathology list and simultaneously added "gender identity disorder of childhood," see Eve Kosofsky Sedgwick, "How to Bring Your Kids Up Gay," in *Tendencies* (Durham: Duke University Press, 1993), pp. 154-164.
4. Rick Reilly, "The Biggest Play of His Life," *Sports Illustrated* 92, 19, p. 114.
5. Carla Golden, "Diversity and Variability in Women's Sexual Identities," in the Boston Lesbian Psychologies Collective, eds., Boston Lesbian Psychologies Collective, *Lesbian Psychologies: Exploration and Challenges* (Chicago: University of Illinois Press, 1987), pp. 19–34.
6. For discussions of causes of sexual orientation and the development of sexual identity see Alan P. Bell and Martin S. Weinberg, *Homosexualities: A Study of Human Diversity* (South Melbourne, Victoria: Macmillan, 1978); Jan Clausen, *Beyond Gay or Straight: Understanding Sexual Orientation* (New York: Chelsea House, 1997); Ronald C. Fox, "Bisexuality in Perspective: A Review of Theory and Research" in Beth A. Firestein, ed., *Bisexuality: The Psychology and Politics of an Invisible Minority* (Thousand Oaks, CA: Sage, 1996), pp. 3–50; Martin S. Weinberg, *Dual Attraction: Understanding Bisexuality* (New York: Oxford University Press, 1994).
7. For a discussion of class and pornography, see Laura Kipnis, "(Male) Desire and (Female) Disgust: Reading *Hustler,*" in Lawrence Grossberg, Cary Nelson, and Paula Treichler, *Cultural Studies* (New York: Routledge, 1992), pp. 373–391. For a presentation of the anti-pornography position in the feminist pornography debate, see Dorchen Leidholdt and Janice G. Raymond, eds., *The Sexual Liberals and the Attack on Feminism* (New York: Pergamon Press, 1990); Laura Lederer and Richard Delgado, eds., *The Price We Pay: The Case against Racist Speech, Hate*

Propaganda, and Pornography (New York: Hill and Wang, 1995). For a discussion of the feminist position in support of pornography, see Lisa Duggan and Nan D. Hunter, eds., *Sex Wars: Sexual Dissent and Political Culture* (New York: Routledge, 1995). For a recent attempt to bridge these two positions see Gail Dines, Robert Jensen, and Ann Russo, *Pornography: The Production and Consumption of Inequality* (New York: Routledge, 1998). For an example from Queer studies of the role of racism in gay pornographic videos, see Richard Fung, "Looking for My Penis: The Eroticized Asian in Gay Video Porn," in Bad Object-Choices, ed., *How Do I Look? Queer Film and Video* (Seattle: Bay Press, 1991).

8. For a discussion of butch-femme roles in the lesbian community, see Joan Nestle, "Butch-Femme Relationships: Sexual Courage in the 1950s," in *A Restricted Country* (Ithaca, NY: Firebrand, 1987), pp. 100–109.
9. For a discussion of sadomasochism, see Robin Ruth Linden et al., eds., *Against Sadomasochism: A Radical Feminist Analysis* (San Francisco: Frog in the Well, 1982); Pat Califia, *Sapphistry: The Book of Lesbian Sexuality* (Tallahassee, FL: Naiad Press, 1980).
10. See Pepper Schwartz and Virginia Rutter, *The Gender of Sexuality* (Thousand Oaks: Pine Forge, 1998), pp. 20–21.
11. Jennifer Babson, "At BU, a fresh look at Viagra—for Women" *Boston Sunday Globe* 254, no. 12 (July 12, 1998), pp. A1, A20.
12. Meika Loe, "Female Sexual Dysfuction: For Women or For Sale?" *The Network News*, January–February 2000, pp. 1, 6 (published by the National Women's Health Network).
13. Pepper Schwartz and Virginia Rutter, *The Gender of Sexuality* (Thousand Oaks, CA: Pine Forge Press, 1998), p. xiv.
14. Aline P. Zoldbrod, *Sex Smart: How Your Childhood Shaped Your Sexual Life and What to Do About It* (Oakland, CA: New Harbinger Publications, 1998).
15. I would like to acknowledge sociologist Gail Dines of Wheelock College for the idea that children are gendered female.
16. Kathleen Barry, *The Prostitution of Sexuality: The Global Exploitation of Women* (New York: NYU Press, 1995).
17. Cynthia Enloe, *Maueuvers: The International Politics of Militarizing Women's Lives* (Berkeley: University of California Press, 2000); Maria Rosa Henson, *Comfort Woman: A Filipina's Story of Prostitution and Slavery Under the Japanese Military* (Lanham, MD: Rowman & Littlefield, 1999).
18. Cynthia Enloe, *Maueuvers: The International Politics of Militarizing Women's Lives* (Berkeley: University of California Press, 2000).
19. Charity Crouse, "Slaves of Chicago: International Sex Trafficking Is Becoming Big Business," *In These Times*, 25, no. 3 (January 8, 2001), pp. 7–8.
20. John Stoltenberg, "Of Microbes and Men" *Ms.* 10, no. 5 (August-September 2000), pp. 60–62.
21. Angela Bonavoglia, "Making Love in the Dark," *Ms.* 10, no. 5 (August-September 2000), pp. 54–59.
22. Jill Lewis, " 'So How Did Your Condom Use Go Last Night, Daddy?' Sex Talk and Daily Life" in Lynne Segal, ed., *New Sexual Agendas* (New York: New York University Press, 1997), pp. 238–252; Carla Willig, "Trust as Risky Practice," in Lynne Segal, ed., *New Sexual Agendas* (New York: New York University Press, 1997), pp. 125–153.
23. Raphael Lewis, "Cleric Calls Condom Use 'Lesser Evil' in HIV Fight," *The Boston Globe* 258, no. 78 (September 16, 2000), p. A1ff.

24. Silvana Paternostro, *In the Land of God and Man: A Latin Woman's Journey* (New York: Penguin Putnam, Inc., 1998).
25. Patricia Hill Collins, *Black Feminist Thought,* 2nd ed. (New York: Routledge, 2000).
26. Connie S. Chan, "Issues of Identity Development among Asian-American Lesbians and Gay Men," *Journal of Counseling and Development* 68, no. 1 (September–October 1989), pp. 16–20; Surina Kahn, "The All-American Queer Pakistani Girl," in Gwen Kirk and Margo Okazawa-Rey, eds., *Women's Lives: Multicultural Perspectives,* 2nd ed. (Mountain View, CA: Mayfield Publishing, 2001).
27. Paula Ross, "What's Race Got to Do with It?" in Karla Jay, ed., *Dyke Life* (New York: Basic Books, 1995), p. 142.
28. Sarah El Deeb, "23 Jailed after Trial for Gay Sex," *The Boston Globe* (November 15, 2001), p. A8.
29. Tatsha Robertson, "Gays Return to the Fold: Many Cite Flaws of 'Conversion'" *The Boston Globe* (September 9, 2000), pp. B1, B4.

32

HOW MEN HAVE (A) SEX

JOHN STOLTENBERG

An address to college students

In the human species, how many sexes are there?
Answer A: *There are two sexes.*
Answer B: *There are three sexes.*
Answer C: *There are four sexes.*
Answer D: *There are seven sexes.*
Answer E: *There are as many sexes as there are people.*

I'd like to take you, in an imaginary way, to look at a different world, somewhere else in the universe, a place inhabited by a life form that very much resembles us. But these creatures grow up with a peculiar knowledge. They know that they have been born in an infinite variety. They know, for instance, that in their genetic material they are born with hundreds of different chromosome formations at the point in each cell that we would say determines their "sex." These creatures don't just come in XX or XY; they also come in XXY and XYY and XXX plus a long list of "mosaic" variations in which some cells in a creature's body have one combination and other cells have another. Some of these creatures are born with chromosomes that aren't even quite X or Y because a little bit of one chromosome goes and gets joined to another. There are hundreds of different combinations, and though all are not fertile, quite a number of them are. The creatures in this world enjoy their individuality; they delight in the fact that they are not divisible into distinct categories. So when another newborn arrives with an esoterically rare chromosomal formation, there is a little celebration: "Aha," they say, "another sign that we are each unique."

These creatures also live with the knowledge that they are born with a vast range of genital formations. Between their legs are tissue structures that vary along a continuum, from clitorises with a vulva through all possible combinations and gradations to penises with a scrotal sac. These creatures live with an understanding that their genitals all developed prenatally from exactly the same little nub of embryonic tissue called a genital tubercle,

---

Jon Stoltenberg, "How Men Have (a) Sex" from *Refusing to Be a Man: Essays on Sex and Justice* (New York: Meridian Books, 1990).

which grew and developed under the influence of varying amounts of the hormone androgen. These creatures honor and respect everyone's natural-born genitalia—including what we would describe as a microphallus or a clitoris several inches long. What these creatures find amazing and precious is that because everyone's genitals stem from the same embryonic tissue, the nerves inside all their genitals got wired very much alike, so these nerves of touch just go crazy upon contact in a way that resonates completely between them. "My gosh," they think, "you must feel something in your genital tubercle that intensely resembles what I'm feeling in my genital tubercle." Well, they don't exactly *think* that in so many words; they're actually quite heavy into their feelings at that point; but they do feel very connected—throughout all their wondrous variety.

I could go on. I could tell you about the variety of hormones that course through their bodies in countless different patterns and proportions, both before birth and throughout their lives—the hormones that we call "sex hormones" but that they call "individuality inducers." I could tell you how these creatures think about reproduction: For part of their lives, some of them are quite capable of gestation, delivery, and lactation; and for part of their lives, some of them are quite capable of insemination; and for part or all of their lives, some of them are not capable of any of those things—so these creatures conclude that it would be silly to lock anyone into a lifelong category based on a capability variable that may or may not be utilized and that in any case changes over each lifetime in a fairly uncertain and idiosyncratic way. These creatures are not oblivious to reproduction; but nor do they spend their lives constructing a self-definition around their variable reproductive capacities. They don't have to, because what is truly unique about these creatures is that they are capable of having a sense of personal identity without struggling to fit into a group identity based on how they were born. These creatures are quite happy, actually. They don't worry about sorting *other* creatures into categories, so they don't have to worry about whether they are measuring up to some category they themselves are supposed to belong to.

These creatures, of course, have sex. Rolling and rollicking and robust sex, and sweaty and slippery and sticky sex, and trembling and quaking and tumultuous sex, and tender and tingling and transcendent sex. They have sex fingers to fingers. They have sex belly to belly. They have sex genital tubercle to genital tubercle. They *have* sex. They do not have *a* sex. In their erotic lives, they are not required to act out their status in a category system—because there *is* no category system. There are no sexes to belong to, so sex between creatures is free to be between genuine individuals—not representatives of a category. They have sex. They do not have a sex. Imagine life like that.

Perhaps you have guessed the point of this science fiction: Anatomically, each creature in the imaginary world I have been describing could be an identical twin of every human being on earth. These creatures, in fact, *are us*—in every way except socially and politically. The way they are born is the way we are born. And we are not born belonging to one or the other of two sexes. We are born into a physiological continuum on which there is no discrete and definite point that you can call "male" and no discrete and definite point that you can call "female." If you look at all the variables in nature that are said to determine human "sex," you can't possibly find one that will unequivocally split the species into two. Each of the so-called criteria of sexedness is itself a continuum—including chromosomal variables, genital and gonadal variations, reproductive capacities, endocrinological proportions, and any other criterion you could think of. Any or all of these different variables may line up in any number of ways, and all of the variables may vary independently of one another.[1]

What does all this mean? It means, first of all, a logical dilemma: Either human "male" and human "female" actually exist in nature as fixed and discrete entities and you can credibly base an entire social and political system on those absolute natural categories, or else the variety of human sexedness is infinite. As Andrea Dworkin wrote in 1974:

> The discovery is, of course, that "man" and "woman" are fictions, caricatures, cultural constructs. As models they are reductive, totalitarian, inappropriate to human becoming. As roles they are static, demeaning to the female, dead-ended for male and female both.[2]

The conclusion is inescapable:

> We are, clearly, a multisexed species which has its sexuality spread along a vast continuum where the elements called male and female are not discrete.[3]

"We are . . . a multisexed species." I first read those words a little over ten years ago—and that liberating recognition saved my life.

All the time I was growing up, I knew that there was something really problematical in my relationship to manhood. Inside, deep inside, I never believed I was fully male—I never believed I was growing up enough of a man. I believed that someplace out there, in other men, there was something that was genuine authentic all-American manhood—the real stuff—but I didn't have it: not enough of it to convince *me* anyway, even if I managed to be fairly convincing to those around me. I felt like an impostor, like a fake. I agonized a lot about not feeling male enough, and I had no idea then how much I was not alone.

Then I read those words—those words that suggested to me for the first time that the notion of manhood is a cultural delusion, a baseless belief, a false front, a house of cards. It's not true. The category I was trying so desperately to belong to, to be a member of in good standing—it doesn't exist. Poof. Now you see it, now you don't. Now you're terrified you're not really part of it; now you're free, you don't have to worry anymore. However removed you feel inside from "authentic manhood," it doesn't matter. What matters is the center inside yourself—and how you live, and how you treat people, and what you can contribute as you pass through life on this earth, and how honestly you love, and how carefully you make choices. Those are the things that really matter. Not whether you're a real man. There's no such thing.

The idea of the male sex is like the idea of an Aryan race. The Nazis believed in the idea of an Aryan race—they believed that the Aryan race really exists, physically, in nature—and they put a great deal of effort into making it real. The Nazis believed that from the blond hair and blue eyes occurring naturally in the human species, they could construe the existence of a separate *race*—a distinct category of human beings that was unambiguously rooted in the natural order of things. But traits do not a race make; traits only make traits. For the idea to be real that these physical traits comprised a race, the race had to be socially constructed. The Nazis inferiorized and exterminated those they defined as "non-Aryan." With that, the notion of an Aryan race began to seem to come true. That's how there could be a political entity known as an Aryan race, and that's how there could be for some people a personal, subjective sense that they belonged to it. This happened through hate and force, through violence and victimization, through treating millions of people as things, then exterminating them. The belief system shared by people who believed they were all Aryan could not exist apart from that force and violence. The force and violence created a racial class system, *and* it created those people's membership in the race considered "superior." The force and violence served their class interests in large part because it created and maintained the class itself. But the idea of an Aryan race could never become metaphysically true, despite all the violence unleashed to create it, because there simply *is* no Aryan race. There is only the idea of it—and the consequences of trying to make it seem real. The male sex is very like that.

Penises and ejaculate and prostate glands occur in nature, but the notion that these anatomical traits comprise a sex—a discrete class, separate and distinct, metaphysically divisible from some other sex, *the* "other sex"—is simply that: a notion, an idea. The penises exist; the male sex does not. The male sex is socially constructed. It is a political entity that flourishes only through acts of force and sexual terrorism. Apart from the global inferiorization and subordination of those who are defined as "nonmale," the idea of personal membership in the male sex class would have no recognizable meaning. It would make no sense. No one could be a member of it and no one would think they *should* be a member of it. There would be no male sex to belong to. That doesn't mean there wouldn't still be penises and ejaculate and prostate glands and such. It simply means that the center of our selfhood would not be required to reside inside an utterly fictitious category—a category that only seems real to the extent that those outside it are put down.

We live in a world divided absolutely into two sexes, even though nothing about human nature warrants that division. We are sorted into one category or another at birth based solely on a visual inspection of our groins, and the only question that's asked is whether there's enough elongated tissue around your urethra so you can pee standing up. The presence or absence of a long-enough penis is the primary criterion for separating who's to grow up male from who's to grow up female. And among all the ironies in that utterly whimsical and arbitrary selection process is the fact that *anyone* can pee both sitting down and standing up.

Male sexual identity is the conviction or belief, held by most people born with penises, that they are male and not female, that they belong to the male sex. In a society predicated on the notion that there are two "opposite" and "complementary" sexes, this idea not only makes sense, it *becomes* sense; the very idea of a male sexual identity produces sensation, produces the meaning of sensation, becomes the meaning of how one's body feels. The sense and the sensing of a male sexual identity is at once mental and physical, at once public and personal. Most people born with a penis between their legs grow up aspiring to feel and act unambiguously male, longing to belong to the sex that is male and daring not to belong to the sex that is not, and feeling this urgency for a visceral and constant verification of their male sexual identity—for a fleshy connection to manhood—as the driving force of their life. The drive does not originate in the anatomy. The sensations derive from the idea. The idea gives the feelings social meaning; the idea determines which sensations shall be sought.

People born with penises must strive to make the idea of male sexual identity personally real by doing certain deeds, actions that are valued and chosen because they produce the desired feeling of belonging to a sex that is male and not female. Male sexual identity is experienced only in sensation and action, in feeling and doing, in eroticism and ethics. The feeling of belonging to a male sex encompasses both sensations that are explicitly "sexual" and those that are not ordinarily regarded as such. And there is a tacit social value system according to which certain acts are chosen because they make an individual's sexedness feel real and certain other acts are eschewed because they numb it. That value system is the ethics of male sexual identity—and it may well be the social origin of all injustice.

Each person experiences the idea of sexual identity as more or less real, more or less certain, more or less true, depending on two very personal phenomena: one's feelings and one's acts. For many people, for instance, the act of fucking makes their sexual identity feel more real than it does at other times, and they can predict from experience that this feeling of greater certainty will last for at least a while after each time they fuck. Fucking is not the only such act, and not only so-called sex acts can result in feelings of certainty about sexual identity; but the act of fucking happens to be a very good example of the correlation between *doing* a specific act in a specific way and *sensing* the specificity of the sexual identity to which one aspires. A person can decide to do certain acts and not others just because some acts will have the payoff of a feeling of greater certainty about sexual identity and others will give the feedback of a feeling of less. The transient reality of one's sexual identity, a person can know, is always a function of what one does and how one's acts make one feel. The feeling and the act must conjoin for the idea of the sexual identity to come true. We all keep longing for surety of our sexedness that we can feel; we all keep striving through our actions to make the idea real.

In human nature, eroticism is not differentiated between "male" and "female" in any clear-cut way. There is too much of a continuum, too great a resemblance. From all that we know, the penis and the clitoris are identically "wired" to receive and retransmit sensations from throughout the body, and the congestion of blood within the lower torso during sexual excitation makes all bodies sensate in a remarkably similar manner. Simply put, we all share all the nerve and blood-vessel layouts that are associated with sexual arousal. Who can say, for instance, that the penis would not experience sensations the way that a clitoris does if this were not a world in which the penis is supposed to be hell-bent on penetration? By the time most men make it through puberty, they believe that erotic sensation is supposed to *begin* in their penis; that if engorgement has not begun there, then nothing else in their body will heat up either. There is a massive interior dissociation from sensations that do not explicitly remind a man that his penis is still there. And not only there as sensate, but *functional and operational.*

So much of most men's sexuality is tied up with gender-actualizing—with feeling like a real man—that they can scarcely recall an erotic sensation that had no gender-specific cultural meaning. As most men age, they learn to cancel out and deny erotic sensations that are not specifically linked to what they think a real man is supposed to feel. An erotic sensation unintentionally experienced in a receptive, communing mode—instead of in an aggressive and controlling and violative mode, for instance—can shut down sensory systems in an instant. An erotic sensation unintentionally linked to the "wrong" sex of another person can similarly mean sudden numbness. Acculturated male sexuality has a built-in fail-safe: Either its political context reifies manhood or the experience cannot be felt as sensual. Either the act creates his sexedness or it does not compute as a sex act. So he tenses up, pumps up, steels himself against the dread that he be found not male enough. And his dread is not stupid; for he sees what happens to people when they are treated as nonmales.

My point is that sexuality does not *have* a gender; it *creates* a gender. It creates for those who adapt to it in narrow and specified ways the confirmation for the individual of belonging to the idea of one sex or the other. So-called male sexuality is a learned connection between specific physical sensations and the idea of a male sexual identity. To achieve this male sexual identity requires that an individual *identify with* the class of males—that is, accept as one's own the values and interests of the class. A fully realized male sexual identity also requires *nonidentification with* that which is perceived to be nonmale, or female. A male must not identify with females; he must not associate with females in feeling, interest, or action. His identity as a member of the sex class men absolutely depends on the extent to which he repudiates the values and interests of the sex class "women."

I think somewhere inside us all, we have always known something about the relativity of gender. Somewhere inside us all, we know that our bodies harbor deep resemblances, that we are wired inside to respond in a profound harmony to the resonance of eroticism inside the body of someone near us. Physiologically, we are far more alike than different. The tissue structures that have become labial and clitoral or scrotal and penile have not forgotten their common ancestry. Their sensations are of the same source. The nerve networks and interlock of capillaries throughout our pelvises electrify and engorge as if plugged in together and pumping as one. That's what we feel when we feel one another's feelings. That's what can happen during sex that is mutual, equal, reciprocal, profoundly communing.

So why is it that some of us with penises think it's sexy to pressure someone into having sex against their will? Some of us actually get harder the harder the person resists. Some of us with penises actually believe that some of us without penises want to be raped. And why is it that some of us with penises think it's sexy to treat other people as objects, as things to be bought and sold, impersonal bodies to be possessed and consumed for our sexual pleasure? Why is it that some of us with penises are aroused by sex tinged with rape, and sex commoditized by pornography? Why do so many of us with penises want such antisexual sex?

There's a reason, of course. We have to make a lie seem real. It's a very big lie. We each have to do our part. Otherwise the lie will look like the lie that it is. Imagine the enormity of what we each must do to keep the lie alive in each of us. Imagine the awesome challenge we face to make the lie a social fact. It's a lifetime mission for each of us born with a penis: to have sex in such a way that the male sex will seem real—and so that we'll feel like a real part of it.

We all grow up knowing exactly what kind of sex that is. It's the kind of sex you can have when you pressure or bully someone else into it. So it's a kind of sex that makes your will more important than theirs. That kind of sex helps the lie a lot. That kind of sex makes you feel like someone important and it turns the other person into someone unimportant. That kind of sex makes you feel real, not like a fake. It's a kind of sex men have in order to feel like a real man.

There's also the kind of sex you can have when you force someone and hurt someone and cause someone suffering and humiliation. Violence and hostility in sex help the lie a lot too. Real men are aggressive in sex. Real men get cruel in sex. Real men use their penises like weapons in sex. Real men leave bruises. Real men think it's a turn-on to threaten harm. A brutish push can make an erection feel really hard. That kind of sex helps the lie a lot. That kind of sex makes you feel like someone who is powerful and it turns the other person into someone powerless. That kind of sex makes you feel dangerous and in control—like you're fighting a war with an enemy and if you're mean enough you'll win but if you let up you'll lose your manhood. It's a kind of sex men have *in order to have* a manhood.

There's also the kind of sex you can have when you pay your money into a profit system that grows rich displaying and exploiting the bodies and body parts of people without penises for the sexual entertainment of people with. Pay your money and watch. Pay your money and imagine. Pay your money and get real turned on. Pay your money and jerk off. That kind of sex helps the lie a lot. It helps support an industry committed to making people with penises believe that people without are sluts who just want to be ravished and reviled—an industry dedicated to maintaining a sex-class system in which men believe themselves sex machines and men believe women are mindless fuck tubes. That kind of sex helps the lie a lot. It's like buying Krugerrands as a vote of confidence for white supremacy in South Africa.

And there's one more thing: That kind of sex makes the lie indelible—burns it onto your retinas right adjacent to your brain—makes you remember it and makes your body respond to it and so it makes you believe that the lie is in fact true: You really are a real man. That slavish and submissive creature there spreading her legs is really not. You and that creature have nothing in common. That creature is an alien inanimate thing, but your penis is completely real and alive. Now you can come. Thank god almighty—you have a sex at last.

Now, I believe there are many who are sick at heart over what I have been describing. There are many who were born with penises who want to stop collaborating in the sex-class system that needs us to need these kinds of sex. I believe some of you want to stop living out the big lie, and you want to know how. Some of you long to touch truthfully. Some of you want sexual relationships in your life that are about intimacy and joy, ecstasy and equality—not antagonism and alienation. So what I have to say next I have to say to you.

When you use sex to have a sex, the sex you have is likely to make you feel crummy about yourself. But when you have sex in which you are not struggling with your partner in order to act out "real manhood," the sex you have is more likely to bring you close.

This means several specific things:

1. *Consent is absolutely essential.* If both you and your partner have not freely given your informed consent to the sex you are about to have, you can be quite certain that the sex you go ahead and have will make you strangers to each other. How do you know if there's consent? You ask. You ask again if you're sensing any doubt. Consent to do one thing isn't consent to do another. So you keep communicating, in clear words. And you don't take anything for granted.
2. *Mutuality is absolutely essential.* Sex is not something you do *to* someone. Sex is not a one-way transitive verb, with a subject, you, and an object, the body you're with. Sex that is mutual is not about doing and being done to; it's about being-with and feeling-with. You have to really be there to experience what is happening between and

within the two of you—between every part of you and within both your whole bodies. It's a matter of paying attention—as if you are paying attention to someone who matters.

3. *Respect is absolutely essential.* In the sex that you have, treat your partner like a real person who, like you, has real feelings—feelings that matter as much as your own. You may or may not love—but you must always respect. You must respect the integrity of your partner's body. It is not yours for the taking. It belongs to someone real. And you do not get ownership of your partner's body just because you are having sex—or just because you have had sex.

For those who are closer to the beginning of your sex lives than to the middle or the end, many things are still changing for you about how you have sex, with whom, why or why not, what you like or dislike, what kind of sex you want to have more of. In the next few years, you are going to discover and decide a lot. I say "discover" because no one can tell you what you're going to find out about yourself in relation to sex—and I say "decide" because virtually without knowing it you are going to be laying down habits and patterns that will probably stay with you for the rest of your life. You're at a point in your sexual history that you will never be at again. You don't know what you don't know yet. And yet you are making choices whose consequences for your particular sexuality will be sealed years from now.

I speak to you as someone who is closer to the middle of my sexual history. As I look back, I see that I made many choices that I didn't know I was making. And as I look at men who are near my age, I see that what has happened to many of them is that their sex lives are stuck in deep ruts that began as tiny fissures when they were young. So I want to conclude by identifying what I believe are three of the most important decisions about your sexuality that you can make when you are at the beginning of your sexual history. However difficult these choices may seem to you now, I promise you they will only get more difficult as you grow older. I realize that what I'm about to give is some quite unsolicited nuts-and-bolts advice. But perhaps it will spare you, later on in your lives, some of the obsessions and emptiness that have claimed the sexual histories of many men just a generation before you. Perhaps it will not help, I don't know; but I hope very much that it will.

First, you can start choosing now not to let your sexuality be manipulated by the pornography industry. I've heard many unhappy men talk about how they are so hooked on pornography and obsessed with it that they are virtually incapable of a human erotic contact. And I have heard even more men talk about how, when they do have sex with someone, the pornography gets in the way, like a mental obstacle, like a barrier preventing a full experience of what's really happening between them and their partner. The sexuality that the pornography industry needs you to have is not about communicating and caring; it's about "pornographizing" people—objectifying and conquering them, not being with them as a person. You do not have to buy into it.

Second, you can start choosing now not to let drugs and alcohol numb you through your sex life. Too many men, as they age, become incapable of having sex with a clear head. But you need your head clear—to make clear choices, to send clear messages, to read clearly what's coming in on a clear channel between you and your partner. Sex is no time for your awareness to sign off. And another thing: Beware of relying on drugs or alcohol to give you "permission" to have sex, or to trick your body into feeling something that it's not, or so you won't have to take responsibility for what you're feeling or for the sex that you're about to have. If you can't take sober responsibility for your part in a sexual encounter, you probably shouldn't be having it—and you certainly shouldn't be zonked out of your mind *in order* to have it.

Third, you can start choosing now not to fixate on fucking—especially if you'd really rather have sex in other, noncoital ways. Sometimes men have coital sex—penetration and thrusting then ejaculating inside someone—not because they particularly feel like it but because they feel they *should* feel like it: It's expected that if you're the man, you fuck. And if you don't fuck, you're not a man. The corollary of this cultural imperative is that if two people don't have intercourse, they have not had real sex. That's baloney, of course, but the message comes down hard, especially inside men's heads: Fucking is *the* sex act, the act in which you act out what sex is supposed to be—and what sex you're supposed to be.

Like others born with a penis, I was born into a sex-class system that requires my collaboration every day, even in how I have sex. Nobody told me, when I was younger, that I could have noncoital sex and that it would be fine. Actually, much better than fine. Nobody told me about an incredible range of other erotic possibilities for mutual lovemaking—including rubbing body to body, then coming body to body; including multiple, nonejaculatory orgasms; including the feeling you get when even the tiniest place where you and your partner touch becomes like a window through which great tidal storms of passion ebb and flow, back and forth. Nobody told me about the sex you can have when you stop working at having a sex. My body told me, finally. And I began to trust what my body was telling me more than the lie I was supposed to make real.

I invite you too to resist the lie. I invite you too to become an erotic traitor to male supremacy.

NOTES

1. My source for the foregoing information about so-called sex determinants in the human species is a series of interviews I conducted with the sexologist Dr. John Money in Baltimore, Maryland, in 1979 for an article I wrote called "The Multisex Theorem," which was published in a shortened version as "Future Genders" in *Omni* magazine, May 1980, pp. 67–73ff.
2. Dworkin, Andrea, *Woman Hating* (New York: Dutton, 1974), p. 174.
3. Dworkin, *Woman Hating,* p. 183.

33

THE MYTH OF THE SEXUAL ATHLETE

DON SABO

The phrase "sexual athlete" commonly refers to male heterosexual virtuosity in the bedroom. Images of potency, agility, technical expertise, and an ability to attract and satisfy women come to mind. In contrast, the few former athletes who have seriously written on the subject, like Dave Meggyesy and Jim Bouton, and films such as *Raging Bull* and *North Dallas Forty,* depict the male athlete as sexually uptight, fixated on early adolescent sexual antics and exploitative of women. The former image of athletic virility, however, remains fixed within the popular imagination. Partly for this reason, little has been said about the *real* connections between sports and male sexuality.

Locker-Room Sex Talk

Organized sports were as much a part of my growing up as Cheerios, television, and homework. My sexuality unfolded within the all-male social world of sports where sex was always a major focus. I remember, for example, when as prepubertal boys I and my friends pretended to be shopping for baseball cards so we could sneak peeks at *Playboy* and *Swank* magazines at the newsstand. After practices, we would talk endlessly about "boobs" and what it must feel like to kiss and neck. Later, in junior high, we teased one another in the locker room about "jerking off" or being virgins, and there were endless interrogations about "how far" everybody was getting with their girlfriends.

Eventually, boyish anticipation spilled into *real* sexual relationships with girls, which, to my delight and confusion, turned out to be a lot more complex than I ever imagined. While sex (kissing, necking, and petting) got more exciting, it also got more difficult to figure out and talk about. Inside, all the boys, like myself, needed to love and be loved. We were awkwardly reaching

---

out for intimacy. Yet we were telling one another to "catch feels," be cool, connect with girls but don't allow yourself to depend on them. When I was a high-school junior, the gang in the weight room once accused me of being wrapped around my girlfriend's finger. Nothing could be further from the truth, I assured them, and to prove it I broke up with her. I felt miserable about this at the time, and I still feel bad about it.

Within the college jock subculture, men's public protests against intimacy sometimes became exaggerated and ugly. I remember two teammates, drunk and rowdy, ripping girls' blouses off at a party and crawling on their bellies across the dance floor to look up skirts. Then there were the late Sunday morning breakfasts in the dorm. We jocks would usually all sit at one table listening to one braggart or another describe his sexual exploits of the night before. Though a lot of us were turned off by such boasting, ego-boosting tactics, we never openly criticized it. Stories of raunchy, or even abusive sex, real or fabricated, were also assumed to "win points." A junior fullback claimed to have defecated on a girl's chest after she passed out during intercourse. There were also some laughing reports of "gang-bangs."

When sexual relationships were "serious," that is, tempered by love and commitment, the unspoken rule was silence. Rarely did we young men share our feeling about women, our uncertainty about sexual performance, or our disdain for the crudeness and insensitivity of some of our teammates. I now see the tragic irony in this: we could talk about casual sex and about using, trivializing, or debasing women, but frank discussions about sexuality that unfolded within a loving relationship were taboo. Within the locker-room subculture, sex and love were seldom allowed to mix. There was a terrible split between our inner needs and outer appearances, between our desire for love from women and our feigned indifference toward them.

Sex as a Sport

Organized sports provide a social setting in which gender (i.e., masculinity and femininity) learning melds with sexual learning. Our sense of "femaleness" or "maleness" influences the ways we see ourselves as sexual beings. Indeed, as we develop, sexual identity emerges as an extension of an already formed gender identity, and sexual behavior tends to conform to cultural norms. To be manly in sports, traditionally, means to be competitive, successful, dominating, aggressive, stoical, goal-directed, and physically strong. Many athletes accept this definition of masculinity and apply it in their relationships with women. Dating becomes a sport in itself, and "scoring," or having sex with little or no emotional involvement, is a mark of masculine achievement. Sexual relationships are games in which women are seen as opponents, and his scoring means her defeat. Too often, women are pawns in men's quests for status within the male pecking order. For many of us jocks, sexual relationships are about man as a hunter and woman as prey.

Why is this? What transforms us from boys who depend on women to men who misunderstand, alienate ourselves from, and sometimes mistreat women? One part of the problem is the expectation that we are supposed to act as though we want to be alone, like the cowboy who always rides off into the sunset alone. In sports, there is only one "most valuable player" on the team.

Too often this prevents male athletes from understanding women and their life experiences. Though women's voices may reach men's ears from the sidelines and grandstands, they remain distant and garbled by the clamor of male competition. In sports, communication gaps between the sexes are due in part to women's historical exclusion, from refusal to allow girls to play along with boys, and coaching practices which quarantine boys from the "feminizing" taint of female influence. One result of this isolation is that sexual myths flourish. Boys end up learning about girls and female sexuality from other males, and the information that gets transmitted within the male network is often inaccurate and downright sexist. As boys, we lacked a vocabulary of intimacy, which would have enabled us to better share sexual experiences with others. The locker-room language that filled our adolescent heads did not exactly foster insights into the true nature of women's sexuality—or our own, for that matter.

Performance and Patriarchy

Traditional gender learning and locker-room sexual myths can also shape men's lovemaking behavior. Taught to be "achievement machines," many athletes organize their energies and perceptions around a performance ethic that influences sexual relations. Men apply their goal-directedness and preoccupation with performance to their lovemaking. In the movie *Joe,* a sexually liberated woman tells her hard-hat lover that "making love isn't like running a fifty-yard dash."

Making intercourse the chief goal of sex limits men's ability to enjoy other aspects of sexual experience. It also creates problems for both men and their partners. Since coitus requires an erection, men pressure themselves to get and maintain erections. If erections do not occur, or men ejaculate too quickly, their self-esteem as lovers and men can be impaired. In fact, sex therapists tell us that men's preoccupation and anxieties about erectile potency and performance can cause the very sexual dysfunctions they fear.

It is important to emphasize that not only jocks swallow this limiting model of male sexuality. Sports are not the only social setting that promotes androcentrism and eroticism without emotional intimacy. Consider how male sexuality is developed in fraternities, motorcycle gangs, the armed forces, urban gangs, pornography, corporate advertising, MTV, magazines like *Playboy* or *Penthouse,* and the movies—to name but a few examples. These are not random and unrelated sources of traditional masculine values. They all originate in patriarchy.

Sexual relations between men and women in Western societies have been conducted under the panoply of patriarchal power. The sexual values that derive from patriarchy emphasize male dominance and the purely physical dimensions of the sex act while reducing women to delectable but expendable objects. An alternative conception of human sexuality, however, is also gaining ascendancy within the culture. Flowing out of women's experiences and based on egalitarian values, it seeks to integrate eroticism with love and commitment. It is deeply critical of the social forces that reduce women (and men) to sex objects, depersonalize relationships, and turn human sexuality into an advertising gimmick or commodity to be purchased. This is the sexual ethos proffered by the women's movement.

Today's young athletes don't seem as hooked as their predecessors on the hypermasculine image traditional sports have provided. Perhaps this is because alternative forms of masculinity and sexuality have begun to enter the locker-room subculture. More girls are playing sports than ever before, and coeducational athletic experiences are more common. As more women enter the traditionally male settings of sports, business, factories, and government, men are finding it more difficult to perceive women in only one dimension. Perhaps we are becoming better able to see them as fellow human beings and, in the process, we are beginning to search for alternative modes of being men.

What Do Men Really Want (or Need)?

Most of us do not really know what it is we want from our sexual lives. Men seem torn between yearning for excitement and longing for love and intimacy. On one side, we feel titillated by the glitter of corporate advertising. Eroticism jolts our minds and bodies. We're sporadically attracted by the simple hedonism of the so-called sexual revolution and the sometimes slick, sometimes sleazy veil of pornography, soft and hard. Many of us fantasize about pursuing eroticism without commitment; some actually live the fantasy. Yet more men are recently becoming aware of genuine needs for intimate relationships. We are beginning to recognize that being independent, always on the make and emotionally controlled, is not meeting our needs. Furthermore, traditional masculine behavior is certainly not meeting women's expectations or satisfying their emotional needs. More and more men are starting to wonder if sexuality can be a vehicle for expressing and experiencing love.

In our culture many men are suffering from sexual schizophrenia. Their minds lead them toward eroticism while their hearts pull them toward emotional intimacy. What they think they want rarely coincides with what they need. Perhaps the uneasiness and the ambivalence that permeate male sexuality are due to this root fact: the traditional certainties that men have used to define their manhood and sexuality no longer fit the realities of their lives. Until equality between the sexes becomes more of a social reality, no new model of a more humane sexuality will take hold.

As for me, I am still exploring and redefining my sexuality. Although I don't have all the answers yet, I do have direction. I am listening more closely to women's voices, turning my head away from the sexist legacy of the locker room, and pursuing a profeminist vision of sexuality. I feel good to have stopped pretending that I enjoy being alone. I never did like feeling alone.

34

USING PORNOGRAPHY

ROBERT JENSEN

How a question is asked has much to do with how it is answered. In investigating heterosexual men's use of pornography and the effects of that use, with a special concern about the possible links to sexual violence against women and children, should we ask, "Does pornography cause rape?" Or, should we ask, "Is pornography implicated in rape?" The form of the question suggests different research methods: The search for causation demands "science," while a concern for pornography's role in rape leaves us more open to listening to stories. Because science has no way to answer the question, predictably the search for causation and the use of science leads most everyone to conclude that we just don't know enough to say for sure. But a shift in emphasis and method offers a way to state not The Truth (or conclude we don't yet know The Truth), but a way to tell true stories and begin to make trustworthy moral and political decisions.

It is those stories I want to focus on in this chapter. I begin by critiquing contemporary culture's faith in science as the only valid route to knowledge about such issues and making a case for a narrative approach. I then present some of the available testimony of women about the role of pornography in their lives, followed by a report on my interviews with male pornography users and sex

---

Robert Jensen, "Using Pornography" from Gail Dines, Robert Jensen, and Ann Russo, *Pornography: The Production and Consumption of Inequality.* Copyright © 1998 by Routledge. Reprinted with the permission of Routledge, Inc., part of The Taylor & Francis Group. This selection contains excerpts from Mimi H. Silbert and Ayala M. Pines, "Pornography and Sexual Abuse of Women" from *Sex Roles* 10(11/12), 1984. Copyright © 1984. Reprinted with the permission of the authors and Plenum Publishing Corporation. Excerpts from Diana E. H. Russell, "Pornography and Violence: What Does the New Research Say?" from *Take Back the Night: Women on Pornography,* edited by Laura Lederer (New York: William Morrow, 1980). Reprinted with the permission of the author.

offenders. From those sources, I make some claims about the way in which pornography is implicated in the sexual abuse of women and children.

Science and Stories

We live in a culture that likes "science" answers provided by "experts," even when the questions are primarily about human values. Not surprisingly, experimental laboratory research has played an important role in the debate over pornography in the past three decades. Some advocates of regulation, both feminist and conservative, commonly cite studies showing links between pornography and violence, while opponents of regulation point to other studies that show no links or are inconclusive.

Experimental research on pornography looks at the effects of viewing or reading sexually explicit material. A typical study might expose groups of subjects to different types or levels of sexually explicit material for comparison to a control group that views nonsexual material. Researchers look for significant differences between the groups on a measure of, for example, male attitudes toward rape. One such measure could be subjects' assessments of the suffering experienced by sexual assault victims or subjects' judgments of the appropriate prison sentence for a rapist. From such controlled testing—measuring the effect of an experimental stimulus (exposure to pornography) on a dependent variable (attitudes toward women or sex) in randomly selected groups—researchers make claims, usually tentative, about causal relationships.

While there is disagreement among researchers about what has been "proved" by these studies (Zillmann, 1989; Linz, 1989), some researchers have drawn tentative conclusions. For example, Weaver (1992) reads the evidence to support the sexual callousness model, which suggests that exposure to pornography activates sexually callous perceptions of women and promotes sexually aggressive behavior by men (Zillman and Bryant, 1982; Zillman and Weaver, 1989). This appears to be the result of both pornography's promotion of a loss of respect for female sexual autonomy and the disinhibition of men's expression of aggression against women (Weaver, 1992, p. 307). A recent comprehensive meta-analysis of the experimental work found that (a) pictorial nudity reduces subsequent aggressive behavior, (b) material depicting nonviolent sexual activity increases aggressive behavior, and (c) depictions of violent sexual activity produce even more aggression (Allen, D'Alessio, and Brezgel, 1995). The researchers concluded that their analysis did not prove causality but made an argument for causality plausible.

Russell (1988, 1993b) makes such an argument. After reviewing the experimental research, she outlined four factors that link pornography to sexual violence. She argues that pornography (1) predisposes some males to desire rape or intensifies this desire; (2) undermines some males' internal inhibitions against acting out rape desires; (3) undermines some males' social inhibitions against acting out rape desires; and (4) undermines some potential victims' abilities to avoid or resist rape.

Taking a different approach, Donnerstein, Linz, and Penrod (1987) argue that only pornography that combines violence and sex has been shown to be harmful, and then only in the sense of immediate effects; they hesitate to speculate on the long term. They conclude there is not enough evidence to show that exposure to nonviolent pornography leads to increases in aggression against women under most circumstances, suggesting "some forms of pornography, under some conditions, promote certain antisocial attitudes and behavior" (Donnerstein, Linz, and Penrod, 1987, p. 171).

Three decades of experimental research on pornography's effects have not answered questions about pornography and sexual violence. Should we hold out hope that more experimental studies will provide answers? Should we privilege that research in the public policy debate over pornography? To do so marginalizes a type of knowledge that holds out much more promise for helping us understand pornography, sexuality, sexism, and violence.

Isolating with any certainty the effect of one particular manifestation of misogyny (pornography) in a culture that is generally misogynist, is hopeless. In fact, the danger of pornography is heightened exactly because it is only one part of a sexist system and because the message it carries about sexuality is reinforced elsewhere. What we learn from the testimony of women and men whose lives have been touched by pornography is how the material is implicated in violence against women and how it can perpetuate, reinforce, and be part of a wider system of woman-hating. Rather than discussing simple causation, we think of how various factors . . . make something inviting. In those terms, pornography does not cause rape but rather helps make rape inviting. Research can examine people's stories about their experiences with pornography and sexual violence to help us determine how close the relationship between the material and the actions is. The work of judging narratives can be difficult and sometimes messy; the process doesn't claim clear, objective standards that experimental research appears to offer. There are no experts to ask for authoritative answers; we all are responsible for building responsible and honest communal practices.

Women's Narratives

As the stories of women about sexual violence have been taken more seriously, society has gained new understandings of stranger and acquaintance rape, the sexual abuse of children, and battering. That same honoring of women's and children's voices is crucial to understanding pornography. The following accounts, taken from scholarly publications and political hearings, have not been given the attention needed to understand pornography. Collecting these narratives in one place helps to overcome the criticism that such evidence is simply anecdotal and of limited value. Placing them next to the narratives of men who have used pornography in the next section brings the picture into clearer focus.

It is important to remember that the feminist anti-pornography critique grew out of these stories. The harms listed in the civil rights ordinance—women coerced into making pornography, forced to view pornography, sexually assaulted in ways connected to pornography, defamed by pornography, and trafficked in pornography—were identified not by experimental research but by taking seriously the lives of women. The following excerpts illustrate these harms.

Silbert and Pines Study

The first few accounts are taken from a study of the sexual abuse of street prostitutes. Of the 200 women interviewed, 73 percent reported being raped, and 24 percent of those women mentioned that their assailants made reference to pornography (Silbert and Pines, 1984). What makes that figure even more significant is that those comments were unsolicited; the research design did not include questions about pornography. Mimi Silbert and Ayala Pines reported that the women's comments about pornography followed a similar pattern: "the assailant referred to pornographic materials he had seen or read and then insisted that the victims not only enjoyed the rape but also the extreme violence" (p. 863).

In a typical comment reported by the victims, an assailant told the woman:

> I know all about you bitches, you're no different; you're like all of them. I seen it in all the movies. You love being beaten. (He then began punching the victim violently.) I just seen it again in that flick. He beat the shit out of her while he raped her and she told him she loved it; you know you love it; tell me you love it (p. 864).

Another woman reported this experience:

> After I told him I'd turn him a free trick if only he'd calm down and stop hurting me, then he just really blew his mind. He started calling me all kinds of names, and then started screaming and shrieking like nothing I'd ever heard. He sounded like a wailing animal. Instead of just slapping me to keep me quiet, he really went crazy and began punching me all over. Then he told me he had seen whores just like me in [three pornographic films mentioned by name], and told me he knew how to do it to whores like me. He knew what whores like me wanted. . . . After he finished raping me, he started beating me with his gun all over. Then he said, "You were in that movie. You were in that movie. You know you wanted to die after you were raped. That's what you want; you want me to kill you after this rape just like [specific pornographic film] did" (p. 865).

The woman suffered vaginal and anal penetration, and a variety of injuries, including broken bones. The rapist also held a loaded pistol at her vagina, threatening to shoot, insisting this was the way she had died in the film he had seen.

Silbert and Pines also summarized the experience of one woman:

> [O]ne of the subjects in the study described a primitive movie projector her father had set up in the garage. He used to show himself and his friends pornographic movies to get them sexually aroused before they would rape her. (She was 9 at the time.) Her brother would also watch the movies when the father was gone; then he also abused her sexually (p. 865).

Russell Study

In her survey of more than 900 women about experiences with sexual violence, Diana E.H. Russell included the question, "Have you ever been upset by anyone trying to get you to do what they'd seen in pornographic pictures, movies, or books?" (Russell, 1980). Ten percent of the women reported at least one such experience. The following are some of the responses to that question (pp. 225–227):

> I was staying at this guy's house. He tried to make me have oral sex with him. He said he'd seen far-out stuff in movies, and that it would be fun to mentally and physically torture a woman. It was physical slapping and hitting. It wasn't a turn-on; it was more a feeling of being used as an object. What was most upsetting was that he thought it would be a turn-on.

> My husband enjoys pornographic movies. He tries to get me to do things he finds exciting in movies. They include twosomes and threesomes. I always refuse. Also, I was always upset with his ideas about putting objects in my vagina, until I learned this is not as deviant as I used to think. He used to force me or put whatever he enjoyed into me.

> He forced me to go down on him. He said he'd been going to porno movies. He'd seen this and wanted me to do it. He also wanted to pour champagne on my vagina. I got beat up because I didn't want to do it. He pulled my hair and slapped me around. After that I went ahead and did it, but there was no feeling in it.

> This guy has seen a movie where a woman was being made love to by dogs. He suggested that some of his friends had a dog and we should have a party and set the dog loose on the women. He wanted me to put a muzzle on the dog and put some sort of stuff on my vagina so that the dog would lick there.

> My old man and I went to a show that had lots of tying up and anal intercourse. We came home and proceeded to make love. He went out and got two belts. He tied my feet together with one, and with the other he kinda beat me. I was in the spirit, I went along with it. But when he tried to penetrate me anally, I couldn't take it, it was too painful. I managed to convey to him verbally to quit it. He did stop, but not soon enough to suit me.

> My boyfriend and I saw a movie in which there was masochism. After that he wanted to gag me and tie me up. He was stoned. I was not. I was really shocked at his behavior. I was nervous and uptight. He literally tried to force me, after gagging me first. He snuck up behind me with a scarf. He was hurting me with it and I started getting upset. Then I realized it wasn't a joke. He grabbed me and shook me by my shoulders and brought out some ropes, and told me to relax, and that I would enjoy it. Then he started putting me down about my feelings about sex, and my inhibitedness. I started crying and struggling with him, got loose, and kicked him in the testicles, which forced him down on the couch. I ran out of the house. Next day he called and apologized, but that was the end of him.

Minneapolis Hearings

The hearings before a committee of the Minneapolis City Council included the testimony of a number of women about how pornography was a part of sexual violence against them. As Catherine MacKinnon stated in her opening remarks at the hearing, "This hearing, this opportunity for our speech is precious and rare and unprecedented" (*Public Hearings,* 1983, p. 2). Opposition to the ordinance also was voiced at the hearings, but the following excerpts are a representative sample of the testimony of women who had been injured by pornography:

Ms. N was 21 years old at the time of the incident she described involving a man she was having a sexual relationship with:

> [My boyfriend] had gone to a stag party, this particular evening I was home alone in my apartment. He called me on the telephone and he said that he had seen several short pornographic films and that he felt very horny. . . . So he asked if he could come over specifically to have sex with me. I said yes because at that time I felt obligated as a girlfriend to satisfy him. I also felt that the refusal would be indicative of sexual, quote-unquote, hangups on my part and that I was not, quote-unquote, liberal enough. When he arrived he informed me that the other men at the party were envious that he had a girlfriend to fuck. They wanted to fuck too after watching the pornography. He informed me of this as he was

> taking his coat off. He then took off the rest of his clothes and had me perform fellatio on him. I did not do this of my own violition. He put his genitals in my face and he said, "Take it all." Then he fucked me on the couch in the living room. All this took about five minutes. And when he was finished, he dressed and went back to the party. I felt ashamed and numb and I also felt very used. This encounter differed from others previous. It was much quicker, it was somewhat rougher, and he was not aware of me as a person. There was no foreplay. It is my opinion that his viewing of the pornography served as foreplay for him (p. 41).

Ms. P described her husband's increasing interest in pornography as their marriage progressed. Out of a sense of duty, she accompanied him to pornographic movies and sex shows, but objected when he wanted to live out some of the pornography-based fantasies he had about group sex:

> He told me if I loved him I would do this. And that, as I could see from the things that he read me in the magazines initially, a lot of times women didn't like it, but if I tried it enough I would probably like it and I would learn to like it. And he would read me stories where women learned to like it. [The husband then tried to initiate sex with a third person.]. . . To prevent more of these group situations, which I found very humiliating and very destructive to my self-esteem and my feeling of self-worth as a person, to prevent these I agreed with him to act out in privacy a lot of those scenarios that he read to me. A lot of them depicting bondage and different sexual acts that I found very humiliating. About this time when things were getting really terrible and I was feeling suicidal and very worthless as a person, at that time any dreams that I had of a career in medicine were just totally washed away. I could not think of myself anymore as a human being. . . . He would read from pornography like a textbook, like a journal. In fact, when he asked me to be bound, when he finally convinced me to do it, he read in the magazine how to tie the knots and how to bind me in a way that I couldn't get out. And most of the scenes that we—most of the scenes where I had to dress up or go through different fantasies were the exact scenes that he had read in the magazines. [After their divorce, her husband remarried.]. . . And at the time I had seen him to finalize things on our divorce and get some of my last possessions, he showed me pictures of [his new wife] and said, "Do you want to see what she looks like?" They were pictures of her naked and in pornographic poses (pp. 43–46).

Ms. Q, a former prostitute, spoke about the ways in which pornography was a part of her life and the lives of other prostitutes in a group to which she belonged. All of them had been introduced to prostitution through pornography. In her testimony, she related the experiences of one of those women:

> Another story is a woman met a man in a hotel room in the 5th Ward. When she got there she was tied up while sitting in a chair nude. She was gagged and left alone in the dark for what she believed to be an hour. The man returned with two other men. They burned her with cigarettes and attached nipple clips to her breasts. They had many S-and-M magazines with them and showed her many pictures of women appearing to consent, enjoy, and encourage this abuse. She was held for 12 hours, continuously raped and beaten (p. 49).

Ms. X, a Native American woman, described how she was raped by two white men who made reference to a pornographic video game called "Custer's Revenge" in which a white Army officer scores points by raping Indian women:

> They held me down and as one was running the tip of his knife across my face and throat he said, "Do you want to play Custer's Last Stand?" It's great. You lose but you don't care, do you? You like a little pain, don't you, squaw?" They both laughed and then he said, "There is a lot of cock in Custer's Last Stand. You should be grateful, squaw, that All-American boys like us want you. Maybe we will tie you to a tree and start a fire around you." They made other comments, "The only good Indian is a dead Indian." "A squaw out alone deserves to be raped." Words that still terrorize me today. It may surprise you to hear stories that connect pornography and white men raping women of color. It doesn't surprise me. I think pornography, racism, and rape are perfect partners. They all rely on hate. They all reduce a living person to an object. A society that sells books, movies, and video games like "Custer's Last Stand" on its street corners gives white men permission to do what they did to me. Like they said, I'm scum. It is a game to track me down, rape and torture me (pp. 66–67).

Attorney General's Commission

No matter what one thinks of the politics of the Attorney General's Commission on Pornography (1986) and the recommendations of its report, the commission was a forum for women to tell about their experiences with pornography. The following excerpts are from the report of the group, which became known as the Meese Commission.

The report contains numerous accounts of how pornography is used to break down the resistance of children, especially girls, to sexual activity with adults. Among those accounts are:

> The father took a *Playboy* magazine and wrote her name across the centerfold. Then he placed it under the covers so she would find it

> when she went to bed. He joined her in bed that night and taught her about sex (p. 775, from letter to the commission from Oklahomans Against Pornography).

> A five year old child told her foster mother, "We have movies at home. Daddy shows them when mother is gone. The people do not wear clothes, and Daddy and I take our clothes off and do the same thing the people in the movies do" (p. 775, from letter to the commission from Oklahomans Against Pornography).

> I was sexually abused by my foster father from the time I was seven until I was thirteen. He had stacks and stacks of *Playboys.* He would take me to his bedroom or his workshop, show me the pictures, and say, "This is what big girls do. If you want to be a big girl, you have to do this, but you can never tell anybody." Then I would have to pose like the women in the pictures. I also remember being shown a *Playboy* cartoon of a man having sex with a child (p. 783, from anonymous letter to Women Against Pornography submitted to the commission).

> The incest started at the age of eight. I did not understand any of it and did not feel that it was right. My dad would try to convince me that it was ok. He would find magazines with articles and/or pictures that would show fathers and daughters and/or mothers, brothers and sisters having sexual intercourse. (Mostly fathers and daughters.) He would say that if it was published in magazines that it had to be all right because magazines could not publish lies.
>
> He would show me these magazines and tell me to look at them or read them and I would turn my head and say no. He would leave them with me and tell me to look later. I was afraid not to look or read them because I did not know what he would do. He would ask me later if I had read them and what they said or if I looked real close at the pictures. He would say, "See, it's okay to do because it's published in magazines" (p. 786, from letter to the commission).

In testimony and letters to the commission, a number of women described how they had been expected to perform specific acts in pornography:

> When I first met my husband, it was in early 1975, and he was all the time talking about *Deep Throat.* After we were married, he on several occasions referred to her performances and suggested I try to imitate her actions. . . . Last January . . . my husband raped me. . . . He made me strip and lie on our bed. He cut our clothesline up . . . and tied my hands and feet to the four corners of the bedframe. (All this was done while our nine month old son watched.) While he held a butcher knife on me threatening to kill me he fed me three strong tranquilizers. I started crying and because the baby got scared and also began crying, he beat my face and my body. I later had welts and bruises. He attempted to smother me with a

> pillow. . . . Then, he had sex with me vaginally, and then forced me to give oral sex to him (p. 775, anonymous letter to the Pornography Resource Center forwarded to the commission).

> I had not realized the extent of the harm that pornography had done to me until a year and a half ago when I was working on a photo montage of the kinds of pornography for an educational forum. I came across a picture of a position that my ex-husband had insisted we try. When we did, I found the position painful, yet he was determined that we have intercourse that way. I hemorrhaged for three days. I finally went to the doctor and I recall the shame I felt as I explained to him what had caused the bleeding (p. 778, from commission hearing in Chicago, Vol. II, p. 241F3).

A number of women also testified about how pornography was made without their consent or under duress. Many of them were young girls at the time, and some were prostitutes, including this woman:

> There was an apartment that I was sent to often. There were usually two to three men there. After I had sex with them, they would take pictures of me in various pornographic poses. When I was a young girl I didn't have the vocabulary to call them pornographers. I used to refer to them as "the photographers."
>
> On another occasion another young girl and myself were taken to an apartment to meet some men. We were told that they were gangsters and that we should be nice to them. When we arrived we were taken into a room that had a large bed at its center surrounded by lighting and film equipment. We were told to act out a "lesbian scene." After about fifteen minutes we were told to get dressed, that they couldn't use us. We were returned to [our city] unpaid. Again, it was only in retrospect as an adult that I realized I had been used in a commercial pornographic film loop (p. 781, from Washington, D.C., hearing, Vol. I, p. 180).

These are excerpts from the narratives of women who have been hurt by pornography. To acknowledge and believe them does not mean we have to pretend there aren't women who see pornography as a positive force in their lives (McElroy, 1995). To point out that some women have pornography forced on them is not to argue that no woman ever chooses to look at pornography. There is no need to pretend the women speak with one voice. We desperately need, however, to listen to these women, to acknowledge that their experiences are real, to acknowledge that they are real, and that they matter.

Men's Narratives

This section reports on 24 interviews I conducted with men about their pornography use. (I refer to men's "use" of pornography rather than their "viewing" of it, to make it more clear that men routinely use pornography as an aid in masturbation.) When analyzed in conjunction with narrative accounts of women's experiences presented in the previous section, these interviews illuminate and provide support for the feminist anti-pornography critique. These narratives give specific examples of how pornography can (1) be an important factor in shaping a male-dominant view of sexuality; (2) contribute to a user's difficulty in separating sexual fantasy and reality; (3) be used to initiate victims and break down their resistance to sexual activity; and (4) provide a training manual for abusers.

Again, it is important to be clear about what narratives can tell us. Such accounts do not prove that pornography causes sexual violence. They do, however, show how pornography is implicated in the abusive behavior of some men. That does not mean that all sex abusers use pornography or that all pornography users will become sex abusers; proponents of the feminist anti-pornography critique have never made such simplistic assertions. But the narratives do suggest that for some sex abusers, pornography is an integral part of their abuse (see also Wyre, 1992).

Pornography Users and Sex Offenders

This project included two sets of interviews. In both cases, subjects were not asked their names, though some wanted me to know their names (all names in this chapter are pseudonyms), and the interviews were tape recorded. The first 11 interviews (the "pornography users" group) were with men who responded to a classified ad in the personals section of the two Minneapolis-St. Paul entertainment weeklies seeking male interview subjects who "read or view any sexually explicit material."

The second set of interviews (the "sex offenders" group) was with 13 residents of the Alpha Human Services sex offender treatment program in Minneapolis. Those subjects volunteered after my project was explained to them by a staff member. Both the Alpha staff and I made it clear that their participation was voluntary, that I had no connection to the program, and that their responses would not affect their status in the program. All the interviews were conducted in an office in the Alpha residence facility.

After some general observations about the interviews, I will focus on several cases in which the links between pornography use and abuse were most clear.

The subjects in both groups were white and came from a variety of class backgrounds and occupations, including students, blue-collar workers, and professionals. The average age of the pornography users group was 34, with a range from 23 to 52. The average age of the sex offenders group was 36, with a range from 21 to 50. In a qualitative study with a small sample, the demographics of the group are not crucial. In general, however, both groups included a fairly even mix of Western religions (Protestant, Catholic, Jewish, and none), political affiliations (conservative, liberal, and no-interest), and marital status (single, married, separated, and divorced). The user group included two gay-identified men and one preoperative male-to-female transsexual, and the offender group included one gay-identified man. The other subjects identified themselves as heterosexual.

Members of the two groups had similar general experiences with pornography. The average age of first viewing for the pornography users group was 10, with a range of 3 to 18. The average age for the sex offenders was 12, with a range from 8 to 19. In the users group, all but one of the men had seen pornography before graduating from high school; in the offenders group, that was true for all but two. As adults, all the men in both groups had viewed the kind of material that is commonly called "hard-core" or "X-rated" pornography: oral, vaginal, and anal sex presented in graphic detail.

For the most part, there were few differences in the history of pornography consumption between users and offenders. The men told similar stories about their entry into the world of pornography, most often through magazines found at home or supplied by friends. The stolen copy of *Playboy* secreted away in a clubhouse or retrieved from dad's drawer was common for men in both groups. The progression from *Playboy* to *Hustler* and more explicit material was also much the same in both groups. The only noticeable difference is that several of the men in the offenders group said they had used overtly violent pornography or child pornography, while none of the men in the users group said they were interested in such material. But in terms of explicitness and frequency of use, both groups had similar ranges of experiences.

One important difference between the two groups is that the stories told by the sex offenders had been filtered through extensive group and individual therapy in the Alpha program. Of specific interest is the program's policy on pornography. Residents are not allowed to keep or use pornography, and such material is confiscated when they arrive. Use of it could result in expulsion from the program, which is a serious sanction; for most of the residents, expulsion would mean a return to jail or prison. In general, pornography is treated as part of a resident's problem in developing a healthy sex life. On rare occasions, counselors present pictures of nude people to residents who are unable to get beyond fantasizing about children. Such material is intended to illustrate more appropriate sex partners and "age their fantasies." These pictures show full nudity but do not depict sexual activity.

Also, acknowledging the harm done to victims and taking responsibility for it are key elements of Alpha treatment. One aspect of that is known as "running a process": When residents begin to fantasize about their abusive behavior, they are asked to take those actions to their logical conclusion and think about the harm the individuals will suffer because of it.

Does this therapy "taint" the interviews with the sex offenders? Of course the therapy affected how they understood their pornography use, just as any framework for understanding our experience affects how we report our experience. However, it is crucial to remember that both sets of interview subjects were working from a well-defined ideology that might "taint" their narratives. With the sex offenders, it was a view of pornography shaped by, among other things, therapy. For the pornography users, it was a view shaped by the general cultural ideology of sexual and expressive freedom, the idea that any sexual activity is, by definition, liberating. (This ideology of sexual liberation obviously exists alongside an ideology of repression that views sex as appropriate only in the context of a culturally sanctioned relationship, such as a heterosexual marriage, and the relative power of each ideology on any individual depends on a variety of factors.) The sex offenders were willing to consider the connections between pornography and their behavior. The pornography users generally didn't consider that as a possibility. If one considers it likely that the sex offenders have been led to certain conclusions by an ideology acquired in therapy, it is at least equally likely that the pornography users were led to their conclusions by a different ideology acquired from contemporary culture. In short, no one has access to an account of their behavior that has not been refracted through ideology. My job as a researcher is to make judgments about which subjects seemed to be making an honest effort to tell their truth as they understand it.

Before concentrating on the stories of several of the men for whom pornography was an important influence on their sexual behavior, it is important to note that most of the pornography users who reported heavy consumption also reported no abusive sexual behavior and that some of the sex offenders reported relatively light consumption and did not see a connection between the pornography and their offenses.

In the pornography user group, only one of the men reported behavior that clearly was abusive, which will be described later. More typical was "Bill," a 39-year-old heterosexual lawyer. He said he began using *Playboy* as a teenager, became a regular viewer of sexually explicit pornographic movies, and used pornographic videos or magazines an average of three times a week. He said his sexual relationships were with consenting adults and that while some of his sexual activity mirrored acts he had seen in pornography, he never purposefully tried to act on fantasies he had about bondage. In Bill's view:

> [T]here's a lot of people like myself who go in with coat and tie, very respectable people who use pornography. If our fantasies are carried out they're carried out only with consenting adults. And we harm no one.

"Pete," a 40-year-old predominantly heterosexual (he reported some sex with men in his past and a continued interest in homosexuality but said he no longer acted on it) office manager, also reported early exposure to pornographic magazines and a long-standing interest in pornographic movies. He said the movies don't spark actual sexual desire in him: "I [have] never sat and watched a movie and thought, God, I got to go jump in bed with a woman."

In the sex offender group, "Brian," a 50-year-old heterosexual insurance salesman who had sexually abused his stepdaughter when she was 10–15 years old, saw *Playboy* as a teenager and continued to occasionally look at pornographic magazines throughout his adult life. His only experience with explicit pornography—renting a half-dozen videos that he watched by himself—came after he had stopped having sex with his stepdaughter. Brian said those videos shaped his fantasies, increased the frequency of masturbation, and reduced the frequency of sexual contact with his wife, but he saw no connection between his earlier sporadic use of pornography and his abusive behavior.

Similarly, "Jack," a 43-year-old heterosexual electronics technician, saw *Playboy* in high school and continued to buy similar magazines as an adult. He reported seeing about a dozen explicit movies in his adult life, usually at the urging of a friend. "After you've seen one or two, you've seen all of them," he said, explaining his lack of interest. Jack said that he didn't want to ignore the possibility that his use of pornography played some role in his sexual abuse of his daughter but that he did not see direct connections.

The other men from the sex offenders group, however, saw some connection between pornography use and abusive acts, even when their use of pornography was not regular or extensive. What follows are more extensive descriptions of, and excerpts from, my interviews with sex offenders and pornography users. These were real cases in which it was most clear that their use of pornography and real-life sexual behavior were linked in some fashion.

Larry

"Larry" was a 41-year-old heterosexual man who had been divorced twice and had two children he had fathered and one stepdaughter. He was a biomedical technician and had two associate degrees. Larry grew up outside a large city and said that as a child he was sexually and emotionally abused by his mother and older sister. He was raised Catholic but had been a member of Lutheran and Baptist churches since then and considered himself Christian. He served in Vietnam as a Marine for two years and called himself an independent-leaning Democrat. Larry was convicted of sexually abusing his stepdaughter. He also said that much of what he considered to be consensual sex when he was a young adult involved force and the use of women who were drunk or stoned.

Larry's first exposure to sexual material came at age 9, when he found his father's *True Detective* magazine with a picture of a woman bound in bra and panties. He saw *Playboy* and other similar magazines sporadically through his teenage years. He saw his first sexually explicit pornographic movies while in the Marines after high school but did not start using pornography heavily until he was out of the service and working. A foreman at his shop introduced him to pornographic novels, especially ones involving bestiality. "And that's when it seemed like my appetite really got out of hand. And it never seemed to be enough," Larry said, describing an escalating use of pornography and an increase of what he called a desire for "deviant sex."

That phase of his life ended temporarily when he married for a second time, but after losing a job and a lot of his self-esteem, Larry said he returned to more heavy pornography use. In this period he began renting and copying sexually explicit videos, amassing a collection of about 15 movies. He said that his wife refused to watch them but that he could manipulate his stepdaughter into watching them, which was part of the process of grooming her for abuse that began when she was 8 years old. He used the tapes to break down her resistance, and he played them while he was abusing her:

> [The movies] played a big role, because I was fantasizing that I was, that my stepdaughter and myself were actually engaging in the same behavior that was on the tape. So, it was more like I was having my own private orgy right there, with the tape, too. And also, it was something for my daughter to concentrate on. It made it more exciting for me.

Elaborating on his use of pornography with his stepdaughter, Larry said the boundaries between the world of pornography and the real world became hazy:

> In fact, when I'd be abusing my daughter, I'd be thinking about some women I saw in a video. Because if I was to open my eyes and see my stepdaughter laying there while I was abusing her, you know, that wouldn't have been very exciting for me. You know, that would bring me back to the painful reality that I'm a child molester, where I'm in this reality of I'm making love or having intercourse with this beautiful woman from the video. The video didn't even come into my mind. It was just this beautiful person who had a beautiful body, and she was willing to do anything I asked.

Larry resisted putting sole, or even primary, blame for his abusive behavior on pornography. But he did see it as contributing to that abuse. He rejected the possibility that pornography could have been a catharsis:

> The pornography actually helped me work into my abuse, I feel. It accelerated that appetite for more. That's what I feel about it. Because, if I wouldn't have been introduced to a lot of this, and got my appetite whetted, then I don't think I'd thought of half the deviant things I've done.

Brad

"Brad" was a 34-year-old heterosexual heating-and-refrigeration service person who attended a vo-tech after high school. He grew up in a rural area, had no religious or political ties, and was separated from his second wife at the time of the interview. Brad said he met his first wife, a Korean woman who was working as a prostitute, while stationed overseas. She came to the United States to continue to work as a prostitute and divorced him. Brad was in the pornography-user group, but in many ways seemed more dangerous to himself and others than most of the men in the sex offender group. He was extremely volatile and seemed capable of violence; this was the only interview during which I felt concerned about my safety.

Brad first saw pornographic magazines at age 3 or 4 with his brothers, who also engaged in sex with him. Although he was not clear about some details, he seemed to have continued to use such magazines through his childhood, and as an adult he has been a regular customer of adult bookstores, using the 25-cent movie booths, renting and buying sexually explicit movies and magazines, calling phone-sex lines, and using prostitutes. He also said that he had videotaped sexual acts with his second wife and that he continued to look at the tapes.

Brad said he had been a shy teenager and avoided women. When he left high school and joined the Army, he began using pornography, from which he got most of his sexual education:

> I didn't know nothing about the world, or women, or, just what I read or saw. I was pretty deluded about women, that's for sure. I'm still fucked up about them. Didn't know how to talk to them or nothing, thought I just knew everything from reading everything.

These excerpts from my interview with Brad reflect the erratic nature of his comments. He alternatively seemed to enjoy and detest his life, sometimes referring to himself as a "sex addict" and other times mocking therapists he had seen. Pornography was a source of both pleasure and shame for him.

Brad said he had grown to prefer things that were rougher and more unusual. He liked pornography to "[s]how some nasty bitches. Be a little more vulgar about it." But after viewing such material, he said he felt ashamed: "As soon as the big excitement's over, I just come down."

Brad described his fantasies as more intense than actual sex with women and said he often had trouble controlling his fantasy life. Often that took the form of thinking of his own life in terms of pornographic scenes and then becoming upset with the resulting fantasy. He described how this affected his relationship with his second wife:

> I just freaked her out a few times, with some of the stuff I'd dream up, or whatever. I'd fantasize stuff that wasn't true, and I'd get myself so hyped up into believing it and calling up phone sex or reading in magazines or something, reading stories or watching stories or hearing stories about somebody's wife screwing around on him, and I'd think, "Yep, she's doing it to me too." Just my imagination.

Although he has thought about stopping his use of pornography, Brad said he often felt helpless. In the course of discussing that question, he often was unclear about whether he thought his actions were harmful to himself or others, again expressing his ambivalence about his sex practices. He described his use of pornography as "pretty much uncontrollable":

> It's like a fucking bee-line to the [adult bookstore]. I'll be thinking about something else and driving along, and all of a sudden there the fuck I am, sitting in front of the place. I've felt like, you know, why control it. Just fucking do what you want to do, and whatever. Pretty much constant my whole life. I think sex is fun and sex is good, stuff like that. I don't see anything wrong with that at all.

Brad put much of the blame for his sexual problems on women, suggesting that they flaunt their sexuality and use it against men: "And these women blame men for pornography and all this, and it's the women out there showing us their pussies, you know, taking all our money like fucking fools." Brad's misogyny was evident throughout the interview, as seen in this exchange:

> Q: Generally, what are the strongest emotions you feel connected with pornographic material? Just the gut-level feelings you have.
> A: Hate.
> Q: Hate for?
> A: Women.

When asked what he usually did after a trip to an adult bookstore, Brad replied, "Just go home and terrorize my wife, maybe," and laughed.

Brad said the attitude toward women in pornography—which he described as "Fucking bitch, man, that's all they're good for"—mirrored his own feelings toward women:

> Pretty much a general attitude toward women. [Sex] is about all they're really good for. That's what the movies and books and pornography tries to put across: The fucking woman is shit. That's what I see. See women screwing a couple different guys. And they have little skits, like, you know, the husband is gone and these guys come over and fuck the shit out of her for a few hours, and you know, stuff like that. I have a hard time with my own imagination without looking at all these other weirdoes' ideas about things.

Brad said he never raped a woman but once tried to force a female hitchhiker he picked up to have sex with him. But when she screamed, he let her go. I asked him twice if he thought he was capable of rape. The first time he replied, "I wouldn't do it, but my mind would say, 'Yea, that sounds exciting.'" The second time he said, "Not unless I was in the wrong mind. In my normal mind, I'm fine, you know. . . . Yea, I could see myself actually doing something like that."

Brad expressed conflicting opinions and emotions about his sex life and pornography use. But it was clear from his statements that pornography had been a part of his own sexual victimization as well as his sexual abuse of women. He had difficulty disengaging from the fantasy world of pornography and often imposed the narratives of pornography on his own life. The anger he felt toward women because of events in his life has been reinforced by the misogyny in pornography. These are particularly tentative conclusions that are hard to completely feel confident about because of Brad's erratic comments. But, I include his story because of the unrestrained way in which he talked about his experiences and my feeling that woven though the story were important illustrations of how pornography can influence a person.

David

"David" was a 37-year-old man who was married but since his arrest had come out as gay. He was divorced, had a daughter and son, and had been convicted of abusing the son from infancy. He had worked in sales and marketing and had completed about three years of college. He grew up in a large city. He said that after his arrest he was reevaluating his former commitment to Catholicism and to "ultra-conservative" political beliefs.

At age 12, David saw his first sexual material, a nudist magazine. He also began using *Playboy* magazines that friends had obtained. David said this was about the time he began playing cruel sexual games with his younger brother and sister. Shortly after that time, he saw explicit pornographic magazines that older boys in the neighborhood had. Those magazines were part of the manipulation and coercion that these 17- and 18-year old boys used to get David to perform oral sex on them: "I remember looking at the magazines and seeing women perform orally on these men, and that's what gave them the idea to have me do that to them." Several years after that, David began molesting male friends while on camping trips, fondling them while they slept in ways that left the friends feeling taken advantage of.

In his early 20s, when he was first married, David stopped using pornography. At about age 24 he started buying gay pornographic magazines, as his fantasy life became completely centered on sex with men. He rejected violent and sadomasochistic pornography, preferring magazines with no overt violence. By not allowing himself to use the material that depicted force:

> that was the way that I gave myself permission, because it didn't involve hurting people. It's part of the denial system I had. Both people wanted to do it, and nobody looked like they were getting hurt. So it was like the gateway into a tremendously hurtful kind of situation.

David said his fantasizing eventually became focused on the son his wife was carrying and that his use of pornography was fuel for those fantasies:

> Prior to [my wife] giving birth to our son, I had masturbated to fantasies of sexually abusing him. So by the time he was born, I had rehearsed over and over in my mind, what I wanted to do. And eventually I acted that out. And intermittently I used pornography to keep my sexual thing going. So, by the time he

> was born, he was a ready-made victim. In my mind, I had done it many times.

Like the other men in the sex offender group, David was reluctant to place blame for his actions on anything or anyone. But he described pornography as "the primary stepping stone that I took to sexually acting out." He used the concept of boundary violations to explain how he thought pornography had functioned in his life. This way of framing the question of pornography's effects was not part of his therapy at Alpha. David said he had been thinking of this on his own and had not discussed it at length with staff members:

> I think what this really is for me, was pornography was a way to begin violating people's boundaries. And it kind of went from there. Where, like when you look at somebody engaging in sex, I think it's a violation of boundaries. That's something that should be private. So, it's like I gave myself permission to voyeur on them. And the more I did that, the more liberties I took to actually act that stuff out. . . . It's a subtle thing. . . . I mean, I didn't realize I was, I didn't even know what boundaries were. I never had any idea of what that was. . . . Well, I brought things into the pornography. There was things in me, that, you know, it's like pornography and I [slapping his hands together], we got bound somehow. And I ended up taking permission over a long period of time to violate boundaries, and I think pornography was the beginning of that violation.

In David's case, his early use of pornography was connected both to his own abuse of his siblings and his abuse at the hands of older boys. In adulthood, pornography was a link in the chain of events that led to his abuse of his son.

Seeing Patterns

The purpose of these narratives is not to suggest that one interview can identify the causes of a person's history of sexual violence. My goal is not to focus on the individual and attempt a psychological profile to explain their actions. Obviously, many of these men experienced abuse as children that played a role in their own abusing, and countless other factors—including the culture's institutionalized misogyny—may have been crucial in leading them to abuse.

However, these interviews can help us identify ways in which pornography is an important actor in the construction of sexuality and gender relations—what men come to see as acceptable, exciting, or necessary sex. Pornography is not the only force in our society constructing sex and gender in these ways, but the use of it is a common experience in the lives of the men interviewed. These interviews identified specific ways in which the use of pornography can be linked to sexual violence. For these men, pornography was an important factor in shaping a male-dominant view of sexuality, and in several cases the material contributed to the men's difficulty in separating fantasy and reality. Pornography also was used by at least one of the men to initiate a victim and break down a young girl's resistance to sexual activity. For several others it was used as a training manual for abuse, as sexual acts and ideas from pornography were incorporated into their sex lives.

REFERENCES

Allen, Mike, Dave D'Alessio, and Keri Brezgel. (1995). A meta-analysis summarizing the effects of pornography II. *Human Communication Research,* 22(2), 258–283.

Attorney General's Commission on Pornography. (1986). *Final Report.* Washington, DC: US Department of Justice. [The report was published commercially as *Final Report of the Attorney General's Commission on Pornography.* (1986). Nashville, TN: Rutledge Hill Press, introduction by Michael J. McManus. Excerpts from the testimony before the commission were published in Phyllis Schlafly (Ed.). (1987). *Pornography's Victims.* Westchester, IL: Crossway Books.]

Donnerstein, Edward, Daniel Linz, and Steven Penrod. (1987). *The Question of Pornography.* New York: The Free Press.

Linz, Daniel. (1989). Exposure to sexually explicit materials and attitudes toward rape: a comparison of study results. *Journal of Sex Research,* 26(1), 50–84.

McElroy, Wendy. (1995) *XXX: A Woman's Right to Pornography.* New York: St. Martin's Press.

Public Hearings on the Proposed Minneapolis Civil Rights Anti-Pornography Ordinance. (1983). Minneapolis: Organizing Against Pornography. The transcript of the hearings was also published as: *Pornography and Sexual Violence: Evidence of the Links.* (1988). London: Everywoman.

Russell, Diana E. H. (1993b). *Against Pornography: Evidence of Harm.* Berkeley: Russell Publications (2018 Shattuck #118; Berkeley, CA 94704).

Russell, Diana E. H. (1988). Pornography and rape: a causal model. *Political Psychology,* 9(1), 41–73.

Russell, Diana E. H. (1980). Pornography and violence: what does the new research say? In Laura Lederer (Ed.), *Take Back the Night: Women on Pornography* (pp. 218–238). New York: William Morrow.

Silbert, Mimi H., and Ayala M. Pines. (1984). Pornography and sexual abuse of women. *Sex Roles,* 10(11/12), 857–869.

Weaver, James. (1992). The social science and psychological research evidence: perceptual and behavioural consequences of exposure to pornography. In Catherine Itzin (Ed.), *Pornography: Women, Violence and Civil Liberties* (pp. 284–309). Oxford: Oxford University Press.

Wyre, Ray. (1992). Pornography and violence: working with sex offenders. In Catherine Itzin (Ed.), *Pornography: Women, Violence and Civil Liberties* (pp. 236–247). Oxford: Oxford University Press.

Zillmann, Dolf. (1989). Pornography research and public policy. In Dolf Zillmann and Jennings Bryant (Eds.), *Pornography: Research Advances and Policy Considerations* (pp. 387–403). Hillsdale, NJ: Lawrence Erlbaum.

Zillmann, Dolf, and James B. Weaver. (1989). Pornography and men's sexual callousness toward women. In Dolf Zillmann and Jenning Bryant (Eds.), *Pornography: Research Advances and Policy Considerations* (pp. 95–125). Hillsdale, NJ: Lawrence Erlbaum.

Zillmann, Dolf, and Jennings Bryant. (1982). Pornography, sexual callousness, and the trivialization of rape. *Journal of Communication,* 32(4), 10–21.

35

THE SEX EXPERTS VERSUS ANN LANDERS

BARRY A. BASS AND SUSAN R. WALEN

Judging from the reaction in the media of our fellow professional sex educators and therapists to the findings of an informal two-question sex survey conducted by Ann Landers, one would have thought that we had all suffered a case of collective sexual amnesia. Not since the publication of the Hite Report in 1976 can we recall such a wave of disbelief and verbal hyperbole. A return to Victorian morality and widespread sexual boredom are but two of the dire predictions made in recent days by media sex experts. All this because Ann Landers reported in her nationally syndicated column that of more than 90,000 women responding to her poll, 72% said they would be willing to forego "the act" in return for being held close and treated tenderly.

One New York sex therapist who hosts a sexual counseling television program was quoted in a Baltimore newspaper (Sex Versus Hugs, 1985) as having said that "this will get us back to the Victorian age. It's dangerous to say a high percentage of women do not expect sexual activity but only caressing." It is unclear from that statement exactly who would be in danger; the woman, the man, their relationship, the species, or the future of sex therapy?

Jim Peterson who writes the Playboy advisor for *Playboy* magazine, said the poll could give people permission to "be boring and just roll over in bed and go to sleep." Here we see quite clearly the not yet discarded sexist belief that if left to the desires of women, sex would be nothing more than a perfunctory goodnight kiss. Women refusing to perform their "conjugal duties" and widespread male sexual frustration is the scenario the enlightened editors at Playboy seem to fear, were the Landers findings to be widely disseminated.

Notwithstanding the obvious methodological flaws and the bias of the sample in the Landers poll, the results should come as no surprise to the readers of this journal. At least since the publication of the first Kinsey survey we have known that for most American couples sex includes much more than the act of intercourse. Respondents to polls commissioned by *Redbook, Playboy,* and Consumers Union have consistently reported that most sexual encounters generally include sexual activities in addition to intercourse. In fact it is not unusual for sex therapists to treat individuals who are needlessly

Barry A. Bass and Susan R. Walen, "The Sex Experts Versus Ann Landers" from *Journal of Sex Education and Therapy* 11, no. 2 (Fall/Winter 1985).

distressed over the fact that they prefer non-coital sex to "the act" itself. Thus, rather than coming as a surprise, the Landers findings only confirm what women and men have been telling us all along—that any given sexual encounter can be satisfying, with or without intercourse.

What troubles us most, however, are comments such as those of one nationally syndicated radio psychologist who was quoted as saying that she "doubts that 72% of all women would be happy without sex" ("Sex Versus Hugs," 1985). The distressing part of that quote is the implied equating of "intercourse" and "sex." If our experience is representative of other therapists, a significant proportion of therapy sessions is spent attempting to disabuse our clients of that very notion. We frequently hear ourselves telling our clients that sex is more than intercourse, more than orgasm, more than any one behavior. We believe sex to be more usefully perceived as a comprehensive term which includes but is not limited to the following concepts: body awareness, sensuality, pleasure seeking, love and caring, sex role and gender identification, cuddling, stroking, hugging, necking, petting, genital arousal, genital pleasuring, intercourse and orgasm. In fact we often begin a course of sex therapy by placing a temporary ban on intercourse, thereby forcing the couple to attend to the multitude of other behaviors available to them in a loving and sensual encounter.

Thus, we believe intercourse is only a small element of "sex" and more importantly, intercourse is not "where it's at" for most women.* Mind you, many women tell us that intercourse can be a lovely experience. When artfully and lovingly done, the woman can feel a closeness with her partner, an appreciation by her partner, a true sense of intimacy with her partner. Holding him inside her body is a very special notion indeed. Unfortunately, however, intercourse is not the best way for most women to achieve sexual release. It is probably no coincidence that in 1976, 70% of Hite's sample said they do not reach orgasm with intercourse and in 1985, 72% of Lander's sample said they could live happily without it.

It is readily rather simple, we tell our clients, if only we would bother to learn our anatomy. Intercourse provides appropriate stimulation to *his* sex organ, timed to *his* rhythmic needs. *Her* sex organ, the clitoris, is usually—and quite literally—left out in the cold. She will need to teach her partner how to provide appropriate stimulation to her sex organ, or more simply, take matters into her own hands.

What is the message we wish to communicate to our fellow sex educators and therapists? Certainly we are not saying that intercourse is not or cannot be an important ingredient of a satisfying sex life. What is or is not sexually satisfying for any particular woman is not the issue here. The more relevant

---

*It is worth noting that after four decades of sex research, data on the percentage of times couples engage in loving and orgasmic sex play that does not include intercourse are not readily available. Even in our "values neutral" surveys, researchers have simply not thought to ask respondents how many of their sexual encounters do not include "the act" of intercourse.

point is that even in the mid 1980s, in the aftermath of the "sexual revolution," our fellow professionals (who frequently serve as the voice for what the rest of society is thinking) can still become irrationally upset when hearing the truth about the way things are for many women. This reaction is a more telling commentary about our sexual enlightenment than any individual finding reported by Kinsey, Masters and Johnson, Hite, or Ann Landers.

REFERENCE

Sex versus hugs: Landers survey raises questions. *Baltimore Sun,* January 16, 1985, pp. 1b; 2b.

36

REPRODUCTIVE RIGHTS
A Disability Rights Issue

MARSHA SAXTON

In recent years, the women's movement has broadened its definition of "reproductive rights" to include not only abortion, but all aspects of sexuality, procreation, and parenthood. The priorities of the National Abortion Reproductive Rights Action League also reveal this broader agenda: protecting adolescent reproductive health, preventing unintended pregnancy and sexually transmitted disease, eliminating restrictive or coercive reproductive health policies, and promoting healthy pregnancy and early childhood health.

Some women may take for granted birth control, reproductive health care, and sex education, forgetting that people with different life experiences based on class, race, or physical or mental ability may not have access to these fundamental aspects of reproductive freedom. But for people with disabilities, *all* the reproductive rights are still at stake.

For centuries, the oppression of people with disabilities has denied us "choice": choice about who should be regarded as "a sexual being," who should have babies, which babies should be born, which babies should be allowed to live after they're born, who should raise these babies into adulthood. These choices were made, for the most part, by others. People with disabilities

Marsha Saxton, "Reproductive Rights: A Disability Rights Issue," from *Sojourner: The Women's Forum* (1995). Reprinted with the permission of the author.

are beginning to demand a say in these decisions now that the Americans with Disabilities Act (ADA) has forced the public to perceive our issues as civil rights issues. In the decades to come, we hope to see a transformation in the public's perception of disability and of people with disabilities. The issue of reproductive rights can serve as a catalyst for this transformation.

The stereotype of asexuality is slowly lifting. There are now a few disabled characters in the popular literature and media who are portrayed as sexual beings participating in intimate activities. (Some of these movie personalities, such as actress Marlee Maitlin, themselves are deaf or have physical disabilities. However, most disabled characters on TV or in the movies are still played by non-disabled actors.)

New and complex issues are emerging in regard to disability and procreation. Many relate to new developments in reproductive technologies. Others reflect changing social values. What follows is a discussion of how these new issues affect people with disabilities.

Reproductive Health Care

Because of patronizing attitudes about disabled people, many medical practitioners and health care facilities do not consider offering reproductive health care services to their patients who have disabilities. Many people with disabilities or with chronic illness, because of the "preexisting condition" exclusion in most health insurance, have been denied access to *any* health care, not only reproductive health care. There are few medical or nursing schools that offer any training on the reproductive health of people with disabilities. Only in the last five years has there been any research on the effects of various birth control methods for people with different kinds of disabilities or chronic illness, and these studies are limited, often focusing only on spinal cord injury. Even people with the more common disabling conditions like diabetes, arthritis, or multiple sclerosis have little or no information about whether they should or shouldn't use particular methods of birth control.

In Chicago, a group of disabled women have created a "disability accessible" gynecological clinic through the Chicago Rehabilitation Institute and the Prentice Women's Hospital, staffed with practitioners who have been trained to serve disabled women. The Health Resource Center for Women with Disabilities is unique. One day a week, it offers accessible core gyn services for women with disabilities and now serves more than 200 women. The staff includes nurse practitioners and midwives; and a nurse who has a disability has been hired. The clinic program plans to expand its resources to include a project director to monitor clinic services and to oversee a library with health-related videos and publications. It will also add an 800 telephone number staffed by a woman with a disability to respond to questions about accessible health care services. The center has initiated research directed at documenting the medical experiences of women with disabilities and improving services for traditionally underserved populations, including developmentally disabled, learning disabled, and mentally retarded women.

Sex Education

Disabled children and adults need information about dating, sex, menstruation, pregnancy, birth control, AIDS, and other sexually transmitted diseases. Attitudes have changed, and increasingly, parents and educators are recognizing that disabled children need sex education. But this is not the norm. Disabled children are still often overprotected by adults who don't know how to teach them about "the facts of life." Questions such as the following tend to provoke confusion: how can blind children be given information about gender anatomy? How should retarded children be told about AIDS? How can deaf children, children who use wheelchairs, or any child who may have felt the stigma of disability be encouraged to interact positively with non-disabled and disabled peers and to learn positive sexual self-esteem? Many disabled adults never received important information about sex. They are vulnerable to confusing or dangerous misinformation and serious difficulties with their own sexuality, difficulties that result not from actual physical limitations but simply from exclusion from information and experience.

Marriage Disincentives

In the United States, people with disabilities who receive certain kinds of Social Security or Medicaid benefits are discouraged from getting married by threat of reduced or eliminated benefits. These "marriage disincentives" (like "employment disincentives," which discourage disabled people from employment by threat of reduced medical coverage) reveal the serious disability discrimination fundamentally built into our disability policies. If an SSI (Supplemental Security Income) recipient marries, his or her spouse's earnings are considered income, thus reducing the recipient's benefits, jeopardizing essential medical and personal care attendant services, and often placing enormous financial burden on the couple to finance prohibitively expensive services or equipment. The current law has the effect of forcing people with disabilities to accept "living together" as temporary sweethearts rather than an adult, community-sanctioned marriage. A recent attempt by disability rights advocates to urge Donna Shalala of the federal Department of Health and Human Services to legislate a more equitable system failed. While the outward rationale for the law is to save taxpayer money on people who could be supported by a spouse (based on the assumption that two can live as cheaply as one), social scientists and disability rights activists suspect that drafters of these marriage disincentive laws were also intending to thwart marriage and potential procreation for disabled people.

"Reproducing Ourselves"

The very idea of disabled persons as parents scares some people and exposes discriminatory attitudes that might otherwise remain hidden. Acceptance of disabled people as parents simply requires the larger community's acceptance of us as human beings. By denying our rights to be mothers and fathers, it is not only our competence to care for our young, but our very existence, our desire to "reproduce ourselves," that is forbidden.

In late 1991, TV news anchor Bree Walker, who has a genetic disability and who was pregnant, became the brunt of a call-in radio talk show when the host Jane Norris asked listeners, "Should disabled people have children?" Callers aired their opinions about whether Walker should have her baby or, as Norris posed the question, "Is it 'fair' to bring a child with a disability into the world?" The incident became the focal point of the disabled women's community's challenge to the idea that people with disabilities should not be born.

Qualifications for Parenthood

The Earls are a married Michigan couple, both severely disabled with cerebral palsy. They had a baby, Natalie, and sought assistance from the Michigan Home Help Program in providing physical care for the infant. Their desire to raise their own child and to demonstrate their competence as loving parents was thwarted by state regulations that bar the personal care assistant (PCA) of a disabled client from touching the client's child during paid work hours. One result of this regulation seems to be that disabled people who rely on the PCA program for help in daily living cannot have children.

Of course, people with disabilities must take seriously the responsibilities of adult sexuality and the potential for pregnancy and parenthood. We must also educate ourselves, the disability community, and our families and friends about what it means to be a parent and be disabled. And we must be prepared to take on the discriminatory policies of a variety of institutions: medical, social services, legal, and media. But we must also do battle within ourselves. We must overcome the voices we've internalized that say, "You can't possibly do this, you can't be good parents, and you don't deserve the benefits or the assistance required to raise your own children."

In Berkeley, California, an agency called Through the Looking Glass offers the first program specifically designed to assist parents with disabilities in skills development, community resources, and peer support. Looking Glass also publishes a newsletter, which can be ordered at [2198 Sixth St., Suite 100, Berkeley, CA 94710].

Custody Struggles

Tiffany Callo is a young woman who wanted to raise her newborn son. Because of her cerebral palsy, the California Department of Social Services challenged her ability to care for the child. Armed with lawyers and court orders, the department refused to allow her to demonstrate her parenting skills in an appropriate environment that would enable her to show the creative approaches she had developed to handle the baby. *Newsweek* reporter Jay Mathews picked up her story, and Callo became a spokesperson for the cause of mothers with disabilities who fight for the right to raise their own children. Social service and child protection agency professionals need training and awareness to allow them to perceive the *abilities* of disabled parents, not only the stereotyped limitations.

Adoption

A large number of children adopted or waiting for adoption are disabled. Many disabled adults were adopted or placed in foster homes. It is still largely the case that adoption agencies do not consider disabled people as prospective parents for either disabled or non-disabled children. We need to challenge this stereotype that people with disabilities cannot be good adoptive parents. A few adoption agencies are changing policies, allowing disabled people to adopt, and in some cases even encouraging disabled adults to adopt children with disabilities. For example, Adoption Resource Associates in Watertown, Massachusetts, has taken a special interest in prospective disabled parents and makes specific mention in their brochure that they do not discriminate on the basis of disability in their placement services.

Sterilization Abuse

Consider this story of a woman with a psychiatric disability: "When I was twenty, I got pregnant by my boyfriend at the state mental school. Of course, there was no birth control for patients. We weren't allowed to have sex, but it went on all the time, even between patients and attendants. A doctor forced my mother to sign a paper giving me an abortion, even though I wanted to give up the baby for adoption. When I woke up, I found out I had had a hysterectomy. Maybe I couldn't take care of the baby then, but nobody even asked me what I wanted to do, or what I hoped for when I got older."

When a guardian or medical professional decides that people labeled retarded, mentally ill, or with other disabilities should not be parents, sterilization without consent may occur. Often, guardians or other decision makers who intervene on behalf of these disabled people have little exposure to the Independent Living Movement, or other community disability resources. As disabled people, we need to be empowered to make our own decisions regarding sexuality and procreation.

Abortion

Women with disabilities have reported significant difficulties with regard to abortion. These include being pressured to undergo an abortion because it is assumed that a disabled woman could not be a good parent, or, conversely, being denied access to abortion because a guardian decides the woman was incapable of making her own reproductive choices. Sometimes, after birth, a disabled woman's child is taken away from her. Women with disabilities experience the same kinds of abortion access difficulties as non-disabled women, but these difficulties are often magnified by disability discrimination.

Prenatal Screening

Scientific advances in the field of genetics have created technologies that can detect an increasing number of genetic conditions in the womb. While the general public seems to regard this medical technology as a wonderful advance and a way to reduce the incidence of disability and improve the quality of life, people with disabilities often have a very different view. As revealed in the Bree Walker case mentioned above, the unchallenged assumption often accompanying the use of these screening tests is that the lives of people with genetically related disabilities (such as muscular dystrophy, Down syndrome, cystic fibrosis, sickle cell anemia, and spina bifida) are simply not worth living and are a burden that families and society would rather not endure. The options to abort a fetus who might die early in life, or to abort in order to preclude the birth of a child with severe disabilities, are framed as "reproductive options." But in this era of health care cost containment, the notion of controlling costs by eliminating births of disabled babies may become a requirement, rather than an option. Then it ceases to be reproductive freedom and becomes quality control of babies—eugenics. The availability of these tests reinforces these notions, and the tests are actually marketed to women and to health care providers on this basis. Women are increasingly pressured to abort a fetus identified as disabled. Real choice must include the right to bear children with disabilities.

We in the disabled community must voice our ideas about selective abortion and attest to the true value of our lives. Only when a valid picture of the quality of our lives is available can prospective parents make choices about the use of tests for genetic disabilities in fetuses.

The Reproductive Rights Movement

The women's movement has begun to reach out to women with disabilities as a group. Women's organizations have begun to understand and challenge their own discriminatory attitudes and behaviors. More and more events in the women's movement are beginning to be wheelchair accessible and interpreted for the hearing impaired. But we have a long way to go to make the women's community fully welcoming of disabled people. This is a good time to get involved and share our thinking and energies. To be fully integrated into society, we must get involved and take leadership in all movements, and the movement for reproductive health care and real choice is an especially important one for people with disabilities to take on.

As disabled people, we have unique perspectives to share. Our views can enlighten everyone about the fundamental issues of sexuality and reproduction. We have gained much knowledge and experience with medical intervention, asking for and effectively managing help, dealing with bureaucracy, and fighting for access and power. Other controversial issues to which we can contribute our thinking include surrogate motherhood, population concerns, birthing technologies, artificial insemination, and *in vitro* fertilization.

The movement for reproductive rights needs to include people with disabilities as much as disabled people need to be included in the movement.

37

THE IMPACT OF MULTIPLE MARGINALIZATION

PAULA C. RUST

One's sexuality is affected not only by the sexual norms of one's culture of origin but also by the position of one's culture of origin vis-à-vis the dominant culture of the United States. For individuals who belong to marginalized racial-ethnic, religious, or socioeconomic groups, the effects are numerous. Marginalized groups sometimes adopt the attitudes of the mainstream; other times, they reject these attitudes as foreign or inapplicable. McKeon (1992) notes that both processes shape the sexual attitudes of the white working class. On the one hand, the working class absorbs the homophobic attitudes promoted by the middle- and upper-class controlled media. At the same time, working-class individuals are rarely exposed to "liberal concepts of tolerance" taught in institutions of higher education which help moderate overclass heterosexism. On the other hand, working-

---

class sexual norms are less centered around the middle-class notion of "propriety" — a value that working-class individuals cannot as readily afford. The result is a set of sexual norms that differs in complex ways from those facing middle- and upper-class bisexuals.

In marginalized racial and ethnic groups, racism interacts with cultural monosexism and heterosexism in many ways. In general, the fact of racism strengthens ethnic communities' desires to preserve ethnic values and traditions, because ethnicity is embodied and demonstrated via the preservation of these values and traditions. Tremble, Schneider, and Appathurai (1989) wrote, "After all, one can abandon traditional values in Portugal and still be Portuguese. If they are abandoned in the New World, the result is assimilation" (p. 225). Thus, ethnic minorities might cling even more tenaciously to traditional cultures than Euro-Americans do, because any cultural change reflects not a change in ethnic culture but a loss of ethnic culture. To the extent that ethnic values and traditions restrict sexual expression to heterosexuality, ethnic minority bisexuals will be under particular pressure to deny same-sex feelings in demonstration of ethnic loyalty and pride. Attempts to challenge these values and traditions by coming out as bisexual will be interpreted as a challenge to ethnic culture and identity in general.

Because homosexuality represents assimilation, it is stigmatized as a "white disease" or, at least, a "white phenomenon." Individuals who claim a bisexual, lesbian, or gay identity are accused of buying into white culture and thereby becoming traitors to their own racial or ethnic group. Previous researchers have found the attitude that lesbian or gay identity is a white thing among African Americans and Hispanics and the attitude that homosexuality is a "Western" behavior among Asian Americans (Chan, 1989; Espin, 1987; H., 1989; Icard, 1986; Matteson, 1994; Morales, 1989). In the current study, the association of gayness with whiteness was reported most often by African American respondents. One African American woman wrote that "when I came out, it was made clear to me that my being queer was in some sense a betrayal of my 'blackness.' Black women just didn't do 'these' kinds of things. I spent a lot of years thinking that I could not be me and be 'really' black too." Morales (1990) found that Hispanic men choose to identify as bisexual even if they are exclusively homosexual, because they see gay identity as representing "a white gay political movement rather than a sexual orientation or lifestyle" (p. 215). A Mexican woman in the current study wrote that she has "felt like . . . a traitor to my race when I acknowledge my love of women. I have felt like I've bought into the White 'disease' of lesbianism." A Puerto Rican woman reported that in Puerto Rico homosexuality is considered an import from the continental States. Chan (1989) found that Asian Americans tend to deny the existence of gays within the Asian American community, Wooden et al. (1983) reported this attitude among Japanese Americans, and Carrier et al. (1992) found denial of the existence of homosexuality among Vietnamese Americans who considered homosexuality the result of seduction by Anglo-Americans. Tremble et al.

(1989) suggested that viewing homosexuality as a white phenomenon might permit ethnic minority families to accept their LesBiGay members, while transferring guilt from themselves to the dominant society.

Ironically, whereas racism can strengthen commitment to ethnic values and traditions, it can also pressure ethnic minorities to conform to mainstream values in an effort to gain acceptance from culturally dominant groups. Because members of ethnic minorities are often perceived by Euro-Americans as representatives of their entire ethnic group, the nonconformist behavior of one individual reflects negatively on the whole ethnic group. For example, African American respondents reported that homosexuality is considered shameful for the African American community because it reflects badly on the whole African American community in the eyes of Euro-Americans. A similar phenomenon exists among lesbians and gays, some of whom chastise their more flamboyant members with "How can you expect heterosexual society to accept us when you act like *that!?*" As one Black bisexual woman put it, "Homosexuality is frowned upon in the black community more than in the white community. It's as if I'm shaming the community that is trying so hard to be accepted by the white community."

The fact of ethnic oppression also interacts with particular elements of ethnic minority culture in ways that affect bisexuals. Specifically, the emphasis on the family found in many ethnic minority cultures is magnified by ethnic oppression in two ways. First, oppression reinforces the prescription to marry and have children among minorities which, for historical reasons, fear racial genocide (Greene, 1994; Icard, 1986). Second, the fact of racism makes the support of one's family even more important for ethnic minority individuals. As Morales (1989) put it, the "nuclear and extended family plays a key role and constitutes a symbol of their ethnic roots and the focal point of their ethnic identity" (p. 225). Ethnic minority individuals learn techniques for coping with racism and maintaining a positive ethnic identity from their families and ethnic communities; to lose the support of this family and community would mean losing an important source of strength in the face of the ethnic hostility of mainstream society (Almaguer, 1993; Chan, 1992; Icard, 1986). Thus, ethnic minority bisexuals have more to lose if they are rejected by their families than do Euro-American bisexuals. At the same time, they have less to gain because of the racism of the predominantly Euro-American LesBiGay community. Whereas Euro-American bisexuals who lose the support of their families can count on receiving support from the LesBiGay community instead (albeit limited by the monosexism of that community), ethnic minority bisexuals cannot be assured of this alternative source of support.

Because of fear of rejection within their own racial, ethnic, or class communities, many bisexuals—like lesbians and gay men—remain in the closet among people who share their racial, ethnic, and class backgrounds. For example, an African American-Chicana "decided to stay in the closet instead of risk isolation and alienation from my communities." Sometimes, individuals who remain closeted in their own racial-ethnic or class communities participate in the mainstream lesbian, gay, and bisexual community, which is primarily a Euro-American middle-class lesbian and gay community. Such individuals have to juggle two lives in two different communities, each of which is a valuable source of support for one aspect of their identity, but neither of which accepts them completely. Among people of their own racial, ethnic, or class background, they are not accepted and often not known as bisexuals, and among Euro-American lesbians and gays, they encounter both monosexism and class and racial prejudice or, at the least, a lack of support and understanding for the particular issues that arise for them because of their race, ethnicity, or class. Simultaneously, like other members of their racial, ethnic, or class community, they have to be familiar enough with mainstream Euro-American heterosexual culture to navigate daily life as a racial or ethnic minority; so they are, in effect, tricultural (Lukes & Land, 1990; Matteson, 1994; Morales, 1989). This situation leads not only to a complex social life but might also promote a fractured sense of self, in which one separates one's sexual identity from one's racial identity from one's American identity and experiences these identities as being in conflict with each other, just as are the communities that support each identity. Some individuals attempt to resolve this dilemma by prioritizing allegiances to these communities (Espin, 1987; Johnson, 1982; Morales, 1989), a response that Morales (1989, 1992) sees as a developmental stage preceding full integration of one's ethnic and sexual identities. More detailed descriptions of the antagonism between ethnic and gay communities and its effect on sexual minority individuals can be found in Gutiérrez and Dworkin (1992), Icard (1986), and Morales (1989, 1992).

Other bisexuals respond to the conflict between their racial/ethnic, class, and sexual communities by leaving their communities of origin in favor of mainstream LesBiGay communities. For most ethnic minority bisexuals, however, this does not solve the problem. For example, an Orthodox Jew who grieves her lost connection to the Jewish community wrote, "I still do not feel that my Jewish life and my queer life are fully integrated and am somewhat at a loss." This is true despite the large numbers of Jewish bisexuals, gays, and lesbians she has met, because "most Jewish people in the queer community are highly assimilated and are no help to me." The identities available for ethnic minorities in the LesBiGay community sometimes consist of racialized sexual stereotypes. Icard (1986), for example, describes the "Super Stud" and "Miss Thing" identities available for African American men in the gay male community. Such stereotypical identities limit and distort the potential for integrated identity development among ethnic minority bisexuals.

Finally, some people from cultures that stigmatize homosexuality choose neither to closet themselves nor to leave their cultures and communities of origin but to remain within their communities as "out" bisexuals, lesbians, or gays to challenge homophobic and biphobic attitudes. In fact, some react positively to their own stigmatization with increased pride. A Korean American immigrant woman explained that the "Asian shun of homosexuality/bisexuality . . . makes me even more defensive yet proud of my orientation." The African American–Chicana mentioned earlier eventually decided to come out within the Latin and African American communities and now uses her "'outness' within [her] communities as a testimony to . . . diversity and to the strength [she has] developed from being raised Latina and African American."

A positive integration of one's racial, ethnic, or class identity with one's sexual identity is greatly facilitated by support from others who share an individual's particular constellation of identities. For some, finding kindred spirits is made difficult by demographic and cultural realities. But as more and more people come out, there are inevitably more "out" members of racial and ethnic minorities and among these, more bisexuals. Many respondents described the leap forward in the development of their sexual identities that became possible when they finally discovered a community of bisexuals, lesbians, or gays with a similar racial or ethnic background. A Jewish Chicana reported that she is "finding more people of my ethnic backgrounds going through the same thing. This is affirming." Similarly, a Chicano is "just now starting to integrate my sexuality and my culture by getting to know other gays/bis of color." An African American woman reported that "it wasn't until I lived in Washington, D.C., for a number of years and met large numbers of Black lesbians that I was able to resolve this conflict for myself." Many Jewish respondents commented on the fact that there are many Jewish bisexuals, lesbians, and gays, and noted that receiving support from these peers was important in the development and maintenance of their positive sexual identities. One man, when asked to describe the effect of his racial or ethnic cultural heritage on his sexuality, said simply, "I'm a Jewish Agnostic Male-oriented Bisexual. There are lots of us." Some Jewish respondents also commented that being racially white facilitated their acceptance in the mainstream LesBiGay community and permitted them to receive support from this community that was not as available to individuals of other racial and ethnic backgrounds. Of course, it is this same assimilationist attitude that caused the Orthodox Jewish woman quoted earlier to find a lack of support among Jewish LesBiGays.

For individuals who belong to racial or ethnic minorities, the discovery that one is bisexual is a discovery that one is a double or triple minority. It is even more the case for bisexuals than for lesbians and gays, because bisexuals are a political and social minority within the lesbian and gay community. Many racial and ethnic minority individuals experience their coming out as a process of further marginalization from the mainstream, that is, as an exacerbation of an already undesirable position. An African American woman described being bi as "just one other negative thing I have to deal with. My race is one and my gender another." This can inhibit coming out for individuals who are reluctant to take on yet another stigmatized identity. For example, Morales (1990) reported that some Hispanic men limit their coming out, because they do not want to risk experiencing double discrimination in their careers and personal lives. A Black woman in the current study said that she is "unwilling to come too far 'out' as I already have so many strikes against me."

Many respondents found, however, that their experiences as racial or ethnic minorities facilitated their recognition and acceptance of their sexuality. This was most common among Jewish respondents, many of whom explained that their history as an oppressed people sensitized them to other issues of oppression. One man wrote, "The Jewish sense of being an outsider or underdog has spurred my rebelliousness; the emphasis on learning and questioning has helped to open my mind." A woman wrote, "My Jewish ethnicity taught me about oppression and the need to fight it. It gave me the tools to be able to assert that the homophobes (like the anti-Semites) are wrong." Some non-Jewish respondents also found that their experiences as ethnic minorities facilitated their coming out as bisexual. For example, a woman of Mexican, Dutch, and Norwegian descent wrote that her cultural background "has made me less afraid to be different." She was already ethnically different, so she was better prepared to recognize and accept her sexual difference. Similarly, an Irish Tsalagi Indian man found being outside the mainstream to be a liberating position; he wrote, "I have always felt alienated from the cultural norm, so I'm only affected in the sense that this alienation has allowed me the freedom to visualize myself on my own terms."

Many bisexuals of mixed race or ethnicity feel a comfortable resonance between their mixed heritage and their bisexuality. In a society where both racial-ethnic and sexual categories are highly elaborated, individuals of mixed heritage or who are bisexual find themselves straddling categories that are socially constructed as distinct from one another. The paradox presented by this position was described by a bisexual woman of Native American, Jewish, and Celtic heritage who wrote, "Because I am of mixed ethnicity, I rotate between feeling 'left out' of every group and feeling 'secretly' qualified for several racial/cultural identities. I notice the same feeling regarding my sexual identity." Other respondents of mixed racial and ethnic backgrounds also saw connections between their ethnic heritage and their bisexuality. For example, an Asian European woman wrote,

> Being multiracial, multicultural has always made me aware of nonbipolar thinking. I have always been outside people's categories, and so it wasn't such a big leap to come out as bi, after spending years explaining my [racial and cultural] identity rather than attaching a single label [to it].

A Puerto Rican who grew up alternately in Puerto Rico and a northeastern state explained,

> The duality of my cultural upbringing goes hand in hand with the duality of my sexuality. Having the best of both worlds (ethnically speaking—I look white but am Spanish) in my everyday life might

> have influenced me to seek the best of both worlds in my sexual life—relationships with both a man and a woman.

A Black Lithuanian Irish Scottish woman with light skin, freckles, red curly hair, and a "Black political identity," who is only recognized as Black by other Blacks, wrote, "As with my race, my sex is not to be defined by others or absoluted by myself. It is a spectrum."

However, individuals whose mixed heritages have produced unresolved cultural difficulties sometimes transfer these difficulties to their bisexuality. A "Latino-Anglo" who was raised to be a "regular, middle-class, all-American," and who later became acculturated to Latin culture, wrote,

> Since I am ethnically confused and pass as different from what I am, as I do in sexual orientation also, I spend a lot of time underground. . . . I think it has definitely been a major factor in the breakup of two very promising long-term relations.

Similarly, a transgendered bisexual respondent of mixed European, Native American, and North African heritage believes that the pressures she feels as a transgenderist and a bisexual are closely related to the fact that her parents "felt it necessary to hide a large part of their ethnic and racial heritage," although she did not elaborate on the nature of these pressures.

In contrast to bisexuals from marginalized racial-ethnic, religious, or class backgrounds, middle- or upper-class Protestant Euro-Americans experience relatively few difficulties integrating their sexual identities with their cultural backgrounds and other identities. Euro-American bisexuals might have difficulty developing a positive bisexual identity in a monosexist culture, but unlike Bisexuals of Color, they have no particular problems integrating their sexual identity with their racial identity, because these identities are already integrated in the LesBiGay community. Being Euro-American gives them the luxury of not dealing with racial identity. Not surprisingly, when asked how their racial-ethnic background had affected their sexuality, most Euro-Americans did not mention their race at all. Instead, Euro-Americans tended to attribute their sexual upbringing to the peculiarities of their parents, their religion, their class, or their geographic location within the United States. One woman explained,

> I do not associate my racial-ethnic cultural background and my sexuality. Undoubtedly I would think and feel differently if I were of a different background but I'm not able to identify the effect of my background on my sexuality.

REFERENCES

Almaguer, T. (1993). Chicano men: A cartography of homosexual identity and behavior. In H. Abelove, M. A. Barale, & D. M. Halperin (Eds.), *The lesbian and gay studies reader.* New York: Routledge.

Carrier, J., Nguyen, B., & Su, S. (1992). Vietnamese American sexual behaviors and HIV infection. *Journal of Sex Research, 29*(4), 547–560.
Chan, C. S. (1989). Issues of identity development among Asian American lesbians and gay men. *Journal of Counseling and Development, 68*(1), 16–21.
Chan, C. S. (1992). Cultural considerations in counseling Asian American lesbians and gay men. In S. H. Dworkin & F. Guitérrez (Eds.), *Counseling gay men and lesbians* (pp. 115–124). Alexandria, VA: American Association for Counseling and Development.
Espin, O. (1987). Issues of identity in the psychology of Latina lesbians. In Boston Lesbian Psychologies Collective (Eds.), *Lesbian psychologies: Explorations and challenges* (pp. 35–51). Urbana: University of Illinois Press.
Greene, B. (1994). Ethnic-minority lesbians and gay men: Mental health and treatment issues. *Journal of Consulting and Clinical Psychology, 62*(2), 243–251.
Guitérrez, F. J., & Dworkin, S. H. (1992). Gay, lesbian, and African American: Managing the integration of identities. In Dworkin & Gutiérrez (Eds.), *Counseling gay men and lesbians* (pp. 141–155).
H., P. (1989). Asian American lesbians: An emerging voice in the Asian American community. In Asian Women United of California (Eds.), *Making waves: An anthology of writings by and about Asian American women* (pp. 282–290). Boston: Beacon.
Icard, L. (1986). Black gay men and conflicting social identities: Sexual orientation versus racial identity. *Journal of Social Work and Human Sexuality, 4*(1/2), 83–92.
Johnson, J. (1982). *The influence of assimilation on the psychosocial adjustment of Black homosexual men.* Unpublished dissertation, California School of Professional Psychology, Berkeley.
Lukes, C. A., & Land, H. (1990, March). Biculturality and homosexuality. *Social Work,* 155–161.
Matteson, D. R. (1994). *Bisexual behavior and AIDS risk among some Asian American men.* Unpublished manuscript.
McKeon, E. (1992). To be bisexual and underclass. In E. R. Weise (Ed.), *Closer to home: Bisexuality & feminism* (pp. 27–34). Seattle, WA: Seal.
Morales, E. S. (1989). Ethnic minority families and minority gays and lesbians. *Marriage and Family Review, 14*(3/4), 217–239.
Morales, E. S. (1990). HIV infection and Hispanic gay and bisexual men. *Hispanic Journal of Behavioral Sciences, 12*(2), 212–222.
Morales, E. S. (1992). Counseling Latino gays and Latina lesbians. In Dworkin, S. H. and Gutiérrez, F. (Eds.), *Counseling gay men and lesbians: Journey to the end of the rainbow* (pp. 125–139).
Tremble, B., Schneider, M., & Appathurai, C. (1989). Growing up gay or lesbian in a multicultural context. *Journal of Homosexuality, 17*(1–4), 253–267.
Wooden, W. S., Kawasaki, H., & Mayeda, R. (1983). Lifestyles and identity maintenance among gay Japanese American males. *Alternative Lifestyles, 5*(4), 236–243.

PART VI
Families

I believe I have as much right in raising a child as she does, but I found a lot of reverse discrimination. . . . Like pediatricians: they speak to my wife, they won't speak to me. . . . The same thing with the nursery school. I went out on all the interviews. They looked at me like, "What're you *doing here?"*

"ERNIE"[1]

Raising Black children – female and male – in the mouth of a racist, sexist, suicidal dragon is perilous and chancy. . . . I wish to raise a Black man who will recognize that the legitimate objects of his hostilty are not women, but the particulars of a structure that programs him to fear and despise women as well as his own Black self.

AUDRE LORDE[2]

The structures of families reflect gender expectations within particular cultures, and cultures themselves are shaped by surrounding social forces, such as sexism, poverty, and homophobia. For example, the wish to have male offspring who are expected to support parents in old age affects whether or not girls even get born in some cultures. In China and in parts of India, sex-selective abortion has changed the gender ratio in favor of boys. An estimated 50 to 80 million more girls and women might be alive today in India and China if discrimination against girls and women had not occurred. One-child policies in China have especially encouraged sex-selective abortions. Sex selection occurs in India even though sex tests on fetuses and sex-selective abortions are illegal there.[3]

Attention to changing gender expectations within families is on many people's minds, even in mainstream U.S. society. People in the women's and men's movements have been talking about this issue for decades, but today people from all walks of life are addressing it. Even the National Conference of Catholic Bishops has urged married couples to move beyond gender stereotypes and develop more equality in marriages through shared decision making, shared household duties when both spouses are employed, fathers who are actively engaged in their children's lives, and the expression of feeling by both spouses.[4] Explicit attention to fathers has increased as more single fathers enjoy and embrace their roles,[5] as divorced fathers fight for custody,[6] and as young fathers join mentoring programs to help them learn parenting skills.[7]

In 1992, 57.8 percent of married women were in the labor force. The task of balancing paid work and family work now affects women across the economic spectrum; it is no longer a challenge only for poor and working-class women, who have always been in the paid workforce. In 1990, for example, 68 percent of women college graduates with a child under one year of age were in the labor force. In 1992, the husband worked outside the home and the wife did unpaid work at home in only 18 percent of families.[8] However, women who work outside the home are most likely to be responsible for arranging child care, and they continue to do most of the housework, working what is frequently referred to as the "second shift" or the "double day."[9]

Family life requires complex negotiations and compromises that are often hidden from view. For example, in a family studied by Arlie Hochschild and Anne Machung, the wife gave up her ideal of a marriage in which household tasks and child care would be shared; she redefined what her husband was willing to do as acceptable, in order to keep the marriage together. He was unwilling to take on much responsibility at home and would have preferred that she work part time so she could handle the work at home with less conflict. Committed to her career, she did not want to work part time. The image of the happy professional mother, her child in one hand and a briefcase in the other, is seldom what it appears to be, even for professional women with enough money to hire people to help at home.[10] The reality of the effects of having children on women's wages has finally hit home, leading researcher Ann Crittendon (Part VIII) to refer to mothers as "society's involuntary philanthropists."[11] The ideology of what sociologist Sharon Hays calls "intensive mothering" reinforces the gender divide since this ideology advises women to spend a lot of time, energy, and money on their children. This frequently results in conflicts with employers, since the ideology of the workplace is at odds with the ideology of intensive mothering.[12]

Sociologist Scott Coltrane, after taking a careful look at changing gender roles in families, concludes that gradually men have begun to share more equally in family life, especially in the area of child care, and he predicts that this trend toward equality in family life will continue, though perhaps gradually and with resistance on both sides.[13] An intergenerational study of Mexican men's roles in the early 1990s by anthropologist Matthew Gutmann found that younger Mexican men were participating more in housework and childrearing as a result of women working outside the home, and were not needing to have a lot of children in order to prove their masculinity.[14] The data in this field are being debated, however, related to changes in men's contributions to housework. Sociologists Julie Press and Eleanor Townsley found that a careful look at two large surveys that have informed the literature on housework participation (not childcare) revealed overreporting of time spent on housework by both husbands and wives. They conclude, also, that ". . . the overreport we document is large enough to cast doubt on the conclusion that husbands have increased their supply of domestic labor to the household in the past 25 years."[15]

The stress and turmoil that poverty imposes on families is well documented.[16] Sociologist Anne R. Roschelle, in an analysis of families of color in the 1987–88 National Survey of Families and Households, argues that one powerful effect of poverty on communities of color has been to weaken support networks, calling into question the assumption that cuts in welfare support will simply force people to lean on their support networks. Those networks, previously documented in the social science literature (see also Collins, this part), appear to have weakened to some extent.[17] The risk of becoming homeless is a pernicious presence for poor families. Many families that are able to escape homelessness function at the margins of the social order, living in crowded conditions and working, at times, in the informal economy—outside the realm of W-2 forms, benefits, and any protection from exploitation by employers.[18] The negative effects of humiliating, illness-inducing work are often brought home in the form of exhaustion, drunkenness, and violence.[19]

In response to the conditions of poor families, especially single mothers with children, professor of education Valerie Polakow asks, ". . . where are our commitments to the existential futures of children as we approach the twenty-first century?" Clearly, the structure of the economy is wreaking havoc in many families, though, as Pokalow argues, homelessness and poverty are often pathologized causing victims of poverty to be labeled and blamed for their conditions. Rather, she argues, society should focus on the economic structure as the source of blame and potential solutions.[20] Political scientist Shirley M. Geiger, examining the public perceptions and public policies concerning African American single mothers argues that their poverty is a result of both conscious action and inaction that is damaging to all poor families, 40 percent of which are headed by white men.[21] Frank F. Furstenberg comes to a similar conclusion regarding poor single fathers, arguing that unless the social order provides adequate incomes for young fathers, most will continue to stay disengaged from their children.[22] Later in this book, the situations of poor families are addressed in more depth (Randy Albelda and Chris Tilly, Part VIII, Roberta Praeger, and Michelle Fine and Lois Weis, Part XI).

The movement to establish the right of gay men and lesbians to marry or at least establish civil unions provides an example of changing attitudes and changing family arrangements in various countries, as discussed in the Introduction to this book. Although many gay and lesbian couples might choose not to marry, their support of the right to do so is strong.[23] In most states (Massachusetts, for example), legislation and/or attorneys have successfully arranged for joint adoptions within same-sex couples so that both partners can become legal parents of the children involved.[24] Gay and lesbian couples still face many challenges, however. In the aftermath of September 11, many surviving partners have gone unrecognized by both their partners' families and by agencies providing financial relief to surviving spouses or next of kin.[25]

The readings in this part address a range of family issues including gender arrangements in working-class families from various ethnic groups (Lillian Rubin); various family and child-care arrangements in African American communities (Patricia Hill Collins); men's experiences as involved fathers (Kathleen Gerson); the challenges of raising an African American son in a lesbian family (Audre Lorde); the challenge of breaking away from a father whose definition of "manhood" is unacceptable (Raul Ybarra); dealing with a homophobic world in the face of disability in a lesbian couple (Nan Hunter); and a cross-cultural study of men's friendships (Walter Williams). The authors in this chapter give voice to many of the challenging aspects of family life today. Embedded in their stories and research are implications for changes in personal relationships and policy, including sharing household and child-rearing tasks; support for fathers' caring involvement in family life; the elimination of poverty; the development of jobs that pay enough to keep families going; the legitimation of various kinds of families; and the development of closer friendships among men.

NOTES

1. Quoted in Kathleen Gerson, *No Man's Land: Men's Changing Commitments to Family and Work* (New York: Basic Books, 1993), p. 249.
2. Audre Lorde, "Man Child: A Black Lesbian Feminist's Response," *Sister Outsider* (Freedom, CA: Crossing Press, 1984), p. 74.
3. Celia W. Dugger, "Modern Asia's Anomoly: The Girls Who Don't Get Born," The *New York Times,* May 6, 2001, p. 4 (WK); Agence France-Presse, "India Cracks Down on Sex Tests for Fetuses," The *New York Times,* May 6, 2001, p. 14 (NE).
4. National Conference of Catholic Bishops, *Follow the Way of Love* (Washington, DC: United States Catholic Conference, 1994), pp. 20–21.
5. Doris Sue Wong, "Single Fathers Embrace Role, Fight Stereotype," *The Boston Globe* (July 5, 1999), p. A1.
6. Kate Zernike, "Divorced Dads Emerge as a Political Force," *The Boston Globe* 253, no. 139 (Tuesday May 19, 1998), p. A1.
7. Erica Thesing, "Mentoring Programs Focusing on Fatherhood," *The Boston Globe* (Saturday June 17, 2000), p. B4.
8. All data in this paragraph are from Barbara Reskin and Irene Padavic, *Women and Men at Work* (Thousand Oaks, CA: Pine Forge Press, 1994), pp. 143–44.
9. Ibid., pp. 149–53. See also Arlie Russell Hochschild with Anne Machung, *The Second Shift: Working Parents and the Revolution at Home* (New York: Avon Books, 1990).
10. Hochschild and Machung, *The Second Shift.*
11. Ann Crittendon, *The Price of Motherhood: Why the Most Important Job in the World is Still the Least Valued.* (New York: Henry Holt and Co., 2001), p. 9.
12. Sharon Hays, *The Cultural Contradictions of Motherhood.* (New Haven: Yale University Press, 1996).
13. Scott Coltrane, "The Future of Fatherhood: Social, Demographic, and Economic Influences on Men's Family Involvements," in William Marsiglio, ed., *Fatherhood: Contemporary Theory, Research, and Social Policy* (Thousand Oaks, CA: Sage, 1995), pp. 255–74.
14. Matthew C. Gutmann, "The Meaning of Macho," in Louise Lamphere, Heléna Ragoné, and Patricia Zavella, eds., *Situated Lives: Gender and Culture in Everyday Life* (New York: Routledge, 1997), pp. 223–34.
15. Julie E. Press and Eleanor Townsley, "Wives' and Husbands' Housework Reporting: Gender, Class, and Social Desirability," *Gender & Society* 12, no. 2 (April 1998), p. 214.

16. Elliot Liebow, *Tell Them Who I Am: The Lives of Homeless Women* (New York: Penguin, 1993); Valerie Polakow, *Lives on the Edge: Single Mothers and Their Children in the Other America* (Chicago: University of Chicago Press, 1994); Doug A. Timmer, Stanley D. Eitzen, and Kathryn D. Talley, *Paths to Homelessness: Extreme Poverty and the Urban Housing Crisis* (Boulder, CO: Westview Press, 1994).
17. Anne R. Roschelle, *No More Kin: Exploring Race, Class, and Gender in Family Networks* (Thousand Oaks, CA: Sage, 1997), pp. 199–202.
18. See, for example, "Patchworking: Households in the Economy," in Nazli Kibria, *Family Tightrope: The Changing Lives of Vietnamese Americans* (Princeton: Princeton University Press, 1993), pp. 73–107.
19. See, for example, Sue Doro, "The Father Poem," in Janet Zandy, ed., *Calling Home: Working-Class Women's Writings: An Anthology* (New Brunswick: Rutgers University Press, 1990), pp. 132–38.
20. Polakow, *Lives on the Edge,* p. 3.
21. Shirley M. Geiger, "African-American Single Mothers: Public Perceptions and Public Policies," in Kim Marie Vaz, ed., *Black Women in America* (Thousand Oaks, CA: Sage, 1995), pp. 244–57.
22. Frank F. Furstenburg, Jr., "Fathering in the Inner City: Paternal Participation and Public Policy," in William Marsiglio, ed., *Fatherhood: Contemporary Theory, Research, and Social Policy* (Thousand Oaks, CA: Sage, 1995), pp. 119–47.
23. Gretchen A. Stiers, *From This Day Forward: Commitment, Marriage, and Family in Lesbian and Gay Relationships* (New York: St. Martin's Griffin, 1999).
24. Associated Press, "N.J. Gay Parents Exchange Vows," *The Boston Globe* (Monday June 22, 1998), p. A4.
25. Kathleen Burge, "Sept. 11 Leaves Same-Sex Partners Adrift," *The Boston Globe,* March 18, 2002, p. B1.

38

THE TRANSFORMATION OF FAMILY LIFE

LILLIAN B. RUBIN

"I know my wife works all day, just like I do," says Gary Braunswig, a twenty-nine-year-old white drill press operator, "but it's not the same. She doesn't *have* to do it. I mean, she *has* to because we need the money, but it's different. It's not really her job to have to be working; it's mine." He stops, irritated with himself because he can't find exactly the words he wants, and asks, "Know what I mean? I'm not saying it right; I mean, it's the man who's supposed to support his family, so I've got to be responsible for that, not her. And that makes one damn big difference."

"I mean, women complain all the time about how hard they work with the house and the kids and all. I'm not saying it's not hard, but that's her responsibility, just like the finances are mine."

"But she's now sharing that burden with you, isn't she?" I remark.

"Yeah, and I do my share around the house, only she doesn't see it that way. Maybe if you add it all up, I don't do as much as she does, but then she doesn't bring in as much money as I do. And she doesn't always have to be looking for overtime to make an extra buck. I got no complaints about that, so how come she's always complaining about me? I mean, she helps me out financially, and I help her out with the kids and stuff. What's wrong with that? It seems pretty equal to me."

Cast that way, his formulation seems reasonable: They're each responsible for one part of family life; they each help out with the other. But the abstract formula doesn't square with the lived reality. For him, helping her adds relatively little to the burden of household tasks he *must* do each day. A recent study by University of Wisconsin researchers, for example, found that in families where both wife and husband work full-time, the women average over twenty-six hours a week in household labor, while the men do about ten.[1] That's because there's nothing in the family system to force him to accountability or responsibility on a daily basis. He may "help her out with the kids and stuff" one day and be too busy or preoccupied the next.

But for Gary's wife, Irene, helping him means an extra eight hours every working day. Consequently, she wants something more consistent from him than a helping hand with a particular task when he has the time, desire, or

---

feels guilty enough. "Sure, he helps me out," she says, her words tinged with resentment. "He'll give the kids a bath or help with the dishes. But only when I ask him. He doesn't have to *ask* me to go to work every day, does he? Why should I have to ask him?"

"Why should I have to ask him?" — words that suggest a radically different consciousness from the working-class women I met twenty years ago. Then, they counted their blessings. "He's a steady worker; he doesn't drink; he doesn't hit me," they told me by way of explaining why they had "no right to complain."[2] True, these words were reminders to themselves that life could be worse, that they shouldn't take these things for granted — reminders that didn't wholly work to obscure their discontent with other aspects of the marriage. But they were nevertheless meaningful statements of value that put a brake on the kinds of demands they felt they could make of their men, whether about the unequal division of household tasks or about the emotional content of their lives together.

Now, the same women who reminded themselves to be thankful two decades ago speak openly about their dissatisfaction with the role divisions in the family. Some husbands, especially the younger ones, greet their wives' demands sympathetically. "I try to do as much as I can for Sue, and when I can't, I feel bad about it," says twenty-nine-year-old Don Dominguez, a Latino father of three children, who is a construction worker.

Others are more ambivalent. "I don't know, as long as she's got a job, too, I guess it's right that I should help out in the house. But that doesn't mean I've got to like it," says twenty-eight-year-old Joe Kempinski, a white warehouse worker with two children.

Some men are hostile, insisting that their wives' complaints are unreasonable, unjust, and oppressive. "I'm damn tired of women griping all the time; it's nothing but nags and complaints," Ralph Danesen, a thirty-six-year-old white factory worker and the father of three children, says indignantly. "It's enough! You'd think they're the only ones who've got it hard. What about me? I'm not living in a bed of roses either."

"Christ, what does a guy have to do to keep a wife quiet these days? What does she want? It's not like I don't do anything to help her out, but it's never enough."

In the past there was a clear understanding about the obligations and entitlements each partner took on when they married. He was obliged to work outside the home; she would take care of life inside. He was entitled to her ministrations, she to his financial support. But this neat division of labor with its clear-cut separation of rights and obligations no longer works. Now, women feel obliged to hold up their share of the family economy — a partnership men welcome. In return, women believe they're entitled to their husbands' full participation in domestic labor. And here is the rub. For while men enjoy the fruits of their wives' paid work outside the home, they have been slow to accept the reciprocal responsibilities — that is, to become real partners in the work inside the home.

The women, exhausted from doing two days' work in one, angry at the need to assume obligations without corresponding entitlements, push their men in ways unknown before. The men, battered by economic uncertainty and by the escalating demands of their wives, feel embattled and victimized on two fronts—one outside the home, the other inside. Consequently, when their wives seem not to see the family work they do, when they don't acknowledge and credit it, when they fail to appreciate them, the men feel violated and betrayed. "You come home and you want to be appreciated a little. But it doesn't work that way, leastwise not here anymore," complains Gary Braunswig, his angry words at odds with the sadness in his eyes. "There's no peace, I guess that's the real problem; there's no peace anywhere anymore."

The women often understand what motivates their husbands' sense of victimization and even speak sympathetically about it at times. But to understand and sympathize is not to condone, especially when they feel equally assaulted on both the home and the economic fronts. "I know I complain a lot, but I really don't ask for that much. I just want him to help out a little more," explains Ralph Danesen's wife, Helen, a thirty-five-year-old office worker. "It isn't like I'm asking him to cook the meals or anything like that. I know he can't do that, and I don't expect him to. But every time I try to talk to him, you know, to ask him if I couldn't get a little more help around here, there's a fight."

One of the ways the men excuse their behavior toward family work is by insisting that their responsibility as breadwinner burdens them in ways that are alien to their wives. "The plant's laying off people left and right; it could be me tomorrow. Then what'll we do? Isn't it enough I got to worry about that? I'm the one who's got all the worries; she doesn't. How come that doesn't count?" demands Bob Duckworth, a twenty-nine-year-old factory worker.

But, in fact, the women don't take second place to their men in worrying about what will happen to the family if the husband loses his job. True, the burden of finding another one that will pay the bills isn't theirs—not a trivial difference. But the other side of this truth is that women are stuck with the reality that the financial welfare of the family is out of their control, that they're helpless to do anything to prevent its economic collapse or to rectify it should it happen. "He thinks I've got it easy because it's not my job to support the family," says Bob's wife, Ruthanne. "But sometimes I think it's worse for me. I worry all the time that he's going to get laid off, just like he does. But I can't do anything about it. And if I try to talk to him about it, you know, like maybe make a plan in case it happens, he won't even listen. How does he think *that* makes me feel? It's my life, too, and I can't even talk to him about it."

Not surprisingly, there are generational differences in what fuels the conflict around the division of labor in these families. For the older couples—those who grew up in a different time, whose marriages started with another set of ground rules—the struggle is not simply around how much men do or about whether they take responsibility for the daily tasks of living without being pushed, prodded, and reminded. That's the overt manifestation of the discord, the trigger that starts the fight. But the noise of the explosion when it comes serves to conceal the more fundamental issue underlying the dissension: legitimacy. What does she have a *right* to expect? "What do I know about doing stuff around the house?" asks Frank Moreno, a forty-eight-year-old foreman in a warehouse. "I wasn't brought up like that. My pop, he never did one damn thing, and my mother never complained. It was her job; she did it and kept quiet. Besides, I work my ass off every day. Isn't that enough?"

For the younger couples, those under forty, the problem is somewhat different. The men may complain about the expectation that they'll participate more fully in the care and feeding of the family, but talk to them about it quietly and they'll usually admit that it's not really unfair, given that their wives also work outside the home. In these homes, the issue between husband and wife isn't only who does what. That's there, and it's a source of more or less conflict, depending upon what the men actually do and how forceful their wives are in their demands. But in most of these families there's at least a verbal consensus that men *ought* to participate in the tasks of daily life. Which raises the next and perhaps more difficult issue in contest between them: Who feels responsible for getting the tasks done? Who regards them as a duty, and for whom are they an option? On this, tradition rules.

Even in families where husbands now share many of the tasks, their wives still bear full responsibility for the organization of family life. A man may help cook the meal these days, but a woman is most likely to be the one who has planned it. He may take the children to child care, but she virtually always has had to arrange it. It's she also who is accountable for the emotional life of the family, for monitoring the emotional temperature of its members and making the necessary corrections. It's this need to be responsible for it all that often feels as burdensome as the tasks themselves. "It's not just doing all the stuff that needs doing," explains Maria Jankowicz, a white twenty-eight-year-old assembler in an electronics factory. "It's worrying all the time about everything and always having to arrange everything, you know what I mean. It's like I run the whole show. If I don't stay on top of it all, things fall apart because nobody else is going to do it. The kids can't and Nick, well, forget it," she concludes angrily.

If, regardless of age, life stage, or verbal consensus, women usually still carry the greatest share of the household burdens, why is it important to notice that younger men grant legitimacy to their wives' demands and older men generally do not? Because men who believe their wives have a right to expect their participation tend to suffer guilt and discomfort when they don't live up to those expectations. And no one lives comfortably with guilt. "I know I don't always help enough, and I feel bad about it, you know, guilty sometimes," explains Bob Beardsley, a thirty-year-old white machine operator, his eyes registering the discomfort he feels as he speaks.

"Does it change anything when you feel guilty?" I ask.

A small smile flits across his face, and he says, "Sometimes. I try to do a little more, but then I get busy with something and forget that she needs me to help out. My wife says I don't pay attention, that's why I forget. But I don't know. Seems like I've just got my mind on other things."

It's possible, of course, that the men who speak of guilt and rights are only trying to impress me by mouthing the politically correct words. But even if true, they display a sensitivity to the issue that's missing from the men who don't speak those words. For words are more than just words. They embody ideas; they are the symbols that give meaning to our thoughts; they shape our consciousness. New ideas come to us on the wings of words. It's words that bring those ideas to life, that allow us to see possibilities unrecognized before we gave them words. Indeed, without words, there is no conscious thought, no possibility for the kind of self-reflection that lights the path of change.[3]

True, there's often a long way between word and deed. But the man who feels guilty when he disappoints his wife's expectations has a different consciousness than the one who doesn't—a difference that usually makes for at least some small change in his behavior. Although the emergence of this changing male consciousness is visible in all the racial groups in this study, there also are differences among them that are worthy of comment.

Virtually all the men do some work inside the family—tending the children, washing dishes, running the vacuum, going to the market. And they generally also remain responsible for those tasks that have always been traditionally male—mowing the lawn, shoveling the snow, fixing the car, cleaning the garage, doing repairs around the house. Among the white families in this study, 16 percent of the men share the family work relatively equally, almost always those who live in families where they and their wives work different shifts or where the men are unemployed. "What choice do I have?" asks Don Bartlett, a thirty-year-old white handyman who works days while his wife is on the swing shift. "I'm the only one here, so I do what's got to be done."

Asian and Latino men of all ages, however, tend to operate more often on the old male model, even when they work different shifts or are unemployed, a finding that puzzled me at first. Why, I wondered, did I find only two Asian men and one Latino who are real partners in the work of the family? Aren't these men subject to the same social and personal pressures others experience?

The answer is both yes and no. The pressures are there, but, depending upon where they live, there's more or less support for resisting them. The Latino and Asian men who live in ethnic neighborhoods—settings where they are embedded in an intergenerational community and where the language and culture of the home country is kept alive by a steady stream of new immigrants—find strong support for clinging to the old ways. Therefore, change comes much more slowly in those families. The men who live outside the ethnic quarter are freer from the mandates and constraints of these often tight-knit communities, and therefore are more responsive to the winds of change in the larger society.

These distinctions notwithstanding, it's clear that Asian and Latino men generally participate least in the work of the household and are the least likely to believe they have much responsibility there beyond bringing home a paycheck. "Taking care of the house and kids is my wife's job, that's all," says Joe Gomez flatly.

"A Chinese man mopping a floor? I've never seen it yet," says Amy Lee angrily. Her husband, Dennis, trying to make a joke of the conflict with his wife, says with a smile, "In Chinese families men don't do floors and windows. I help with the dishes sometimes if she needs me to or," he laughs, "if she screams loud enough. The rest, well, it's pretty much her job."

The commonly held stereotype about black men abandoning women and children, however, doesn't square with the families in this study. In fact, black men are the most likely to be real participants in the daily life of the family and are more intimately involved in raising their children than any of the others. True, the men's family work load doesn't always match their wives', and the women are articulate in their complaints about this. Nevertheless, compared to their white, Asian, or Latino counterparts, the black families look like models of egalitarianism.

Nearly three-quarters of the men in the African-American families in this study do a substantial amount of the cooking, cleaning, and child care, sometimes even more than their wives do. All explain it by saying one version or another of: "I just figure it's my job, too"—which simply says what is, without explaining how it came to be that way.

To understand that, we have to look at family histories that tell the story of generations of African-American women who could find work and men who could not, and to the family culture that grew from this difficult and painful reality. "My mother worked six days a week cleaning other people's houses, and my father was an ordinary laborer, when he could find work, which wasn't very often," explains thirty-two-year-old Troy Payne, a black waiter and father of two children. "So he was home a lot more than she was, and he'd do what he had to do around the house. The kids all had to do their share, too. It seemed only fair, I guess."

Difficult as the conflict around the division of labor is, it's only one of the many issues that have become flash points in family life since mother went to work. Most important, perhaps, is the question: Who will care for the children? For the lack of decent, affordable facilities for the care of the children creates unbearable problems and tensions for these working-class families.

It's hardly news that child care is an enormous headache and expense for all two-job families. In many professional middle-class families, where the child-care bill can be $1,500–2,000 a month, it competes with the mortgage payment as the biggest single monthly expenditure. Problematic as this may be, however, these families are the lucky ones when compared to working-class families, many of whom don't earn much more than the cost of child care for these upper-middle-class families. Even the families in this study at the highest end of the earnings scale, those who earn $42,000 a year, can't dream of such costly arrangements.

For most working-class families, therefore, child care often is patched together in ways that leave parents anxious and children in jeopardy. "Care for the little ones, that's a real big problem," says Beverly Waldov, a thirty-year-old white mother of three children—the youngest two; products of a second marriage, under three years old. "My oldest girl is nine, so she's not such a problem. I hate the idea of her being a latchkey kid, but what can I do? We don't even have the money to put the little ones in one of those good day-care places, so I don't have any choice with her. She's just *got* to be able to take care of herself after school," she says, her words a contest between anxiety and hope.

"We have a kind of complicated arrangement for the little kids. Two days a week, my mom takes care of them. We pay her, but at least I don't have to worry when they're with her; I know it's fine. But she works the rest of the time, so the other days we take them to this woman's house. It's the best we can afford, but it's not great because she keeps too many kids, and I know they don't get good attention. Especially the little one; she's just a baby, you know." She pauses and looks away, anguished. "She's so clingy when I bring her home; she can't let go of me, like nobody's paid her any mind all day. But it's not like I have a choice. We barely make it now; if I stop working, we'd be in real trouble."

Even such makeshift solutions don't work for many families. Some speak of being unable to afford day care at all. "We couldn't pay our bills if we had to pay for somebody to take care of the kids."

Some say they're unwilling to leave the children in the care of strangers. "I just don't believe someone else should be raising our kids, that's all."

Some have tried a variety of child-care arrangements, only to have them fail in a moment of need. "We tried a whole bunch of things, and maybe they work for a little while," says Faye Ensey, a black twenty-eight-year-old office worker. "But what happens when your kid gets sick? Or when the baby sitter's kids get sick? I lost two jobs in a row because my kids kept getting sick and I couldn't go to work. Or else I couldn't take my little one to the baby sitter because her kids were sick. They finally fired me for absenteeism. I didn't really blame them, but it felt terrible anyway. It's such a hassle, I sometimes think I'd be glad to just stay home. But we can't afford for me not to work, so we had to figure out something else."

For such families, that "something else" is the decision to take jobs on different shifts—a decision made by one-fifth of the families in this study. With one working days and the other on swing or graveyard, one parent is home with the children at all times. "We were getting along okay before Daryl junior was born, because Shona, my daughter, was getting on. You know, she didn't need somebody with her all the time, so we could both work days," explains Daryl Adams, a black thirty-year-old postal clerk with a ten-year-old daughter and a nine-month-old son. "I used to work the early shift—seven to three—so I'd get home a little bit after she got here. It worked out okay. But then this here big surprise came along." He stops, smiles down fondly at his young son and runs his hand over his nearly bald head.

"Now between the two of us working, we don't make enough money to pay for child care and have anything left over, so this is the only way we can manage. Besides, both of us, Alesha and me, we think it's better for one of us to be here, not just for the baby, for my daughter, too. She's growing up and, you know, I think maybe they need even more watching than when they were younger. She's coming to the time when she could get into all kinds of trouble if we're not here to put the brakes on."

But the cost such arrangements exact on a marriage can be very high. When I asked these husbands and wives when they have time to talk, more often than not I got a look of annoyance at a question that, on its face, seemed stupid to them. "Talk? How can we talk when we hardly see each other?" "Talk? What's that?" "Talk? Ha, that's a joke."

Mostly, conversation is limited to the logistics that take place at shift-changing time when children and chores are handed off from one to the other. With children dancing around underfoot, the incoming parent gets a quick summary of the day's or night's events, a list of reminders about things to be done, perhaps about what's cooking in the pot on the stove. "Sometimes when I'm coming home and it's been a hard day, I think: Wouldn't it be wonderful if I could just sit down with Leon for half an hour and we could have a quiet beer together?" thirty-one-year-old Emma Guerrero, a Latina baker, says wistfully.

But it's not to be. If the arriving spouse gets home early enough, there may be an hour when both are there together. But with the pressures of the workday fresh for one and awaiting the other, and with children clamoring for parental attention, this isn't a promising moment for any serious conversation. "I usually get home about forty-five minutes or so before my wife has to leave for work," says Ralph Jo, a thirty-six-year-old Asian repairman, whose children, ages three and five, are the product of a second marriage. "So we try to take a few minutes just to make contact. But it's hard with the kids and all. Most days the whole time gets spent with taking care of business—you know, who did what, what the kids need, what's for supper, what bill collector was hassling her while I was gone—all the damn garbage of living. It makes me nuts."

Most of the time even this brief hour isn't available. Then the ritual changing of the guard takes only a few minutes—a quick peck on the cheek in greeting, a few words, and it's over. "It's like we pass each other. He comes in; I go out; that's it."

Some of the luckier couples work different shifts on the same days, so they're home together on weekends. But even in these families there's so little time for normal family life that there's hardly any room for anyone or anything outside. "There's so much to do when I get home that there's no time for anything but the chores and the kids," says Daryl's wife, Alesha Adams. "I never get to see anybody or do anything else anymore and, even so, I'm always feeling upset and guilty because there's not enough time for them. Daryl leaves a few minutes after I get home, and the rest of the night is like a blur—Shona's homework, getting the kids fed and down for the night, cleaning up, getting everything ready for tomorrow. I don't know; there's always something I'm running around doing. I sometimes feel like—What do you call them?—one of those whirling dervishes, rushing around all the time and never getting everything done.

"Then on the weekends, you sort of want to make things nice for the kids—and for us, too. It's the only time we're here together, like a real family, so we always eat with the kids. And we try to take them someplace nice one of the days, like to the park or something. But sometimes we're too tired, or there's too many other catch-up things you have to do. I don't even get to see my sister anymore. She's been working weekends for the last year or so, and I'm too busy week nights, so there's no time.

"I don't mean to complain; we're lucky in a lot of ways. We've got two great kids, and we're a pretty good team, Daryl and me. But I worry sometimes. When you live on this kind of schedule, communication's not so good."

For those whose days off don't match, the problems of sustaining both the couple relationship and family life are magnified enormously. "The last two years have been hell for us," says thirty-five-year-old Tina Mulvaney, a white mother of two teenagers. "My son got into bad company and had some trouble, so Mike and I decided one of us had to be home. But we can't make it without my check, so I can't quit.

"Mike drives a cab and I work in a hospital, so we figured one of us could transfer to nights. We talked it over and decided it would be best if I was here during the day and he was here at night. He controls the kids, especially my son, better than I do. When he lays down the law, they listen." She interrupts her narrative to reflect on the difficulty of raising children. "You know, when they were little, I used to think about how much easier it would be when they got older. But now I see it's not true; that's when you really have to begin to worry about them. This is when they need someone to be here all the time to make sure they stay out of trouble."

She stops again, this time fighting tears, then takes up where she left off. "So now Mike works days and I work graveyard. I hate it, but it's the only answer; at least this way somebody's here all the time. I get home about 8:30 in the morning. The kids and Mike are gone. It's the best time of the day because it's the only time I have a little quiet here. I clean up the house a little, do the shopping and the laundry and whatever, then I go to sleep for a couple of hours until the kids come home from school.

"Mike gets home at five; we eat; then he takes over for the night, and I go back to sleep for another couple of hours. I try to get up by 9 so we can all have a little time together, but I'm so tired that I don't make it a lot of times. And by 10, he's sleeping because he has to be up by 6 in the morning.

So if I don't get up, we hardly see each other at all. Mike's here on weekends, but I'm not. Right now I have Tuesday and Wednesday off. I keep hoping for a Monday–Friday shift, but it's what everybody wants, and I don't have the seniority yet. It's hard, very hard; there's no time to live or anything," she concludes with a listless sigh.

NOTES

1. James Sweet, Larry Bumpass, and Vaugn Call, *National Survey of Families and Households* (Madison, Wisc.: Center for Demography and Ecology, University of Wisconsin, 1988). This study featured a probability sample of 5,518 households and included couples with and without children. See also Joseph Pleck, *Working Wives/Working Husbands* (Beverly Hills: Sage Publications, 1985), who summarizes time-budget studies; and Iona Mara-Drita, "The Effects of Power, Ideology, and Experience on Men's Participation in Housework," unpublished paper (1993), whose analysis of Sweet, Bumpass, and Call's data shows that when housework and employment hours are added together, a woman's work week totals 69 hours, compared to 52 hours for a man.
2. Lillian Rubin, *Worlds of Pain* (New York: Basic Books, 1992), p. 93.
3. See Daniel Stern, *The Interpersonal World of the Infant* (New York: Basic Books, 1985), who argues that a child's capacity for self-reflection coincides with the development of language.

39

BLOODMOTHERS, OTHERMOTHERS, AND WOMEN-CENTERED NETWORKS

PATRICIA HILL COLLINS

In many African-American communities, fluid and changing boundaries often distinguish biological mothers from other women who care for children. Biological mothers, or bloodmothers, are expected to care for their children. But African and African-American communities have also recognized that vesting one person with full responsibility for mothering a child may not be wise or possible. As a result, othermothers—women who assist bloodmothers by sharing mothering responsibilities—traditionally have been central to the institution of Black motherhood (Troester 1984).

Patricia Hill Collins, "Bloodmothers, Othermothers, and Women-Centered Networks" from *Black Feminist Thought* (New York: Routledge, 2000), pp. 178–83. Reprinted with permission.

The centrality of women in African-American extended families reflects both a continuation of African-derived cultural sensibilities and functional adaptations to intersecting oppressions of race, gender, class, and nation (Tanner 1974; Stack 1974; Martin and Martin 1978; Sudarkasa 1981b; Reagon 1987). Women's centrality is characterized less by the *absence* of husbands and fathers than by the significance of women. Though men may be physically present or have well-defined and culturally significant roles in the extended family, the kin unit tends to be woman-centered. Bebe Moore Campbell's (1989) parents separated when she was small. Even though she spent the school year in the North Philadelphia household maintained by her grandmother and mother, Campbell's father assumed an important role in her life. "My father took care of me," Campbell remembers. "Our separation didn't stunt me or condemn me to a lesser humanity. His absence never made me a fatherless child. I'm not fatherless now" (p. 271). In woman-centered kin units such as Campbell's—whether a mother-child household unit, a married couple household, or a larger unit extending over several households—the centrality of mothers is not predicated on male powerlessness (Tanner 1974, 133).

Organized, resilient, women-centered networks of bloodmothers and othermothers are key in understanding this centrality. Grandmothers, sisters, aunts, or cousins act as othermothers by taking on child-care responsibilities for one another's children. Historically, when needed, temporary child-care arrangements often turned into long-term care or informal adoption (Stack 1974; Gutman 1976). These practices continue in the face of changing social pressures. Andrea Hunter's (1997) research on Black grandmothers explores how Black parents rely on grandmothers for parenting support. This traditional source of support became even more needed in the 1980s and 1990s, when increasing numbers of Black mothers saw their teenage children fall victim to drugs and the crime associated with it. Many witnessed their sons killed or incarcerated, while their daughters became addicts. In many cases, these young men and women left behind children, who often ended up in foster care. Other children did not, primarily because their grandmothers took responsibility for raising them, often under less than optimal conditions.

In many African-American communities these women-centered networks of community-based child care have extended beyond the boundaries of biologically related individuals to include "fictive kin" (Stack 1974). Civil rights activist Ella Baker describes how informal adoption by othermothers functioned in the rural Southern community of her childhood:

> My aunt who had thirteen children of her own raised three more. She had become a midwife, and a child was born who was covered with sores. Nobody was particularly wanting the child, so she took the child and raised him . . . and another mother decided she didn't want to be bothered with two children. So my aunt took one and raised him . . . they were part of the family. (Cantarow 1980, 59)

Stanlie James recounts how othermother traditions work with notions of fictive kin within her own extended family. James notes that the death of her grandmother in 1988 reunited her family, described as a host of biological and fictive kin. James's rendition of how one female family member helped James's nine-year-old daughter deal with the loss of her great-grandmother illustrates the interactions among women-centered extended kin networks, fictive kin, and othermother traditions. The woman who helped James's daughter was not a blood relative but had been "othermothered" by James's grandmother and was a full member of the extended family. James's grandmother believed that because all children must be fed, clothed, and educated, if their biological parents could not discharge these obligations, then some other member of the community should accept that responsibility. As James points out, "This fictive kin who stepped in to counsel my daughter was upholding a family tradition that had been modeled by my grandmother some fifty years before" (James 1993, 44).

Even when relationships are not between kin or fictive kin, African-American community norms traditionally were such that neighbors cared for one another's children. Sara Brooks, a Southern domestic worker, describes the importance that the community-based child care a neighbor offered her daughter had for her: "She kept Vivian and she didn't charge me nothin either. You see, people used to look after each other, but now its not that way. I reckon its because we all was poor, and I guess they put theirself in the place of the person that they was helpin'" (Simonsen 1986, 181). Brooks's experiences demonstrate how the African-American cultural value placed on cooperative child care traditionally found institutional support in the adverse conditions under which so many Black women mothered.

Othermothers can be key not only in supporting children but also in helping bloodmothers who, for whatever reason, lack the preparation or desire for motherhood. In confronting racial oppression, maintaining community-based child care and respecting othermothers who assume child-care responsibilities can serve a critical function in African-American communities. Children orphaned by sale or death of their parents under slavery, children conceived through rape, children of young mothers, children born into extreme poverty or to alcoholic or drug-addicted mothers, or children who for other reasons cannot remain with their bloodmothers have all been supported by othermothers, who, like Ella Baker's aunt, take in additional children even when they have enough of their own.

Young women are often carefully groomed at an early age to become othermothers. As a 10-year-old, Ella Baker learned to be an othermother by caring for the children of a widowed neighbor: "Mama would say, 'You must take the clothes to Mr. Powell's house, and give so-and-so a bath.' The children were running wild. . . . The kids . . . would take off across the field. We'd chase them down, and bring them back, and put 'em in the tub, and wash 'em off, and change clothes, and carry the dirty ones home, and wash them. Those kind of things were routine" (Cantarow 1980, 59).

Many Black men also value community-based child care but historically have exercised these values to a lesser extent. During slavery, for example, Black children under age 10 experienced little division of labor. They were dressed alike and performed similar tasks. If the activities of work and play are any indication of the degree of gender role differentiation that existed among slave children, "then young girls probably grew up minimizing the difference between the sexes while learning far more about the differences between the races" (D. White 1985, 94). Because they are often left in charge of younger siblings, many young Black men learn how to care for children. Geoffrey Canada (1995) recounts how he had to learn how to fight in his urban neighborhood. The climate of violence that he and his two brothers encountered mandated developing caretaking skills, especially since his single mother had to work and could not offer them the protection that they needed. Thus, differences among Black men and women in behaviors concerning children may have more to do with male labor force patterns and similar factors. As Ella Baker observes, "My father took care of people too, but . . . my father had to work" (Cantarow 1980, 60).

Historically, within Black diasporic societies, community-based child care and the relationships among bloodmothers and othermothers in women-centered networks have taken diverse institutional forms. In some polygynous West African societies, the children of the same father but different mothers referred to one another as brothers and sisters. While a strong bond existed between the biological mother and her child—one so strong that, among the Ashanti for example, "to show disrespect toward one's mother is tantamount to sacrilege" (Fortes 1950, 263)—children could be disciplined by any of their "mothers." Cross-culturally, the high status given to othermothers and the cooperative nature of child-care arrangements among bloodmothers and othermothers in Caribbean and other Black diasporic societies gives credence to the importance that people of African descent place on mothering (Sudarkasa 1981a).

Although the political economy of slavery brought profound changes to Africans enslaved in the United States, beliefs in the importance of motherhood and the value of cooperative approaches to child care continued. During slavery, while older women served as nurses and midwives, their most common occupation was caring for the children of parents who worked (D. White 1985). Informal adoption of orphaned children reinforced the importance of social motherhood in African-American communities (Gutman 1976). The relationship between bloodmothers and othermothers also survived the transition from a slave economy to post-emancipation Southern rural agriculture. Children in Southern rural communities were not solely the responsibility of their biological mothers. Aunts, grandmothers, and others who had time to supervise children served as othermothers (Dougherty 1978). The significant status that women enjoyed in family networks and in African-American communities continued to be linked to their bloodmother and othermother activities.

In the 1980s, the entire community structure of bloodmothers and othermothers came under assault. Racial desegregation as well as the emergence of class-stratified Black neighborhoods greatly altered the fabric of Black civil society. African-Americans of diverse social classes found themselves in new residential, school, and work settings that tested this enduring theme of bloodmothers, othermothers, and woman-centered networks. In many inner-city, working-class neighborhoods, the very fabric of African-American community life eroded when crack cocaine flooded the streets. African-American children and youth often formed the casualties of this expanding market for drugs, from the increasing number of Black children in foster care (Nightingale 1993), to children threatened by violence (Canada 1995), to those killed. Residents of Central Harlem interviewed by anthropologist Leith Mullings repeatedly expressed concern about losing the community's children, leading Mullings to observe, "The depth of worry about children growing up in these conditions is difficult to convey" (Mullings 1997, 93). Given this situation, it is remarkable that even in the most troubled communities, remnants of the othermother tradition endure. Bebe Moore Campbell's 1950s North Philadelphia neighborhood underwent startling changes in the 1980s. Increases in child abuse and parental neglect left many children without care. But some residents, such as Miss Nee, continued the othermother tradition. After raising her younger brothers and sisters and five children of her own, Miss Nee cared for three additional children whose families fell apart. Moreover, on any given night Miss Nee's house may have been filled by up to a dozen children because she had a reputation for never turning away a needy child ("Children of the Underclass" 1989).

Black middle-class women and their families found challenges from another direction. In some fundamental ways, moving into the middle class means adopting the values and lifestyles of White middle-class families. While the traditional family ideal is not the norm, the relative isolation of such families from others is noteworthy. U.S. middle-class family life is based on privatization—buying a big house so that one need not cooperate with one's neighbors, or even see them. American middle-class families participate in the privatization of everything, from schools and health care, to for-fee health clubs and private automobiles. Working-class African-Americans who experience social mobility thus may encounter a distinctly different value system. Not only are woman-centered networks of bloodmothers and othermothers much more difficult to sustain structurally—class-stratified residential and employment patterns mean that middle-class Black women often see working-class and poor Black women only as their employees or clients—such ideas are often anathema to the ethos of achievement. From the security firms that find ways to monitor nannies, to the gated-communities of suburbia, purchasing services appears to be the hallmark of American middle-class existence. In this context, stopping to help others to whom one is not related and doing it for free can be seen as rejecting the basic values of the capitalist market economy.

In this context, these relationships among bloodmothers and othermothers and the persistence of woman-centered networks may have greater theoretical importance than currently recognized. The traditional family ideal assigns mothers full responsibility for children and evaluates their performance based on their ability to procure the benefits of a nuclear family household. Within this capitalist marketplace model, those women who "catch" legal husbands, who live in single-family homes, who can afford private school and music lessons for their children, are deemed better mothers than those who do not. In this context, those African-American women who continue community-based child care challenge one fundamental assumption underlying the capitalist system itself: that children are "private property" and can be disposed of as such. Under the property model that accompanies the traditional family ideal, parents may not literally assert that their children are pieces of property, but their parenting may reflect assumptions analogous to those they make in connection with property. For example, the exclusive parental "right" to discipline children as parents see fit, even if discipline borders on abuse, parallels the widespread assumption that property owners may dispose of their property without consulting members of the larger community.

By seeing the larger *community* as responsible for children and by giving othermothers and other nonparents "rights" in child rearing, those African-Americans who endorse these values challenge prevailing capitalist property relations. In Harlem, for example, Black women are increasingly the breadwinners in their families, and rates of households maintained by single mothers remain high. These families are clearly under stress, yet to see the household formation itself as an indication of decline in Black family organization misreads a more complex situation. Leith Mullings suggests that many of these households participate in fluid, familylike networks that have different purposes. Women activate some networks for socialization, reproduction, and consumption, and others for emotional support, economic cooperation, and sexuality. The networks may overlap, but they are not coterminous (Mullings 1997, 74).

The resiliency of women-centered family networks and their willingness to take responsibility for Black children illustrates how African-influenced understandings of family have been continually reworked to help African-Americans as a collectivity cope with and resist oppression. Moreover, these understandings of woman-centered kin networks become critical in understanding broader African-American understandings of community. At the same time, the erosion of such networks in the face of the changing institutional fabric of Black civil society points to the need either to refashion these networks or develop some other way of supporting Black children. For far too many African-American children, assuming that a grandmother or "fictive kin" will care for them is no longer a reality.

REFERENCES

Campbell, Bebe Moore. 1989. *Sweet Summer: Growing Up with and without My Dad.* New York: Putnam.

Canada, Geoffrey. 1995. *First Stick Knife Gun: A Personal History of Violence in America.* Boston: Beacon.

Cantarow, Ellen. 1980. *Moving the Mountain: Women Working for Social Change.* Old Westbury, NY: Feminist Press.

"Children of the Underclass." 1989. *Newsweek.* September 11, 16–27.

Dougherty, Molly C. 1978. *Becoming a Woman in Rural Black Culture.* New York: Holt, Rinehart and Winston.

Fortes, Meyer. 1950. "Kinship and Marriage among the Ashanti." In *African Systems of Kinship and Marriage,* ed. A. R. Radcliffe-Brown and Daryll Forde, 252–84. New York: Oxford University Press.

Gutman, Herbert, 1976. *The Black Family in Slavery and Freedom,* 1750–1925. New York: Random House.

Hunter, Andrea. 1997. "Counting on Grandmothers: Black Mothers' and Fathers' Reliance on Grandmothers for Parenting Support." *Journal of Family Issues* 18 (3): 251–69.

James, Stanlie. 1993. "Mothering: A Possible Black Feminist Link to Social Transformation?" In *Theorizing Black Feminisms: The Visionary Pragmatism of Black Women,* ed. Stanlie James and Abena Busia, 44–54. New York: Routledge.

Martin, Elmer, and Joanne Mitchell Martin. 1978. *The Black Extended Family.* Chicago: University of Chicago Press.

Mullings, Leith. 1997. *On Our Own Terms: Race, Class, and Gender in the Lives of African American Women.* New York: Routledge.

Nightingale, Carl Husemoller. 1993. *On the Edge: A History of Poor Black Children and Their American Dreams.* New York: Basic Books.

Reagon, Bernice Johnson. 1987. "African Diaspora Women: The Making of Cultural Workers." In *Women in Africa and the African Diaspora,* ed. Rosalyn Terborg-Penn, Sharon Harley, and Andrea Benton Rushing, 167–80. Washington, D.C.: Howard University Press.

Simonsen, Thordis, ed. 1986. *You May Plow Here: The Narrative of Sara Brooks.* New York: Touchstone.

Stack, Carol D. 1974. *All Our Kin: Strategies for Survival in a Black Community.* New York: Harper and Row.

Sudarkasa, Niara. 1981a. "Female Employment and Family Organization in West Africa." In *The Black Woman Cross-Culturally,* ed. Filomina Chioma Steady, 49–64. Cambridge, MA: Schenkman.

Tanner, Nancy. 1974. "Matrifocality in Indonesia and Africa and among Black Americans." In *Woman, Culture, and Society,* ed. Michelle Z. Rosaldo and Louise Lamphere, 129–56. Stanford, CA: Stanford University Press.

Troester, Rosalie Riegle. 1984. "Turbulence and Tenderness: Mothers, Daughters, and 'Othermothers' in Paule Marshall's *Brown Girl, Brownstones.*" *Sage: A Scholarly Journal on Black Women* 1 (2): 13–16.

White, Deborah Gray. 1985. *Ar'n't I a Woman? Female Slaves in the Plantation South.* New York: W. W. Norton.

40

DILEMMAS OF INVOLVED FATHERHOOD

KATHLEEN GERSON

Work's a necessity, but the things that really matter are spending time with my family. If I didn't have a family, I don't know what I would have turned to. That's why I say you're rich in a lot of ways other than money. I look at my daughter and think, "My family is everything."

– CARL, A THIRTY-FOUR-YEAR-OLD UTILITIES WORKER

Social disapproval and economic inequality put full-time domesticity out of reach for almost all men. Yet most also found that economic necessity and employer intransigence made anything less than full-time work an equally distant possibility. Few employers offered the option of part-time work, especially in male-dominated fields. Arthur, a married sanitation worker planning for fatherhood, complained:

> If it was feasible, I would love to spend more time with my child. That would be more important to me than working. I'd love to be able to work twenty-five hours a week or four days a week and have three days off to spend with the family, but most jobs aren't going to accommodate you that way.

Yet, even if part-time work were available, involved fathers still needed the earnings that only full-time and overtime work could offer. Lou, the sewage worker who worked the night shift in order to spend days with his young daughter, could not accept lower wages or fewer benefits:

> If I knew that financially everything would be set, I'd stay home. I'd like to stay more with my daughter. It's a lot of fun to be with a very nice three-year-old girl. But if I work less, I would equate it to less money and then I wouldn't be taking care of my family. If it meant less work and the same or more money, I'd say, "Sure!" I'd be dumb if I didn't.

Dean, the driver for a city department of parks, agreed that his economic obligations could not take a backseat to his nurturing ones:

> It always comes down to the same thing: I would like to have more time to spend with my children, but if I didn't have money, what's the sense of having time off? If I could work part-time and make enough money, that would be fine and dandy.

Since involved fathers tried to nurture as well as support their children, they made an especially hard choice between money and time. Like many mothers, they had to add caretaking onto full-time workplace responsibilities, but employers are generally reluctant to recognize male (or female) parental responsibility as a legitimate right or need.[1] Worse yet, paternal leaves are rarely considered a legitimate option for men even if they formally exist. Involved fathers wished to take time off for parenting, but like most men they were reluctant to do so for fear of imperiling their careers.[2] And even though most employers allow health-related leaves with impunity, they have not been so flexible when it comes to the job of parenting. Workers receive the message that illness is unavoidable, but parenting is voluntary—an indication of a lack of job commitment. Our current corporate culture thus makes parenting hazardous to anyone's career, and choosing a "daddy track" can be just as dangerous as the much-publicized "mommy track." Juan, a financial analyst, knew he could not pull back from his job for more than a few days or a week without jeopardizing his job security. To parental leave,

> I'd say yes, but realistically no. It would be a problem because it's very difficult for me to tell my boss that I have to leave at such a time. I have deadlines to meet. If I leave the office for two or three months, my job is in jeopardy.

Because employers did not offer flexible options for structuring work on a daily basis or over the course of a career, some involved fathers looked to self-employment or home-based work for more flexibility and control. Craig, the ex-dancer currently working in an office, hoped he would be able to integrate work and parenting by working at home:

> I would like to find myself in the situation where I'm not locked into a nine-to-five schedule. Ultimately, I hope I'm doing consulting on my own at home, which means time close to the family. So that in the middle of my own workday, at the house, I'm available. I can just put my work aside and play Daddy.

Most could not even entertain this option. They had to fit parenting in around the edges of their work lives.[3]

Domestic arrangements also impede full equality. Child rearing remains an undervalued, isolating, and largely invisible accomplishment for *all* parents. This has fueled women's flight from domesticity and also dampened men's motivation to choose it. Russell, the legal-aid attorney and father of two, recognized that child rearing was less valued than employment:

> I think I would feel somewhat meaningless to not be engaged in any form of productive work—although certainly raising children is productive work. But I couldn't be responsible for that on a full-time basis. While I love my guys, I don't think I could be around them all the time.

Child rearing can be invisible as well as undervalued. Unlike the size of a paycheck or the title one holds at work, there are few socially recognized rewards for the time a parent devotes to raising a child or the results it produces. This made only the most dedicated, like Hank, willing to consider full-time parenting:

> Nobody will know the time and the effort I put in the family. They will look down on it. I would devote time, hours, and nobody will be happy with it except me because I'll know what I was trying for.

The forces pulling women out of the home are stronger than the forces pulling men into it. Since the social value of public pursuits outstrips the power and prestige of private ones, men are likely to resist full-time domesticity even as women move toward full-time employment. This process is similar to the one pulling women into male-dominated occupations while leaving men less inclined to enter female-dominated ones. In addition, just as women in male-dominated occupations face prejudice and discrimination, fathers who become equal or primary parents are stigmatized—treated as "tokens" in a female-dominated world.[4] Roger shied away from the pervasive questioning about his life as a custodial parent:

> I think I've become somewhat more introverted than I used to be—because I get tired of explaining my situation at home. . . . The thing that blows all the kids' minds—they're all living with Mommy and my kids are living with Daddy.

In the face of such disincentives, most involved fathers rejected staying home for the same reasons many women do and more. Female breadwinning and male homemaking did not seem acceptable even when they made economic sense. Robin, a stockbroker, rejected domesticity precisely because his poor work prospects left him in no state to bear the additional stigma of becoming a househusband. Although he was making a lot less money than his wife was, he felt too "demoralized" to consider staying home. "I'm not secure enough, I guess, to stay home and be a househusband."

Of course, involved fathers actively resisted the discrimination they encountered. They asserted their nurturing competence and insisted on being taken as seriously as female parents are. The prevailing skepticism about men's parental abilities, however, made this an uphill battle. Ernie complained:

> I believe I have as much right in raising the child as she does, but I found a lot of reverse discrimination—people assuming that the

> mother takes care of the child. It's a lot of stereotyping, a lot that's taken for granted. Like pediatricians: they speak to my wife; they won't speak to me. I say, "Hey, I take care of her, too." They look at me like I'm invisible. The same thing with the nursery school. I went out on all the interviews. They looked at me like, "What're *you* doing here?"

Economic, social, and ideological arrangements thus made involved fatherhood difficult. The lack of workplace and domestic supports diluted and suppressed the potential for involvement even among the most motivated men. In the absence of these hurdles, fathers who wished to be involved might have participated far more than they actually did. They might, in fact, have made choices that now remain open to a rapidly diminishing number of women. Ernie wished he had options that only full-time mothers enjoy:

> I'm not the type that has career aspirations and is very goal-oriented. If I didn't have to work, I wouldn't. But I would volunteer. I would work in a nursery school. I would do a lot more volunteer work with my daughter's school. I would love to go on trips like the mothers who don't work, be more active in the P.T.A. I would love that. But I can't.

As the supports for homemaking mothers erode, supports for equal and primary fathers have not emerged to offset the growing imbalance between children's needs and families' resources. Fathers have had to depend on paid help, relatives, and already overburdened wives even when they did not wish to do so.

These obstacles not only left mothers giving up more. They also made involved fathers appear heroic about *whatever* they did. Comparisons with other men could be used to ward off complaints and resist further change. Ernie maintained:

> Sometimes she didn't think I did enough. I couldn't stand that because I thought I was doing too much. I really felt I was doing more than I should, whatever that means. I told her to go talk to some of her friends and see what their husbands are doing.

Nurturing fathers faced deeply rooted barriers to full equality in parenting. Social arrangements at work and in the home dampened even willing men's ability to share equally. The truncated range of choices open to most of these men limited the options of their wives, ex-wives, and partners as well. We can only guess how many mothers' helpers would become equal parents if these obstacles did not exist or, better yet, were replaced by positive supports for involved fatherhood.

Benefiting from the Loss of Privilege: Incentives for Change

If full equality remained beyond the reach of most involved fathers, they nevertheless moved a notable distance toward it. They were not simply forced to make concessions; nor were they just being altruistic. They also perceived offsetting, if unheralded, benefits. After all, parenting can be its own reward—offering intrinsic pleasures and a powerful sense of accomplishment. Rick explained:

> I have an extremely close relationship with my kids, and that makes me feel good. The fact that they're both doing very well in school—I know that at least a little bit of that comes from having been with them when they were young. So there's all those interactions in seeing them on their way to being healthy and vibrant kids.

These feelings took on added significance when other avenues for building self-esteem were blocked. Todd, the aspiring actor who became a construction worker, hoped his talents could be channeled toward his daughter instead of his job:

> If there's any Creator at all up there, She or It or They're going to ask for some sort of accounting at the end. They're going to be pleased if they gave you a certain amount of gifts and you were able to do something with them. I'd still like to be a part of something more meaningful than putting in a new fire hydrant—I guess through my influence on this little one's life.

If children offered a source of pride for those whose workplace aspirations had not been met, this was not just a concern for passing on genes or the family name. Contributions of time and emotions counted more. Carl, who chose utility repair work so that he could care for his daughter after school, saw his "investment" reflected in her talents and achievements:

> I've had a lot of compliments on her, and I take them as a compliment also. It's something that became part of you—teaching them different things, helping them grow up. They'll do something, and it's like seeing a reflection of you.

As work opportunities stall in an age of stagnant economic growth, parenting offers men another avenue for developing self-esteem. But economically successful fathers also reaped benefits from involvement because it balanced lives that would otherwise have been more narrowly focused on paid work. For Charles, the attorney with a young son, caretaking provided a legitimate reason for limiting the demands of work: "I'm working a little less hard, taking on fewer responsibilities. . . . But I think it's great. I don't need all the other shit."

Children also provided the hope of permanence in an age of divorce. Even happily married fathers came to see their children as the bedrock of stability in a shaky world, the one bond that could not be severed or assailed. Having been reared by a single mother, Juan viewed his children rather than his wife as the best chance for enduring emotional ties: "What if one day my wife and I get sick of each other after so many years? So I would like to have children."

Involved fatherhood also provided emotional supports by creating a bond between husbands and wives. Married men were less likely to feel rejected by their wives and excluded from the new relationships that form with the birth of a child. Timothy, the worker at a city dump, could not understand why less-involved fathers complained of being rejected when a new baby arrived:

> They have these books about how fathers are supposed to go through blues because the wife is giving her attention to the child. Is this some kind of maniac that wrote this? I take care of him just as much as she does.

Sharing the load of caring for a newborn also seemed to decrease the chances that a mother would feel overwhelmed and alone during a critical, and trying, turning point in a marriage.[5] Carlos hoped that sharing the caretaking would help him avoid the hostility that he felt unequal arrangements would generate:

> I think it's a great burden to have one parent do all the caretaking. It would burn out that person, and they're not going to be able to respond to you. Then I would start feeling resentment towards her and possibly the child. So the only way I could see avoiding that is by sharing the responsibility.

Since involved fathers believed that a satisfying relationship depended on both partners being able to meet their needs, thwarting a partner's dreams by refusing to participate seemed to be a Pyrrhic victory. The costs of not sharing appeared greater than the costs of sharing. Carl was pleased to escape his parents' pattern:

> My parents are the old school. He never really touched a dish. I like what I'm doing better. The older way, I feel the woman will think, "I never really had an opportunity to do things." She will become resentful later on. Where my wife can't say nothing because she's had her freedom, she's worked, she's not stayed in the kitchen barefoot and pregnant, and I did what I had to do. I feel in the long run it pays off. The other way, maybe she would have left.

Involved fatherhood thus offered two ways of coping with the risks of marriage in an era of divorce. It provided another source of emotional sustenance in the event that the marital bond did not survive. And it offered a way to build less rancorous relationships by reducing wives' resentment. Indeed, there is growing evidence that egalitarian relationships do provide benefits to husbands and wives. In one report, wives whose husbands participate in domestic duties showed lower rates of depression than those with husbands who don't, while another found that the more housework a husband does, the lower are the chances that his wife has considered divorce.[6]

Emotional gratification and marital peace were not the only payoffs. In agreeing to share the domestic load, men can also share the economic load. Their wives' income lessens the pressure to work long hours and take on second jobs. Wesley was pleased to exchange extra hours at work for domestic sharing:

> If Cindy wants to be home, she can stay home. But that would probably mean I would have to either get myself another job or work overtime on the job I have. I would do it. She knows that. But she doesn't want me to. We spend more time with each other this way.

Involved fathers also believed their children would benefit in both the short and long runs—perceptions that research on both married and divorced fathers supports.[7] Larry observed:

> Having spent a lot of time with both of us, she's not really dependent on either one of us. Mommy's like daddy; daddy's like mommy. At times I am her mother. It's good to switch roles. She don't run to mommy or run to daddy. She runs to both of us.

They hoped their example would help their daughters and sons develop a flexible approach to building their own lives. Ernie decided his involvement created a better domestic environment for his daughter:

> The sharing—it's a good role model for her. She sees me cook. I'm trying to teach her baking, and I think it's nice my daughter is learning baking from her father. So I'm hoping she sees that it's split and not that just the wife does this and the man does that.

He also hoped his participation would give his daughter a sense of self-reliance, agreeing with a growing group of psychologists who argue that girls no less than boys need their fathers. Both sexes identify in varying degrees with both parents, and girls look to fathers as well as mothers to provide models for living:[8]

> Raising my child, that is my priority—seeing that she's raised well in the sense of preparing her to face the world, trying to get her exposed as much as possible, so she may find out what she likes to pursue. I hope she has a career. I hope she finds something she really likes and works for it.

These men concluded that their domestic arrangements would also benefit their sons, echoing recent research showing that sons of involved fathers are likely to show a more developed capacity for empathy.[9] Wesley thus concluded that his two sons "feel close to the two of us. Maybe when they get married, they'll share in the house."

Just as these fathers created families that differed from the households in which they were reared, so their children will take the lessons of their childhood into unknown futures. Involved fathers' belief in the advantages of domestic sharing cannot guarantee a similar response in their children, but it can and did strengthen their own resolve to create a more egalitarian household. As more fathers become involved, their growing numbers should prompt wider social acceptance of egalitarian households, bolstering the option to make such choices.

Ultimately, however, men's movement toward domestic equality will depend on their ability to overcome the obstacles to change and their desire to resist the social pressures to conform. Equal fathers were willing and able to defy social expectations, to overcome social constraints, and to reject the pathways of the past. There is good reason to believe that their outlooks and choices reflect a simmering mood among many American men, who long for more work flexibility and fewer work demands. There is even reason to believe many would be willing to relinquish some earnings in exchange for spending more time with their families. A *Time* survey found that 56 percent of a random sample of men said they would forfeit up to one-fourth of their salaries "to have more family and personal time," and 45 percent "said they would probably refuse a promotion that involved sacrificing hours with their families."[10] Carl reflects this mood:

> It's amazing how many people don't understand the way I feel. I would prefer to be home than work overtime, where they would kill to get it. They say, "What are you, rich?" No, but you only need a certain amount of money to live. God forbid you walk down the street and get struck by a car, or whatever, and it's over. I don't want to say, "Why didn't I spend more time with my family?" It's not going to happen to me. You can control it.

By focusing on the advantages and discounting the drawbacks of their choices, men are able to overcome some of the social and ideological barriers to equal parenting. In adding up the sacrifices and the gains, Larry spoke for the group: "I've given some things up, sure, but the changes in my lifestyle are eighty or ninety percent in the positive."

Though few in number, equal fathers demonstrate that men can discover or acquire nurturing skills and find pleasure in using them. Those men who did find support for being an equal father made contingent choices just like those who did not. In both instances, different circumstances could easily have produced different outcomes. It is not surprising that Rick found his rare and unexpected path to be a matter of chance:

I have very conservative attitudes in many respects. The fact that we got married and had children was very conservative. The fact that within those parameters, we shared, co-shared, work and family—that was not conservative. We've never discussed it, but I feel that the outcome is built much more on chance. I may not have always felt that way, but my own experiences confirmed it.

Chance, however, is just another way of saying that his choice was based on unusual and unexpected opportunities. Given how rare are the supports for involved fathering and how pervasive the obstacles, its rise is even more significant than its limited nature. For the potential of the many men who wish to be more involved to be realized, however, the unusual circumstances that now prompt only a small fraction of men to become equal parents must become real for a much larger group.

NOTES

1. See Lawson, Carol. 1991. "Baby Beckons: Why Is Daddy at Work?" *New York Times* (May 16); C1, C8. The Family Leave Act that finally became law in 1993 is an important first step, but much more will be needed for men to feel able to choose equal parenting.
2. Joseph H. Pleck. 1983. "Husbands' Paid Work and Family Roles: Current Research Trends," *Research in the Interweave of Social Roles: Jobs and Families* 3: 251–333.
3. Barbara J. Risman and Maxine P. Atkinson. 1990. "Gender in Intimate Relationships: Toward a Dialectical Structural Theory." Paper presented at the National Council on Family Relations Theory, Construction, and Research Methodology Workshop (November), Seattle, Washington. According to Risman and Atkinson: "No matter how involved 'new feminist' fathers become in child-care, they . . . are expected to work harder and are constrained from leaving less than optimal jobs because of their economic responsibilities. When they do care for their children after work, they are praised highly by friends, family members, and wives as wonderful, modern, 'involved' fathers" (pp. 15–16).
4. Hal Strauss. 1989. "Freaks of Nature." *American Health* (January–February): 70–71; Rosabeth M. Kanter. 1977. *Men and Women of the Corporation*. New York: Basic Books; Bryan E. Robinson. 1986. "Men Caring for the Young: A Profile." In *Men's Changing Roles in the Family*, pp. 151–61. Edited by Robert A. Lewis and Marvin B. Sussman. New York: Haworth Press. Men who become primary parents face barriers similar to those faced by the first female managers, who had to cope with being "tokens." Strauss discusses the stigmatization and social isolation of househusbands. Kanter analyzes how the first female managers were tokens in the corporation. Robinson, 1986, reports that male caregivers who work in nursery schools and day-care programs also faced discrimination and stigma from employers, co-workers, and even parents.
5. See Alice A. Rossi. 1960. "Transition to Parenthood." *Journal of Marriage and the Family* 30: 26–39.
6. Joan Huber and Glenna Spitze. 1983. *Sex Stratification: Children, Housework, and Jobs*. New York: Academic Press; Catherine E. Ross, John Mirowsky, and Joan Huber. 1983. "Dividing Work, Sharing Work, and In-Between: Marriage Patterns and Depression." *American Sociological Review* 48 (6) (December): 809–23; See also

Michael E. Lamb, Joseph H. Pleck, and James A. Levine. 1987. "Effects of Increased Paternal Involvement on Fathers and Mothers." In *Reassessing Fatherhood: New Observations on Fathers and the Modern Family,* pp. 103–25. Edited by Charlie Lewis and Margaret O'Brien. Newberry Park, CA: Sage Publications; Arlie R. Hochschild with Anne Machung. 1989. *The Second Shift: Working Parents and the Revolution at Home.* New York: Viking.

7. See Frank F. Furstenberg, Jr., S. Phillip Morgan, and Paul D. Allison. 1987. "Paternal Participation and Children's Well-Being After Marital Dissolution." *American Sociological Review* 52(5):695–701; Shirley M. H. Hanson. 1986. "Father/Child Relationships: Beyond *Kramer vs. Kramer.*" In *Men's Changing Roles in the Family,* pp. 135–50. Edited by Robert A. Lewis and Marvin B. Sussman. New York: Haworth Press; Michael E. Lamb, ed. 1976. *The Role of the Father in Child Development.* New York: Wiley; J. W. Santrock and R. A. Warshak. 1979. "Father Custody and Social Development in Boys and Girls." *Journal of Social Issues* 32: 112–25; J. W. Santrock, R. A. Warshak, and G. L. Elliot. 1982. "Social Development and Parent-Child Interaction in Father-Custody and Stepmother Families." In *Nontraditional Families: Parenting and Child Development,* pp. 289–314. Edited by Michael E. Lamb. Hillside, NJ: Lawrence Erlbaum.
8. Victoria Secunda. 1992. *Women and Their Fathers: The Sexual and Romantic Impact of the First Man in Your Life.* New York: Delacorte Press.
9. Daniel Goleman. 1990. "Surprising Findings about the Development of Empathy in Children." *New York Times* (July 10): C1.
10. Reported in Judith Stacey. 1991. "Backwards toward the Post-Modern Family." In *America at Century's End,* pp. 17–34. Edited by Alan Wolfe. Berkeley and Los Angeles: University of California Press. See also Phyllis Moen and Donna I. Dempster-McClain. 1987. "Employed Parents: Role Strain, Work Time, and Preferences for Working Less." *Journal of Marriage and the Family* 49 (3): 579–90; Eli Chinoy. 1955. *Automobile Workers and the American Dream.* New York: Random House. If Chinoy found that automobile workers in the 1950s dreamed about retiring, inheriting wealth, or opening their own businesses as an alternative to dead-end factory jobs, then the decline of well-paying, secure manufacturing jobs over the last decade has given this dream of independence through self-employment new life.

41

MAN CHILD
A Black Lesbian Feminist's Response

AUDRE LORDE

This article is not a theoretical discussion of Lesbian Mothers and their Sons, nor a how-to article. It is an attempt to scrutinize and share some pieces of that common history belonging to my son and to me. I have two children: a fifteen-and-a-half-year-old daughter Beth, and a fourteen-year-old son Jonathan. This is the way it was/is with me and Jonathan, and I leave the theory to another time and person. This is one woman's telling.

I have no golden message about the raising of sons for other lesbian mothers, no secret to transpose your questions into certain light. I have my own ways of rewording those same questions, hoping we will all come to speak those questions and pieces of our lives we need to share. We are women making contact within ourselves and with each other across the restrictions of a printed page, bent upon the use of our own/one another's knowledges.

The truest direction comes from inside. I give the most strength to my children by being willing to look within myself, and by being honest with them about what I find there, without expecting a response beyond their years. In this way they begin to learn to look beyond their own fears.

All our children are outriders for a queendom not yet assured.

My adolescent son's growing sexuality is a conscious dynamic between Jonathan and me. It would be presumptuous of me to discuss Jonathan's sexuality here, except to state my belief that whomever he chooses to explore this area with, his choices will be nonoppressive, joyful, and deeply felt from within, places of growth.

One of the difficulties in writing this piece has been temporal; this is the summer when Jonathan is becoming a man, physically. And our sons must become men—such men as we hope our daughters, born and unborn, will be pleased to live among. Our sons will not grow into women. Their way is more difficult than that of our daughters, for they must move away from us, without us. Hopefully, our sons have what they have learned from us, and a howness to forge it into their own image.

Our daughters have us, for measure or rebellion or outline or dream; but the sons of lesbians have to make their own definitions of self as men. This

---

Audre Lorde, "Man Child: A Black Lesbian Feminist's Response" from *Sister Outsider: Essays and Speeches.* Reprinted with the permission of The Crossing Press.

is both power and vulnerability. The sons of lesbians have the advantage of our blueprints for survival, but they must take what we know and transpose it into their own maleness. May the goddess be kind to my son, Jonathan.

Recently I have met young Black men about whom I am pleased to say that their future and their visions, as well as their concerns within the present, intersect more closely with Jonathan's than do my own. I have shared vision with these men as well as temporal strategies for our survivals and I appreciate the spaces in which we could sit down together. Some of these men I met at the First Annual Conference of Third World Lesbians and Gays held in Washington, D.C., in October, 1979. I have met others in different places and do not know how they identify themselves sexually. Some of these men are raising families alone. Some have adopted sons. They are Black men who dream and who act and who own their feelings, questioning. It is heartening to know our sons do not step out alone.

When Jonathan makes me angriest, I always say he is bringing out the testosterone in me. What I mean is that he is representing some piece of myself as a woman that I am reluctant to acknowledge or explore. For instance, what does "acting like a man" mean? For me, what I reject? For Jonathan, what he is trying to redefine?

Raising Black children—female and male—in the mouth of a racist, sexist, suicidal dragon is perilous and chancy. If they cannot love and resist at the same time, they will probably not survive. And in order to survive they must let go. This is what mothers teach—love, survival—that is, self-definition and letting go. For each of these, the ability to feel strongly and to recognize those feelings is central: how to feel love, how to neither discount fear nor be overwhelmed by it, how to enjoy feeling deeply.

I wish to raise a Black man who will not be destroyed by, nor settle for, those corruptions called *power* by the white fathers who mean his destruction as surely as they mean mine. I wish to raise a Black man who will recognize that the legitimate objects of his hostility are not women, but the particulars of a structure that programs him to fear and despise women as well as his own Black self.

For me, this task begins with teaching my son that I do not exist to do his feeling for him.

Men who are afraid to feel must keep women around to do their feeling for them while dismissing us for the same supposedly "inferior" capacity to feel deeply. But in this way also, men deny themselves their own essential humanity, becoming trapped in dependency and fear.

As a Black woman committed to a liveable future, and as a mother loving and raising a boy who will become a man, I must examine all my possibilities of being within such a destructive system.

Jonathan was three and one half when Frances, my lover, and I met; he was seven when we all began to live together permanently. From the start, Frances' and my insistence that there be no secrets in our household about the fact that we were lesbians has been the source of problems and strengths for both children. In the beginning, this insistence grew out of the knowledge, on both parts, that whatever was hidden out of fear could always be used either against the children or ourselves—one imperfect but useful argument for honesty. The knowledge of fear can help make us free.

> for the embattled
> there is no place
> that cannot be
> home
> nor is.[1]

For survival, Black children in America must be raised to be warriors. For survival, they must also be raised to recognize the enemy's many faces. Black children of lesbian couples have an advantage because they learn, very early, that oppression comes in many different forms, none of which have anything to do with their own worth.

To help give me perspective, I remember that for years, in the name-calling at school, boys shouted at Jonathan not—"your mother's a lesbian"—but rather—"your mother's a nigger."

When Jonathan was eight years old and in the third grade, we moved, and he went to a new school where his life was hellish as a new boy on the block. He did not like to play rough games. He did not like to fight. He did not like to stone dogs. And all this marked him early on as an easy target.

When he came in crying one afternoon, I heard from Beth how the corner bullies were making Jonathan wipe their shoes on the way home whenever Beth wasn't there to fight them off. And when I heard that the ringleader was a little boy in Jonathan's class his own size, an interesting and very disturbing thing happened to me.

My fury at my own long-ago impotence, and my present pain at his suffering, made me start to forget all that I knew about violence and fear, and blaming the victim, I started to hiss at the weeping child. "The next time you come in here crying . . . ," and I suddenly caught myself in horror.

This is the way we allow the destruction of our sons to begin—in the name of protection and to ease our own pain. *My* son get beaten up? I was about to demand that he buy that first lesson in the corruption of power, that might makes right. I could hear myself beginning to perpetuate the age-old distortions about what strength and bravery really are.

And no, Jonathan didn't have to fight if he didn't want to, but somehow he did have to feel better about not fighting. An old horror rolled over me of being the fat kid who ran away, terrified of getting her glasses broken.

About that time a very wise woman said to me, "Have you ever told Jonathan that once you used to be afraid, too?"

The idea seemed far-out to me at the time, but the next time he came in crying and sweaty from having run away again, I could see that he felt shamed at having failed me, or some image he and I had created in his head of mother/woman. This image of woman being able to handle it all was bolstered by the fact that he lived in a household with three strong women, his lesbian parents and his forthright older sister. At home, for Jonathan, power was clearly female.

And because our society teaches us to think in an either/or mode—kill or be killed, dominate or be dominated—this meant that he must either surpass or be lacking. I could see the implications of this line of thought. Consider the two western classic myth/models of mother/son relationships: Jocasta/Oedipus, the son who fucks his mother, and Clytemnestra/Orestes, the son who kills his mother.

It all felt connected to me.

I sat down on the hallway steps and took Jonathan on my lap and wiped his tears. "Did I ever tell you about how I used to be afraid when I was your age?"

I will never forget the look on that little boy's face as I told him the tale of my glasses and my after-school fights. It was a look of relief and total disbelief, all rolled into one.

It is as hard for our children to believe that we are not omnipotent as it is for us to know it, as parents. But that knowledge is necessary as the first step in the reassessment of power as something other than might, age, privilege, or the lack of fear. It is an important step for a boy, whose societal destruction begins when he is forced to believe that he can only be strong if he doesn't feel, or if he wins.

I thought about all this one year later when Beth and Jonathan, ten and nine, were asked by an interviewer how they thought they had been affected by being children of a feminist.

Jonathan said that he didn't think there was too much in feminism for boys, although it certainly was good to be able to cry if he felt like it and not to have to play football if he didn't want to. I think of this sometimes now when I see him practicing for his Brown Belt in Tae Kwon Do.

The strongest lesson I can teach my son is the same lesson I teach my daughter: how to be who he wishes to be for himself. And the best way I can do this is to be who I am and hope that he will learn from this not how to be me, which is not possible, but how to be himself. And this means how to move to that voice from within himself, rather than to those raucous, persuasive, or threatening voices from outside, pressuring him to be what the world wants him to be.

And that is hard enough.

Jonathan is learning to find within himself some of the different faces of courage and strength, whatever he chooses to call them. Two years ago, when Jonathan was twelve and in the seventh grade, one of his friends at school who had been to the house persisted in calling Frances "the maid." When Jonathan corrected him, the boy then referred to her as "the cleaning woman." Finally Jonathan said, simply, "Frances is not the cleaning woman, she's my mother's lover." Interestingly enough, it is the teachers at this school who still have not recovered from his openness.

Frances and I were considering attending a Lesbian/Feminist conference this summer, when we were notified that no boys over ten were allowed. This presented logistic as well as philosophical problems for us, and we sent the following letter:

> Sisters:
>
> Ten years as an interracial lesbian couple has taught us both the dangers of an oversimplified approach to the nature and solutions of any oppression, as well as the danger inherent in an incomplete vision.
>
> Our thirteen-year-old son represents as much hope for our future world as does our fifteen-year-old daughter, and we are not willing to abandon him to the killing streets of New York City while we journey west to help form a Lesbian-Feminist vision of the future world in which we can all survive and flourish. I hope we can continue this dialogue in the near future, as I feel it is important to our vision and our survival.

The question of separatism is by no means simple. I am thankful that one of my children is male, since that helps to keep me honest. Every line I write shrieks there are no easy solutions.

I grew up in largely female environments, and I know how crucial that has been to my own development. I feel the want and need often for the society of women, exclusively. I recognize that our own spaces are essential for developing and recharging.

As a Black woman, I find it necessary to withdraw into all-Black groups at times for exactly the same reasons—differences in stages of development and differences in levels of interaction. Frequently, when speaking with men and white women, I am reminded of how difficult and time-consuming it is to have to reinvent the pencil every time you want to send a message.

But this does not mean that my responsibility for my son's education stops at age ten, any more than it does for my daughter's. However, for each of them, that responsibility does grow less and less as they become more woman and man.

Both Beth and Jonathan need to know what they can share and what they cannot, how they are joined and how they are not. And Frances and I, as grown women and lesbians coming more and more into our power, need to relearn the experience that difference does not have to be threatening.

When I envision the future, I think of the world I crave for my daughters and my sons. It is thinking for survival of the species—thinking for life.

Most likely there will always be women who move with women, women who live with men, men who choose men. I work for a time when women with women, women with men, men with men, all share the work of a world that does not barter bread or self for obedience, nor beauty, nor love. And in that world we will raise our children free to choose how best to fulfill themselves. For we are jointly responsible for the care and raising of the young, since *that* they be raised is a function, ultimately, of the species.

Within that tripartite pattern of relating/existence, the raising of the young will be the joint responsibility of all adults who choose to be associated with children. Obviously, the children raised within each of these three relationships will be different, lending a special savor to that eternal inquiry into how best can we live our lives.

Jonathan was three and a half when Frances and I met. He is now fourteen years old. I feel the living perspective that having lesbian parents has brought to Jonathan is a valuable addition to his human sensitivity.

Jonathan has had the advantage of growing up within a nonsexist relationship, one in which this society's pseudo-natural assumptions of ruler/ruled are being challenged. And this is not only because Frances and I are lesbians, for unfortunately there are some lesbians who are still locked into patriarchal patterns of unequal power relationships.

These assumptions of power relationships are being questioned because Frances and I, often painfully and with varying degrees of success, attempt to evaluate and measure over and over again our feelings concerning power, our own and others'. And we explore with care those areas concerning how it is used and expressed between us and between us and the children, openly and otherwise. A good part of our biweekly family meetings are devoted to this exploration.

As parents, Frances and I have given Jonathan our love, our openness, and our dreams to help form his visions. Most importantly, as the son of lesbians, he has had an invaluable model—not only of a relationship—but of relating.

Jonathan is fourteen now. In talking over this paper with him and asking his permission to share some pieces of his life, I asked Jonathan what he felt were the strongest negative and the strongest positive aspects for him in having grown up with lesbian parents.

He said the strongest benefit he felt he had gained was that he knew a lot more about people than most other kids his age that he knew, and that he did not have a lot of the hang-ups that some other boys did about men and women.

And the most negative aspect he felt, Jonathan said, was the ridicule he got from some kids with straight parents.

"You mean, from your peers?" I said.

"Oh no," he answered promptly. "My peers know better. I mean other kids."

NOTE

1. From "School Note" in *The Black Unicorn* (W. W. Norton and Company, New York, 1978), p. 55.

42

I AM A MAN

RAUL E. YBARRA

Even though it was difficult, I continued working as a janitor at night and went to school during the day. On weekends I worked out in the fields doing anything from planting the crops to irrigating, to harvesting, and anything in between. I was not able to keep any of the money, however. My father took most of it. "For room and board," he'd say. Then he'd give me about forty dollars back. Then he'd tell me to give half of the forty to my brothers. My younger brothers did not have to work; all they needed to do was go to school. In addition, I had to go looking for my younger brothers when they were off at football or basketball games, dances, or whatever.

Whenever my father saw that I was the only one in my room, he asked me where my brothers were. "I don't know," was my usual answer. "Ve a buscarlos. And don't come back until you find them," was his usual command.

I'd get in his little, light blue Chevy Luv and go into town. Most of the time I didn't have any idea where to look for them, so I'd drive around until I got tired or ran low on gas. Then I'd stop at the local 7-11 store for a Diet Pepsi and play video games.

As soon as I stepped inside the store, the sales clerk, who was usually a high school student, would jokingly say "No, they're not here," and laugh.

I'd laugh along with him even though I didn't like it. But I knew that there was nothing I could do. Most of the students knew who I was and what I was doing. So I'd put a burrito in the microwave and eat it while I played games.

"Eating frozen burritos again?" the boy behind the counter joked. "Why don't you tell your mother to make you some? Be a man about it."

I'd just ignore him and continue playing Pac Man or Star Blaster. All the time I was there, I knew I was the butt of many jokes about looking for my brothers and eating food made by a machine. Sometimes I did know where my brothers were, but I still didn't look for them, even though I knew I was going to get in trouble for not finding them.

"¡Estúpido!" my father called me as soon as he saw me get out of the pickup alone. I knew what would follow before he even said it. "Did you look for them? Why couldn't you find them? You go to school, and you can't do anything right!"

All the time he yelled at me, I didn't say anything back. I just stared at him, at his feet. They were swollen with a couple of toenails missing, and their color was more yellow than the rest of his skin.

"Tu no sabes hacer nada," he continued yelling. "You're useless. Go to bed."

Then I'd slowly walk to my bedroom, angry—angry at my brothers for getting me into trouble, angry at my father for making me do his work, angry at myself for being too scared to say anything back. I'd just lie in my bed listening to my breathing as I slowly calmed down. Later I'd hear my brothers come home giggling and laughing, and I'd pretend to be asleep. The noise, however, usually woke my father up. "Raul, why can't you keep them quiet?" he'd yell. That was enough most of the time to calm my brothers down, so I didn't have to say anything. But one night I answered back, "Because they're not my sons."

The entire house suddenly became quiet. My brothers' breathing became very loud as they pretended to be asleep. The floor creaked louder and louder as my father walked toward our bedroom. When the door opened, it seemed to whine. The color of my father's skin made it difficult for me to see him clearly, but I made out his outline standing in the doorway. He was in his white underwear with a belt in his hand.

"¿Que dijites?" he asked.

"Nada," I answered, also shaking my head.

"Levantate."

I slowly pulled the blanket off of me and stood.

"¡Mentiroso!" he said as he swung his belt across my face. "I don't want lies." Then he left the room.

Tears poured down my face, stinging the mark on my cheek, as I stood clenching my teeth and gripping the bedpost. "Hombres no lloran," I remembered my father saying. I wanted to prove I was a man. I didn't want to cry, so I closed my eyes, but that only made the tears come faster. I got back in bed without turning, pulled the blanket over me and stared at the bunk above, forcing myself not to think of anything.

Back then I wondered why my younger brothers didn't have to work, why I started working at ten years of age and they didn't. I had no idea. Now I do. Albert and I were the older ones. We had to support our younger brothers. But Albert wasn't there; I was. I was quiet, didn't complain, kept my grades up. My brothers did none of these. I wanted to leave, to do what Albert and my sisters did, but I didn't. And I knew the reason. My father was a big man to me still. I was scared.

A month later, I graduated from high school and, according to my father, it was time to go and work like a man. I started the summer like the summers before: weeds in June, sweet potatoes in July, and grapes in August. In late August, I wanted to start college, but my father took me with him to knock almonds. He began by banging the trees with a rubber mallet, and I followed with a twenty-foot bamboo pole in my hands, knocking the almonds that clung to the tree. We worked fifteen hours a day that week. We started at eight to give the sun time to dissipate the moisture and worked until eleven at night, using spotlights after dark. At the end of the day, we went home tired, sweaty, and covered with dust. I just wanted to clean myself up and go to bed.

On Saturday, after we had gotten off work, I sat down in a chair, thankful that the next day was Sunday. I didn't have to get up. I started taking off my shoes when my father whistled. I thought about pretending I didn't hear, but I realized that would just get him angry. I got up slowly and dragged myself over to him.

"Tráigame una cerveza," he said.

I was tired, tired of working long hours, tired of following his orders. I wanted to say, "No. Go get it yourself," but I went to the kitchen, grabbed a beer, and started taking it to him.

I was almost to him when he yelled, "¡Andale pronto!"

All I could think about was how my father treated me. I realized I wasn't a man to him. He never wanted me to be a man, only a slave like my mother. I was there to bring him his beer, bring him his shoes, work for him. Now I saw why my brother and sisters had left. They too didn't like the way they were treated, and they too were scared of him. But they left anyway. I realized now why Anna let herself get pregnant, why Margaret went to live with a man, why Albert just left without saying anything to anybody, why he never bothered to tell anybody where he went. Fear. I knew why I was still there, still being his slave. . . . I didn't say anything; I didn't go anywhere; I followed orders. Gripping the beer can tightly, I gave it to him. He didn't even look at me. Instead, he reached down and patted Tico.

I was angry, angry at the dog. He was better treated, petted when he did something right. I never got that attention.

I don't remember everything that happened next. I do remember white foam splashing from the can that hit the floor. I remember Jose coming between us pushing me away as I went for my father.

"Pinche Perro. Hijo de perra," my father kept yelling at me over and over.

Jose and Richard held me back, while I yelled, "Fuck you! Fuck you!" at the same time struggling to break loose. "I ain't your fucking slave no more." Then I saw my mother crying, holding onto my father's arm, trying to calm him down.

My brothers were holding me back, telling me, "Calm down, man. Calm down. Man, what's you trying to do?"

"Let go," I yelled, trying to free myself from their grip. But they just held tighter, too afraid to let go for fear I'd attack my father. My mother walked over, stopped in front of me, and slapped my face.

I looked at her. I saw the dog jumping wildly, barking. I looked at my father. He was the same height as I was, his skin a dull brown, his hair now more grey than black. He didn't look proud or menacing with his belly sticking out and his shoulders slouched. I realized then that this was my father, the man I had patterned myself after, the man I had wanted to be.

After they saw I was calm enough, my brothers let me go. I turned to leave, and one of them gave me a helping push. I quickly shoved the arm away and glared at them.

I heard my mother say "ya no Raul." I walked out the door and down the street, kicking and hitting anything in my way. I ended up at a house of a friend, Don Mier, one of the few instructors who had helped me through high school.

By the time I got there, my right hand was swollen to where I couldn't close it, but I was calm enough to start worrying about where I was going to stay. Don wasn't at home, so I sat on his patio table to think about what I was going to do next. When I woke, it was already daylight, and Don still wasn't home, so I broke into his house, washed up, ate, and was gone before he came. The next night I did the same thing, slept on the patio table, but he saw me in the morning. He never asked any questions. He just told me I could stay there as long as I wanted, but I would have to pay rent when I could afford it.

"I only need a couple of days," I remember telling him, "to figure out what I'm going to do."

43

SEXUAL DISSENT AND THE FAMILY
The Sharon Kowalski Case

NAN D. HUNTER

No connection between family, marriage, or procreation on the one hand and homosexual activity on the other has been demonstrated.

SUPREME COURT, BOWERS V. HARDWICK, 1986

Sharon Kowalski is the child of a divorce between her consanguineous family and her family of affinity, the petitioner Karen Thompson. . . . That Sharon's family of affinity has not enjoyed societal recognition in the past is unfortunate.

MINNESOTA STATE DISTRICT COURT
IN RE: GUARDIANSHIP OF SHARON KOWALSKI, WARD, 1991

In the effort to end second-class citizenship for lesbian and gay Americans, no obstacle has proved tougher to surmount than the cluster of issues surrounding "the family." The concept of family functions as a giant cultural screen. Projected onto it, contests over race, gender, sexuality and a range of other "domestic" issues from crime to taxes constantly create and recreate a newly identified zone of social combat, the politics of the family. Activists of all persuasions eagerly seek to enter the discursive field, ever ready to debate and discuss: Who counts as a family? Which "family values" are the authentic ones? Is there a place in the family for queers? As battles are won and lost in this cultural war, progressives and conservatives agree on at least one thing—the family is highly politicized terrain.

For lesbians and gays, these debates have dramatic real-life consequences, probably more so than with any other legal issue. Relationship questions touch almost every person's life at some point, in a way that military issues, for example, do not. Further, the unequal treatment is blatant, *de jure* and universal, as compared with the employment arena, where discrimination may be more subtle and variable. No state allows a lesbian or gay couple to marry. No state recognizes (although a number of counties and

---

Nan D. Hunter, "Sexual Dissent and the Family: The Sharon Kowalski Case" from *The Nation* (October 7, 1991). Reprinted with permission.

cities do) domestic partnership systems under which unmarried couples (gay or straight) can become eligible for certain benefits usually available only to spouses. The fundamental inequity is that, barring mental incompetence or consanguinity, virtually any straight couple has the option to marry and thus establish a next-of-kin relationship that the state will enforce. No lesbian or gay couple can. Under the law, two women or two men are forever strangers, regardless of their relationship.

One result is that every lesbian or gay man's nightmare is to be cut off from one's primary other, physically incapacitated, stranded, unable to make contact, without legal recourse. It is a nightmare that could not happen to a married couple. But it did happen to two Minnesota women, Sharon Kowalski and Karen Thompson, in a remarkable case that threaded its way through the courts for seven years.

Sharon Kowalski, notwithstanding the Minnesota State District Court's characterization of her as a "child of divorce," is an adult with both a committed life partner and parents who bitterly refuse to acknowledge either her lesbianism or her lover. Kowalski is a former physical education teacher and amateur athlete, whose Minnesota women's high school shot-put record still stands. In 1983, she was living with her lover, Thompson, in the home they had jointly purchased in St. Cloud. Both women were deeply closeted; they exchanged rings with each other but told virtually no one of their relationship. That November, Kowalski suffered devastating injuries in a car accident, which left her unable to speak or walk, with arms deformed and with major brain damage, including seriously impaired short-term memory.

After the accident, both Thompson and Kowalski's father petitioned to be appointed Sharon's guardian; initially, an agreement was entered that the father would become guardian on the condition that Thompson retain equal rights to visit and consult with doctors. By the summer of 1985, after growing hostilities, the father refused to continue the arrangement, and persuaded a local court that Thompson's visits caused Kowalski to feel depressed. One doctor hired by the father wrote a letter stating that Kowalski was in danger of sexual abuse. Within twenty-four hours after being named sole guardian, the father cut off all contact between Thompson and Kowalski, including mail. By this time, Kowalski had been moved to a nursing home near the small town where she grew up in the Iron Range, a rural mining area in northern Minnesota.

Surely one reason the Kowalski case is so compelling is that, for millions of parents, learning that one's son is gay or daughter is lesbian would be *their* worst nightmare. That is all the more true in small-town America, among people who are religiously observant and whose expectations for a daughter are primarily marriage and motherhood. "The good Lord put us here for reproduction, not that kind of way," Donald Kowalski told the *Los Angeles Times* in 1988. "It's just not a normal life style. The Bible will tell you that." Karen Thompson, he told other reporters, was "an animal" and was lying about his daughter's life. "I've never seen anything that would make me believe" that his daughter is lesbian, he said to the *New York Times* in 1989. How much less painful it must be to explain a lesbian daughter's life as seduction, rather than to experience it as betrayal.

In 1988, Thompson's stubborn struggle to "bring Sharon home" entered a new stage. A different judge, sitting in Duluth, ordered Kowalski moved to a new facility for medical evaluation. Soon thereafter, based on staff recommendations from the second nursing facility, the court ordered that Thompson be allowed to visit. The two women saw each other again in the spring of 1989, after three and a half years of forced separation. Kowalski, who can communicate by typing on a special keyboard, said that she wanted to live in "St. Cloud with Karen."

In May 1990, citing a heart condition for which he had been hospitalized, Donald Kowalski resigned as his daughter's guardian. This resignation set the stage for Thompson to file a renewed petition for appointment as guardian, which she did. But in an April 1991 ruling, Minnesota State District Court Judge Robert Campbell selected as guardian Karen Tomberlin—a friend of both Kowalski and her parents, who supported Tomberlin's request. On the surface, the court sought balance. The judge characterized the Kowalski parents and Karen Thompson as the "two wings" of Sharon Kowalski's family. He repeatedly asserted that both must have ample access to visitation with Kowalski. He described Tomberlin as a neutral third party who would not exclude either side. But the biggest single reason behind the decision, the one that he characterized as "instrumental," seemed to be the judge's anger at Thompson for ever telling Kowalski's parents (in a private letter), and then the world at large, that she and Kowalski were lovers.

The court condemned Thompson's revelation of her own relationship as the "outing" of Sharon Kowalski. Thompson did write the letter to Kowalski's parents without telling Kowalski (who was at the time just emerging from a three-month coma after the accident) and did build on her own an active political organization around the case, composed chiefly of disability and lesbian and gay rights groups. Of course, for most of that period, she could not have consulted Kowalski because the two were cut off from each other.

In truth, though, the judge's concern seemed to be more for the outing of Kowalski's parents. He describes the Kowalskis as "outraged and hurt by the public invasion of Sharon's privacy and their privacy," and he blames this outing for the bitterness between Thompson and the parents. Had Thompson simply kept this to herself, the court implies, none of these nasty facts would ever have had to be discussed. The cost, of course, would have been the forfeiture of Thompson's relationship with her lover.

An openly stated preference for ignorance over knowledge is remarkable in a judicial opinion. One imagines the judge silently cursing Thompson for her arrogance in claiming the role of spouse, and for her insistence on shattering the polite fiction of two gym teachers living and buying a house together as just good friends. Women, especially, aren't supposed to be so stubborn or uppity. One can sense the court's empathetic response of shared embarrassment with the parents, of the desire not to be told and thus not to be forced to speak on this subject.

The final chapter in the Kowalski case vindicated Karen Thompson's long struggle. The Minnesota Court of Appeals granted Thompson's guardianship petition in December, 1991, reversing the trial judge on every point.

The conflict in the Kowalski case illustrates one of the prime contradictions underlying all the cases seeking legal protection for lesbian and gay couples. This culture is deeply invested with a notion of the ideal family as not only a zone of privacy and a structure of authority (preferably male in the conservative view) but also as a barrier against sexuality unlicensed by the state. Even many leftists and progressives, who actively contest male authority and at least some of the assumptions behind privacy, are queasy about constructing a family politics with queerness on the inside rather than the outside.

When such sexuality is culturally recognized *within* family bounds, "the family" ceases to function as an enforcer of sexual norms. That is why the moms and dads in groups like P-FLAG, an organization primarily of parents supportive of their lesbian and gay children, make such emotionally powerful spokespersons for the cause of civil rights. Parents who welcome sexual dissenters within the family undermine the notion that such dissent is intrinsically antithetical to deep human connection.

The theme of cultural anxiety about forms of sexuality not bounded and controlled by the family runs through a series of recent judicial decisions. In each case, the threat to norms did not come from an assault on the prerogatives of family by libertarian outsiders, a prospect often cited by the right wing to trigger social anxieties. Instead, each court faced the dilemma of how to repress, at least in the law, the anomaly of unsanctioned sexuality within the family.

In a stunning decision in 1989, the Supreme Court ruled in *Michael H. v. Gerald D.* that a biological father had no constitutionally protected right to a relationship with his daughter, despite both paternity (which was not disputed) and a psychological bond that the two had formed. Instead, the Court upheld the rule that because the child's mother—who had had an affair with the child's biological father—was married to another man, the girl would be presumed to be the husband's child. It was more important, the Court declared, to protect the "unitary family," that is, the marriage, than to subject anyone to "embarrassment" by letting the child and her father continue to see each other. The Court ruled that a state could properly force the termination of that bond rather than "disrupt an otherwise harmonious and apparently exclusive marital relationship." We are not bound, the Court said, to protect what it repeatedly described as "adulterous fathers."

In *Hodgson v. Minnesota,* the Supreme Court upheld a Minnesota requirement that a pregnant teenager had to notify both of her parents—even if they were divorced or if there was a threat of violence from her family—

prior to obtaining an abortion, so long as she had the alternative option to petition a court. The decision was read primarily as an abortion decision and a ruling on the extent of privacy protection that will be accorded a minor who decides to have an abortion. But the case was also, at its core, about sex in the family and specifically about whether parents could rely on the state for assistance in learning whether a daughter is sexually active.

In two very similar cases in 1991, appellate courts in New York and California ruled that a lesbian partner who had coparented a child with the biological mother for some years had no standing to seek visitation after the couple split up. Both courts acknowledged that the best interests of the child would be served by allowing a parental relationship to continue, but both also ruled that the law would not recognize what the New York court called "a biological stranger." Such a person could be a parent only if there had been a marriage or an adoption.

Indeed, perhaps the most important point in either decision was the footnote in the California ruling that invited lesbian and gay couples to adopt children jointly: "We see nothing in these [statutory] provisions that would preclude a child from being jointly adopted by someone of the same sex as the natural parent." This opens the door for many more such adoptions, at least in California, which is one of six states where lesbian- or gay-couple adoption has occurred, although rarely. The New York court made no such overture.

The effort to legalize gay marriage will almost certainly emerge as a major issue in the next decade. Lawsuits seeking a right to marry have been filed in the District of Columbia and Hawaii, and activists in other states are contemplating litigation. In 1989, the Conference of Delegates of the State Bar of California endorsed an amendment of that state's law to permit lesbian and gay couples to marry.

The law's changes to protect sexual dissent within the family will occur at different speeds in different places, which might not be so bad. Family law has always been a province primarily of state rather than federal regulation, and often has varied from state to state; grounds for divorce, for example, used to differ dramatically depending on geography. What seems likely to occur in the next wave of family cases is the same kind of variability in the legal definition of the family itself. Those very discrepancies may help to denaturalize concepts like "marriage" and "parent," and to expose the utter contingency of the sexual conventions that, in part, construct the family.

44

THE RELATIONSHIP BETWEEN MALE-MALE FRIENDSHIP AND MALE-FEMALE MARRIAGE
American Indian and Asian Comparisons

WALTER L. WILLIAMS

Very often popular critics complain about problems of alienation resulting from men's inability to develop intimate friendships. Humans, like other social animals, need and want intimacy, yet many men feel an inability to express that part of their being freely. This lack of close friendship is decried by many (see, for example, Brod, 1987; Franklin, 1984; Kilgore, 1984; Kimmel & Messner, 1989; Miller, 1983; Pleck & Pleck, 1980). Yet suggestions for change are inevitably greeted with a chorus of disbelievers who dismiss such relationships among men as being utopian, unrealistic, or even "unnatural." Given our observation of the way most American men act, we tend to think that this is the only way men *can* behave and still be "men." We might acknowledge, and even admire, the intense friendships that often exist among gay men, but this intensity itself seems to suggest that such friendships are not part of the standard masculine pattern. If men wish to retain their sense of being masculine, if they wish to be successful, if they wish to keep from being "emasculated," then close friendship seems to be the inevitable casualty.

Such a viewpoint is understandable, given our ignorance of other realistic alternatives. If the only point of reference is from within contemporary American culture, this viewpoint is easy to accept because so few "successful" white heterosexual men seem to challenge it. When examining men's friendship from the perspective of other cultures, however, it is the American style that seems strange.

Not enough research has been done on this subject to draw valid generalizations but what investigation has been done on male friendships shows a quite different pattern from one culture to another. And within any particular culture, there is variation based on class, ethnic background, sexuality, and other differences. Masculinity, no less than other aspects of personality, is a socially constructed achieved status (Gilmore, 1990). The lack of

---

intimacy and demonstrated affection among American men is quite unlike the situation in many other cultures. Many Americans may be aware, from newspaper photographs, that the acceptable style of formal greeting for men in France, Russia, and other European cultures is to embrace and kiss each other. Some of us may even be aware that Arab leaders often are seen walking arm in arm, or holding hands as they talk. Yet most of us are so ignorant of men's daily behavior in much of the non-Western world that we do not realize the peculiarity of men's interactions in the United States. In short, contemporary American mainstream masculinity is rather unique in its suppression of displays of affection, and of close and intimate friendships, between adult men.

Most of human history has occurred in small-scale societies where people know one another much more closely than in modern cities. For about 99% of our history as a species, humans existed in small hunter-gatherer bands. In more recent epochs, pastoral herdsmen or settled agriculture villages emerged. Only within the last century, and only in certain areas of the world, have urban populations surpassed rural ones. Perhaps it is time for us to examine the ways of life of these various social patterns and to see what lessons we might learn about how better to conduct our own social relations. This chapter focuses on male friendship patterns in other cultures, using select examples as a means of demonstrating not only that intimate relationships among men are realistic and possible but also that these kinds of relationships have indeed existed in many other times and places.

Friendship across Cultures

To understand the differences between friendship in other cultures and friendship in contemporary America, it is necessary to look at some diverse examples; however, very little ethnographic data exist. While marriage patterns have been analyzed exhaustively by ethnographers, hardly any anthropological attention has been devoted to friendship—even though friendship is universal behavior. Friendships are often unstructured and spontaneous, thus fitting poorly with anthropologists' theories about the structures of society (Leyton, 1974). Gilmore (1990) has recently written the first cross-cultural study of manhood as an institutionalized social category; but despite the importance of his work, there is still a lack of cross-cultural focus on men's friendships.

The most extensive anthropological study of friendship remains *Friends and Lovers,* by Robert Brain (1976). Based largely on his fieldwork in Africa, Brain's book provides numerous examples where friendships are encouraged by being ceremonialized and formalized in society. In southern Ghana, for example, same-sex best friends go through a marriage ceremony similar to that performed for husbands and wives. This same-sex marriage, for members of the noble class as well as commoners, includes the payment of "brideprice" to the parents of the younger friend. Among the Bangwa of

Cameroon, where Brain did most of his research, social pressure is directed to every child to encourage him to pair up with a best friend, much in the same way that other societies pressure everyone to find a spouse. Cautionary myths are told about the misfortunes falling to a self-centered person who neglects to make a friend. A major theme of popular songs is the celebration of friendships, in contrast to Western pop music, which emphasizes heterosexual romance and sex. In fact, Bangwa same-sex friendships are even more durable than male-female marriages. These friendships typically last from adolescence through old age, while marriages commonly split up when children reach adulthood.

Once a year, in the major Bangwa ceremony at the king's palace, men exchange gifts and formally proclaim their friendships as continuing for another year. When a man dies, his funeral ceremony is paid for by his best friend rather than his family. The friend's public mourning is treated even more seriously than the lament of the deceased's widow and children. Throughout the life course, friendship is publicly recognized and ceremonialized among the Bangwa in multiple ways that are not even verbalized among most American men (Brain, 1976).

The institution of "godparenthood," so often commented upon by anthropologists as a form of "fictive kinship" to give a child the advantage of an extra set of parents, is also often a means of formally recognizing friendships. Godparenthood institutionalizes the relationship between the parents of the child and their best friend. In some areas of Latin America, two men will perform a rite of baptism that makes them "godbrothers" (Brain, 1976). Such ceremonies formalize and give social and religious respect to friendship in a way that modern American society does not. Even though the mythic basis for such a ceremony in Judeo-Christian cultures exists in the Biblical story of Jonathan and David, there is a noticeable lack of ritual in Protestant Christian churches that celebrates close friendships. The Catholic Church even warns its priests and seminary students against forming "particular friendships," thus depriving its unmarried clergy of *any* form of intimate relationship. On the sports field, probably the place most encouraging of same-sex camaraderie in modern America, the emphasis is on team loyalty, competition, and success—rather than on particular friendships.

North American Indian Friendships

How do other cultures manage to encourage these intense friendships among men? In order to understand the important role of such friendships, I turn to my own research with North American Indians. As with many other cultures, same-sex friendships among aboriginal North Americans were emotionally intense because marriages were not the center of a person's emotional life. Marriage was primarily an economic arrangement between women and men to produce offspring and gather food. This arrangement had its basis in a division of labor by gender. Although wide ranges of activities were open for both women and men, in most pre-Columbian American societies there existed a basic division between masculine tasks and feminine tasks. While some individual males or females had the option of doing the tasks usually associated with the other sex, by taking on a highly respected *berdache* gender role that mixed the masculine and feminine aspects together, most people limited their skills to either masculine or feminine ones (Williams, 1986).

By dividing the necessary tasks of each family into "men's work" and "women's work," people only had to learn half of the necessary skills, and gained the expertise of their spouse in tasks that were different from their own skills. Because many Native American societies did not have social taboos against homosexual behavior, same-sex marriages were also recognized, just as long as one of the spouses took on a berdache role and agreed to do the labor of the other sex. The emphasis of the culture was to encourage marriage and parenthood (either by procreation or adoption), not to try to dictate what kind of sexual behavior a person should engage in. As a result, homosexually inclined individuals were not alienated, and family ties were quite strong. By marrying, a person could gain the assistance and support of the spouse's kin group, and thus could double the number of relatives to whom one could turn for support in time of need.

For American Indian societies, as with most societies in all of human history, marriage has primarily been an economic arrangement. Marriage partners in many of these situations might or might not be sexually attracted to each other, but they did expect to be able to depend on each other and their kinsmen for economic support. They had little expectation that they would be each other's best friend. Other than when they were engaging in sex, husbands and wives kept a certain respectful emotional distance from each other. They would bring their resources home to provide food for their spouse and children; they would eat at home and sleep there (at least some of the time). But American Indian men, like those in many other cultures, would not spend much of their leisure time at home. In some native societies husbands and wives did not even sleep together. Among groups as disparate as the Cherokees in the Southeast and Yupik Eskimos of Alaska, males above age 10 regularly slept in the village "men's house," a sort of community center for males that doubled as the men's sleeping quarters, while the women and small children slept in their own individual houses.

Friendships in such sex-segregated societies followed the same pattern. For friendship, men's primary psychological needs would be met by their long-term friends from childhood. And those friendships were, of course, with persons of the same gender. Men usually had deep feelings of love for their mothers, aunts, grandmothers, and sisters, based on their intimacy in early childhood, but the only adult male who would experience continued close friendships with women was the androgynous berdache, who moved back and forth between the separated gender worlds of men and women. Because of their in-between gender status, berdaches (or their masculined female counterpart) often served as a go-between to negotiate agreements or settle disputes between men and women. In some groups, like the Cheyenne Indians of the Plains, men were so shy around women that they would often ask berdaches to negotiate proposals of marriage.

In such a situation, where each sex felt such shyness in dealing with the other, they each turned to same-sex friends for primary intimacy needs. Early Western explorers often commented upon the especially warm friendships that existed between an Indian man and his "blood brother." A nineteenth-century United States Army officer, for example, reported about "brothers by adoption" that he observed from his years on the frontier. Speaking of Indian male pairs, he pointed out the contrast with more reserved friendships among white men. He said that Arapaho males "really seem to 'fall in love' with men; and I have known this affectionate interest to live for years." The union of two men was often publicly recognized in a Friendship Dance that they would do together (Trumbull, 1894, pp. 71–72, 165–166).

One of these friendships among Lakotas was described by Francis Parkman, who met the two men during his journey on the Oregon Trail in 1846. They were, he wrote:

> [I]nseperable; they ate, slept, and hunted together, and shared with one another almost all that they possessed. If there be anything that deserves to be called romantic in the Indian character, it is to be sought for in friendships such as this, which are common among many of the prairie tribes. (Parkman, 1969, pp. 280–283)

This is not to suggest that these special friendships should be equated with homosexuality. The emphasis for the Indian men was a close emotional bond, which might well be nonsexual in many or maybe most of these friendships. If two close friends engaged in sexual activity, that would be considered their own private business, which would not be publicly mentioned. Even if they were known to be sexual with each other, they would not be labeled as a distinct category like "homosexual." As long as they continued to follow a masculine lifestyle, they would not be socially defined as a berdache. And they certainly would not be stigmatized for their erotic acts. The socially recognized part of their relationship was their deep friendship; native communities honored that. What this meant is that Native American men were allowed to develop intense friendships, and even to be able to express their love for their blood brother friend, without worry that they would be stigmatized. Except for the berdache, any concept like "homosexual" was foreign to the thinking and social world of American Indians.

Friendship and Marriage: Andalusia and Java

The pattern of friendship that traditionally existed among Native Americans, where a man gets his intimate needs met more by his male friends than by his wife, is quite common in various areas of the world. When Brandes

(1987) did his field research in rural areas of Andalusia, Spain, he found that both men and women feel more comfortable revealing their deeper thoughts to a same-sex friend than to their spouse. Brandes was told by his male informants that the home is basically women's space; for men it is "only for eating and sleeping." Men in Andalusia spend most of their leisure time with their male friends at the local tavern. When their teenaged sons become old enough to be brought into the men's friendship sphere, then the men take over the raising of the adolescent males; otherwise men are not much involved in the rearing of younger children. Except for harvest season, when adults are busy working long hours, a man is expected to spend several hours each day with his best friend. He goes home only in the evening for a late dinner just before bedtime. Since any association between an unrelated woman and a man would arouse suspicion of adultery, men and women avoid close social interaction with the other sex.

It should be noted that these intense male-male friendships in Andalusia are not seen as a threat to the family in any way. Marriage is strong, but is kept within its bounds of economic co-dependence, food consumption, sex, and sleeping. Marriage relationships between husbands and wives are close, but are not expected to answer one's personal intimacy needs, which are met by one's same-sex friends. As a result of this system, people have two types of close bonds: the structured mixed-sex marriage-kinship system, and the unstructured same-sex friendships networks. These two bonds strengthen and complement each other, providing supportive allegiances and psychological outlets from the pressures of life. Rather than threaten each other, each of these two bonds has its restricted area and does not try to impose on the other. The two together work better than either marriage or friendship would by itself (Brandes, 1987).

My thinking on the complementary relationship between close friendships and marriage partnerships has also been influenced by my fieldwork on the island of Java, which is the most populous island in the archipelago of Indonesia. In 1987 and 1988 I lived in the classical court city of Yogyakarta, where Javanese culture remains strong. Javanese people show a strong sense of reserve in terms of public interactions between women and men, even when they are married. A scandal would ensue if a husband and wife kissed in public, and except for younger urbanites, who have been influenced by American movies and television shows to adopt more Westernized lifestyles, it is rare even to see a Javanese man and woman holding hands in public. This reserve is part of a larger pattern of the limits placed on male-female intimacy. One reason that such reserve exists has to do with arranged marriages. Traditionally, there was no such thing as dating between proper young women and men in Java. Marriages were arranged by parents, with the bride and groom often meeting each other for the first time at their wedding ceremony. Before marriage, people spend most of their time with same-sex friends rather than in heterosexual dating.

Many Americans are shocked to hear of such a custom as arranged marriages, yet our shock is no greater than the shock felt by Javanese who observe American patterns of relationships. I have had several fascinating conversations with Indonesians on this topic. While they admire the material wealth of the United States, Indonesians often wonder "why Americans seem so intent on making themselves miserable." After watching American movies together, I noticed how often they expressed puzzlement about the way Americans experience so much stress by falling in and out of love. "Why," they asked me, "do Americans experience such fragile personal relationships?" One Indonesian spoke for many when he told me that he had the impression that "Americans don't seem to have a hold on anything. They don't seem committed—to their relationships, their friends, or to anything else." It is obvious to them that Western romanticism and traditional forms of family life are not working for many Americans.

In the United States, various groups have called for a "return to the traditional family" as a cure for society's ills. Yet, the nuclear family seems to be less and less able to deal with the realities of the stresses facing people in modern America. Progressive voices have not really articulated a vision for the future, beyond merely accepting the fact that divorce and singlehood are becoming more and more common. The question is, are there other alternatives to the patriarchal nuclear family that will help to prevent an increasing sense of alienation in the lifestyle of the twenty-first century? The extended family is long gone from the American scene, and the nuclear family seems likewise destined. One-to-one relationships continue to be made and broken in fairly similar patterns among both heterosexual couples and homosexual couples. Can people live comfortably with the uncertainty of not knowing how long their partnership will last? These are questions that terrify many, and people are pulled between their desires for the adventure of love and the security of a long-term relationship. Magazines are filled with articles telling worried spouses "how to keep your husband/wife in love with you."

No one seems to be asking the question that maybe it is precisely the romantic ideal of "being in love" that is itself the problem with contemporary marriages. It is in this regard that we might be able to learn something from Indonesian patterns. It became quite evident to me, during my time in Java, that Indonesian husbands and wives do not seem to feel the necessity of "being in love" all the time. In their view, such romantic ideals only lead to grief, because they promote so much longing that families are broken apart.

In Indonesia, under the influence of Westernization, younger people are beginning to choose their marriage partners by "falling in love," but the older generation questions the ideal of romantic love as the primary basis for one's emotional life. I interviewed elderly husbands and wives whose marriages had been arranged by their parents, asking them how they could have adjusted to life together without getting to know each other and falling in love beforehand. They told me it was precisely *because* of their nonromantic approach that their marriage worked. They pointed out that even if two young people know each other intimately for several years, and think that they are completely right for each other, they are so inexperienced in human relationships that they cannot possibly know anything definite about the other person. Plus, individuals change so much over the life course that it does not matter much what kind of person the other one was at that moment. The important advantage of an arranged marriage, in the Javanese view, is that the two young people are *not* "in love," and therefore they are not disillusioned later when they fall out of love. (For interviews with elderly Javanese, where they detail their thoughts about arranged marriages and friendship patterns, see Williams, 1991.)

Such nonemotional marriages work because they are complemented by people's emotional needs being met by same-sex friendships. The strong balance between marriage and friendship is most strikingly presented in the context of wedding ceremonies that I observed in Java. The most obvious difference from an American wedding was that all the men sat on one side of the room while the women sat together on the other side of the room. The seating pattern was consciously designed to reflect the separateness of women and men. Weddings are a big event in the villages, reflecting the importance of the family in Javanese culture.

In contrast to an American wedding, which focuses on the love between the bride and groom, a Javanese wedding ceremony emphasizes the economic and social obligations of the new couple to each other, to their future children, to their parents and other relatives, and to the community as a whole. The couple sits down together on the wedding seat, the bride on the women's side, and the groom on the men's, indicating that they retain their closeness to their same-sex friends, even while becoming husband and wife.

Throughout the ceremony, the major emphasis is the economic obligation of the bride and groom. Nowhere does "love," or any expression of emotion between the two partners, put in an appearance. After thinking about the meaning of this ceremony, and talking with Javanese people about the role of marriage, love, and friendship in their lives, I think that perhaps this deliberate deemphasis on love in a marriage is—ironically, to us—one of the reasons for its stability. Instead of an ideal of romantic love, Indonesians seem to have more realistic expectations for a marriage, keeping it more or less restricted to its economic and procreative functions. (For further elaboration of the Javanese wedding ceremony, see Williams, 1991.)

In the Javanese view, marriage should not be too intimate. To them, a person's intimacies are best kept where they were already located before two people got married: with their same-sex friends. A man continues to have his relatives and male age-mates as his most intimate friends, and a woman does likewise with her female friends and relatives. They do not expect that their spouse will be either some knight in shining armor or a princess in perpetual beauty, and so they are not disappointed later. As in Andalusia, friendship is not antipathetic to the marriage bond, but they are complementary to each other. One's sexual partner is not expected to also be one's best friend. Given the economic importance of marriage in Javanese village life, the exaltation of friendship among one's same-sex friends serves as a balancing point.

As their separated seating at the Javanese wedding ceremony makes clear, women are not expected to separate themselves from other women and give all their emotional support to their husbands. Both they and their husbands are getting many of their emotional needs met by their same-sex friends. If husbands and wives do not sit together at a ceremony as symbolic as a wedding, why should it be expected for them to be together otherwise? In their workday, men and women are likewise often separated. Women spend much of their time at the market, selling their family's food produce to other women. Markets for food sales are primarily women's spaces, with men seldom involved. At their domestic work, women are either in the kitchen or at the riverbank, washing their clothes in company with other women. Men are off plowing with the oxen, or working in all-male labor gangs in the fields or the irrigation canals.

During the evening hours in a typical Javanese village, after the day's work is completed, husbands and wives will each go their separate ways. Women will visit and chat with other women, while the men will gather among themselves. They may be involved with an arts organization or a dance group, and each of these groups is either all-male or all-female. Men may play musical instruments, or women may join a singing group, but there is little overlap between the sexes in many of their leisure activities.

The Future of Friendship

Strong extended family kinship networks have often not been able to survive the extensive geographical mobility characteristic of modern America. Relatives are separated as the capitalist job market has forced many people to migrate to other locations. Under these pressures, "the family" has been reduced from its original extended form (the most common type of family among humans) to a mere nuclear remnant of parents and children. In modern America, a person's "significant other" has now become practically the sole person with whom he or she can be intimate. For many couples, this is too much to ask of their relationships, as the significant other is expected simultaneously to be sexual playmate, economic partner, kinship system, best friend, and everything else. Because of the dictatorship of the romantic ideal, many Americans expect their spouse to meet all their emotional needs. That is doubly difficult to do while both partners are also holding down full-time employment outside of the home.

As more American marriages become households where both spouses have jobs outside the home, there is less energy left for being emotionally supportive of one's partner. Even these rump nuclear family marriages are, therefore, in increasing numbers of cases, falling apart. The flip side of the American ideal of individual freedom and progress is thus often a legacy of individual alienation and loneliness.

In contrast, by not expecting the marriage relationship to fulfill all of a person's needs, many other cultures allow people more emotional closeness to same-sex friends. To take one example, in some cultures, families are not often broken up over the issue of homosexuality. In such a situation, in fact, there is not as much emotional need for homosexually inclined individuals to construct a separate homosexual identity. There will, of course, still be a certain percentage of people who erotically prefer a same-sex partner, but that inclination may be fulfilled within the friendship bond. There is no social pressure for persons to leave their marriage just because they desire same-sex erotic contacts. Sexual desires may have little to do with family bonding, because the marriage is not assumed to be sexually exclusive.

Same-sex friendships need not, of course, include a sexual component, but as far as the society is concerned, the important factor is the friendship rather than the sexual behavior. The person might be sexually involved with a same-sex friend while also being heterosexually married. Both forms of bonding occur, and a person does not have to choose one over the other. This flexibility resolves to the advantage of society and the individual. There is a looseness and an adaptiveness that allow for close intimate interaction with both sexes within the dual bonds of marriage and friendship.

In cultures that do not stigmatize same-sex eroticism, and do not divide up people into "homosexuals" and "heterosexuals," there is remarkable freedom from worry among males that others will perceive them to be members of a distinct "homosexual" category. This freedom from worry demonstrates that much of the inhibition that contemporary American men feel about their friendships is due to the fear that others might categorize them as homosexual. This can most clearly be seen by contrasting behavior of late twentieth-century Indian men with their nonhomophobic ancestors. As contemporary Indian people have absorbed more and more mainstream white American values, through Christian missionaries, government schools, off-reservation residence, and television, they have become more homophobic. On reservations today, friendships are not as intense as among past generations. American Indian men's alienation from each other is a "miner's canary" to warn us of the even more extreme alienation going on among mainstream Americans. Friendships among heterosexual men are one of the main casualties of homophobia.

Given all these pressures, which restrict men's expressions of their feelings and increase their stress levels, it will be valuable to get some concrete ideas as to how we can get beyond some of these dilemmas facing American men. A cross-cultural analysis is one possible source of knowledge regarding how men can conceptualize their intimacy needs.

First, it is necessary to move beyond the view that every person is either exclusively heterosexual or exclusively homosexual. Two facts emerge from the anthropological literature: (a) There is a diversity in individual sexual inclinations, with some persons clearly preferring the other sex and some clearly preferring the same sex, but many (probably a majority) having a mixture of erotic feelings for both sexes; and (b) for most people, healthy human operation requires the spreading around of intimacy to a wider circle of people. This is the most common pattern, in the extended family networks and the close friendships, of probably the majority of cultures, yet this is precisely what twentieth-century American culture has failed to do. Since our geographical mobility precludes the reestablishment of extended family kinship systems for most Americans, it behooves us to reexamine the cross-cultural data on friendships and to try to start building alternative forms of relationships on this basis.

Perhaps it is time for us to begin a more fundamental public discourse questioning the primacy of the male-female romantic ideal (i.e., "the traditional family") as sufficient for meeting human intimacy needs by itself. Many Americans know that something is wrong with their lives, but the only solution they hear is popular music's refrain that they should fall in love, and the allied heterosexist "pro-family" rhetoric. Perhaps a new rhetoric of friendship needs to be emphasized. It is not an exaggeration to say that there has been a denigration of friendship in the United States. The pro-heterosexual, pro-marriage discourse has almost obliterated intense same-sex friendships. This is not to suggest that people should abandon their sexual partners, but that they should expect less of such a partner than his or her total emotional support.

In the 1970s, radical feminist separatists' and gay men's friendship networks emerged as never before. New possibilities seemed to be emerging. By the 1980s, however, as a drive for social respectability set in, fueled by the AIDS crisis, gay men and lesbians tended to settle into same-sex couplehoods that mirror the American heterosexual marriage rather than the more widespread intimacy patterns of many other cultures.

As we prepare for a new century, a revitalization of the psychological and social importance of friendship should become a high priority. Ironically, the AIDS crisis has brought out the importance of friendship "buddy" networks, as well as domestic partners, as caregivers within the gay and lesbian community. In the non-gay community as well, more attention must be given to ceremonializing and ritualizing friendship relationships in the same way that romantic relationships and marriages have been. More serious respect can be given, from one's partner as well as by society at large, for the importance of friends. Since sexual attractions are often subject to change over the years, maybe more people will be living the slogan that "lovers come and go, but friends remain."

Certainly, these suggestions do not imply that all people will evolve new kinds of relationships, but they do imply the need for equal social respect being given for a variety of friendship types. They imply that, rather than regretting the passing of a traditional form of marriage that has already disappeared for many people, Americans will be better served by paying more attention to our needs for close intimate friendships. The problem is not the breakdown of marriage as much as it is the need to develop wider distributions of individuals to whom we can express our intimacy. In this society, women are doing this much more successfully than are men. Before American men dismiss the possibility of anything different, they might educate themselves to the necessity of getting over barriers to intimacy with friends, whether this is due to homophobia or to a competitive ethos at the workplace. We already have, in the examples from other cultures, many functioning models that have well served the emotional needs of men for centuries. These models bear further investigation. Those who have highly developed friendships can recognize the power of these relationships to carry us forward into the future. For at least some of us, maybe this is a better place to focus our intimacies, rather than placing all our hopes on some romantic love that might later turn sour and then become so disruptive in our lives.

If our society is to survive, when traditional family patterns are evolving and geographical mobility strains the limits of intergenerational connections, it is up to innovative individuals to search out new forms for intimate relationships beyond sexual partnerships. We need to analyze and nurture our long-term close friendship networks as the best possible base on which to build an emotionally satisfying future.

REFERENCES

Brain, R. (1976). *Friends and lovers.* New York: Basic Books.

Brandes, S. (1987). Sex roles and anthropological research in rural Andalusia. *Women's Studies,* 13, 357–372.

Brod, H. (Ed.). (1987). *The making of masculinities: The new men's studies.* Boston: Allen & Unwin.

Franklin, C. (1984). *The changing definition of masculinity.* New York: Plenum.

Gilmore, D. (1990). *Manhood in the making: Cultural concepts of masculinity.* New Haven, CT: Yale University Press.

Kilgore, J. (1984). *The intimate man: Intimacy and masculinity in the 80s.* Nashville, TN: Abingdon.

Kimmel, M., & Messner, M. (Eds.). (1989). *Men's lives.* New York: Macmillan.

Leyton, E. (Ed.). (1974). *The compact: Selected dimensions of friendship* (Newfoundland Social and Economic Papers No. 3). Toronto: University of Toronto Press and Memorial University of Newfoundland.

Miller, S. (1983). *Men and friendship.* Boston: Houghton Mifflin.

Parkman, F. (1969). *The Oregon Trail.* Madison: University of Wisconsin Press.

Pleck, E. H., & Pleck, J. H. (1980). *The American man.* Englewood Cliffs, NJ: Prentice-Hall.

Trumbull, H. C. (1894). *Friendship the master passion.* Philadelphia: Wattles.

Williams, W. L. (1986). *The spirit and the flesh: Sexual diversity in American Indian culture.* Boston: Beacon.

Williams, W. L. (1991). *Javanese lives: Women and men in modern Indonesian society.* New Brunswick, NJ: Rutgers University Press.

PART VII
Education

While race differences in educational attainment have virtually disappeared, and women attain slightly more education than men, both minorities and women remain "less equal" than men – that is, on average they earn less income than white males with comparable educational credentials.

ROSLYN MICKELSON AND STEPHEN SMITH[1]

"Why are women's brains smaller than men's?" asked a surgeon of a group of male medical students in the doctor's lounge. . . . "Because they're missing logic!"

ADRIENNE FUGH-BERMAN[2]

There is substantial agreement in the United States that equal opportunity is something worth providing to our citizens and that the education system is the central institution that should prepare people for equal opportunity.[3] Even in the face of tension and competition between various racial and ethnic groups, the value of an adequate education for all is shared by nearly everyone. For example, in a 1994 survey conducted by the National Conference of Christians and Jews (now called the National Conference for Community and Justice), about 90 percent of the 3,000 Asian, Black, Latino, and white respondents said they would be willing to work with members of other racial or ethnic groups, even those with whom they felt the least in common, in order to "help schools teach kids what they really need to learn to succeed."[4]

Many changes in the U.S. education system during the past several decades have been implemented with the goal of eliminating the education gap between white students and students of color, between poor children and wealthier ones, and between boys and girls and men and women. Sociologist Roslyn Mickelson and political scientist Stephen Smith have taken a close look at the effects of some of these changes. Programs designed to increase the education level of poor children have helped to equalize levels of education. For example, compensatory education (such as Head Start), and various other initiatives, have helped to create a situation where Black and white women and men, on average, achieve similar levels of education (about 13 years), in spite of the fact that a majority of children in the United States still attend schools segregated by race, ethnicity, and class. A look at income, however, reveals continuing disparity, with whites earning more than Blacks and men earning more than women. And a close look at class issues within groups reveals large differences. For example, in the eighties, a child of a Black farmer completed less than 9 years of schooling, while children of Black professionals averaged 14 years of schooling.[5]

Mickelson and Smith consider three issues related to inequality: equality, equality of educational opportunity, and equality of educational outcomes.

They conclude that the United States has no interest in equality and has failed to establish equality of educational outcomes. Thus, as a country we support equal educational opportunity but have not designed an economy that would guarantee a living wage for everyone who achieves a certain level of education.

On an individual level, research demonstrates that race, class, and gender continue to affect students' experiences in spite of efforts to the contrary. Jonathan Kozol, for example, describes how race and poverty intersect in brutally impoverished schools in several U.S. cities, severely limiting learning.[6] Jorge Noriega looks at the history of American Indian education in the United States and concludes that it has been, and continues to be (with minor exceptions), a cultural disaster, designed primarily for indoctrination to the white majority culture and limiting career options to vocational ones.[7]

A series of reports on gender and education reveal troublesome results for students of both genders. A report entitled *How Schools Shortchange Girls*, commissioned by the American Association of University Women Educational Foundation, documents how gender, race, and class all affect educational achievement. Some of the data suggest that class is the most important of these three variables.[8] Bernice Sandler, director of the Project on the Status and Education of Women at the Association of American Colleges and Universities, discovered that men in college were given both overt and subtle support, whereas women were undermined in both overt and subtle ways. Studying interaction in classrooms, Sandler found frequent cases of disparaging remarks about women, such as sexist jokes made by male professors, and she found subtle differences in the treatment of male and female students, such as men being called on more frequently than women, by faculty of both genders.[9]

Educators David and Myra Sadker, concluding overall that girls experience discrimination in schools, nevertheless observed that although boys receive more attention than girls at both the elementary and secondary levels, that attention does not necessarily lead to success. They reported that boys are more likely to receive lower grades, to suffer from learning disabilities, to be assigned to special education classes, to be suspended, and to drop out than are girls.[10] Similar findings have been reported by other researchers working on the situations of boys.[11] Some of these writers and educators are exploring ways to allow boys to express their traditionally high energy without pathologizing it. Some suggest all-boy environments to support and nurture boys, a suggestion that troubles others who have fought for coeducation at all levels. Recent federal guidelines on single-sex education allow the development of single-sex schools as long as comparable course work and facilities are available for both sexes.[12]

What these data on boys obscure, however, is the reality that boys generally achieve higher grades on standardized tests and are more economically successful into adulthood, in spite of the difficult time that some of them have in school. Clearly, some boys need more help than others. Although women outnumber men as college students, this gender discrepancy is most pronounced at lower-status institutions; men tend to major in more lucrative fields like engineering, computer science, business and physics; and the five occupations most likely to be held by women include secretary, receptionist, bookkeeper, nurse, and hairdresser/cosmetologist.[13] In short, all children need more effective educations in contexts that promote equality related to gender, class, race, ability, and culture.

The choice of which fields women and men pursue is obviously a crucial aspect of education as it relates to occupational outcomes. Thus, some scholars have attempted to analyze the effects of race and gender on educational outcomes while others have looked at the experience of women and people of color in various careers.[14] Programs designed to encourage the study of math and science by boys and girls of color and white girls have also emerged with the goal of addressing the underrepresentation of white women and women and men of color in mathematical and scientific careers.[15] Programs designed to support white female graduate students and graduate students of color in math and science have also emerged in recent years.[16]

Other educators have documented ways that subtle and overt stereotypes are reinforced in the curriculum, and many have worked toward eliminating them. For example, substantial attention has been given to gendered images in children's books, and now attention is focusing on the intersections of gender with other factors.[17] Other scholars are examining the success or failure of the testing system for various groups. For example, in a recent finding that helps explain why bright Black students do not perform as well as expected on tests, Claude Steele, a social psychologist at Stanford University, identified what he calls "stereotype vulnerability"—the tendency for group members to perform badly when they think their performance is a reflection of their group. Concerned that even highly qualified Black students tended to earn increasingly lower grades as they progressed through college, Steele set out to identify the cause. He found that when Black Stanford University undergraduates were given a difficult verbal test, those who were told that it was a "genuine test of your verbal abilities and limitations" received lower scores than the white students also being tested. But when another group of Black students taking the same test was told that it was designed to study "psychological factors involved in solving verbal problems," they performed as well as the white students. Steele repeated this experiment in various places and formats, documenting that stereotype vulnerability also affected women when they were told that a given math test showed "gender differences." It even affected white men who were told that Asians tended to outperform whites on a difficult math test.[18]

The context of test taking is just one aspect of the hidden curriculum—the myriad messages, subtle and obvious, that affect students' attitudes and performance, apart from course content. Classroom interaction has been the subject of much research, as educators attempt to establish more gender-equal classrooms.[19] Other scholars observe the social environment on campuses. In an ethnographic study of Black and white women on two college campuses, anthropologists Dorothy Holland and Margaret Eisenhart found that peer culture eroded career plans for many women in both groups as romance became more important than their studies.[20]

Pressure to conform in K-12 classrooms puts pressure on many kinds of young people, from girls who are "too masculine," to Black girls who are "too loud," to boys who are "too feminine." Students who fail to conform to white heterosexist hegemonic expectations, for whatever reasons, are defined as "other" and pay a high price. Anthropologist Signithia Fordham argues that educators need to accept a range of behavior in students and not expect conformity to narrow standards; after intensive research in an urban school in Washington DC, she was especially concerned about Black children who were expected to conform to white expectations ("acting white"), rather than be supported to develop their own ways of expressing themselves within the context of a challenging academic program.[21]

Pressure for gender conformity can be especially difficult. In a study of schooling in England, educator Máirtín Mac an Ghaill recounts an incident in a schoolyard that shook the gender rules: a male student, happy over passing his exams, brought flowers to Mac an Ghaill. Mac an Ghaill was scolded for the incident.[22] In two recently reported cases in the United States, boys who were acting "too effeminate" were the subject of ridicule in schools. In one case, the boy was expelled from his private school for cross-dressing.[23] In another case, the Center for Constitutional Rights helped a grandmother intervene in a situation in which her grandson had been referred to as a girl and called "girlish" by his teacher and his peers. The intervention succeeded in convincing the teacher to apologize and in convincing the school to institute seminars on sexual harassment and gender-based name calling for fifth and sixth graders.[24] According to the Supreme Court, schools receiving federal funds are responsible for student-on-student harassment if they know about it and do not intervene, and if it is severe enough to interfere with the victim's education.[25] As a result, schools are becoming more proactive in preventing harassment, including harassment of gay and lesbian young people.[26] In yet another case, a Massachusetts child who is physically male and diagnosed as transgendered challenged a school's decision to disallow female dress. Many months later, the city finally agreed to allow her to come to school in female attire.[27] Transgendered teachers are an issue as well, as schools and parents grapple with whether or not to support the hiring or continued employment of transgendered teachers, and as states debate whether transgender rights deserve protection.[28]

Frequently, prejudice against gay teenagers is so strong that these teenagers drop out of school. The Hetrick-Martin Institute in New York City was founded to serve lesbian and gay youth, offering an alternative high school for those who cannot tolerate mainstream schooling. Hetrick-Martin also provides a wide array of other programs including a planned shelter to house some of the estimated 8,000 homeless gay and lesbian youth in New York City who have been kicked out of their homes because they are gay.[29] In Massachusetts, state law has mandated support for gay and lesbian students in high schools in order to create a climate that will be more welcoming, especially given the high suicide rate of gay teens. K-12 schools, it seems, have become a primary battleground for gay, lesbian, and transgender rights.[30]

College campuses serve as a battleground for gender equality as well. The September 2000 issue of *Men's Health* ranked colleges based on how male-friendly they were; issues such as the presence of a large women's studies department were cause for a low ranking.[31] A woman who wanted to play football at Duke University was awarded $2 million in damages when she was cut from the team by a coach who had suggested that she participate in beauty pageants instead of football.[32]

Affirmative action, which requires employers and educational institutions to "actively seek inclusion of qualified minorities among their pool of applicants,"[33] is another issue affecting higher education. Laws, voter petitions and executive orders in various parts of the United States have undercut or eliminated affirmative action programs, arguing that they are no longer necessary. An effect in some areas of the country is "resegregation."[34] Ironically, once the state of Texas eliminated affirmative action, the state legislature passed a law mandating that all students in the top 10 percent of their high school class be granted automatic admission to institutions of higher education in Texas. Because of the high level of school segregation in Texas, the effect of the legislation has been to increase the level of diversity in undergraduate colleges in Texas. In states with more integrated schools, this sort of alternative to affirmative action would not succeed in diversifying the student body. Some colleges are changing admissions procedures to include examining a range of factors such as SAT score, class rank, race/ethnicity, and life experience. The goal is to have a diverse student body for educational purposes (supporting a university's mission), rather than to right past discrimination.[35]

The Texas alternative did not affect graduate schools. With the elimination of affirmative action, applications to the University of Texas School of Law dropped among Blacks, Mexican Americans, Asian Americans, and whites, with the largest decline occurring among Blacks—66 percent. Admissions of Black and Latino students to law school in both Texas and California—the two states that had eliminated affirmative action at the time of the study—have dropped considerably. This has provoked attorney Robert J. Grey, chair of the House of Delegates of the American Bar Association, to express concern over the decline in minority lawyers that will result if fewer people of color continue to apply to law school.[36] In the midst of fluctuations in application by students of color, the legality of taking race into account as one factor in admission is currently in the courts, related to two lawsuits against the University of Michigan. These and other related cases are likely to be finally settled by the Supreme Court, since various circuit courts are in disagreement over the use of race as a factor in admissions.[37]

While the truth-seeking traditions outlined in the introduction to this book have led to a voluminous literature designed to eliminate the invisibility of many groups in the curriculum at the university level, many members of those groups now risk being shut out of higher education. The likelihood of changing the low proportion of people of color and white women at the upper ranks of higher education is not high if people of color and white women are not allowed into institutions of higher education, especially at the graduate level.[38] And, once there, these institutions are frequently not the most welcoming of environments for white women and people of color.[39]

The readings in this part of the book address issues in both K-12 and higher education. Interactions of boys and girls in elementary schools (Barrie Thorne), the experience of Black boys (Ann Arnett Ferguson), conflicts and discrimination on college campuses (Ruth Sidel and bell hooks), and the importance of men's studies (Harry Brod) are addressed. The messages in this chapter echo many that have been heard throughout this book so far: people need validation of their varied experiences; knowledge is incomplete without a broad range of voices and perspectives; and discrimination greatly interferes with people's abilities to move freely in the world and achieve their goals. Some of these themes will be heard again in Part VIII in the context of paid work and unemployment.

NOTES

1. Roslyn Arlin Mickelson and Stephen Samuel Smith, "Education and the Struggle against Race, Class, and Gender Inequality," in Berch Berberoglu, ed., *Critical Perspectives in Sociology: A Reader* (Dubuque, IA: Kendall-Hunt, 1991).
2. Adrienne Fugh-Berman, "Tales Out of Medical School," *The Nation* (January 20, 1992), p. 54.
3. Mickelson and Smith, "Education and the Struggle."
4. "Taking America's Pulse: A Summary Report of the National Conference Survey on Inter-Group Relations" (New York: paper from the National Conference of Christians and Jews, 1994), p. 11.
5. Mickelson and Smith, "Education and the Struggle."
6. Jonathan Kozol, *Savage Inequalities* (New York: Crown, 1991).
7. Jorge Noriega, "American Indian Education in the United States: Indoctrination for Subordination to Colonialism," in M. Annette Jaimes, ed., *The State of Native America* (Boston: South End Press, 1992), pp. 371–402.
8. American Association of University Women Educational Foundation, *How Schools Shortchange Girls* (New York: Marlowe & Company, 1995).
9. Bernice Resnick Sandler, "The Classroom Climate: Still a Chilly One for Women," in Carol Lasser, ed., *Educating Men and Women Together: Coeducation in a Changing World* (Urbana: University of Illinois Press in conjunction with Oberlin College, 1987). Reprinted in Karin Bergstrom Costello, *Gendered Voices: Readings from the American Experience* (New York: Harcourt Brace, 1996), pp. 359–68. Sandler does not discuss the intersections of gender with other factors.

10. Myra Sadker and David Sadker, *Failing at Fairness: How Our Schools Cheat Girls* (New York: Simon & Schuster, 1994).
11. Carey Goldberg, "After Girls Get Attention, Focus Shifts to Boys' Woes," *The New York Times* (April 22, 1998), p. A1; Christina Hoff Sommers, *The War Against Boys: How Misguided Feminism is Harming Our Young Men* (New York: Simon & Schuster, 2000).
12. Greg Toppo, "US to boost single-sex schools: Education Dept. offers rules to encourage growth," *The Boston Globe* (May 9, 2002), p. A4.
13. David Sadker, "Gender Games," *The Washington Post* (July 31, 2000), p. A19.
14. Lisa M. Frehill, "Subtle Sexism in Engineering," in Nijole V. Benokraitis, ed., *Subtle Sexism: Current Practices and Prospects for Change* (Thousand Oaks, CA: Sage, 1997), pp. 117–35.
15. David Johnson, ed., *Minorities and Girls in School: Effects on Achievement and Performance* (Thousand Oaks, CA: Sage, 1997).
16. For a description of one such program, contact the New England Board of Higher Education, 45 Temple Place, Boston, MA 02111.
17. For a recent look at gendered images in children's books and references to prior work in this area, see Roger Clark, Rachel Lennon, and Leanna Morris, "Of Caldecotts and Kings: Gendered Images in Recent American Children's Books by Black and Non-Black Illustrators," *Gender & Society 7,* no. 2 (June 1993), pp. 227–45.
18. See Claude Steele and Joshua Aronson, "Stereotype Threat and the Intellectual Test Performance of African Americans," *Journal of Personality and Social Psychology 69,* no. 5 (Fall 1995), pp. 797ff. For a discussion of bias, especially gender bias, in standardized college entrance tests (PSAT and SAT), see Myra Sadker and David Sadker, "Test Drive," in Sadker and Sadker, eds., *Failing at Fairness.*
19. Magda Lewis, "Interrupting Patriarchy: Politics, Resistance, and Transformation in the Feminist Classroom, *Harvard Educational Review 60,* no. 4 (November 1990), pp. 467–88; Sara N. Davis, Mary Crawford, and Jadwiga Sebrechts, eds., *Coming Into Her Own: Educational Success in Girls and Women* (San Francisco: Jossey-Bass, 1999); Berenice Malka Fisher, *No Angel in the Classroom* (Lanham, MD: Rowman & Littlefield, 2001); Sharon Bernstein, "Feminist Intentions: Race, Gender and Power in a High School Classroom," *NWSA Journal 7,* no. 2 (1995), pp. 18–34.
20. Dorothy C. Holland and Margaret A. Eisenhart, *Educated in Romance: Women, Achievement, and College Culture* (Chicago: University of Chicago Press, 1990).
21. Signithia Fordham, *Blacked Out: Dilemmas of Race, Identity and Success at Capital High* (Chicago: Chicago University Press, 1996).
22. For an extended discussion of this see Máirtín Mac an Ghaill, *The Making of Men: Masculinities, Sexualities and Schooling* (Buckingham, UK: Open University Press, 1994).
23. "Feminine Boy Shakes Up Small School" *New York Times* (October 29, 1998).
24. Margaret Carey, "In re Minor Child," *Center for Constitutional Rights Docket* (New York: Center for Constitutional Rights, 1998), p. 76.
25. Mary Leonard, "Schools Can Be Liable if Pupils Harass," *The Boston Globe* (May 25, 1999), p. A1.
26. Anna Gorman, "Educators Taking Steps to Protect Homosexual Pupils," *The Boston Globe 258,* no. 77 (September 15, 2000), p. A29.
27. Rick Klein, "Brockton Boy Still at Home: Talks Continue on Class Return," *The Boston Globe* (October 18, 2000), p. B2; "Student Allowed to Wear Female Clothing," *The Boston Globe* (May 17, 2001), p. B2.

28. Stephanie Simon, "Transgender Protection Debated in Minn.," *The Boston Globe* (April 10, 1999), p. A9.
29. For more information contact the Hetrick-Martin Institute, 2 Astor Place, New York, NY 10003.
30. Eric Rofes, "Gay Issues, Schools, and the Right-Wing Backlash," *Resist 8,* no. 5 (June 1999), pp. 1–3.
31. Lawrence Roy Stains, "The Best and Worst Colleges for Men." *Men's Health 15,* no. 3, p. 120.
32. "Title IX Victory," *Outlook,* 95, no. 1, (2001), p. 9.
33. A. E. Sadler, ed., *Affirmative Action* (San Diego, CA: Greenhaven Press, 1996), p. 6.
34. Doreen Iudica Vigue, "Schools Segregating Anew, Harvard Researchers Report," *The Boston Globe* (June 12, 1999), p. A3.
35. Arthur L. Coleman, "'Affirmative Action' Through a Different Looking Glass," *Diversity Digest 5,* no. 3 (Spring 2001), pp. 1ff.
36. Evelyn Apgar, "Impact of California, Texas Decisions," *The New Jersey Lawyer* (Sept. 7, 1998), p. 1.
37. Maryanne George, "Judges Weigh Race in Mich. Admission," *The Boston Globe* (December 7, 2001), p. A10; Mary Leonard, "Diversity Benefits Whites, Project Finds: Research Called 'Long Overdue,'" *The Boston Globe* (May 18, 2001), p. A8.
38. For a look at the numbers of women at various levels of academia, including students and faculty, see Margaret L. Andersen, *Thinking about Women: Sociological Perspectives on Sex and Gender,* 3rd ed. (New York: Macmillan, 1993), p. 64. Andersen draws on data from Charles J. Andersen, Deborah J. Carter, and Andrew Malizio, *1989–90 Fact Book on Higher Education* (New York: Macmillan, 1989).
39. Judith E. Owen Blakemore, Jo Young Switzer, Judith A. DiLorio, David L. Fairchild, "Exploring the Campus Climate for Women Faculty," in Nijole V. Benokraitis, ed., *Subtle Sexism: Current Practices and Prospects for Change* (Thousand Oaks, CA: Sage, 1997), pp. 54–71; Teresa Córdova, "Power and Knowledge: Colonialism in the Academy," in Carla Trujillo, ed., *Living Chicana Theory* (Berkeley, CA: Third Woman Press, 1998), pp. 17–45.

45

GIRLS AND BOYS TOGETHER . . . BUT MOSTLY APART
Gender Arrangements in Elementary School

BARRIE THORNE

Throughout the years of elementary school, children's friendships and casual encounters are strongly separated by sex. Sex segregation among children, which starts in preschool and is well established by middle childhood, has been amply documented in studies of children's groups and friendships (e.g., Eder & Hallinan, 1978; Schofield, 1981) and is immediately visible in elementary school settings. When children choose seats in classrooms or the cafeteria, or get into line, they frequently arrange themselves in same-sex clusters. At lunchtime, they talk matter-of-factly about "girls' tables" and "boys' tables." Playgrounds have gendered turfs, with some areas and activities, such as large playing fields and basketball courts, controlled mainly by boys, and others—smaller enclaves like jungle-gym areas and concrete spaces for hopscotch or jump rope—more often controlled by girls. Sex segregation is so common in elementary schools that it is meaningful to speak of separate girls' and boys' worlds.

Studies of gender and children's social relations have mostly followed this "two worlds" model, separately describing and comparing the subcultures of girls and of boys (e.g., Lever, 1976; Maltz & Borker, 1983). In brief summary: Boys tend to interact in larger, more age-heterogeneous groups (Lever, 1976; Waldrop & Halverson, 1975; Eder & Hallinan, 1978). They engage in more rough and tumble play and physical fighting (Maccoby & Jacklin, 1974). Organized sports are both a central activity and a major metaphor in boys' subcultures; they use the language of "teams" even when not engaged in sports, and they often construct interaction in the form of contests. The shifting hierarchies of boys' groups (Savin-Williams, 1976) are evident in their more frequent use of direct commands, insults, and challenges (Goodwin, 1980).

Fewer studies have been done of girls' groups (Foot, Chapman, & Smith, 1980; McRobbie & Garber, 1975), and—perhaps because categories for description and analysis have come more from male than from female experience—researchers have had difficulty seeing and analyzing girls' social relations. Recent work has begun to correct this skew. In middle childhood, girls' worlds are less public than those of boys; girls more often interact in private places and in smaller groups or friendship pairs (Eder & Hallinan, 1978; Waldrop & Halverson, 1975). Their play is more cooperative and turn-taking (Lever, 1976). Girls have more intense and exclusive friendships, which take shape around keeping and telling secrets, shifting alliances, and indirect ways of expressing disagreement (Goodwin, 1980; Lever, 1976; Maltz & Borker, 1983). Instead of direct commands, girls more often use directives which merge speaker and hearer, e.g., "let's" or "we gotta" (Goodwin, 1980).

Although much can be learned by comparing the social organization and subcultures of boys' and of girls' groups, the separate worlds approach has eclipsed full, contextual understanding of gender and social relations among children. The separate worlds model essentially involves a search for group sex differences, and shares the limitations of individual sex difference research. Differences tend to be exaggerated and similarities ignored, with little theoretical attention to the integration of similarity and difference. Statistical findings of difference are often portrayed as dichotomous, neglecting the considerable individual variation that exists; for example, not all boys fight, and some have intense and exclusive friendships. The sex difference approach tends to abstract gender from its social context, to assume that males and females are qualitatively and permanently different (with differences perhaps unfolding through separate developmental lines). These assumptions mask the possibility that gender arrangements and patterns of similarity and difference may vary by situation, race, social class, region, and subculture.

Sex segregation is far from total, and is a more complex and dynamic process than the portrayal of separate worlds reveals. Erving Goffman (1977) has observed that sex segregation has a "with-then-apart" structure; the sexes segregate periodically, with separate spaces, rituals, and groups, but they also come together and are, in crucial ways, part of the same world. This is certainly true in the social environment of elementary schools. Although girls and boys do interact as boundaried collectivities—an image suggested by the separate worlds approach—there are other occasions when they work or play in relaxed and integrated ways. Gender is less central to the organization and meaning of some situations than others. In short, sex segregation is not static, but is a variable and complicated process.

To gain an understanding of gender which can encompass both the "with" and the "apart" of sex segregation, analysis should start not with the individual, nor with a search for sex differences, but with social relationships. Gender should be conceptualized as a system of relationships rather than as an immutable and dichotomous given. Taking this approach, I have organized my research on gender and children's social relations around questions like the following: How and when does gender enter into group formation? In a given situation, how is gender made more or less salient or infused with particular meanings? By what rituals, processes, and forms of social organization and conflict do "with-then-apart" rhythms get enacted? How are these processes affected by the organization of institutions (e.g., different types of schools, neighborhoods, or summer camps), varied settings (e.g., the constraints and possibilities governing interaction on playgrounds vs. classrooms), and particular encounters?

Methods and Sources of Data

This study is based on two periods of participant observation. In 1976–1977 I observed for 8 months in a largely working-class elementary school in California, a school with 8% Black and 12% Chicana/o students. In 1980 I did fieldwork for 3 months in a Michigan elementary school of similar size (around 400 students), social class, and racial composition. I observed in several classrooms—a kindergarten, a second grade, and a combined fourth–fifth grade—and in school hallways, cafeterias, and playgrounds. I set out to follow the round of the school day as children experience it, recording their interactions with one another, and with adults, in varied settings.

Participant observation involves gaining access to everyday, "naturalistic" settings and taking systematic notes over an extended period of time. Rather than starting with preset categories for recording, or with fixed hypotheses for testing, participant-observers record detail in ways which maximize opportunities for discovery. Through continuous interaction between observation and analysis, "grounded theory" is developed (Glaser & Strauss, 1967).

The distinctive logic and discipline of this mode of inquiry emerges from: (1) theoretical sampling—being relatively systematic in the choice of where and whom to observe in order to maximize knowledge relevant to categories and analysis which are being developed; and (2) comparing all relevant data on a given point in order to modify emerging propositions to take account of discrepant cases (Katz, 1983). Participant observation is a flexible, open-ended and inductive method, designed to understand behavior within, rather than stripped from, social context. It provides richly detailed information which is anchored in everyday meanings and experience.

Daily Processes of Sex Segregation

Sex segregation should be understood not as a given, but as the result of deliberate activity. The outcome is dramatically visible when there are separate girls' and boys' tables in school lunchrooms, or sex-separated groups on playgrounds. But in the same lunchroom one can also find tables where girls and boys eat and talk together, and in some playground activities the sexes mix. By what processes do girls and boys separate into gender-defined and relatively boundaried collectivities? And in what contexts, and through what processes, do boys and girls interact in less gender-divided ways?

In the school settings I observed, much segregation happened with no mention of gender. Gender was implicit in the contours of friendship, shared interest, and perceived risk which came into play when children chose companions—in their prior planning, invitations, seeking-of-access, saving-of-places, denials of entry, and allowing or protesting of "cuts" by those who violated the rules for lining up. Sometimes children formed mixed-sex groups for play, eating, talking, working on a classroom project, or moving through space. When adults or children explicitly invoked gender—and this was nearly always in ways which separated girls and boys—boundaries were heightened and mixed-sex interaction became an explicit arena of risk.

In the schools I studied, the physical space and curricula were not formally divided by sex, as they have been in the history of elementary schooling (a history evident in separate entrances to old school buildings, where the words "Boys" and "Girls" are permanently etched in concrete). Nevertheless, gender was a visible marker in the adult-organized school day. In both schools, when the public address system sounded, the principal inevitably opened with "Boys and girls . . . ," and in addressing clusters of children, teachers and aides regularly used gender terms ("Heads down, girls"; "The girls are ready and the boys aren't"). These forms of address made gender visible and salient, conveying an assumption that the sexes are separate social groups.

Teachers and aides sometimes drew upon gender as a basis for sorting children and organizing activities. Gender is an embodied and visual social category which roughly divides the population in half, and the separation of girls and boys permeates the history and lore of schools and playgrounds. In both schools—although through awareness of Title IX, many teachers had changed this practice—one could see separate girls' and boys' lines moving, like caterpillars, through the school halls. In the fourth–fifth grade classroom the teacher frequently pitted girls against boys for spelling and math contests. On the playground in the Michigan school, aides regarded the space close to the building as girls' territory, and the playing fields "out there" as boys' territory. They sometimes shooed children of the other sex away from those spaces, especially boys who ventured near the girls' area and seemed to have teasing in mind.

In organizing their activities, both within and apart from the surveillance of adults, children also explicitly invoked gender. During my fieldwork in the Michigan school, I kept daily records of who sat where in the lunchroom. The amount of sex segregation varied: It was least at the first grade tables and almost total among sixth graders. There was also variation from classroom to classroom within a given age, and from day to day. Actions like the following heightened the gender divide:

> In the lunchroom, when the two second-grade tables were filling, a high-status boy walked by the inside table, which had a scattering of both boys and girls, and said loudly, "Oooo, too many girls," as he headed for a seat at the far table. The boys at the inside table

> picked up their trays and moved, and no other boys sat at the inside table, which the pronouncement had effectively made taboo.

In the end, that day (which was not the case every day), girls and boys ate at separate tables.

Eating and walking are not sex-typed activities, yet in forming groups in lunchrooms and hallways children often separated by sex. Sex segregation assumed added dimensions on the playground, where spaces, equipment, and activities were infused with gender meanings. My inventories of activities and groupings on the playground showed similar patterns in both schools: Boys controlled the large fixed spaces designated for team sports (baseball diamonds, grassy fields used for football or soccer); girls more often played closer to the building, doing tricks on the monkey bars (which, for sixth graders, became an area for sitting and talking) and using cement areas for jumprope, hopscotch, and group games like four-square. (Lever, 1976, provides a good analysis of sex-divided play.) Girls and boys most often played together in kickball, and in group (rather than team) games like four-square, dodgeball, and handball. When children used gender to exclude others from play, they often drew upon beliefs connecting boys to some activities and girls to others:

> A first-grade boy avidly watched an all-female game of jump rope. When the girls began to shift positions, he recognized a means of access to the play and he offered, "I'll swing it." A girl responded, "No way, you don't know how to do it, to swing it. You gotta be a girl." He left without protest.

Although children sometimes ignored pronouncements about what each sex could or could not do, I never heard them directly challenge such claims.

When children had explicitly defined an activity or a group as gendered, those who crossed the boundary—especially boys who moved into female-marked space—risked being teased. ("Look! Mike's in the girls' line!" "That's a girl over there," a girl said loudly, pointing to a boy sitting at an otherwise all-female table in the lunchroom.) Children, and occasionally adults, used teasing—especially the tease of "liking" someone of the other sex, or of "being" that sex by virtue of being in their midst—to police gender boundaries. Much of the teasing drew upon heterosexual romantic definitions, making cross-sex interaction risky, and increasing social distance between boys and girls.

Relationships between the Sexes

Because I have emphasized the "apart" and ignored the occasions of "with," this analysis of sex segregation falsely implies that there is little contact between girls and boys in daily school life. In fact, relationships between girls and boys—which should be studied as fully as, and in connection with, same-sex relationships—are of several kinds:

1. "Borderwork," or forms of cross-sex interaction which are based upon and reaffirm boundaries and asymmetries between girls' and boys' groups;
2. Interactions which are infused with heterosexual meanings;
3. Occasions where individuals cross gender boundaries to participate in the world of the other sex; and
4. Situations where gender is muted in salience, with girls and boys interacting in more relaxed ways.

Borderwork

In elementary school settings boys' and girls' groups are sometimes spatially set apart. Same-sex groups sometimes claim fixed territories such as the basketball court, the bars, or specific lunchroom tables. However, in the crowded, multifocused, and adult-controlled environment of the school, groups form and disperse at a rapid rate and can never stay totally apart. Contact between girls and boys sometimes lessens sex segregation, but gender-defined groups also come together in ways which emphasize their boundaries.

"Borderwork" refers to interaction across, yet based upon and even strengthening gender boundaries. I have drawn this notion from Fredrik Barth's (1969) analysis of social relations which are maintained across ethnic boundaries without diminishing dichotomized ethnic status.[1] His focus is on more macro, ecological arrangements; mine is on face-to-face behavior. But the insight is similar: Groups may interact in ways which strengthen their borders, and the maintenance of ethnic (or gender) groups can best be understood by examining the boundary that defines the group, "not the cultural stuff that it encloses" (Barth, 1969, p. 15). In elementary schools there are several types of borderwork: contests or games where gender-defined teams compete; cross-sex rituals of chasing and pollution; and group invasions. These interactions are asymmetrical, challenging the separate-but-parallel model of "two worlds."

Contests Boys and girls are sometimes pitted against each other in classroom competitions and playground games. The fourth–fifth grade classroom had a boys' side and a girls' side, an arrangement that reemerged each time the teacher asked children to choose their own desks. Although there was some within-sex shuffling, the result was always a spatial moiety system—boys on the left, girls on the right—with the exception of one girl (the "tomboy" whom I'll describe later), who twice chose a desk with the boys and once with the girls. Drawing upon and reinforcing the children's self-segregation, the teacher often pitted the boys against the girls in spelling and math competitions, events marked by cross-sex antagonism and within-sex solidarity:

> The teacher introduced a math game; she would write addition and subtraction problems on the board, and a member of each team would race to be the first to write the correct answer. She wrote two scorekeeping columns on the board: "Beastly boys". . . "Gossipy Girls." The boys yelled out, as several girls laughed, "Noisy girls! Gruesome girls!" The girls sat in a row on top of their desks; sometimes they moved collectively, pushing their hips or whispering "pass it on." The boys stood along the wall, some reclining against desks. When members of either group came back victorious from the front of the room, they would do the "giving five" handslapping ritual with their team members.

On the playground a team of girls occasionally played against a team of boys, usually in kickball or team two-square. Sometimes these games proceeded matter-of-factly, but if gender became the explicit basis of team solidarity, the interaction changed, becoming more antagonistic and unstable:

> Two fifth-grade girls against two fifth-grade boys in a team game of two-square. The game proceeded at an even pace until an argument ensued about whether the ball was out or on the line. Karen, who had hit the ball, became annoyed, flashed her middle finger at the other team, and called to a passing girl to join their side. The boys then called out to other boys, and cheered as several arrived to play. "We got five and you got three!" Jack yelled. The game continued, with the girls yelling, "Bratty boys! Sissy boys!" and the boys making noises—"weee haw" "ha-ha-ha"—as they played.

Chasing Cross-sex chasing dramatically affirms boundaries between girls and boys. The basic elements of chase and elude, capture and rescue (Sutton-Smith, 1971) are found in various kinds of tag with formal rules, and in informal episodes of chasing which punctuate life on playgrounds. These episodes begin with a provocation (taunts like "You can't get me!" or "Slobber monster!," bodily pokes, or the grabbing of possessions). A provocation may be ignored, or responded to by chasing. Chaser and chased may then alternate roles. In an ethnographic study of chase sequences on a school playground, Christine Finnan (1982) observes that chases vary in the number of chasers to chased (e.g., one chasing one, or five chasing two); form of provocation (a taunt or a poke); outcome (an episode may end when the chased outdistances the chaser, or with a brief touch, being wrestled to the ground, or the recapturing of a hat or a ball); and in use of space (there may or may not be safety zones).

Like Finnan (1982), and Sluckin (1981), who studied a playground in England, I found that chasing has a gendered structure. Boys frequently chase one another, an activity which often ends in wrestling and mock fights. When girls chase girls, they are usually less physically aggressive; they less often, for example, wrestle one another to the ground.

Cross-sex chasing is set apart by special names—"girls chase the boys"; "boys chase the girls"; "the chase"; "chasers"; "chase and kiss"; "kiss chase"; "kissers and chasers"; "kiss or kill"—and by children's animated talk about the activity. The names vary by region and school, but contain both gender and sexual meanings (this form of play is mentioned, but only briefly analyzed, in Finnan, 1982; Sluckin, 1981; Parrott, 1972; and Borman, 1979).

In "boys chase the girls" and "girls chase the boys" (the names most frequently used in both the California and Michigan schools) boys and girls become, by definition, separate teams. Gender terms override individual identities, especially for the other team ("Help, a girl's chasin' me!"; "C'mon Sarah, let's get that boy"; "Tony, help save me from the girls"). Individuals may call for help from, or offer help to, others of their sex. They may also grab someone of their sex and turn them over to the opposing team: Ryan grabbed Billy from behind, wrestling him to the ground. "Hey, girls, get 'im," Ryan called.

Boys more often mix episodes of cross-sex with same-sex chasing. Girls more often have safety zones, places like the girls' restroom or an area by the school wall, where they retreat to rest and talk (sometimes in animated postmortems) before new episodes of cross-sex chasing begin.

Early in the fall in the Michigan school, where chasing was especially prevalent, I watched a second-grade boy teach a kindergarten girl how to chase. He slowly ran backwards, beckoning her to pursue him, as he called, "Help, a girl's after me." In the early grades chasing mixes with fantasy play, e.g., a first-grade boy who played "sea monster," his arms outflung and his voice growling, as he chased a group of girls. By third grade, stylized gestures—exaggerated stalking motions, screams (which only girls do), and karate kicks—accompany scenes of chasing.

Names like "chase and kiss" mark the sexual meanings of cross-sex chasing, a theme I return to later. The threat of kissing—most often girls threatening to kiss boys—is a ritualized form of provocation. Cross-sex chasing among sixth graders involves elaborate patterns of touch and touch avoidance, which adults see as sexual. The principal told the sixth graders in the Michigan school that they were not to play "pom-pom," a complicated chasing game, because it entailed "inappropriate touch."

Rituals of Pollution Cross-sex chasing is sometimes entwined with rituals of pollution, as in "cooties," where specific individuals or groups are treated as contaminating or as carrying "germs." Children have rituals for transferring cooties (usually touching someone else and shouting "You've got cooties!"), for immunization (e.g., writing "CV" for "cootie vaccination" on their arms), and for eliminating cooties (e.g., saying "no gives" or using "cootie catchers" made of folded paper described in Knapp & Knapp, 1976). While girls may give cooties to girls, boys do not generally give cooties to one another (Samuelson, 1980).

In cross-sex play, either girls or boys may be defined as having cooties, which they transfer through chasing and touching. Girls give cooties to boys more often than vice versa. In Michigan, one version of cooties is called "girl stain"; the fourth graders whom Karkau (1973) describes used the phrase "girl touch." "Cootie queens," or "cootie girls" (there are no "kings" or "boys") are female pariahs, the ultimate school untouchables, seen as contaminating not only by virtue of gender, but also through some added stigma such as being overweight or poor.[2] That girls are seen as more polluting than boys is a significant asymmetry, which echoes cross-cultural patterns, although in other cultures female pollution is generally connected to menstruation, and not applied to prepubertal girls.

Invasions Playground invasions are another asymmetric form of borderwork. On a few occasions I saw girls invade and disrupt an all-male game, most memorably a group of tall sixth-grade girls who ran onto the playing field and grabbed a football which was in play. The boys were surprised and frustrated, and, unusual for boys this old, finally tattled to the aide. But in the majority of cases, boys disrupt girls' activities rather than vice versa. Boys grab the ball from girls playing four-square, stick feet into a jump rope and stop an ongoing game, and dash through the area of the bars, where girls are taking turns performing, sending the rings flying. Sometimes boys ask to join a girls' game and then, after a short period of seemingly earnest play, disrupt the game:

> Two second-grade boys begged to "twirl" the jumprope for a group of second-grade girls who had been jumping for some time. The girls agreed, and the boys began to twirl. Soon, without announcement, the boys changed from "seashells, cockle bells" to "hot peppers" (spinning the rope very fast), and tangled the jumper in the rope. The boys ran away laughing.

Boys disrupt girls' play so often that girls have developed almost ritualized responses: They guard their ongoing play, chase boys away, and tattle to the aides. In a playground cycle which enhances sex segregation, aides who try to spot potential trouble before it occurs sometimes shoo boys away from areas where girls are playing. Aides do not anticipate trouble from girls who seek to join groups of boys, with the exception of girls intent on provoking a chase sequence. And indeed, if they seek access to a boys' game, girls usually play with boys in earnest rather than breaking up the game.

A close look at the organization of borderwork—or boundaried interactions between the sexes—shows that the worlds of boys and girls may be separate but they are not parallel, nor are they equal. The worlds of girls and boys articulate in several asymmetric ways:

1. On the playground, boys control as much as ten times more space than girls, when one adds up the area of large playing fields and compares it with the much smaller areas where girls predominate. Girls, who play closer to the building, are more often watched over and protected by the adult aides.

2. Boys invade all-female games and scenes of play much more than girls invade boys'. This, and boys' greater control of space, correspond with other findings about the organization of gender, and inequality, in our society: compared with men and boys, women and girls take up less space, and their space, and talk, are more often violated and interrupted (Henley, 1977).
3. Although individual boys are occasionally treated as contaminating (e.g., a third-grade boy who [to] both boys and girls was "stinky" and "smelled like pee"), girls are more often defined as polluting. This pattern ties to themes that I discuss later: It is more taboo for a boy to play with (as opposed to invade) girls, and girls are more sexually defined than boys.

A look at the boundaries between the separated worlds of girls and boys illuminates within-sex hierarchies of status and control. For example, in the sex-divided seating in the fourth–fifth grade classroom, several boys recurringly sat near "female space": their desks were at the gender divide in the classroom, and they were more likely than other boys to sit at a predominantly female table in the lunchroom. These boys—two nonbilingual Chicanos and an overweight "loner" boy who was afraid of sports—were at the bottom of the male hierarchy. Gender is sometimes used as a metaphor for male hierarchies; the inferior status of boys at the bottom is conveyed by calling them "girls":

> Seven boys and one girl were playing basketball. Two younger boys came over and asked to play. While the girl silently stood, fully accepted in the company of players, one of the older boys disparagingly said to the younger boys, "You girls can't play."[3]

In contrast, the girls who more often travel in the boys' world, sitting with groups of boys in the lunchroom or playing basketball, soccer, and baseball with them, are not stigmatized. Some have fairly high status with other girls. The worlds of girls and boys are asymmetrically arranged, and spatial patterns map out interacting forms of inequality.

Heterosexual Meanings

The organization and meanings of gender (the social categories "woman/man," "girl/boy") and of sexuality vary cross-culturally (Ortner & Whitehead, 1981)—and, in our society, across the life course. Harriet Whitehead (1981) observed that in our (Western) gender system, and that of many traditional North American Indian cultures, one's choice of a sexual object, occupation, and one's dress and demeanor are closely associated with gender. However, the "center of gravity" differs in the two gender systems. For Indians, occupational pursuits provide the primary imagery of gender; dress and demeanor are secondary, and sexuality is least important. In our system, at least for adults, the order is reversed: heterosexuality is central to our definitions of "man" and "woman" ("masculinity"/"femininity") and the relationships that obtain between them, whereas occupation and dress/demeanor are secondary.

Whereas erotic orientation and gender are closely linked in our definitions of adults, we define children as relatively asexual. Activities and dress/demeanor are more important than sexuality in the cultural meanings of "girl" and "boy." Children are less heterosexually defined than adults, and we have nonsexual imagery for relations between girls and boys. However, both children and adults sometimes use heterosexual language—"crushes," "like," "goin' with," "girlfriends," and "boyfriends"—to define cross-sex relationships. This language increases through the years of elementary school; the shift to adolescence consolidates a gender system organized around the institution of heterosexuality.

In everyday life in the schools, heterosexual and romantic meanings infuse some ritualized forms of interaction between groups of boys and girls (e.g., "chase and kiss") and help maintain sex segregation. "Jimmy likes Beth" or "Beth likes Jimmy" is a major form of teasing, which a child risks in choosing to sit by or walk with someone of the other sex. The structure of teasing, and children's sparse vocabulary for relationships between girls and boys, are evident in the following conversation, which I had with a group of third-grade girls in the lunchroom:

> Susan asked me what I was doing, and I said I was observing the things children do and play. Nicole volunteered, "I like running, boys chase all the girls. See Tim over there? Judy chases him all around the school. She likes him." Judy, sitting across the table, quickly responded, "I hate him. I like him for a friend." "Tim loves Judy," Nicole said in a loud, sing-song voice.

In the younger grades, the culture and lore of girls contain more heterosexual romantic themes than those of boys. In Michigan, the first-grade girls often jumped rope to a rhyme which began: "Down in the valley where the green grass grows, there sat Cindy (name of the jumper), as sweet as a rose. She sat, she sat, she sat so sweet. Along came Jason, and kissed her on the cheek . . . first comes love, then comes marriage, then along comes Cindy with a baby carriage . . . " Before a girl took her turn at jumping, the chanters asked her, "Who do you want to be your boyfriend?" The jumper always proffered a name, which was accepted matter-of-factly. In chasing, a girl's kiss carried greater threat than a boy's kiss; "girl touch," when defined as contaminating, had sexual connotations. In short, starting at an early age, girls are more sexually defined than boys.

Through the years of elementary school, and increasing with age, the idiom of heterosexuality helps maintain the gender divide. Cross-sex interactions, especially when children initiate them, are fraught with the risk of being teased about "liking" someone of the other sex. I learned of several close cross-sex friendships, formed and maintained in neighborhoods and church, which went underground during the school day.

By the fifth grade a few children began to affirm, rather than avoid, the charge of having a girlfriend or a boyfriend; they introduced the heterosexual courtship rituals of adolescence:

> In the lunchroom in the Michigan school, as the tables were forming, a high-status fifth-grade boy called out from his seat at the table: "I want Trish to sit by me." Trish came over, and almost like a king and queen, they sat at the gender divide—a row of girls down the table on her side, a row of boys on his.

In this situation, which inverted earlier forms, it was not a loss, but a gain in status to publicly choose a companion of the other sex. By affirming his choice, the boy became unteasable (note the familiar asymmetry of heterosexual courtship rituals: the male initiated). This incident signals a temporal shift in arrangements of sex and gender.

Traveling in the World of the Other Sex

Contests, invasions, chasing, and heterosexually defined encounters are based upon and reaffirm boundaries between girls and boys. In another type of cross-sex interaction, individuals (or sometimes pairs) cross gender boundaries, seeking acceptance in a group of the other sex. Nearly all the cases I saw of this were tomboys—girls who played organized sports and frequently sat with boys in the cafeteria or classroom. If these girls were skilled at activities central in the boys' world, especially games like soccer, baseball, and basketball, they were pretty much accepted as participants.

Being a tomboy is a matter of degree. Some girls seek access to boys' groups but are excluded; other girls limit their "crossing" to specific sports. Only a few—such as the tomboy I mentioned earlier, who chose a seat with the boys in the sex-divided fourth–fifth grade—participate fully in the boys' world. That particular girl was skilled at the various organized sports which boys played in different seasons of the year. She was also adept at physical fighting and at using the forms of arguing, insult, teasing, naming, and sports-talk of the boys' subculture. She was the only Black child in her classroom, in a school with only 8% Black students; overall that token status, along with unusual athletic and verbal skills, may have contributed to her ability to move back and forth across the gender divide. Her unique position in the children's world was widely recognized in the school. Several times, the teacher said to me, "She thinks she's a boy."

I observed only one boy in the upper grades (a fourth grader) who regularly played with all-female groups, as opposed to "playing at" girls' games and seeking to disrupt them. He frequently played jumprope and took turns with girls doing tricks on the bars, using the small gestures—for example, a helpful push on the heel of a girl who needed momentum to turn her body around the bar—which mark skillful and earnest participation. Although I never saw him play in other than an earnest spirit, the girls often chased him away from their games, and both girls and boys teased him. The fact that girls seek and have more access to boys' worlds than vice versa, and the fact that girls who travel with the other sex are less stigmatized for it, are obvious asymmetries, tied to the asymmetries previously discussed.

Relaxed Cross-Sex Interactions

Relationships between boys and girls are not always marked by strong boundaries, by heterosexual definitions, or by interacting on the terms and turfs of the other sex. On some occasions girls and boys interact in relatively comfortable ways. Gender is not strongly salient nor explicitly invoked, and girls and boys are not organized into boundaries collectively. These "with" occasions have been neglected by those studying gender and children's relationships, who have emphasized either the model of separate worlds (with little attention to their articulation) or heterosexual forms of contact.

Occasions where boys and girls interact without strain, where gender wanes rather than waxes in importance, frequently have one or more of the following characteristics:

1. The situations are organized around an absorbing task, such as a group art project or creating a radio show, which encourages cooperation and lessens attention to gender. This pattern accords with other studies finding that cooperative activities reduce group antagonism (e.g., Sherif & Sherif, 1953, who studied divisions between boys in a summer camp; and Aronson et al., 1978, who used cooperative activities to lessen racial divisions in a classroom).
2. Gender is less prominent when children are not responsible for the formation of the group. Mixed-sex play is less frequent in games like football, which require the choosing of teams, and more frequent in games like handball or dodgeball, which individuals can join simply by getting into a line or a circle. When adults organize mixed-sex encounters—which they frequently do in the classroom and in physical education periods on the playground—they legitimize cross-sex contact. This removes the risk of being teased for choosing to be with the other sex.
3. There is more extensive and relaxed cross-sex interaction when principles of grouping other than gender are explicitly involved—for example, counting off to form teams for spelling or kickball, dividing lines by hot lunch or cold lunch, or organizing a work group on the basis of interests or reading ability.
4. Girls and boys may interact more readily in less public and crowded settings. Neighborhood play, depending on demography, is more often sex and age integrated than play at school, partly because with

fewer numbers, one may have to resort to an array of social categories to find play partners or to constitute a game. And in less crowded environments there are fewer potential witnesses to "make something of it" if girls and boys play together.

Relaxed interactions between girls and boys often depend on adults to set up and legitimize the contact.[4] Perhaps because of this contingency—and the other, distancing patterns which permeate relations between girls and boys—the easeful moments of interaction rarely build to close friendship. Schofield (1981) makes a similar observation about gender and racial barriers to friendship in a junior high school.

Implications for Development

I have located social relations within an essentially spatial framework, emphasizing the organization of children's play, work, and other activities within specific settings, and in one type of institution, the school. In contrast, frameworks of child development rely upon temporal metaphors, using images of growth and transformation over time. Taken alone, both spatial and temporal frameworks have shortcomings; fitted together, they may be mutually correcting.

Those interested in gender and development have relied upon conceptualizations of "sex role socialization" and "sex differences." Sexuality and gender, I have argued, are more situated and fluid than these individualist and intrinsic models imply. Sex and gender are differently organized and defined across situations, even within the same institution. This situational variation (e.g., in the extent to which an encounter heightens or lessens gender boundaries, or is infused with sexual meanings) shapes and constrains individual behavior. Features which a developmental perspective might attribute to individuals, and understand as relatively internal attributes unfolding over time, may, in fact, be highly dependent on context. For example, children's avoidance of cross-sex friendship may be attributed to individual gender development in middle childhood. But attention to varied situations may show that this avoidance is contingent on group size, activity, adult behavior, collective meanings, and the risk of being teased.

A focus on social organization and situation draws attention to children's experiences in the present. This helps correct a model like "sex role socialization" which casts the present under the shadow of the future, or presumed "endpoints" (Speier, 1976). A situated analysis of arrangements of sex and gender among those of different ages may point to crucial disjunctions in the life course. In the fourth and fifth grades, culturally defined heterosexual rituals ("goin' with") begin to suppress the presence and visibility of other types of interaction between girls and boys, such as nonsexualized and comfortable interaction, and traveling in the world of the other sex. As "boyfriend/girlfriend" definitions spread, the fifth-grade tomboy I described had to work to sustain "buddy" relationships with boys. Adult women who were tomboys often speak of early adolescence as a painful time when they were pushed away from participation in boys' activities. Other adult women speak of the loss of intense, even erotic ties with other girls when they entered puberty and the rituals of dating, that is, when they became absorbed into the institution of heterosexuality (Rich, 1980). When Lever (1976) describes best-friend relationships among fifth-grade girls as preparation for dating, she imposes heterosexual ideologies onto a present which should be understood on its own terms.

As heterosexual encounters assume more importance, they may alter relations in same-sex groups. For example, Schofield (1981) reports that for sixth- and seventh-grade children in a middle school, the popularity of girls with other girls was affected by their popularity with boys, while boys' status with other boys did not depend on their relations with girls. This is an asymmetry familiar from the adult world; men's relationships with one another are defined through varied activities (occupations, sports), while relationships among women—and their public status—are more influenced by their connections to individual men.

A full understanding of gender and social relations should encompass cross-sex as well as within-sex interactions. "Borderwork" helps maintain separate, gender-linked subcultures, which, as those interested in development have begun to suggest, may result in different milieux for learning. Daniel Maltz and Ruth Borker (1983), for example, argue that because of different interactions within girls' and boys' groups, the sexes learn different rules for creating and interpreting friendly conversation, rules which carry into adulthood and help account for miscommunication between men and women. Carol Gilligan (1982) fits research on the different worlds of girls and boys into a theory of sex differences in moral development. Girls develop a style of reasoning, she argues, which is more personal and relational; boys develop a style which is more positional, based on separateness. Eleanor Maccoby (1982), also following the insight that because of sex segregation, girls and boys grow up in different environments, suggests implications for gender-differentiated prosocial and antisocial behavior.

This separate worlds approach, as I have illustrated, also has limitations. The occasions when the sexes are together should also be studied, and understood as contexts for experience and learning. For example, asymmetries in cross-sex relationships convey a series of messages: that boys are more entitled to space and to the nonreciprocal right of interrupting or invading the activities of the other sex; that girls are more in need of adult protection, and are lower in status, more defined by sexuality, and may even be polluting. Different types of cross-sex interaction—relaxed, boundaried, sexualized, or taking place on the terms of the other sex—provide different contexts for development.

By mapping the array of relationships between and within the sexes, one adds complexity to the overly static and dichotomous imagery of separate worlds. Individual experiences vary, with implications for development. Some children prefer same-sex groupings; some are more likely to cross the gender boundary and participate in the world of the other sex; some children (e.g., girls and boys who frequently play "chase and kiss") invoke heterosexual meanings, while others avoid them.

Finally, after charting the terrain of relationships, one can trace their development over time. For example, age variation in the content and form of borderwork, or of cross- and same-sex touch, may be related to differing cognitive, social, emotional, or physical capacities, as well as to age-associated cultural forms. I earlier mentioned temporal shifts in the organization of cross-sex chasing, for mixing with fantasy play in the early grades to more elaborately ritualized and sexualized forms by the sixth grade. There also appear to be temporal changes in same- and cross-sex touch. In kindergarten, girls and boys touch one another more freely than in fourth grade, when children avoid relaxed cross-sex touch and instead use pokes, pushes, and other forms of mock violence, even when the touch clearly couches affection. This touch taboo is obviously related to the risk of seeming to *like* someone of the other sex. In fourth grade, same-sex touch begins to signal sexual meanings among boys, as well as between boys and girls. Younger boys touch one another freely in cuddling (arm around shoulder) as well as mock violence ways. By fourth grade, when homophobic taunts like "fag" become more common among boys, cuddling touch begins to disappear for boys, but less so for girls.

Overall, I am calling for more complexity in our conceptualization of gender and of children's social relationships. Our challenge is to retain the temporal sweep, looking at individual and group lives as they unfold over time, while also attending to social structure and context, and to the full variety of experiences in the present.

Acknowledgement

I would like to thank Jane Atkinson, Nancy Chodorow, Arlene Daniels, Peter Lyman, Zick Rubin, Malcolm Spector, Avril Thorne, and Margery Wolf for comments on an earlier version of this paper. Conversations with Zella Luria enriched this work.

NOTES

1. I am grateful to Frederick Erickson for suggesting the relevance of Barth's analysis.
2. Sue Samuelson (1980) reports that in a racially mixed playground in Fresno, California, Mexican-American but not Anglo children gave cooties. Racial as well as sexual inequality may be expressed through these forms.
3. This incident was recorded by Margaret Blume, who, for an undergraduate research project in 1982, observed in the California school where I earlier did field-

work. Her observations and insights enhanced my own, and I would like to thank her for letting me cite this excerpt.

4. Note that in daily school life, depending on the individual and the situation, teachers and aides sometimes lessened and at other times heightened sex segregation.

REFERENCES

Aronson, F., et al. (1978). *The jigsaw classroom.* Beverly Hills, CA: Sage.

Barth, F. (Ed.). (1969). *Ethnic groups and boundaries.* Boston: Little, Brown.

Borman, K. M. (1979). Children's interactions in playgrounds. *Theory into Practice, 18,* 251–257.

Eder, D., & Hallinan, M. T. (1978). Sex differences in children's friendships. *American Sociological Review, 43,* 237–250.

Finnan, C. R. (1982). The ethnography of children's spontaneous play. In G. Spindler (Ed.), *Doing the ethnography of schooling* (pp. 358–380). New York: Holt, Rinehart & Winston.

Foot, H. C., Chapman, A. J., & Smith, J. R. (1980). *Introduction. In Friendship and social relations in children* (pp. 1–14). New York: Wiley.

Gilligan, C. (1982). *In a different voice: Psychological theory and women's development.* Cambridge, MA: Harvard University Press.

Glaser, B. G., & Strauss, A. L. (1967). *The discovery of grounded theory.* Chicago: Aldine.

Goffman, E. (1977). The arrangement between the sexes. *Theory and Society, 4,* 301–336.

Goodwin, M. H. (1980). Directive-response sequences in girls' and boys' task activities. In S. McConnell-Ginet, R. Borker, & N. Furman (Eds.), *Women and language in literature and society* (pp. 157–173). New York: Praeger.

Henley, N. (1977). *Body politics: Power, sex, and nonverbal communication.* Englewood Cliffs, NJ: Prentice-Hall.

Karkau, K. (1973). *Sexism in the fourth grade* [Pamphlet]. Pittsburgh: KNOW, Inc.

Katz, J. (1983). *A theory of qualitative methodology: The social system of analytic fieldwork.* In R. M. Emerson (Ed.), *Contemporary field research* (pp. 127–148). Boston: Little, Brown.

Knapp, M., & Knapp, H. (1976). *One potato, two potato: The secret education of American children.* New York: W. W. Norton.

Lever, J. (1976). Sex differences in the games children play. *Social Problems, 23,* 478–487.

Maccoby, E. (1982). *Social groupings in childhood: Their relationship to prosocial and antisocial behavior in boys and girls.* Paper presented at conference on the Development of Prosocial and Antisocial Behavior. Voss, Norway.

Maccoby, E., & Jacklin, C. (1974). *The psychology of sex differences.* Stanford, CA: Stanford University Press.

Maltz, D. N., & Borker, R. A. (1983). A cultural approach to male-female miscommunication. In J. J. Gumperz (Ed.), *Language and social identity* (pp. 195–216). New York: Cambridge University Press.

McRobbie, A., & Garber, J. (1975). Girls and subcultures. In S. Hall and T. Jefferson (Eds.), *Resistance through rituals* (pp. 209–223). London: Hutchinson.

Ortner, S. B., & Whitehead, H. (1981). *Sexual meanings.* New York: Cambridge University Press.

Parrott, S. (1972). Games children play: Ethnography of a second-grade recess. In J. P. Spradley & D. W. McCurdy (Eds.), *The cultural experience* (pp. 206–219). Chicago: Science Research Associates.

Rich, A. (1980). Compulsory heterosexuality and lesbian existence. *Signs, 5,* 631–660.

Samuelson, S. (1980). The cooties complex. *Western Folklore, 39,* 198–210.
Savin-Williams, R. C. (1976). An ethological study of dominance formation and maintenance in a group of human adolescents. *Child Development, 47,* 972–979.
Schofield, J. W. (1981). Complementary and conflicting identities: Images and interaction in an interracial school. In S. R. Asher & J. M. Gottman (Eds.), *The development of children's friendships* (pp. 53–90). New York: Cambridge University Press.
Sherif, M., & Sherif, C. (1953). *Groups in harmony and tension.* New York: Harper.
Sluckin, A. (1981). *Growing up in the playground.* London: Routledge and Kegan Paul.
Speier, M. (1976). The adult ideological viewpoint in studies of childhood. In A. Skolnick (Ed.), *Rethinking childhood* (pp. 168–186). Boston: Little, Brown.
Sutton-Smith, B. (1971). A syntax for play and games. In R. E. Herron and Brian Sutton-Smith (Eds.), *Child's play* (pp. 298–307). New York: Wiley.
Waldrop, M. F., & Halverson, C. F. (1975). Intensive and extensive peer behavior: Longitudinal and cross-sectional analyses. *Child Development, 46,* 19–26.
Whitehead, H. (1981). The bow and the burden strap: A new look at institutionalized homosexuality in native America. In S. B. Ortner and H. Whitehead (Eds.), *Sexual meanings* (pp. 80–115). New York: Cambridge University Press.

46

DREAMS

ANN ARNETT FERGUSON

The purpose of education, finally, is to create in a person the ability to look at the world for himself, to make his own decisions, to say to himself this is black or this is white, to decide for himself whether there is a God in heaven or not. To ask questions of the universe, and then learn to live with those questions, is the way he achieves his own identity. But no society is really anxious to have that kind of person around. What societies really, ideally, want is a citizenry which will simply obey the rules of society. If a society succeeds in this, that society is about to perish.

—*JAMES BALDWIN, "A TALK TO TEACHERS"*

This book [*Bad Boys*] began with an anecdote about the school's vice principal identifying a small boy as someone who had a jail-cell with his name on it. I started with this story to illustrate how school personnel made predictive decisions about a child's future based on a whole ensemble of negative assumptions about African American males and their life-chances. The kids, however, imagined their future in a more positive light. They neither saw themselves as being "on the fast track to prison," as predicted by school personnel, nor did they see themselves as working at low-level service jobs as adults. The boys, in fact, had a decidedly optimistic view about their future.

This scenario, at such variance with that of the administrator's, became clear to me in my final semester at Rosa Parks, when the sixth-graders wrote an essay on the jobs they would like to have as adults. As I scanned these written accounts of students' dreams, I became conscious of a striking pattern. The overwhelming majority of the boys aspired to be professional athletes—playing basketball, baseball, or football—when they grew up. The reasons they gave for this choice were remarkably similar: the sport was something they were good at; it was work they would enjoy doing; and they would make a lot of money.[1] They acknowledged it would be extremely difficult to have such a career, but, they argued, if you worked hard and had the talent, you could make it.

These youthful essays confirmed what the boys had told me in interviews about the adult occupations they imagined for themselves. While a few had mentioned other options such as becoming a stand-up comedian, a Supreme Court justice, or a rap musician, almost all expressed the desire to play on an NBA or NFL team. This was not just an empty fantasy. Most of the boys with whom I had contact in my research were actively and diligently involved in after-school sports, not just as play, but in the serious business of preparing themselves for adult careers. This dream was supported in tangible ways by parents who boasted about their sons' prowess, found time to take them to practice, and cheered their teams on at games. I had assumed initially that these after-school sports activities were primarily a way of parents keeping kids busy to guard against their getting into drugs and sex. However, after talking to parents and kids I realized that what I observed was not just about keeping boys out of trouble but was preparation for future careers.

The occupational dreams of these boys are not at all unique. A survey by Northeastern University's Center for the Study of Sport in Society found that two-thirds of African American males between the ages of thirteen and eighteen believe they can earn a living playing professional sports.[2] Nor is this national pattern for black youth really surprising. For African American males, disengagement from the school's agenda for approval and success is a psychic survival mechanism; so imagining a future occupation for which schooling seems irrelevant is eminently rational. A career as a professional athlete represents the possibility of attaining success in terms of the dominant society via a path that makes schooling seem immaterial, while at the same time affirming central aspects of identification.

I have argued that the boys distance themselves from the school's agenda to avoid capitulating to its strategies for fashioning a self for upward mobility—strategies requiring black youth to distance themselves from family and neighborhood, to reject the language, the style of social interaction, the connections in which identities are grounded. From the highly idealized viewpoint of youth, a career in sports does not appear to require these strategic detachments. Their heroes—players like Michael Jordan, Scottie Pippen, Dennis Rodman, Rickey Henderson, to name just a few—have achieved the highest reaches of success without disguising or eradicating their Blackness.

But these are only dreams, for the chances of getting drafted by professional teams are slim to nonexistent. The probability has been calculated as somewhere in the region of one in ten thousand that a youth will end up in pro football or basketball.[3] Based on these facts, a plethora of popular and scholarly literature, as well as fiction and documentary films, have underscored how unrealistic such ambitions are, making the point that few youths who pour their hearts, energy, and schooling into sports will actually make it to the professional teams where the glory lies and the money is made.[4] They point out this discouraging scenario in order to persuade young black males to rechannel their energies and ambitions into conventional school learning that allows for more "realistic" career options.

Yet, in reality, for these youth efforts to attain high-status occupations through academic channels are just as likely to fail, given the conditions of their schooling and the unequal distribution of resources across school systems.[5] Children attending inner-city public schools are more likely to end up in dead-end, minimum-wage, service sector jobs because they do not have the quality of education available in the suburban public or elite private schools. Today's dreams will be transformed into tomorrow's nightmares.

Nightmares

While I rejected the labeling practices of the school vice principal, in my opening chapter, I also reluctantly admitted that by the end of the school year I, too, had come to suspect that a prison cell might have a place in the future of many Rosa Parks students. In contrast to the vice principal, this foreboding was not by any means rooted in a conclusion I had come to about individual children's proclivity for a life of crime, nor was it grounded in any evidence that, as some labeling theories hold, individuals stigmatized as deviant come to internalize this identity and adopt delinquent behaviors at rates higher than other youth. Rather it emanated from my increased awareness of the way that racial bias in institutions external to school, such as the media and criminal justice system, mirrored and converged with that of the educational system. This convergence intensifies and weights the odds heavily in favor of a young black male ending up in jail. School seems to feed into the prison system, but what exactly is the connection between the two? What are the practical links between the punishing rooms, jailhouses, and dungeons of educational institutions and the cells of local, state, and federal prison systems? There are both long-term causal links as well as visible, immediate connections.

There are serious, long-term effects of being labeled a Troublemaker that substantially increase one's chances of ending up in jail. In the daily experience of being so named, regulated, and surveilled, access to the full resources of the school are increasingly denied as the boys are isolated in nonacademic spaces in school or banished to lounging at home or loitering on the streets. Time in the school dungeon means time lost from classroom learning; suspension, at school or at home, has a direct and lasting negative effect on the continuing growth of a child. When removal from classroom life begins at an early age, it is even more devastating, as human possibilities are stunted at a crucial formative period of life. Each year the gap in skills grows wider and more handicapping, while the overall process of disidentification that I have described encourages those who have problems to leave school rather than resolve them in an educational setting.

There is a direct relationship between dropping out of school and doing time in jail: the majority of black inmates in local, state, and federal penal systems are high school dropouts.[6] Therefore, if we want to begin to break the ties between school and jail, we must first create educational systems that foster kids' identification with school and encourage them not to abandon it.

One significant but relatively small step that could be taken to foster this attachment would be to reduce the painful, inhospitable climate of school for African American children through the validation and affirmation of Black English, the language form that many of the children bring from home/neighborhood. As I pointed out earlier, the denigration of this form and the assumptions made about the academic potential of speakers of Ebonics pose severe dilemmas of identification for black students—especially for males. The legitimation of Black English in the world of the school would not only enrich the curriculum but would undoubtedly provide valuable lessons to all students about sociolinguistics and the contexts in which standard and nonstandard forms are appropriate. The necessary prerequisite for this inclusion would be a mandatory program for teachers and school administrators to educate them about the nature and history of Ebonics. This was of course the very change called for by the Oakland School Board in 1996. However, it is clear from the controversy that ensued and the highly racialized and obfuscatory nature of the national media's coverage of the Oakland Resolution that there is serious opposition to any innovations that appear to challenge the supremacy of English.[7]

There is also an immediate, ongoing connection between school and jail. Schools mirror and reinforce the practices and ideological systems of other institutions in the society. The racial bias in the punishing systems of the school reflects the practices of the criminal justice system. Black youth are caught up in the net of the juvenile justice system at a rate of two to four times that of white youth.[8] Does this mean that African American boys are more prone to criminal activity than white boys? There is evidence that this is not the case. A study by Huizinga and Elliott demonstrates that the contrast in incarceration statistics is the result of a different *institutional response* to the race of the youth rather than the difference in actual behavior. Drawing on a representative sample of youth between the ages of eleven and seventeen, they compare the delinquent acts individual youth admit to committing in annual self-report interviews with actual police records of delinquency in the areas in which the boys live. Based on the self-reports, they conclude that there were few, if any, differences in the number or type of delinquent acts perpetrated by the two racial groups. What they did find, however, was that there was a substantially and significantly higher risk that the minority youth would be apprehended and charged for these acts by police than the whites who reported committing the same kind of offenses. They conclude that "minorities appear to be at greater risk for being charged with more serious offenses than whites involved in comparable levels of delinquent behavior, a factor which may eventually result in higher incarceration rates among minorities."[9]

Images of black male criminality and the demonization of black children play a significant role in framing actions and events in the justice system in a way that is similar to how these images are used in school to interpret the behavior of individual miscreants. In both settings, the images result in differential treatment based on race. Jerome G. Miller, who has directed juvenile justice detention systems in Massachusetts and Illinois, describes how this works:

> I learned very early on that when we got a black youth, virtually everything—from arrest summaries, to family history, to rap sheets, to psychiatric exams, to "waiver" hearings as to whether or not he would be tried as an adult, to final sentencing—was skewed. If a middle-class white youth was sent to us as "dangerous," he was more likely actually to be so than the black teenager given the same label. The white teenager was more likely to have been afforded competent legal counsel and appropriate psychiatric and psychological testing, tried in a variety of privately funded options, and dealt with more sensitively and individually at every stage of the juvenile justice processing. For him to be labeled "dangerous," he had to have done something very serious indeed. By contrast, the black teenager was more likely to be dealt with as a stereotype from the moment the handcuffs were first put on—easily and quickly relegated to the "more dangerous" end of the "violent-nonviolent" spectrum, albeit accompanied by an official record meant to validate each of a biased series of decisions.[10]

Miller indicates that racial disparities are most obvious at the very earliest and the latest stages of processing of youth through the juvenile justice system, and African American male youth are more likely to be apprehended and caught up in the system in the very beginning. They are also more likely "to be waived to adult court, and to be adjudicated delinquent.

If removed from their homes by the court, they were less likely to be placed in the better-staffed and better-run private-group home facilities and more likely to be sent into state reform schools."[11]

Given the poisonous mix of stereotyping and profiling of black males, their chances of ending up in the penal system as a juvenile is extremely high. Even if a boy manages to avoid getting caught within the juvenile justice system through luck or the constant vigilance of parents, his chances of being arrested and jailed are staggeringly high as an adult. A 1995 report by the Sentencing Project finds that nearly one in three African Americans in his twenties is in prison or jail, on probation or parole, on any given day.[12]

The school experience of African American boys is simultaneously replicated in the penal system through processes of surveillance, policing, charges, and penalties. The kids recognize this; the names they give to disciplinary spaces are not just coincidence. They are referencing the chilling parallels between the two.

A systematic racial bias is exercised in the regulation, control, and discipline of children in the United States today. African American males are apprehended and punished for misbehavior and delinquent acts that are overlooked in other children. The punishment that is meted out is usually more severe than that for other children. This racism that systematically extinguishes the potential and constrains the world of possibilities for black males would be brutal enough if it were restricted to school, but it is replicated in other disciplinary systems of the society, the most obvious parallel being the juvenile justice system.

Open Endings

Whenever I give a talk about my research, I am inevitably asked what ideas or recommendations I have for addressing the conditions that I describe. What do I think should be done, listeners want to know? The first few times this happened I felt resentful partly because I knew my colleagues who did research on subjects other than schooling were rarely asked to come up with policy recommendations to address the problems they had uncovered. This request for solutions is made on the assumption that schools, unlike the family and workplace, are basically sound albeit with flaws that need adjusting.

My hesitation to propose solutions comes from a conviction that minor inputs, temporary interventions, individual prescriptions into schools are vastly inadequate to remedy an institution that is fundamentally flawed and whose goal for urban black children seems to be the creation of "a citizenry which will simply obey the rules of society." I stand convinced that a restructuring of the entire educational system is what is urgently required if we are to produce the thoughtful, actively questioning citizens that Baldwin describes in the epigraph to this chapter. To make the point, however, that small programs at Rosa Parks school such as PALS—always underfunded, always dependent on grants of "soft" money that required big promises of quick fixes—served always too few and would inevitably disappear entirely or be co-opted by the institution, was so disheartening, so paralyzing that I am forced to rethink my reply. Is it all or nothing? Can we eradicate forms of institutional racism in school without eliminating racism in the society at large? Are the alternatives either quick hopeless fixes or paralysis because small changes cannot make a difference in the long run? How can the proliferation of local initiatives that spring up, in hope and with enthusiasm, be sustained without taking on institutional goals and attitudes? How can emergent forms appear alongside and out of the old? Most important of all, will attention be paid to the counterdiscourse of the Troublemakers themselves?

When I asked the kids, Schoolboys and Troublemakers, how they thought schooling might be improved, they looked at me blankly. I think they shared my sense of despair. The responses that I wrung out of them seemed trivial, even frivolous. It was all about play, about recreation: a longer recess, bigger play areas, playgrounds with grass not asphalt—and so on. The list that I had dreamed up was the opposite of frivolous. It was all about curriculum: smaller classes, Saturday tutoring, year-round school, antiracist training for student teachers, mutual respect between adults and youth. One thing I am convinced of is that more punitive measures, tighter discipline, greater surveillance, more prisons—the very path that our society seems to be determined to pursue—is not the approach to take. Perhaps, allowing ourselves to imagine the possibilities—what could, should, and must be—is an indispensable first step.

NOTES

1. It is interesting to note that the girls in the class all responded in a stereotypical way. The vast majority wanted to have "helping" careers in traditional female occupations: teachers, nurses, psychologists. None of the girls gave money as a reason for their choice.
2. Survey reported in *U.S. News and World Report,* March 24, 1997, 46.
3. Raymie E. McKerrow and Norinne H. Daly, "The Student Athlete," *National Forum* 71, no. 4 (1990): 44.
4. For examples see Gary A. Sailes, "The Exploitation of the Black Athlete: Some Alternative Solutions," *Journal of Negro Education* 55 no. 4 (1986); Robert M. Sellers and Gabriel P. Kuperminc, "Goal Discrepancy in African-American Male Student-Athletes' Unrealistic Expectations for Careers in Professional Sports," *Journal of Black Psychology* 23, no. 1 (1997); Alexander Wolf, "Impossible Dream," *Sports Illustrated,* June 2, 1997; and John Hoberman, *Darwin's Athletes: How Sport Has Damaged Black America and Preserved the Myth of Race* (Boston: Houghton Mifflin, 1997).
5. For a shocking demonstration of the difference between schools see Kozol, *Savage Inequalities.*
6. United States Department of Justice, *Profile of Jail Inmates* (Washington, D.C.: U.S. Government Printing Office, 1980). Two-thirds of the black inmates have less than a twelfth-grade education, while the rate of incarceration drops significantly for those who have twelve or more years of schooling.

7. For an excellent overview of the debate that ensued over the Oakland School Board's resolution and a discussion of Ebonics, see Theresa Perry and Lisa Delpit, eds. *The Real Ebonics Debate: Power, Language, and the Education of African American Children* (Boston: Beacon Press, 1998).
8. Miller, *Search and Destroy,* 73.
9. David Huizinga and Delbert Elliot, "Juvenile Offenders: Prevalence, Offender Incidence, and Arrest Rates by Race," paper presented at "Race and the Incarceration of Juveniles," *Racine,* Wisconsin, December 1986, quoted in ibid., 72.
10. Ibid., 78.
11. Ibid., 73.
12. Sentencing Project, *Young Black Americans and the Criminal Justice System: Five Years Later* (Washington, D.C.: Sentencing Project, 1995). This unprecedented figure reflects an increase from the 1990 Sentencing Project findings that one in four black males in their twenties was under the supervision of the criminal justice system.

REFERENCES

Kozol, Jonathan. *Savage Inequalities: Children in America's Schools.* New York: HarperCollins, 1991.

Miller, Jerome G. *Search and Destroy: African American Males in the Criminal Justice System.* New York: Cambridge University Press, 1996.

47

CONFLICT WITHIN THE IVORY TOWER

RUTH SIDEL

Either/or dichotomous thinking categorizes people, things, and ideas in terms of their difference from one another. . . . This emphasis on quantification and categorization occurs in conjunction with the belief that either/or categories must be ranked. The search for certainty of this sort requires that one side of a dichotomy be privileged while its other is denigrated. Privilege becomes defined in relationship to its other.[1]

PATRICIA HILL COLLINS,
BLACK FEMINIST THOUGHT:
KNOWLEDGE, CONSCIOUSNESS, AND THE
POLITICS OF EMPOWERMENT

Admission to college or university is, as has been noted, a first but crucial step in an individual's preparation for meaningful participation in the social, economic, and political life of postindustrial America. But admission is merely the first hurdle a student must clear in higher education. Financing college education, achieving academically, and maneuvering around the multitude of social, psychological, and political obstacles that impede the path to a bachelor's degree are often much higher hurdles than admission. Among the barriers that many students have had to face in recent years are virtually continuous clashes stemming from prejudice, ethnocentrism, and fear—fear of the unknown, of the stranger among us. At root these clashes are about entitlement and power, and about students' concerns with the precariousness of their position in the social structure.

Although colleges and universities have since the end of the Second World War been to a considerable extent transformed from elite bastions of privilege to increasingly open, heterogeneous communities, a wave of overt intolerance has recently swept over the academic community. There is little doubt that students today are more tolerant than their grandparents and their parents, yet clashes—some involving vocal or written assaults, some involving violence—continue to plague academic institutions and to shock observers. One of the reasons these so-called hate incidents are so shocking is the increasing unacceptability of overtly racist, sexist, anti-Semitic, and homophobic language and behavior in much of the wider society; another is the contrast between the violence of these incidents and the open expression of hatred and bigotry on the one hand, and the expectation of at least minimal civility in academic settings on the other.

Two relatively recent incidents that deal with the incendiary combination of race and gender point up the depth and pervasiveness of intergroup hostility on campuses all over the country. In the small rural town of Olivet, Michigan, at Olivet College, a school founded in 1844 by the abolitionist minister the Reverend John Shipherd as a "bastion of racial tolerance,"[2] a "racial brawl" involving approximately forty white students and twenty black students broke out one night in early April 1992. According to one report:

> Racial epithets were shouted at the black students as the two sides rumbled on the gray linoleum. Two students, one black, one white, were injured and briefly hospitalized.
>
> Afterward, blacks and whites who had crammed together for midterms and shared lunch money and dormitory rooms could not look each other in the face and were no longer on speaking terms.[3]

This incident was the culmination of increasing hostility among black and white students at Olivet. In the months prior to the incident, white male students had become more openly resentful of black men dating white women. Then, on April 1, a white female student claimed she had been attacked by four black students and left unconscious in a field near the campus. She was not hospitalized, and, despite a police investigation, no arrests were made. College officials were said to be skeptical about her accusations. Nonetheless, word spread, and later that night two trash cans were set on fire outside the dormitory rooms of black student leaders.

The specific incident that precipitated the brawl occurred the next night and again involved a white female student and black male students. Three male students, two black and one white, knocked on a female student's door to ask about a paper she was typing for one of the black students. The men later described the conversation as "civil." The woman, a sorority member, called her brother fraternity for help, saying she was being harassed by some male students. Within a few minutes, about fifteen members of the white fraternity Phi Alpha Pi arrived and confronted the two black men. More whites joined in, and black female students called more black males to even the numbers. Who threw the first punch is unclear; black students claim it was a white fraternity member. "What is clear," according to one report of the incident, "is that instead of seeing a roommate or a fellow sophomore, the students saw race."[4] Davonne Pierce, a dormitory resident assistant who is black, stated that his white friends shouted racial epithets at him as he was trying to break up the fight. He said to them, "How can you call me that when we were friends, when I let you borrow my notes?" But, he later recalled, "At that point, it was white against black. It was disgusting."[5]

After the incident, most of the fifty-five black students, who said they feared for their safety, left the college and went home. They made up 9 percent of the student body. Davonne Pierce stayed on campus but stated, "Obviously they don't want us here."[6] Dave Cook, a white junior who was one of the fraternity members involved in the fight, later said, "There were a lot of bonds that were broken that didn't need to be broken." He talked about his friendship with a black female student: "We would high-five each other and study for tests. But I don't know what she thinks about me. I don't know whether she's hating me or what. I didn't say one word to her, and she didn't say one word to me. Now she's gone."[7]

Racist behavior on college campuses is, of course, not limited to students. An incident involving a campus in New York State reveals the deep-seated stereotyping and bigotry of some college administrators, police officers, and citizens in communities all over the country. In the early morning of September 4, 1992, a seventy-seven-year-old woman was attacked in the small town of Oneonta, New York. She told the state police that she thought her attacker was a black man who used a "stiletto-style" knife and that his hands and arms were cut when she fended him off.[8] In response to a request from the police, the State University of New York at Oneonta gave the police a list of all of the black and Hispanic males registered at the college. Armed with the list, state and city police, along with campus security, tracked down the students "in their dormitories, at their jobs and in the shower." Each student was asked his whereabouts at the time the attack occurred, and each had to show his hands and his arms.

Michael Christian, the second of five children from a family headed by a single mother, grew up in the Bronx. His mother encouraged him to go to Oneonta to get him away from the problems of the city. Shortly after the attack, two state-police officers and representatives of campus security went to his dormitory room and woke him at 10:00 A.M. After asking him where he was at the time of the attack and demanding to see his hands, they said they wanted to question him downtown, and then they left. His roommate, Hopeton Gordon, a Jamaican student who had gone to high school in the Bronx with Mr. Christian, was questioned in front of other students from their dormitory. When the police asked to see his hands and he demanded their reasons, they responded, "Why? Do you have something to hide?" He said that he had felt humiliated in front of his suite mates and in front of female students.

This is not the first time black students, faculty, and administrators have been humiliated and have seen their civil rights trampled in Oneonta. Edward I. (Bo) Whaley, who went to the small town in upstate New York in 1968 as a student, remained, and is currently an instructor and counselor in the school's Educational Opportunity Program for disadvantaged students, recalls being followed by salespeople in Oneonta shops because they feared he would shoplift. He remembers the two minority ball players—one of whom he was trying to recruit—who were picked up as suspects in a rape case and had to pay for DNA testing even though someone else was convicted for the crime.

An admissions coordinator, Sheryl Champen, who is also black, was herself stopped by the state police the night of the attack. They demanded to see her identification before she could board a bus to New York City. It is unclear why the police questioned her and three other black women traveling with children, who also had to show identification before boarding the bus, since the attacked woman had reported that the person who assaulted her was a man. Their only common characteristic was race. When she heard about the treatment of the students of color, Ms. Champen said, "I was devastated, ashamed of being an admissions coordinator. Am I setting them up?" She feels that the behavior of the police was not an example of overeagerness to solve a crime. After recounting thirteen years of incidents that had begun when she was a first-year student at SUNY/Oneonta, she stated, "I know what it was. It was a chance to humiliate niggers."[9]

The release of the names of the 125 black and Hispanic students not only violated their privacy (and their right to be presumed innocent until proven guilty) but also violated the Family Educational Rights and Privacy Act of 1974 (also known as the Buckley Amendment). Following the incident, the vice-president who authorized the release of the names was suspended for one month without pay and demoted. The president of SUNY/Oneonta called using the list in the investigation "an affront to individual dignity and human rights."[10]

Though each of these events is unique and a product of the particular social environment, demographics, personalities, and stresses at the particular institution, during the late 1980s and early 1990s campuses were rife with similar episodes. A Brown student describes one incident at her university:

> It was April 25, 1989, the end of spring term. . . . Students . . . were preparing for Spring Weekend, an annual fling before final exams. That day, found scrawled in large letters across an elevator door in Andrews dormitory were the words, NIGGERS GO HOME. Over the next 24 hours, similar racial epithets were found on the doors of several women of color living in that hall; on the bathroom doors WOMEN was crossed out and replaced with NIGGERS, MEN was crossed out, replaced with WHITE. And in that same women's bathroom, a computer-printed flyer was found a day later which read: "Once upon a time Brown was a place where a white man could go to class without having to look at little black faces or little yellow faces or little brown faces except when he went to take his meals. Things have been going downhill since the kitchen help moved into the classroom. Keep white supremcy [sic] alive! Join the Brown Chapter of the KKK."[11]

Seven years earlier, the *Dartmouth Review* had set the standard for racist denigration by publishing an article ridiculing black students. The article was entitled "Dis Sho' Ain't No Jive, Bro," and read in part: "Dese boys be saying that we be comin hee to Dartmut an' not takin' the classics. . . . We be culturally 'lightened, too. We be takin hard courses in many subjects, like Afro-Am studies . . . and who bee mouthin' bout us not bein' good read?"[12]

During the late 1980s, the University of Michigan experienced several racist incidents. One of the most infamous took place in 1988, when a poster mocking the slogan of the United Negro College Fund was hung in a classroom. It read "Support the K.K.K. College Fund. A mind is a terrible thing to waste—especially on a nigger."[13]

Violent behavior has also been part of the cultural climate over the past decade. In February 1991, two black students from the University of Maine were allegedly assaulted by nine white men. The two students, both twenty-one, were driving in downtown Orono when approximately a dozen white men attacked their car and shouted, "Nigger, get out of here." When they got out of the car to see what was going on, the two men were kicked and beaten. Three students from the university were among those who attacked the students.[14]

Incidents have not been limited to one kind of school, but have occurred at private as well as public, urban and rural, large and small, at Ivy League as well as less prestigious, little-known institutions. . . .

According to the Anti-Defamation League, anti-Semitic incidents on college campuses have risen sharply in recent years, from fifty-four in 1988 to over double that number, 114, in 1992.[15] In February 1990, at American University in Washington, D.C., anti-Semitic graffiti were spray-painted on the main gate and on a residence hall. On the gate were painted a Star of David, an equal sign, and a swastika. On the dormitory was sprayed an expletive followed by "Israel Zionist."[16] In 1991, at California State University at Northridge, a ceremonial hut used to celebrate the Jewish holiday of Sukkoth was vandalized with anti-Semitic writing. In addition to swastikas, "Hi' [sic] Hitler" and "Fuckin [sic] Jews" defaced the informative signs and flyers that decorated the hut.[17] Two months earlier, Dr. Leonard Jeffries, Jr., then chair of the African-American Studies department at the City College of New York, delivered a speech at a black cultural festival in which he spoke of "a conspiracy, planned and plotted and programmed out of Hollywood" by "people called Greenberg and Weisberg and Trigliani." He went on to say that "Russian Jewry had a particular control over the movies and their financial partners, the Mafia, put together a financial system of destruction of black people."[18]

Gay bashing has also been widely visible on college campuses. A Syracuse University fraternity, Alpha Chi Rho, was suspended by its national organization in 1991 for selling T-shirts with antihomosexual slogans, including one advocating violence against gays. On the front the shirts said "Homophobic and Proud of It!" and on the back, "Club Faggots Not Seals!" The picture illustrating the words was of a muscled crow, the fraternity's symbol, holding a club and standing over a faceless figure lying on the ground. Next to them is a seal hoisting a mug of beer.[19]

During the same year, *Peninsula,* a conservative campus magazine at Harvard, published an issue entirely devoted to the subject of homosexuality. The magazine called homosexuality a "bad alternative" to heterosexuality and stated in its introduction that "homosexuality is bad for society."[20] Within one hour of the magazine's distribution, the door of a gay student's room was defaced with antihomosexual words.

But, of course, discrimination does not need to be physical or perpetrated by students to wound, and to exclude some from mainstream college life. The football coach at the University of Colorado has called homosexuality "an abomination" and has supported a statewide group working to limit gay rights.[21] In 1992, the governor of Alabama signed legislation prohibiting gay student groups from receiving public money or using buildings at state universities.[22]

Sexual harassment and assault have been reported on campuses across the country. . . . Perhaps the most disturbing account of sexual harassment has been described by Carol Burke, currently an associate dean at Johns Hopkins University, about events at the U.S. Naval Academy, where she taught for seven years.[23] Marching chants—or "cadence calls," as they are called in the navy—provide a window into the macho male culture fostered at the academy, a culture that simultaneously celebrates the power of men and violence toward women. As Burke states:

> Cadence calls not only instill mutual solidarity but resurrect the Casey Jones of American ballad tradition as a brave pilot who survives the crash of his plane only to subdue women with greater ferocity:
>
> Climbed all out with his dick in his hand.
> Said, "Looky here, ladies, I'm a hell of a man."
> Went to his room and lined up a hundred . . .
> Swore up and down he'd fuck everyone.
> Fucked ninety-eight till his balls turned blue.
> Then he backed off, jacked off, and fucked the other two.

Members of the academy's Male Glee Club while away the hours on bus trips back from concerts by singing a particularly sadistic version of the song "The Candy Man":

> THE S&M MAN
>
> Who can take a chain saw,
> Cut the bitch in two,
> Fuck the bottom half
> and give the upper half to you. . . .
>
> The S&M Man, the S&M Man
> The S&M Man cause he mixes it with love
> and makes the hurt feel good!

Who can take a bicycle,
Then take off the seat,
Set his girlfriend on it
Ride her down a bumpy street. . . .

Who can take an ice pick
Ram it through her ear
Ride her like a Harley,
As you fuck her from the rear. . . .

Lest we think that such lyrics are sung only at the U.S. Naval Academy, the following incident took place at the Phi Kappa Psi fraternity at UCLA in 1992:

> A group of fraternity brothers waited outside the door. They serenaded the rape victim inside, cheering a brother on as if it were a football game. To the tune of "The Candy Man," they sang, "Who can take his organ / Dip it in vaseline / Ram it up inside you till it tickles your spleen / The S and M man, the S and M man / The S and M man can / cause he mixes it with love and / makes the hurtin feel good."
>
> UCLA's administration looked the other way this spring as Phi Kappa Psi fraternity brothers distributed a songbook with lyrics glorifying necrophilia, rape and violent torture of women. Although a 1991 suspension for violation of alcohol and other policies forced the fraternity to implement pledge education programs and forums on sexism and homophobia, the recent songbook controversy reveals the inadequacies of such programs.[24]

In March 1992, *Together,* a feminist magazine at UCLA, "exposed" the songbook that was left anonymously in their office.[25] When asked about the songs, an assistant vice-chancellor of the university first responded, "What's the problem? They are just erotic lyrics." Later, when questioned by the media, he stated, "I was horrified, revolted, shocked and embarrassed. This book is sexist, homophobic and promoted violence." The president of Phi Kappa Psi claimed that the "lyrics are a joke [and] so exaggerated that it is . . . ridiculous to say these songs promote violence against women."

Nevertheless, it is clear that fraternities have been in the forefront of bias-related incidents. Among the most serious incidents occurred at a University of Rhode Island fraternity. An eighteen-year-old female first-year student claimed she was raped during a fraternity party while at least five other men watched. During the investigation a former student committed suicide just hours before he was to be questioned by the police. In this case, as in many others, not only had the fraternity members been drinking heavily but often the victims as well. . . .[26]

Over the past several years, an increasing number of rapes have been reported at campuses across the country. . . . Most studies indicate that alcohol is involved, on the part of the victim as well as the perpetrator. A national study of women at thirty-two institutions of higher education in the U.S. found that 15 percent of college women said they had experienced attempted intercourse by the threat of force and 12 percent said they had experienced attempted intercourse by the use of alcohol or drugs.[27] Recent data plus in-depth studies of individual cases have made it clear that acquaintance rape is far more common than stranger rape in the United States. According to David Beatty, the public-policy director of the National Victim Center, a Washington-based advocacy group, "There is no question that acquaintance rape is more common than stranger rape. No one has the exact numbers, but the consensus is that probably in 80 to 85 percent of all rape cases, the victim knows the defendant."[28]

Many questions have been raised about acquaintance rape since the surge of reported cases has been noted across the country. Notorious cases such as the one involving William Kennedy Smith, in which rape was not proved, and the one involving Mike Tyson, in which the verdict was guilty, have also raised many questions: What is rape? Must physical force be used? When does "no" mean "no" and when is it part of a mating ritual? What about plying a woman with drugs or alcohol and then, when she is too inebriated or out of control to protest effectively, having sex with her? Is that rape?

An incident that came to be known as the "St. John's case" is a vivid and heart-wrenching example of the difficulties of establishing the parameters of acquaintance rape and of prosecuting the alleged perpetrators:

> As she recalled it, the evening of March 1, 1990, a Thursday, began ordinarily enough: the St. John's University student took target practice with another member of the school's rifle club and bantered with him and the coach about everything from the coach's shabby clothing to the other student's love life.
>
> But when the evening ended about seven hours later, as the 22-year-old woman later testified, she had been "forced" to drink nearly three cups of mixture of orange soda and vodka and had been disrobed, ogled, fondled, berated and sodomized by at least seven St. John's students, including her acquaintance from the rifle club. The debauchery began in a house near the Jamaica, Queens, campus; then she was transported, semiconscious and disheveled, to a second house where a party was underway and the assault continued.
>
> Later, she said, she heard the men debating what to do with her. One asked, "What if she talks?" Another replied: "So what? Remember Tawana Brawley? Nobody believed her. Nobody will believe this one."[29]

And, of course, he was partially right. After months of publicity and an extensive trial, after two students pleaded guilty to lesser charges while essentially corroborating the young woman's story, three of the defendants were found not guilty and the final defendant interrupted his trial to plead guilty to sharply reduced charges but, in so doing, admitted that he had done everything he had been accused of.

As newspaper accounts stressed, the case "rocked" the ten-thousand-student university, the country's largest Roman Catholic institution of higher education, and the surrounding community. Adding to the explosive nature of the accusations—that someone the female student knew took her back to a house where several of the accused lived and plied her with alcohol, and then, when she was on the couch with her eyes closed, appearing helpless, he and other male students fondled the woman and made her perform oral sex on them—all six defendants were white and the young woman was black. None of the six defendants were convicted of the original felony charges against them.

Perhaps the most disturbing analysis of rape on college campuses is anthropologist Peggy Reeves Sanday's shocking study of fraternity gang rape. Also known as "gang banging," the phenomenon of "pulling train" refers to a "group of men lining up like train cars to take turns having sex with the same woman."[30] Bernice Sandler, one of the authors of a report issued in 1985 by the American Association of American Colleges, has reported finding more than seventy-five documented cases of gang rape in recent years. These incidents, which occurred at all kinds of institutions—"public, private, religiously affiliated, Ivy League, large and small"—share a common pattern:

> A vulnerable young woman, one who is seeking acceptance or who is high on drugs or alcohol, is taken to a room. She may or may not agree to have sex with one man. She then passes out, or is too weak or scared to protest, and a train of men have sex with her. Sometimes the young woman's drinks are spiked without her knowledge, and when she is approached by several men in a locked room, she reacts with confusion and panic. Whether too weak to protest, frightened, or unconscious, as has been the case in quite a number of instances, anywhere from two to eleven or more men have sex with her.[31]

The specific case that is the centerpiece of Sanday's study involves a young woman, Laurel, who was known to have serious drinking and drug problems. The evening in question, she was drunk on beer and had taken "four hits of LSD" before going to a fraternity-house party. According to her account, she fell asleep after the party in a room on the first floor. When she awoke, she was undressed. One of the fraternity members dressed her and carried her upstairs, where she claimed she was raped by five or six "guys." She said, in Sanday's words, that she was "barely conscious and lacked the strength to push them off her."[32] This account was corroborated by another woman, a friend of the fraternity members, who felt that, because Laurel was incapable of consenting to sex, she had been raped. The fraternity brothers never publicly admitted to any wrongdoing; they claimed throughout the investigation that Laurel had "lured" them into a "gang bang," which they preferred to call an "express."

In this study, Sanday claims that "coercive sexual behavior" is prevalent on college campuses and that rape is "the means by which men programmed for violence and control use sexual aggression to display masculinity and to induct younger men into masculine roles."[33] Sanday continues her analysis:

> [The] male participants brag about their masculinity and . . . [the] female participants are degraded to the status of what the boys call "red meat" or "fish." The whole scenario joins men in a no-holds-barred orgy of togetherness. The woman whose body facilitates all of this is sloughed off at the end like a used condom. She may be called a "nympho" or the men may believe that they seduced her—a practice known as "working a yes out"—through promises of becoming a little sister, by getting her drunk, by promising her love, or by some other means. Those men who object to this kind of behavior run the risk of being labeled "wimps" or, even worse in their eyes, "gays" or "faggots."[34]

As we have seen, a variety of groups have been perceived and treated as "the Other"—in Patricia Hill Collins' words, "viewed as an object to be manipulated and controlled"[35]—on college campuses over the past few years. Though many of the bias incidents have involved racial enmity and misunderstanding, anti-Semitism, homophobia, and blatant sexism have also been catalysts for hostile acts. Many academic institutions, concerned about overtly demeaning, sometimes violent behavior as well as the far more subtle denigration of women and other minority groups, have attempted to address these problems through a variety of measures: speech codes; orientation programs for entering students that stress respect for diversity and the importance of civility; curriculum changes that focus on multiculturalism; hiring policies whose goals are to increase the number of women and members of minority groups on the faculty and staff of the institution; and the recruitment of more students of color. These measures, often employed to counter the ignorance, ethnocentrism, and anger within the college community, have themselves become the subject of controversy and debate. Both academic and popular discourse have focused far more on political correctness, on affirmative action, and on changes in the curriculum than on the hate incidents and violence that continue to occur. Speech codes at the universities of Wisconsin and Michigan became front-page news; discussions of what and who was p.c. seemed ubiquitous; and the pros and cons of a multicultural curriculum have been debated in university governing bodies and editorial meetings across the country.

NOTES

1. Patricia Hill Collins, *Black Feminist Thought: Knowledge, Consciousness, and the Politics of Empowerment* (Boston: Unwin Hyman, 1990), pp. 68, 225.
2. Isabel Wilkerson, "Racial Tension Erupts Tearing a College Apart," *New York Times,* April 13, 1992.
3. Ibid.
4. Ibid.

5. Ibid.
6. Ibid.
7. Ibid.
8. Diana Jean Schemo, "Anger over List Divides Blacks and College Town," *New York Times,* September 27, 1992.
9. Ibid.
10. "College Official Who Released List of Black Students Is Demoted," *New York Times,* September 18, 1992.
11. N'Tanya Lee, "Racism on College Campuses," *Focus* (monthly magazine of the Joint Center for Political Studies), Special Social Policy Issue, August/September 1989.
12. Ibid.
13. Michele Collison, "For Many Freshmen, Orientation Now Includes Efforts to Promote Racial Understanding," *Chronicle of Higher Education,* September 7, 1988.
14. Denise Goodman, "Racial Attack Jolts U. of Maine," *Boston Globe,* February 23, 1991.
15. "ADL 1992 Audit of Anti-Semitic Incidents: Overall Numbers Decrease but Campus Attacks Are Up," *On the Frontline* (monthly newsletter published by the Anti-Defamation League), March 1993.
16. "Anti-Semitic Slurs Are Painted: Campus Reacts," *New York Times,* February 11, 1990.
17. Sharon Kaplan, "Hillel Hut Vandalized with Anti-Semitic Graffiti," *Daily Sundial* (California State University, Northridge), September 26, 1991.
18. James Barron, "Professor Steps off a Plane into a Furor over His Words," *New York Times,* August 15, 1991.
19. "Anti-Gay Shirts Oust Syracuse Fraternity," *USA Today,* June 28, 1991.
20. "Magazine Issue on Homosexuality Leads to Rallies," *New York Times,* December 22, 1991.
21. Dirk Johnson, "Coach's Anti-Gay Stand Ignites Rage," *New York Times,* March 15, 1992.
22. "Alabama Denies Aid to Gay Student Groups," *New York Times,* May 16, 1992.
23. Carol Burke, "Dames at Sea," *New Republic,* August 17, 24, 1992, pp. 16–20.
24. Katrina Foley, "Terror on Campus: Fraternities Training Grounds for Rape and Misogyny," *New Directions for Women,* September/October 1992, pp. 15, 29.
25. Ibid.
26. William Celis, 3d, "After Rape Charge, 2 Lives Hurt and 1 Destroyed," *New York Times,* November 12, 1990.
27. Peggy Reeves Sanday, *Fraternity Gang Rape: Sex, Brotherhood, and Privilege on Campus* (New York: New York University Press, 1990), pp. 23–24.
28. Tamar Lewin, "Tougher Laws Mean More Cases Are Called Rape," *New York Times,* May 27, 1991.
29. E. R. Shipp, "St. John's Case Offers 2 Versions of Events," *New York Times,* July 6, 1991.
30. Sanday, *Fraternity Gang Rape,* p. 1.
31. Ibid., pp. 1–2.
32. Ibid., p. 6.
33. Ibid., pp. 8–9.
34. Ibid., p. 11.
35. Collins, *Black Feminist Thought,* p. 69.

48

BLACK AND FEMALE
Reflections on Graduate School

bell hooks

Searching for material to read in a class about women and race, I found an essay in *Heresies: Racism is the Issue* that fascinated me. I realized that it was one of the first written discussions of the struggles black English majors (and particularly black women) face when we study at predominantly white universities. The essay, "On Becoming A Feminist Writer," is by Carole Gregory. She begins by explaining that she has been raised in racially segregated neighborhoods but that no one had ever really explained "white racism or white male sexism." Psychically, she was not prepared to confront head-on these aspects of social reality, yet they were made visible as soon as she registered for classes:

> Chewing on a brown pipe, a white professor said, "English departments do not hire Negroes or women!" Like a guillotine, his voice sought to take my head off. Racism in my hometown was an economic code of etiquette which stifled Negroes and women.
>
> "If you are supposed to explain these courses, that's all I want," I answered. Yet I wanted to kill this man. Only my conditioning as a female kept me from striking his volcanic red face. My murderous impulses were raging.

Her essay chronicles her struggles to pursue a discipline which interests her without allowing racism or sexism to defeat and destroy her intellectual curiosity, her desire to teach. The words of this white male American Literature professor echo in her mind years later when she finds employment difficult, when she confronts the reality that black university teachers of English are rare. Although she is writing in 1982, she concludes her essay with the comment:

> Many years ago, an American Literature professor had cursed the destiny of "Negroes and women." There was truth in his ugly words. Have you ever had a Black woman for an English teacher in the North? Few of us are able to earn a living. For the past few years, I have worked as an adjunct in English. Teaching brings me great satisfaction; starving does not. . . . I still remember the red

bell hooks, "Black and Female: Reflections on Graduate School" from *Talking Back: Thinking Feminist, Thinking Black.* Reprinted with the permission of South End Press and Between the Lines.

color of the face which said, "English departments do not hire Negroes or women." Can women change this indictment? These are the fragments I add to my journal.

Reading Carole Gregory's essay, I recalled that in all my years of studying in English department classes, I had never been taught by a black woman. In my years of teaching, I have encountered students both in English classes and other disciplines who have never been taught by black women. Raised in segregated schools until my sophomore year of high school, I had wonderful black women teachers as role models. It never occurred to me that I would not find them in university classrooms. Yet I studied at four universities—Stanford, University of Wisconsin, University of Southern California, and the University of California, Santa Cruz—and I did not once have the opportunity to study with a black woman English professor. They were never members of the faculty. I considered myself lucky to study with one black male professor at Stanford who was visiting and another at the University of Southern California even though both were reluctant to support and encourage black female students. Despite their sexism and internalized racism, I appreciated them as teachers and felt they affirmed that black scholars could teach literature, could work in English departments. They offered a degree of support and affirmation, however relative, that countered the intense racism and sexism of many white professors.

Changing hiring practices have meant that there are increasingly more black professors in predominantly white universities, but their presence only mediates in a minor way the racism and sexism of white professors. During my graduate school years, I dreaded talking face-to-face with white professors, especially white males. I had not developed this dread as an undergraduate because there it was simply assumed that black students, and particularly black female students, were not bright enough to make it in graduate school. While these racist and sexist opinions were rarely directly stated, the message was conveyed through various humiliations that were aimed at shaming students, at breaking our spirit. We were terrorized. As an undergraduate, I carefully avoided those professors who made it clear that the presence of any black students in their classes was not desired. Unlike Carole Gregory's first encounter, they did not make direct racist statements. Instead, they communicated their message in subtle ways—forgetting to call your name when reading the roll, avoiding looking at you, pretending they do not hear you when you speak, and at times ignoring you altogether.

The first time this happened to me I was puzzled and frightened. It was clear to me and all the other white students that the professor, a white male, was directing aggressive mistreatment solely at me. These other students shared with me that it was not likely that I would pass the class no matter how good my work, that the professor would find something wrong with it. They never suggested that this treatment was informed by racism and sexism; it was just that the professor had for whatever "unapparent" reason decided to dislike me. Of course, there were rare occasions when taking a course meant so much to me that I tried to confront racism, to talk with the professor; and there were required courses. Whenever I tried to talk with professors about racism, they always denied any culpability. Often I was told, "I don't even notice that you are black."

In graduate school, it was especially hard to choose courses that would not be taught by professors who were quite racist. Even though one could resist by naming the problem and confronting the person, it was rarely possible to find anyone who could take such accusations seriously. Individual white professors were supported by white-supremacist institutions, by racist colleagues, by hierarchies that placed the word of the professor above that of the student. When I would tell the more supportive professors about racist comments that were said behind closed doors, during office hours, there would always be an expression of disbelief, surprise, and suspicion about the accuracy of what I was reporting. Mostly they listened because they felt it was their liberal duty to do so. Their disbelief, their refusal to take responsibility for white racism made it impossible for them to show authentic concern or help. One professor of 18th century literature by white writers invited me to his office to tell me that he would personally see to it that I would never receive a graduate degree. I, like many other students in the class, had written a paper in a style that he disapproved of, yet only I was given this response. It was often in the very areas of British and American literature where racism abounds in the texts studied that I would encounter racist individuals.

Gradually, I began to shift my interest in early American literature to more modern and contemporary works. This shift was influenced greatly by an encounter with a white male professor of American literature whose racism and sexism was unchecked. In his classes, I, as well as other students, was subjected to racist and sexist jokes. Any of us that he considered should not be in graduate school were the objects of particular scorn and ridicule. When we gave oral presentations, we were told our work was stupid, pathetic, and were not allowed to finish. If we resisted in any way, the situation worsened. When I went to speak with him about his attitude, I was told that I was not really graduate school material, that I should drop out. My anger surfaced and I began to shout, to cry. I remember yelling wildly, "Do you love me? And if you don't love me then how can you have any insight about my concerns and abilities? And who are you to make such suggestions on the basis of one class?" He of course was not making a suggestion. His was a course one had to pass to graduate. He was telling me that I could avoid the systematic abuse by simply dropping out. I would not drop out. I continued to work even though it was clear that I would not succeed, even as the persecution became more intense. And even though I constantly resisted.

In time, my spirits were more and more depressed. I began to dream of entering the professor's office with a loaded gun. There I would demand that he listen, that he experience the fear, the humiliation. In my dreams I could hear his pleading voice begging me not to shoot, to remain calm. As soon as I put the gun down he would become his old self again. Ultimately in the dream the only answer was to shoot, to shoot to kill. When this dream became so consistently a part of my waking fantasies, I knew that it was time for me to take a break from graduate school. Even so I felt as though his terrorism had succeeded, that he had indeed broken my spirit. It was this feeling that led me to return to graduate school, to his classes, because I felt I had given him too much power over me and I needed to regain that sense of self and personal integrity that I allowed him to diminish. Through much of my graduate school career, I was told that "I did not have the proper demeanor of a graduate student." In one graduate program, the black woman before me, who was also subjected to racist and sexist aggression, would tell me that they would say she was not as smart as me but she knew her place. I did not know my place. Young white radicals began to use the phrase "student as nigger" precisely to call attention to the way in which hierarchies within universities encouraged domination of the powerless by the powerful. At many universities the proper demeanor of a graduate student is exemplary when that student is obedient, when he or she does not challenge or resist authority.

During graduate school, white students would tell me that it was important not to question, challenge, or resist. Their tolerance level seemed much higher than my own or that of other black students. Critically reflecting on the differences between us, it was apparent that many of the white students were from privileged class backgrounds. Tolerating the humiliations and degradations we were subjected to in graduate school did not radically call into question their integrity, their sense of self-worth. Those of us who were coming from underprivileged class backgrounds, who were black, often were able to attend college only because we had consistently defied those who had attempted to make us believe we were smart but not "smart enough"; guidance counselors who refused to tell us about certain colleges because they already knew we would not be accepted; parents who were not necessarily supportive of graduate work, etc. White students were not living daily in a world outside campus life where they also had to resist degradation, humiliation. To them, tolerating forms of exploitation and domination in graduate school did not evoke images of a lifetime spent tolerating abuse. They would endure certain forms of domination and abuse, accepting it as an initiation process that would conclude when they became the person in power. In some ways they regarded graduate school and its many humiliations as a game, and they submitted to playing the role of subordinate. I and many other students, especially non-white students from non-privileged backgrounds, were unable to accept and play this "game." Often we were ambivalent about the rewards promised. Many of us were not seeking to be in a position of power over others. Though we wished to teach, we did not want to exert coercive authoritarian rule over others. Clearly those students who played the game best were usually white males and they did not face discrimination, exploitation, and abuse in many other areas of their lives.

Many black graduate students I knew were concerned about whether we were striving to participate in structures of domination and were uncertain about whether we could assume positions of authority. We could not envision assuming oppressive roles. For some of us, failure, failing, being failed began to look like a positive alternative, a way out, a solution. This was especially true for those students who felt they were suffering mentally, who felt that they would never be able to recover a sense of wholeness or well-being. In recent years, campus awareness of the absence of support for international students who have many conflicts and dilemmas in an environment that does not acknowledge their cultural codes has led to the development of support networks. Yet there has been little recognition that there are black students and other non-white students who suffer similar problems, who come from backgrounds where we learned different cultural codes. For example, we may learn that it is important not to accept coercive authoritarian rule from someone who is not a family elder—hence we may have difficulties accepting strangers assuming such a role.

Not long ago, I was at a small party with faculty from a major liberal California university, which until recently had no black professors in the English department who were permanent staff, though they were sometimes visiting scholars. One non-white faculty member and myself began to talk about the problems facing black graduate students studying in English departments. We joked about the racism within English departments, commenting that other disciplines were slightly more willing to accept study of the lives and works of non-white people, yet such work is rarely affirmed in English departments, where the study of literature usually consists of many works by white men and a few by white women. We talked about how some departments were struggling to change. Speaking about his department, he commented that they have only a few black graduate students, sometimes none, that at one time two black students, one male and one female, had been accepted and both had serious mental health problems. At departmental meetings, white faculty suggested that this indicated that black students just did not have the wherewithal to succeed in this graduate program. For a time, no black students were admitted. His story revealed that part of the burden these students may have felt, which many of us have felt, is that our performance will have future implications for all black students and this knowledge heightens one's performance anxiety from the very beginning. Unfortunately, racist biases often lead departments to see the behavior of one black student as an indication of the way all black students will perform academically. Certainly, if individual white students have difficulty adjusting or succeeding within a graduate program, it is not seen as an indication that all other white students will fail.

The combined forces of racism and sexism often make the black female graduate experience differ in kind from that of the black male experience. While he may be subjected to racial biases, his maleness may serve to mediate the extent to which he will be attacked, dominated, etc. Often it is assumed that black males are better able to succeed at graduate school in English than black females. While many white scholars may be aware of a black male intellectual tradition, they rarely know about black female intellectuals. African-American intellectual traditions, like those of white people, have been male-dominated. People who know the names of W.E.B. Du Bois or Martin Delaney may have never heard of Mary Church Terrell or Anna Cooper. The small numbers of black women in permanent positions in academic institutions do not constitute a significant presence, one strong enough to challenge racist and sexist biases. Often the only black woman white professors have encountered is a domestic worker in their home. Yet there are no sociological studies that I know of which examine whether a group who has been seen as not having intellectual capability will automatically be accorded respect and recognition if they enter positions that suggest they are representative scholars. Often black women are such an "invisible presence" on campuses that many students may not be aware that any black women teach at the universities they attend.

Given the reality of racism and sexism, being awarded advanced degrees does not mean that black women will achieve equity with black men or other groups in the profession. Full-time, non-white women comprise less than 3 percent of the total faculty on most campuses. Racism and sexism, particularly on the graduate level, shape and influence both the academic performance and employment of black female academics. During my years of graduate work in English, I was often faced with the hostility of white students who felt that because I was black and female I would have no trouble finding a job. This was usually the response from professors as well if I expressed fear of not finding employment. Ironically, no one ever acknowledged that we were never taught by any of these black women who were taking all the jobs. No one wanted to see that perhaps racism and sexism militate against the hiring of black women even though we are seen as a group that will be given priority, preferential status. Such assumptions, which are usually rooted in the logic of affirmative action hiring, do not include recognition of the ways most universities do not strive to attain diversity of faculty and that often diversity means hiring one non-white person, one black person. When I and other black women graduate students surveyed English departments in the United States, we did not see masses of black women and rightly felt concerned about our futures.

Moving around often, I attended several graduate schools but finally finished my work at the University of California, Santa Cruz, where I found support despite the prevalence of racism and sexism. Since I had much past experience, I was able to talk with white faculty members before entering the program about whether they would be receptive and supportive of my desire to focus on African-American writers. I was given positive reassurance that proved accurate. More and more, there are university settings where black female graduate students and black graduate students can study in supportive atmospheres. Racism and sexism are always present, yet they do not necessarily shape all areas of graduate experience. When I talk with black female graduate students working in English departments, I hear that many of the problems have not changed, that they experience the same intense isolation and loneliness that characterized my experience. This is why I think it is important that black women in higher education write and talk about our experiences, about survival strategies. When I was having a very difficult time, I read *Working It Out.* Despite the fact that the academics who described the way in which sexism had shaped their academic experience in graduate school were white women, I was encouraged by their resistance, by their perseverance, by their success. Reading their stories helped me to feel less alone. I wrote this essay because of the many conversations I have had with black female graduate students who despair, who are frustrated, who are fearful that the experiences they are having are unique. I want them to know that they are not alone, that the problems that arise, the obstacles created by racism and sexism are real—that they do exist—they do hurt but they are not insurmountable. Perhaps these words will give solace, will intensify their courage, and renew their spirit.

49

SCHOLARLY STUDIES OF MEN
The New Field Is an Essential Complement to Women's Studies

HARRY BROD

In something of a turn of the tables, scholars in women's studies are having to decide what to do about a new field that is emerging in academe. The new kid asking to enter the club is "men's studies."

For some feminist scholars, the phenomenon seems either preposterous or dangerous, or more likely both. After all, the traditional curriculum that women's studies sought to reform was, in essence, men's studies. Other feminists, however, believe that the new field of men's studies is really a welcome extension of feminism's intellectual insights into hitherto male terrain. I believe that the field of men's studies is not only compatible with women's studies, but also an essential complement.

Men's studies begin by accepting as valid feminism's critique of traditional scholarship for its androcentric bias in generalizing from men to all human beings. The field adds the perspective that this bias not only excludes women and/or judges them to be deficient, but also ignores whatever may be specific to men *as men,* rather than as generic humans. The field also invokes feminist concepts that "gender" is not natural difference, but constructed power, to argue that the multiple forms of masculinities and femininities need to be re-examined.

The field of men's studies, for most of us anyway, thus is rooted in a feminist commitment to challenge existing concepts of gender. The debate within our still-nascent field over that commitment, however, has made some feminists skeptical about our entire enterprise. They see in the call for a new "gender studies" focused on both men and women the possibility that women's priorities and standpoints will again be subsumed and ignored under generic labels. Other feminists, though, find that the idea of a broadly conceived "gender studies," in which "gender" describes power and not just difference, does reflect the underlying conceptualization of their field. We should recognize, however, that the meaning of terms is still in flux. At my own institution, for example, our current solution is to develop a program in "Women's and Gender Studies."

Feminists' legitimate fear of once again having women's discourse subordinated to men's should not blind us to the very real and much-needed intellectual project that the field of men's studies is undertaking. To simplify a more extended argument, I believe the field is an essential complement to women's studies because neither gender ultimately can be studied in isolation. Gender is, itself, a relational concept: Masculinities and femininities are not isolated "roles," but contested relationships.

But it does not follow from my argument for men's studies as an intellectual enterprise that the field must be established in any particular form in academic institutions. Such decisions should be made by women in women's studies. And any efforts to divert resources from women's studies to men's studies must be resisted; funds for the new men's studies must come from the old.

The new field has important implications for scholarship. For example, many explanations of the "gender gap" in political voting patterns have failed to see that it takes two to make a gap. Having noted the appearance of a "gap," social scientists have rushed to explain the changes in women that have produced it. Yet some of the evidence shows that the gap was produced more by a shift in men's than in women's political identification and voting patterns. By trying to understand the mutability and diversity of masculinities, men's studies avoid the pitfall of associating change only with women while assuming male constancy—a sexist bias.

By pointedly taking up the question of power relations among men in addition to those between the sexes, the new field also allows for a more differentiated conception of patriarchy. For the power of the real and symbolic father is not simply that of male over female, but also that of heterosexual over homosexual, one generation over another, and other constellations of authority. The field forces us to ask, Why does society privilege some men over others, even as it gives all men power over women? Why do so many of our founding myths contain fathers willing to kill their sons—the violence committed and permitted by Abraham against Isaac, Laius against Oedipus, the Christian God the Father against Jesus?

Further, the field of men's studies is not simply calling for sensitivity to diversity, though it surely does that, but also tries to apply an understanding of difference gained from radical feminism to men, arguing that sexuality is as socially constructed as identity. The field therefore is also forging special links to gay studies.

Two current phenomena show the need for men's studies to transcend a white, middle-class origin and orientation: the large number of suicides among Vietnam-era veterans and the huge number of college-age black men in prison rather than in college. When we speak of men's issues, there really is more to consider than the existential anxieties of middle-aged, middle-class executives and fathers, popular media treatments notwithstanding.

A final example from my own experience highlights the way feminism has helped me to ask new questions about men. I have noticed in recent years that many of the female political activists I know have devoted increasing attention to women's issues, for example moving from the peace movement to the women's peace movement or from environmentalism to the fusion of ecological and feminist concerns called ecofeminism.

At first, I simply contrasted this to the conventional wisdom that people become more conservative, *i.e.*, more "mature," with age. But I also recalled that the women's movement has been said to differ from others precisely because its members tend to become more radical as they age; it took only brief reflection to identify the conventional dictum as a male norm. Accordingly, I then asked myself what it was about women's lives that made them different. As I was coming up with various plausible answers I suddenly caught myself. I realized that I was committing the usual error of looking only to women to explain difference. In fact, as I started to see, if one believes as I do that there is validity in various radical social critiques, then the women's pattern should be the norm, as life experiences increasingly validate early perceptions of biased treatment of certain groups. Thus the question should not be, "What happens to women to radicalize them?" but rather "What happens to men to deradicalize them?" That question, more for men's studies than for women's studies, can open up fruitful areas of inquiry.

Indeed, I believe that any strategy for fundamental feminist transformation requires a more informed understanding of men. By exposing and demystifying the culture of male dominance from the inside out, the field of men's studies offers both women and subordinated men the empowerment such knowledge brings.

By elucidating the many and varied prices of male power—the drawbacks and limitations of traditional roles—the field helps motivate men to make common cause with feminist struggles, though not, it must be said, on the basis of any simple cost-benefit analysis, since the price men pay still purchases more than it pays for.

The field of men's studies, then, emerges not as some counterweight or corrective to women's studies, but as the extension and radicalization of women's studies. For it is the adoption of thoroughly women-centered perspectives, taking women as norm rather than "other," that helps us ask new questions about men.

PART VIII
Paid Work and Unemployment

Nearly a quarter of all the children in the United States under the age of six live in poverty.

U.S. CENSUS BUREAU[1]

. . . women have been catching up with men in earnings at a rate of one-third of a percent a year. At this rate of progress, the sexes will receive equal pay in the year 2083.

BARBARA RESKIN AND IRENE PADAVIC[2]

Equality of educational opportunity, as discussed previously in the introduction to the readings on education, cannot produce equality in society. Once people enter or attempt to enter the workforce, they face three major obstacles. First, the economic structure blocks many people from finding any type of work at all. Second, the economic structure fails to provide enough jobs that pay a decent wage. Third, discrimination in the workplace limits the progress of many, either by keeping people out or by blocking their upward mobility. Our economic system privileges a small proportion of the population with large amounts of wealth and leaves a huge proportion with varying degrees of economic difficulty, including brutal poverty. For example, the richest fifth of the U.S. population holds 79 percent of household wealth (houses, cars, stocks, bonds, cash, and so on). At the other end of the spectrum, a fifth of U.S. children and 15 percent of the entire population live in poverty.[3] Many women on welfare struggle to provide basic needs for themselves and their children and face cutoffs when they reach the maximum time allowed on Temporary Assistance for Needy Families (TANF), the 1996 replacement for Aid to Families with Dependent Children (AFDC).

Progressive economists debate ways to redistribute U.S. wealth more fairly, by creating a more socialistic economic structure, closing tax loopholes that benefit the rich, or redistributing some of the defense budget to social services and education. But politicians continue to support benefits for the rich and to cut social services. This situation has been exacerbated following September 11, 2001, as a larger proportion of federal and state budgets is now spent on defense and security, and as tax revenues dropped following the downturn in the stock market.

Many people face the effects of discrimination in the workplace on the basis of gender, race, ability, sexual orientation, or other factors. This discrimination includes sexual and other harassment, blocked access to jobs or promotions, or wage gaps that privilege the earnings of certain groups over others. For example, occupations dominated by women or people of color generally have lower pay scales.[4] Discrimination and prejudice are sometimes confusingly subtle, but often there nonetheless.[5] Disability or being gay or lesbian can serve as the kiss of death in some work situations.[6] Some recent examples include women earning 76.5 percent of men's wages for the same full-time work in 1999;[7] the exclusion of women from roles as ministers in the Southern Baptist Convention in June 2000;[8] the persistently different experiences of Black and white women in the business world;[9] the persistent harassment of gays and lesbians in the military, leading to more discharges than before the "don't ask, don't tell" policy;[10] and the dismal record of hiring women in most fire departments (not to mention the harassment the few women firefighters typically receive).[11] Around the world, the use of computers has left women segregated at the bottom of the technology hierarchy, as they have become the "data and keyboard drones" of the information world.[12]

The dearth of high-paying jobs combined with systematic discrimination against many groups leaves large numbers of people in the United States either without work or without adequate income. Even middle-class people are struggling to hold their own, no longer able to assume that they will do as well as their parents. In fact, many people cannot afford to buy houses like the ones they grew up in, and others cannot buy houses at all.[13]

Sexual harassment in the workplace is a very common experience for women and affects some men as well. In a study of women physicians, 32 percent reported unwanted sexual attention and 48 percent reported the use of sexist teaching materials during their training.[14] In a 1991 survey by the U.S. Navy, 44 percent of enlisted women and 33 percent of women officers reported sexual harassment within the year prior to responding to the survey. By comparison, 8 percent of enlisted men and 2 percent of male officers reported sexual harassment in the same time period.[15] Work contexts obviously vary in relation to this issue, ranging from a pervasive sexualized atmosphere aimed at many women (as in the Mitsubishi case that settled for $34 million[16]), to isolated cases of harassment. The Supreme Court decided for the first time in 1998 that a male-male case of sexual harassment did qualify as sexual harassment under federal law, and other cases followed,[17] even though some people question the appropriateness of that definition of sexual harassment.[18]

Where a person is situated in the workplace affects their perception and experience of how fair the workplace is. In the Navy survey just mentioned, men perceived the equal opportunity climate in the Navy to be more positive than did women; white male officers had the most positive perceptions, with African American women holding the least positive perceptions; and women who had been sexually harassed had more negative perceptions of the climate than did those who had not been sexually harassed. In another study that compared Black and white women in professional and managerial positions, sociologists Lynn Weber and Elizabeth Higginbotham found that the vast majority of white women perceived no race discrimination in their various workplaces, whereas a large majority of Black women did.[19]

By contrast, some equality gains have been made as Israeli women in 2000 won the right to serve in any army position, including combat units;[20] as

Japanese women won, in 2000, a sex discrimination case related to promotion and pay that was filed in 1987;[21] as boys have braved teasing and ridicule to become ballet dancers;[22] and as Pride at Work, a national organization of gay, lesbian, bisexual and transgendered labor activists, became an official constituency group of the AFL-CIO in August 1997.[23]

The conflict between work and family is a persistent and unresolved issue facing parents who work outside the home. Women's increased participation in the workforce has exacerbated this.[24] Some corporations are developing "family friendly" policies including such options as flex time, job sharing, child care, and paid family leave. But according to a recent study of one of the top 100 companies for working mothers identified by *Working Woman* magazine, policies that look good on paper are frequently not available to all workers; often this is a result of mothers being pressured not to use the policies.[25] Sociologist Arlie Hochschild, in her recent book *The Time Bind,* looks at the relationship between work and family and concludes that corporate culture, with its pressure to put in long hours at the office, is to blame for the bind most families are in. She argues for new social values that would encourage spending less time at work and more time with children, family, and community. In support of her position, she cites corporate experiments that have increased efficiency while saving time.[26]

The situation of women workers around the world varies depending on the social support offered by governments. Within Europe, for example, the number of women in paid work is highest in Scandinavia, apparently because of the availability of publicly funded child care. Women in Sweden and Finland had more children than in other European countries for the same reason.[27] On the other hand, some analysts observe that the presence of supportive family leave policies can reinforce gender segregation in the workplace.[28]

Globalization has had a huge impact on workers worldwide. U.S. corporations have moved many factories to parts of the world where wages are lower (see Enloe, this part). The plight of women who cannot earn a decent living in their home countries and who come to the United States as domestic workers is gaining attention, revealing situations in which the workers live isolated, lonely lives while someone else cares for their children far away in their home countries.[29] These immigrants share many of the experiences of invisibility and disempowerment experienced by Black domestic workers in the United States as described by sociologist Judith Rollins.[30]

An estimated 50,000 undocumented workers are trafficked to the United States each year to work as prostitutes, agricultural workers, sweatshop laborers, or domestic workers. Many are enslaved by their employers, have few rights, and often fear for their lives. Only in the late 1990s was there a serious move to prosecute perpetrators of involuntary servitude, especially sexual slavery.[31] Many women work in sweatshop conditions in both the United States and abroad, particularly in the garment industry.[32]

This part of this book looks at welfare (Randy Albeda and Chris Tilly), the effects of motherhood on earnings (Ann Crittendon), workplace discrimination (Ben Fong-Torres and Stan Gray), affirmative action (Barbara Reskin), and the global sneaker industry (Cynthia Enloe). Implied or stated in these pieces are suggestions for empowerment at personal, group, and policy levels.

NOTES

1. Cited in Greg Mantsios, "Class in America: Myths and Realities," in Paula S. Rothenberg, ed., *Race, Class, and Gender in the United States: An Integrated Study,* 3rd ed. (New York: St. Martin's Press, 1995), p. 133.
2. Barbara Reskin and Irene Padavic, *Women and Men at Work* (Thousand Oaks, CA: Pine Forge Press, 1994), p. 126.
3. Mantsios, *Class in America,* p. 133.
4. Reskin and Padavic, *Women and Men at Work,* pp. 110–26.
5. Yanick St. Jean and Joe R. Feagin, "Racial Masques: Black Women and Subtle Gendered Racism," in Nijole V. Benokraitis, ed., *Subtle Sexism: Current Practices and Prospects for Change* (Thousand Oaks, CA: Sage, 1997), pp. 179–200.
6. For a discussion of discrimination against gay men in the workforce, see Martin P. Levine, "The Status of Gay Men in the Workplace," in Michael S. Kimmel and Michael A. Messner, eds., *Men's Lives,* 3rd ed. (Boston: Allyn & Bacon, 1995), pp. 212–24. Michelle Fine and Adrienne Asch report that it is estimated that between 65 and 76 percent of women with disabilities are unemployed: "Disabled Women: Sexism without the Pedestal," in Mary Jo Deegan and Nancy A. Brooks, eds., *Women and Disability: The Double Handicap* (New Brunswick, NJ: Transaction, 1985), pp. 6–22.
7. Associated Press, "Women Said to Earn 76.5% of Men's Wage," *The Boston Globe* (May 27, 2000), p. A10.
8. Brad Liston and Michael Paulson, "Southern Baptists Deliver a 'No' on Women as Pastors," *The Boston Globe* 257, no. 167 (June 15, 2000), p. A1.
9. Ella J. E. Bell and Stella M. Nkomo, *Our Separate Ways: Black and White Women and the Struggle for Professional Identity* (Boston: Harvard Business School Press, 2001).
10. Debbie Emery, "The Mother of All Witch Hunts," *Out,* June 1996, p. 176.
11. Joseph P. Kahn, "Under Fire," *The Boston Globe Magazine* (December 7, 1997), pp. 19ff; David Armstrong, "Brotherhood Under Fire: Big-City Departments Facing Reform of Closed Culture and Old-Boy Traditions," *The Boston Globe* (January 9, 2000), pp. A1ff.
12. Christa Wichterich, *The Globalized Woman: Reports from a Future of Inequality* (New York: Zed Books, 2000), p. 47.
13. Katherine S. Newman, *Declining Fortunes: The Withering of the American Dream* (New York: Basic Books, 1993).
14. M. Catherine Vukovich, "The Prevalence of Sexual Harassment Among Female Family Practice Residents in the United States," *Violence and Victims* 11, no. 2 (1996), pp. 175–80.
15. Carol E. Newell, Paul Rosenfeld, and Amy L. Culbertson, "Sexual Harassment Experiences and Equal Opportunity Perceptions of Navy Women," *Sex Roles: A Journal of Research,* 32 no. 3–4 (February 1995), pp. 159–68.
16. Harriet Brown, "After the Suit, How Do Women Fit in at Mitsubishi?" *Ms.* IX, no. 2 (September/October 1998), pp. 32–36.
17. Thomas M. Sipkins and Joseph G. Schmitt, "Same-Sex Harassers Get Equal Time; After 'Oncale,' Employers Should Consider Implementing Sexual Harassment Policies That Deal with Same-Sex Perpetrators," *The National Law Journal* 20 no. 41

(June 8, 1998), p. B7, col. 1; Stephanie Ebbert, "Man Wins Same-Sex Lawsuit Judgment," *The Boston Globe* (June 19, 1998), p. D40.

18. Elizabeth Pryor Johnson and Michael A. Puchades, "Same-Gender Sexual Harassment: But Is It Discrimination Based on Sex?" *Florida Bar Journal* (December, 1995), pp. 79–160.
19. Lynn Weber and Elizabeth Higginbotham, "Black and White Professional-Managerial Women's Perceptions of Racism and Sexism in the Workplace," in Elizabeth Higginbotham and Mary Romero, eds., *Women and Work: Exploring Race, Ethnicity, and Class* (Thousand Oaks, CA: Sage, 1997), pp. 153–75.
20. Associated Press, "Israeli Law Lifts Barriers for Women Soldiers," *The Boston Globe* (January 5, 2000), p. 14.
21. Yuri Kageyama, "Women Win Bias Case in Japan," *The Boston Globe* (December 23, 2000), p. A16.
22. Stephen Kiehl, "Difficult Journey of Dance: Braving Taunts, More Boys Turn to Art of Ballet," *The Boston Globe* (August 2, 1998), p. B1.
23. Carol Schachet, "Gay and Lesbian Labor Gains a Voice: Pride at Work is Officially Recognized by the AFL-CIO," *Resist* 7, no. 5 (June 1998), pp. 1–3.
24. For a history of women's participation in the paid labor force see Elizabeth Higginbotham, "Introduction" in Elizabeth Higginbotham and Mary Romero, eds., *Women and Work: Exploring Race, Ethnicity, and Class* (Thousand Oaks, CA: Sage, 1997), pp. xv–xxxii.
25. Jane Kiser, "Behind the Scenes at a 'Family Friendly' Workplace," *Dollars and Sense*, no. 215 (January/February 1998), pp. 19–21.
26. Arlie Russell Hochschild, *The Time Bind: When Work Becomes Home and Home Becomes Work* (New York: Metropolitan Books, 1997).
27. Christa Wichterich, *The Globalized Woman: Reports from a Future of Inequality* (New York: Zed Books, 2000), p. 99.
28. Deborah Figart and Ellen Mutari, "It's About Time: Will Europe Solve the Work/Family Dilemma?" *Dollars and Sense* (January/February 1998), pp. 27–31.
29. Pierette Hondagneu-Sotelo, *Doméstica: Immigrant Workers Cleaning and Caring in the Shadows of Affluence* (Berkeley, CA: University of California Press, 2001); Rhacel Salazar Parreñas, *Servants of Globalization: Women, Migration, and Domestic Work* (Stanford, CA: Stanford University Press, 2001); Grace Chang, *Disposable Domestics: Immigrant Women Workers in the Global Economy* (Boston: South End Press, 2000).
30. Judith Rollins, *Between Women: Domestics and Their Employers* (Philadelphia: Temple University Press, 1985).
31. Michelle Herrera Mulligan, "Fields of Shame," *Latina* (May 2000), pp. 110 ff.
32. Miriam Ching Yoon Louie, *Sweatshop Warriors: Immigrant Women Workers Take on the Global Factory* (Boston: South End Press, 2001).

50

IT'S A FAMILY AFFAIR
Women, Poverty, and Welfare

RANDY ALBELDA AND CHRIS TILLY

Hating poor women for being poor is all the rage—literally. Radio talk show hosts, conservative think tanks, and many elected officials bash poor single mothers for being too "lazy," too "dependent," and too fertile. Poor mothers are blamed for almost every imaginable economic and social ill under the sun. Largely based on anecdotal information, mythical characterizations, and a recognition that the welfare system just isn't alleviating poverty, legislatures across the land and the federal government are proposing and passing draconian welfare "reform" measures.

It is true that current welfare policies do not work well—but not for the reasons usually presented. Welfare "reform" refuses to address the real issues facing single-mother families, and is heavily permeated by myths.

Aid to Families with Dependent Children (AFDC), the government income transfer program for poor non-elder families in the United States, serves only about 5 percent of the population at any given time, with over 90 percent of those receiving AFDC benefits being single mothers and their children. In 1993, 14 million people (two-thirds of them children) in the United States received AFDC. That same year, just under 40 million people were poor. Despite garnering a lion's share of political discussion, AFDC receives a minuscule amount of funding: It accounts for less than 1 percent of the federal budget and less than 3 percent of the state budgets.

Single mothers work. Not only do they do the unpaid work of raising children, they also average the same number of hours in the paid labor force as other mothers do—about 1,000 hours a year (a full-

---

Randy Albelda and Chris Tilly, "It's a Family Affair: Women, Poverty, and Welfare" from *For Crying Out Loud: Women's Poverty in the United States,* edited by Diane Dujon and Ann Withorn. Reprinted with the permission of South End Press.

Author's Note: Although this essay was written prior to the death of AFDC in 1996, it is included here because of the authors' analysis of the causes and realities of poverty as well as their understanding of the characteristics and experiences of women on welfare.

time, year-round job is about 2,000 hours a year).[1] And while close to 80 percent of all AFDC recipients are off in two years, over half of those return at some later point—usually because their wages in the jobs that got them off welfare just didn't match the cost of health care and childcare needed so they could keep the jobs. In fact, most AFDC recipients "cycle" between relying on families, work, and AFDC benefits to get or keep their families afloat.[2] That means that, for many single mothers, AFDC serves the same function as unemployment insurance does for higher-paid, full-time workers.

And, contrary to a highly volatile stereotype, welfare mothers, on average, have fewer kids than other mothers. And once on AFDC, they are less likely to have another child.

Poverty and the "Triple Whammy"

Poverty is a persistent problem in the United States. People without access to income are poor. In the United States, most people get access to income by living in a family with one or more wage-earners (either themselves or others). Income from ownership (rent, dividends, interest, and profits) provides only a few families with a large source of income. Government assistance is limited—with elders getting the bulk of it. So wages account for about 80 percent of all income generated in the United States. Not surprisingly, people whose labor market activity is limited, or who face discrimination, are the people most at risk for poverty. Children, people of color, and single mothers are most likely to be poor (see Boxes).

In 1993, 46 percent of single-mother families in the United States were living in poverty, but only 9 percent of two-adult families with children were poor.[3]

Why are so many single-mother families poor? Are they lazy, do they lack initiative, or are they just unlucky? The answer to all of these is a resounding "No." Single-mother families have a very hard time generating enough income to keep themselves above the poverty line for a remarkably straightforward reason: One female adult supports the family—and one female adult usually does not earn enough to provide both childcare expenses and adequate earnings.

To spell it out, single mothers face a "triple whammy." First, like all women, when they do paid work they often face low wages—far lower than men with comparable education and experience. In 1992, the median income (the midpoint) for all women who worked full-time was $13,677. That means that about 40 percent of all working women (regardless of their marital status) would not have made enough to support a family of three above the poverty line. Even when women work year-round full-time, they make 70 percent of what men do.

Second, like all mothers, single mothers must juggle paid and unpaid work. Taking care of healthy and, sometimes, sick children, and knowing where they are when at work, requires time and flexibility that few full-time jobs afford. All mothers are more likely to earn less and work less than other women workers because of it.

BOX 1
Who's Poor in the United States?

In 1993, one person in six was living below the official poverty line. The poverty line is an income threshold determined annually by the Department of Commerce's Census Bureau. The dollar amount is based on the price-adjusted determination of the 1960s cash value of a minimum adequate diet for families of different sizes multiplied by three (at the time, budget studies indicated that low-income families spent one-third of their incomes on food.) In 1993, the poverty threshold for a family of four is about $11,631.

While 10 percent of all men are poor, 16 percent of women and 25 percent—a full quarter—of all children in the United States are poor. Further, 36 percent of all black persons and 34 percent of Latinos are poor, versus 17 percent of Asians and 13 percent of white persons. Does education help stave off poverty? Yes—but not very evenly. Consider the table in Box 2. Those with low levels of education are much more likely to be poor—but gender matters. For men, getting a high school diploma cuts the chances of being poor by half—20 percent versus 10 percent. For women, poverty rates are more than halved by getting that degree, but the rates are still high—15 percent. For women to lower their likelihood of poverty to that of men with high school diplomas means getting some college education.

Percent Poor Persons in the United States (All Ages) by Selected Characteristics, 1993

	All	Men	Women	Children
All	**16.4%**	**10.2%**	**16.1%**	**25.2%**
By race				
White	13.2%	8.6%	13.2%	19.8%
Black	35.9%	20.6%	34.5%	50.8%
Asian	17.0%	14.3%	17.4%	20.0%
By ethnicity				
Non-Latino	14.5%	8.9%	14.5%	22.0%
Latino	33.7%	22.2%	32.5%	45.2%
By residence				
City	24.1%	14.4%	22.6%	38.8%
Suburb	11.4%	7.1%	11.2%	17.4%
Rural	18.1%	11.8%	18.4%	25.9%

Source: U.S. Census Bureau, Current Population Survey, 1994.

BOX 2
Poverty Rates for Adults in the United States by Educational Attainment, 1993

Years of Education	All Adults	Men	Women
8 or less	31.6%	26.4%	36.7%
9–11	27.5%	19.9%	34.3%
12	13.1%	10.0%	15.6%
13–15	9.0%	6.8%	10.9%
16	4.3%	3.8%	4.8%
17+	2.9%	2.8%	3.1%

Source: U.S. Census Bureau, Current Population Survey, 1994.

Finally, *unlike* married mothers, many single mothers must juggle earning income and taking care of children without the help of another adult. Single-mother families have only one adult to send into the labor market. And that same adult must also make sure children get through their day.

The deck is stacked—but not just for single mothers. All women with children face a job market which has little sympathy for their caregiving responsibilities and at the same time places no economic value on their time spent at home. The economic activity of raising children is one that no society can do without. In our society, we do not recognize it as work worth paying mothers for. For a married mother, this contradiction is the "double day." For a single mother, the contradiction frequently results in poverty for her and her children.

Denying the Real Problems

The lack of affordable childcare, the large number of jobs that fail to pay living wages, and the lack of job flexibility are the real problems that face all mothers (and increasingly everyone). For single mothers, these problems compound into crisis.

But instead of tackling these problems head on, politicians and pundits attack AFDC. Why? One reason is that non-AFDC families themselves are becoming more desperate, and resent the limited assistance that welfare provides to the worst-off. With men's wages falling over the last 30 years, fewer and fewer families can get by with only one wage earner. The government is not providing help for many low-income families who are struggling but are still above the AFDC eligibility threshold. This family "speed-up" has helped contribute to the idea that if both parents in a two-parent household can work (in order to be poor), then all AFDC recipients should have to work too.

Instead of facing the real problems, debates about welfare reform are dominated by three dead ends. First, politicians argue that single mothers must be made to work in the paid labor market. But most single mothers already work as much as they can. Studies confirm that AFDC recipients already do cycle in and out of the labor force. Further, as surveys indicate, mothers receiving AFDC would like to work. The issue is not whether or not to work, but whether paid work is available, how much it pays, and how to balance work and childcare.

Second, there is a notion of replacing the social responsibilities of government assistance with individual "family" responsibilities: Make men pay child support, demand behavioral changes of AFDC recipients, or even pressure single women to get married. While child support can help, for most single mothers it offers a poor substitute for reliable government assistance. Penalizing women and their children for ascribed behaviors (such as having more children to collect welfare) that are supported by anecdotes but not facts is at best mean-spirited.

Third, there is an expectation that people only need support for a limited amount of time—many states and some versions of federal welfare reform limit families to 24 months of aid over some period of time (from a lifetime to five years). Yet limiting the amount of time women receive AFDC will not reduce or limit the need for support. Children do not grow up in 24 months, nor will many women with few skills and little education necessarily become job ready. But more important, many women who do leave AFDC for the workplace will not make enough to pay for childcare or the health insurance they need to go to work.

In short, welfare "reform" that means less spending and no labor market supports will do little beyond making poor women's lives more miserable.

Beyond Welfare Reform

What could be done instead? Welfare reform in a vacuum can solve only a small part of the problem. To deal with poverty among single-mother families, to break the connection between gender and poverty, requires changing the world of work, socializing the costs of raising children, and providing low-wage supports.

If we as a nation are serious about reducing the poverty of women and children, we need to invest in seven kinds of institutional changes:

- *Create an income-maintenance system that recognizes the need for full-time childcare.* Policies that affect families must acknowledge the reality of children's needs. To truly value families means to financially support those (women or men) who must provide full-time childcare at home or to provide dependable, affordable, and caring alternative sources of childcare for those who work outside the home.

- *Provide support for low-wage workers.* If leaving welfare and taking a job means giving up health benefits and childcare subsidies, the loss to poor families can be devastating. Although high-salary workers receive (or can afford) these benefits, low-wage workers often don't. Government should provide these supports; universal heath care and higher earned income tax credits (EITC) are a first step in the right direction.
- *Close the gender pay gap.* One way to achieve pay equity is to require employers to re-evaluate the ways that they compensate comparable skills. Poor women need pay equity the most, but all women need it. Another way to close the pay gap is to increase the minimum wage. Most minimum-wage workers are women. An increase from the current $4.25 an hour to $5.50 would bring the minimum wage to 50 percent of the average wage.
- *Create jobs.* Create the opportunity to work, for poor women and poor men as well. Full employment is an old idea that still makes sense.
- *Create jobs that don't assume you have a "wife" at home to perform limitless unpaid work.* It's not just the welfare system that has to come to terms with family needs; it's employers as well. With women making up 46 percent of the workforce—and men taking on more childcare responsibilities as well—a change in work styles is overdue.
- *Make education and training affordable and available for all.* In an economy where the premium on skills and education is increasing, education and training are necessary for young people and adults, women and men.
- *Fix the tax structure.* Many of these proposals require government spending consistent with the ways our industrial counterparts spend money. Taxes must be raised to pay for these programs: the alternative—not funding child allowances, health care, and training—will prove more costly to society in the long run. But it is critically important to make the programs universal, and to fund them with a *fairer* tax system. Federal, state, and local governments have taxed middle- and low-income families for too long without assuring them basic benefits. Taxes paid by the wealthiest families as a percentage of their income have fallen dramatically over the last 15 years, while the burden on the bottom 80 percent has risen; it's time to reverse these trends.

The changes proposed are sweeping, but no less so than those proposed by the Republican Contract with America. With one out of every four children in this nation living in poverty, all our futures are at stake.

NOTES

1. These data, and others throughout the paper, were calculated by the authors using current population survey tapes.

2. Five recent studies have looked at welfare dynamics and all come to these conclusions. LaDonna Pavetti, "The Dynamics of Welfare and Work: Exploring the Process by Which Young Women Work Their Way Off Welfare," paper presented at the APPAM Annual Research Conference, 1992; Kathleen Harris, "Work and Welfare Among Single Mothers in Poverty," *American Journal of Sociology* vol. 99 (2), September 1993, pp. 317–52; Roberta Spalter-Roth, Beverly Burr, Heidi Hartmann, and Lois Shaw, "Welfare That Works: The Working Lives of AFDC Recipients," Institute for Women's Policy Research, 1995; Rebecca Blank and Patricia Ruggles, "Short-Term Recidivism Among Public Assistance Recipients," *American Economic Review,* vol. 84 (2), May 1994, pp. 49–53; and Peter David Brandon, "Vulnerability to Future Dependence Among Former AFDC Mothers," Institute for Research on Poverty discussion paper DP1005-95, University of Wisconsin, Madison, Wis., 1995.
3. U.S. Department of Commerce, Census Bureau, "Income, Poverty and Valuation of Noncash Benefits," *Current Populations Reports,* 1995, pp. 60–188, p. D-22.

51

SIXTY CENTS TO A MAN'S DOLLAR

ANN CRITTENDEN

In the Bible, in Leviticus, God instructs Moses to tell the Israelites that women, for purposes of tithing, are worth thirty shekels while men are worth fifty—a ratio of 60 percent.[1] For fifty years, from about 1930 to 1980, the value of employed women eerily reflected that biblical ratio: The earnings of full-time working women were only 60 percent of men's earnings. In the 1980s, that ratio began to change. By 1993, women working full-time were earning an average of seventy-seven cents for every dollar men earned. (In 1997, the gap widened again, as the median weekly earnings of full-time working women fell to 75 percent of men's earnings.)

But lo and behold, when we look closer, we find the same old sixty cents to a man's dollar. The usual way to measure the gender wage gap is by comparing the hourly earnings of men and women who work full-time year-round. But this compares only the women who work like men with men—a method that neatly excludes most women. As we have seen, only about half of the mothers of children under eighteen have full-time, year-round paying jobs.[2]

To find the real difference between men's and women's earnings, one would have to compare the earnings of all male and female workers, both full- and part-time. And guess what one discovers? The average earnings of *all* female workers in 1999 were 59 percent of men's earnings.[3] Women who work for pay are still stuck at the age-old biblical value put on their labor.

My research turned up other intriguing reflections of the 60 percent ratio: A survey of 1982 graduates of the Stanford Business School found that ten years after graduation, the median income of the full- and part-time employed female M.B.A.s amounted to $81,300, against the men's median income of $139,100. Again, the women's share is 58 percent. Another study, of 1974 graduates of the University of Michigan Law School, revealed that in the late 1980s the women's average earnings were 61 percent of the men's—despite the fact that 96 percent of the women were working, and that the men and women were virtually identical in terms of training. The authors of this study concluded that the women's family responsibilities were "certainly the most important single cause of sex differences in earnings."[4]

Conservatives frequently tout women's economic gains in order to charge that women's advocates who haven't folded their tents and gone home must be making up things to complain about. In a polemic titled *Who Stole Feminism?* Christina Hoff Sommers lambasts feminist activists for wearing a button stating that women earn fifty-nine cents to a man's dollar, which, she claims, is "highly misleading and now egregiously out of date."[5] Sommers is right if we skim over what she calls such "prosaic matters" as the fact that people who have primary responsibility for a child have different work patterns from people without caring responsibilities. But if we are interested in the real differences in the earnings of employed men and women, those buttons still tell the real story.

The Cost of Being a Mother

A small group of mostly female academic economists has added another twist to the story. Their research reveals that working mothers not only earn less than men, but also less per hour than childless women, even after such differences as education and experience are factored out. The pay gap between mothers and nonmothers under age thirty-five is now larger than the wage gap between young men and women.

The first comprehensive estimates of the cost of motherhood in terms of lost income were made in England by Heather Joshi of the City University in London and Hugh Davies of Birkbeck College of the University of London. The two economists estimated that a typical middle-class British mother of two forfeits almost *half* of her potential lifetime earnings.[6]

In the United States, similar work has been done by Jane Waldfogel at Columbia University. Waldfogel set out to assess the opportunity cost of motherhood by asking exactly how much of the dramatic wage gains made by women in the 1980s went to women without family responsibilities. How many of the female winners in the 1980s were people like Donna Shalala, Janet Reno, Elizabeth Dole, and Carole Bellamy, the director of UNICEF: childless women whose work patterns were indistinguishable from those of traditional males.

Back in the late 1970s, Waldfogel found, the difference between men's and women's pay was about the same for all women. Nonmothers earned only slightly higher wages. But over the next decade things changed.[7] By 1991, thirty-year-old American women without children were making 90 percent of men's wages, while comparable women with children were making only 70 percent. Even when Waldfogel factored out all the women's differences, the disparity in their incomes remained—something she dubbed the "family wage gap."[8]

Why do working mothers earn so much less than childless women? Academic researchers have worried over this question like a dog over a bone but haven't turned up a single, definitive answer.[9]

Waldfogel argues that the failure of employers to provide paid maternity leaves is one factor that leads to the family wage gap in the United States. This country is one of only six nations in the world that does not require a paid leave. (The others are Australia, New Zealand, Lesotho, Swaziland, and Papua New Guinea.)[10] With no right to a paid leave, many American mothers who want to stay at home with a new baby simply quit their jobs, and this interruption in employment costs them dearly in terms of lost income. Research in Europe reveals that when paid maternity leaves were mandated, the percentage of women remaining employed rose, and women's wages were higher, unless the leaves lasted more than a few months.[11]

In the United States as well, women who are able to take formal paid maternity leave do not suffer the same setback in their wages as comparably placed women who do not have a right to such leaves. This is a significant benefit to mothers in the five states, including California, New York, and New Jersey, that mandate temporary disability insurance coverage for pregnancy and childbirth.[12]

Paid leaves are so valuable because they don't seem to incur the same penalties that employers impose on even the briefest of unpaid career interruptions. A good example is the experience of the 1974 female graduates of the University of Michigan Law School. During their first fifteen years after law school, these women spent an average of only 3.3 months out of the workplace, compared with virtually no time out for their male classmates. More than one-quarter of the women had worked part-time, for an average of 10.1 months over the fifteen years, compared with virtually no part-time work among the men. While working full-time, the women put in only 10 percent fewer hours than full-time men, again not a dramatic difference.

But the penalties for these slight distinctions between the men's and women's work patterns were strikingly harsh. Fifteen years after graduation, the women's average earnings were not 10 percent lower, or even 20 percent lower, than the men's, but almost 40 percent lower. Fewer than one-fifth of the women in law firms who had worked part-time for more than six months had made partner in their firms, while more than four-fifths of the mothers with little or no part-time work had made partner.[13]

Another survey of almost 200 female M.B.A.s found that those who had taken an average of only 8.8 months out of the job market were less likely to reach upper-middle management and earned 17 percent less than comparable women who had never had a gap in their employment.[14]

Working-class women are also heavily penalized for job interruptions, although these are the very women who allegedly "choose" less demanding occupations that enable them to move in and out of the job market without undue wage penalties. The authors of one study concluded that the negative repercussions of taking a little time out of the labor force were still discernible after twenty years.[15] In blue-collar work, seniority decides who is eligible for better jobs, and who is "bumped" in the event of layoffs. Under current policies, many women lose their seniority forever if they interrupt their employment, as most mothers do. Training programs, required for advancement, often take place after work, excluding the many mothers who can't find child care.[16]

Mandatory overtime is another handicap placed on blue-collar mothers. Some 45 percent of American workers reported in a recent survey that they had to work overtime with little or no notice.[17] In 1994 factory workers put in the highest levels of overtime ever reported by the Bureau of Labor Statistics in its thirty-eight years of tracking the data. Where does that leave a woman who has to be home in time for dinner with the kids? Out of a promotion and maybe out of a job. Increasingly in today's driven workplace, whether she is blue- or white-collar, a woman who goes home when she is supposed to go home is going to endanger her economic well-being.

The fact that many mothers work part-time also explains some of the difference between mother's and comparable women's hourly pay. (About 65 percent of part-time workers are women, most of whom are mothers.)[18] Employers are not required to offer part-time employees equal pay and benefits for equal work. As a result, nonstandard workers earn on average about 40 percent less an hour than full-time workers, and about half of that wage gap persists even for similar workers in similar jobs.

Many bosses privately believe that mothers who work part-time have a "recreational" attitude toward work, as one Maryland businessman assured me. Presumably, this belief makes it easier to justify their exploitation. But the working conditions they face don't sound very much like recreation. A recent survey by Catalyst, a research organization focused on women in business, found that more than half of the people who had switched to part-time jobs and lower pay reported that their workload stayed the same. Ten percent reported an increase in workload after their income had been reduced. Most of these people were mothers.[19]

Another factor in the family wage gap is the disproportionate number of mothers who operate their own small businesses, a route often taken by women who need flexibility during the child-rearing years. Female-owned small businesses have increased twofold over small businesses owned by men in recent years.[20] In 1999, women owned 38 percent of all U.S. businesses, compared with only 5 percent in 1972, a remarkable increase that is frequently cited as evidence of women's economic success. One new mother noted that conversations at play groups "center as much on software and modems as they do on teething and ear infections."[21]

Less frequently mentioned is the fact that many of these women-owned businesses are little more than Mom-minus-Pop operations: one woman trying to earn some money on the side, or keep her career alive, during the years when her children have priority. Forty-five percent of women-owned businesses are home-based. And the more than one-third of businesses owned by women in 1996 generated only 16 percent of the sales of all U.S. businesses in that year.[22]

In 1997, although women were starting new businesses at twice the rate of men, they received only 2 percent of institutional venture capital, a principal source of financing for businesses with serious prospects for growth. Almost one-quarter of female business owners financed their operations the same way that they did their shopping: with their credit cards.[23]

Some researchers have suggested that mothers earn less than childless women because they are less productive. This may be true for some mothers who work at home and are subject to frequent interruptions, or for those who are exhausted from having to do most of the domestic chores, or distracted by creaky child-care arrangements. But the claim that mothers have lower productivity than other workers is controversial and unproven. It is easier to demonstrate that working mothers face the same old problem that has bedeviled women in the workplace for decades.

It's Discrimination, Stupid

It is revealing that those occupations requiring nurturing skills, such as child care, social work, and nursing, are the most systematically underpaid, relative to their educational and skill demands.[24] These are also, of course, the occupations with the highest percentage of females. But men who are primary caregivers also pay a heavy price: a "daddy tax," if you will. This suggests that at least part of the huge tax on mothers' earnings is due to work rules and practices and habits of mind that discriminate against anyone, of either sex, who cannot perform like an "unencumbered" worker. In other words, discrimination against all good parents, male or female.

Surveys have found that wives may adore husbands who share the parenting experience, but employers distinctly do not. A majority of managers believe that part-time schedules and even brief parental leaves are inappropriate for men.[25] When Houston Oiler David Williams missed one Sunday game to be with his wife after the birth of their first child, he was docked $111,111.

A survey of 348 male managers at twenty Fortune 500 companies found that fathers from dual-career families put in an average of *two* fewer hours per week—or about 4 percent less—than men whose wives were at home. That was the only difference between the two groups of men. But the fathers with working wives, who presumably had a few more domestic responsibilities, earned almost 20 percent less. There it is again: a 20 percent family wage gap.[26]

"Face time still matters as much or more than productivity in many companies," Charles Rodgers, a management consultant in Boston, said. Rodgers told me about a man in a high-tech company who regularly came to work two hours early so that he could occasionally leave early for Little League games with his son. He was given a poor performance rating.[27]

Such discrimination is hard to quantify, but it is potentially a powerful political issue. When the Clinton administration announced that it was banning employment discrimination against *parents* working in the federal government, there were so many calls to a White House staffer assigned to the case that her machine stopped taking messages.

Only eight states currently have laws prohibiting discrimination against parents in the workplace. Examples include taking a primary parent off a career track out of an assumption that the individual couldn't do the work; hiring someone without children over a more qualified person with children; forcing a primary parent to work overtime, or else; and refusing to hire a single parent, though the employer hires single, childless people. In the course of my reporting, I encountered numerous mothers who felt that their employer's refusal to arrange a shorter workweek, particularly after the birth of a second baby, amounted to career-destroying discrimination.

NOTES

1. Amity Shales, "What Does Woman Want?" *Women's Quarterly* (summer 1996): 10.
2. According to June O'Neill, an economist and former head of the Congressional Budget Office, "Full-time year-round workers are not likely to be representative of all workers. Women are less likely to be in this category than men." See June O'Neill and Solomon Polachek, "Why the Gender Gap in Wages Narrowed in the 1980s," *Journal of Labor Economics* 2, no. 1, pt. 1 (1993): 208–9.
3. U.S. Bureau of the Census, Current Population Reports, *Money Income in the U.S.: 1995,* Washington, D.C., March 2000, P60-209, pp. 46–49.
4. Robert G. Wood, Mary E. Corcoran, and Paul N. Courant, "Pay Differentials Among the Highly-Paid: The Male-Female Earnings Gap in Lawyers' Salaries," *Journal of Labor Economics* 11, no. 3 (1993): 417–41.

5. Christina Hoff Sommers, *Who Stole Feminism?* (New York: Simon & Schuster, 1994), p. 240.
6. The estimate of a 47 percent loss of lifetime earnings was presented by Hugh Davies at a session of the Allied Social Science Association in New York City on January 4, 1999. It is based on the British Household Poll Survey of 1994. Using earlier data, Davies and Joshi calculated that the mommy tax on a typical British secretary was the equivalent of $324,000—not counting lost pension benefits. See Heather Joshi, "Sex and Motherhood as Handicaps in the Labour Market," in *Women's Issues in Social Policy,* ed. Mavis Maclean and Dulcie Grove (London: Routledge, 1991), p. 180. See also Heather Joshi, "The Cost of Caring," in *Women and Poverty in Britain: The 1990's,* ed. Carol Glendenning and Jane Millar (New York: Harvester Wheatsheaf, 1992), p. 121. Also see Heather Joshi and Pierella Paci, *Unequal Pay for Men and Women* (Cambridge, Mass.: M.I.T. Press, 1998).
7. Jane Waldfogel, "Women Working for Less: Family Status and Women's Pay in the US and UK," Malcolm Wiener Center for Social Policy Working Paper D-94-1, Harvard University, 1994.
8. Jane Waldfogel, "Understanding the 'Family Gap' in Pay for Women with Children," *Journal of Economic Perspectives* 12, no. 1 (winter 1998): 137–56. See also Waldfogel, "The Family Gap for Young Women in the United States and Britain," *Journal of Labor Economics* 11 (1998): 505–19. Looking at two different cohorts of young women, one averaging age thirty in 1981 and the other about thirty in 1990, Waldfogel found that the nonmothers' wages rose from 72 percent to 90 percent of men's between 1981 and 1990. But the wages of mothers rose less, from 60 percent to only 70 percent of men the same age during the same period. The more children a woman had, the lower her earnings, even with all other factors being equal.

   Waldfogel also uncovered a wage gap of 20 percentage points for young women in the United Kingdom. Nonmothers at age thirty-three earn 84 percent of men's pay, while mothers earn only 64 percent. See Jane Waldfogel, "The Family Gap for Young Women in the US and UK: Can Maternity Leave Make a Difference?" Malcolm Wiener Center for Social Policy, Harvard University, October 1994, pp. 1, 20.
9. See Paula England and Michelle Budig, "The Effects of Motherhood on Wages in Recent Cohorts: Findings from the National Longitudinal Survey of Youth," unpublished paper, 1999.
10. Elizabeth Olson, "U.N. Surveys Paid Leave for Mothers," *New York Times,* February 16, 1998.
11. Christopher J. Ruhm, "The Economic Consequences of Parental Leave Mandates: Lessons from Europe," *Quarterly Journal of Economics* CXIII, no. 1 (1998): 285–317. Ruhm found that longer leaves (of nine months or more) were associated with a slight reduction in women's relative wages, but Waldfogel discovered that mothers in Britain who exercised their right to a ten-month paid maternity leave and returned to their original employer had wages no different from those of childless women.

    See also "Working Mothers Then and Now: A Cross-Cohort Analysis of the Effects of Maternity Leave on Women's Pay," in *Gender and Family Issues in the Workplace,* ed. Francine Blau and Ronald Ehrenberg (New York: Russell Sage Foundation, 1997).
12. Heidi Hartmann, Institute for Women's Policy Research, personal communication, January 8, 1995. Hartmann's research has shown that fully 11 percent of women who have no paid leave have to go on public assistance during their time with a new baby.
13. Wood, Corcoran, and Courant, "Pay Differentials," pp. 417–28.

14. This 1993 study was coauthored by Joy Schneer of Rider University's College of Business Administration and Frieda Reitman, professor emeritus at Pace University's Lubin School of Business.
15. Joyce Jacobsen and Arthur Levin, "The Effects of Intermittent Labor Force Attachment on Female Earnings," *Monthly Labor Review* 118, no. 9 (September 1995): 18.
16. For a good discussion of the obstacles to mothers' employment in relatively well-paying blue-collar work, see Joan Williams, *Unbending Gender: Why Family and Work Conflict and What to Do About It* (New York: Oxford University Press, 2000), pp. 76–81.
17. This survey of 1,000 workers was conducted by researchers at the University of Connecticut and Rutgers University, and was reported in the *Wall Street Journal,* May 18, 1999.
18. A survey of more than 2,000 people in four large corporations found that 75 percent of the professionals working part-time were women who were doing so because of child-care obligations. Only 11 percent of the male managers surveyed expected to work part-time at some point in their careers, compared with 36 percent of women managers. *A New Approach to Flexibility: Managing the Work/Time Equation* (New York: Catalyst, 1997), pp. 25–26.
19. There is other evidence that many so-called part-timers are increasingly working what used to be considered full-time—thirty-five to forty hours a week—for lower hourly pay than regular full-timers. See Reed Abelson, "Part-time Work for Some Adds Up to Full-Time Job," *New York Times,* November 2, 1998.
20. In the five years from 1988 through 1992, the number of women-owned sole proprietorships, partnerships, and similar businesses soared 43 percent, compared with overall growth of 26 percent in such businesses. *Wall Street Journal,* January 29, 1996.
21. Tracy Thompson, "A War Inside Your Head," *Washington Post Magazine,* February 15, 1998, p. 29.
22. Information on women-owned businesses provided by the National Foundation for Women Business Owners in Washington, D.C., September 2000.
23. Noelle Knox, "Women Entrepreneurs Attract New Financing," *New York Times,* July 26, 1998.
24. For the relatively low value placed on the caring professions, see Paula England, George Farkas, Barbara Kilbourne, Kurt Beron, and Dorothea Weir, "Returns to Skill, Compensating Differentials, and Gender Bias: Effects of Occupational Characteristics on Wages of White Women and Men," *American Journal of Sociology* 100, no. 3 (November 1994): 689–719.
25. On corporate attitudes toward part-time work for men, see the study cited in note 17. Another study found that 63 percent of large employers thought it was inappropriate for a man to take *any* parental leave, and another 17 percent thought it unreasonable unless the leave was limited to two weeks or less. Martin H. Malin, "Fathers and Parental Leave," *Texas Law Review* 72 (1994): 1047, 1089; cited in Williams, *Unbending Gender,* p. 100
26. This study, by Linda Stroh of Loyola University, was reported by Tamar Lewin, "Fathers Whose Wives Stay Home Earn More and Get Ahead, Studies Find," *New York Times,* October 12, 1994.
27. Charles Rodgers, personal communication, October 1993.

52

WHY ARE THERE NO MALE ASIAN ANCHOR*MEN* ON TV?

BEN FONG-TORRES

Connie Chung, the best-known Asian TV newswoman in the country, is a co-anchor of *1986,* a prime-time show on NBC. Ken Kashiwahara, the best-known Asian TV newsman, has been chief of ABC's San Francisco bureau for seven years; his reports pop up here and there on ABC's newscasts and other news-related programs.

Wendy Tokuda, the best-known Asian TV newswoman in the Bay Area, is a co-anchor of KPIX's evening news. David Louie, the most established Asian TV newsman, is a field reporter, covering the Peninsula for KGO.

And that's the way it is: among Asian American broadcasters, the glamour positions—the anchor chairs, whose occupants earn more than $500,000 a year in the major markets—go to the women; the men are left outside, in the field, getting by on reporters' wages that top out at about $80,000.

The four Bay Area television stations that present regular newscasts (Channels 2, 4, 5 and 7) employ more than 40 anchors. Only two are Asian Americans: Tokuda and Emerald Yeh, a KRON co-anchor on weekends. There is no Asian male in an anchor position, and there has never been one. (Other Asian women who have anchored locally are Linda Yu [KGO] and Kaity Tong [KPIX], now prime-time anchors in Chicago and New York.)

None of the two dozen broadcasters this reporter spoke to could name a male Asian news anchor working anywhere in the United States.

Don Fitzpatrick, a TV talent headhunter whose job it has been for four years to help television stations find anchors and reporters, maintains a video library in his San Francisco office of 9000 people on the air in the top 150 markets.

There are, in fact, several reasons proposed by broadcasters, station executives, talent agents and others.

Ben Fong-Torres, "Why Are There No Male Asian Anchor*men* on TV?" from *San Francisco Chronicle* (July 13, 1986). Reprinted with permission.

- Asian men have been connected for generations with negative stereotypes. Asian women have also been saddled with false images, but, according to Tokuda, "In this profession, they work for women and against men."
- Asian women are perceived as attractive partners for the typical news anchor: a white male. "TV stations," says Henry Der, director of Chinese for Affirmative Action, "have discovered that having an Asian female with a white male is an attractive combination." And, adds Sam Chu Lin, a former reporter for both KRON and KPIX, "they like the winning formula. If an Asian woman works in one market, then another market duplicates it. So why test for an Asian male?"
- Asian women allow television stations to fulfill two equal-opportunity slots with one hiring. As Mario Machado, a Los Angeles-based reporter and producer puts it, "They get two minorities in one play of the cards. *They* hit the jackpot."
- Asian males are typically encouraged by parents toward careers in the sciences and away from communications.
- Because there are few Asian men on the air, younger Asian males have no racial peers as role models. With few men getting into the profession, news directors have a minuscule talent pool from which to hire.

And, according to Sumi Haru, a producer at KTLA in Los Angeles, the situation is worsening as stations are being purchased and taken over by large corporations. At KTTV, the ABC affiliate, "The affirmative action department was the first to go." At her own station, the public affairs department is being trimmed. "We're concerned with what little Asian representation we have on the air," said Haru, an officer of the Association of Asian-Pacific American Artists.

Honors Thesis

Helen Chang, a communications major at UC Berkeley now working in Washington, DC, made the missing Asian anchorman the subject of her honors thesis. Chang spoke with Asian anchorwomen in Los Angeles, Chicago and New York as well as locally. "To capsulize the thesis," she says, "it is an executive decision based on a perception of an Asian image. On an executive decision level, the image of the Asian woman is acceptable."

"It's such a white bread medium; it's the survival of the blandest," says a male Asian reporter who asked to remain anonymous. A native San Franciscan, this reporter once had ambitions to be an anchor, but after several static years at his station, "I've decided to face reality. I have a white man's credentials but it doesn't mean a thing. I'm not white. How can it not be racism?"

"Racism is a strong word that scares people," says Tokuda.

"But whatever's going on here is some ugly animal. It's not like segregation in the south. What it is is very subtle . . . bias."

To Mario Machado, it's not that subtle. Machado, who is half Chinese and half Portuguese, is a former daytime news anchor in Los Angeles who's had the most national television exposure after Kashiwahara. Being half Chinese, he says, has given him no advantage in getting work. "It's had no bearing at all. There's a move on against Asians, period, whether part-Asian or full-Asian."

TV executives, he charges, "don't really want minority males to be totally successful. They don't want minority men perceived as strong, bright, and articulate. We can be cute second bananas, like Robert Ito on *Quincy.* But having an Asian woman—that's always been the feeling from World War II, I guess. You bring back an Asian bride, and she's cute and delicate. But a strong minority man with authority and conviction—I don't think people are ready for that."

War Image

Bruno Cohen, news director at KPIX, agrees that "for a lot of people, the World War II image of Japanese, unfortunately, is the operative image about what Asian males are all about."

That image, says Serena Chen, producer and host of *Asians Now!* on KTVU, was one of danger. "They may be small, but they're strong. So watch out, white women!"

The Vietnam war and recent movies like *Rambo,* Machado says, add to the historic negativity. "You never went to war against Asian women," he says. "You always went to war against Asian men."

Today, says Tokuda, Asian men are saddled with a twin set of stereotypes. "They're either wimpy—they have real thick glasses and they're small and they have an accent and they're carrying a lot of cameras—or they're a murderous gangster." "Or," says Les Kumagai, a former KPIX intern now working for a Reno TV station, "they're businessmen who are going to steal your jobs."

"The Asian woman is viewed as property, and the Asian male has been denied sexuality," says Chen. "Eldridge Cleaver created a theory of the black male being superglorified in the physical and superdecreased in the mental. It's very difficult for people to see a successful black male unless he's an athlete or a performer. If he's in a corporate situation, everyone says, 'Wow, he's the product of affirmative action.' That theory holds that in this society, people who have potential to have power have to be male, and have both mental and physical [strength] to be the superior male. In this society, they took away the black male's mental and gave him his physical. The Asian male has been denied the physical and given the mental."

Veteran KRON reporter Vic Lee listens to a tally of stereotypes and images associated with Asian men. "All those reasons limit where an Asian American can work. I've always said to my wife, if I'm fired here, there're only a couple of cities I can go to and get a job based on how well I do my work, not how I look or what color my skin is. There are cities with Asian

American populations, and you can count them on one hand: Seattle, Los Angeles, New York, Boston, and possibly Washington.

"The rest of the country? You might as well forget Detroit. They *killed* a [Chinese] guy just 'cause he looked Japanese." Lee is referring to Vincent Chin, who was beaten to death by two white auto workers who mistook him for a Japanese and blamed him for their unemployment.

"Exotic" Females

In contrast to the threatening Asian male, says Les Kumagai, "Females are 'exotic.' They're not threatening to non-Asian females and they're attractive to non-Asian males. You're looking to draw the 18-to-45-year-old female demographic for advertising. You just won't get that draw from an Asian male."

To Tokuda, the Asian woman's persisting stereotype is more insidious than exotic. "It's the Singapore girl: not only deferential but submissive. It's right next to the geisha girl."

At KGO, says one newsroom employee, "somebody in management was talking about [recently hired reporter] Janet Yee and blurted out, 'Oh, she's so cute.' They don't care about her journalistic credentials. . . . That type of thinking still persists."

Aggressive

Janet Yee says she can take the comment as a compliment, but agrees that it is "a little dehumanizing." Yee, who is half Chinese and half Irish-Swedish, says she doesn't get the feeling, at KGO, that she was hired for her looks. Stereotypes "are the things I've fought all my life," she says, adding that she isn't at all submissive and deferential. "I'm assertive and outgoing, and I think that's what got me the job."

Emerald Yeh, who worked in Portland and at CNN (Cable News Network) in Atlanta before joining KRON, says she's asked constantly about the part being an Asian woman played in her landing a job. "The truth is that it's a factor, but at the same time, there is absolutely no way I can keep my job virtually by being Asian."

Despite the tough competition for jobs in television, Yeh, like Tokuda and several peers in Los Angeles, is vocal about the need to open doors to Asian men. "People think Asians have done so well," she says, "but how can you say that if one entire gender group is hardly visible?"

George Lum, a director at KTVU who got into television work some 30 years ago at Channel 5, has a theory of his own. "The Asian male is not as aggressive as the Asian female. In this business you have to be more of an extrovert. Men are a little more passive."

Headhunter Don Fitzpatrick agrees. "Watching my tapes, women in general are much more aggressive than men. . . . My theory on that is that—say a boy and girl both want to get into television, and they have identical SATs and grade point averages. Speakers tell them, you'll go to Chico or Medford and start out making $17,000 to $18,000 a year. A guy will say, 'This is bull. If I stay in school and get into accounting or law . . . ' And they have a career change. A woman will go to Chico or Medford and will get into LA or New York."

"In Helen Chang's paper," recalls Tokuda, "she mentions the way Asian parents have channeled boys with a narrow kind of guidance."

"With Japanese kids," says Tokuda, "right after the war, there was a lot of pressure on kids to get into society, on being quiet and working our way back in." In Seattle, she says, "I grew up with a whole group of Asian American men who from the time they were in junior high knew that they were going to be doctors—or at least that they were gonna be successful. There was research that showed that they were very good in math and sciences and not good in verbal skills. With girls there's much less pressure to go into the hard sciences."

Most of the men who do make it in broadcasting describe serendipitous routes into the field, and all of them express contentment with being reporters. "Maybe I'm covering my butt by denying that I want to anchor," says Kumagai, "but I do get a bigger charge being out in the field."

Still, most Asian male reporters do think about the fame and fortune of an anchor slot. Those thoughts quickly meet up against reality.

David Louie realizes he has little chance of becoming the 6 o'clock anchor. "I don't have the matinee idol look that would be the most ideal image on TV. Being on the portly side and not having a full head of hair, I would be the antithesis of what an anchorman is supposed to look like."

Kind of like KPIX's Dave McElhatton? Louie laughs. "But he's white," he says, quickly adding that McElhatton also has 25 years of experience broadcasting in the Bay Area.

At least Louie is on the air. In Sacramento, Lonnie Wong was a reporter at KTXL (Channel 40), and Jan Minagawa reported and did part-time anchoring at KXTV (Channel 10). Both have been promoted into newsroom editing and production jobs. And neither is thrilled to be off the air.

Wong, who says he was made an assignment editor because, among reporters, he had "the most contacts in the community," says his new job is "good management experience. But I did have a reservation. I was the only minority on the air at the station; and I know that's valuable for a station."

Minagawa's station, KXTV, does have an Asian on the air: a Vietnamese woman reporter named Mai Pham. "That made the decision easier," says Minagawa, who had been a reporter and fill-in anchor for seven years. A new news director, he says, "had a different idea of what should be on the air" and asked him to become a producer. "I didn't like it, but there was nothing I could do."

Mitch Farris rejects any notion of a conspiracy by news directors against Asian American men. In fact, he says they are "desperate" for Asian male applicants. "Just about any news director would strive to get an Asian on the air and wouldn't mind a man."

To which Machado shouts, "We're here! We're here! We're looking for work."

53

SHARING THE SHOP FLOOR

STAN GRAY

On an October evening in 1983, a group of women factory workers from Westinghouse came to the United Steelworkers hall in Hamilton, Ontario, to tell their story to a labor federation forum on affirmative action. The women told of decades of maltreatment by Westinghouse—they had been confined to job ghettoes with inferior conditions and pay, and later, when their "Switchgear" plant was shut down, they had fought to be transferred to the other Westinghouse plants in the city. They had to battle management and the resistance of some, though not all, of their brothers in the shops. They won the first round, but when the recession hit, many were laid off regardless of seniority and left with little or no income in their senior years.

By the night of the forum I had worked at Westinghouse for ten years and had gone through the various battles for equality in the workplace. As I listened to the women, I thought of how much their coming into our plant had changed me, my fellow workers, and my brother unionists.

The women were there to tell their own story because the male staff officials of their union, United Electrical Workers, had prevented the women's committee of the local labor council from presenting their brief. The union claimed it was inaccurate, the problems weren't that bad, and it didn't give union officials the credit for leading the fight for women's rights. The Westinghouse women gave their story and then the union delivered a brief of its own, presenting a historical discussion of male-female relations in the context of the global class struggle, without mentioning Westinghouse or Hamilton or any women that it represented.[1]

This kind of thing happens in other cities and in other unions. The unanimous convention resolutions in support of affirmative action tend to mask a male resistance within the unions and on the shop floor. Too many men pay lip service to women's rights but leave the real fighting to the women. They don't openly confront the chauvinism of their brothers on the shop floor and in the labor movement. Yet an open fight by men against sexism is an important part of the fight for sexual equality. It is also important because sexism is harmful for working men, in spite of whatever benefits they gain in the short term; it runs counter to their interests and undermines the quality of their trade unionism.

Stan Gray, "Sharing the Shop Floor" from *Canadian Dimension* (June 18, 1984). Reprinted with the permission of *Canadian Dimension* magazine, 91 Alberta Street, Room 2B, Winnipeg, Manitoba R3B 1G5, Canada.

I was one of those unionists who for years sat on the fence in this area until sharp events at work pushed me off. I then had to try to deal with these issues in practice. The following account of the debates and struggles on the shop floor at Westinghouse concentrates on the men rather than on the women's battle; it focuses on the men's issues and tries to bring out concretely the interests of working men in the fight against sexism.

My Education Begins

My education in the problems of the Westinghouse women began in November 1978, when I was recalled to work following a bitter and unsuccessful five-month strike. The union represented eighteen hundred workers in three plants that produced turbines, motors, transformers, and switchgear equipment. When I was recalled to work it wasn't to my old Beach Road plant—where I had been a union steward and safety rep—but to an all-female department in the Switchgear plant and to a drastic drop in my labor grade. The plant was mostly segregated; in other words, jobs (and many departments) were either male or female. There were separate seniority lists and job descriptions. The dual-wage, dual-seniority system was enshrined in the collective agreement signed and enforced by both company and union.

At Switchgear I heard the complaints of the women, who worked the worst jobs in terms of monotony, speed, and work discipline but received lower pay, were denied chances for promotion, and were frequently laid off. They complained too of the union, accusing the male leadership of sanctioning and policing their inferior treatment. In cahoots with management, it swept the women's complaints under the carpet. From the first day it was obvious to me that the company enforced harsher standards for the women. They worked harder and faster, got less break time, and were allowed less leeway than the men. When I was later transferred to the all-male machine shop, the change was from night to day.

Meanwhile the men's club that ran the union made its views known to me early and clearly. The staff rep told me that he himself would never work with women. He boasted that he and his friends in the leadership drank in the one remaining all-male bar in the city. The local president was upset when he heard that I was seriously listening to the complaints of the women workers. He told me that he always just listened to their unfounded bitching, said "yes, yes, yes," and then completely ignored what he had been told. I ought to do the same, was his advice. Although I had just been elected to the executive in a rank-and-file rebellion against the old guard, he assumed that a common male bond would override our differences. When I persisted in taking the women's complaints seriously, the leadership started to ridicule me, calling me "the Ambassador" and saying they were now happy that I was saving them the distasteful task of listening to the women's bitching.

Then in 1979 the boom fell at Switchgear: the company announced it would close the plant. For the women, this was a serious threat. In the new contract the seniority and wage lists had been integrated, thanks to a new Ontario Human Rights Code. But would the women be able to exercise their seniority and bump or transfer to jobs in the other Hamilton plants, or would they find themselves out in the street after years at Switchgear?

Divide and Conquer

By this time I had been recalled to my old department at the Beach Road plant, thanks to shop-floor pressure by the guys. There was a lot of worry in the plants about the prospect of large-scale transfers of women from Switchgear. A few women who had already been transferred had met with harassment and open hostility from the men. Some of us tried to raise the matter in the stewards' council, but the leadership was in no mood to discuss and confront sexism openly. The union bully boys went after us, threatening, shouting, breast beating, and blaming the women for the problems.

Since the union structures weren't going to touch the problem, we were left to our own resources in the shop. I worked in the Transformer Division, which the management was determined to keep all male. As a steward I insisted that the Switchgear women had every right to jobs in our department, at least to training and a trial period as stipulated by seniority. Since this was a legal and contractual right, management developed a strategy of Divide and Rule: present the women as a threat to men's jobs; create splits and get the hourly men to do the bosses' dirty work for them. Management had a secondary objective here, which was to break our shop-floor union organization. Since the trauma of the strike and post-strike repression, a number of stewards and safety reps had patiently rebuilt the union in the plant, block by block—fighting every grievance, hazard, and injustice with a variety of tactics and constructing some shop-floor unity. We did so in the teeth of opposition from both company and union, whose officials were overly anxious to get along peacefully with each other. A war of the sexes would be a weapon in management's counteroffensive against us.

For months before the anticipated transfers, foremen and their assorted rumor mongers stirred up the pot with the specter of the Invasion of the Women. Two hundred Switchgear women would come and throw all Beach Road breadwinners out in the street; no one's job would be safe. Day after day, week after week, we were fed the tales: for example, that fourteen women with thirty years' seniority were coming to the department in eight days and no male would be protected. Better start thinking now about unemployment insurance.

In the department next to mine a few transfers of women were met with a vicious response from the men. Each side, including the militant steward, ended up ratting on the other to the boss. The men were furious and went all over the plant to warn others against allowing any "cunts" or "bitches" into their departments.

Meanwhile I had been fighting for the women to be called into new jobs opening up in the iron-stacking area of my department. The union's business agent had insisted that women couldn't physically handle those and other jobs. But I won the point with the company. The major influx of women would start here.

For weeks before their arrival, the department was hyper-alive, everyone keyed to the Invasion of the Women. I was approached by one of the guys, who said that a number of them had discussed the problem and wanted me, as their steward, to tell management the men didn't want the women in here and would fight to keep them out.

The moment was a personal watershed for me. As I listened to him, I knew that half measures would no longer do. I would now have to take the bull by the horns.

Over the years I had been dealing with male chauvinism in a limited fashion. As a health and safety rep, I had to battle constantly with men who would knowingly do dangerous work because it was "manly" to do so and because it affirmed their masculine superiority. The bosses certainly knew how to use guys like that to get jobs done quickly. With a mixture of sarcasm, force, and reason, I would argue, "It's stupidity not manliness to hurt yourself. Use your brains, don't be a hero and cripple yourself; you're harming all of us and helping the company by breaking the safety rules we fought so hard to establish, rules that protect all of us."

From this I was familiar with how irrational, self-destructive, and anti-collective the male ego could be. I also felt I had learned a great deal from the women's movement, including a never-ending struggle with my own sexism. Off and on I would have debates with my male co-workers about women's liberation. But all this only went so far. Now with the approaching invasion and the Great Fear gripping the department, I had to deal with an angry male sexism in high gear. I got off the fence.

I told this guy, "No. These women from Switchgear are our sisters, and we have fought for them to come into our department. They are our fellow workers with seniority rights, and we want them to work here rather than get laid off. If we deny them their seniority rights, it hurts us, for once that goes down the drain, none of us has any protection. It is our enemies, the bosses, who are trying to do them out of jobs here. There's enough work for everyone; even if there weren't, seniority has to rule. For us as well as for them. The guys should train the women when they come and make them feel welcome."

And with that reply, the battle was on. For the next few weeks the debate raged hot and heavy, touching on many basic questions, drawing in workers from all over the plant. Many men made the accusation that the women would be the bosses' fifth column and break our unity. They would side with the foremen, squeal on us, outproduce us, and thereby force speedups. The women were our enemy, or at least agents of the enemy, and would be used by *them* against *us*. Many of them pointed to the experience of the next department over, where, since the influx of a few women, the situation had been steadily worsening.

The reply was that if we treated the women as sisters and friends they'd side with us, not the boss. Some of us had worked in Switchgear and knew it was the *men* there who got favored treatment. What's more, our own shop-floor unity left a lot to be desired and many of our male co-workers engaged in squealing and kowtowing to the boss. Some of us argued sarcastically that women could never equal some of our men in this area.

We argued that we had common class interests with our sisters against the company, particularly in protecting the seniority principle.

It was easy to tease guys with the contradictions that male double standards led them to. Although they were afraid the women would overproduce, at the same time they insisted that women wouldn't be physically strong enough to do our "man's work." Either they could or they couldn't was the answer to that one, and if they could, they deserved the jobs. It would be up to us to initiate them into the department norms. Many of the guys said that the women would never be able to do certain of the heavy and rotten jobs. As steward and safety rep I always jumped on that one: we shouldn't do those jobs either. Hadn't we been fighting to make them safer and easier for ourselves? Well, they answered, the women would still not be able to do all the jobs. Right, I would say, but how many guys here have we protected from doing certain jobs because of back or heart problems, or age, or simply personal distaste? If the women can't do certain jobs, we treat them the same way as men who can't. We don't victimize people who can't do everything the company wants them to. We protect them: as our brothers, and as our sisters.

By pointing out the irrationalities of the sexist double standards, we were pushing the guys to apply their class principles—universal standards of equal treatment. Treat the women just as we treat men regarding work tasks, seniority, illness, and so on.

Countering Sexism

Male sexist culture strives to degrade women to nothing but pieces of flesh, physical bodies, mindless animals . . . something less than fully human, which the men can then be superior to. Name-calling becomes a means of putting women in a different category from *us,* to justify different and inferior treatment.

Part of the fight to identify the women as co-workers was therefore the battle against calling them "cunts" or "bitches." It was important to set the public standard whereby the women were labeled as part of us, not *them.* I wouldn't be silent with anyone using these sexist labels and pushed the point very aggressively. Eventually everyone referred to "the women."

After a while most of the men in the department came to agree that having the women in and giving them a chance was the right thing to do by any standard of fairness, unionism, or solidarity, and was required by the basic human decency that separates *us* from *them.* But then the focus shifted to other areas. Many men came back with traditional arguments against women in the workforce. They belong at home with the kids, they're robbing male breadwinners of family income, and so forth. But others disagreed: most of the guys' wives worked outside the home or had done so in the past; after all, a family needed at least two wages these days. Some men answered that in bad times a family should have only one breadwinner so all would have an income. Fine, we told them, let's be really fair and square: you go home and clean the house and leave your wife at work. Alright, they countered, they could tolerate women working who supported a family, but not single women. And so I picked out four single men in our department and proposed they be immediately sacked.

Fairness and equality seemed to triumph here too. The guys understood that everyone who had a job at Westinghouse deserved equal protection. But then, some men found another objection. As one, Peter, put it, "I have no respect for any women who could come in to work here in these rotten conditions." The comeback was sharp: "What the hell are *you* putting up with this shit for? Why didn't you refuse to do that dirty job last month? Don't *you* deserve to be treated with respect?"[2]

As the Invasion Date approached I got worried. Reason and appeals to class solidarity had had a certain impact. Most of the guys were agreeing, grudgingly, to give the women a chance. But the campaign had been too short; fear and hostility were surfacing more and more. I was worried that there would be some ugly incident the first day or two that would set a pattern.

Much of the male hostility had been kept in check because I, as the union steward, had fought so aggressively on the issue. I decided to take this one step further and use some intimidation to enforce the basics of public behavior. In a tactic I later realized was a double-edged sword, I puffed myself up, assumed a cocky posture, and went for the jugular. I loudly challenged the masculinity of any worker who was opposed to the women. What kind of man is afraid of women? I asked. Only sissies and wimps are threatened by equality. A *real man* has nothing to be afraid of; he wants strong women. Any man worth his salt doesn't need the crutch of superiority over his sisters; he fears no female. A real man lives like an equal, doesn't step on women, doesn't degrade his sisters, doesn't have to rule the roost at home in order to affirm his manhood. Real men fight the boss, stand up with self-respect and dignity, rather than scapegoat our sisters.

I was sarcastic and cutting with my buddies. "This anti-woman crap of yours is a symbol of weakness. Stand up like a real man and behave and work as equals. The liberation of the women is the best thing that ever came along. . . . It's in *our* interests." To someone who boasted of how he made his wife cook his meals and clean his floors, I'd ask if she wiped his ass too? To the porno addicts I'd say, "You like that pervert shit? What's wrong with the real thing? Can you only get it up with those fantasies and cartoon women? Afraid of a real woman?" I'd outdo some of the worst guys in verbal intimidation and physical feats. Then I'd lecture them on women's equality and on welcoming our sisters the next week. I zeroed in on one or two of the sick types and physically threatened them if they pulled off anything with the women.

All of this worked, as I had hoped. It established an atmosphere of intimidation; no one was going to get smart with the women. Everyone would stand back for a while, some would cooperate, some would be neutral, and those I saw as "psycho-sexists" would keep out.

The tactic was effective because it spoke directly to a basic issue. But it was also effective because it took a leaf from the book of the psycho-sexists themselves.

At Westinghouse as elsewhere, some of the men were less chauvinistic and more sensible than others, but they often kept quiet in a group. They allowed the group pattern to be set by the most sexist bullies, whose style of woman baiting everyone at least gave in to. The psycho-sexists achieved this result because they challenged, directly or by implication, the masculinity of any male who didn't act the same way. All the men, whatever their real inclinations, are intimidated into acting or talking in a manner degrading to women. I had done the same thing, but in reverse. I had challenged the masculinity of any worker who would oppose the women. I had scared them off.

The Day the Women Arrived

The department crackled with tension the morning The Women arrived. There were only two of them to start with. The company was evidently scared by the volatile situation it had worked so hard to create. They backed off a direct confrontation by assigning my helper George and me to work with the women.

The two women were on their guard: Betty and Laura, in their late thirties, were expecting trouble. They were pleasantly shocked when I said matter-of-factly that we would train them on the job. They were overjoyed when I explained that the men had wanted them in our department and had fought the bosses to bring them here.

It was an unforgettable day. Men from all corners of the plant crept near the iron-stacking area to spy on us. I explained the work and we set about our tasks. We outproduced the standard rate by just a hair so that the company couldn't say the women weren't able to meet the normal requirements of the job.

My strategy was to get over the hump of the first few days. I knew that once the guys got used to the women being there, they'd begin to treat them as people, not as "women," and their hysteria would go away. It was essential to avoid incidents. Thus I forced the guys to interact with them. Calling over one of the male opponents, I introduced him as Bruce the Slinger who knew all the jobs and was an expert in lifts and would be happy to help them if asked and could always be called on to give a hand. This put him on the spot. Finally he flashed a big smile, and said, "Sure, just ask and I'd be pleased to show you anything, and to begin with, here's what to watch out for. . . ."

The morning went by. There were no incidents. From then on it was easy. More guys began to talk to the two women. They started to see them as Betty with four kids who lived on the mountain and knew wiring and was always cheerful; or Laura, who was a friend of John's uncle and was cranky early in the morning, who could easily operate the crane but had trouble with the impact gun, and who liked to heat up meat pies for lunch. After all, these men lived and worked with women all of their lives outside the plant—mothers, sisters, wives, in-laws, friends, daughters, and girlfriends. Having women at work was no big deal once they got over the trauma of the invasion of this male preserve. Just like helping your sister-in-law hang some wallpaper.

As the news spread, more and more women applied to transfer to our department. They were integrated with minimum fuss. The same thing happened in several adjoining departments. Quickly, men and women began to see each other as people and co-workers, not as enemies. Rather than man vs. woman it was John, Mary, Sue, Peter, Alice, George, and Laura. That Christmas we had a big party at someone's home—men and women of the department, drinking and dancing. The photos and various raucous tales of that night provided the basis for department storytelling for the next three months.

Was this, then, peace between the sexes? The integration of men and women as co-workers in the plant? Class solidarity triumphing over sex antagonism? Not quite. Although they were now together, it was not peace. The result was more complicated, for now the war between the sexes was being extended from the community into the workplace.

Workplace Culture

As our struggle showed, sexism coexists and often is at war with class consciousness and with the trade union solidarity that develops among factory men. Our campaign was successful to the extent that it was able to sharply polarize and push the contradictions between these two tendencies in each individual. With most of the men, their sense of class solidarity triumphed over male chauvinism.

Many of the men had resisted the female invasion of the workplace because for them it was the last sanctum of male culture. It was somewhere they could get away from the world of women, away from responsibility and children and the civilized society's cultural restraints. In the plant they could revel in the rough and tumble of a masculine world of physical harshness, of constant swearing and rough behavior, of half-serious fighting and competition with each other and more serious fighting with the boss. It was eight hours full of filth and dirt and grease and grime and sweat—manual labor and a manly atmosphere. They could be vulgar and obscene, talk about football and car repairs, and let their hair down. Boys could be boys.

The male workplace culture functions as a form of rebellion against the discipline of their society. Outside the workplace, women are the guardians of the community. They raise the kids and enforce some degree of family and collective responsibility. They frequently have to force this upon men, who would rather go drinking or play baseball while the women mind the kids, wash the family's clothes, attend to problems with the neighbors and in-laws, and so on. Like rebellious teenage sons escaping mother's control, male wage earners enter the factory gates, where in their male culture they feel free of the restraints of these repressive standards.

Even if all factory men don't share these attitudes, a large proportion do, to a greater or lesser degree.

The manly factory culture becomes an outlet for accumulated anger and frustration. But this is a vicious circle because the tedious work and the subordination to the bosses is in large part the very cause of the male worker's dissatisfaction. He is bitter against a world that has kept him down, exploited his labor power, bent him to meet the needs of production and profit, cheated him of a better life, and made the daily grind so harsh. Working men are treated like dirt everywhere: at work they are at the bottom of the heap and under the thumb of the boss; outside they are scorned by polite society. But, the men can say, we are better than them all in certain ways; we're doing men's work; it's physically tough; women can't do it; neither can the bankers and politicians. Tough work gives a sense of masculine superiority that compensates for being stepped on and ridiculed. All that was threatened by the Women's Invasion.

However, this male workplace culture is not one-sided, for it contains a fundamentally positive sense of class value. The working men contrast themselves to other classes and take pride in having a concrete grasp of the physical world around them. The big shots can talk fancy and manipulate words, flout their elegance and manners. But we control the nuts and bolts of production, have our hands on the machines and gears and valves, the wires and lathes and pumps, the furnaces and spindles and batteries. We're the masters of the real and the concrete; we manipulate the steel and the lead, the wood, oil, and aluminum. What we know is genuine, the real and specific world of daily life. Workers are the wheels that make a society go round, the creators of social value and wealth. There would be no fancy society, no civilized conditions if it were not for our labor.

The male workers are contemptuous of the mild-mannered parasites and soft-spoken vultures who live off our daily sweat: the managers and directors, the judges and entertainers, the lawyers, the coupon clippers, the administrators, the insurance brokers, the legislators . . . all those who profit from the shop floor, who build careers for themselves with the wealth we create. All that social overhead depends upon our mechanical skills, our concrete knowledge, our calloused hands, our technical ingenuity, our strained muscles and backs.

The Dignity of Labor, but society treats us like a pack of dumb animals, mere bodies with no minds or culture. We're physical labor power; the intelligence belongs to the management class. Workers are sneeringly regarded as society's bodies, the middle class as society's mind. One is inferior; the other is superior and fully human. The workers are less than human, close to animals, society's beasts of burden.

The male workplace culture tends to worship this self-identity of vulgar physicalness. It is as if the men enjoy wallowing in a masculine filth. They brag of being the wild men of the factory. Say it loud: I'm a brute and I'm proud.

Sexism thus undermines and subverts the proud tradition of the dignity of labor. It turns a class consciousness upside down by accepting and then glorifying the middle-class view of manual labor and physical activity as inferior, animalistic, and crude. When workers identify with the savages that the bosses see them as, they develop contempt for themselves. It is self-contempt to accept the scornful labels, the negative definitions, the insulting dehumanized treatment, the cartoon stereotypes of class chauvinism: the super-masculine menials, the industrial sweat hogs.

Remember Peter, who couldn't respect a woman who would come to work in this hellhole. It was obviously a place where he felt he had lost his own self-respect. My reply to him was that he shouldn't put up with that rotten treatment, *that the men also deserved better.* We should be treated with dignity. Respect yourself—fight back like a man, not a macho fool who glorifies that which degrades him.

Everything gets turned inside out. It is seen as manly to be treated as less than a man, as just a physical, instinctual creature. But this is precisely how sexist society treats women: as mindless bodies, pieces of flesh . . . "biology is destiny." You would think that male factory workers and the women's movement would be natural allies, that they'd speak the same language. They share a common experience of being used as objects, dehumanized by those on top. Men in the factory are treated not as persons, but as bodies, replaceable numbers, commodities, faceless factors of production. The struggles of working men and of women revolve around similar things. The right to choice on abortion, for example, revolves around the right for women to control their own bodies. Is this not what the fight for health and safety on the shop floor is all about? To have some control over our bodies, not to let the bastards do what they want with our lives and limbs, to wreck us in their search for higher profits.

But male chauvinism turns many working men away from their natural allies, away from a rational and collective solution to their problems, diverting them from class unity with their sisters into oppressors and degraders of their sisters. Robbed of their real manhood—their humanity as men—they get a false sense of manhood by lording over women.

Playing the Foreman at Home

Many men compensate for their wage-labor status in the workplace by becoming the boss at home. Treated terribly in the factory, he plays foreman after work and rules with authority over his wife and kids. He thus gains at home that independence he loses on the shop floor. He becomes a part-time boss himself with women as his servants. This becomes key to his identity and sense of self-esteem. Working-class patriarchs, rulers of the roost.

This sense of authority has an economic underpinning. The male worker's role as primary breadwinner gives him power over the family and status in society. It also makes him the beneficiary of the woman's unpaid labor in the household.

A wage laborer not only lacks independence, he also lacks property, having nothing but his labor power to sell. Sexism gives him the sense of property, as owner of the family. His wife or girlfriend is his sexual property. As Elvis sang, "You are my only possession, you are my everything." This domination and ownership of a woman are basic to how he sees himself.

These things are powerful pressures toward individualism, a trait of the business class: foreman of the family, man of property, possessiveness. They elevate the wage earner above the category of the downtrodden common laborer, and in doing so divert him from the collective struggle with his brothers and sisters to change their conditions. Capitalism is based on competitiveness and encourages everyone to be better than the next guy, to rise up on the backs of your neighbors. Similarly the male chauvinist seeks superiority over others, of both sexes. Men tend to be competitive, always putting one another down, constantly playing one-upmanship. Men even express appreciation and affection for each other through good-natured mutual insults.

Sexist culture thus undermines the working-class traditions of equality and solidarity and provides a recruiting ground for labor's adversaries. Over the years at Westinghouse I had noticed that a high proportion of workers who became foremen were extreme chauvinists—sexual braggarts, degraders of women, aggressive, individualistic, ambitious, ever willing to push other workers around. Male competition is counterproductive in the shop or union, where we ought to cooperate as equals and seek common solutions. The masculine ego makes for bad comradeship, bad brotherhood. It also makes it difficult for chauvinistic men to look at and deal objectively with many situations because their fragile egos are always on the line. They have to keep up a facade of superiority and are unable to handle criticism, no matter how constructive. Their chauvinistic crutches make them subjective, irrational, unreliable, and often self-destructive, as with men who want to work or drive dangerously.

Working men pay a high price for the limited material benefits they get from sexist structures. It is the bosses who make the big bucks and enjoy the real power from the inferior treatment of women.

The Next Round and a Peek into the Women's World

Battles continued about the women getting a crack at the more skilled and high-paying assembly jobs up the floor. Next we won the fight against the company, which was trying to promote junior men. This time women were there to fight for themselves, and there were male stewards from other departments who backed them up. The shop floor was less hostile, many of the men being sympathetic or neutral.

But despite the general cooperation, most men still maintained that the women were inferior workers. The foremen did their best to foster sex divisions by spreading stories of all the mistakes the women supposedly made. They would reserve the worst jobs for the men, telling them the women couldn't do them. The men would thus feel superior while resenting the women's so-called privileges and the women would feel grateful for not having to do these jobs. The supervisors forged a common cause with some of the guys against the women. They fed their male egos and persuaded them to break safety rules, outproduce, and rat on other workers. The male bond often proved stronger than the union bond, and our collective strength suffered as a result.

As for myself, I was learning and changing a lot as a result of my experiences. I would often meet with the women at the lunch table to plan strategy. These sessions affected me in many ways. They were good talks, peaceful and constructive, with no fighting and argument, no competition, all of us talking sensibly about a common problem and figuring out how to handle it as a group. It was a relaxed and peaceful half hour, even when we had serious differences.

This was in marked contrast to the men's lunch tables, which were usually boisterous and raucous during those months. There was a lot of yelling and shouting, mutual insults, fists pounding, and throwing things at one another. When you ate at the women's table, you sat down to rest and relax. When you ate at the men's table, you sat down to fight.

I had read and heard a lot from my feminist friends about this so-called woman's world of warmth, cooperation, and friendship, as contrasted to men's norm of aggression, violence, and competition. Although I had always advocated women's liberation and respected the women's movement, I paid only lip service, if that, to this distinction, and was in fact more often scornful of this "women's world." Over the years I had become a more aggressive male, which I saw as distinct from being a chauvinist or sexist male. In the world of constant struggle, I thought, you had to be aggressive or go under. We'd have peace and love in the socialist future, some distant day.

As a unionist it became very clear to me that the women almost automatically acted like a collective. And in those months of going back and forth between the men's and women's tables, I took a long and serious look at this women's world. It was an unnerving but pleasant experience to sit down among friends, without competition and put-downs, not to have to watch out for flying objects, not to be on the alert for nerve-shattering noises, to be in a non-threatening atmosphere. There was obviously something genuine there and it seemed to offer a better way. It also became obvious to me that the gap between the sexes was enormous and that men and women were far from speaking a common language.

New Struggles and the Recession

In the months ahead there were new struggles. There was the fight to form a women's committee in the union in order to bring women's demands to the fore, to combat sexism among the male workers, and to give women a forum for developing their own outlook, strategy, and leadership. We launched that fight in the fall of 1981, with Mary, a militant woman in our rank-and-file group, in the lead. The old guard, led by the union's national president, fought us tooth and nail. The battle extended over a number of months and tumultuous membership meetings, and we eventually lost as the leadership railroaded through its chauvinistic policy. No women's committee was formed. In time, however, the leadership came to support women's rights formally, even though they did little to advance the cause in practice.

In the spring of 1982 the recession finally caught up with us at Westinghouse and there were continuous layoffs in every division. Our bargaining power shrank, everyone was afraid for his or her own job, and the contract became little more than a piece of paper as the company moved aggressively to roll back the clock on our hard-won traditions on seniority rules, health and safety regulations, and so on. Bitterness and frustration were everywhere.

The company went after the women. Their seniority rights were blatantly ignored as they were transferred to "chip and grind" duties—the least skilled, the heaviest, dirtiest, and most unpleasant jobs. The progress the men had made also seemed to vanish. From the first day of the layoff announcements, many rallied to the call of "Get the women out first." Those most hostile to women came back out in the open and campaigned full blast. They found many sympathetic responses on the shop floor: protect the breadwinners and, what's more, no women should be allowed to bump a male since they're not physically capable of doing the jobs anyway. It was the war of the sexes all over again, but far worse now because the situation allowed little leeway. There was some baiting of the women, and the plant became a tension-ridden, hateful place for all workers.

The bosses managed to seize back many of the powers the shop floor had wrenched away from them over the years, and even to create newer and deeper divisions within the workforce. But the recession was not all-powerful. We still managed to win all our battles on health and safety, and the shop floor continued to elect our militant shop stewards.

Some of the women gave in to the inevitable and were laid off despite their seniority. But others fought back and fought well. Some of them were even able to gain the sympathy of the male workers who had at first stood aside or resisted them. In some cases, the men joined in and helped the women retain their jobs.

Obviously, things had changed a great deal amongst the men since the first women began to come into the division. *When the chips were down, many men took their stand with their sisters against the company—despite the recession. . . .*

Working men share basic common interests with our sisters. When more of us recognize this, define and speak about these interests in our own way, and act in common with women, then we will be able to start moving the mountains that stand in our way.

NOTES

1. United Electrical Workers (UEW) is a union whose militant rhetoric is rarely matched by its actual behavior. For example, it has passed resolutions at its national conventions favoring the formation of women's committees at the national and local levels, but what is on paper often does not match daily reality. Some leaders have a habit of advocating a position that suits the political needs of the moment rather than consistent principles. These limitations are not peculiar to UEW, which is much like the rest of the labor movement, despite its sometimes radical rhetoric. Like most of the labor movement, it has its good and its bad locals, its good and its bad leaders. Like a lot of other unions it has moved toward a better position on "women's" issues, although with a lot of sharp contradictions and see-saws in behavior along the way, given its authoritarian style.
2. The names of the plant workers in this article are not their real ones.

54

THE EFFECTS OF AFFIRMATIVE ACTION ON OTHER STAKEHOLDERS

BARBARA RESKIN

Affirmative action policies and practices reduce job discrimination against minorities and white women, although their effects have not been large. Some critics charge that affirmative action's positive effects have been offset by its negative effects on white men, on productivity, and on the merit system. The research examined in this chapter shows that affirmative action rarely entails reverse discrimination, and neither hampers business productivity nor unduly increases the costs of doing business. Both theoretical and empirical research suggest that it enhances productivity by encouraging employment practices that better utilize workers' skills.

Reverse Discrimination

For many people, the most troubling aspect of affirmative action is that it may discriminate against majority-group members (Lynch 1997). According to 1994 surveys, 70 to 80 percent of whites believed that affirmative action sometimes discriminates against whites (Steeh and Krysan 1996, p. 139). Men are more likely to believe that a woman will get a job or promotion over an equally or more qualified man than they are to believe that a man will get a promotion over an equally or more qualified women (Davis and Smith 1996). In short, many whites, especially white men, feel that they are vulnerable to reverse discrimination (Bobo and Kluegel 1993). When asked whether African Americans or whites were at greater risk of discrimination at work, respondents named whites over African Americans by a margin of two to one (Steeh and Krysan 1996, p. 140). In addition, 39 percent of respondents to a 1997 *New York Times*/CBS News poll said that whites losing out because of affirmative action was a bigger problem than African Americans losing out because of discrimination (Verhovek 1997, p. 32).

Barbara F. Reskin, "The Effects of Affirmative Action on Other Stakeholders" from *The Realities of Affirmative Action in Employment*. Reprinted with the permission of the American Sociological Association.

Several kinds of evidence indicate that whites' fears of reverse discrimination are exaggerated. Reverse discrimination is rare both in absolute terms and relative to conventional discrimination.[1] The most direct evidence for this conclusion comes from employment-audit studies: On every measured outcome, African-American men were much more likely than white men to experience discrimination, and Latinos were more likely than non-Hispanic men to experience discrimination (Heckman and Siegelman 1993, p. 218). Statistics on the numbers and outcomes of complaints of employment discrimination also suggest that reverse discrimination is rare.

According to national surveys, relatively few whites have experienced reverse discrimination. Only 5 to 12 percent of whites believe that their race has cost them a job or promotion, compared to 36 percent of African Americans (Steeh and Krysan 1996, pp. 139–40). Of 4,025 Los Angeles workers, 45 percent of African Americans and 16 percent of Latinos said that they had been refused a job because of their race, and 16 percent of African Americans and 8 percent of Latinos reported that they had been discriminated against in terms of pay or a promotion (Bobo and Suh 1996, table 1). In contrast, of the 863 whites surveyed, less than 3 percent had ever experienced discrimination in pay or promotion, and only one mentioned reverse discrimination. Nonetheless, two-thirds to four-fifths of whites (but just one-quarter of African Americans) surveyed in the 1990s thought it likely that less qualified African Americans won jobs or promotions over more qualified whites (Taylor 1994a; Davis and Smith 1994; Steeh and Krysan 1996, p. 139).[2]

Alfred Blumrosen's (1996, pp. 5–6) exhaustive review of discrimination complaints filed with the Equal Employment Opportunity Commission offers additional evidence that reverse discrimination is rare. Of the 451,442 discrimination complaints filed with the EEOC between 1987 and 1994, only 4 percent charged reverse discrimination (see also Norton 1996, pp. 44–5).[3] Of the 2,189 discrimination cases that Federal appellate courts decided between 1965 and 1985, less than 5 percent charged employers with reverse discrimination (Burstein 1991, p. 518).

Statistics on the more than 3,000 cases that reached district and appeals courts between 1990 and 1994 show an even lower incidence of reverse-discrimination charges: Less than 2 percent charged reverse discrimination (U.S. Department of Labor, Employment Standards Administration n.d., p. 3). The small number of reverse discrimination complaints by white men does not appear to stem from their reluctance to file complaints: They filed more than 80 percent of the age discrimination complaints that the EEOC received in 1994. Instead, as former EEOC chair Eleanor Holmes Norton (1996, p. 45) suggested, white men presumably complain most about the kind of discrimination that they experience most and least about discrimination they rarely encounter.

Allegations of reverse discrimination are less likely than conventional discrimination cases to be supported by evidence. Of the approximately 7,000 reverse-discrimination complaints filed with the EEOC in 1994, the EEOC found only 28 credible (Crosby and Herzberger 1996, p. 55). Indeed, U.S. district and appellate courts dismissed almost all the reverse-discrimination cases they heard between 1990 and 1994 as lacking merit.

Although rare, reverse discrimination does occur. District and appellate courts found seven employers guilty of reverse discrimination in the early 1990s (all involved voluntary affirmative action programs), and a few Federal contractors have engaged in reverse discrimination, according to the Office of Federal Contract Compliance Program's (OFCCP) director for Region II (Stephanopoulos and Edley 1995, section 6.3).[4]

The actions and reports of Federal contractors are inconsistent with the belief that goals are *de facto* quotas that lead inevitably to reverse discrimination. In the first place, the fact that contractors rarely meet their goals means that they do not view them as quotas (Leonard 1990, p. 56). Second, only 2 percent of 641 Federal contractors the OFCCP surveyed in 1994 complained that the agency required quotas or reverse discrimination (Stephanopoulos and Edley 1995, section 6.3).

How can we reconcile the enormous gulf between whites' perceptions that they are likely to lose jobs or promotions because of affirmative action and the small risk of this happening? The white men who brought reverse discrimination suits presumably concluded that their employers' choices of women or minorities could not have been based on merit, because men are accustomed to being selected for customarily male jobs (*New York Times*, March 31, 1995).[5] Most majority-group members who have not had a first-hand experience of competing unsuccessfully with a minority man or woman or a white woman cite media reports as the source of their impression that affirmative action prompts employers to favor minorities and women (Hochschild 1995, pp. 144, 308).[6] It seems likely that politicians' and the media's emphasis on "quotas" has distorted the public's understanding of what is required and permitted in the name of affirmative action (Entman 1997). It is also likely that the public does not distinguish affirmative action in employment from affirmative action in education which may include preferences or in the awarding of contracts which have included set-asides.

Affirmative Action and American Commerce

Does affirmative action curb productivity, as some critics have charged? On the one hand, affirmative action could impede productivity if it forces employers to hire or promote marginally qualified and unqualified workers, or if the paperwork associated with affirmative action programs is burdensome. On the other hand, employers who assign workers to jobs based on their qualifications rather than their sex or race should make more efficient use of workers' abilities and hence should be more productive than those who use discriminatory employment practices (Becker 1971; Leonard 1984c; Donohue 1986). Affirmative action could also increase profitability by introducing varied points of view or helping firms broaden their markets (Cox and Blake 1991; Watson, Kumar, and Michaelsen 1993).

Effects on Productivity

There is no evidence that affirmative action reduces productivity or that workers hired under affirmative action are less qualified than other workers. In the first place, affirmative action plans that compromise valid educational and job requirements are illegal. Hiring unqualified workers or choosing a less qualified person over a more qualified one because of their race or sex is illegal and is not condoned in the name of affirmative action (U.S. Department of Labor, Employment Standards Administration n.d., p. 2). Second, to the extent that affirmative action gives women and minority men access to jobs that more fully exploit their productive capacity, their productivity and that of their employers should increase.

Although many Americans believe that affirmative action means that less qualified persons are hired and promoted (Verhovek 1997, p. 32), the evidence does not bear this out. According to a study of more than 3,000 workers hired in entry-level jobs in a cross-section of firms in Atlanta, Boston, Detroit, and Los Angeles, the performance evaluations of women and minorities hired under affirmative action did not differ from those of white men or female or minority workers for whom affirmative action played no role in hiring (Holzer and Neumark 1998). In addition, Columbus, Ohio, female and minority police officers hired under an affirmative action consent decree performed as well as white men (Kern 1996). Of nearly 300 corporate executives surveyed in 1979, 72 percent believed that minority hiring did not impair productivity (*Wall Street Journal* 1979); 41 percent of CEOs surveyed in 1995 said affirmative action improved corporate productivity (Crosby and Herzberger 1996, p. 86).[7]

Of the handful of studies that address the effect of affirmative action on productivity, none suggests a negative affect of the employment of women or minorities on productivity. First, the increasing representation of female and minority male workers between 1966 and 1977 and between 1984 and 1988 did not affect firms' productivity (Leonard 1984c; Conrad 1995). Second, in the context of policing, the proportions of minority or female officers are unrelated to measures of departments' effectiveness (Lovrich, Steel, and Hood 1986, p. 70; Steel and Lovrich 1987, p. 67). Third, according to a sophisticated analysis of 1990 data on establishments' and workers' characteristics, there is no relationship between firms' employment of women and their productivity in smaller plants, but in plants with more market power (and hence the capacity to discriminate), the more women plants employed, the better the firms' performance (Hellerstein, Neumark, and Troske 1998).

Studies assessing the effect of firms' racial makeup on their profits also show no effects of affirmative action on productivity. An analysis of 100 of Chicago's largest firms over a 13-year period found no statistically significant relationship between the firms' share of minority workers and their profit margins or return on equity (McMillen 1995). This absence of an association is inconsistent with companies using lower standards when hiring African American employees. Finally, according to a study that compared the market performance of the 100 firms with best and worst records of hiring and promoting women and minorities, the former averaged an 18-percent return on investments, whereas the latter's average returns were below 8 percent (Glass Ceiling Commission 1995, pp. 14, 61).[8]

Costs to Business

Estimates of the price tag of affirmative action range from a low of hundreds of millions of dollars to a high of $26 billion (Brimelow and Spencer 1993).[9] More realistic estimates put enforcement and compliance costs at about $1.9 billion (Leonard 1994, p. 34; Conrad 1995, pp. 37–8). According to Andrew Brimmer (1995, p. 12), former Governor of the Federal Reserve Board, the inefficient use of African Americans' productive capacity (as indicated by their education, training, and experience) costs the economy 70 times this much: about $138 billion annually, which is about 2.15 percent of the gross national product. Adding the cost of sex discrimination against white women would substantially increase the estimated cost of discrimination because white women outnumber African American men and women in the labor force by about three to one. The more affirmative action reduces race and sex discrimination, the lower its costs relative to the savings it engenders.

The affirmative action that the Federal executive order requires of Federal contractors adds to their paperwork. Companies with at least $50,000 in Federal contracts that employ at least 50 employees must provide written affirmative action plans that include goals and timetables, based on an annual analysis of their utilization of their labor pool. They must also provide specified information to the OFFCP and keep detailed records on the composition of their jobs and job applicants by race and sex. In response to an OFCCP survey soliciting their criticisms of the program, about one in eight Federal contractors complained about the paperwork burden (Stephanopoulos and Edley 1995, section 6.3). Keeping the records required by the OFCCP encourages the bureaucratization of human resource practices. As noted, informal employment practices, while cheaper in the short run, are also more subject to discriminatory bias and hence cost firms efficiency. Thus, implicit in the logic of the OFCCP's requirements is the recognition that formalizing personnel practices helps to reduce discrimination.

Business Support

U.S. business has supported affirmative action for at least 15 years. The Reagan administration's efforts to curtail the contract compliance program in the early 1980s drew strong opposition from the corporate sector (Bureau of National Affairs 1986). Among the groups that went on record as opposing cutbacks in Federal affirmative action programs was the National Association of Manufacturers, a major organization of U.S. employers (*The San Diego Union-Tribune* 1985, p. AA-2). All but six of 128 heads of major corporations indicated that they would retain their affirmative action plans if the Federal government ended affirmation action (Noble 1986, p. B4). A 1996 survey showed similar levels of corporate support for affirmative action: 94 percent of CEOs surveyed said that affirmative action had improved their hiring procedures, 53 percent said it had improved marketing, and—as noted above—41 percent said it had improved productivity (Crosby and Herzberger 1996, p. 86). The business community's favorable stance toward affirmative action is also seen in the jump in stock prices for firms recognized by the OFCCP for their effective affirmative action programs (Wright et al. 1995, p. 281).

Perhaps the most telling sign of business support for affirmative action is the diffusion of affirmative action practices from Federal contractors to noncontractors. As noncontractors have recognized the efficiency or market payoffs associated with more objective employment practices and a more diverse workforce, many have voluntarily implemented some affirmative action practices (Fisher 1985).

Affirmative Action and Other Stakeholders

The consequences of affirmative action reach beyond workers and employers by increasing the pools of skilled minority and female workers. When affirmative action prompts employers to hire minorities or women for positions that serve the public, it can bring services to communities that would otherwise be underserved. For example, African-American and Hispanic physicians are more likely than whites and Anglos to practice in minority communities (Komaromy et al. 1996). Graduates of the Medical School at the University of California at San Diego who were admitted under a special admissions program were more likely to serve inner-city and rural communities and saw more poor patients than those admitted under the regular procedures (Penn, Russell, and Simon 1986).

Women's and minorities' employment in nontraditional jobs also raises the aspirations of other members of excluded groups by providing role models and by signaling that jobs are open to them. Some minorities and women do not pursue jobs or promotions because they expect to encounter discrimination (Mayhew 1968, p. 313). By reducing the perception that discriminatory barriers block access to certain lines of work, affirmative action curtails this self-selection (Reskin and Roos 1990, p. 305). In addition, the economic gains provided by better jobs permit beneficiaries to invest in the education of the next generation.

Affirmative Action, Meritocracy, and Fairness

Affirmative action troubles some Americans for the same reasons discrimination does: They see it as unfair and inconsistent with meritocracy (Nacoste 1990). The evidence summarized above indicates that employers very rarely use quotas and that affirmative action does not lead to the employment of unqualified workers. We know too that many employers implement affirmative action by expanding their recruiting efforts, by providing additional training, and by formalizing human resource practices to eliminate bias. By eliminating cronyism, drawing on wider talent pools, and providing for due process, these practices are fairer to all workers than conventional business practices (*Harvard Law Review* 1989, pp. 668–70; Dobbin et al. 1993, pp. 401–6). After all, managers who judge minority and female workers by their race or sex instead of their performance may judge white workers by arbitrary standards as well (Rand 1996, p. 72).

Available research does not address how often employers take into account race and gender in choosing among equally qualified applicants. Although the courts have forbidden race- and gender-conscious practices in layoffs, they have allowed employers to take into account race or gender in selecting among qualified applicants in order to remedy the consequences of having previously excluded certain groups from some jobs. Such programs trouble some Americans, as we can see from the research evidence presented in the next section.

Americans' Views of Affirmative Action

The passage of the 1996 California Civil Rights Initiative, which barred this state from engaging in affirmative action, has been interpreted as signaling mounting public opposition to affirmative action. In reality, whites' and African Americans' views of affirmative action are both more nuanced and more positive than the California election result suggests. People's responses to opinion polls depend largely on how pollsters characterize affirmative action (Kravitz et al. 1997).[10] About 70 percent of Americans support affirmative action programs that pollsters describe as not involving "quotas" or "preferences" (Steeh and Krysan 1996, pp. 132, 134; Entman 1997, p. 37). Like a red flag, the term "quota" also triggers strong negative reactions. This happens because people view quotas as inconsistent with merit-based hiring and because quotas provoke fear of unfairly losing a job or promotion by members of groups that are not covered by affirmative action. As a result, most whites and African Americans oppose quotas (Bobo and Kluegel, 1993; Steeh and Krysan 1996, pp. 132–3, 148).

A casual reading of newspaper reports indicates considerable instability in Americans' attitudes toward affirmative action and a fair amount of opposition to affirmative action. For example, fewer than one in eight Americans surveyed in a 1995 Gallup poll approved of affirmative action programs that involve hiring quotas, and only 40 to 50 percent of Americans endorsed affirmative action programs designed to give African Americans or women preferential treatment (Moore 1995). However, polls that show low levels of support for affirmative action in the workplace typically ask about practices that are illegal and hence rare in actual affirmative action programs (Kravitz et al. 1997, p. xi). When pollsters ask about affirmative action in general or about the practices that actual affirmative action programs include, the majority of whites and African Americans are supportive.

In national polls conducted in the mid-1990s, about 70 percent of respondents endorsed affirmative action either as currently practiced or with reforms (Entman 1997, p. 37). For example, almost three-quarters of the respondents to a 1995 Gallup poll approved of employers using outreach efforts to recruit qualified minorities and women (Steeh and Krysan 1996, pp. 132, 134). Most whites and African Americans support such practices as targeted recruitment, open advertising, monitoring diversity, job training, and educational assistance designed to allow minorities to compete as individuals (e.g., training programs). More than three out of four white respondents and 85 percent of African-American respondents to a 1991 Harris survey agreed that "as long as there are no rigid quotas, it makes sense to give special training and advice to women and minorities so that they can perform better on the job" (Bobo and Kluegel 1993; Bruno 1995, p. 24).

We do not know how Americans feel about the kinds of race- or gender-conscious affirmative action that EEOC guidelines and Supreme Court rulings allow. When asked about "preferential hiring," most Americans disapprove. For example, only one-sixth to one-fifth of respondents surveyed during the 1990s favored the preferential hiring and promotion of African Americans because of past discrimination (about 10 to 17 percent of whites and about half to three-quarters of African Americans; Steeh and Krysan 1996, pp. 146–7). Just one survey phrased the question so that it approximately corresponded to what race- and gender-conscious affirmative action entails: giving a preference to a woman or minority over an equally qualified white man. Three-quarters of respondents did not view this practice as discriminatory (Roper Center for Public Opinion 1995).

Overall, the public is less concerned with affirmative action than media accounts would have us believe (Entman 1997). For example, respondents to a 1996 *Wall Street Journal*/NBC News poll ranked affirmative action second to last in importance out of 16 issues.[11] As Robert Entman (1997) argued, the media's framing of affirmative action as controversial exaggerates white opposition to and public discord over it.

In sum, the polls reveal that the majority of whites and African Americans have supported affirmative action since the early 1970s. Most Americans support the affirmative action procedures that employers actually use, such as taking extra efforts to find and recruit minorities and women. The broadest support is for practices that expand the applicant pool, but ignore race or gender in the selection process. Thus, Americans' first choice is enhancing equal opportunity without using race- or gender-conscious mechanisms. What most Americans oppose is quotas, an employment remedy that courts impose only under exceptional circumstances. Thus, the kinds of affirmative action practices most Americans support are in synch with what most affirmative action employers do.

Conclusion

Some critics charge that any positive effects of affirmative action come at too high a price. However, the evidence suggests that the predominant effects of affirmative action on American enterprise are neutral, and some are positive. Contrary to popular opinion, reverse discrimination is rare. Workers for whom affirmative action was a hiring consideration are no less productive than other workers. There is no evidence that affirmative action impairs productivity, and there is some evidence that, when properly implemented, affirmative action increases firms' efficiency by rationalizing their business practices. These neutral to positive effects of affirmative action contribute to the broad support it enjoys in corporate America. The affirmative action practices that appear to be most common—such as special training programs or efforts to expand recruitment pools (Bureau of National Affairs 1986)—have the support of the majority of whites and people of color.

Although most affirmative action practices are neutral with respect to race and gender (e.g., eliminating subjectivity from evaluation systems), some employers take into account race and sex as "plus factors" in choosing among qualified candidates in order to reduce imbalances stemming from their past employment practices. Race- and gender-conscious practices are legal if they are part of court-ordered or voluntary affirmative action programs designed to correct a serious imbalance resulting from past exclusionary practices and as long as they are properly structured so that they do not unnecessarily or permanently limit the opportunities of groups not protected under affirmative action. At least one in four Americans oppose such race- and gender-conscious practices. More generally, any departure from strict reliance on merit troubles some Americans. Others favor taking into account group membership in order to eradicate America's occupational caste system, enhance equal opportunity, and strengthen the U.S. democracy (Steinberg 1995).

The tension between affirmative action and merit is the inevitable result of the conflict between our national values and what actually occurs in the nation's workplaces. As long as discrimination is more pervasive than affirmative action, it is the real threat to meritocracy. But because no one will join the debate on behalf of discrimination, we end up with the illusion of a struggle between affirmative action and merit.

NOTES

1. Lynch's (1989, p. 53) search for white male Southern Californians who saw themselves as victims of reverse discrimination turned up only 32 men.
2. Younger whites, those from more privileged backgrounds, and those from areas with larger black populations—especially black populations who were relatively well off—were most likely to believe that blacks benefited from preferential treatment (Taylor 1994b).

3. Two percent were by white men charging sex, race, or national origin discrimination (three-quarters of these charged sex discrimination), and 1.8 percent were by white women charging race discrimination (Blumrosen 1996, p. 5).
4. In the early years of affirmative action, some federal contractors implemented quotas; since then the OFCCP has made considerable effort to ensure that contractors understand that quotas are illegal.
5. Occupational segregation by sex, race, and ethnicity no doubt contribute to this perception by reinforcing the notion that one's sex, color, or ethnicity is naturally related to the ability to perform a particular job.
6. The disproportionate number of court-ordered interventions to curtail race and sex discrimination in cities' police and fire departments (Martin 1991) and the large number of court challenges by white men (Bureau of National Affairs 1995, pp. 5–12) probably contributed to the public's impression that hiring quotas are common.
7. No data were provided on the proportion who believed that affirmative action hampered productivity.
8. Although firms' stock prices fall after the media report a discrimination suit, they rebound within a few days (Hersch 1991; Wright et al. 1995).
9. The $26 billion estimate includes the budgets of the OFCCP, the EEOC, other federal agencies' affirmative action–related activities, and private firms' compliance costs estimated at $20 million for each million of public funds budgeted for enforcement (Brimelow and Spencer 1993). Arguably, the EEOC's budget—indeed all enforcement costs—should be chalked up to the cost of discrimination, not the cost of affirmative action.
10. Several factors affect Americans' response to surveys about affirmative action in the workplace: whether their employer practices affirmative action (Taylor 1995), their own conception of what affirmative action means (one-third of white respondents to a 1995 CBS/*New York Times* poll acknowledged that they were not sure what affirmative action is; Steeh and Krysan 1996, p. 129), whether the question also asks about affirmative action in education, whether the question asks about race- or sex-based affirmative action (although contractors are also obliged to provide affirmative action for Vietnam-era veterans and disabled persons, these groups are invisible in opinion polls), the respondents' own race and sex, the reasons respondents think racial inequality exists, and their level of racial prejudice (Bobo and Kluegel 1993). For full reviews, see Steeh and Krysan (1996) and Kravitz et al. (1997).
11. Only 1 percent of respondents named affirmative action as the most important problem our country faces (Entman 1997, p. 38).

REFERENCES

Becker, Gary S. 1971. *A Theory of Discrimination.* 2d ed. Chicago, IL: University of Chicago Press.

Blumrosen, Alfred W. 1996. *Declaration.* Statement submitted to the Supreme Court of California in Response to Proposition 209, September 26.

Bobo, Lawrence and James R. Kluegel. 1993. "Opposition to Race Targeting." *American Sociological Review* 58:443–64.

Bobo, Larry and Susan A. Suh. 1996. "Surveying Racial Discrimination: Analyses from a Multi-Ethnic Labor Market." Working Paper No. 75, Russell Sage Foundation, New York.

Brimelow, Peter and Leslie Spencer. 1993. "When Quotas Replace Merit, Everybody Suffers." *Forbes,* February 15, pp. 80–102.

Brimmer, Andrew F. 1995. "The Economic Cost of Discrimination against Black Americans." Pp. 11–29 in *Economic Perspectives on Affirmative Action,* edited by M. C. Simms. Washington, DC: Joint Center for Political and Economic Studies.

Bruno, Andorra. 1995. *Affirmative Action in Employment.* CRS Report for Congress. Washington, DC: Congressional Research Service.

Bureau of National Affairs. 1986. *Affirmative Action Today: A Legal and Political Analysis. A BNA Special Report.* Washington, DC: The Bureau of National Affairs.

———. 1995. *Affirmative Action after Adarand: A Legal, Regulatory, Legislative Outlook.* Washington, DC: The Bureau of National Affairs.

Burstein, Paul. 1991. "'Reverse Discrimination' Cases in the Federal Courts: Mobilization by a Countermovement." *Sociological Quarterly* 32:511–28.

Conrad, Cecilia. 1995. "The Economic Cost of Affirmative Action." Pp. 33–53 in *Economic Perspectives on Affirmative Action,* edited by M. C. Simms. Washington, DC: Joint Center for Political and Economic Studies.

Cox, Taylor H. and Stacy Blake. 1991. "Managing Cultural Diversity: Implications for Organizational Competitiveness." *Academy of Management Executive* 5:45–56.

Crosby, Faye J. and Sharon D. Herzberger. 1996. "For Affirmative Action." Pp. 3–109 in *Affirmative Action: Pros and Cons of Policy and Practice,* edited by R. J. Simon. Washington, DC: American University Press.

Davis, James A. and Tom W. Smith. 1994. *General Social Survey* [MRDF]. Chicago IL: National Opinion Recearch Center [producer, distributor].

———. 1996. *General Social Survey* [MRDF]. Chicago IL: National Opinion Research Center [producer, distributor].

Dobbin, Frank, John Sutton, John Meyer, and W. Richard Scott. 1993. "Equal Opportunity Law and the Construction of Internal Labor Markets." *American Journal of Sociology* 99:396–427.

Donohue, John J. 1986. "Is Title VII Efficient?" *University of Pennsylvania Law Review* 134:1411–31.

Entman, Robert M. 1997. "Manufacturing Discord: Media in the Affirmative Action Debate." *Press/Politics* 2:32–51.

Fisher, Ann B. 1985. "Businessmen Like to Hire by the Numbers." *Fortune Magazine,* September 16, pp. 26, 28–30.

Glass Ceiling Commission. See U.S. Department of Labor, Office of Federal Contract Compliance Programs, Glass Ceiling Commission.

Harvard Law Review. 1989. "Rethinking Weber: The Business Response to Affirmative Action." *Harvard Law Review* 102:658–71.

Heckman, James J. and Peter Siegelman. 1993. "The Urban Institute Audit Studies: Their Methods and Findings." Pp. 187–229 in *Clear and Convincing Evidence: Measurement of Discrimination in America,* edited by M. Fix and R. J. Struyk. Washington, DC: The Urban Institute.

Hellerstein, Judith K., David Neumark, and Kenneth R. Troske. 1998. "Market Forces and Sex Discrimination." Department of Sociology, University of Maryland, College Park. Unpublished manuscript.

Hersch, Joni. 1991. "Equal Employment Opportunity Law and Firm Profitability." *Journal of Human Resources* 26:139–53.

Hochschild, Jennifer. 1995. *Facing Up to the American Dream.* Princeton, NJ: Princeton University Press.

Holzer, Harry J. and David Neumark. Forthcoming 1998. "Are Affirmative Action Hires Less Qualified? Evidence from Employer-Employee Data on New Hires." *Journal of Labor Economics.*

Kern, Leesa. 1996. "Hiring and Seniority: Issues in Policing the Post-Judicial Intervention Period." Department of Sociology, Ohio State University, Columbus, OH: Unpublished manuscript.

Kormaromy, Miriam, Kevin Grumbach, Michael Drake, Karen Vranizan, Nicole Lurie, Dennis Keane, and Andrew Bindman. 1996. "The Role of Black and Hispanic Physicians in Providing Health Care in Underserved Populations." *New England Journal of Medicine* 334:1305–10.

Kravitz, David A., David A. Harrison, Marlene E. Turner, Edward L. Levine, Wanda Chaves, Michael T. Brannick, Donna L. Denning, Craig J. Russell, and Maureen A. Conrad. 1997. *Affirmative Action: A Review of Psychological and Behavioral Research.* Bowling Green, OH: Society for Industrial and Organizational Psychology.

Leonard, Jonathan S. 1984c. "Anti-Discrimination or Reverse Discrimination: The Impact of Changing Demographics, Title VII, and Affirmative Action on Productivity" *Journal of Human Resources* 19:145–74.

———. 1990. "The Impact of Affirmative Action Regulation and Equal Employment Law on Black Employment." *Journal of Economic Perspectives* 4:47–63.

———. 1994. "Use of Enforcement Techniques in Eliminating Glass Ceiling Barriers." Report to the Glass Ceiling Commission, April, U.S. Department of Labor, Washington, DC.

Lovrich, Nicholas P., Brent S. Steel, and David Hood. 1986. "Equity versus Productivity: Affirmative Action and Municipal Police Services." *Public Productivity Review* 39:61–72.

Lynch, Frederick R. 1989. *Invisible Victims: White Males and the Crisis of Affirmative Action.* New York: Greenwood.

———. 1997. *The Diversity Machine: The Drive to Change the White Male Workplace.* New York: Free Press.

Martin, Susan E. 1991. "The Effectiveness of Affirmative Action: The Case of Women in Policing." *Justice Quarterly* 8:489–504.

Mayhew, Leon. 1968. *Law and Equal Opportunity: A Study of Massachusetts Commission against Discrimination.* Cambridge, MA: Harvard University Press.

McMillen, Liz. 1995. "[Affirmative Action] Policies Said to Help Companies Hire Qualified Workers at No Extra Cost." *Chronicle of Higher Education,* November 17, p. A7.

Moore, David W. 1995. "Americans Today Are Dubious about Affirmative Action." *The Gallup Poll Monthly,* March, pp. 36–8.

Nacoste, Rupert Barnes. 1990. "Sources of Stigma: Analyzing the Psychology of Affirmative Action." *Law & Policy* 12:175–95.

New York Times. 1995. "Reverse Discrimination Complaints Rare, Labor Study Reports." *New York Times,* March 31, p. A23.

Noble, Kenneth. 1986. "Employers Are Split on Affirmative Goals." *New York Times,* March 3, p. B4.

Norton, Elenor Holmes. 1996. "Affirmative Action in the Workplace." Pp. 39–48 in *The Affirmative Action Debate,* edited by G. Curry. Reading, MA: Addison-Wesley.

Penn, Nolan E., Percy J. Russell, and Harold J. Simon. 1986. "Affirmative Action at Work: A Survey of Graduates of the University of California at San Deigo Medical School." *American Journal of Public Health* 76:1144–46.

Rand, A. Barry. 1996. "Diversity in Corporate America." Pp. 65–76 in *The Affirmative Action Debate,* edited by G. Curry. Reading, MA: Addison-Wesley.

Reskin, Barbara F. and Patricia Roos. 1990. *Job Queues, Gender Queues.* Philadelphia, PA: Temple University Press.

Roper Center for Public Opinion. 1995. *Poll Database:* Question ID USGALLUP.95MRW1.R32[MRDF]. Storrs, Ct: Roper Center for Public Opinion [producer, distributor].

San Diego Union-Tribune. 1985. "Groups at Odds Over Affirmative Action Revisions." *San Diego Union-Tribune,* September 13, p. AA-2.

Steeh, Charlotte, and Maria Krysan. 1996. "The Polls—Trends: Affirmative Action and the Public, 1970–1995." *Public Opinion Quarterly* 60:128–58.

Steel, Brent S. and Nicholas P. Lovrich. 1987. "Equality and Efficiency Tradeoffs in Affirmative Action—Real or Imagined? The Case of Women in Policing." *Social Science Journal* 24:53–70.

Steinberg, Steven. 1995. *Turning Back: Retreat from Racial Justice in American Thought.* Boston, MA: Beacon.

Stephanopoulos, George and Christopher Edley, Jr. 1995. "Affirmative Action Review." *Report to the President,* Washington, DC.
Taylor, Marylee C. 1994a. "Beliefs about the Preferential Hiring of Black Applicants: Sure It Happens, But I've Never Seen It." Pennsylvania State University, University Park, PA. Unpublished manuscript.
———. 1994b. "Impact of Affirmative Action on Beneficiary Groups: Evidence from the 1990 General Social Survey." *Basic and Applied Social Psychology* 15:143–78.
———. 1995. "White Backlash to Workplace Affirmative Action: Peril or Myth?" *Social Forces* 73:1385–1414.
U.S. Department of Labor, Employment Standards Administration, Office of Federal Contract Compliance Programs [cited as OFCCP]. n.d. "The Rhetoric and the Reality about Federal Affirmative Action at the OFCCP." Washington, DC: U.S. Department of Labor.
U.S. Department of Labor, Office of Federal Contract Compliance Programs, Glass Ceiling Commission. 1995. *Good for Business: Making Full Use of the Nation's Human Capital/The Environmental Scar.* Washington, DC: U.S. Government Printing Office.
Verhovek, Sam Howe. 1997. "In Poll, Americans Reject Means but Not Ends of Racial Diversity." *New York Times,* December 14, pp. 1, 32.
Wall Street Journal. 1979. "Labor Letter: A Special News Report on People and Their Jobs in Offices, Fields, and Factories: Affirmative Action Is Accepted by Most Corporate Chiefs." *Wall Street Journal,* April 3, p. 1.
Watson, Warren E., Kamalesh Kumar, and Larry K. Michaelsen. 1993. "Cultural Diversity's Impact on Interaction Process and Performance: Comparing Homogeneous and Diverse Task Groups." *Academy of Management Journal* 36:590–602.
Wright, Peter, Stephen P. Ferris, Janine S. Hiller, and Mark Kroll. 1995. "Competitiveness through Management of Diversity: Effects on Stock Price Valuation." *Academy of Management Journal* 38:272–87.

55

THE GLOBETROTTING SNEAKER

CYNTHIA ENLOE

Four years after the fall of the Berlin Wall marked the end of the Cold War, Reebok, one of the fastest-growing companies in United States history, decided that the time had come to make its mark in Russia. Thus it was with considerable fanfare that Reebok's executives opened their first store in downtown Moscow in July 1993. A week after the grand opening, store managers described sales as well above expectations.

Cynthia Enloe, "The Globetrotting Sneaker" from *Ms.* (September/October 1995) and "Sneak Attack" from *Ms.* (December 2001). Both reprinted with the permission of the publisher.

Author's Note: This article draws from the work of South Korean scholars Hyun Sook Kim, Seung-kyung Kim, Katherine Moon, Seungsook Moon, and Jeong-Lim Nam.

Reebok's opening in Moscow was the perfect post-Cold War scenario: commercial rivalry replacing military posturing; consumerist tastes homogenizing heretofore hostile peoples; capital and managerial expertise flowing freely across newly porous state borders. Russians suddenly had the "freedom"to spend money on U.S. cultural icons like athletic footwear, items priced above and beyond daily subsistence: at the end of 1993, the average Russian earned the equivalent of $40 a month. Shoes on display were in the $100 range. Almost 60 percent of single parents, most of whom were women, were living in poverty. Yet in Moscow and Kiev, shoe promoters had begun targeting children, persuading them to pressure their mothers to spend money on stylish, Western sneakers. And as far as strategy goes, athletic shoe giants have, you might say, a good track record. In the U.S. many inner-city boys who see basketball as a "ticket out of the ghetto" have become convinced that certain brand-name shoes will give them an edge.

But no matter where sneakers are bought or sold, the potency of their advertising imagery has made it easy to ignore this mundane fact: Shaquille O'Neal's Reeboks are stitched by someone; Michael Jordan's Nikes are stitched by someone; so are your roommate's, so are your grandmother's. Those someones are women, mostly Asian women who are supposed to believe that their "opportunity" to make sneakers for U.S. companies is a sign of their country's progress—just as a Russian woman's chance to spend two months' salary on a pair of shoes for her child allegedly symbolizes the new Russia.

As the global economy expands, sneaker executives are looking to pay women workers less and less, even though the shoes that they produce are capturing an ever-growing share of the footwear market. By the end of 1993, sales in the U.S. alone had reached $11.6 billion. Nike, the largest supplier of athletic footwear in the world, posted a record $298 million profit for 1993—earnings that had nearly tripled in five years. And sneaker companies continue to refine their strategies for "global competitiveness"—hiring supposedly docile women to make their shoes, changing designs as quickly as we fickle customers change our tastes, and shifting factories from country to country as trade barriers rise and fall.

The logic of it all is really quite simple; yet trade agreements such as the North American Free Trade Agreement (NAFTA) and the General Agreement of Tariffs and Trade (GATT) are, of course, talked about in a jargon that alienates us, as if they were technical matters fit only for economists and diplomats. The bottom line is that all companies operating overseas depend on trade agreements made between their own governments and the regimes ruling the countries in which they want to make or sell their products. Korean, Indonesian, and other women workers around the world know this better than anyone. They are tackling trade politics because they have learned from hard experience that the trade deals their governments sign do little to improve the lives of workers. Guarantees of fair, healthy labor practices, of the rights to speak freely and to organize independently, will usu-

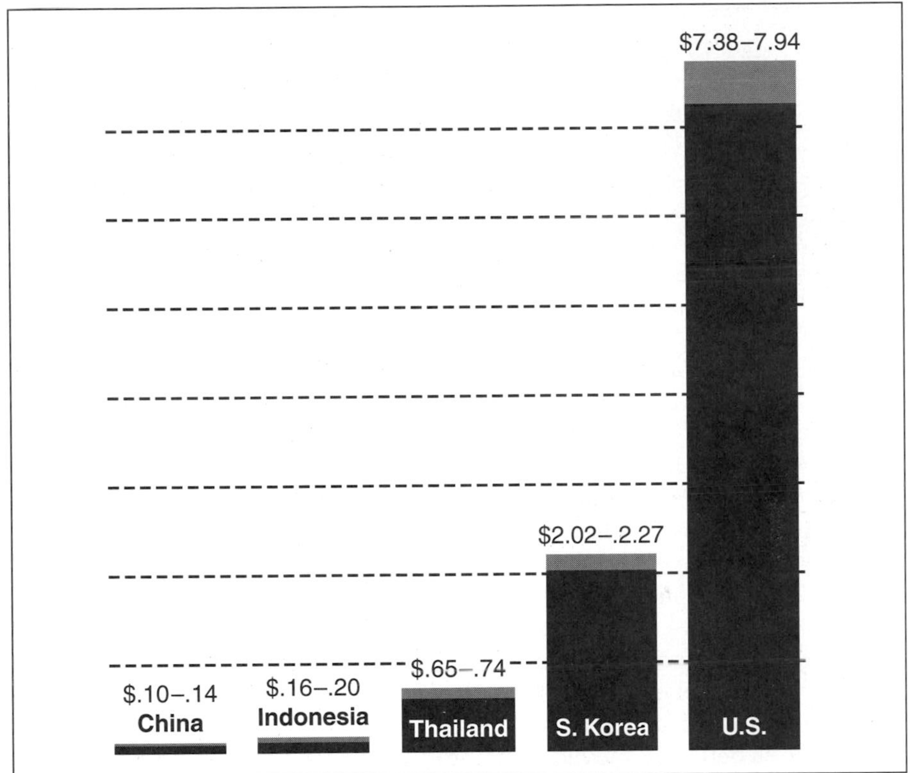

FIGURE 1 Hourly Wages in Athletic Footwear Factories

ally be left out of trade pacts—and women will suffer. The recent passage of both NAFTA and GATT ensures that a growing number of private companies will now be competing across borders without restriction. The result? Big business will step up efforts to pit working women in industrialized countries against much lower-paid working women in "developing" countries, perpetuating the misleading notion that they are inevitable rivals in the global job market.

All the "New World Order" really means to corporate giants like athletic shoemakers is that they now have the green light to accelerate long-standing industry practices. In the early 1980s, the field marshals commanding Reebok and Nike, which are both U.S.-based, decided to manufacture most of their sneakers in South Korea and Taiwan, hiring local women. L.A. Gear, Adidas, Fila, and Asics quickly followed their lead. In short time, the coastal city of Pusan, South Korea, became the "sneaker capital of the world." Between 1982 and 1989 the U.S. lost 58,500 footwear jobs to cities like Pusan, which attracted sneaker executives because its location facilitated international transport. More to the point, South Korea's military government had

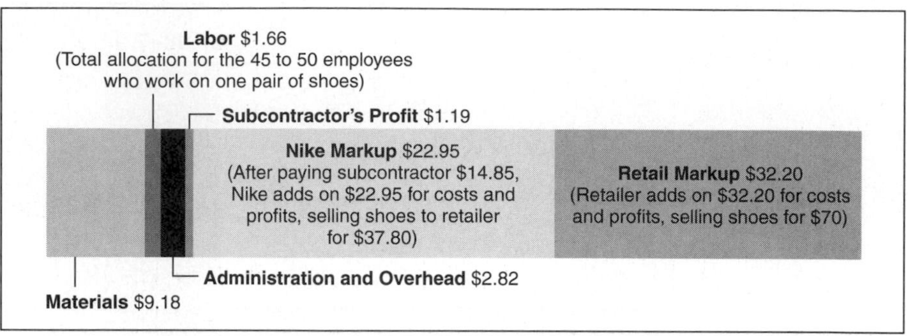

FIGURE 2 A $70 Pair of Nike Pegasus: Where the Money Goes

an interest in suppressing labor organizing, and it had a comfortable military alliance with the U.S. Korean women also seemed accepting of Confucian philosophy, which measured a women's morality by her willingness to work hard for her family's well-being and to acquiesce to her father's and husband's dictates. With their sense of patriotic duty, Korean women seemed the ideal labor force for export-oriented factories.

U.S. and European sneaker company executives were also attracted by the ready supply of eager Korean male entrepreneurs with whom they could make profitable arrangements. This fact was central to Nike's strategy in particular. When they moved their production sites to Asia to lower labor costs, the executives of the Oregon-based company decided to reduce their corporate responsibilities further. Instead of owning factories outright, a more efficient strategy would be to subcontract the manufacturing to wholly foreign-owned—in this case, South Korean—companies. Let them be responsible for workers' health and safety. Let them negotiate with newly emergent unions. Nike would retain control over those parts of sneaker production that gave its officials the greatest professional satisfaction and the ultimate word on the product: design and marketing. Although Nike was following in the footsteps of garment and textile manufacturers, it set the trend for the rest of the athletic footwear industry.

But at the same time, women workers were developing their own strategies. As the South Korean pro-democracy movement grew throughout the 1980s, increasing numbers of women rejected traditional notions of feminine duty. Women began organizing in response to the dangerous working conditions, daily humiliations, and low pay built into their work. Such resistance was profoundly threatening to the government, given the fact that South Korea's emergence as an industrialized "tiger" had depended on women accepting their "role" in growing industries like sneaker manufacture. If women reimagined their lives as daughters, as wives, as workers, as citizens, it wouldn't just rattle their employers; it would shake the very foundations of the whole political system.

At the first sign of trouble, factory managers called in government riot police to break up employees' meetings. Troops sexually assaulted women workers, stripping, fondling, and raping them "as a control mechanism for suppressing women's engagement in the labor movement," reported Jeong-Lim Nam of Hyosung Women's University in Taegu. It didn't work. It didn't work because the feminist activists in groups like the Korean Women Workers Association (KWWA) helped women understand and deal with the assaults. The KWWA held consciousness-raising sessions in which notions of feminine duty and respectability were tackled along with wages and benefits. They organized independently of the male-led labor unions to ensure that their issues would be taken seriously, in labor negotiations and in the pro-democracy movement as a whole.

The result was that women were at meetings with management, making sure that in addition to issues like long hours and low pay, sexual assault at the hands of managers and health care were on the table. Their activism paid off: in addition to winning the right to organize women's unions, their earnings grew. In 1980, South Korean women in manufacturing jobs earned 45 percent of the wages of their male counterparts; by 1990, they were earning more than 50 percent. Modest though it was, the pay increase was concrete progress, given that the gap between women's and men's manufacturing wages in Japan, Singapore, and Sri Lanka actually widened during the 1980s. Last, but certainly not least, women's organizing was credited with playing a major role in toppling the country's military regime and forcing open elections in 1987.

Without that special kind of workplace control that only an authoritarian government could offer, sneaker executives knew that it was time to move. In Nike's case, its famous advertising slogan—"Just Do It"—proved truer to its corporate philosophy than its women's "empowerment" ad campaign, designed to rally women's athletic (and consumer) spirit. In response to South Korean women workers' newfound activist self-confidence, the sneaker company and its subcontractors began shutting down a number of their South Korean factories in the late 1980s and early 1990s. After bargaining with government officials in nearby China and Indonesia, many Nike subcontractors set up shop in those countries, while some went to Thailand. China's government remains nominally Communist; Indonesia's ruling generals are staunchly anti-Communist. But both are governed by authoritarian regimes who share the belief that if women can be kept hard at work, low paid, and unorganized, they can serve as a magnet for foreign investors.

Where does all this leave South Korean women—or any woman who is threatened with a factory closure if she demands decent working conditions and a fair wage? They face the dilemma confronted by thousands of women from dozens of countries. The risk of job loss is especially acute in relatively mobile industries; it's easier for a sneaker, garment, or electronics manufacturer to pick up and move than it is for an automaker or a steel producer. In the case of South Korea, poor women had moved from rural villages into the cities searching for jobs to support not only themselves, but parents and siblings. The exodus of manufacturing jobs has forced more women into the growing "entertainment" industry. The kinds of bars and massage parlors offering sexual services that had mushroomed around U.S. military bases during the Cold War have been opening up across the country.

But the reality is that women throughout Asia are organizing, knowing full well the risks involved. Theirs is a long-term view; they are taking direct aim at companies' nomadic advantage, by building links among workers in countries targeted for "development" by multinational corporations. Through sustained grassroots efforts, women are developing the skills and confidence that will make it increasingly difficult to keep their labor cheap. Many are looking to the United Nations conference on women in Beijing, China, this September [1995], as a rare opportunity to expand their cross-border strategizing.

The Beijing conference will also provide an important opportunity to call world attention to the hypocrisy of the governments and corporations doing business in China. Numerous athletic shoe companies followed Nike in setting up manufacturing sites throughout the country. This included Reebok—a company claiming its share of responsibility for ridding the world of "injustice, poverty, and other ills that gnaw away at the social fabric," according to a statement of corporate principles.

Since 1988, Reebok has been giving out annual human rights awards to dissidents from around the world. But it wasn't until 1992 that the company adopted its own "human rights production standards"—after labor advocates made it known that the quality of life in factories run by its subcontractors was just as dismal as that at most other athletic shoe suppliers in Asia. Reebok's code of conduct, for example, includes a pledge to "seek" those subcontractors who respect workers' rights to organize. The only problem is that independent trade unions are banned in China. Reebok has chosen to ignore that fact, even though Chinese dissidents have been the recipients of the company's own human rights award. As for working conditions, Reebok now says it sends its own inspectors to production sites a couple of times a year. But they have easily "missed" what subcontractors are trying to hide—like 400 young women workers locked at night into an overcrowded dormitory near a Reebok-contracted factory in the town of Zhuhai, as reported last August in the *Asian Wall Street Journal Weekly.*

Nike's cofounder and CEO Philip Knight has said that he would like the world to think of Nike as "a company with a soul that recognizes the value of human beings." Nike, like Reebok, says it sends in inspectors from time to time to check up on work conditions at its factories; in Indonesia, those factories are run largely by South Korean subcontractors. But according to Donald Katz in a recent book on the company, Nike spokesman Dave Taylor told an in-house newsletter that the factories are "[the subcontractors'] business to run." For the most part, the company relies on regular reports from subcontractors regarding its "Memorandum of Understanding," which managers must sign, promising to impose "local government standards" for wages, working conditions, treatment of workers, and benefits.

In April, the minimum wage in the Indonesian capital of Jakarta will be $1.89 *a day*—among the highest in a country where the minimum wage varies by region. And managers are required to pay only 75 percent of the wage directly; the remainder can be withheld for "benefits." By now, Nike has a well-honed response to growing criticisms of its low-cost labor strategy. Such wages should not be seen as exploitative, says Nike, but rather as the first rung on the ladder of economic opportunity that Nike has extended to workers with few options. Otherwise, they'd be out "harvesting coconut meat in the tropical sun," wrote Nike spokesman Dusty Kidd, in a letter to the *Utne Reader.* The all-is-relative response craftily shifts attention away from reality: Nike didn't move to Indonesia to help Indonesians; it moved to ensure that its profit margin continues to grow.And that is pretty much guaranteed in a country where "local standards" for wages rarely take a worker over the poverty line. A 1991 survey by the International Labor Organization (ILO) found that 88 percent of women working at the Jakarta minimum wage at the time—slightly less than a dollar a day—were malnourished.

A woman named Riyanti might have been among the workers surveyed by the ILO. Interviewed by the *Boston Globe* in 1991, she told the reporter who had asked about her long hours and low pay: "I'm happy working here. . . . I can make money and I can make friends." But in fact, the reporter discovered that Riyanti had already joined her coworkers in two strikes, the first to force one of Nike's Korean subcontractors to accept a new women's union and the second to compel managers to pay at least the minimum wage. That Riyanti appeared less than forthcoming about her activities isn't surprising. Many Indonesian factories have military men posted in their front offices who find no fault with managers who tape women's mouths shut to keep them from talking among themselves. They and their superiors have a political reach that extends far beyond the barracks. Indonesia has all the makings for a political explosion, especially since the gap between rich and poor is widening into a chasm. It is in this setting that the government has tried to crack down on any independent labor organizing—a policy that Nike has helped to implement. Referring to a recent strike in a Nike-contracted factory, Tony Nava, Nike representative in Indonesia, told the *Chicago Tribune* in November 1994 that the "troublemakers" had been fired. When asked about Nike policy on the issue, spokesman Keith Peters struck a conciliatory note: "If the government were to allow and encourage independent labor organizing, we would be happy to support it."

Indonesian workers' efforts to create unions independent of governmental control were a surprise to shoe companies. Although their moves from South Korea have been immensely profitable [see chart], they do not have the sort of immunity from activism that they had expected. In May 1993, the murder of a female activist outside Surabaya set off a storm of local and international protest. Even the U.S. State Department was forced to take note in its 1993 worldwide human rights report, describing a system similar to that which generated South Korea's boom 20 years earlier: severely restricted union organizing, security forces used to break up strikes, low wages for men, lower wages for women—complete with government rhetoric celebrating women's contribution to national development.

Yet when President Clinton visited Indonesia last November, he made only a token effort to address the country's human rights problem. Instead, he touted the benefits of free trade, sounding indeed more enlightened, more in tune with the spirit of the post–Cold War era than do those defenders of protectionist trading policies who coat their rhetoric with "America first" chauvinism. But "free trade" as actually being practiced today is hardly *free* for any workers—in the U.S. or abroad—who have to accept the Indonesian, Chinese, or Korean workplace model as the price of keeping their jobs.

The not-so-new plot of the international trade story has been "divide and rule." If women workers and their government in one country can see that a sneaker company will pick up and leave if their labor demands prove more costly than those in a neighbor country, then women workers will tend to see their neighbors not as regional sisters, but as competitors who can steal their precarious livelihoods. Playing women off against each other is, of course, old hat. Yet it is as essential to international trade politics as is the fine print in GATT.

But women workers allied through the networks like the Hong Kong–based Committee for Asian Women are developing their own post–Cold War foreign policy, which means addressing women's needs: how to convince fathers and husbands that a woman going out to organizing meetings at night is not sexually promiscuous; how to develop workplace agendas that respond to family needs; how to work with male unionists who push women's demands to the bottom of their lists; how to build a global movement.

These women refuse to stand in awe of the corporate power of the Nike or Reebok or Adidas executive. Growing numbers of Asian women today have concluded that trade politics have to be understood by women on their own terms. They will be coming to Beijing this September [1995] ready to engage with women from other regions to link the politics of consumerism with the politics of manufacturing. If women in Russia and Eastern Europe can challenge Americanized consumerism, if Asian activists can solidify their alliances, and if U.S. women can join with them by taking on trade politics—the post–Cold War sneaker may be a less comfortable fit in the 1990s.

PART IX
Violence

. . . two Asian women were gang raped by fraternity brothers in two separate incidents. One of the rapes was part of a racially targeted game called the "Ethnic Sex Challenge," in which the fraternity men followed an ethnic checklist indicating what kind of women to gang rape.

HELEN ZIA[1]

As an American, a woman, a feminist, and a Jew, I have to recognize that the Bin Ladens of the world hate me and would like me dead; if they had power over me, they would make my life a living hell.

ROSALIND P. PETCHESKY[2]

Violence and abuse pervade U.S. society and put millions of people at risk for direct or indirect attack. When we combine the numbers of people who have been victims of violence with those whose loved ones have been victims and those who fear victimization, nearly everyone in this society is touched by violence. Add to that the attacks on the United States on September 11, 2001, and the anthrax dispersion that followed, and we have a society infused with real or potential terror. However, as with the other issues addressed in this book, people's position in the matrix of domination and privilege affects their experiences.

A recent survey in Asian American communities suggests that domestic abuse is a major problem, with 69 percent of respondents reporting being hit by their parents while growing up and many people believing that divorce is not an option even in violent marriages. A code of silence seems to prevail about the violence.[3] A study of poor and working-class white women found that 92 percent had experiences with childhood and/or adult abuse and most told no one, again controlled by a code of silence. In the latter study, 68 percent of African American women reported domestic violence but were much more likely to have taken action in response to it by telling someone, finding alternate shelter, or getting the abuser out of the home.[4]

Although some people attempted to deny the reality of violence in the United States prior to September 11, 2001, it had become increasingly difficult to do so in the face of the many mass shootings in schools by white boys; whatever sense of safety that existed in suburban and rural areas has been shaken. And in all communities, many children are terrorized by adults, often by their parents or other family members, sometimes by pedophiles and kidnappers outside their families. Women are physically and sexually attacked and terrorized in many social contexts, especially in their own homes, primarily by men. Boys and men are frequently attacked and terrorized by each other, starting with school-yard fights, and continuing in violent sports, military training, street violence, gangs, war, and physically dangerous jobs. People and communities of color, Jewish communities, gay men, lesbians, bisexuals, and transgendered people are often victims of hate crimes.[5] Institutions and the people within them are increasingly becoming victims of terrorism, as evidenced by attacks on abortion clinics (including years of anthrax threats), on doctors who perform abortions, and on government institutions such as in the case of the 1995 Oklahoma City bombing, and, of course, by the events of September 11.[6] Worldwide, women's low status correlates with high rates of rape, abuse, discrimination, death in childbirth, sexual slavery, sexually transmitted diseases, infanticide, and genital mutilation, all in a context of inadequate legal protection.[7] An estimated two out of five women in the United States will be physically or sexually assaulted in their lifetimes.[8]

Based on an analysis of the 1991 Federal Government's Uniform Crime Reports, attorney Sherri L. Schornstein reports that women are 10 times more likely than men to become victimized by intimates. Men, on the other hand, are much more likely to be victimized by someone outside their families, with only 5 percent of violent victimizations against men caused by family members. She reminds us of former Surgeon General C. Everett Koop's conclusion that domestic violence in the 1980s was the most serious health risk facing women, causing more injuries to women than car accidents, muggings, and rapes combined.[9] The crucial role of judges in granting restraining orders and helping to protect battered women is being examined, with the goal of making the judicial process more accountable to battered women.[10]

The daily crime reports in all urban areas and many suburban and rural ones suggest a country at war with itself. Many urban children are growing up in war zones, caught in the emotional and literal cross fire between warring teenagers and adults; many will, unfortunately, be pressed into gangs as their only option for a sense of meaning in life and into violence as their only means of self-defense.[11] Ironically, while gender socialization teaches women to fear violence and be vulnerable and teaches men to not fear it and be strong, men are at higher risk for every type of violence except sexual assault. Simultaneously, women are taught to fear attacks by strangers but, in fact, are much more likely to be attacked by people they know.[12] Children, too, taught to fear strangers, are most likely to be sexually assaulted by a relative or an acquaintance such as a teacher.[13] Recent outrage at the extent to which the Boston Archdiocese protected pedophile priests at children's expense may actually lead to some constructive changes as Massachusetts considers requiring clergy to become mandatory reporters of child abuse and as the Catholic Church is pressed to play a proactive role in sexual abuse prevention within its ranks.[14]

Although the rate of violent crime has gone down to some extent or stayed stable in recent years,[15] the rate of prison construction and imprisonment has gone up significantly, leading to what is now referred to as the prison-industrial complex in the United States. The United States now has the highest incarceration rate in the world.[16] Critics of this system focus especially on the physical, emotional, and sexual abuse that inmates, both men and women, experience, and on the reality that prison is more apt to punish than "correct" in spite of the alleged philosophy of many departments of correction. Some critics also raise questions about why so many prisons are being built, suggesting that there are economic rather than correctional reasons behind the prison boom (e.g., creation of jobs).[17] The fact that community-based programs for male batterers are more effective than criminal justice interventions (lowering the incidence of violent incidents and controlling behaviors) suggests that more such alternative programs might make more sense than construction of new prisons.[18] A recent study of women of color and law enforcement finds that the growth of law enforcement (including activity of the Immigration and Naturalization Service) has disproportionately affected women of color, leading to increased incarceration and detainment, abuse within these settings, and denial of reproductive and sexual autonomy. According to the study, between 1985 and 1996 the number of women of color imprisoned tripled and that of women detained by the INS doubled. The two fastest growing inmate populations are U.S.-born women of color and immigrants of color.[19]

A movement toward a new system of justice, called restorative justice, is gaining ground as people in various places in the judicial system along with community activists attempt to move toward community solutions to crime rather than punitive ones. With the goals of holding offenders accountable and also integrating them into the community rather than sending them to prison, meetings occur between offenders and their victims in an effort to educate offenders and provide an opportunity for them to "make things right" with the support of community members. The needs of people on both sides of the offense are addressed.[20]

The recent study of trauma has shed much light on violence and its effects on victims. Focusing on victims of war, torture, rape, incest, domestic violence, and other horrors, psychiatrist Judith Lewis Herman describes the dynamics of abuse and identifies symptoms experienced by survivors, including posttraumatic stress, addictions, suicidal feelings, suicide attempts, and general life upheaval.[21] The rates of violence against women, for example, are even more upsetting when we consider the devastating pain, loss of time, and loss of quality of life that results from such violence. Most women who have been raped, for example, take at least a few months or, more frequently, several years to recover.[22] Thousands of veterans of the Vietnam and other wars have not been able to get their lives together since their war experience. When I think about the profound waste of human potential and life due to violence, I often wonder how different the world would be without it. And it is not just the victims who suffer; their families and friends, as well as the families of the perpetrators of violence, are forced to turn their attention to violence rather than to more productive concerns. An estimated 325,000 children in the United States are sexually abused each year, and hundreds of thousands are involved as sex workers worldwide. These children are frequently left with permanent scars.[23]

Many institutions are blamed for violence against women. They include the system of gender inequality that creates an image of women as inferior objects worthy of disrespect; pornography, which sexualizes women's inferior status and presents women as fair game for sexual abuse; privacy, since it encourages a lot of violence to remain behind closed doors; women's unemployment and poverty, which keeps women from leaving abusive men; and men's participation in sports.[24] The latter is a growing problem, according to writer Jeff Benedict, former director of research for the Center for the Study of Sport in Society. In his study of both publicized and unpublicized cases of violence against women by college and professional athletes, he concludes that athletes commit more violence against women than their numbers would predict and expresses dismay at the fact that so many athlete role models are setting a poor example for boys and young men.[25]

The case of the gang rape of a retarded girl by a group of high school athletes in Glen Ridge, New Jersey, led writer Bernard Lefkowitz to conclude that the rape might only have been prevented if the community had taken a close look at what it was modeling for its children:

> Adults might have forstalled the unfolding tragedy in their town if they had questioned their own values, if they had challenged the assumptions of the culture that defined how people treated one another in Glen Ridge. . . . What happened to Leslie Faber is important because it reveals the extreme outcome of the behavior of young men who are made to feel omnipotent. If a culture is measured by how it treats its weakest members, the Glen Ridge case, first to last, revealed American culture at its basest.[26]

Another important theme to mention here is the high rate of civilian violence that men perpetrate against each other, particularly in prisons, in street warfare—gangs, etc.—and in other masculine institutions that involve initiations and hazing such as fraternities and sports. Violence against gay men and transgendered people by (presumably heterosexual) men, as in the recent murders of Matthew Shepard and Navajo gay/two-spirit teen Fred C. Martinez, is another aspect of men's violence against men, representing extreme and tragic examples of Kimmel's hypothesis that masculinity is essentially about homophobia (Part II).[27]

Finally, there is a growing literature on women's roles as perpetrators of violence, surrounded by much debate over many aspects of this issue. Researchers and activists are concerned with how to compute valid rates of female violence, how to understand the causes of violence, how to measure its effects in terms of harm and death, and the need to examine the purpose of the violence (e.g., women tend to use violence to stop or attempt to stop a violent event or relationship, whereas men tend to use violence as a means of control). Included in such discussions is the tendency for women to be more likely than men to admit to having used force against another person, therefore skewing the data.[28]

Prevention of violence is a central aspect of studies of violence at all levels (interpersonal, intergroup, and international). A "culture of peace" perspective on violence explores new ways of approaching violence prevention, and an examination of causes of male violence is a central aspect of this work.[29] Attention to men and boys as victims of violence, as mentioned in the introduction to this text, has received increasing attention, including within the culture of peace framework. Thus, in a Norwegian study that attempted to explain men's violence against women, Holter found that the predictors of male violence against women related not so much to their relationships with women or to masculine identity but to their relationships to men. They were more likely to be aggressive toward women if they had been bullied, especially in childhood or youth by boys or men or if they had experienced violence in the family of origin, particularly from their fathers. Holter also found that when men engage in care work (child care, etc.) they are more likely to have a positive attitude toward it and to be less violent. Men in Norway have the option of a month of paid paternity leave and most take it.[30]

The education and nurturance of boys and young men is a primary approach to violence prevention. The goals include helping boys to recognize their needs, learn alternatives to violence, and develop caring relationships with people of both sexes. The Oakland Men's Project in California has run anti-violence workshops for boys and men around the United States (see Robert Allen in Part XI). The Canadian White Ribbon Campaign to end violence against women has sponsored workshops in schools, corporations, and trade unions across Canada.[31] Women in many parts of the world are actively engaged in peace efforts as they attempt to end war in Bosnia, Northern Ireland, and Israel/Palestine. In these situations, women from different sides of the conflicts have come together to work toward peace (see Gila Svirsky, Part XI).[32]

This part of this book addresses everyday violence in a range of contexts as well as the events of September 11. Self-defense for women (Melanie Kaye/Kantrowitz), a portrait of a school killer (Jonah Blank), trafficking in women (Jan Goodwin), racism and hate crimes (Helen Zia), and rape of men in prison (Terry Kupers) provide a look at some of the ways that women and men are victims of violence on an ongoing basis. Following these essays are several pieces related to the attacks on September 11, including an overview of issues involved (Rosalind Petchesky), a look at recent history in Afghanistan (Rina Amiri), gender and militarization (Cynthia Enloe), and a perspective on safety in the United States (Desiree Taylor).

NOTES

1. Helen Zia, "Where Race and Gender Meet: Racism, Hate Crimes and Pornography," in Laura Lederer and Richard Delgado, eds., *The Price We Pay: The Case Against Racist Speech, Hate Propaganda, and Pornography* (New York: Hill & Wang, 1995), p. 234.

2. Rosalind P. Petchesky, "Phantom Towers: Feminist Reflections on the Battle between Global Capitalism and Fundamentalist Terrorism," *The Women's Review of Books* XIX, no. 2 (November 2001), p. 3.
3. "Asian Family Violence Report Calls for Action," *New Moon: The Newsletter of the Asian Task Force against Domestic Violence,* 11, no. 2 (2000), pp. 1, 3–5; "Asian Family Violence Report," www.atask.org.
4. Michelle Fine and Lois Weis, "Disappearing Acts: The State and Violence against Women in the Twentieth Century," *Signs* 25, no. 4 (Summer 2000), pp. 1139 ff.
5. "Bias Incidents Reported During 1994," *Klanwatch Intelligence Report* 77 (March 1995), pp. 14 ff.
6. For articles on clinic violence and the ongoing commitment to providing abortion to women who want one, see *Ms.* (May/June 1995), pp. 42–66; and (no author), "Welcome to My World," an interview with Merle Hoffman, founder and president of Choices Women's Medical Center in Queens, NY, *Women's Review of Books* XIX, no. 3 (December 2000), pp. 8–9; and Ruth Rosan, "Blind, Unpredictable Terror," *San Francisco Chronicle* (October 29, 2001). For a discussion of recent militia activity that threatens public officials, see "Extremists Pose Increasing Threat of Violence to Police, Other Public Officials," *Klanwatch Intelligence Report* 80 (October 1995), pp. 1 ff.
7. Lyndsay Griffiths, "Hardships Plague Women Worldwide, UN Report Says," *The Boston Globe* (Thursday September 21, 2000), p. A14; Beth Gardiner, "Torture of Women Said to Be 'Global,'" *The Boston Globe* (Wednesday March 21, 2001), p. A12; *Miami Herald,* "Man Pleads Guilty to Sex-Slave Operation," 97th year, no. 124 (Saturday January 16, 1999), p. 5B.
8. Associated Press, "2 of 5 Women Encounter Sexual or Physical Abuse, Study Finds," *The Boston Globe* (Thursday May 6, 1999), p. A25.
9. Sherri L. Schornstein, *Domestic Violence and Health Care: What Every Professional Needs to Know* (Thousand Oaks: Sage Publications, 1997), p. 2.
10. James Ptacek, *Battered Women in the Courtroom: The Power of Judicial Responses* (Boston: Northeastern University Press, 1999).
11. For a moving autobiography of gang life see Luis Rodríguez, *Always Running* (New York: Simon & Schuster, 1993).
12. Jocelyn A. Hollander, "Vulnerability and Dangerousness: The Construction of Gender through Conversation about Violence," *Gender & Society* 15, no. 1 (February 2001), pp. 83–109; Jordana Hart, "Statistics Say Abuse Hits Close to Home: Most Young Victims Know Their Molester," *The Boston Globe* (Tuesday May 30, 2000), pp. B1, B8.
13. Raymond Hernandez, "Children's Sexual Exploitation Underestimated, Study Finds," *New York Times on the Web* (September 10, 2001), http://www.nytimes.com/2001/01/10/national/10CHIL.html?todaysheadlines=&pagewanted=print9/10/01; Lee H. Bowker, "The Coaching Abuse of Teenage Girls," in Lee H. Bowker, ed., *Masculinities and Violence* (Thousand Oaks, CA: Sage, 1998).
14. Walter V. Robinson, "Scores of Priests Involved in Sex Abuse Cases: Settlements Kept Scope of Issue Out of Public Eye," *The Boston Globe* 261, no. 31 (January 31, 2002), pp. A1 ff; Stephen Kurkjian and Farah Stockman, "DA Sees Lack of Priest Controls: Archdiocese Had No Rule on Abuse," *The Boston Globe* 261, no. 32 (February 1, 2002), pp. B1 ff.
15. Eric Lichtblau, "Attacks between Partners Fall: Justice Dept. Data Seen as Encouraging," *The Boston Globe* (Thursday May 18, 2000), p. A3.
16. Silja J. A. Talvi, "The Craze of Incarceration," *The Progressive* (May 2001), pp. 40–4.

17. For a disturbing look at treatment of male inmates in a maximum security prison see Mara Taub, "Super-Max Punishment in Prison," *Resist Newsletter* 9, no. 1, pp. 1–2. See also John Raymond Cook, *Asphalt Justice: A Critique of the Criminal Justice System in America* (Westport, CT: Praeger, 2001); Joseph T. Hallinan, *Going Up the River: Travels in a Prison Nation* (New York: Random House, 2001); Sue Pleming, "Abuse of Women Inmates Seen Rampant: Misconduct Found in All but One State, Amnesty USA says," *The Boston Globe* (Wednesday March 7, 2001), p. A7; and Don Sabo, Terry A. Kupers, and Willie London, eds., *Prison Masculinities* (Philadelphia: Temple University Press, 2001).
18. R. Emerson Dobash, Russell P. Dobash, Kate Cavanagh, and Ruth Lewis, *Changing Violent Men* (Thousand Oaks, CA: Sage: 2000).
19. Anannya Bhattacharjee, *Whose Safety? Women of Color and the Violence of Law Enforcement* (Philadelphia, PA: American Friends Service Committee, Committee on Women, Population, and the Environment. 2001). Available full-text on line at www.afsc.org/JusticeVisions.htm
20. Kay Pranis, "Peacemaking Circles: Restorative Justice in Practice Allows Victims and Offenders to Begin Repairing the Harm," *Corrections Today* 59, no. 7 (December 1997), pp. 72ff; Howard Zehr, "A Restorative Lens" in *Changing Lenses* (Waterloo, Ontario: Herald Press, 1990), pp. 177–214.
21. Judith Lewis Herman, *Trauma and Recovery* (New York, Basic Books, 1992).
22. Herman cites several studies of rape victims in *Trauma and Recovery*, pp. 47–8. See also Catherine Cameron, *Resolving Childhood Trauma: A Long-Term Study of Abuse Survivors* (Thousand Oaks, CA: Sage, 2000).
23. Raymond Hernandez, "Children's Sexual Exploitation Underestimated, Study Finds," *New York Times on the Web* (September 10, 2001). http://www.nytimes.com/2001/01/10/national/10CHIL.html?todaysheadlines=&pagewanted=print9/10/01; Grant Peck, "Sex Trade Lures More Children, UN Says," *The Boston Globe* (Saturday December 8, 2001), p. A5; Marian Uhlman, "Sex Trade Targeting the Young Is Called Hidden Epidemic," *The Boston Globe* (Thursday September 11, 2001), p. A6.
24. For a look at debates about these alleged causes of violence see Karin L. Swisher, Carol Wekesser, and William Barbour, eds., *Violence against Women* (San Diego, CA: Greenhaven Press, 1994).
25. Jeff Benedict, *Public Heroes, Private Felons: Athletes and Crimes against Women* (Boston: Northeastern University Press, 1997).
26. Bernard Lefkowitz, *Our Guys* (New York: Vintage Books, 1997), pp. 493–4.
27. For a range of essays on men and violence against women, children, and men, see Lee H. Bowker, ed., *Masculinities and Violence* (Thousand Oaks, CA: Sage, 1998).
28. For a discussion of these issues see Walter D. Keseredy and Martin D. Schwartz, *Women Abuse on Campus: Results of the Canadian National Survey* (Thousand Oaks, CA: Sage, 1998); Nancy Worcester, "What Is the Battered Women's Movement Saying about Women Who Use Force?" *Wisconsin Coalition against Domestic Violence Newsletter* 20, no. 1 (Spring 2001), pp. 2–5, 16–17.
29. Ingeborg Breines, Robert Connell and Ingrid Eide, eds., *Male Roles, Masculinities and Violence: A Culture of Peace Perspective* (Paris: United Nations Educational, Scientific and Cultural Organization, 2000).
30. Øystein Gullvåg Holter, "Masculinities in Context: On Peace Issues and Patriarchal Orders," in Ingeborg Breines, Robert Connell, and Ingrid Eide, eds., *Male Roles, Masculinities and Violence: A Culture of Peace Perspective* (Paris: United Nations Educational, Scientific and Cultural Organization, 2000), pp. 61–83.

31. Paul Kivel, *Boys Will Be Men: Raising Our Sons for Courage, Caring and Community* (Gabriola Island, B.C., Canada: New Society Publishers, 1999); Michael Kaufman, "Working with Men and Boys to Challenge Sexism and End Men's Violence," in Ingeborg Breines, Robert Connell, and Ingrid Eide, eds., *Male Roles, Masculinities and Violence: A Culture of Peace Perspective* (Paris: United Nations Educational, Scientific and Cultural Organization, 2000), pp. 213–22.
32. Cynthia Cockburn, *The Space between Us: Negotiating Gender and National Identities in Conflict* (New York: Zed Books, 1998).

56

WOMEN, VIOLENCE, AND RESISTANCE[1]

MELANIE KAYE/KANTROWITZ

Blocks to Resistance

Imagination: To Consider Violence

A woman raped by a landlord showing her an apartment remarks, "The only degrading thing I can recall about it is simply not being able to hit the guy. I just really wanted to sock him in the teeth."[2]

> Another woman, awakened and raped with a knife at her throat: . . . You never forget it and you're never the same. . . . It hits you where you're most vulnerable. . . . About six months to a year later some of the vulnerability disappeared. It was replaced by rage. Oh, I wish now I had hit him. Or killed him.[3]

Listen to women cheer at karate demonstrations simulating attack when the woman playing "victim" strikes back. Think about women's reaction to *Thelma & Louise*.[4] In response to violence, it's natural to consider violence.

Yet as a movement, we don't.

If a woman is abused and strikes back, we often work for her defense. We respond to her risk. But we do not ourselves shoulder it, even as a movement. Nor do we encourage women to avail ourselves of violence as a serious, perhaps effective option.

Why?

Obvious response #1: *Violence is wrong.*
Obvious response #2: *Violence won't work.*

What do we mean, *wrong?* What do we mean, *work?* When women are prepared to use violence, they are less likely to get raped, abused, and murdered.

Listen.

> . . . all of a sudden he got this crazy look in his eye and he said to me, "Now I'm going to kill you." Then I started saying my prayers. I knew there was nothing I could do. He started to hit me—I still

Melanie Kaye/Kantrowitz, excerpt from "Women, Violence and Resistance" from *The Issue Is Power: Essays on Women, Jews, Violence and Resistance.* Reprinted with the permission of Aunt Lute Books.

> wasn't sure if he wanted to rape me at this point—or just to kill me. He was hurting me, but hadn't yet gotten me into a strangle-hold because he was still drunk and off balance. Somehow we pushed into the kitchen where I kept looking at this big knife. But I didn't pick it up. Somehow no matter how much I hated him at that moment, I still couldn't imagine putting the knife in his flesh, and then I was afraid he would grab it and stick it into me. . . .[5]

I couldn't imagine.
I was afraid.

I couldn't imagine corresponds to *it's wrong.* Sticking the knife into his flesh is unimaginable, too horrible.

This horror, this failure of imagination might have cost her life. Her life against his, and she chooses his.

I was afraid corresponds to *it won't work.* Using the knife might make it worse. But how much worse could it get? He's already threatened to kill her.

Is this in women's interest?

If we avoid the question of using violence because it makes us uncomfortable, many men have no such compunctions. They continue to rape, mutilate, beat and kill us. So we are not avoiding violence, only the guilt we associate with using it. Something about innocence is dangerous here. We are innocent because helpless. As long as we insist on maintaining our innocence, we lock ourselves into helplessness. In this way we become complicit with our oppression.

A few feminists have touched on the question. Phyllis Chesler, M. F. Beal, Karen Haglund conclude similarly; in Chesler's words:

> Women, like men, must be capable of violence or self-defense before their refusal to use violence constitutes a free and moral choice rather than "making the best of a bad bargain."[6]

But how do we become capable? What if we are already capable? And what if we don't refuse?

Let us begin to imagine putting the knife in his flesh. If we choose not to, let the reason *not* be that we couldn't imagine doing it. The women who wrote the excellent *Women's Gun Pamphlet* have an answer to the *violence is wrong* voice:

> The only way I've figured out to try and eliminate the all-nurturing masochist in each of us is to remember that the man or men who attack, rape, mutilate, and try to kill you, have done and will do the same to as many women as they can. While you defend yourself, bear in your mind all the women you love that you are fighting for, especially those you know who have been attacked.[7]

Violence and Power Yes, I'm talking about violence. But the violence did not originate with us. If we submit, evade, fight back directly or indirectly—

no matter what we do we are responding to a violence that already is. Janet Koenig has described how the oppressor's violence

> becomes routinized and ritualized. It becomes so part of the environment, of the school, factory, prison, and family that it is barely perceived consciously. Ideology distorts the perception of violence. The source of violence now appears to be not the system but those who rebel against it.[8]

And Assata Shakur succinctly remarks:

> Women have been raped throughout history, and now when we fight back, now that we have the consciousness to fight back—they call us violent.[9]

To avoid this conceptual error, Ti-Grace Atkinson would call responsive violence, the violence of rebellion, by another name:

> When "violence" appears *against* "oppression," it is a *negation of institutionalized* violence. "Violence," these opening blows are a positive humane act—under such circumstances. Such acts are *acts of bravery* . . . It is a betrayal of humanity, and of hope, to represent such acts as shameful, or regrettable.[10]

Not to deny the horror of violence. Or to invalidate or mock the part in us that does not want to harm. We have an honorable past on this subject. Often life has been preserved solely because of our efforts to feed, wash, clothe, and keep our families in health. We have been active in movements to stop slavery, wars, imperialism, lynching, and abuse of all kinds.

It's hard to transform such concerns into a willingness to cut down another woman's son.

Nor am I saying violence should be leapt to lightly. But the situation is hardly light. I am saying only that using violence should be thinkable. And that the grounds on which we decide whether or not to commit violence against men be *our* grounds: *is it in our interest?*

Violence is an aspect of power. In a conflictual society, where power imbalance exists, so does the possibility of physical force to meet physical threat. "Women," Karen Hagberg points out,

> are called violent (indeed, we actually consider ourselves violent) whenever we assert ourselves in the smallest ways. One woman recently described the verbal challenging of men on the streets as an act of violence.[11]

This is absurd or tragic. Yet the piece of embedded truth is that any woman's challenge to male power—from a calm "I'm not interested" to an assertive "please turn down your stereo"—may be perceived as aggressive and met with violence. Most of us know we risk danger in even a mild confrontation with a man. Every male-female interaction assumes: *in a physical fight he will win*. Every man assumes this about every woman. This is the assumption behind rape. As Ellen Willis remarked in 1968, *Men don't take us seriously because they're not physically afraid of us.*

An Analog: African American Liberation from Slavery Recent scholarship about African Americans in the South during and after the Civil War sheds intriguing light on the relationship between violence and freedom. When the war began, the great abolitionist and former slave Frederick Douglass

> immediately called for the enlistment of slaves and free blacks into a "liberating army" that would carry the banner of emancipation through the South. Within thirty days, Douglass believed, 10,000 black soldiers could be assembled. "One black regiment alone would be, in such a war, the full equal of two white ones. The very fact of color in this case would be more terrible than powder and balls. The slaves would learn more as to the nature of the conflict from the presence of one such regiment, than from a thousand preachers."[12]

But Northern white men were not so sure. As they debated the question of arming Blacks—slaves or freedmen—three fears were repeated. They feared slave insurrections against slaveholders who, though the enemy, were, after all, white. They feared Black incompetence; no less a personage than President Lincoln speculated that, if Blacks were armed, "in a few weeks the arms would be in the hands of the rebels." But perhaps the deepest and most revealing fear was that Blacks would prove competent. As one Union congressman noted,

> If you make him the instrument by which your battles are fought, the means by which your victories are won, you must treat him as a victor is entitled to be treated, with all decent and becoming respect.[13]

In the South, the same debate was much more anxiety-laden: would armed slaves turn on their masters? (The transparency of the "happy slave" myth is evident in these musings.) What would happen if distinctions were levelled? "The day you make soldiers of them is the beginning of the end of the revolution," warned General Howell Cobb. "If slaves will make good soldiers, our whole theory of slavery is wrong."[14]

In fact, Black soldiers were crucial to the North, and their performance in the Union army, by all accounts courageous and impressive as Douglass had predicted, revealed that "the whole theory of slavery" was more resilient than General Cobb had imagined, surviving as it did the institution of slavery itself. But whether violence is a tool, a back-up to power, a psychological release or an inevitable response to oppression,[15] *being able* to use violence may be a critical aspect of freedom. Listen to Felix Haywood, a former slave in Texas:

> If everymother's son of a black had thrown 'way his hoe and took up a gun to fight for his own freedom along with the Yankees, the war'd been over before it began. But we didn't do it. We couldn't help stick to our masters. We couldn't no more shoot 'em than we could fly. My father and me used to talk 'bout it. We decided we was too soft and freedom wasn't goin' to be much to our good even if we had an education.[16]

Couldn't shoot them. Soft. The definition of manliness that depends on murder may be the saddest comment on patriarchy anyone can dredge up. As W.E.B. Du Bois remarked with some disgust,

> How extraordinary, and what a tribute to ignorance and religious hypocrisy, is that fact that in the minds of most people, even those of liberals, only murder makes men. The slave pleaded; he was humble; he protected the women of the South, and the world ignored him. The slave killed white men; and behold, he was a man.[17]

What about the women? Slave women were vulnerable to sexual abuse by white and Black men alike, though solidarity between enslaved women and men appears to have been very strong.[18] Many women resisted, sometimes with violence. Rose Williams tells of taking a poker to the man chosen by her master for her to marry (i.e., breed with), and of capitulating only after her owner threatened her with a whipping.[19] Cherry Loguen used a stick to knock out a man armed with a knife who tried to rape her. Two women attacked by an overseer waited till he undressed and "pounced upon him, wrestled him to the ground, and then ran away."[20] It's likely that women were able to resist assaults and unwanted attention more forcefully from other slaves than from their owners, though Linda Brent's excruciating narrative of resistance to her owner's sexual demands demonstrates the lengths to which some women went to preserve their sexual integrity.[21]

Did women resist enslavement? During the Middle Passage, women, unlike men, were not chained or confined to the hold. While this freedom left them vulnerable to sexual abuse by the ship's crews, it also left them freer to rebel, and there are several reported instances of women inciting or assisting insurrections at sea.[22] On the plantations,

> Some murdered their masters, some were arsonists, and still others refused to be whipped. . . . Equipped with a whip and two healthy dogs, an Alabama overseer tied a woman named Crecie to a stump with intentions of beating her. To his pain and embarrassment, she jerked the stump out of the ground, grabbed the whip, and sent the overseer running.[23]

A Union official recorded several women entering the Union camp with marks of severe whipping. The whipper was caught and a male slave first lashed him twenty times, and then the women, one after another, gave him twenty lashes, according to the official, "to remind him that they were no longer his";[24] but maybe also because releasing rage where it belongs is one step towards healing.[25] There are also instances of women fighting against their men being taken away.[26]

The ability to defend oneself, one's people, one's dignity, to struggle for one's own liberation, is clearly a survival skill. As Robert Falls, former slave, summed it up: "If I had my life to live over, I would die fighting rather than be a slave again. . . ."[27]

Observations by Black and white, Southerners and Northerners indicate that the Black soldiery affected everyone strongly. Blacks felt pride. Whites felt fear. Both groups recognized that consciousness changed radically when the Black divisions marched through.

And not only consciousness. In New Orleans free Blacks formed two regiments for the Confederacy, in part to improve their status and esteem by learning firearms (though they were never called for combat duty).[28] We could argue the absurdity and tragedy of such a stance, not unlike the arguments that have swirled around Black police or military today. Yet Blacks understood that a Black soldiery might be fair, might protect them, would not automatically assume they were chattel and without rights. A Black soldiery gave Black—and white—people a vision of a differently ordered world: a hint that perhaps the whole theory of slavery was, indeed, wrong.

The analogy is suggestive. Women police officers, fire fighters, soldiers do challenge "the whole theory of slavery,"[29] as do women athletes and construction workers, as well as physicists. But particularly since physical domination so characterizes male-female relations under patriarchy, if women were to defend ourselves and other women, could avail ourselves of violence when needed; and if this potential for self-defense became an expectation, a norm, then patriarchal definitions of male and female would be shaken. Not only minds would change, but reality. Would men begin to wonder if *perhaps the whole theory of patriarchy is wrong?* Would women?

Fear of the Self/Fear of Our Power[30]

If in a patriarchal system violence is an aspect of power, if capacity for violence is a basis for resistance, it's obvious whose interests are served by *it won't work* and *it's wrong;* by the implied fear and horror.

Women often learn to see with the eyes of the dominant culture: male eyes. Especially middle-class heterosexual white women are taught to fear strong women, women with power, women with physical strength, angry women who express that anger forcefully. *It isn't ladylike. It isn't nice.* Even those of us who have long rejected these norms (or accepted our inability to live inside them) still may fear the explosiveness of anger—though this fear obscures the reason for our deep anger, which is our powerlessness. Instead of learning to cherish this rage and to direct it effectively, we often try to suppress it, in ourselves and in others. It's exactly as if we have an army we're afraid to mobilize, train, and use.

Yet we are not always victims. We can be violent. How have we managed to avoid noticing? The idea that men are inherently violent, women inherently non-violent, is dangerous, not only because it is a doctrine of biological superiority, and such doctrines have supported genocide.[31]

The idea that women are inherently non-violent is also dangerous because it's not true. Any doctrine that idealizes us as the non-violent sex idealizes our victimization and institutionalizes who men say we are: intrinsically nurturing, inherently gentle, intuitive, emotional. They think; we feel. They have power; we won't touch it with a ten-foot pole. Guns are for them; let's suffer in a special kind of womanly way.

Such an analysis dooms us to inappropriate kindness and passivity; overlooks both our capacity for and experience with violence; ignores in fact everything about us that we aren't sure we like, including how we sometimes abuse each other. Whatever we disapprove of, we call *theirs,* and then say, when women do these things—talk loud, use reason, fuck hard, act insensitive or competitive, ride motorcycles, carry weapons, explode with rage, fight—they are acting like men.[32]

But who defines "like men," "like women"? On what basis? Remember Sojourner Truth's challenge to restrictive definition: *ain't I a woman?* All women defined as deviant might well echo her words. We may be numerous enough to redefine the "norm." When we find many of us doing what only men are supposed to do, and nearly all of us expressing in some form what is supposed to be a male behavior, then maybe we need to enlarge our notion of who *we* are. The woman who is violent is not acting like a man. She may be announcing a host of contradictions: that her condition is intolerable; that she is or isn't afraid; that she feels entitled; that she has nothing to lose or something to protect; that she needs physical release; that she's a bully; that she has lost or given over or seeks control. But always, in addition, she announces that women are not who men say we are.

> TO SEE WOMEN'S VIOLENCE AS A FIELD INCLUDING:
> SLASHING YOUR WRISTS STANDING UP TO A THREATENING
> LANDLORD KILLING A RAPIST ATTACKING A WOMAN AT
> THE BAR FIGHTING AN ABUSIVE HUSBAND PUNCHING
> YOUR LOVER PUNCHING A MAN WHO MOUTHS OFF AT
> YOU LEARNING KARATE KICKING A DOG SHOOTING UP
> WRESTLING FOR MONEY DRINKING TOO MUCH ALCOHOL
> WRESTLING FOR FUN BEATING YOUR CHILD KILLING
> ANOTHER WOMAN'S RAPIST

To see women's violence as a wide range of behavior which can serve, protect, endanger, or violate women and children—or be neutral.[33] To expose the taboo which clothes even our questions about violence. To admit that when we don't fight back against men's violence, it's not because we're passive, not even because we're good: but because we're afraid of what they'll do back.

And for good reason. Consider these words from two married women:

> Sometimes I get so mad I wish I could hit him. I did once, but he hit me back, and he can hurt me more than I can hurt him.
>
> When he's so much bigger and stronger, and you got four kids to take care of, what's a woman supposed to do?[34]

Consider the implications of the fact that in the late seventies a full 40% of the women imprisoned for homicide in Chicago's Cook County jail had killed men in response to physical abuse by these men.[35] Even though judges in some states have ruled to release women serving time on such convictions, many women still remain in prison.

The fact is, fighting back, even supporting women who fight back, can be dangerous. The wife who feigns sleep when her husband comes home drunk; the child who lies to avoid getting beaten; these are tactics based on experience. Sometimes evasion works better than confrontation. At least it has sometimes kept us alive.

We worry about making things worse. "If you do what I say, I won't hurt you," says the rapist, but the woman who trusts him forgets, in her desperation and terror, that he is, after all, a rapist: hardly a basis for trust. With the husband or mate, while appeasement may be plausible, it's hardly desirable as a way of life.

What happens to women who actively resist violence? The facts, especially about street violence, flatly contradict the usual police/male advice of "don't fight it." When a woman resists a rape *in any way*—saying NO like she means it, screaming, kicking, running, fighting—her chance of escaping ranges from 60–80%.[36]

Whereas *if she doesn't resist her chance of getting raped is 100%.*

Women and Guns

From my journal, 1978:

> For three or four years I've dreamed about rape regularly. The can't run dreams. The can't scream ones. Dreams where I'm being attacked and I have a knife in my pocket but I can't get it, or I'm afraid to use it. The dream that keeps extending into more complication, more danger, until there he is again, "my" rapist. I even had a dream where I'm sitting by a lake and a man swims up, sticks his head out of the water, and says: "I'm your rapist."
>
> In many of these dreams, I don't recognize the danger early enough to respond.
>
> Since I bought a gun and have learned to use it, my dreams have changed. Whatever the situation, whatever the form of attack, I simply

whip out my gun. Sometimes I shoot. Sometimes I don't even need to shoot, I just aim and he is suddenly harmless. The man who called himself "my rapist " laughs at me when I draw my gun; he says, "The hospital can suck those bullets out in no time." But I know, and he doesn't, that it's a .38 I'm holding, and I shoot, confident that the bullets will do the job.

If resistance alleviates abuse and increases dramatically our chances of escape, how can we increase our ability to resist? The most certain way to refuse violation would be to keep a gun handy.

Many women immediately reject this option. Some call guns "masculine." Many are simply terrified of guns' murderous power. But aside from fears of legal repercussions or male retaliation, fears which are realistic and need to be addressed—is a gun really more dangerous than, for example, a car? Is owning a gun more dangerous than not owning one? Past the realistic fears is, I believe, a fear of our own selves.

I've talked with many women about getting a gun and learning to shoot.

R. tells me, "I'm afraid I'd kill my husband."

Not to dismiss killings that happen in rage because a gun is handy (though how many of these killings are committed by women?) But to recognize that in her mind she's protected against killing her husband only because she lacks the means.

K. says she's afraid she'd shoot the first man she saw acting like an asshole.

I ask what she means by "an asshole." She says, "Like some man beating up on some woman." Again, she is protected (from her best impulses) only by her inability to act.

N. says she's afraid she'd shoot her nose off.

As if a woman who has learned to cook, play the recorder, ride the subway, drive a car, and change a diaper couldn't learn to shoot.

H., B., C., E., many many women say, "I'm afraid if I have a gun it'll get used against me."

Of course this is exactly what men tell us. For example, in Boston in 1979, after the sixth Black woman in as many weeks had been killed, police still advised Black women against carrying weapons because they could be used against them. Yet what alternatives did the police offer?

In fact I've rarely heard of a real-life woman's weapon being used against her, though I've seen it happen over and over again on TV and in the movies. I've heard of a 14-year-old woman who shot her assailant with his gun, a 17-year-old who sliced her attacker's jugular vein with his knife, a mother who shot with his gun the policeman who threatened her child—she killed him and wounded his partner.[37] Maybe it's men who shouldn't carry weapons. But no one tells them that.

I also discover among my friends women who aren't afraid of guns. L., who teaches me to shoot, grew up around guns in rural Oregon. P. learned to shoot in the army. F.'s father hunted. M.'s grandfather was a gangster. Against the dominant experience of women—which is to have little acquaintance with deadly weapons—an alternative perspective emerges: that of women who were taught to shoot as girls; country women who'd as soon live without a knife in the kitchen as a gun in the bedroom; women who recognize a gun as a tool: useful, dangerous but controllable, like a book of matches.

The first time L. took me shooting with a handgun, I tried a .22 pistol for a while, practiced aiming again and again till it came easy. Then I tried the .38. Fire leaped from the barrel, my hand jumped. TV and movies lie about the sound of guns: it is unbelievably loud. The noise, even with earplugs, shook me. After the first round I sat down, took a deep breath, and said, "I feel like I can't control it."

"It feels like that," L. said, "you just have to get used to how it feels."

After a few minutes, I got up to try again. I started to hit the target.

A learning experience, like a million others in a woman's life. Yet so many of us consider ourselves tiny children when it comes to guns. We're afraid a gun—a source of possible protection—will be turned against us. This fear deprives us of strength, lest our strength benefit them, not us. We're afraid what we'd do *if we could*—which, again, keeps us powerless, lest we use our power badly.

To fear ourselves is to use them as model:

they abuse their power, therefore we would too

is to imagine only helplessness keeps us in line:

the more choices we have, the worse we'll be

is to insist in some hidden corner of the body:

we need oppression

Like, *you can't take the law into your own hands.*
But what better hands to take the law into?

Our fear of ourselves then is fear of ourselves empowered. As we worry about what we'd do if we could, we are undermined in our attempts to end our oppression. We are partly afraid we can't be trusted with freedom.

NOTES

1. I want to acknowledge general indebtedness to the work that preceded or has accompanied the writing of this essay. The first feminist speak-out on rape, in New York City in 1971, was documented in Noreen Connell and Cassandra Wilson, *Rape: The First Sourcebook for Women* (1974). Susan Griffin, *Rape: The Power of Consciousness* (1979) includes her earlier essay, which is still one of the best discus-

sions of the issue. Andrea Medea and Kathleen Thompson, *Against Rape* (1974) remains useful, as does Susan Brownmiller, *Against Our Will: Men, Women and Rape* (1975)—the classic, limited but essential. Early work on battering includes Erin Pizzey, *Scream Quietly or the Neighbors Will Hear You* (1974), Betsy Warrior, *Battered Lives* (1974) and Del Martin, *Battered Wives* (1976). Susan Schechter, *Women and Male Violence: The Visions and Struggles of the Battered Women's Movement* (1982) remains the best single text on battering to combine service-provider and activist consciousness. On incest, Florence Rush's early work is included in the Sourcebook noted above, and her book *The Best Kept Secret: Sexual Abuse of Children* (1980) contains the earliest discussion of how Freud suppressed information and revised his theory, based on his women patients' experience of incestuous abuse by male relatives, in favor of his oedipal theory that women fantasized this abuse. Sandra Butler, *Conspiracy of Silence: The Trauma of Incest* (1978) remains one of the clearest treatments built from women's experience, compassionate and politically savvy. Also, Judith Lewis Herman, with Lisa Hirschman, *Father-Daughter Incest* (1981). General books on violence against women: Andrea Dworkin's *Woman Hating* (1974) and *Our Blood* (1976); Kathleen Barry's *Female Sexual Slavery* (1979); and Frederique Delacorte and Felice Newman, eds., *Fight Back! Feminist Resistance to Male Violence* (1981). Pauline B. Bart and Patricia H. O'Brien, *Stopping Rape: Successful Survival Strategies* (1985), and Evelyn C. White, *Chain Chain Change: For Black Women Dealing with Physical and Emotional Abuse* (1985) are extremely useful.

I want also to acknowledge general indebtedness to numerous conversations in the late seventies with Paula King and Michaele Uccella, and to the many thinkers and activists with whom I worked in the Portland, Oregon movement to stop violence against women. Many women have read pieces of this essay over the years and shared their responses with me: Gloria Anzaldúa, Margaret Blanchard, Sandy Butler, Chrystos, Irena Klepfisz, Helena Lipstadt, Fabienne McPhail-Grant, Bernice Mennis, Maureen O'Neill, Linda Vance, and Judy Waterman, in addition, of course, to Joan Pinkvoss, my editor and publisher at Aunt Lute. I alone am responsible for its weaknesses.

2. *Sourcebook,* note 1, 49.
3. Brownmiller, note 1, 363.
4. Interesting that in patriarchal western culture, revenge is considered practically a sacred duty for men, Hamlet and Orestes being only two of the more obvious examples (both sons avenging their fathers in part against their mothers). But women are not even supposed to entertain vengeful feelings.
5. Griffin, *Consciousness,* note 1, 21.
6. Phyllis Chesler, *Women and Madness* (1973), 292; see also M. F. Beal, *S.A.F.E. House* (1976) and Karen Hagberg, "Why the Women's Movement Cannot Be Non-Violent," *Heresies 6: Women and Violence* (1979), 44, from Nadia Telsey and Linda Maslanko, with the help of the Women's Martial Art Union, Self-Defense for Women (1974).
7. *The Women's Gun Pamphlet by and for Women* (1975), 3.
8. Janet Koenig, "The Social Meaning of Violence," *Heresies 6,* note 6, 91.
9. Assata Shakur, from an interview in *Plexus* by Women Against Prison, quoted in Beal, note 7, 111.
10. Ti-Grace Atkinson, *Amazon Odyssey* (1974), ccxlix. The term *violence* she reserves to represent "a class function," available as a *tactic* only to the oppressor class (200).
11. Hagberg, note 6, 44.
12. Leon Litwack, *Been in the Storm So Long: The Aftermath of Slavery* (1980), 65–66.

13. Litwack, note 12, 66.
14. Litwack, note 12, 43. What is being said here? First, the "whole theory of slavery" boiled down to an assumption of African inferiority, less-than-humanness. Second, military prowess dominated patriarchal notions of humanness: only competent soldiers, i.e., men who could act like "real men," were equal human beings. Consider that slaves were not an unknown people but the very people who not only performed necessary physical labor, but also raised white Southern children and tended the white Southern sick; obviously, tenderness, intelligence, caring, etc. did not challenge "the whole theory of slavery." See Deborah Gray White, *Ar'n't I a Woman: Female Slaves in the Plantation South* (1985).
15. Frantz Fanon, *The Wretched of the Earth* (1963), discusses the political implications of the oppressed's psychological need to release rage.
16. Litwack, note 12, 46.
17. W.E.B. Du Bois, *Black Reconstruction* (1935), quoted in Litwack, note 12, 64.
18. See Angela Davis, "The Legacy of Slavery: Standards for a New Womanhood," in *Women, Race, and Class* (1981), 3–29, and Linda Brent, *Incidents in the Life of a Slave Girl* (1973; 1st pub. 1861), which depicts extreme sexual harassment and abuse suffered by enslaved Black women from white men, and solidarity among Black women and men, both enslaved and free. Of course Brent was writing an abolitionist document.

    It appears that women employed all the forms of resistance used by men, direct and indirect. But unlike the men, the women had no access to the military, no institutional focus through which to transform capacity for violence into organized strength. And if "manliness," as Du Bois caustically remarked, meant murder, "womanliness" translated into what Black women were deprived of, the right to be protected by their men, and to raise their own babies.
19. White, *Ar'n't I a Woman,* note 14, 102–3, citing B. A. Botkin, ed., *Lay My Burden Down: A Folk History of Slavery* (1945), 160–62.
20. White, note 14, 78.
21. Brent, note 18.
22. White, note 14, 63–64.
23. White, note 14, 77–78.
24. Litwack, note 12, 65.
25. Toni Morrison's *Beloved* (1987) and Sherley Anne William's *Dessa Rose* (1986) both imagine permutations of violence from enslaved women.
26. Litwack, note 12, 76, 114.
27. Litwack, note 12, 46.
28. Litwack, note 12, 42.
29. Susan Brownmiller argued in *Against Our Will* for the critical importance of integrating by gender the military and the police. Though we have seen some signal changes as some gender integration occurs, and though women police and soldiers may improve their individual status, challenge stereotypes, and offer better service or protection to women, it's no more an adequate solution to rape than Black soldiers were an adequate solution to racist violence. The missing link in Brownmiller's argument is the role of the army and police in the U.S., which is to safeguard the interests of the powerful at home and abroad. This means men. Until or unless male institutions truly serve our interest, we can't adequately fight for women through them. During the Civil War and Reconstruction the interests of northern capitalists uniquely coincided with the interests of the slaves.

30. An earlier version of part of this chapter appeared in *Fight Back,* note 1, co-authored by me and Michaele Uccella. The ideas emerged in our discussions; the actual writing was done by me.
31. Andrea Dworkin argued this in "Biological Superiority: The World's Most Dangerous and Deadly Idea," *Heresies 6,* note 6, 46.
32. "The belief that violence is somehow gender-linked is amazingly prevalent throughout all literature, even feminist literature. . . . Obviously it would be stupid and cruel to say that women are not brutally victimized, systematically, institutionally, across all age, class, and race barriers. Quite the contrary. But the assumption that women are inherently incapable of violence is something else. My own inquiry into the matter has shown me that this assumption is simply not true." Michaele Uccella, *Lesbian Violence,* presented at Goddard College and at the Montpelier (Vermont) Women's Center, September, 1978.
33. The theory that a woman's capacity for doing violence (however covert or unacceptable the expression) is also a capacity for resistance was developed by Michaele Uccella in *Lesbian Violence.*
34. Two women quoted in Lillian Rubin, *Worlds of Pain: Life in the Working Class Family* (1976), 117, 42.
35. C. McCormick, "Battered Women" (1977), cited by Schneider, Jordan, and Arguedas, "Representation of Women Who Defend Themselves," in *Heresies 6,* note 12, 100ff.
36. Police statistics from Portland, Oregon, 1976, indicated a 60% rate of escape for women who use some form of resistance. Considering that many women who get away don't bother to report to the police, the higher rate of 80% indicated by other studies seems plausible. (Of course many many women who don't escape also refuse to report to the police, perhaps as many as 90% of all women who get raped.) Bart, note 1, has compiled resistance strategies from women who escaped.
37. The first escape was recorded in the *Portland Oregonian* sometime in 1979; the second came from the *New York Post,* 1/31/79. Neither of these women was charged. Also note the following divine judgment: "An axwielding Portland youth was killed early Friday when he accidentally struck himself in the side of the neck while allegedly threatening two girls in the parking lot of a convenience market." *Oregon Journal,* 7/19/78.

57

THE KID NO ONE NOTICED

JONAH BLANK

Paducah, Ky.—When Michael Carneal warned friends last Thanksgiving to stay away from their high school lobby, it was not, he now says, because he knew that a tragedy would occur there once the long weekend came to an end. "Just about every day I told people that something was going to happen on Monday." He had developed a habit of making frequent but empty threats, he says, after logging onto a Web site called "101 Ways to Annoy People."

This week, Michael Carneal pleads guilty but mentally ill to three counts of murder and five of attempted murder—the result of a threat that proved anything but empty. When he gunned down eight clasmates at a prayer circle in the lobby of Heath High School last December 1, he was a frail 14-year-old, a little over 5 feet tall and weighing 110 pounds. Now, at 15, he is a few inches taller and 20 pounds heavier. He has spent the past 10 months in juvenile detention, which he prefers to high school. He likes the food, sleeps well, and, he says, "people respect me now."

Of all the school shootings that made headlines in America over the past year, the Paducah killings may be the most baffling. Nearly every theory trotted out at the time of the tragedy now seems hollow: the obsession of a gun nut or the revenge of a bully's victim, atheistic nihilism or the influence of violent movies, the traumas of a dysfunctional childhood or the ravages of criminal insanity—all important social problems but, in this case, each a dead end. What's striking about Michael Carneal is how ordinary he is. But he had an extraordinary craving for "respect."

U.S. News has obtained a copy of the psychiatric report prepared as evidence for his trial—an evaluation by doctors who spent several days interviewing him, his family, and five of his friends. "Michael Carneal was not mentally ill nor mentally retarded at the time of the shootings," the doctors found. His lawyers agree that he was not legally insane at the time but say he is mentally ill and needs treatment. The Carneal quotes in this [reading] come from the psychiatric report.

In school shootings from Mississippi to Arkansas to Oregon, an inner darkness seems to have preceded the mayhem: membership in a satanic cult, a history of torturing animals, or a fanatical fascination with firearms and ex-

---

plosives. But whatever demons may have lurked in Michael's heart remain well hidden. Examine the psychiatric reports and the police records, talk to anyone in Paducah who is still willing to talk, and a picture gradually comes into focus: Michael Carneal is, and was, insecure, self-centered, and hungry for attention, a boy wrestling with the frustrations of puberty and desiring the approval of his peers—hardly different from millions of kids across America. In some ways, though, he seemed younger than most teenagers. While his contemporaries were listening to gangsta rap, Michael still liked Smurfs. On Heath High's social ladder, he was barely clinging to the lower rungs.

Heroes A few Friday nights ago, while Michael read a Stephen King book in his cell, his ex-schoolmates donned camouflage fatigues. The Heath Pirates were playing a football archrival, the Ballard Bombers, and the kids were decked out in military garb to show their school spirit. Even after a 35–0 defeat, Heath High's heroes were clearly the boys in football gear. They were the ones who would be talked about until the next Friday, the ones for whom the cheerleaders cheered, for whom the band played. Until the shooting, Michael was a band member, a skinny freshman with a baritone horn.

Once he wrote a secret story, a tale in which a shy kid named Michael was picked on by "preps"—the popular kids—but was saved by a brother with a gun. "Michael" gave the corpses of the slain preps to his mother as a gift. The story might have set off alarms, but it remained hidden until after the shootings.

The actual Michael Carneal had no heroic brother, no fictional alter ego to save him from a threat that seemed quite real. He felt alienated, pushed around, picked on. "I didn't like to go to school," he said. "I didn't feel as if anyone really liked me." But he cited little evidence of bullying. Once in middle school, someone pulled his pants down; friends say such things were happening to kids all the time. In his own view, however, he was a castaway, at the mercy of cruel Pirates.

He was never very close to his father, a lawyer. His older sister, Kelly, got much of the family's attention. A popular girl, she became the school valedictorian half a year after the shootings. "He tries to be as good as me," she told psychiatrists, "and he can never size up." Michael compensated by becoming a class clown, what one friend called an "energetic prankster who would get attention any way he could." Michael later told doctors he stole CDs, sold parsley to a classmate as marijuana, and downloaded Internet pornography, which he passed around the school.

He was not a gun enthusiast; he may have handled firearms only a few times in his life. His friends noticed no pronounced interest in violent movies, music, TV, or video games. He dismissed the media-spread notion that his rampage was inspired by a scene in the movie *The Basketball Diaries,* which he described as boring. "I don't know why it happened, but I know it wasn't a movie."

One possible element was hardly mentioned at the time: unrequited love, or unrequited lust. Gwen Hadley, mother of one of the victims, confirms to *U.S. News* what many students had suspected: "Michael was in love with my daughter Nicole, and Nicole had no interest in him." Michael told his doctors he liked Nicole but said they never dated. Gwen Hadley says he had phoned Nicole almost nightly in the weeks before the shootings, ostensibly to discuss chemistry.

Their photos tell the whole story: Nicole was tall, pretty, and, in a school where many a girl seems to be a bottle blond, she had enough self-assurance to remain a defiant [brunette]. But Michael, with his thick glasses, had the owlish aspect of a pubescent Steve Forbes. Nicole played in the band with Michael and did not treat him with disdain. On a few occasions, they did homework together in his home.

Michael told psychiatrists he had begun to date but had never so much as kissed a girl. He was upset when students called him a "faggot," and he almost cried when a school gossip sheet labeled him gay. Classmates now say kids toss such taunts around freely, but, for Michael, the barbs stung. Alone in his room, with his Internet porn for company, the lack of a girlfriend was a source of physical frustration and social embarrassment. When he fired into the prayer circle, his first bullet struck Nicole Hadley.

The why may never be fully explained, but the what of those final days is now tragically clear. On Thanksgiving, Michael stole two shotguns, two semiautomatic rifles, a pistol, and 700 rounds of ammunition from a neighbor's garage. He hauled the cache home on his bike and sneaked it through a bedroom window. "I was feeling proud, strong, good, and more respected," he would tell the psychiatrists. "I had accomplished something. I'm not the kind of kid who accomplishes anything. This is the only adventure I've ever had."

The next day, he stole two more shotguns, these from his parents' bedroom. A day later, on Saturday, he took "the best" guns to a friend's house; the boys admired the longarms and shot targets with a pistol. On Sunday, after church and homework, he wrapped his arsenal in a blanket. He did not plan to shoot anyone, he said, but just wanted to show the guns off. "Everyone would be calling me and they would come over to my house or I would go to their house. I would be popular. I didn't think I would get into trouble."

On Monday, he put the bundle into the trunk of his sister's Mazda. In his backpack was a Ruger .22 pistol. He rode with Kelly to school and found his friends, as usual, hanging out in the front lobby. A few feet away, the morning prayer circle was ending. His moment had arrived: He announced what was in the blanket and waited for the adulation he was certain would follow.

The boys talked about the guns for a minute or two but were not especially impressed. In western Kentucky, firearms are a part of everyday life. As the discussion turned to new CDs, Michael reached into his backpack. He put plugs in his ears and rammed the ammo clip into his Ruger. "I pulled it out," he recalled, "and nobody noticed." Witnesses thought they were merely watching the class clown. Three shots killed three girls who had played beside Michael in the band: Nicole Hadley, Kayce Steger, and Jessica James. The remaining five shots wounded five other students.

"I Had Guns." When he opened fire, Michael said, he was trying to get people to notice him: "I don't know why I wasn't bluffing this time. I guess it was because they ignored me. I had guns, I brought them to school, I showed them to them, and they were still ignoring me." He didn't think the light-calibered Ruger could kill, he said, nor did he aim at anyone in particular. But after another student—a football player—talked him into dropping the gun, the meaning of his actions sank in. "I said, 'Kill me, please, Please kill me.' I wanted to die. I knew what I had done."

Now, the families of his victims are searching for a sliver of meaning. At a two-day quilting bee, where they stitched together panels of sympathy sent from as far away as France and Japan, mothers and fathers grasped at the hope of preventing the next schoolyard shooting.

"We've got to teach parents to love and respect their kids," said Jessica James's father, Joe, who took up quilting especially for the occasion. "We don't have homes anymore," added his wife, Judy. "We only have places where kids come to sleep." Yet the Carneal family, by all external appearances and the judgment of several psychiatrists, was in no way dysfunctional.

The families see Michael as a cold, deliberate killer and believe the sure threat of harsh punishment might have prevented the tragedy. But Michael, who faces a life sentence with no chance of parole for 25 years, seems not to have pondered the consequences of his actions. His best explanation for pulling the trigger is pathetically childish: "I just wanted the guys to think I was cool."

Gwen Hadley, for all her efforts at positive renewal, knows that her daughter won't be the last schoolgirl cut down for no reason. "It's going to happen again," she said. "This can happen anywhere, at any time." Then she put another stitch in the quilt of hope.

58

THE ULTIMATE GROWTH INDUSTRY Trafficking in Women and Girls

JAN GOODWIN

The California travel agency brochure could not be more blunt: "Sex Tours to Thailand, Real Girls, Real Sex, Real Cheap," it reads. "These women are the most sexually available in the world. Did you know you can actually buy a virgin girl for as little as $200? You could fuck a different girl every night for the rest of your life." There is even a prize for the man that has sex with the most girls during the tour. As for AIDS, the brochure continues, "Thailand is safe. And all the places we visit are police protected."

What the ad copy doesn't say is that these "virgin girls" are frequently children who have been kidnapped or sold into brothels. Forced into prostitution, sometimes even chained to their beds, they lead lives that are brutal, and frequently short. Averaging 15 customers a day, they work all but two days a month. They must perform any act demanded by their customers, most of whom refuse to wear condoms. If they object, the brothel owners beat them into submission. According to human rights activists working in Thailand, a large percentage of the prostitutes there are under 15, and girls as young as eight are sold into the industry. Within six months of being sold into the sex trade, a girl is commonly HIV-infected.

But you don't have to travel to Asia; sexual servitude can be found here in the U.S. too, as an 18-month undercover investigation by the Global Survival Network discovered. For example, women from the former Soviet Union can be found in brothels in New York, Bethesda, Maryland, and Los Angeles. Fleeing a collapsing economy at home, these women pay up to $3,000 in "processing fees" for what they are promised will be good jobs abroad; instead, they are sold into sexual slavery. The industry is tightly controlled by the Russian mafia, whose contacts with their own government and immigration officials facilitate the acquisition of the necessary visas and passports. Women trying to escape have been murdered, and the threat that family members back home will be beaten to death is also used to keep women in line.

According to GSN, which is based in Washington, D.C., every year trafficking in women and girls puts billions of dollars into the coffers of crimi-

Jan Goodwin, "The Ultimate Growth Industry: Trafficking in Women and Girls" from *On the Issues: The Progressive Woman's Quarterly* (Fall 1998). Reprinted with the permission of the author.

nal syndicates worldwide—an amount rivaling their incomes from drugs and guns. And there is another plus in trading in human flesh: dope and weapons can only be sold once; a woman or girl can be sold again and again.

As the disparities in the global economy widen, girl children and young women are increasingly seen as currency and quick profits. The United Nations estimates that, around the world, some 200 million people are forced to live as sexual or economic slaves, the latter often involving sexual exploitation as well. In Southeast Asia alone, a reported 60 to 70 million women and children have been sold in the sex industry in the last decade. "Slavery is one of the most undesirable consequences of globalization," says a UN spokesman, adding, "We regret that this is not considered a priority by any country at the moment."

Nor is trafficking in women and girls limited to prostitution; it is also used to supply the forced-marriage industry. In China today, for example, there are now three males for every two females in the population over the age of 15. This as a result of the government's "one child, one couple" policy, combined with the traditional, and still powerful, requirement for a son. If the first child is a girl, the fetus may be aborted, or the infant abandoned or even killed. As a consequence, young women and girls are being sold into marriage, in a revival of a once-standard feudal practice. According to Chinese government reports, in the first 10 months of 1990 alone, trafficking in brides increased by 60 percent over the previous year. Either kidnapped or sold by impoverished families, the young women are purchased by potential bridegrooms for up to $600. The government's Office for the Eradication of the Kidnapping and Sale of Women acknowleges some 50,000 such kidnappings per year (although human rights organizations believe the real numbers are much higher). And the profits are enormous. In a five-year period from 1991 to 1996, Chinese police freed 88,000 women and children who had been kidnapped for this purpose.

Particularly disturbing is the violence to which these forced brides are subjected. The abducted women, who can be as young as 13 or 14, are frequently gang-raped by the slave traders before being sold, a practice that is intended to terrify them into passivity, and is no doubt effective in many cases. Those who try to run from their new husbands are violently punished, even maimed, by the traffickers in ways that are too sickening to be printed here.

In some cases, sex tours from the U.S. to the Third World are offered as a means by which lonely men can find a mate. Norman Barabash, who runs Big Apple Oriental Tours out of Queens, New York, views his tours as a social development program. Until recently, $2,200 bought 10 days and 11 nights of "paradise" in the Philippines; since last year, when Big Apple was banned from doing business in that country, Barabash has been sending American men to Thailand. Women in these countries have no jobs, and are dying to get American husbands, he says. "They are so set on landing one, they will do anything their conscience allows." According to Barabash, some 20 to 25 percent of his clients end up marrying women they meet on the tours.

Big Apple is only one of some 25 or 30 similar operations in the U.S. that ride on—and promote—the myth that "exotic oriental women are thrilled to meet American men, and know how to please and serve them," says Ken Franzblau, a lawyer for Equality Now, a human rights organization. Franzblau went underground for almost two years to investigate sex-tour companies in the U.S. "I posed as a shy man who felt insecure around women, and inquired about taking such a trip," he says. "I was told that all kinds of kinky sex would be available, and that the tour guides would negotiate prices for me with the pimps."

Franzblau points out that the operations demean women at both ends of their business. Reads one brochure: "Had enough of American bitches who won't give you the time of day, and are only interested in your bank account? In Asia you'll meet girls who will treat you with respect and appreciation, unlike their American counterparts." These operators insist that American women are unloving, feminist manhaters, he says. "At the destination end, sex tours create the ever-increasing demand to bring young women and girls into the sex industry."

In the Philippines and Thailand, prostitution is illegal. Here in the U.S., as well as in Germany, the Netherlands, Sweden, and Australia—all countries where sex tours originate—such "tourism" is likewise illegal, although in this country, the law applies only to traveling with the intent to engage in a sexual act with a juvenile, which is punishable for up to 10 years imprisonment. In the four years this law has been in force, however, there have been no prosecutions.

It is also illegal in virtually every state of America (including New York, where Big Apple operates) to promote prostitution, or knowingly profit from it. Yet sex-tour operators openly advertise in magazines and on the Internet, and the websites of many feature hardcore pornographic photographs of promised "delights." So, too, do the videos they send potential customers. An hour-long video sent to men interested in going on a Big Apple tour and viewed by *On the Issues* shows what is described as a wet T-shirt contest, but in reality is more a sex circus in which young women are stripped, and a mob of raucous overweight, aging American men suck on their nipples, perform oral sex, and otherwise explore their body cavities as they are passed around the crowd. The video also offers "daily introductions to the ladies of your choice who will be your companion for the night or around the clock." As two young women are shown cavorting naked in a jacuzzi, the voice-over cautions that if viewers don't take a tour, they will "miss an afternoon at a sex motel with two lovely ladies."

There is nothing subtle or obscure about the promotional video and its customer come-ons, but in a letter to Democratic Senator Catherine Abate last September, Queens County District Attorney Richard Brown wrote: "Our investigation [of Big Apple Oriental Tours], which has been quite extensive and included the use of undercover operatives as well as assistance provided by the FBI and the US Customs Service, has disclosed no provable violations of New York's criminal laws." At the time the decision not to pursue an indictment was made, the DA's office was in possession of the video.

After that ruling, Equality Now met with the DA, and offered additional evidence, including records of Franzblau's conversations with Big Apple's owner, and the reports of the two men who took the tours. The DA has subsequently reopened his investigation of the company.

Many other countries are also lax about cracking down on trafficking. The Japanese not only appear to condone the industry, they actively obstruct interference in it. Due to massive unemployment in the Philippines, even for those with college degrees, some 80,000 Filipinos work in Japan; 95 percent of them are women employed as "dance entertainers." Commonly, the passports of these "guest workers" are confiscated on arrival and their salaries withheld; according to Mizuho Matsuda, the director of HELP, the only shelter for abused migrant women workers in Tokyo, many are forced into prostitution. Japan's criminal syndicate, the Yazuka, is heavily involved in trafficking women for the country's sex-and-entertainment industry, and like their Russian counterpart, have contacts in the government, and therefore often enjoy its protection.

A grisly side of a grim industry is highlighted by the death of 22-year old Maricris Siosin, a graduate in modern dance. Five months after arriving in Tokyo, she was sent home in a closed coffin, with a death certificate stating she had died of hepatitis. When her family opened the coffin for the funeral, they discovered that she had been beaten and stabbed. An autopsy conducted by the Philippines National Bureau of Investigation and confirmed, at the request of Equality Now, by a leading pathologist in the U.S., showed that a double-edged sword had been thrust into her vagina.

In Japan, S&M has a long tradition, and extremely violent S&M comics are readily available. Many male commuters openly read them instead of newspapers as they travel to and from work. One theory is that Maricris was forced to participate in a "snuff" movie (a porno flick in which the woman is actually killed).

A Philippine government mission which was sent to Japan to investigate the murder was turned away by Japanese authorities. Similarly, Maricris' family has been denied access to medical documents and police records. Some 33 Filipino workers died in Japan the same year Maricris was killed. At least 12 of these deaths took place under "suspicious circumstances."

In other countries, local authorities facilitate sex trafficking. In the southern Thai town of Ranong, for example, brothels are surrounded by electrified barbed wire and armed guards to keep girls from escaping. The local police chief condones the practice, describing the brothels as an important part of the local economy. And while prostitution is illegal in Thailand, customers and owners alike have no fear of arrest. The police can be bought off, or accept payment in kind—free use of the brothels; a number of them also act as procurers for the traffickers.

The government periodically promises to crack down on the industry, but because of the amount of money it generates, invariably looks the other way. Of the five million annual visitors to Thailand on tourist visas, three out of four are men traveling alone, many of whom are from Europe, the Middle East, Japan, and the U.S. When raids are planned, the police often alert the brothels ahead of time. The only people arrested are the young prostitutes. Tragically, they are then frequently "recycled," often with the assistance of the local police, who resell them to agents of a different brothel. And so the tragic circle remains unbroken, until the girls become too sick to work, or die on the job, like the five young prostitutes on Phuket island, a popular vacation resort for foreigners in southern Thailand: When fire broke out in the brothel where they worked, they burned to death because they were chained to their beds and unable to escape.

Tourism in Thailand generates $3 billion annually, and the country's international image as a sexual paradise has made prostitution one of its most valuable economic subsectors. That international reputation is one even the U.S. Navy has recognized. The first port of call and liberty shore leave for much of the U.S. fleet after the Gulf War was Pattaya, a beach resort notorious as a center of Thailand's sex industry. This apparent reward for service was given despite the fact that at the time at least 50 percent of the prostitutes in the region were HIV-positive. Another major destination for sex traffickers is India, where an estimated 15 million women and girls, many of whom have been sold into it from impoverished Nepal, Bangladesh, and Pakistan, work in the sex industry.

"Women and girls are moved between a lot of different countries," says a spokesman for Human Rights Watch. Moreover, trafficking is not only a global phenomenon, it is a "hidden one." For example, the organization reported recently, the U.S. gives Thailand $4 million a year to control the traffic in narcotics, but no U.S. aid is aimed at curtailing sex trafficking there. It is imperative that the U.S. government "recognize the severity of the problem," says Human Rights Watch. "And the United Nations also needs to be very aggressive in fighting this modern form of slavery."

59

WHERE RACE AND GENDER MEET
Racism, Hate Crimes, and Pornography

HELEN ZIA

There is a specific area where racism, hate crimes, and pornography intersect, and where current civil rights law fails: racially motivated, gender-based crimes against women of color. This area of bias-motivated sexual assault has been called "ethnorape"; I refer to it as "hate rape."

I started looking into this issue after years of organizing against hate killings of Asian Americans. After a while, I noticed that all the cases I could name concerned male victims. I wondered why. Perhaps it was because Asian-American men came into contact with perpetrator types more often or because they are more hated and therefore more often attacked by racists. But the subordination and vulnerability of Asian-American women, who are thought to be sexually exotic, subservient, and passive, argued against that interpretation. So where were the Asian-American women hate-crime victims?

Once I began looking, I found them, in random news clippings, in footnotes in books, through word of mouth. Let me share with you some examples I unearthed of bias-motivated attacks and sexual assaults:

- In February 1984, Ly Yung Cheung, a nineteen-year-old Chinese woman who was seven months pregnant, was pushed in front of a New York City subway train and decapitated. Her attacker, a white male high school teacher, claimed he suffered from "a phobia of Asian people" and was overcome with the urge to kill this woman. He successfully pleaded insanity. If this case had been investigated as a hate crime, there might have been more information about his so-called phobia and whether it was part of a pattern of racism. But it was not.
- On December 7, 1984, fifty-two-year-old Japanese American Helen Fukui disappeared in Denver, Colorado. Her decomposed body was found weeks later. Her disappearance on Pearl Harbor Day, when anti-Asian speech and incidents increase dramatically, was considered

---

significant in the community. But the case was not investigated as a hate crime and no suspects were ever apprehended.

- In 1985 an eight-year-old Chinese girl named Jean Har-Kaw Fewel was found raped and lynched in Chapel Hill, North Carolina—two months after Penthouse featured pictures of Asian women in various poses of bondage and torture, including hanging bound from trees. Were epithets or pornography used during the attack? No one knows—her rape and killing were not investigated as a possible hate crime.
- Recently a serial rapist was convicted of kidnapping and raping a Japanese exchange student in Oregon. He had also assaulted a Japanese woman in Arizona, and another in San Francisco. He was sentenced to jail for these crimes, but they were never pursued as hate crimes, even though California has a hate statute. Was hate speech or race-specific pornography used? No one knows.
- At Ohio State University, two Asian women were gang raped by fraternity brothers in two separate incidents. One of the rapes was part of a racially targeted game called the "Ethnic Sex Challenge," in which the fraternity men followed an ethnic checklist indicating what kind of women to gang rape. Because the women feared humiliation and ostracism by their communities, neither reported the rapes. However, campus officials found out about the attacks, but did not take them up as hate crimes, or as anything else.

All of these incidents could have been investigated and prosecuted either as state hate crimes or as federal civil rights cases. But they were not. To have done so would have required one of two things: awareness and interest on the part of police investigators and prosecutors—who generally have a poor track record on race and gender issues—or awareness and support for civil rights charges by the Asian-American community—which is generally lacking on issues surrounding women, gender, sex, and sexual assault. The result is a double-silencing effect on the assaults and deaths of these women, who become invisible because of their gender and their race.

Although my research centers on hate crimes and Asian women, this silence and this failure to provide equal protection have parallels in all of the other classes protected by federal civil rights and hate statutes. That is, all other communities of color have a similar prosecution rate for hate crimes against the women in their communities—namely, zero. This dismal record is almost as bad in lesbian and gay antiviolence projects: the vast preponderance of hate crimes reported, tracked, and prosecuted concern gay men—very few concern lesbians. So where are all the women?

The answer to this question lies in the way our justice system was designed, and the way women are mere shadows in the existing civil rights framework. But in spite of this history, federal and state law do offer legal avenues for women to be heard. Federal civil rights prosecutions, for example, can be excellent platforms for high-visibility community education on the harmful impact of hate speech and behavior. When on June 19, 1982, two white auto workers in Detroit screamed racial epithets at Chinese-American Vincent Chin and said, "It's because of you motherfuckers that we're out of work," a public furor followed, raising the level of national discourse on what constitutes racism toward Asian Americans. Constitutional law professors, and members of the American Civil Liberties Union and the National Lawyers Guild had acted as if Asian Americans were not covered by civil rights law. Asian Americans emphatically corrected that misconception.

Hate crimes remedies can be used to force the criminal justice bureaucracy to adopt new attitudes. Patrick Purdy went to an elementary school in Stockton, California, in which 85 percent of the students came from Southeast Asia. When he selected that school as the place to open fire with his automatic weapon and killed five eight-year-olds and wounded thirty other children, the police and the media did not think it was a bias-motivated crime. Their denial reminds me of the response by the Montreal officials to the anti-feminist killings of fourteen women students there. But an outraged Asian-American community forced a state investigation into the Purdy incident and uncovered hate literature in the killer's effects. As a result, the community was validated, and, in addition, the criminal justice system and the media acquired a new level of understanding.

Imagine if a federal civil rights investigation had been launched in the case of the African-American student at St. John's University who was raped and sodomized by white members of the school lacrosse team, who were later acquitted. Investigators could have raised issues of those white men's attitudes toward the victim as a black woman, found out whether hate speech or race-specific pornography was present, investigated the overall racial climate on campus, and brought all of the silenced aspects of the incident to the public eye. Community discourse could have been raised to a high level.

Making these investigations happen will not be an easy road. Hate-crime efforts are generally expended on blatant cases, with high community consensus, not ones that bring up hard issues like gender-based violence. Yet these intersections of race and gender hatred are the very issues we must give voice to.

There is a serious difficulty with pushing for use of federal and state hate remedies. Some state statutes have been used against men of color: specifically, on behalf of white rape victims against African-American men. We know that the system, if left unchecked, will try to use antihate laws to enforce unequal justice. On the other hand, state hate statutes could be used to prosecute men of color who are believed to have assaulted women of color of another race—interminority assaults are increasing. Also, if violence against women generally were made into a hate crime, women of color could seek prosecutions against men in their own community for their gender-based violence—even if this would make it harder to win the support of men in communities of color, and of women in those communities who would not want to be accused of dividing the community.

But at least within the Asian-American antiviolence community, this discourse is taking place now. Asian-American feminists in San Francisco have prepared a critique of the Asian movement against hate crimes and the men of that movement are listening. Other communities of color should also examine the nexus between race and gender for women of color, and by extension, for all women.

The legal system must expand the boundaries of existing law to include the most invisible women. There are hundreds of cases involving women of color waiting to be filed. Activists in the violence-against-women movement must reexamine current views on gender-based violence. Not all sexual assaults are the same. Racism in a sexual assault adds another dimension to the pain and harm inflicted. By taking women of color out of the legal shadows, out of invisibility, all women make gains toward full human dignity and human rights.

60

HOMOPHOBIA IN STRAIGHT MEN

TERRY A. KUPERS

A few years ago I toured a high-security prison in the Midwest as an expert witness in litigation concerning the effects of prison conditions on prisoners' mental health. When I stepped into the main entry area of the prison, I saw a woman milling around with the men a short distance down one of the halls. She was blond, slim, very feminine—or so I thought on first glance. Actually, "she" was a young man, perhaps 21, dressed as a woman. Blond, blue-eyed, slight and sensuous, he played the part very well. He wore a flowing red gown that reached the floor, had a shawl draped across his chest in a way that did not permit one to assess the size of his breasts, wore make-up, and sported a very seductive female pose. I was surprised to see an attractive woman roaming around in a men's prison. One of the attorneys accompanying me on the tour told me with a wink that "she" was a he, and asked if I would like to talk to him.

The inmate told me he was not really gay, and certainly did not believe he would dress as a woman again after he was released, but on "the inside" it's the only way for him to survive unless he "locks up"; that is, asks for protective custody in a segregated section of the prison where inmates who do not feel safe on the "mainline" are housed, including those identified as "snitches" and child molesters. When this man arrived at the prison at 19 he was beat up and raped a number of times, and on several other occasions prison toughs fought with each other for the opportunity to use him sexually. He learned that it was safer to become the "woman" of a tough prisoner, that way he would not be beaten nor be the object of rivalries between prison toughs. He would become the passive sexual partner of one dominant man.

Later that day I met with a group of security officers. One mentioned the young man. I said I had met him. The officer asked if I'd like to hear the bit of advice he would have given that slight and fair young man if he had seen him when he entered the prison. Before I had a chance to answer, he blurted out:

> What you want to do is the first time you go out on the yard you break off a metal bed post and shove it down your trouser leg. Then, when a big guy comes up and pinches your ass or makes a lewd remark, you pull out the metal stick and smack him as hard as you can across the face. You'll both get thrown in the hole for ten days. Then, when you get out, everyone will respect you as a "crazy" and no one will hassle you for sex any more.

In prison, "butt-fucking" is the symbol of dominance. The strong do it, the weak must submit. Homosexual rape is a constant threat for those who cannot prove they are "man enough." According to Tom Cahill (1990), a survivor of prison rape: "We are victims of a system in which those who are dominated and humiliated come to dominate and humiliate others" (p. 33). Perhaps this explains why prisoners do so much body-building.

Free men do a lot of toughening, too. If it is not the physique it's the mind, or it's the reputation or the financial empire, but men are always building something that they believe will keep them off the bottom of the heap, out of range of those who would "shaft" them. This is not a complete explanation of men's competitiveness and defensiveness—competition is built into our social relations—but men's subjective dread of "being shafted" plays a part in sustaining those competitive social relations. The prison drama reverberates in the male psyche. It is as if men do not want to appear incapable of defending themselves against rape at any time. We stiffen our bodies when approached by other men who want to touch or hug and we keep men at a certain distance—where we can watch them and be certain that closeness and dependency will not make us too vulnerable.

61

PHANTOM TOWERS
Feminist Reflections on the Battle between Global Capitalism and Fundamentalist Terrorism

ROSALIND P. PETCHESKY

These are trying times, hard times to know where we are from one day to the next. The attack on the World Trade Center has left many kinds of damage in its wake, not the least of which is a gaping ethical and political confusion in the minds of many Americans who identify in some way as "progressive"—meaning, anti-racist, feminist, democratic (small d), anti-war. While we have a responsibility to those who died in the disaster and their loved ones, and to ourselves, to mourn, it is urgent that we also begin the work of thinking through what kind of world we are now living in and what it demands of us. And we have to do this, even while we know our understanding at this time can only be very tentative and may well be invalidated a year or even a month or a week from now by events we can't foresee or information now hidden from us.

So I want to try to draw a picture or a kind of mapping of the global power dynamics as I see them at this moment, including their gendered and racialized dimensions. I want to ask whether there is some alternative, more humane and peaceable way out of the two unacceptable polarities now being presented to us: the permanent war machine (or permanent security state) and the regime of holy terror.

Let me make very clear that, when I pose the question whether we are presently facing a confrontation between global capitalism and an Islamist-fundamentalist brand of fascism, I do not mean to imply their equivalence. If, in fact, the attacks of September 11 were the work of bin Laden's Al-Qaeda network or something related and even larger—and for the moment I think we can assume this as a real possibility—then most of us in this room are *structurally positioned* in a way that gives us little choice about our identities. (For the Muslim-Americans and Arab-Americans among us, who are both

---

Rosalind P. Petchesky, "Phantom Towers: Feminist Reflections on the Battle Between Global Capitalism and Fundamentalist Terrorism" from *Women's Review of Books* (November 2001).

This essay originated in a presentation given at the Hunter College Political Science Department Teach-In, New York City, September 25, 2001.

opposed to terrorism and terrified to walk in our streets, the moral dilemma must be, I imagine, much more agonizing.) As an American, a woman, a feminist, and a Jew, I have to recognize that the bin Ladens of the world hate me and would like me dead; or, if they had power over me, would make my life a living hell. I have to wish them—these "perpetrators," "terrorists," whatever they are—apprehended, annulled, so I can breathe in some kind of peace. This is quite different from living at the very center of global capitalism—which is more like living in a very dysfunctional family that fills you with shame and anger for its arrogance, greed, and insensitivity but is, like it or not, your home and gives you both immense privileges and immense responsibilities.

Nor, however, do I succumb to the temptation of casting our current dilemma in the simplistic, Manichean terms of cosmic Good versus Evil. Currently this comes in two opposed but mirror-image versions: the narrative, advanced not only by the terrorists and their sympathizers but also by many on the left in the United States and around the globe, that blames U.S. cultural imperialism and economic hegemony for the "chickens coming home to roost"; versus the patriotic, right-wing version that casts U.S. democracy and freedom as the innocent target of Islamist madness. Both these stories erase all the complexities that we must try to factor into a different, more inclusive ethical and political vision. The Manichean, apocalyptic rhetorics that echoed back and forth between Bush and bin Laden in the aftermath of the attacks—the pseudo-Islamic and the pseudo-Christian, the jihad and the crusade—both lie.

So, while I do not see terrorist networks and global capitalism as equivalents or the same, I do see some striking and disturbing parallels between them. I picture them as the phantom Twin Towers arising in the smoke clouds of the old—fraternal twins, not identical, locked in a battle over wealth, imperial aggrandizement and the meanings of masculinity. It is a battle that could well end in a stalemate, an interminable cycle of violence that neither can win because of their failure to see the other clearly. Feminist analysts and activists from many countries—whose voices have been inaudible thus far in the present crisis—have a lot of experience to draw from in making this double critique. Whether in the UN or national settings, we have been challenging the gender-biased and racialized dimensions of *both* neoliberal capitalism and various fundamentalisms for years, trying to steer a path between their double menace. The difference now is that they parade onto the world stage in their most extreme and violent forms. I see six areas where their posturing overlaps:

1. Wealth—Little needs to be said about the United States as the world's wealthiest country nor the ways in which wealth-accumulation is the holy grail, not only of our political system (think of the difficulty we have even in reforming campaign finance laws), but of our national ethos. We are the headquarters of the corporate and financial mega-empires that dominate global capitalism and influence the policies of the international financial institutions (IMF, World Bank, WTO) that are its main governing bodies. This reality resonates around the globe in the symbolic pantheon of what the United States stands for—from the McDonald's and Kentucky Fried Chicken ads sported by protestors in Genoa and Rawalpindi to the WTC towers themselves. Acquisitiveness, whether individual or corporate, also lurks very closely behind the values that Bush and Rumsfeld mean when they say our "freedoms" and our "way of life" are being attacked and must be defended fiercely. (Why, as I'm writing this, do unsolicited messages about Wall Street investment opportunities or low fares to the Bahamas come spewing out of my fax machine?)

Wealth is also a driving force behind the Al-Qaeda network, whose principals are mainly the beneficiaries of upper-middle-class or elite financing and education. bin Laden himself derives much of his power and influence from his family's vast fortune, and the cells of Arab-Afghan fighters in the 1980s war against the Soviets were bankrolled not only by the Pakistani secret police and the CIA—$3 billion writes Katha Pollitt in *The Nation,* "more money and expertise than for any other cause in CIA history"—but also by Saudi oil money. More important than this, though, are the values behind the terrorist organizations, which include—as bin Laden made clear in his famous 1998 interview—defending the "honor" and "property" of Muslims everywhere and "[fighting] the governments that are bent on attacking our religion and on stealing our wealth. . . ." Political scientist Paul Amar, in a recent talk at Hunter College, rightly urges us not to confuse these wealthy networks—whose nepotism and ties to oil interests eerily resemble those of the Bush family—with impoverished and resistant social movements throughout the Middle East and Asia. There is no evidence that economic justice or equality figure anywhere in the terrorist program.

2. *Imperialist Nationalism*—The Bush administration's initial reaction to the attacks exhibited the behavior of a superpower that knows no limits, that issues ultimatums under the cover of "seeking cooperation." "Every nation in every region has a decision to make," pronounced Bush in his speech to the nation that was really a speech to the world; "Either you are with us or you are with the terrorists." "This is the world's fight, this is civilization's fight"—the United States, then, becoming the leader and spokesman of "civilization," relegating not only the terrorists but also those who refuse to join the fight to the ranks of the uncivilized. To the Taliban and to every other regime that "harbors terrorists," he was the sheriff stonewalling the cattle rustlers: "Hand over all the terrorists or you will share in their fate." And a few days later we read "the American announcement that it *would* use Saudi Arabia as a headquarters for air operations against Afghanistan." As the war campaign progresses, its aims seem more openly imperialist: "Washington wants to offer [the small, also fundamentalist, drug-dealing *mujahedeen* mostly routed by the Taliban] a role in governing Afghanistan after the conflict," according to The *New York Times* of September 24, as if this were

"Washington's" official role. Further, it and its allies are courting the octogenarian, long-forgotten Afghan king (now exiled in Italy) to join in a military operation to oust the Taliban and set up—what? a kind of puppet government? Nothing here about internationally monitored elections, nothing about the UN, or any concept of the millions of Afghan people—within the country or in exile—as anything but voiceless, downtrodden victims and refugees.

Clearly, this offensive involves far more than rooting out and punishing terrorists. Though I don't want to reduce the situation to a crude Marxist scenario, one can't help wondering how it relates to the longstanding determination of the United States to keep a dominant foothold in the gulf region and to maintain control over oil supplies. At least one faction of the Bush "team," clamoring to go after Saddam Hussein as well, is clearly in this mindset. And let's not forget Pakistan and its concessions to U.S. demands for cooperation in return for lifting of United States economic sanctions—and now, the assurance of a sizable IMF loan. In the tradition of neo-imperial power, the United States does not need to dominate countries politically or militarily to get the concessions it wants; its economic influence backed up by the capacity for military annihilation is sufficient. And, spurred by popular rage over the WTC attacks, all this is wrapped in the outpouring of nationalist patriotism and flag-waving that now envelops the American landscape.

Though lacking the actual imperial power of the United States, the bin Laden forces mimic its imperial aspirations. If we ask, what are the terrorists seeking?, we need to recognize their worldview as an extreme and vicious form of nationalism—a kind of fascism, I would argue, because of its reliance on terror to achieve its ends. In this respect, their goals, like those of the United States, go beyond merely punishment. Amar says the whole history of Arab and Islamic nationalism has been one that transcended the colonially imposed boundaries of the nation-state, one that was always transnational and pan-Arabic, or pan-Muslim, in form. Although the terrorists have no social base or legitimacy in laying claim to this tradition, they clearly seek to usurp it. This seems evident in bin Laden's language invoking "the Arab nation," "the Arab peninsula," and a "brotherhood" reaching from Eastern Europe to Turkey and Albania, to the entire Middle East, South Asia and Kashmir. Their mission is to drive out "the infidels" and their Muslim supporters from something that looks like a third of the globe. Provoking the United States to bomb Afghanistan and/or attempt ousting the Taliban would likely destabilize Pakistan and possibly catapult it into the hands of Taliban-like extremists, who would then control nuclear weapons—a big step toward their perverted and hijacked version of the pan-Muslim dream.

*3. **Pseudo-Religion***—As many others have commented, the "clash of religions" or "clash of cultures" interpretation of the current scenario is utterly specious. What we have instead is an appropriation of religious symbolism and discourse for predominantly political purposes, and to justify permanent war and violence. So bin Laden declares a jihad, or holy war, against the United States, its civilians as well as its soldiers; and Bush declares a crusade against the terrorists and all who harbor or support them. Bin Laden declares himself the "servant of Allah fighting for the sake of the religion of Allah" and to protect Islam's holy mosques, while Bush declares Washington the promoter of "infinite justice" and predicts certain victory, because "God is not neutral." (The Pentagon changed the "Operation Infinite Justice" label to "Operation Enduring Freedom" after Muslim-Americans objected and three Christian clergymen warned that "infinite" presumed divinity, the "sin of pride.") But we have to question the authenticity of this religious discourse on both sides, however sincere its proponents. A "Statement from Scholars of the Islamic Religion," circulated after the attacks, firmly denounces terrorism—the wanton killing of innocent civilians—as contrary to Sh'aria law. And Bush's adoption of this apocalyptic discourse can only be seen as substituting a conservative, right-wing form of legitimation for the neoliberal internationalist discourse that conservatives reject. In either case, it is worth quoting the always wise Eduardo Galeano, writing in Mexico's *La Jornada:* "In the struggle of Good against Evil, it's always the people who get killed."

***4. Militarism*—**Both the Bush administration and the bin Laden forces adopt the methods of war and violence to achieve their ends, but in very different ways. U.S. militarism is of the ultra-high-tech variety that seeks to terrorize by the sheer might, volume and technological virtuosity of our armaments. Of course, as the history of Vietnam and the survival of Saddam Hussein attest, this is an illusion of the highest order. (Remember the "smart bombs" in the Gulf War that headed for soda machines?) But our military technology is also a vast and insatiable industry for which profit, not strategy, is the driving rationale. As Jack Blum, a critic of U.S. foreign policy, pointed out recently in the *Sacramento Bee,* "the national defense game is a systems and money operation" that has little if any relevance to terrorism. Missiles were designed to counter hostile states with their own fixed territories and weapons arsenals, not terrorists who sneak around the globe and whose "weapons of mass destruction" are human bodies and hijacked planes; nor the famously impervious terrain and piles of rubble that constitute Afghanistan. Even George W., in one of his most sensible comments to date, remarked that we'd know better than to aim "a $2 billion cruise missile at a $10 empty tent." And yet four days after the attack the Democrats in Congress piled madness atop madness and withdrew their opposition to Bush's costly and destructive "missile shield," voting to restore $1.3 billion in spending authority for this misconceived and dangerous project. And the armaments companies quickly started lining up to receive their big orders for the impending next war—the war, we are told, that will last a long time, maybe the rest of our lives. U.S. militarism is not about rationality—not even about fighting terrorism—but about profits.

The war-mania and rallying around the flag exhibited by the American people express desire, not for military profits, but for something else, something harder for feminist and anti-war dissidents to understand. Maybe it's just the need to vent anger and feel avenged, or the more deep-rooted one to experience some sense of community and higher purpose in a society where we are so atomized and isolated from one another and the world. On September 25, Barbara Kingsolver wrote in the *San Francisco Chronicle* that she and her husband reluctantly sent their 5-year-old daughter to school dressed in red, white and blue like the other kids because they didn't want to let jingoists and censors "steal the flag from us." Their little girl probably echoed the longings of many less reflective grownups when she said, wearing the colors of the flag "means we're a country; just people all together."

The militarism of the terrorists is of a very different nature—based on the mythic figure of the Bedouin warrior, or the Ikhwan fighters of the early 20th century who enabled Ibn Saud to consolidate his dynastic state. Their hallmark is individual courage and ferocity in battle; Malise Ruthven's *Islam in the World* quotes one Arab witness who described them, foreshadowing reports of Soviet veterans from the 1980s Afghan war, as: "utterly fearless of death, not caring how many fall, advancing rank upon rank with only one desire—the defeat and annihilation of the enemy." Of course, this image too, like every hyper-nationalist ideology, is rooted in a mythic golden past and has little to do with how real terrorists in the 21st century are recruited, trained and paid off. And, like high-tech militarism, terrorist low-tech militarism is also based in an illusion—that millions of believers will rise up, obey the fatwa, and defeat the infidel. It's an illusion because it grossly underestimates the most powerful weapon in global capitalism's arsenal—not "infinite justice" or even nukes but infinite Nikes and CD's. And it also underestimates the local power of feminism, which the fundamentalists mistakenly confuse with the West. Iran today, in all its internal contradictions, shows the resilience and globalized/localized variety of both youth cultures and women's movements.

5. ***Masculinism***—Militarism, nationalism, and colonialism as terrains of power have always been in large part contests over the meanings of manhood. Feminist political scientist Cynthia Enloe remarks that "men's sense of their own masculinity, often tenuous, is as much a factor in international politics as is the flow of oil, cables, and military hardware." In the case of bin Laden's Taliban patrons, the form and excessiveness of the misogyny that goes hand in hand with state terrorism and extreme fundamentalism have been graphically documented. Just go to the website of the Revolutionary Association of the Women of Afghanistan (RAWA), at www.rawa.org, to view more photos of atrocities against women (and men) for sexual offenses, dress code offenses, and other forms of deviance than you'll be able to stomach. According to John Burns, writing in the *NY Times Magazine* in 1990, the "rebel" leader in the Afghan war who received "the lion's share of American money and weapons"—and was not a Taliban—had been reputed to have "dispatched followers [during his student movement days] to throw vials of acid into the faces of women students who refused to wear veils."

In the case of transnational terrorists and bin Laden himself, their model of manliness is that of the Islamic "brotherhood," the band of brothers bonded together in an agonistic commitment to fighting the enemy to the death. The CIA-Pakistani-Saudi-backed camps and training schools set up to support the "freedom fighters" (who later became "terrorists") in the anti-Soviet war were breeding grounds not only of a worldwide terrorist network but also of its masculinist, misogynist culture. Bin Laden clearly sees himself as a patriarchal tribal chief whose duty is to provide for and protect, not only his own retinue, wives and many children, but also his whole network of lieutenants and recruits and their families. He is the legendary Arabic counterpart of the Godfather.

In contrast to this, can we say that the United States as standard-bearer of global capitalism is "gender-neutral"? Don't we have a woman—indeed an African-American woman—at the helm of our National Security Council, the president's right hand in designing the permanent war machine? Despite reported "gender gaps" in polls about war, we know that women are not inherently more peace-loving than men. Remember all those suburban housewives with their yellow ribbons in midwestern airports and shopping malls during the Gulf War? Global capitalist masculinism is alive and well but concealed in its Eurocentric, racist guise of "rescuing" downtrodden Afghan women from the misogynist regime it helped bring to power. Feminists around the world, who have tried for so long to call attention to the plight of women and girls in Afghanistan, cannot feel consoled by the prospect of U.S. warplanes and U.S.-backed guerrilla chiefs coming to "save our Afghan sisters." Meanwhile, the U.S. will send single mothers who signed up for the National Guard when welfare ended to fight and die in its holy war; U.S. media remain silent about the activism and self-determination of groups like RAWA, Refugee Women in Development and NEGAR; and the U.S. military establishment refuses accountability before an International Criminal Court for the acts of rape and sexual assault committed by its soldiers stationed across the globe. Masculinism and misogyny take many forms, not always the most visible.

6. Racism—Of course, what I have named fascist fundamentalism, or transnational terrorism, is also saturated in racism, but of a very specific, focused kind—which is anti-semitism. The WTC towers symbolized not only American capitalism, not only finance capitalism, but, for the terrorists, *Jewish* finance capitalism. We can see this in the reported misreporting of the September 11 attacks in Arabic language newspapers in the Middle East as probably the work of the Israelis; their erroneous allegation that not a single person among the dead and missing was Jewish, so Jews must have had advance warning, etc. In his 1998 interview, bin Laden constantly refers to "Jews," not Israelis, in his accusations about plans to take over the whole Arab peninsula. He asserts that "the Americans and the Jews . . . represent the spearhead with which the members of our religion have been slaughtered. Any effort directed against America and the Jews yields positive and direct results." And finally, he rewrites history and collapses the diversity of Muslims in a warning to "Western governments" to sever their ties to Jews: "the enmity between us and the Jews goes far back in time and is deep rooted. There is no question that war between the two of us is inevitable. For this reason it is not in the interest of Western governments to expose the interests of their people to all kinds of retaliation for almost nothing." (I cringe to realize I am part of the "nothing.")

U.S. racism is much more diffuse but just as insidious; the pervasive racism and ethnocentrism that fester under the American skin always boil to the surface at times of national crisis. As Sumitha Reddy put it in a recent teach-in, the targeting of Sikhs and other Indians, Arabs, and even tan Latinos and African-Americans in the wave of violent and abusive acts throughout the country since the disaster signals an enlargement of the "zone of distrust" in American racism beyond the usual black-white focus. Women who wear headscarves or saris are particularly vulnerable to harassment, but Arab and Indian men of all ages are the ones being murdered. The state pretends to abhor such incidents and threatens their full prosecution. But this is the same state that made the so-called Anti-Terrorism Act, passed in 1995 after the Oklahoma City bombing (an act committed by native white Christian terrorists), a pretext for rounding up and deporting immigrants of all kinds; and that is now once again waiving the civil liberties of immigrants in its zealous anti-terrorist manhunt. Each day The *New York Times* publishes its rogues' gallery of police photos of the suspects, so reminiscent of those eugenic photographs of "criminal types" of an earlier era and imprinting upon readers' minds a certain set of facial characteristics they should now fear and blame. Racial profiling becomes a national pastime.

If we look only at terrorist tactics and the world's revulsion against them, then we might conclude rather optimistically that thuggery will never win out in the end. But we ignore the context in which terrorism operates at our peril, and that context includes not only racism and Eurocentrism but many forms of social injustice. In thinking through a moral position on this crisis, we have to distinguish between *immediate causes* and *necessary conditions.* Neither the United States (as a state) nor the corporate and financial power structure that the World Trade Centers symbolized *caused* the horrors of September 11. Without question, the outrageous, heinous murder, maiming and orphaning of so many innocent people—who were every race, ethnicity, color, class, age, gender, and some 60-odd nationalities—deserve some kind of just redress. On the other hand, the *conditions* in which transnational terrorism thrives, gains recruits, and lays claim to moral legitimacy include many for which the United States and its corporate/financial interests are directly responsible even if they don't for a minute excuse the attacks. It is often asked lately, why does the Third World hate us so much? Put another way, why do so many people including my own friends in Asia, Africa, Latin

America and the Middle East express so much ambivalence about what happened, both lamenting an unforgivable criminal act and at the same time taking some satisfaction that Americans are finally suffering too? We make a fatal mistake if we attribute these mixed feelings only to envy or resentment of our wealth and freedoms and ignore a historical context of aggression, injustice and inequality. Consider these facts:

1. The United States is still the only country in the world to have actually *used* the most infamous weapons of mass destruction in the nuclear bombing of innocent civilians—in Hiroshima and Nagasaki.
2. The United States persists to this day in bombing Iraq, destroying the lives and food supplies of hundreds of thousands of civilian adults and children there. We bombed Belgrade—a dense capital city—for 80 straight days during the war in Kosovo and supported bombing that killed untold civilians in El Salvador in the 1980s. In the name of fighting Communism, our CIA and military training apparatus sponsored paramilitary massacres, assassinations, tortures and disappearances in many Latin American and Central American countries in Operation Condor and the like in the 1970s and has supported corrupt, authoritarian regimes in the Middle East, Southeast Asia, and elsewhere—the Shah of Iran, Suharto in Indonesia, the Saudi dynasty, and let's not forget the Taliban regime itself. September 11 is also the date of the coup against the democratically elected Allende government in Chile and the beginning of the 25-year Pinochet dictatorship, again thanks to U.S. support. Yes, a long history of state terrorism.
3. In the Middle East, which is the microcosm of the current conflagration, billions in annual U.S. military aid and the Bush administration's refusal to pressure the Sharon government are the sine qua non of continued Israeli government policies of attacks on villages, demolition of homes, destruction of olive orchards, restrictions on travel, continual human rights abuses of Palestinians and even Arab citizens, assassination of political leaders, building of roads and enlarging of settlements—all of which exacerbate Palestinian despair and suicide bombings. The United States thereby contributes to deepening the illegal occupation and "bantustanizing" the Palestinian territories, and thus perpetuating hostilities.
4. Despite its pretense to uphold women's rights, the U.S. is one of only around two dozen countries that have failed to ratify the UN Convention on the Elimination of All Forms of Discrimination Against Women, and the only country in the world [as of April 2002, when Somalia finally agreed to sign] that refuses to sign the UN Convention on the Rights of the Child. It is the most vocal opponent of the statute establishing an International Criminal Court as well as the treaties banning land mines and germ warfare; a principal subverter of a new multilateral treaty to combat illegal small arms trafficking; and the

sole country in the world to threaten an unprecedented space-based defense system and imminent violation of the ABM treaty. So who is the "outlaw," the "rogue state"?

5. The United States is the only major industrialized country to refuse signing the final Kyoto Protocol on Global Climate Change, despite compromises in that document designed to meet U.S. objections. Meanwhile, a new global scientific study shows that the countries whose productivity will benefit most from climate change are Canada, Russia and the United States, while the biggest losers will be the countries that have contributed least to global climate change—i.e., most of Africa.
6. As even the World Bank and the United Nations Development Programme attest, two decades of globalization have resulted in enlarging rather than shrinking the gaps between rich and poor, both within countries and among countries. The benefits of global market liberalization and integration have accrued disproportionately to wealthy Americans and Europeans (as well as small elites in the Third World). Despite the presumed democratizing effects of the Internet, a middle-class American "needs to save a month's salary to buy a computer; a Bangladeshi must save all his wages for eight years to do so." And despite its constant trumpeting of "free-trade" rhetoric, the United States remains a persistent defender of protectionist policies for its farmers and steel and textile manufacturers. Meanwhile small producers throughout Asia, Africa and the Caribbean—a great many of whom are women—are squeezed out by U.S. imports and relegated to the informal economy or sweatshop labor for multinationals.
7. The G-8 countries, of which the United States is the senior partner, dominate decision-making in the IMF and the World Bank, whose structural adjustments and conditionalities for loans and debt relief help to keep many poor countries and their citizens locked in poverty.
8. In the aftermath of the September 11 attacks, the U.S. Congress was able to come up with an immediate $40 billion for "anti-terrorism" activities, another $40 billion to bail out the airlines, and a 20-year contract with Lockheed to produce military aircraft for $200 billion—enough to eliminate contagious diseases from the face of the earth. Yet our foreign assistance appropriations (except for military aid) have shrunk; we, the world's richest country, contribute only 1/7 of 1 percent of our GNP to foreign aid—the least of any industrialized country. A recent WHO report tells us the total cost of providing safe water and sanitation to all of sub-Saharan Africa would be only $11 billion, only no one can figure out where the money will come from; and the UN is still a long way off from raising a similar amount for its proclaimed Global Fund to combat AIDS, malaria and TB. What kind of meanness is this? And what does it say about forms of racism, or "global apartheid," that value some lives—those in the United States and Europe—far more than others in other parts of the globe?

And the list goes on, with McDonald's, Coca-Cola, CNN and MTV and all the uninvited commercial detritus that proliferates everywhere on the face of the earth and offends the cultural and spiritual sensibilities of so many—including transnational feminist travelers like me, when we find pieces of our local shopping mall transplanted to central Manila, Kampala or Bangalore. But worse than the triviality and bad taste of these cultural and commercial barrages is the arrogant presumption that our "way of life" is the best on earth and ought to be welcome everywhere; or that our power and supposed advancement entitle us to dictate policies and strategies to the rest of the world. This is the face of imperialism in the 21st century.

None of this reckoning can comfort those who lost loved ones on September 11, or the thousands of attack victims who lost their jobs, homes and livelihoods; nor can it excuse the hideous crimes. As the Palestinian poet Mahmoud Darwish writes, "nothing, nothing justifies terrorism." Still, in attempting to understand what has happened and think how to prevent it happening again (which is probably a vain wish), we Americans have to take all these painful facts into account. The United States as the command center of global capitalism will remain ill equipped to "stop terrorism" until it begins to recognize its own past and present responsibility for many of the conditions I've listed and to address them in a responsible way. But this would mean the United States becoming something different from itself, transforming itself, including abandoning the presumption that it should unilaterally police the world. This problem of transformation is at the heart of the vexing question of finding solutions different from all-out war. So let me turn to how we might think differently about power. Here is what I propose, tentatively, for now:

1. The slogan "War Is Not the Answer" is a practical as well as an ontological truth. Bombing or other military attacks on Afghanistan will not root out networks of terrorists, who could be hiding deep in the mountains or in Pakistan or Germany or Florida or New Jersey. It will only succeed in destroying an already decimated country, killing untold numbers of civilians as well as combatants and creating hundreds of thousands more refugees. And it is likely to arouse so much anger among Islamist sympathizers as to destabilize the entire region and perpetuate the cycle of retaliation and terrorist attacks. All the horror of the 20th century surely should teach us that war feeds on itself and that armed violence reflects, not an extension of politics by other means, but the failure of politics; not the defense of civilization, but the breakdown of civilization.
2. Tracking down and bringing the perpetrators of terrorism to justice, in some kind of international police action, is a reasonable aim but one fraught with dangers. Because the United States is the world's only "superpower," its declaration of war against terrorism and its supporters everywhere says to other countries that we are once again taking over as global policeman, or, as Fidel Castro put it, a "world military dictatorship under the exclusive rule of force, irrespective of any

international laws or institutions." Here at home a "national emergency" or "state of war"—*especially* when defined as different from any other war—means the curtailment of civil liberties, harassment of immigrants, racial profiling, and withholding of information (censorship) or feeding of disinformation to the media, all without any time limits or accountability under the dubious Office of Homeland Security and the "USA Patriot Act." We should oppose both U.S. unilateralism and the permanent security state. We should urge our representatives in Congress to diligently defend the civil liberties of all.

3. I agree with the Afro-Asian Peoples Solidarity Organization (AAPSO) in Cairo that "this punishment should be inflicted according to the law and only upon those who were responsible for these events," and that it should be organized within the framework of the United Nations and international law, not unilaterally by the United States. This is not the same as the United States getting unanimous approval from the Security Council to commandeer global security, which is a first step at best. Numerous treaties against terrorism and money-laundering already exist in international law. The International Criminal Court, whose establishment the U.S. government has so stubbornly opposed, would be the logical body to try terrorist cases, with the cooperation of national police and surveillance systems. *We should demand that the United States ratify the ICC statute.* In the meantime, a special tribunal under international auspices, like the ones for the former Yugoslavia and Rwanda, could be set up as well as an international agency to coordinate national police and intelligence efforts, with the United States as one participating member. This is the power of international engagement and cooperation.
4. No amount of police action, however cooperative, can stop terrorism without addressing the conditions of misery and injustice that nourish and aggravate terrorism. The United States has to undertake a serious reexamination of its values and its policies with regard not only to the Middle East but also to the larger world. It has to take responsibility for being in the world, including ways of sharing its wealth, resources and technology; democratizing decisions about global trade, finance, and security; and assuring that access to "global public goods" like health care, housing, food, education, sanitation, water, and freedom from racial and gender discrimination is given priority in international relations. What we even mean by "security" has to encompass all these aspects of well-being, of "human security," and has to be universal in its reach.

Let me again quote from the poet Mahmoud Darwish's statement, which was published in the Palestinian daily *Al Ayyam* on September 17 and signed by many Palestinian writers and intellectuals.

> "We know that the American wound is deep and we know that
> this tragic moment is a time for solidarity and the sharing of pain.
> But we also know that the horizons of the intellect can traverse

> landscapes of devastation. Terrorism has no location or boundaries, it does not reside in a geography of its own; its homeland is disillusionment and despair.
>
> "The best weapon to eradicate terrorism from the soul lies in the solidarity of the international world, in respecting the rights of all peoples of this globe to live in harmony and by reducing the ever increasing gap between north and south. And the most effective way to defend freedom is through fully realizing the meaning of justice."

What gives me hope is that this statement's sentiments are being voiced by growing numbers of groups here in the United States, including the National Council of Churches, the Green Party, a coalition of 100 entertainers and civil rights leaders, huge coalitions of peace groups and student organizations, New Yorkers Say No to War, black and white women celebrities featured on Oprah Winfrey's show, parents and spouses of attack victims, as well as some 500 petitioners from women's peace groups here and across the globe calling on the UN Security Council to "Stop the War, Rebuild a Just Society in Afghanistan, and Support Women's Human Rights." Maybe out of the ashes we will recover a new kind of solidarity; maybe the terrorists will force us not to mirror them, but to see the world and humanity as a whole.

62

COMPREHENDING THE AFGHAN QUAGMIRE

RINA AMIRI

> *"Has Afghanistan always been this way?"*
> *"Is the violence in your country due to the feudal, tribalistic culture?"*
> *"Are violence and war in the Afghan genes?"*
> *"Why should we go clean up the Afghan mess? Why are we contributing food and aid to our enemies—the people who harbor terrorists in Afghanistan?"*°

Many questions and comments have been directed at me these last weeks by those who have struggled to grasp the situation in Afghanistan today—the decades of war, the radicalism, and the tragic situation of the people. I have taken on the role of responding and trying to put a human face on the conflict. Time is the only factor that distinguishes me from the Afghans you see on TV,

---

those desperately fleeing Afghanistan with their few belongings and children strapped to a mule, or trudging on foot through the rugged terrain, tugging at the arms of their exhausted and hungry children. More than twenty years ago, I was one of those confused children, clutching the hands of my parents, bewildered by why we were leaving our country all of a sudden.

My family was among the first waves of refugees who traversed the well-trodden Khyber Pass in the 1970s after the Afghan King, Zahir Shah, was overthrown by his cousin, Sardar Daoud. Like the refugees of today in Afghanistan and throughout the world, overnight we were branded as the enemy of the state and became countryless and homeless as a result of other people's wars and other people's politics.

Prior to the coup d'etat in 1973, Afghanistan was a normal place, with ordinary people living routine lives under modest conditions. In Kabul, women made up 60 percent of the educational force and were employed as professionals; secular law and the Islamic Sharia law co-existed as legal mechanisms to address violations; and Afghanistan had not been involved in a war since fighting against British invaders in the 1880s.

What happened, and how has Afghanistan become a victim of an endless cycle of violence and war? There are a multitude of answers capturing the kaleidoscope of truths about Afghanistan. The common element in all of these explanations are two factors: foreign intervention and the internal and external struggle to control Afghanistan.

While Afghanistan has consistently been one of the most underdeveloped and poorest nations in the world, it has also been considered geopolitically one of the most strategic countries to control. It is the boundary between land power and sea power, the meeting point between Central Asia, Iran, India, and the Persian Gulf. Controlling Afghanistan is the key to maintaining influence over these trade routes.

Foreign great powers have always been keenly aware of this. In the nineteenth century, Afghanistan's history was shaped by the British and Russian empires' struggle for domination in what Kipling coined "The Great Games." The twentieth century only continued this trend, with the Soviet Union, the United States, and regional neighbors imposing their respective interests onAfghanistan.

Many Afghans would agree that the beginning of the twentieth-century Great Game can be traced back to the overthrow of the Afghan king in 1973. Seeking revenues to modernize Afghanistan, President Daoud turned to the United States and the Soviet Union for financial support. The United States turned Afghanistan down largely because of the U.S. alliance with Pakistan. Pakistan and Afghanistan had always had contentious relations because of a territorial dispute.

Aid Equals Intervention

The Soviet Union had been looking for this opportunity and immediately agreed to provide financial and infrastructure support. Foreign aid soon became foreign intervention. Once Daoud realized the gamble that he had made, it was too late. The Soviets became entrenched in Afghanistan, initially in the unsuccessful propping up of the minority Afghan communist parties, and finally with the official invasion of Afghanistan in 1979.

For the next ten years, the Soviets pummeled Afghanistan, mining the country, and terrorizing and slaughtering its people. America responded by throwing $2 to $3 billion into the Afghan war against the Soviets, relying on Pakistan to help shape the U.S. strategy. Because of its territorial disputes with Afghanistan, Pakistan has never been a proponent of Afghan nationalism. Instead, Pakistan encouraged an Islamic fundamentalist approach to mobilizing against the Soviets. Harnessing the anger of the Muslim world over the invasion, the United States and Pakistan supported an Islamic war against the Soviet Union. It worked. Fundamentalists from throughout the Muslim world, including Osama bin Laden, poured into Pakistan and Afghanistan. The "Afghan" freedom fighters, "the Mujadheddin," were fierce, driven by anger, moral zeal, and Western arms. Ten years later, in 1989, the Soviets withdrew and the Cold War was won.

For Afghans, the results of this war were devastating: 1.5 million dead, 5 million refugees, the exodus or death of its intellectual community, more than a million landmines, 500,000 widows, hundreds of thousands of orphans, and extremist Islamic groups in Afghanistan armed with some of the deadliest American weapons. The ground was ripe for disaster, but the world looked away from the impending crisis. Buoyed over the collapse of communism, and suddenly disinterested in the messy Afghan aftermath, the West allowed a political vacuum to develop in Afghanistan between 1989 and 1992.

Geopolitics of Oil Interests

The internal "Great Games" in Afghanistan emerged within the context of this void. With the collapse of the Soviet Union, the stakes for controlling Afghanistan had become increasingly higher. Afghanistan was positioned to become an important potential opening to the sea for the landlocked new states of Central Asia. The presence of large oil and gas deposits in the area soon attracted countries like Russia and China, not to mention Pakistan and India, and multinational oil conglomerates like Unocal and Bridas.

Between 1992 and 1996, the "heroic" Mujaheddin turned against each other and their people, playing the ethnic card and engaging in a bloodbath to control Afghanistan. The enemy was now within, with warlords raping, pillaging, looting, and killing their own people indiscriminately. The results were dramatic: another mass exodus of Afghan refugees and an opening for the extremist nominally Islamic group—the Taliban—to take over.

The Taliban, largely comprising war orphans raised in strictly male societies and educated in Pakistani *madrassas* (Islamic religious schools), were able to take over 95 percent of Afghanistan because they promised law and order. They delivered law and order, of the severest kind, and killed the last of what Afghanistan had—our culture and our heritage. They forbade music, dancing, and every form of Afghan cultural display. They created an international outcry when they destroyed one of our most magnificent historical monuments, the 1,500-year-old Bamiyan Buddhas, this year.

Among other things, the Taliban forced men into the armed forces against the Northern Alliance. While the women did not face the risk of being combatants, they faced harsh repressive measures and the loss of their future and livelihood. Girls and women of all ages were thrown out of school and deprived of the right to work. These measures impacted the 500,000 war widows, who had an average of five children each, the hardest. Many of these women resorted to begging and some resorted to prostitution to feed their children.

Consequences of Extremism

For the last several years, Afghans have tried to alert the international community to the role of the Taliban in supporting the use of Afghan territory as a breeding ground for an international network of terrorists. The international community knew of this situation, but left it unattended, perhaps because it did not seem to be an imminent danger to the West's interests. The 1993 bombing of the World Trade Center in New York, the 1998 bombings of American embassies in Africa, and last year's attack on the U.S.S. Cole in Yemen showed that this was an illusion. Sanctions were applied against the Taliban, but the one-pronged approach proved to be disastrous.

On September 11, the world was brutally shown the devastating consequences of the extremism bred in Afghan terrorist camps and the deadly threat it posed to the international community.

And now we—we the global community—stand facing a situation filled with contradictions and complexities. There are no simple answers. Terrorists have used Afghanistan as one of their bases, but none of the suspects in the World Trade Center attack are Afghans. The United States is at war with Afghanistan, allied with the Northern Alliance faction against the Taliban and Osama bin Laden. But the people of Afghanistan have been the brutalized victims of the Taliban, the Northern Alliance, and the bin Laden terrorist network. Afghanistan is being bombed, but the Afghan people are receiving U.S. and Western humanitarian aid.

The world gazes from the CNN precipice, getting a bird's eye view of the collapse of Afghanistan, marveling at the destruction, stunned by the human devastation that has gone on in Afghanistan over twenty years. Pity for the refugees is intertwined with anger that the phantoms of the Soviet-Afghan war have come back to haunt us all in the shape of bin Laden, terrorist networks, and a violent brand of extremism that has spread to every layer of our society in the international community. Like the Afghan refugees who stand desperately at closed borders, we have nowhere to run. The threat of terrorism is everywhere.

I have tried to respond to the questions posed to me and now I will end by asking questions of my own:

Will we look for easy answers, dividing the world into neat compartments of Islamic terrorists and Western victims, or will we see that terrorism is a minority extremist group, spreading from the Al Qaeda network in the Middle East to the Timothy McVeighs in the United States, and that these people threaten Muslims, Christians, and Jews alike?

Will we once again pick the winners in an Afghan war and walk away, without thinking about the long-term implications of what they will breed in Afghanistan and the international community?

Will we finally recognize that the political and humanitarian conditions of such oil- and resource-poor countries as Afghanistan matter geopolitically, strategically, and morally to the type of future we envision for our world?

63

SNEAK ATTACK
The Militarization of U.S. Culture

CYNTHIA ENLOE

Things start to become militarized when their legitimacy depends on their associations with military goals. When something become militarized, it appears to rise in value. Militarization is seductive.

But it is really a process of loss. Even though something seems to gain value by adopting an association with military goals, it actually surrenders control and gives up the claim to its own worthiness.

Militarization is a sneaky sort of transformative process. Sometimes it is only in the pursuit of *de*militarization that we become aware of just how far down the road of complete militarization we've gone. Representative Barbara Lee (D.-Calif.) pulled back the curtain in the aftermath of the September 11 attacks when she cast the lone vote against giving George W. Bush carte blanche to wage war. The loneliness of her vote suggested how far the militarization of Congress—and its voters back home—has advanced. In

---

Cynthia Enloe, "The Globetrotting Sneaker" from *Ms.* (September/October 1995) and "Sneak Attack" from *Ms.* (December 2001). Both reprinted with the permission of the publisher.

fact, since September 11, publicly criticizing militarization has been widely viewed as an act of disloyalty.

Whole cultures can be militarized. It is a militarized U.S. culture that has made it easier for Bush to wage war without most Americans finding it dangerous to democracy. Our cultural militarization makes war-waging seem like a comforting reconfirmation of our collective security, identity, and pride.

Other sectors of U.S. culture have also been militarized:

- **Education.** School board members accept Jr. ROTC programs for their teenagers, and social studies teachers play it safe by avoiding discussions of past sexual misconduct by U.S. soldiers overseas. Many university scientists pursue lucrative Defense Department weapons research contracts.
- **Soldiers' girlfriends and wives.** They've been persuaded that they are "good citizens" if they keep silent about problems in their relationships with male soldiers for the sake of their fighting effectiveness.
- **Beauty.** This year, the Miss America Pageant organizers selected judges with military credentials, including a former Secretary of the Navy and an Air Force captain.
- **Cars.** The Humvee ranks among the more bovine vehicles to clog U.S. highways, yet civilians think they will be feared and admired if they drive them.

Then there is the conundrum of the flag. People who reject militarization may don a flag pin, unaware that doing so may convince those with a militarized view of the U.S. flag that their bias is universally shared, thus deepening the militarization of culture.

The events of post–September 11 have also shown that many Americans today may be militarizing non-U.S. women's lives. It was only after Bush declared "war on terrorists and those countries that harbor them" that the violation of Afghan women's human rights took center stage. Here's the test of whether Afghan women are being militarized: if their well-being is worthy of our concern only because their lack of well-being justifies the U.S.'s bombing of Afghanistan, then we are militarizing Afghan women—as well as our own compassion. We are thereby complicit in the notion that something has worth only if it allows militaries to achieve their missions.

It's important to remember that militarization has its rewards, such as newfound popular support for measures formerly contested. For example, will many Americans now be persuaded that drilling for oil in the Alaskan wilderness is acceptable because it will be framed in terms of "national security"? Will most U.S. citizens now accept government raids on the Social Security trust fund in the name of paying for the war on terrorism?

Women's rights in the U.S. and Afghanistan are in danger if they become mere by-products of some other cause. Militarization, in all its seductiveness and subtlety, deserves to be bedecked with flags wherever it thrives—fluorescent flags of warning.

64

HOW SAFE IS AMERICA?

DESIREE TAYLOR

I saw a picture in a magazine in which a woman is walking away from the collapsed World Trade Center towers covered in orange dust from head to toe. Her face is twisted into a shocked and horrifying expression and she is turned around slightly looking back at the photographer as she walks away from the scene. What strikes me about this picture is that I have never seen another like it, such an elegant and stylish depiction of war. The woman is so immaculately dressed, her hair so stylishly cut, that the whole scene looks like a clever fashion spread from an upscale magazine. This just couldn't be real, but it is. Looking at this picture, I try to really see the woman in it. I try to feel the horror of her experience, but as I do I can also see that she is not from my America. She is from an America that before September 11 was in many ways safer and freer than mine before or after that day.

On September 12, the day after the attack on the United States, I watched the media coverage and a very middle-class looking woman interviewed on the street said she "no longer felt safe in America." I was born and have grown up in this country. As a mixed race, half Black, half white woman born into poverty, I have never felt safe here.

In America, life within one class is nothing at all like it is in another. On September 11 thousands of people died in the collapsed World Trade towers. They were not alone. Every day in this country people die from exploitation that originates right here at home. Some who toil and slave in service to a system of wealth and prestige, who don't even earn a living for their trouble, slit their wrists out of desperation and pain. Some die used up and exhausted, in hospital beds with two dollars and eighty-five cents in their purse, like my own mother. Some people work two or more jobs and try to fit some kind of life in between, maybe an education, which gets harder and harder as they lose out on more and more sleep. The amount of safety one can truly feel in America is directly related to how much money you have.

Safety Depends on Money

I think about these people who were and are anything but safe here. I think about those who sweat out unappreciated labor to make the American Dream seem so real, to make the consumer culture function. I wonder if the woman in the picture ever looked as closely at the people who are dying in the class war here at home as I do at her.

It enrages me to hear people saying they no longer feel safe here. The United States that is being attacked is the one the woman in the picture belongs to. It is the prosperous, comfortable United States. It is not my United States. But all of a sudden we are all in it together. The flags are brought out and everybody sings, "I'm proud to be an American."

But it's impossible for me to suddenly forget that the United States empire was built upon and is still maintained by abuses against the poor and minorities. I think about those who will fight and die in this war. I think about all the poor, and often Black, students from my high school who enlisted in the armed services to earn money for college. I think about all the students who wouldn't have been caught dead joining the armed forces, kids for whom the military was not one of their few options to move out of poverty. I think about how many low-income families are worrying right now about the lives of their enlisted children. I wonder what proportion of persons who will fight in this war will be those who are not sharing in the "American Dream." I believe that it will be disproportionally high.

Poor Invisible to Mainstream

The plight of low-income people in this country is invisible to mainstream America. This invisible other America, the poor, enters through side and back doors of hotels, through the servants' entrances. They live in segregated neighborhoods, and work jobs in which they are unseen even though they are in plain view.

For example, I went to Walgreens the other day and was handed a receipt that read at the top: "I'm Laqueeta [name changed]. I'm here to serve you." The message continued on the next line: "with our seven service basics." A middle-class person in this corporation decided that Laqueeta should hand this message out on every one of her receipts. What made someone earning a good salary think that this was a good idea? We're not even told what those seven service basics are, and they don't really matter. What matters is that the plantation-type American Dream is being acted out here. I, as a consumer, am for a moment in the seat of power with someone to serve me. This is meant to register with me, but the server is not. She doesn't matter. If she did, she would be able to survive doing this kind of work.

I decided to inquire about a cashier's job at Walgreens. The pay rate, I was told, is $6.75 an hour in Boston. When I worked hourly wage jobs in retail stores I learned that employers would keep employees just under 40 hours a week, so that officially they were not full-time and therefore not entitled by law to benefits. I do not know if Walgreens does this, but the practice is widespread. For 39 hours of work at $6.75 an hour, that is $263.25 a week before taxes and $758.16 per month after taxes. After subtracting $35 for a subway pass and at least $460 a month for rent and bills (and for rent this low that means living in a hovel with probably four other people she doesn't know), that leaves Laqueeta just $65.79 a week for food, clothing, savings, entertainment, household expenses, healthcare, and any other expense that might come up, including saving for college and a computer. I hope she doesn't have a child. How safe is Laqueeta in America? Does anybody care? The appearance of America's bounty is maintained by the exploitation of people right here at home who are in positions to be easily misused.

The United States feels very much to me like several countries made up of separate social/economic classes, who don't and perhaps won't take the time to really look at each other; they can't feel each other's pains, cannot relate, and largely live in separate worlds. Now that we're at war with outside forces, we are supposed to come together within the United States. We are all supposed to feel the same hurts and the same threats. We are all supposed to feel each other's pain. We are all supposed to defend justice and freedom.

During the past few weeks we have heard over and over again that these acts of terrorism are not only attacks on the United States, but on everything the country stands for. They tell us these are attacks on freedom and justice itself. But how is this possible when here at home justice, freedom, and the American Dream are denied to so many?

PART X
Health and Illness

As a middle-class, educated, bilingual Asian-American woman, I was aware of the importance of having the choice to have an abortion. . . . I had been unaware of how the right to have an abortion is also a right to survival in this country if you are a poor, uneducated, non-English-speaking immigrant.

CONNIE CHAN[1]

A recent study . . . concluded that men in western countries today have sperm counts less than half as high as their grandfathers had at the same age.

PETER MONTAGUE[2]

Women and men face different challenges related to health and illness. Gender-linked illnesses correlate with both genetic/biological differences between women and men and with socialized differences in the form of masculine and feminine behavior. Thus, women don't get testicular cancer and the vast majority of lung cancer patients were men before women earned the right to smoke.[3] The structure of sex-segregated work and the widely shared assumption that men should engage in risky physical behavior put many women and men at different risks for various injuries and illnesses. These differences probably explain why women live longer than men in the United States.[4] They probably also explain why women are more likely than men to become addicted to prescription drugs and are more likely to report feeling depressed.[5]

Even when women and men suffer from the same diseases, the causes and experiences of the disease may differ. For example, alcoholic women tend to respond differently to their alcohol addiction than do alcoholic men in various ways. They are more likely to hide their addictions, to be diagnosed later than men, to feel depressed and suicidal in the midst of the disease, and to feel low levels of self-esteem since addiction and femininity are not ordinarily compatible.[6] Finally, they are more likely to be survivors of physical and sexual abuse than are male alcoholics.[7]

New research on the effects of environmental toxins on male and female reproductive systems suggests that these toxins create different kinds of illnesses in men than in women. For instance, Janet Raloff examined the impact of environmental toxins on men's reproductive health and concluded that toxins are linked to such reproductive issues as low sperm counts, testicles that fail to descend, and male urinary tract defects.[8]

Other factors, such as sexual orientation and race, intersect with gender to put different groups at higher or lower risk for illness and injury. The AIDS epidemic, for example, thus far has affected primarily men in the United States, in part because the majority of early victims of this epidemic were gay men and intravenous drug users (unlike in Africa, for example, where AIDS has primarily been a heterosexually transmitted disease). Few lesbians, on the other hand, have contracted AIDS.[9] The faces of people with HIV infection and AIDS are changing, however, as the epidemic spreads (see Campo, this part). Heterosexual women are now the fastest-growing group with AIDS in the United States.[10] Teenage girls, especially girls of color, are at particularly high risk; in some regions, they have higher rates of HIV infection than boys.[11]

Race interacts with gender to create vast disparities in the health issues of Blacks and whites in the United States. African American women face higher rates of violence and childbirth-related illness and death than do white women.[12] Both Black and white men die from homicide at higher rates than Black and white women. Although both Black and white men die in automobile accidents at similar rates, Black men are more likely than white men to die in other kinds of accidents.[13] Among young men, Black men aged 15–24 are six times more likely than white men to die of homicide, and homicide is the principal cause of death for Black men in this age group.[14] Men are more likely than women to commit suicide, and among both women and men, whites are twice as likely as Blacks to do so.[15] The suicide gap between Black and white teens is narrowing, however, as more Black male teens commit suicide. White men are much more likely than men of color to contract testicular cancer.[16] Black men are twice as likely as white men to die of prostate cancer.[17]

The kinds of discrimination and oppression described throughout this book are present in the health care system as well. People who deviate from a Caucasian able-bodied, male norm are at higher risk for inadequate care. For example, the Institute of Medicine, an independent research institute that advises Congress, released a report in March 2002 that addressed racial disparities in health care. Unlike most prior studies, this one looked only at people who had health insurance, and concluded that racial discrepancies in quality of care persist even when people have similar insurance coverage. The report lists a wide array of suggestions, including increasing the number of underrepresented health care professionals and better education of both professionals (especially) and consumers.[18] In addition to race and ethnicity, other factors affect health care. Women with disabilities, for example, are presumed by most doctors to not be sexual and not want to be mothers.[19] Lesbians and gay men have health needs that many physicians fail to understand, related to feeling uncomfortable with homophobic practitioners (and therefore avoiding health care) and related to partners' rights in the face of illness or disability.[20] Disabled lesbians are hard pressed to find treatment facilities that can address their full array of medical needs when sexism, ableism and homophobia intersect.[21] Trans liberationist Leslie Feinberg was ordered out of a hospital emergency room in the midst of a life-threatening illness when the physician discovered that although she appeared to be male, her body was female.[22] Fat women and men are frequently refused various kinds of treatment "until they lose weight," which is usually not feasible. The pressure on this group to take weight loss medication is high, with many women, especially, risking their health in order to try to get health care.[23]

Apart from differences in the kinds of health risks faced by various groups, the issue of access to health care is becoming increasingly serious in the United States. People who hold low-paying jobs without health insurance frequently cannot afford to buy it. Women are more likely than men to hold such jobs and are more likely than men to be the primary caretakers of children who need coverage.[24] A recent estimate put the number of uninsured people nationwide at 45 million.[25] Managed care is also interfering with health care in many cases, as doctors and patients must submit requests for treatment to third parties who do not know the individual patients involved. Without major structural reform of the health care system, this situation is very likely to worsen, since individual and small collective efforts at empowerment cannot really change the system.

The privacy and autonomy of pregnant women continues to be an issue. Debates about abortion persist, as anti-choice advocates lobby for restricted access to abortion and pro-choice advocates lobby to keep abortion easily accessible, safe, and legal. Ironically, it appears that states with the strongest restrictions on abortions are less likely to provide resources for children in need than do states with stronger abortion access.[26] The privacy rights of pregnant women have also come under attack in recent years, leading to the arrest of pregnant women for behavior perceived as threatening to their fetuses. The Supreme Court rendered some of this policing activity illegal in March 2001, as it struck down a South Carolina statute that required drug testing of pregnant women at a public hospital and the subsequent arrest of those found to be using drugs.[27] Advocates for children and women's health argue for supportive intervention and treatment when a fetus is allegedly placed at risk (for drug use, smoking, alcohol use, etc.), rather than arrest and incarceration.

The women's health movement has worked to address women's health concerns for the past 30 years. In the face of unresponsive health care systems, women have opened health clinics for women, have provided clandestine abortions when abortion was illegal, have lobbied for health-related legislation and research funding, and have written extensively about women's health. The success of the many editions of *Our Bodies Our Selves* since it was first published in 1970 attests to women's need for straightforward information about their bodies. Various editions of *Our Bodies Our Selves* have been translated into a total of 17 languages and a recent version in Spanish has not simply been translated but has been revised to be more culturally appropriate for women in Latin America.[28] Organizations such as the National Women's Health Network (Washington, DC), the National Black Women's Health Project (Atlanta, GA), the National Asian Women's Health Organization (San Francisco, CA), the National Latina Health Organization (Oakland, CA), and the Native American Women's Health Education Resource Center have all supported the movement for better health care for women via a wide range of health services, support, research, publications, education, and effective lobbying.

Organizations for men, such as the Prostate Cancer Action Network, have also lobbied for more attention to male-specific illnesses. Conflicting analyses over which gender has received more attention in health research has been the subject of much debate. Following an analysis of subjects in medical research published in a medical journal, the National Institutes of Health recently retracted a 1997 statement that "women were routinely excluded from medical research supported by NIH." Lobbying seems to have been effective in raising the number of women in clinical trials and some critics argue that there was never a "gender gap."[29] Obviously, issues specific to both men and women (not to mention people who are gay, lesbian, or transgender) each need specific attention in order to assure effective, humane, and accessible health care for everyone.

Literature on health and illness explores the links between illness or death and gender socialization, including the ways that various women and men cope with illness.[30] The readings in this chapter address several aspects of this large and growing field of study, focusing on men's health (Don Sabo), African American women's health and reproductive freedom (Evelyn L. Barbee and Marilyn Little), the importance of access to abortion for low-income women of color (Connie S. Chan), environmental toxins (Sandra Steingraber), and AIDS (Rafael Campo). The voices in this chapter make powerful pleas for decent health care for all people in a nontoxic world.

NOTES

1. Connie S. Chan, "Reproductive Issues Are Essential Survival Issues for the Asian-American Communities, in Marlene Gerber Fried, ed., *From Abortion to Reproductive Freedom* (Boston: South End Press, 1990), p. 176.
2. Peter Montague, "Are Environmental Chemicals Causing Men to Lose Their Essential Masculinity?" *Rachel's Hazardous Waste News* 343 (June 23, 1993), p. 1.
3. Ingrid Waldron, "Contributions of Changing Gender Differences in Behavior and Social Roles to Changing Gender Differences in Mortality," in Donald Sabo and David Frederick Gordon, eds., *Men's Health and Illness: Gender, Power, and the Body* (Thousand Oaks, CA: Sage, 1995), p. 27; Robert Weissman, "Women and Tobacco," *The Network News* (National Women's Health Network) (March/April 2001), pp. 1, 4, 5.
4. Will H. Courtenay, "Behavioral Factors Associated with Disease, Injury, and Death among Men: Evidence and Implications for Prevention," *The Journal of Men's Studies 9,* no. 1 (Fall 2000), pp. 81 ff; Judith M. Stillion, "Premature Death among Males: Extending the Bottom Line of Men's Health," in Sabo and Gordon, *Men's Health and Illness,* pp. 46–67.
5. Regarding addictions, see "Addictive Behaviors from the Women's Health Data Book," reprinted in Nancy Worcester and Marianne Whatley, eds., *Women's Health: Readings on Social, Economic, and Political Issues,* 2nd ed. (Dubuque, IA: Kendall/Hunt, 1994), pp. 153–57. Regarding depression, see Marian Murphy, "Women and Mental Health," reprinted in Worcester and Whatley, eds., *Women's Health,* pp. 127–32.
6. Rokelle Lerner, "What Does Female Have to Do with It?" *Professional Counselor* (August 1995), p. 20.

7. Willie Langeland and Christina Hartgers, "Child Sexual and Physical Abuse and Alcoholism: A Review," *Journal of Alcohol Studies* 59, no. 3 (May 1998), pp. 336–48.
8. Janet Raloff, "That Feminine Touch; Are Men Suffering from Prenatal or Childhood Exposures to 'Hormonal' Toxicants?" *Science News* 145 (January 22, 1994), pp. 56–8.
9. Ruth L. Schwartz, "New Alliances, Strange Bedfellows: Lesbians, Gay Men and AIDS," in Arlene Stein, ed., *Sisters, Sexperts, and Queers: Beyond the Lesbian Nation* (New York: Plume, 1993), pp. 230–44.
10. M. Wolfe, "Women and HIV/AIDS Education," paper prepared for the NEA Health Information Network, Atlanta, 1991. Cited in the American Association of University Women Educational Foundation, *How Schools Shortchange Girls* (New York: Marlowe, 1992), p. 137.
11. L. D'Angelo, et al., "HIV Infection in Adolescents: Can We Predict Who Is at Risk?," poster presentation at the Fifth International Conference on AIDS, June 1989. Data from Washington, DC, was reported. Cited in the American Association of University Women Educational Foundation, *How Schools Shortchange Girls*, p. 137.
12. Paul Simao, "Pregnancy Death Highest for Black Women, US Study Shows," *The Boston Globe* (Friday May 11, 2002), p. A27; Evelyn L. Barbee and Marilyn Little, "Health, Social Class, and African-American Women," in Stanlie M. James and Abena P. A. Buscia, eds., *Theorizing Black Feminisms: The Visionary Pragmatism of Black Women* (New York: Routledge, 1993).
13. Stillion, "Premature Death among Males," p. 52.
14. Jewell Taylor Gibbs, "Anger in Young Black Males: Victims or Victimizers?" in Richard G. Majors & Jacob U. Gordon, eds., *The American Black Male: His Status and His Future* (Chicago: Nelson-Hall, 1994), p. 128.
15. Stillion, "Premature Death among Males," p. 53.
16. David Frederick Gordon, "Testicular Cancer and Masculinity," in Sabo and Gordon, *Men's Health and Illness.*
17. National Cancer Institute, *Cancer among Blacks and Other Minorities: Statistical Profiles* (Washington, DC: U.S. Department of Health and Human Services, NIH Publication #86-2785, 1986), p. 10.
18. Brian D. Smedley, Adrienne Y. Stith, & Alan R. Nelson, eds. *Unequal Treatment: Confronting Racial and Ethnic Disparities in Health Care.* Washington, DC Institute of Medicine, 2002.
19. Carol J. Gill, "Editorial: When Is a Woman Not a Woman?" *Sexuality and Disability* 12, no. 2 (1994), pp. 117–9; Carrie Killoran, "Women with Disabilities Having Children: It's Our Right Too," *Sexuality and Disability* 12, no. 2 (1994), pp. 121–26.
20. Ann Pollinger Haas, "Lesbian Health Issues: An Overview," in Alice J. Dan, ed., *Reframing Women's Health: Multidisciplinary Research and Practice* (Thousand Oaks, CA: Sage Publications, 1994), pp. 339–56.
21. Corbett Joan O'Toole, "Disabled Lesbians: Challenging Monocultural Constructs," *Sexuality and Disability* 14, no. 3 (1996), pp. 221–36.
22. Leslie Feinberg, *Trans Liberation: Beyond Pink or Blue* (Boston: Beacon Press, 1998), p. 2.
23. Pat Lyons, "The Great Weight Debate: Where Have All the Feminists Gone?" *The Network News* 23, no. 5 (September/October, 1998), pp. 1 ff.
24. I recently saw an advertisement in Boston offering health insurance for children. Parents had the option to insure their children when they could not afford to insure the whole family.
25. Ellen R. Shaffer, "Universal Health Care: A Proposal for the New Millennium," *The Network News* (January/February 2000), pp. 3–4.

26. Jean Reith Schroedel, *Is the Fetus a Person? A Comparison of Policies across the Fifty States* (Ithaca: Cornell University Press, 2000).
27. Lynn P. Paltrow, "South Carolina: Where Pregnancy Is a Crime" *The Network News* (National Women's Health Network) (July/August 2000), pp. 3–4; Jean Reith Schroedel, *Is the Fetus a Person?;* Lyle Denniston, "Drug Test Ruling Backs Pregnant Women's Privacy," *The Boston Globe* (Thursday March 22, 2001), p. A3.
28. For the most recent edition in English, see Boston Women's Health Book Collective, *Our Bodies Our Selves for the New Century.* (New York: Simon & Schuster, 1998). In Spanish: La Colectiva del Libro de Salud de las Mujeres de Boston, Nuestos Cuerpos, *Nuestras Vidas: La Guía Definitive para la Salud de la Mujer Latina* (Nueva York/New York: Siete Cuentos Editorial/Seven Stories Press, 2000). For an example of an early groundbreaking book in the women's health movement that was important enough to be republished 25 years later, see Barbara Seaman, *The Doctor's Case Against the Pill,* 25th Anniversary Edition (Alameda, CA: Hunter House, 1995).
29. Cathy Young, "It's Time to End the Gender Gap in Health Care," *The Boston Globe* (Wednesday November 15, 2000), p. A27.
30. For more information on women's and men's health, see Sabo and Gordon, *Men's Health and Illness,* Worcester and Whatley, eds., *Women's Health;* Evelyn C. White, ed., *The Black Women's Health Book* (Seattle: Seal Press, 1990).

65

MASCULINITIES AND MEN'S HEALTH
Moving toward Post–Superman Era Prevention

DON SABO

My grandfather used to smile and say, "Find out where you're going to die and stay the hell away from there." Grandpa had never studied epidemiology (the study of variations in health and illness in society), but he understood that certain behaviors, attitudes, and cultural practices can put individuals at risk for accidents, illness, or death. This chapter presents an overview of men's health that proceeds from the basic assumption that aspects of traditional masculinity can be dangerous to men's health (Sabo & Gordon, 1995; Harrison, Chin, & Ficarrotto, 1992). First, I identify some gender differences in relation to morbidity (sickness) and mortality (death). Next, I examine how the risk for illness varies from one male group to another. I then discuss an array of men's health issues and a preventative strategy for enhancing men's health.

Gender Differences in Health and Illness

When British sociologist Ashley Montagu put forth the thesis in 1953 that women were biologically superior to men, he shook up the prevailing chauvinistic beliefs that men were stronger, smarter, and better than women. His argument was partly based on epidemiological data that show males are more vulnerable to mortality than females from before birth and throughout the life span.

Mortality

From the time of conception, men are more likely to succumb to prenatal and neonatal death than females. Men's chances of dying during the prenatal

---

stage of development are about 12% greater than those of females and, during the neonatal (newborn) stage, 130% greater than those of females. A number of neonatal disorders are common to males but not females, such as bacterial infections, respiratory illness, digestive diseases, and some circulatory disorders of the aorta and pulmonary artery. Table 1 compares male and female infant mortality rates across historical time. Though the infant mortality rate decreases over time, the persistence of the higher rates for males than females suggests that biological factors may be operating. Data also show that males have higher mortality rates than females in every age category, from "under one year" through "over 85" (National Center for Health Statistics, 1992). In fact, men are more likely to die in 9 out of the 10 leading causes of death in the United States. (See Table 2.)

Females have greater life expectancy than males in the United States, Canada, and postindustrial societies (Verbrugge and Wingard, 1987; Wal-

TABLE 1 Infant Mortality Rate

Year	Both Sexes	Males	Females
1940	47.0	52.5	41.3
1950	29.2	32.8	25.5
1960	26.0	29.3	22.6
1970	20.0	22.4	17.5
1980	12.6	13.9	11.2
1989	9.8	10.8	8.8

Note: Rates are for infant (under 1 year) deaths per 1,000 live births for all races.
Sources: Adapted from *Monthly Vital Statistics Report,* Vol. 40, No. 8. Supplement 2, January 7, 1992, p. 41.

TABLE 2 Death Rates by Sex and 10 Leading Causes: 1989

	Age-Adjusted Death Rate Per 100,000 Population			
Cause of Death	**Total**	**Male**	**Female**	**Sex Differential**
Diseases of the heart	155.9	210.2	112.3	1.87
Malignant neoplasms	133.0	163.4	111.7	1.45
Accidents and adverse effects	33.8	49.5	18.9	2.62
Cerebrovascular disease	28.0	30.4	26.2	1.16
Chronic liver disease, cirrhosis	8.9	12.8	5.5	2.33
Diabetes	11.5	2.0	11.0	1.09
Suicide	11.3	18.6	4.5	4.13
Homicide and legal intervention	9.4	14.7	4.1	3.59

Sources: Adapted from the *U.S. Bureau of the Census: Statistical Abstracts of the United States:* 1992 (112th ed., p. 84), Washington, DC.

dron, 1986). This fact suggests a female biological advantage, but a closer analysis of changing trends in the gap between women's and men's life expectancy indicates that social and cultural factors related to lifestyle, gender identity, and behavior are operating as well. Life expectancy among American females is about 78.3 years but 71.3 years for males (National Center for Health Statistics, 1990). As Waldron's (1995) analysis of shifting mortality patterns between the sexes during the 20th century shows, however, women's relative advantage in life expectancy over men was rather small at the beginning of the 20th century. During the mid-20th century, female mortality declined more rapidly than male mortality, thereby increasing the gender gap in life expectancy. Whereas women benefited from decreased maternal mortality, the midcentury trend toward a lowering of men's life expectancy was slowed by increasing mortality from coronary heart disease and lung cancer that were, in turn, mainly due to higher rates of cigarette smoking among males.

The most recent trends show that differences between women's and men's mortality decreased during the 1980s; that is, female life expectancy was 7.9 years greater than that of males in 1979 and 6.9 years in 1989 (National Center for Health Statistics, 1992). Waldron explains that some changes in behavioral patterns between the sexes, such as increased smoking among women, have narrowed the gap between men's formerly higher mortality rates from lung cancer, chronic obstructive pulmonary disease, and ischemic heart disease. In summary, it appears that both biological and sociocultural factors are involved with shaping patterns of men's and women's mortality. In fact, Waldron (1976) suggests that gender-related behaviors rather than strictly biogenic factors account for about three-quarters of the variation in men's early mortality.

Morbidity

Whereas females generally outlive males, females report higher morbidity rates, even after controlling for maternity. National health surveys show that females experience acute illnesses such as respiratory conditions, infective and parasitic conditions, and digestive system disorders at higher rates than males do; however, males sustain more injuries (Givens, 1979; Cypress, 1981; Dawson & Adams, 1987). Men's higher injury rates are partly owed to gender differences in socialization and lifestyle, such as learning to prove manhood through recklessness, involvement in contact sports, and working in risky blue-collar occupations.

Females are generally more likely than males to experience chronic conditions such as anemia, chronic enteritis and colitis, migraine headaches, arthritis, diabetes, and thyroid disease. However, males are more prone to develop chronic illnesses such as coronary heart disease, emphysema, and gout. Although chronic conditions do not ordinarily cause death, they often limit activity or cause disability.

After noting gender differences in morbidity, Cockerham (1995) asks whether women really do experience more illness than men—or could it be that women are more sensitive to bodily sensations than men, or that men are not as prone as women to report symptoms and seek medical care? He concludes, "The best evidence indicates that the overall differences in morbidity are real" and, further, that they are due to a mixture of biological, psychological, and social influences (p. 42).

Masculinities and Men's Health

There is no such thing as masculinity; there are only masculinities (Sabo & Gordon, 1995). A limitation of early gender theory was its treatment of "all men" as a single, large category in relation to "all women" (Connell, 1987). The fact is, however, that all men are not alike, nor do all male groups share the same stakes in the gender order. At any given historical moment, there are competing masculinities—some dominant, some marginalized, and some stigmatized—each with its respective structural, psychosocial, and cultural moorings. There are substantial differences between the health options of homeless men, working-class men, lower-class men, gay men, men with AIDS, prison inmates, men of color, and their comparatively advantaged middle- and upper-class, white, professional male counterparts. Similarly, a wide range of individual differences exists between the ways that men and women act out "femininity" and "masculinity" in their everyday lives. A health profile of several male groups is discussed below.

Adolescent Males

Pleck, Sonenstein, and Ku (1992) applied critical feminist perspectives to their research on problem behaviors and health among adolescent males. A national sampling of adolescent, never-married males aged 15–19 were interviewed in 1980 and 1988. Hypothesis tests were geared to assessing whether "masculine ideology" (which measured the presence of traditional male role attitudes) put boys at risk for an array of problem behaviors. The researchers found a significant, independent association with seven of ten problem behaviors. Specifically, traditionally masculine attitudes were associated with being suspended from school, drinking and use of street drugs, frequency of being picked up by the police, being sexually active, the number of heterosexual partners in the last year, and tricking or forcing someone to have sex. These kinds of behaviors, which are in part expressions of the pursuit of traditional masculinity, elevate boys' risk for sexually transmitted diseases, HIV transmission, and early death by accident or homicide. At the same time, however, these same behaviors can also encourage victimization of women through men's violence, sexual assault, unwanted teenage pregnancy, and sexually transmitted diseases.

Adolescence is a phase of accelerated physiological development, and good nutrition during this period is important to future health. Obesity puts adults at risk for a variety of diseases such as coronary heart disease, diabetes mellitus, joint disease, and certain cancers. Obese adolescents are also apt to become obese adults, thus elevating long-term risk for illness. National Health and Nutrition Examination Surveys show that obesity among adolescents increased by 6% during 1976–80 and 1988–91. During 1988–91, 22% of females of 12–18 years were overweight, and 20% of males in this age group were as well (*Morbidity and Mortality Weekly Report,* 1994a).

Males form a majority of the estimated 1.3 million teenagers who run away from home each year in the United States. For both boys and girls, living on the streets raises the risk of poor nutrition, homicide, alcoholism, drug abuse, and AIDS. Young adults in their 20s comprise about 20% of new AIDS cases and, when you calculate the lengthy latency period, it is evident that they are being infected in their teenage years. Runaways are also more likely to be victims of crime and sexual exploitation (Hull, 1994).

Clearly, adolescent males face a spectrum of potential health problems—some that threaten their present well-being, and others that could take their toll in the future.

Men of Color

Patterns of health and illness among men of color can be partly understood against the historical and social context of economic inequality. Generally, because African Americans, Hispanics, and Native Americans are disproportionately poor, they are more apt to work in low-paying and dangerous occupations, reside in polluted environments, be exposed to toxic substances, experience the threat and reality of crime, and worry about meeting basic needs. Cultural barriers can also complicate their access to available health care. Poverty is correlated with lower educational attainment, which, in turn, mitigates against adoption of preventative health behaviors.

The neglect of public health in the United States is particularly pronounced in relation to African Americans (Polych & Sabo, 1996). For example, in Harlem, where 96% of the inhabitants are African American and 41% live below the poverty line, the survival curve beyond the age of 40 for men is lower than that of men living in Bangladesh (McCord & Freeman, 1990). Even though African American men have higher rates of alcoholism, infectious diseases, and drug-related conditions, for example, they are less apt to receive health care, and when they do, they are more apt to receive inferior care (Bullard, 1992; Staples, 1995). Statistics like the following led Gibbs (1988) to describe young African American males as an "endangered species":

- The number of young African American male homicide victims in 1977 (5,734) was higher than the number killed in the Vietnam War during 1963–72 (5,640) (Gibbs, 1988:258).

- Homicide is the leading cause of death among young African American males. The probability of a black man dying from homicide is about the same as that of a white male dying from an accident (Reed, 1991).
- More than 36% of urban African American males are drug and alcohol abusers (Staples, 1995).
- In 1993 the rate of contracting AIDS for African American males aged 13 and older was almost 5 times higher than the rate for white males (*Morbidity and Mortality Weekly Report,* 1994b).

The health profile of Native Americans and Native Canadians is also poor. For example, alcohol is the number-one killer of Native Americans between the ages of 14 and 44 (May, 1986), and 42% of Native American male adolescents are problem drinkers, compared to 34% of same-age white males (Lamarine, 1988). Native Americans (10–18 years of age) comprise 34% of inpatient admissions to adolescent detoxification programs (Moore, 1988). Compared to the "all race" population, Native American youth exhibit more serious problems in the areas of depression, suicide, anxiety, substance use, and general health status (Blum et al., 1992). The rates of morbidity, mortality from injury, and contracting AIDS are also higher (Sugarman et al., 1993; Metler et al., 1991).

Like those of many other racial and ethnic groups, the health problems facing American and Canadian natives correlate with the effects of poverty and social marginalization, such as dropping out of school, a sense of hopelessness, the experience of prejudice, poor nutrition, and lack of regular health care. Those who care about men's health, therefore, need to be attuned to the potential interplay between gender, race/ethnicity, cultural differences, and economic conditions when working with racial and ethnic minorities.

Gay and Bisexual Men

Gay and bisexual men are estimated to constitute 5% to 10% of the male population. In the past, gay men have been viewed as evil, sinful, sick, emotionally immature, and socially undesirable. Many health professionals and the wider public have harbored mixed feelings and homophobic attitudes toward gay and bisexual men. Gay men's indentity, their lifestyles, and the social responses to homosexuality can impact the health of gay and bisexual men. Stigmatization and marginalization, for example, may lead to emotional confusion and suicide among gay male adolescents. For gay and bisexual men who are "in the closet," anxiety and stress can tax emotional and physical health. When seeking medical services, gay and bisexual men must often cope with the homophobia of health care workers or deal with the threat of losing health care insurance if their sexual orientation is made known.

Whether they are straight or gay, men tend to have more sexual contacts than women do, which heightens men's risk for contracting sexually transmitted diseases (STDs). Men's sexual attitudes and behaviors are closely tied to the way masculinity has been socially constructed. For example, real men are taught to suppress their emotions, which can lead to a separation of sex from feeling. Traditionally, men are also encouraged to be daring, which can lead to risky sexual decisions. In addition, contrary to common myths about gay male effeminacy, masculinity also plays a powerful role in shaping gay and bisexual men's identity and behavior. To the extent that traditional masculinity informs sexual activity of men, masculinity can be a barrier to safer sexual behavior among men. This insight leads Kimmel and Levine (1989) to assert that "to educate men about safe sex, then, means to confront the issues of masculinity" (p. 352). In addition to practicing abstinence and safer sex as preventive strategies, therefore, they argue that traditional beliefs about masculinity be challenged as a form of risk reduction.

Men who have sex with men remain the largest risk group for HIV transmission. For gay and bisexual men who are infected by the HIV virus, the personal burden of living with an AIDS diagnosis is made heavier by the stigma associated with homosexuality. The cultural meanings associated with AIDS can also filter into gender and sexual identities. Tewksbury's (1995) interviews with 45 HIV positive gay men showed how masculinity, sexuality, stigmatization, and interpersonal commitment mesh in decision making related to risky sexual behavior. Most of the men practiced celibacy in order to prevent others from contracting the disease; others practiced safe sex, and a few went on having unprotected sex.

Prison Inmates

There are 1.3 million men imprisoned in American jails and prisons (Nadelmann & Wenner, 1994). The United States has the highest rate of incarceration of any nation in the world, 426 prisoners for every 100,000 people (American College of Physicians, 1992), followed by South Africa and the former Soviet Union (Mauer, 1992). Racial and ethnic minorities are overrepresented among those behind bars. Black and Hispanic males, for example, comprise 85% of prisoners in the New York State prison system (Green, 1991).

The prison system acts as a pocket of risk, within which men already at high risk of having a preexisting AIDS infection are exposed to conditions that further heighten the risk of contracting HIV (Toepell, 1992) or other infections such as tuberculosis (Bellin, Fletcher, & Safyer, 1993) or hepatitis. The corrections system is part of an institutional chain that facilitates transmission of HIV and other infections in certain North American populations, particularly among poor, inner-city, minority males. Prisoners are burdened not only by social disadvantage but also by high rates of physical illness, mental disorder, and substance abuse that jeopardize their health (Editor, *Lancet*, 1991).

AIDS prevalence is markedly higher among state and federal inmates than in the general U.S. population, with a known aggregate rate in 1992 of

202 per 100,000 population (Brewer & Derrickson, 1992) compared to a total population prevalence of 14.65 in 100,000 (American College of Physicians, 1992). The cumulative total of American prisoners with AIDS in 1989 was estimated to be 5,411, a 72% increase over the previous year (Belbot & del Carmen, 1991). The total number of AIDS cases reported in U.S. corrections as of 1993 was 11,565 (a minimum estimate of the true cumulative incidence among U.S. inmates) (Hammett; cited in Expert Committee on AIDS and Prisons, 1994). In New York State, at least 10,000 of the state's 55,000 prisoners are believed to be infected (Prisoners with AIDS/HIV Support Action Network, 1992). In Canadian federal penitentiaries, it is believed that 1 in 20 inmates is HIV infected (Hankins; cited in Expert Committee on AIDS and Prison, 1994).

The HIV virus is primarily transmitted between adults by unprotected penetrative sex or by needle sharing, without bleaching, with an infected partner. Sexual contacts between prisoners occur mainly through consensual unions and secondarily though sexual assault and rape (Vaid; cited in Expert Committee on AIDS and Prisons, 1994). The amount of IV drug use behind prison walls is unknown, although it is known to be prevalent and the scarcity of needles often leads to sharing of needles and sharps (Prisoners with AIDS/HIV Support Action Network, 1992).

The failure to provide comprehensive health education and treatment interventions in prisons not only puts more inmates at risk for HIV infection, but also threatens the public at large. Prisons are not hermetically sealed enclaves set apart from the community but an integral part of society (Editor, *Lancet,* 1991). Prisoners regularly move in and out of the prison system. In 1989, prisons in the United States admitted 467,227 persons and discharged 386,228 (American College of Physicians, 1992). The average age of inmates admitted to prison in 1989 was 29.6, with 75% between 18 and 34 years; 94.3% were male. These former inmates return to their communities after having served an average of 18 months inside (Dubler & Sidel, 1989). Within three years, 62.5% will be rearrested and jailed. Recidivism is highest among poor black and Hispanic men. The extent to which the drug-related social practices and sexual activities of released or paroled inmates who are HIV positive are putting others at risk upon return to their communities is unresearched and unknown.

Male Athletes

Injury is everywhere in sport. It is evident in the lives and bodies of athletes who regularly experience bruises, torn ligaments, broken bones, aches, lacerations, muscle tears, and so forth. For example, about 300,000 football-related injuries per year require treatment in hospital emergency rooms (Miedzian, 1991). Critics of violent contact sports claim that athletes are paying too high a physical price for their participation. George D. Lundberg (1994), editor of the *Journal of the American Medical Association,* has called for a ban on boxing in the Olympics and in the U.S. military. His editorial entreaty, though based on clinical evidence for neurological harm from boxing, is also couched in a wider critique of the exploitative economics of the sport.

Injuries are basically unavoidable in sports, but, in traditional men's sports, there has been a tendency to glorify pain and injury, to inflict injury on others, and to sacrifice one's body in order to "win at all costs." The "no pain, no gain"philosophy, which is rooted in traditional cultural equations between masculinity and sports, can jeopardize the health of athletes who conform to its ethos (Sabo, 1994).

The connections between sport, masculinity, and health are evidenced in Klein's (1993) study of how bodybuilders use anabolic steroids, overtrain, and engage in extreme dietary practices. He spent years as an ethnographic researcher in the muscled world of the bodybuilding subculture, where masculinity is equated to maximum muscularity and men's striving for bigness and physical strength hides emotional insecurity and low self-esteem.

A nationwide survey of American male high school seniors found that 6.6% used or had used anabolic steroids. About two-thirds of this group were athletes (Buckley et al., 1988). Anabolic steroid use has been linked to health risks such as liver disease, kidney problems, atrophy of the testicles, elevated risk of injury, and premature skeletal maturation.

Klein lays bare a tragic irony in American subculture—the powerful male athlete, a symbol of strength and health, has often sacrificed his health in pursuit of ideal masculinity (Messner & Sabo, 1994).

Men's Health Issues

Advocates of men's health have identified a variety of issues that impact directly on men's lives. Some of these issues may concern you or men you care about.

Testicular Cancer

The epidemiological data on testicular cancer are sobering. Though relatively rare in the general population, it is the fourth most common cause of death among males of 15–35 years, accounting for 14% of all cancer deaths for this age group. It is the most common form of cancer affecting males of 20–34 years. The incidence of testicular cancer is increasing, and about 6,100 new U.S. cases were diagnosed in 1991 (American Cancer Society, 1991). If detected early, the cure rate is high, whereas delayed diagnosis is life threatening. Regular testicular self-examination (TSE), therefore, is a potentially effective means for ensuring early detection and successful treatment. Regrettably, however, most physicians do not teach TSE techniques (Rudolf & Quinn, 1988).

Denial may influence men's perceptions of testicular cancer and TSE (Blesch, 1986). Studies show that most males are not aware of testicular cancer, and even among those who are aware, many are reluctant to examine their testicles as a preventive measure. Even when symptoms are recognized, men sometimes postpone seeking treatment. Moreover, men who are taught TSE are often initially receptive, but their practice of TSE decreases over time. Men's resistance to TSE has been linked to awkwardness about touching themselves, associating touching genitals with homosexuality or masturbation, or the idea that TSE is not a manly behavior. And finally, men's individual reluctance to discuss testicular cancer partly derives from the widespread cultural silence that envelops it. The penis is a cultural symbol of male power, authority, and sexual domination. Its symbolic efficacy in traditional, male-dominated gender relations, therefore, would be eroded or neutralized by the realities of testicular cancer.

Disease of the Prostate

Middle-aged and elderly men are likely to develop medical problems with the prostate gland. Some men may experience benign prostatic hyperplasia, an enlargement of the prostate gland that is associated with symptoms such as dribbling after urination, frequent urination, or incontinence. Others may develop infections (prostatitis) or malignant prostatic hyperplasia (prostate cancer). Prostate cancer is the third leading cause of death from cancer in men, accounting for 15.7 deaths per 100,000 population in 1989. Prostate cancer is now more common than lung cancer (Martin, 1990). One in 10 men will develop this cancer by age 85, with African American males showing a higher prevalence rate than whites (Greco & Blank, 1993).

Treatments for prostate problems depend on the specific diagnosis and may range from medication to radiation and surgery. As is the case with testicular cancer, survival from prostate cancer is enhanced by early detection. Raising men's awareness about the health risks associated with the prostate gland, therefore, may prevent unnecessary morbidity and mortality. Unfortunately, the more invasive surgical treatments for prostate cancer can produce incontinence and impotence, and there has been no systematic research on men's psychosocial reactions and adjustment to sexual dysfunction associated with treatments for prostate cancer.

Alcohol Abuse

Although social and medical problems stemming from alcohol abuse involve both sexes, males comprise the largest segment of alcohol abusers. Some researchers have begun exploring the connections between the influence of the traditional male role on alcohol abuse. Isenhart and Silversmith (1994) show how, in a variety of occupational contexts, expectations surrounding masculinity encourage heavy drinking while working or socializing during after-work or off-duty hours. Some predominantly male occupational groups, such as longshoremen (Hitz, 1973), salesmen (Cosper, 1979), and members of the military (Pursch, 1976), are known to engage in high rates of alcohol consumption. Mass media play a role in sensationalizing links between booze and male bravado. Postman, Nystrom, Strate, and Weingartner (1987) studied the thematic content of 40 beer commercials and identified a variety of stereotypical portrayals of the male role that were used to promote beer drinking: reward for a job well done; manly activities that feature strength, risk, and daring; male friendship and esprit de corps; romantic success with women. The researchers estimate that, between the ages of 2 and 18, children view about 100,000 beer commercials.

Findings from a Harvard School of Public Health (1994) survey of 17,600 students at 140 colleges found that 44% engaged in "binge drinking," defined as drinking five drinks in rapid succession for males and four drinks for females. Males were more apt to report binge drinking during the past two weeks than females: 50% and 39% respectively. Sixty percent of the males who binge three or more times in the past two weeks reported driving after drinking, compared to 49% of their female counterparts, thus increasing the risk for accident, injury, and death. Compared to non–binge drinkers, binge drinkers were seven times more likely to engage in unprotected sex, thus elevating the risk for unwanted pregnancy and sexually transmitted disease. Alcohol-related automobile accidents are the top cause of death among 16- to 24-year-olds, especially among males (Henderson & Anderson, 1989). For all males, the age-adjusted death rate from automobile accidents in 1991 was 26.2 per 100,000 for African American males and 24.2 per 100,000 for white males, 2.5 and 3.0 times higher than for white and African American females respectively (*Morbidity and Mortality Weekly Report,* 1994d). The number of automobile fatalities among male adolescents that results from a mixture of alcohol abuse and masculine daring is unknown.

Men and AIDS

Human immunodeficiency virus (HIV) infection became a leading cause of death among males in the 1980s. Among men aged 25–44 in 1990, HIV infection was the second leading cause of death, compared to the sixth leading cause of death among same-age women (*Morbidity and Mortality Weekly Report,* 1993a). Among reported cases of acquired immunodeficiency syndrome (AIDS) for adolescent and adult men in 1992, 60% were men who had sex with other men, 21% were intravenous drug users, 4% were exposed through heterosexual sexual contact, 6% were men who had sex with men and injected drugs, and 1% were transfusion recipients. Among the cases of AIDS among adolescent and adult women in 1992, 45% were intravenous drug users, 39% were infected through heterosexual contact, and 4% were transfusion recipients (*Morbidity and Mortality Weekly Report,* 1993a).

Because most AIDS cases have been among men who have sex with other men, perceptions of the epidemic and its victims have been tinctured by sexual attitudes. In North American cultures, the stigma associated with AIDS is fused with the stigma linked to homosexuality. Feelings about men with AIDS can be mixed and complicated by homophobia.

Thoughts and feelings about men with AIDS are also influenced by attitudes toward race, ethnicity, drug abuse, and social marginality. Centers for Disease Control data show, for example, that men of color aged 13 and older constituted 51% (45,039) of the 89,165 AIDS cases reported in 1993. Women of color made up 71% of the cases reported among females aged 13 and older (*Morbidity and Mortality Weekly Report,* 1994b). The high rate of AIDS among racial and ethnic minorities has kindled racial prejudices in some minds, and AIDS is sometimes seen as a "minority disease." Although African American or Hispanic males may be at a greater risk of contracting HIV/AIDS, just as yellow fingers do not cause lung disease, it is not race or ethnicity that confers risk, but the behaviors they engage in and the social circumstances of their lives.

Perceptions of HIV/AIDS can also be influenced by attitudes toward poverty and poor people. HIV infection is linked to economic problems that include community disintegration, unemployment, homelessness, eroding urban tax bases, mental illness, substance abuse, and criminalization (Wallace, 1991). For example, males comprise the majority of homeless persons. Poverty and homelessness overlap with drug addiction, which, in turn, is linked to HIV infection. Of persons hospitalized with HIV in New York City, 9–18% have been found to be homeless (Torres et al, 1990). Of homeless men tested for HIV at a New York City shelter, 62% of those who took the test were seropositive (Ron & Rogers, 1989). Among runaway or homeless youth in New York City, 7% tested positive, and this rate rose to 15% among the 19- and 20-year-olds. Of homeless men in Baltimore, 85% admitted to substance use problems (Weinreb & Bassuk, 1990).

Suicide

The suicide rates for both African American and white males increased between 1970 and 1989, whereas female rates decreased. Indeed, males are more likely than females to commit suicide from middle childhood until old age (Stillion, 1985, 1995). Compared to females, males typically deploy more violent means of attempting suicide (e.g., guns or hanging rather than pills) and are more likely to complete that act. Men's selection of more violent methods to kill themselves is consistent with traditionally masculine behavior (Stillion, White, McDowell, & Edwards, 1989).

Canetto (1995) interviewed male survivors of suicide attempts in order to better understand sex differences in suicidal behavior. Although she recognizes that men's psychosocial reactions and adjustments to nonfatal suicide vary by race/ethnicity, socioeconomic status, and age, she also finds that gender identity is an important factor in men's experiences. Suicide data show that men attempt suicide less often than women but are more likely to die than women. Canetto indicates that men's comparative "success" rate points toward a tragic irony that, consistent with gender stereotypes, men's failure even at suicide undercuts the cultural mandate that men are supposed to succeed at everything. A lack of embroilment in traditionally masculine expectations, she suggests, may actually increase the likelihood of surviving a suicide attempt for some men.

Elderly males in North America commit suicide significantly more often than elderly females. Whereas white women's lethal suicide rate peaks at age 50, white men age 60 and older have the highest rate of lethal suicide, even surpassing that rate for younger males (Manton et al., 1987). Canetto (1992) argues that elderly men's higher suicide mortality is chiefly owed to gender differences in coping. She writes,

> Older women may have more flexible and diverse ways of coping than older men. Compared to older men, older women may be more willing and capable of adopting different coping strategies—"passive" or "active," "connected" or "independent"—depending on the situation (p. 92).

She attributes men's limited coping abilities to gender socialization and development.

Erectile Disorders

Men often joke about their penises or tease one another about penis size and erectile potency ("not getting it up"). In contrast, they rarely discuss their concerns about impotence in a serious way. Men's silences in this regard are regrettable in that many men, both young and old, experience recurrent or periodic difficulties getting or maintaining an erection. Estimates of the number of American men with erectile disorders range from 10 million to 30 million (Krane, Goldstein, & Saenz de Tejada, 1989; National Institutes of Health, 1993). The Massachusetts Male Aging Study of the general population of noninstitutionalized, healthy American men between ages 40 and 70 years found that 52% reported minimal, moderate, or complete impotence (Feldman et al., 1994). The prevalence of erectile disorders increased with age, and 9.6% of the men were afflicted by complete impotence.

During the 1960s and 1970s, erectile disorders were largely thought to stem from psychological problems such as depression, financial worries, or work-related stress. Masculine stereotypes about male sexual prowess, phallic power, or being in charge of lovemaking were also said to put too much pressure to perform on some males (Zilbergeld, 1993). In contrast, physiological explanations of erectile disorders and medical treatments have been increasingly emphasized since the 1980s. Today diagnosis and treatment of erectile disorders should combine psychological and medical assessment (Ackerman & Carey, 1995).

Men's Violence

Men's violence is a major public health problem. The traditional masculine stereotype calls on males to be aggressive and tough. Anger is a by-product of aggression and toughness and, ultimately, part of the inner terrain of traditional masculinity (Sabo, 1993). Images of angry young men are compelling vehicles used by some males to separate themselves from women and to measure their status in respect to other males. Men's anger and violence derive, in part, from sex inequality. Men use the threat or application of violence to maintain their political and economic advantage over women and lower-status men. Male socialization reflects and reinforces these larger patterns of domination.

Homicide is the second leading cause of death among 15- to 19-year-old males. Males aged 15–34 years made up almost half (49%, or 13,122) of homicide victims in the United States in 1991. The homicide rate for this age group increased by 50% from 1985 to 1991 (*Morbidity and Mortality Weekly Report,* 1994c).

Women are especially victimized by men's anger and violence in the form of rape, date rape, wife beating, assault, sexual harassment on the job, and verbal harassment (Thorne-Finch, 1992). That the reality and potential of men's violence impact women's mental and physical health can be surely assumed. However, men's violence also exacts a toll on men themselves in the forms of fighting, gang clashes, hazing, gay-bashing, intentional infliction of injury, homicide, suicide, and organized warfare.

Summary

It is ironic that two of the best-known actors who portrayed Superman have met with disaster. George Reeves, who starred in the original black-and-white television show, committed suicide, and Christopher Reeve, who portrayed the "man of steel" in recent film versions, was paralyzed by an accident during a high-risk equestrian event. Perhaps one lesson to be learned here is that, behind the cultural facade of mythic masculinity, men are vulnerable. Indeed, as we have seen in this chapter, some of the cultural messages sewn into the cloak of masculinity can put men at risk for illness and early death. A sensible preventive health strategy for the 1990s calls upon men to critically evaluate the Superman legacy, that is, to challenge the negative aspects of traditional masculinity that endanger their health, while hanging on to the positive aspects of masculinity and men's lifestyles that heighten men's physical vitality.

The promotion of men's health also requires a sharper recognition that the sources of men's risks for many diseases do not strictly reside in men's psyches, gender identities, or the roles that they enact in daily life. Men's roles, routines, and relations with others are fixed in the historical and structural relations that constitute the larger gender order. As we have seen, not all men or male groups share the same access to social resources, educational attainment, and opportunity that, in turn, can influence their health options. Yes, men need to pursue personal change in order to enhance their health, but without changing the political, economic, and ideological structures of the gender order, the subjective gains and insights forged within individuals can easily erode and fade away. If men are going to pursue self-healing, therefore, they need to create an overall preventive strategy that at once seeks to change potentially harmful aspects of traditional masculinity and meets the health needs of lower-status men.

REFERENCES

Ackerman, M. D., & Carey, P. C. (1995). *Journal of Counseling & Clinical Psychology, 63*(6), 862–876.

American Cancer Society (1991). Cancer Facts and Figures—1991. Atlanta, GA: American Cancer Society.

American College of Physicians. (1992). The crisis in correctional health care: The impact of the national drug control strategy on correctional health services. *Annals of Internal Medicine, 117*(1), 71–77.

Belbot, B. A., & del Carmen, R. B. (1991). AIDS in prison: Legal issues. *Crime and Delinquency, 31*(1), 135–153.

Bellin, E. Y., Fletcher, D. D., & Safyer, S. M. (1993). Association of tuberculosis infection with increased time in or admission to the New York City jail system. *Journal of the American Medical Association, 269*(17), 2228–2231.

Blesch, K. (1986). Health beliefs about testicular cancer and self-examination among professional men. *Oncology Nursing Forum, 13*(1), 29–33.

Blum, R., Harman, B., Harris, L., Bergeissen, L., & Restrick, M. (1992). American Indian–Alaska native youth health. *Journal of American Medical Association, 267*(12), 1637–1644.

Brewer, T. F., & Derrickson, J. (1992). AIDS in prison: A review of epidemiology and preventive policy. *AIDS, 6*(7), 623–628.

Buckley, W. E., Yesalis, C. E., Friedl, K. E., Anderson, W. A., Steit, A. L., & Wright, J. E. (1988). Estimated prevalence of anabolic steroid use among male high school seniors. *Journal of the American Medical Association, 260*(23), 3441–3446.

Bullard, R. D., (1992). Urban infrastructure: Social, environmental, and health risks to African Americans. In B. J. Tidwell (Ed.), *The State of Black America* (pp. 183–196). New York: National Urban League.

Canetto, S. S. (1995). Men who survive a suicidal act: Successful coping or failed masculinity? In D. Sabo & D. Gordon (Eds.), *Men's health and illness* (pp. 292–304). Newbury Park, CA: Sage.

Canetto, S. S. (1992). Gender and suicide in the elderly. *Suicide and Life-Threatening Behavior, 22*(1), 80–97.

Cockerham, W. C. (1995). *Medical sociology.* Englewood Cliffs, NJ: Prentice Hall.

Connell, R. W. (1987). *Gender and power.* Stanford: Stanford University Press.

Cosper, R. (1979). Drinking as conformity: A critique of sociological literature on occupational differences in drinking. *Journal of Studies on Alcoholism, 40,* 868–891.

Cypress, B. (1981). Patients' reasons for visiting physicians: National ambulatory medical care survey, U. S. 1977–78. DHHS Publication No. (PHS) 82-1717, Series 13, No. 56. Hyattsville, MD: National Center for Health Statistics, December, 1981a.

Dawson, D. A., & Adams, P. F. (1987). Current estimates from the national health interview survey: U.S. 1986. Vital Health Statistics Series, Series 10, No. 164. DHHS Publication No. (PHS) 87-1592, Public Health Service. Washington, DC: U. S. Government Printing Office.

Dubler, N. N., & Sidel, V. W. (1989). On research on HIV infection and AIDS in correctional institutions. *The Milbank Quarterly, 67*(1–2), 81–94.

Editor. (1991, March 16). Health care for prisoners: Implications of "Kalk's refusal." *Lancet, 337,* 647–648.

Expert Committee on AIDS and Prison. (1994). *HIV/AIDS in prisons: Summary report and recommendations to the Expert Committee on AIDS and Prisons* (Ministry of Supply and Services Canada Catalogue No. JS82-68/2-1994). Ottawa, Ontario, Canada: Correctional Service of Canada.

Feldman, H. A., Goldstein, I., Hatzichristou, D. G., Krane, R. J., & McKinlay, J. B. (1994). Impotence and its medical and psychosocial correlates: Results of the Massachusetts Male Aging Study. *Journal of Urology, 151,* 54–61.

Gibbs, J. T. (Ed.) (1988). *Young, black, and male in America: An endangered species.* Dover, MA: Auburn House.

Givens, J. (1979). Current estimates from the health interview survey: U.S. 1978. DHHS Publications No. (PHS) 80-1551, Series 10, No. 130. Hyattsville, MD: Office of Health Research Statistics, November 1979.

Greco, K. E., & Blank, B. (1993). Prostate-specific antigen: The new early detection test for prostate cancer. *Nurse Practitioner, 18*(5), 30–38.

Green, A. P. (1991). Blacks unheard. *Update* (Winter), New York State Coalition for Criminal Justice, 6–7.

Harrison, J., Chin, J., & Ficarrotto, T. (1992). Warning: Masculinity may be dangerous to your health. In M. S. Kimmel & M. A. Messner (Eds.), *Men's lives* (pp. 271–285). New York: Macmillian.

Harvard School of Public Health. Study reported by Wechsler, H., Davenport, A., Dowdall, G., Moeykens, B., & Castillo, S. (1994). Health and behavioral consequences of binge drinking in college: A national survery of students at 140 campuses. *Journal of the American Medical Association, 272*(21), 1672–1677.

Henderson, D. C., & Anderson, S. C. (1989). Adolescents and chemical dependency. *Social Work in Health Care, 14*(1), 87–105.

Hitz, D. (1973). Drunken sailors and others: Drinking problems in specific occupations. *Quarterly Journal of Studies on Alcohol, 34,* 496–505.

Hull, J. D. (1994, November 21). Running scared. *Time, 144*(2), 93–99.

Isenhart, C. E., & Silversmith, D. J. (1994). The influence of the traditional male role on alcohol abuse and the therapeutic process. *Journal of Men's Studies, 3*(2), 127–135.

Kimmel, M. S., and Levine, M. P. (1989). Men and AIDS. In M. S. Kimmel & M. A. Messner (Eds.), *Men's lives* (pp. 344–354). New York: Macmillian.

Klein, A. (1993). Little big men: Bodybuilding subculture and gender construction. Albany, NY: SUNY Press.

Krane, R. J., Goldstein, I., Saentz de Tejada, I. (1989). Impotence. *New England Journal of Medicine, 321,* 1648–1659.

Lamarine, R. (1988). Alcohol abuse among Native Americans. *Journal of Community Health, 13*(3), 143–153.

Lundberg, G. D. (1994, June 8). Let's stop boxing in the Olympics and the United States military. *Journal of the American Medical Association, 271*(22), 1990.

Manton, K. G., Blazer, D. G., & Woodbury, M. A. (1987). Suicide in middle age and later life: Sex and race specific life table and cohort analysis. *Journal of Gerontology, 42,* 219–227.

Martin, J. (1990). Male cancer awareness: Impact of an employee education program. *Oncology Nursing Forum, 17*(1), 59–64.

Mauer, M. (1992). Men in American prisons: Trends, causes, and issues. *Men's Studies Review, 9*(1), 10–12. A special issue on men in prison, edited by Don Sabo and Willie London.

May, P. (1986). Alcohol and drug misuse prevention programs for American Indians: Needs and opportunities. *Journal of Studies of Alcohol, 47*(3), 187–195.

McCord, C., & Freeman, H. P. (1990). Excess mortality in Harlem. *New England Journal of Medicine, 322*(22), 1606–1607.

Messner, M. A., & Sabo, D. (1994). *Sex, violence, and power in sports: Rethinking masculinity.* Freedom. CA: Crossing Press.

Metler, R., Conway, G. & Stehr-Green, J. (1991). AIDS surveillance among American Indians and Alaskan natives. *American Journal of Public Health, 81*(11), 1469–1471.

Miedzian, M. (1991). *Boys will be boys: Breaking the link between masculinity and violence.* New York: Doubleday.

Montagu, A. (1953). *The natural superiority of women.* New York: Macmillian.

Moore, D. (1988). Reducing alcohol and other drug use among Native American youth. *Alcohol Drug Abuse and Mental Health, 15*(6), 2–3.

Morbidity and Mortality Weekly Report. (1993a). Update: Mortality attributable to HIV infection/AIDS among persons aged 25–44 years—United States, 1990–91. *42*(25), 481–486.

Morbidity and Mortality Weekly Report. (1994a). Prevalence of overweight among adolescents—United States, 1988–91, *43*(44), 818–819.

Morbidity and Mortality Weekly Report. (1994b). AIDS among racial/ethnic minorities—United States, 1993, *43*(35), 644–651.

Morbidity and Mortality Weekly Report. (1994c). Homicides among 15–19-year-old males—United States, *43*(40), 725–728.

Morbidity and Mortality Weekly Report. (1994d). Deaths resulting from firearm- and motor-vehicle-related injuries—United States, 1968–1991. *43*(3), 37–42.

Nadelmann, P., & Wenner, L. (1994, May 5). Toward a sane national drug policy [Editorial]. *Rolling Stone,* 24–26.

National Center for Health Statistics. (1990). *Health, United States, 1989.* Hyattsville, MD: Public Health Service.

National Center for Health Statistics. (1992). Advance report of final mortality statistics, 1989. *Monthly Vital Statistics Report, 40* (Suppl. 2) (DHHS Publication No. [PHS] 92-1120).

National Institutes of Health. (1993). Consensus development panel on impotence. *Journal of the American Medical Association, 270,* 83–90.

Pleck, J., Sonenstein, F. L., & Ku, L. C. (1992). In R. Ketterlinus, & M. E. Lamb (Eds.), *Adolescent problem behaviors.* Hillsdale, NJ: Larwence Erlbaum Associates.

Polych, C., & Sabo, D. (1996). Gender politics, pain, and illness: The AIDS epidemic in North American prisons. In D. Sabo & D. Gordon (Eds.), *Men's health and illness* (pp. 139–157), Newbury Park, CA: Sage.

Postman, N., Nystrom, C., Strate, L., & Weingartner, C. (1987). *Myths, men and beer: An analysis of beer commercials on broadcast television,* 1987. Falls Church, VA: Foundation for Traffic Safety.

Prisoners with AIDS/HIV Support Action Network. (1992). *HIV/AIDS in prison systems: A comprehensive strategy* (Brief to the Minister of Correctional Services and the Minister of Health). Toronto: Prisoners with AIDS/HIV Support Action Network.

Pursch, J. A. (1976). From quonset hut to naval hospital: The story of an alcoholism rehabilitation service. *Journal of Studies on Alcohol, 37,* 1655–1666.

Reed, W. L. (1991). Trends in homicide among African Americans. *Trotter Institute Review, 5,* 11–16.

Ron, A., & Rogers, D. E. (1989). AIDS in New York City: The role of intravenous drug users. *Bulletin of the New York Academy of Medicine, 65*(7), 787–800.

Rudolf, V., & Quinn, K. (1988). The practice of TSE among college men: Effectiveness of an educational program. *Oncology Nursing Forum, 15*(1), 45–48.

Sabo, D., & Gordon, D. (1995). *Men's health and illness: Gender, power, and the body.* Newbury Park, CA: Sage.

Sabo, D. (1994). The body politics of sports injury: Culture, power, and the pain principle. A paper presented at the annual meeting of the National Athletic Trainers Association, Dallas, TX, June 6, 1994.

Sabo, D. (1993). Understanding men. In Kimball G. (Ed.), *Everything you need to know to succeed after college,* (pp. 71–93), Chico, CA: Equality Press.

Staples, R. (1995). *Health and illness among African-American males.* In D. Sabo and D. Gordon (Eds.), *Men's health and illness,* (pp. 121–138), Newbury Park, CA: Sage.

Stillion, J. (1985). *Death and the sexes: An examination of differential longevity, attitudes, behaviors, and coping skills.* New York: Hemisphere.

Stillion, J. (1995). Premature death among males: Rethinking links between masculinity and health. In D. Sabo and D. Gordon (Eds.), *Men's health and illness,* (pp. 46–67), Newbury Park, CA: Sage.

Stillion, J., White, H., McDowell, E. E., & Edwards, P. (1989). Ageism and sexism in suicide attitudes. *Death Studies, 13,* 247–261.

Sugarman, J., Soderberg, R., Gordon, J., & Rivera, F. (1993). Racial misclassifications of American Indians: Its effects on injury rates in Oregon, 1989–1990. *American Journal of Public Health, 83*(5), 681–684.

Tewksbury, R. (1995). Sexual adaptation among gay men with HIV. In D. Sabo and D. Gordon (Eds.), *Men's health and illness,* (pp. 222–245), Newbury Park, CA: Sage.

Thorne-Finch, R. (1992). *Ending the silence: The origins and treatment of male violence against women.* Toronto: University or Toronto Press.

Toepell, A. R. (1992). *Prisoners and AIDS: AIDS education needs assessment.* Toronto: John Howard Society of Metropolitan Toronto.

Torres, R. A., Mani, S., Altholz, J., & Brickner, P. W. (1990). HIV infection among homeless men in a New York City shelter. *Archives of Internal Medicine, 150,* 2030–2036.

Verbrugge, L. M., & Wingard, D. L. (1987). Sex differentials in health and mortality. *Women's Health, 12,* 103–145.

Waldron, I. (1995). Contributions of changing gender differences in mortality. In D. Sabo and D. Gordon (Eds.), *Men's health and illness,* (pp. 22–45), Newbury Park, CA: Sage.

Waldron, I. (1986). What do we know about sex differences in mortality? *Population Bulletin of the U.N., No. 18-1985,* 59–76.

Waldron, I. (1976). Why do women live longer than men? *Journal of Human Stress, 2,* 1–13.

Wallace, R. (1991). Traveling waves of HIV infection on a low dimensional "sociogeographic" network. *Social Science Medicine, 32*(7), 847–852.

Weinreb, L. F., & Bassuk, E. L. (1990). Substance abuse: A growing problem among homeless families. *Families and Community Health, 13*(1), 55–64.

Zilbergeld, B. (1993). *The new male sexuality.* New York: Bantam.

66

HEALTH, SOCIAL CLASS AND AFRICAN-AMERICAN WOMEN

EVELYN L. BARBEE AND MARILYN LITTLE

The litany of health problems which plague African-American women at rates disproportionate to their percentage of the US population is familiar: hypertension, lupus, diabetes, maternal mortality, cervical cancer, etc. Of these problems, the success rate in terms of maintenance (in cases of chronic diseases) and cure (in cases of episodic illnesses) is affected by the constant circumscribing effect of being an African-American female in a white, patriarchal, racist society. This chapter asserts that being African-American and female constitutes a unique position in American society. The position of African-American women in American society is unique because the same ideology used during slavery to justify the roles of Black women underlies the external, controlling images of contemporary African-American women (Collins, 1990). As a result, the multiple jeopardies (King, 1988) and externally imposed images of African-American women interact in ways that serve to compromise their health status.

Consequently, the health needs of the African-American woman cannot be met by reformulation or "reform" of racist health policies or sexist health policies; rather her needs will only be addressed by looking at the point where the two sets of policies converge and form a barrier to her mental, emotional and physical well-being. Although we agree with King's (1988) conclusion that scholarly descriptions that concentrate on our multiple oppressions "have confounded our ability to discover and appreciate the ways in which African-American women are not victims," one area that has not been adequately explored, an area in which African-American women currently and historically have been victimized, is the "health care" arena.

In 1988 an estimated 30.3 million African-Americans represented more than 12 percent of the population (US Bureau of the Census, 1989a). More than 52 percent of these 30.3 million people were female. Within the African-American population the ratio of women to men is 110 to 100. The respective Euro-American sex ratio is 104 females for every 100 males. Although African-American males outnumber females up until the age of 20 years,

---

after the age of 20 years the number of African-American women to men increases to the extent that the ratio at ages 65 years and over is 149:100 (US Bureau of the Census, 1989a).

In terms of family structure, 51 percent of African-American families were married couples; 43 percent were female householders, no husband present; and 6 percent were male householders, no wife present (US Bureau of the Census, 1989b). The respective median incomes for these households were: $27,182, $9,710 and $17,455. Among families that included children under 18 years of age, those households headed by women were four times more likely to be poor than those of two-parent families (US Bureau of the Census, 1988).

The Position of African-American Women

Contemporary efforts to explain the position of African-American women in the USA were built upon the notion of "double jeopardy" (Beale, 1970). Beale's idea recognized that African-American women faced double discrimination because of their race and sex. Lewis's (1977) exploration of the structural position of African-American women was premised on "double jeopardy." "While inequality is *manifested* in the exclusion of a group from public life, it is actually *generated* in the group's unequal access to power and resources in a hierarchically arranged social order" (Lewis, 1977:343). Because African-American women have membership in two subordinate groups, African-American and women, they lack access to authority and resources in society and are in structural opposition with the dominant racial/ethnic group (Euro-American) and the dominant sexual group (male) (Lewis, 1977).

In her critique of the concepts of double jeopardy and triple jeopardy (racism, sexism and classism), King (1988) noted that because each conceptualization presumes direct independent effect on status, neither was able to deal with the interactive effects of sexism, racism and classism. African-American women are subjected to several, simultaneous oppressions which involve multiplicative relationships. The importance of any one factor in explaining African-American women's circumstances varies and is dependent upon the particular aspect of life under consideration and the reference group to whom African-American women are being compared (King, 1988). In regard to health, the multifaceted influences of race, gender and often social class interact in ways that render African-American women less healthy and more vulnerable to sickness than Euro-American women. Furthermore, they have to contend with their illness at the same time that they seek care from the racist, sexist and class-based system of American medicine.

While African-American women may be invisible in many spheres of life (hooks, 1981), their visibility vis-à-vis the medical establishment appears to be dependent upon procedures that need to be practiced (e.g., hysterectomies) and drugs that need to be tested (e.g., birth control). Elsewhere Barbee (1992) argued that the externally produced images of African-American women profoundly influence how medical and social professionals treat African-American women when these women are victims of violence. Here it is argued that these same images influence the kind of medical care or treatment given or not given to African-American women.

Images of African-American Women

Because of the interactions among racism, sexism and often classism, African-American women occupy a structural position in which they are viewed as subordinate to all other women and men in this society. Beliefs, myths and stereotypes about African-American women have served to intensify their status as "other." This view of the African-American woman as an object encourages the deployment of externally applied images and makes it particularly difficult to be viewed as a person, let alone an individual, by medical practitioners. As Christensen (1988: 191) noted: "No other woman has suffered physical and mental abuse, degradation, and exploitation on North American shores comparable to that experienced by the Black female."

In pointing out that race, class and gender oppression depend on powerful ideological justification for their existence, Collins (1990) identifies four externally defined, socially constructed, controlling images that are applied to African-American women. These images are mammy, the faithful, obedient domestic servant; the matriarch; the welfare mother and the Jezebel. The prevailing images of mammy, matriarch, welfare mother; and Jezebel provide the ideological justification for racial oppression, gender subordination and economic exploitation (Collins, 1990). Each of these images contributes to society's and consequently medicine's view of African-American women.

The mammy image, the faithful, obedient servant, was created to justify the economic exploitation of Black women during slavery. As a social construction, its persistence is due to a need to rationalize the long-standing restriction of Black women to domestic service (Collins, 1990). In general, medical workers are not receptive to questions from clients and patients. Those who subscribe to the mammy image are even less receptive to questions from African-American women. An additional danger is that those African-American women who internalize the mammy image may consciously and unconsciously sustain gender and racial exploitation in a number of ways. One of the more dangerous consequences may be a tendency to agree voluntarily to medical procedures because they believe in obeying the doctor.

Matriarchs are considered to be overly aggressive, emasculating, strong, independent, unfeminine women. The matriarch image implies the actuality of a social order in which women exercise social and political power. This image is central to the interlocking systems of race, class and gender oppression. The matriarch image allows the dominant group to blame African-American women for the success or failure of their children (Collins, 1990). An additional effect of this image is that it allows "helping" professionals to ignore African-American women when they need assistance. It is difficult to acknowledge that an African-American woman needs medical assistance when she is constantly referred to as being "strong."

Equally damaging is the welfare mother image. This is essentially an updated version of the breeder image that was created during slavery (Collins, 1990). Welfare mothers are viewed as being too lazy to work and thus are content to sit around and collect their welfare checks. This current objectification of African-American women as welfare mothers serves to label their fertility as unnecessary and dangerous. The welfare mother image provides Euro-Americans (and some African-Americans who have embraced these images without understanding their underlying ideology) with ideological justification for restricting the fertility of some African-American women because they are producing too many economically non-productive children (Davis, 1983).

The Jezebel image is one of a whore or a sexually aggressive woman (Collins, 1990). As Collins (1990) notes, the whore image is a central link in the Euro-American elite male's images of African-American women because attempts to control African-American women's sexuality lie at the heart of African-American women's oppression. Historically, the sexually promiscuous stereotype was used to contrast African-American women with the "virtuous" Euro-American woman. It also provided the rationale that justified the sexual assaults on Black women by Euro-American men (Collins, 1990; hooks, 1981). In contemporary times the Jezebel image is used as reason both for the sexual denigration of African-American women and for ignoring or minimizing such sexual abuse. The repercussions of these images on African-American women are most clearly seen in health statistics. While these "facts" are in and of themselves tragic enough, the real tragedy lies in how they have been used in an attempt to undermine the self-esteem of African-American women.

Health Statistics and the Right to Privacy

One of the first things a poor person loses is the right to privacy. She must surrender information about her private life in exchange for a modicum of basic needs which the state grudgingly provides. The fact that the information extracted often goes beyond what is required for service is of little use to her. She is powerless and in need. *They* have the ability to determine her ineligible and consequently to affect her physical survival.

The vulnerability of the poor is ruthlessly exploited in the name of science. Countless graduate students in the health sciences have benefited from this vulnerability. Innumerable theses and dissertations have been written based on data collected from the poor. The informants were usually corralled at points of defenselessness: while waiting for WIC tickets (a nutritional supplement program for poor women and children), for emergency medical care, etc. Many of these women probably had no idea that it was unnecessary to submit to the questions. Some may have been given an option but believed compliance would improve their future service.

The data collected are never returned to the informants in a way that is useful. The original reports are written for the intellectual elite. The final dissemination of the data is through the mass media and only then if the results are newsworthy (i.e., sensational). Results are deemed newsworthy when they support the prevailing myths of our system. The master myth relevant to health is the inherent (i.e., genetic) instability of African-Americans' minds, bodies and "culture."

The right to privacy is predicated by income and mediated by race. The vast numbers of poor whites have not been an issue of interest for the intellectual elite. There has been historically a conscious choice to analyze health data by race, not by income. The impact of this decision is manifested by our present inability to relieve the health problems of many Americans as we remain the only industrialized society outside of South Africa not to have a national health insurance plan. It is unquestionable that the same obstacles as in South Africa exist in the USA: the unwillingness to provide adequate health care to all regardless of color or income.

Public health statistics support the resistance to a national health insurance as they imply an inequity in health problems. When they suggest that only certain segments of the population suffer from certain diseases, and then are used to promote interventions for another segment of the population, health statistics are used as instruments of oppression. For example, although health statistics clearly indicate that coronary heart disease (CHD) is and has been a very serious problem for African-American women, public intervention programs imply that it is primarily a problem for Euro-American males. African-American women's death rate from CHD exceeds that of Euro-American women (Myers, 1986). Although there are different types of heart disease, the different types share common risk factors. For African-American women these risk factors include cigarette smoking, hypertension, obesity and diabetes. The social and structural risk factors include higher life stresses (Harburg *et al.*, 1973), truncated medical care access and lower-quality care (Yellin *et al.*, 1983).

A comparison of other CHD impact variables attributable to smoking (deaths, related lost years of life, cases, related hospital days, related days of restricted activity and related medical expenditures) between African-American and Euro-American women concluded that there were no "racial" differences (Kumanyika and Savage, 1986: 243). However, these comparisons did not take into account the fact that a large number of African-American women are heads of households and often responsible for young children. The sociocultural impact of CHD on African-American women is much greater for them and their families than it is for Euro-American women.

The prevalence of hypertension in African-American women increases with age and is 1.7 to 3 times higher in African-American women than Euro-American women in every age group (Kumanyika and Savage, 1986). In addition to being a risk factor for heart disease and heart failure, hypertension leads to pathological changes which can cause kidney disease or stroke. Demographically the highest levels of blood pressure for African-American women are in the South and the West. A major structural risk factor for hypertension is stress. Urban women's blood pressures are lower than those of rural women (Kumanyika and Savage, 1986). The aetiology for these demographic differences is unknown. Hypertension is often associated with another health problem of African-American women, obesity.

Obesity, an excess of body fat, can range from mild (120 percent) to severe (more than 200 percent) of the desirable or ideal body weight (Moore, 1990). Overweight, a weight in excess of the desirable body weight (Moore, 1990), is often confused with obesity. Because the prevalence of overweight in African-American women is higher than that of comparable groups of Euro-American women (Gillum, 1987), fat is a feminist issue that affects large numbers of African-American women.

Research-identified variables that make it more difficult for African-American women to lose weight are: (1) education below college level, (2) marriage and (3) low family income (Kahn *et al.,* 1991). Narratives from African-American women reveal entirely different factors:

> I work for General Electric making batteries, and from the stuff they suit me up in, I know it's killing me. My home life is not working. My old man is an alcoholic. My kids got babies. Things are not well with me. And the one thing I know I can do when I come home is to cook me a pot of food and sit down in front of the TV and eat it. And you can't take that away from me until you're ready to give me something in its place. (Avery, 1990: 7)

What confounds the issue in regard to weight and African-American women are Eurocentric notions about attractiveness, biomedical determinations about health and African-American cultural ideas about beauty. Many of the negative traits associated with obesity, lack of control, unattractiveness and slovenliness, have long been associated with African-Americans as a "race." On the one hand, Eurocentric ideas about obesity tend to equate fat with unattractiveness. Consequently, those African-American women who subscribe to Euro-American standards of beauty are placed in a double bind in which one culturally evaluated trait (obesity) reinforces this society's negative view of their physical appearance. On the other hand, in African-American communities, a certain level of obesity is considered attractive. Historically, African-Americans have associated degrees of overweight with well-being. To be thin was to be "poor." The African-American community's preference for "healthy" women has resulted in much lower rates of anorexia and bulimia for African-American women. However, the close relationship between adult onset diabetes and obesity requires that African-American women closely monitor their weight.

Diabetes is a disease that has particularly severe consequences for African-American women. Data from the 1981 National Health Interviews demonstrated that African-American women's diabetes rate was 38.2 per 1,000. One of the ten leading causes of death in 1988 was diabetes mellitus, and African-American women's death rate from this was 27.3 versus 17.6 for Euro-American women (National Center for Health Statistics, 1990). An additional problem for African-American women is that the associations among obesity, diabetes and hypertension increase the risk for heart disease.

Comparison health statistics between African-American and Euro-American women that illustrate less, little or no difference in incidence between them for a specific disease sometimes serve to mask the enormity of certain problems for African-American women. Breast cancer statistics are a case in point. For years the focus on the lower incidence of breast cancer in African-American versus Euro-American women effectively served to mask the fact that African-American women have a higher death rate from breast cancer than Euro-American women. Although the breast cancer rate for African-American women is less than that for Euro-American women, their mortality rate for this disease exceeds that of any other group of women (National Center for Health Statistics, 1990). Some of the reasons given for this disparity in mortality rates are socioeconomic status (SES), later stage at diagnosis, and delay in detection and treatment, treatment differences and biological/constitutional factors (Report of the Secretary's Task Force, 1986). Since biological/constitutional factors are neither defined nor discussed in the report, they can be dismissed as factors. SES, later stage at diagnosis and delay in treatment are related to problems of access. Poverty is a major factor in both later diagnosis and delay in treatment. The poor have not benefited from the various advances in cancer prevention, detection and treatment (American Cancer Society, 1990). However, poverty is not the only factor. McWhorter and Mayer (1987) found that when age, stage of cancer and histology were adjusted, African-American women received less aggressive surgical treatment, were less likely to be treated surgically and were more likely to be treated nonsurgically than Euro-American women.

Human Immunodeficiency Virus (HIV)/Autoimmunodeficiency Disease (AIDS)

AIDS is a national problem that is wreaking devastation in the African-American community. It is one of the ten leading causes of death for the African-American population (National Center for Health Statistics, 1990). African-Americans accounted for 25 percent of the AIDS deaths in 1988 (National Center for Health Statistics, 1990). HIV affects African-American women in a number of ways. First, African-American women and their children are part of the fastest-growing population of AIDS victims. Second, if diagnosed with AIDS, in addition to being concerned about herself, the woman has to be concerned with the effect of her death on her children. Third, the case definition of AIDS is based upon a male profile. As a result the profile does not take into account gynecological manifestations of HIV. As Anastos and Marte note: "If women's disease manifests with the same infections as it does in men, it may be recognized and reported as AIDS; if the infections, still HIV related, are different, the women are not considered to have AIDS" (1989: 6). Since eligibility for Supplemental Security Income (SSI) is based upon a diagnosis of AIDS, many women with AIDS are deemed ineligible for SSI benefits. Fourth, if a woman is pregnant and HIV positive, she is concerned with transmitting the disease to her newborn. Fifth, if she is diagnosed as HIV positive, her chances of contracting AIDS are higher and she will die sooner than her Euro-American sister. This disparity is usually accounted for by the mode of transmission. Many African-American women are exposed to HIV through intravenous drug use. As a result, the virus reaches their bloodstream much faster than it does when the virus is transmitted through sexual contact. Sixth, if someone in a woman's family, i.e., her child or partner, contracts the disease, in all likelihood she will be responsible for taking care of them.

Mental Health

In 1979, African-American women reported a lower level of well-being than African-American males, white females and white males (Institute for Urban Affairs and Research, 1981). One third of the women surveyed reported a level of distress comparable with that of an independent sample of mental health patients (Institute for Urban Affairs and Research, 1981). Although the research on depression in African-American women reports high rates of depressive symptomatology and depression (Carrington, 1980; Dressler, 1987; Dressler and Badger, 1985; Gary *et al.*, 1985), African-American women are less likely to be medically diagnosed as depressive than Euro-American females (Smith, 1981).

Among African-Americans the highest rates of depression occur in women under 45 years of age; the lowest rates are in African-Americans aged 45 years and older. At all ages and income levels, women's depressive symptomatology is greater than men's (Gary *et al.*, 1985). Factors that increase the risk of depression in younger African-American women are: being poor, being between 18 and 45 years of age, being unemployed, high school education or less, the presence of minor children in the household, and being divorced or separated (Brown, 1990).

There is some evidence that suggests that support networks as traditionally viewed are not as useful to African-American women when they are depressed. In an examination of the relationships among economic stressors, extended kin support, active coping and depressive symptoms in a sample of 285 African-American households in a southern community, Dressler (1987) found a positive relationship between extended kin support and depressive symptoms. Women who reported higher active coping strategies reported fewer depressive symptoms. In addition to the previously discussed medical conditions two other conditions that disproportionally affect the health of African-American women are reproductive rights and violence.

Reproductive Rights versus Reproductive Freedom

We take issue with the notion of reproductive rights, particularly as it concerns African-American women. The national debate on reproductive rights is one that almost totally eclipses the interest and needs of African-American women. The debate, from its intellectual framework to its proposed goals, does not address the serious health problems of marginalized groups. The philosophical boundaries of the debate are seriously compromised. To talk in terms of "reproductive rights" is an intellectual abdication to a legal system primarily concerned with property rights, *not* human rights. The phrase is an oxymoron. Human reproduction is not a right; it is a biological possibility. The two major opponents in the debate have chosen or accepted the media terms of "pro choice" and "right to life." The right to life seems to presume the "right" begins with conception, is most vibrant during gestation and ends at birth. The success of neither of the two will significantly improve the plight of Black females who have historically suffered disproportionally from the institutionalized attack on the Black family and "Third World" rates of infant mortality.

Tervalon (1988) notes that there are three interconnected aspects of reproductive rights: access to abortion, infant mortality and forced sterilization. Rather than talking about reproductive rights, it would be more accurate to speak of reproductive freedom. Reproductive freedom is defined here as unrestrained access to the medical knowledge (information) available in one's society that is necessary for the optimum maintenance of one's reproductive health. In addition to the aspects referred to by Tervalon, reproductive freedom would include safe, effective, affordable forms of birth control, family planning, sexual education, freedom from forced sterilization (Ditzion and Golden, 1984), the right of consenting adults to conduct their sex lives as they choose, reduction in African-American infant and maternal mortality rates, and affordable access to diagnosis and treatment of sexually transmitted diseases (STDs).

The lack of reproductive freedom has resulted in disastrous consequences for African-American women. These consequences include being three times more likely than Euro-American women to die of causes associated with pregnancy, childbirth and the puerperium (the period during and immediately after childbirth), an infant mortality rate of 17.6 (National

Center for Health Statistics, 1990) and sterilization. Sterilization of African-American women encompasses a broad range of issues: (1) the right of African-American women to give informed consent to surgical procedures; (2) the racism that underlies the actions of physicians and surgeons who treat African-American women; and (3) the need for African-American women to be informed about a broad range of gynecological problems which may lead to hysterectomies or other sterilizing procedures (Black Women's Community Development Foundation, 1974). Data on sterilization in the USA demonstrate that a higher percentage of African-American women are sterilized and that the rate of sterilization of African-American women is increasing (Mosher and Pratt, 1990). The respective figures for African-American and Euro-American women's sterilization in 1982 and 1988 were 38.1 percent versus 26.1 percent and 30 percent versus 22.1 percent (Mosher and Pratt, 1990).

This high rate of sterilization underscores African-American women's lack of basic human rights. It sends a clear message about the links between African-American women's sexuality, fertility and roles within the political economy (Collins, 1990). Under slavery Black women were reproducers of human capital; slave women who reproduced often were rewarded (Giddings, 1984). Over time, changes in the political economy have transformed African-American women's fertility from a necessity for an economy in need of cheap labor to a costly threat to political and economic stability (Collins, 1990). As a result, the fertility of African-American women, particularly those who carry the image of welfare mothers, must be controlled. Additional issues of sterilization include: the relationship of African-American women to the pro- and anti-abortion movements, the role that African-American women should play in policy-making around these issues, the genocide issue, and the effort of African-American women to balance their right not to have unwanted children with their fears of genocidal national and international policies (Black Women's Community Development Foundation, 1974).

The year 1990 was to have been the target date for the completion of the "second public health revolution" (US Department of Health, Education and Welfare, 1979: vii). Goals were set to improve the health conditions of all ages of the US populace. A primary goal was to reduce the national infant mortality rate to 9 deaths per 1,000 live births. The ability of the USA as a nation to execute a second revolution was in doubt from the beginning. Joseph A. Califano in the foreword of the report which listed the goals wrote: "What is in doubt is whether we have the personal discipline and political will to solve these problems" (US Department of Health, Education and Welfare, 1979: viii). Some communities in the USA have reached the goal of "9 by 90." Other communities, poor, marginalized and dark in hue, have infant mortality rates exceeding 30 per 1,000. When the debate over reproductive rights is over, the debate that begins at the birth of each African-American child will still rage: can s/he survive? Will this child be allowed to thrive?

Violence

Although violence in African-American communities is disproportional in its effects upon women, the continued focus has been on the African-American male homicide rate. This exclusive focus on males serves to mask the violence to which African-American women are constantly exposed. For African-American women crime statistics are also health statistics. Homicide is one of the ten leading causes of death for African-American women. The reported rape rate for African-American women is almost three times that of Euro-American women (US Department of Justice, 1991). Once raped, African-American women have a harder time getting police and medical professionals to believe them.

In popular African-American magazines rape, a crime of violence usually perpetrated against women, is explained by African-American male authorities as being caused by male frustration. Although one would like to believe that African-American male physicians might bring more sensitivity and awareness to the problems of African-American women, often male physicians are unwilling or unable to recognize either their own sexism or their own inability to understand that sexual violence transcends race. Thus in an article about rape in *Ebony* magazine, Alvin Poussaint, an African-American male psychiatrist, concluded that the high rate of rape of African-American women was due to the "feelings of rejection" of African-American males and to their need to bolster their self-esteem (Norment, 1991: 96).

Poussaint's apologist stance comes dangerously close to the rationale used historically by Euro-American males to justify their sexual abuse of African-American women. He joins the long line of African-American males who do not believe that Black males should be held responsible for their violence against African-American women (Lorde, 1990). Most rapes are planned (Amir, 1971), which suggests premeditation and hence responsibility. African-American male psychiatrists are not the only ones to beg the issue on the subject of rape in African-American communities. Ironically, Davis (1983) in an entire chapter on rape, in a book about women, while appropriately criticizing Euro-American women's treatises about the African-American male rapist, ignores the high rape rate of African-American women in African-American communities.

In addition to the high rape rate, there is also a high prevalence of sexual abuse. According to the empirical literature, African-American women are more frequently victims of sexual abuse than Euro-American women (Katz and Mazur, 1979). Furthermore, African-American women are at risk of rape and child sexual abuse across all age groups (Amir, 1971; Peters, 1976; Kercher and McShane, 1984). Wyatt (1985) found that African-American preteens were most likely to experience abuse in their homes from male nuclear or extended family members. African-American women reported more incidence of sexual abuse involving stepfathers, mothers' boyfriends, foster fathers, male cousins and other relatives than did Euro-American women (Wyatt, 1985).

Although battering is a strong concern of African-American women, Coley and Beckett (1988) in a twenty-year (1967–87) review of the empirical literature in counseling, psychology, social work and sociology, found only two sources on battering and African-American women. In addition to being physically battered, African-American women are also psychologically battered through music. The lyrics in some rap songs or hip hop music are especially violent toward and degrading of women. In an interesting combination of blaming the victim, transforming violence to sexism and holding women accountable for male behavior, a hip hop expert writes:

> As I once told a sister, hip hop lyrics are, among other things, what a lot of Black men say about Black women when Black women aren't around. In this sense the music is no more or less sexist than your fathers, brothers, husbands, friends and lovers and in many cases more upfront. As an unerringly precise reflection of the community, hip hop's sexist thinking will change when the community changes. Because women are the ones best able to define sexism, they will have to challenge the music—tell it how to change and make it change—if change is to come. (Allen, 1989: 117)

If males are creating and perpetuating violent, sexist lyrics, why is it women's responsibility to change them? Another question is why would African-American women take part in such music? African-American women who participate in and create women-abusing rap lyrics, have essentially embraced the external controlling images and are participating in their own oppression.

Hospitals Are Dangerous

In addition to having to deal with the danger in the communities, African-American women are exposed to added dangers when they seek medical care. The vulnerability of African-American women is only too apparent. Dr. Norma Goodwin (1990: 12) in her analysis of why African-Americans die six to seven years earlier than their white counterparts listed two factors central to the dilemma of black females: "the lack of culturally sensitive health information" and "decreased access to high quality care." These factors are excruciatingly sensitive to the economic status of the individual. The African-American woman all too often finds herself on Medicaid (health insurance for the poor), not Medicare (health insurance for the elderly). The reluctance of private physicians to accept Medicaid is not even apologetic. Even so, those individuals are better off than the estimated 35 million Americans without any form of health insurance (Edelman, 1987).

The absence of a national health insurance means that many African-American women receive their basic health care from public health clinics and county hospitals. The other historical source of health care is the university research hospital. Most of the major university hospitals in the country are located in economically distressed areas. For centuries marginalized groups have served the medical establishment as disease models, guinea pigs and cadavers. The ever-present vulnerability of African-American women was brought back to our memories with the exposé of medical research at Cook County Hospital in Chicago in 1988.

More than 200 pregnant women were given a drug, Dilantin, without their knowledge. Fortunately, to date, the drug, used normally to treat epilepsy, has not caused damage to the resulting offspring or their mothers. The fact that such blatant abuses of human rights can occur in a publicly monitored setting only indicates the probability of what is occurring in private practices. According to the Public Citizen Health Research Group, the trend is for clinical trials to be conducted in doctors' offices (1990b: 1). That African-American women will continue to be guinea pigs sacrificed to the US medical establishment is a foregone conclusion. In 1989, the Food and Drug Administration found that there were irregularities in the informed consent forms in 75 percent of the investigations of drug trials conducted in doctors' offices, outpatient clinics and hospitals (Public Citizen Health Research Group, 1990b: 1). Those same factors elucidated by Goodwin suggest who is most likely to participate in experimental drug trials.

Summary

Lewis suggested in 1977 that the structural position of African-American women would cause them to become more responsive to feminist issues. One area in which Lewis's prophecy has materialized is in the area of African-American women's health. One of the first conferences exclusively devoted to African-American women's health was sponsored by the Black Women's Community Development Foundation. As B. Smith pointed out: "The health of Black women is a subject of major importance for those of us who are committed to learning, teaching, and writing about our sisters" (1982: 103).

Although there is a greater awareness of African-American women's health problems, the massive budget cuts for social and health programs under the Reagan-Bush administrations have only served to undermine the progress of and place pressure on local African-American women's health initiatives. At the state level, redefinition of the eligibility requirements for Medicaid have reduced or eliminated medical coverage for large numbers of African-American women and their children. At a time when we should be concentrating on thriving, we are still concerned with survival. However, as Collins (1990: 92) noted: "Resisting by doing something that 'is not expected' could not have occurred without Black women's long-standing rejection of mammies, matriarchs, and other controlling images." The development of the National Black Women's Health Project and the organization of the First

National Conference on Black Women's Health exemplifies doing the "unexpected." The Black Women's Health Project's first conference on Black women's health received an overwhelming response. In addition the Black Women's Health Project has developed regional networks that provide an environment that encourages African-American women to define and respond to their own health problems.

At the First National Conference on Black Women's Health Issues, Christmas, an African-American woman physician, made the following points about African-American women's health: (1) we must not accept the blame for our condition; (2) we must be responsible for ourselves and at the same time hold the medical community and community agencies accountable, and (3) we must demand affordable, accessible, responsive facilities and medical providers (Butler, 1984). The life we want is one in which basic health care is assured. African-American women need and have a right to health. The state must try to provide safe living and workplace conditions, a safe environment, primary health care and adequate nutrition throughout life to its citizens. These rights which the state could guarantee are not on the table for debate.

REFERENCES

Allen, H. (1989) "Rap Is Our Music!" *Essence* 20 (12): 78–80, 114, 117, 119.

American Cancer Society (1990) *Cancer and the Poor: A Report to the Nation,* Atlanta, GA: American Cancer Society.

Amir, M. (1971) *Patterns of Forcible Rape,* Chicago: University of Chicago Press.

Anastos, K. and Marte, K. (1989) "Women—The Missing Persons in the AIDS Epidemic," *Health/PAC Bulletin* 19 (4): 6–11.

Avery, B. Y. (1990) "Breathing Life into Ourselves: The Evolution of the Black Women's Health Project," in E. White (ed.) *The Black Women's Health Book: Speaking for Ourselves,* Seattle: Seal Press: 4–10.

Barbee, E. L. (1992) "Ethnicity and Woman Abuse in the United States," in C. Sampselle (ed.) *Violence Against Women: Nursing Research, Practice and Education Issues,* Washington, DC: Hemisphere: 153–66.

Beale, F. (1970) "Double Jeopardy: To Be Black and Female," in T. Cade (ed.) *The Black Female,* New York: New American Library: 90–100.

Black Women's Community Development Foundation (1974) *Miniconsultation on the Mental and Physical Health Problem of Black Women,* Washington, DC: Black Women's Community Development Foundation.

Brown, D. R. (1990) "Depression Among Blacks," in D. S. Ruiz (ed.) *Handbook of Mental Health and Mental Disorder Among Black Americans,* New York: Greenwood Press: 71–93.

Butler, E. (1984) "The First National Conference on Black Women's Health Issues," in N. Worcester and M. H. Whatley (eds.) *Women's Health: Readings in Social, Economic & Political Issues,* Dubuque, IA: Kendall/Hunt: 37–42.

Carrington, C. H. (1980) "Depression in Black Women: A Theoretical Appraisal," in L. F. Rodgers-Rose (ed.) *The Black Woman,* Beverly Hills, CA: Sage: 265–71.

Christensen, C. P. (1988) "Issues in Sex Therapy with Ethnic and Racial Minority Women," *Women & Therapy* 7: 187–205.

Coley, S. M. and Beckett, J. O. (1988) "Black Battered Women: A Review of the Literature," *Journal of Counseling and Development* 66: 266–70.

Collins, P. H. (1990) *Black Feminist Thought: Knowledge, Consciousness, and the Politics of Empowerment,* Boston, Mass.: Unwin Hyman.

Davis, A. Y. (1983) *Women, Race and Class,* New York: Vintage Books.

Ditzion, J. and Golden, J. (1984) "Introduction," in Boston Women's Health Book Collective, *The New Our Bodies Ourselves,* New York: Simon & Schuster: 201–2.

Dressler, W. W. (1987) "The Stress Process in a Southern Black Community: Implications for Prevention Research," *Human Organization* 46: 211–20.

Dressler, W. W. and Badger, L. W. (1985) "Epidemiology of Depressive Symptoms in Black Communities," *Journal of Nervous and Mental Disease* 173: 212–20.

Edelman, M. W. (1987) *Families in Peril,* Cambridge, Mass.: Harvard University Press.

Gary, L. E., Brown, D. R., Milburn, N. G., Thomas, V. G. and Lockley, D. S. (1985) *Pathways: A Study of Black Informal Support Networks,* Washington, DC: Institute for Urban Affairs and Research, Howard University.

Giddings, P. (1984) *When and Where I Enter . . . : The Impact of Black Women on Race and Sex in America,* Toronto: Bantam Books.

Gillum, R. F. (1987) "Overweight and Obesity in Black Women: A Review of Published Data from the National Center for Health Statistics," *Journal of the National Medical Association* 79: 865–71.

Goodwin, N. J. (1990) "Health and the African American Community," *Crisis* 97 (8): 12 and 50.

Harburg, E., Erfurt, J. C., Chape, L. S., Hauestein, L. S., Schull, W. J. and Schork, M. A. (1973) "Socioecological Stress Areas and Black-White Blood Pressure: Detroit," *Journal of Chronic Diseases* 26: 595–611.

hooks, bell (1981) *Ain't I a Woman: Black Women and Feminism;* Boston, Mass.: South End Press.

Institute for Urban Affairs and Research. (1981) *Statistical Profile of the Black Female,* Washington, DC: Howard University 7 (1): 1–4.

Kahn, H. S., Williamson, D. F. and Stevens, J. A. (1991) "Race and Weight Change in US Women: The Roles of Socioeconomic and Marital Status," *American Journal of Public Health* 81: 319–23.

Katz, S. and Mazur, M. (1979) *Understanding the Rape Victim: A Synthesis of Research Findings,* New York: Wiley.

Kercher, G. and McShane, M. (1984) "The Prevalence of Child Sexual Abuse Victimization in an Adult Sample of Texas Residents," *Child Abuse and Neglect* 8: 495–502.

King, D. K. (1988) "Multiple Jeopardy, Multiple Consciousness: The Context of a Black Feminist Ideology," *Signs: Journal of Women in Culture and Society* 14 (1) (August): 42–72.

Kumanyika, S. and Savage, D. D. (1986) "Ischemic Heart Disease Risk Factors in Black Americans," in Report of the Secretary's Task Force on Black & Minority Health, Vol. IV, *Cardiovascular and Cerebrovascular Disease, Part 2,* US Department of Health and Human Services, Washington, DC: US Government Printing Office: 229–90.

Lewis, D. (1977) "A Response to Inequality: Black Women, Racism and Sexism," *Signs: Journal of Women in Culture and Society* 3: 339–405.

Lorde, A. (1990) *Need: a Chorale for Black Woman Voices,* Latham, NY: Kitchen Table Press.

McWhorter, W. P. and Mayer, W. J. (1987) "Black/White Differences in Type of Initial Breast Cancer Treatment and Implications for Survival," *American Journal of Public Health* 77: 1515–17.

Moore, M. C. (1990) "Nutritional Alterations," in P. G. Beare and J. L. Myers (eds.) *Principles and Practices of Adult Health Nursing,* St Louis, MO: Mosby: 343–84.

Mosher, W. D. and Pratt, W. F. (1990) *Contraceptive Use in the United States, 1973–88, Advance data from vital and health statistics;* no. 182, Hyattsville, MD: National Center for Health Statistics.

Myers, H. F. (1986) "Coronary Heart Disease in Black Populations: Current Research, Treatment and Prevention Needs," in Report of the Secretary's Task Force on Black & Minority Health, Vol. IV, *Cardiovascular and Cerebrovascular Disease, Part 2,* US Department of Health and Human Services, Washington, DC: US Government Printing Office: 303–44.

National Center for Health Statistics (1990) *Advance Report of Final Mortality Statistics, 1988,* Monthly Vital Statistics report; Vol. 39, no. 7, supplement, Hyattsville, MD: Public Health Service.

Norment, L. (1991) "What's Behind the Dramatic Rise in Rapes?" *Ebony* 46 (11) (September): 92, 94, 96–8.

Peters, J. J. (1976) "Children Who Are Victims of Sexual Assault and the Psychology of Offenders," *American Journal of Psychotherapy* 30: 393–421.

——— (1990b) *Health Letter* 6 (11).

Report of the Secretary's Task Force on Black & Minority Health (1986) Vol. III, *Cancer* US Department of Health and Human Services, Washington, DC: US Government Printing Office.

Smith, B. (1982) "Black Women's Health: Notes for a Course," in G. T. Hull, P. Bell-Scott and B. Smith (eds.) *All the Women Are White, All the Blacks Are Men, But Some of Us Are Brave,* Old Westbury, NY: Feminist Press: 103-14.

Smith, E. J. (1981) "Mental Health and Service Delivery Systems for Black Women," *Journal of Black Studies* 17: 126–41.

Tervalon, M. (1988) "Black Women's Reproductive Rights," in N. Worcester and M. H. Whatley (eds.) *Women's Health: Readings in Social, Economic & Political Issues,* Dubuque, IA: Kendall/Hunt: 136–7.

US Bureau of the Census Current Population Reports (1988) series P-60, no. 161, *Money, Income and Poverty Status in the United States: 1987,* Washington, DC: US Government Printing Office: August.

US Bureau of the Census Current Population Reports (1989a) series P-25, no. 1018, *Projection of the Population of the United States by Age, Sex and Race: 1988 to 2080,* Washington, DC: US Government Printing Office: January.

US Bureau of the Census Current Population Reports (1989b) series P-20, no. 433, *Marital Status and Living Arrangements: March, 1988,* Washington, DC: US Government Printing Office: January.

US Department of Health, Education and Welfare (1979) *Healthy People,* Washington, DC: US Government Printing Office.

US Department of Justice, Office of Justice Programs, Bureau of Justice Statistics (1991) *Criminal Victimization in the United States: 1973–88 Trends,* Washington, DC: US Government Printing Office: July.

Wyatt, G. E. (1985) "The Sexual Abuse of Afro-American and White Women in Childhood," *Child Abuse and Neglect* 9: 507–19.

Yellin, E. H., Kramer, I. S. and Epstein, W. V. (1983) "Is Health Care Use Equivalent Across Social Groups? A Diagnosis-Based Study," *American Journal of Public Health* 73: 563–71.

67

REPRODUCTIVE ISSUES ARE ESSENTIAL SURVIVAL ISSUES FOR THE ASIAN-AMERICAN COMMUNITIES

CONNIE S. CHAN

When the Asian-American communities in the United States list their priorities for political action and organizing, several issues concerning basic survival are usually included: access to bilingual education, housing, health care, and child care, among others. Yet the essential survival issue of access to reproductive counseling, education, and abortions is frequently missing from the agenda of Asian-American community organizations. Why is the reproductive issue perceived as unimportant to the Asian-American communities? I think there are several reasons—ignorance, classism, sexism, and language barriers. Of course, these issues are interrelated, and I'll try to make the connections between them.

First, let me state that I am not an "expert" on the topic of reproductive issues in the Asian-American communities, but I do have first-hand experiences which have given me some insight into the problems. Several years ago, I was a staff psychologist at a local community health center serving the greater Boston Asian population. Most of our patients were recent immigrants from China, Vietnam, Cambodia, Laos, and Hong Kong. Almost all of these new immigrants understood little or no English. With few resources (financial or otherwise), many newcomers struggled to make sense of life in the United States and to survive in whatever fashion they could.

At the health center, the staff tried to help by providing information and advocacy in getting through our confusing system. I thought we did a pretty good job until I found out that neither our health education department nor our ob-gyn department provided *any* counseling or information about birth control or abortion services. The medical department had interpreted our federal funding regulations as prohibiting not only the performance of abortions on-site, but also the dissemination of information which might lead to, or help patients to obtain, an abortion.

Needless to say, as a feminist and as an activist, I was horrified. When I found out that pregnant women who inquired about abortions were given only a name of a white, English-speaking ob-gyn doctor and sent out alone, it

Connie Chan, "Reproductive Issues Are Essential Survival Issues for Asian-American Communities" from *From Abortion to Reproductive Freedom,* edited by Marlene Gerber Fried. Reprinted with the permission of South End Press.

seemed a morally and ethically neglectful practice. One of the nurse-midwives agreed with me and suggested that I could serve as an interpreter/advocate for pregnant women who needed to have abortions, or at least wanted to discuss the option with the English-speaking ob-gyn doctor. The only catch was that I would have to do it on my own time, I could not claim any affiliation with the health center, and I could not suggest follow-up care at the health center.

Not fully knowing the nature of what I was volunteering for, I agreed to interpret and advocate for Cantonese-speaking pregnant women at their appointments with the obstetrician. It turned out that over the course of three years I interpreted during at least a hundred abortions for Asian immigrant women who spoke no English. After the first few abortions, the obstetrician realized how essential it was to have an interpreter present, and began to require that all non-English-speaking women have an interpreter during the abortion procedure.

As a middle-class, educated, bilingual Asian-American woman, I was aware of the importance of having the choice to have an abortion, and the necessity of fighting for the right to choose for myself. I had been unaware of how the right to have an abortion is also a right to survival in this country if you are a poor, uneducated, non-English-speaking immigrant.

The women I interpreted for were, for the most part, not young. Nor were they single. They ranged in age from 25 to 45, with a majority in their late twenties and early thirties. Almost all were married and had two or more children. Some had as many as five or six children. They needed to have abortions because they had been unlucky enough to have gotten pregnant after arriving in this country. Their families were barely surviving on the low wages that many new immigrant workers earned as restaurant workers, garment factory workers, or domestic help. Almost all of the women worked full-time: the ones who had young children left them with older, retired family members or did piece-work at home; those with older children worked in the factories or hotels. Without fail each woman would tell me that she needed to have an abortion because their family could not afford another mouth to feed, that the family could not afford to lose her salary contribution, not even for a few months, to care for an infant. In some ways, one could not even say that these women were choosing to have abortions. The choice had already been made for them, and it was a choice of basic survival.

Kai Ling was one of the women for whom I interpreted. A 35-year-old mother of four children, ages 2 to 7, she and her husband emigrated to the United States from Vietnam. They had no choice; in their emigration, they were refugees whose village had been destroyed and felt fortunate to escape with their lives and all four of their children. Life in the United States was difficult, but they were scraping by, living with another family in a small apartment where their entire family slept in one room. Their hope was that their children would receive an education and "make it" in American society; they lived with the deferred dream for the next generation.

When Kai Ling found out that she was pregnant, she felt desperate. Because she and her husband love children and live for their children, they wanted desperately to keep this child, this one who would be born in America and be an American citizen from birth. Yet they sadly realized that they could not afford another child, they could not survive on just one salary, they could not feed another one. Their commitment was to the children they already had, and to keeping their family together.

When I accompanied Kai Ling to her abortion, she was saddened but resigned to what she had to do. The $300 that she brought to the clinic represented almost a month of wages for her; she had borrowed the money from family and friends. She would pay it back, she said, by working weekends for the next ten weeks. Their major regret was that she would not be able to buy any new clothes for her children this year because of this unexpected expense.

Kai Ling spoke very little English. She did not understand why she had to go to a white American doctor for her abortion instead of receiving services from her Asian doctor at the health center. She had no real understanding of reproductive rights issues, of *Roe v. Wade,* or of why there were demonstrators waving pictures of fetuses and yelling at her as we entered the clinic. Mercifully, she did not understand the questions they shouted at her in English, and she did not ask me what they had said, remarking only that the protesters seemed very angry at someone. She felt sure, I think, that they were not angry at her. She had done nothing to provoke anyone's anger. She was merely trying to survive in this country under this country's rules.

It is a crime and an injustice that Kai Ling could not receive counseling in her language and services from her doctors at the Asian neighborhood health center. It is a crime that she had to borrow $300 to pay for her own abortion, that her Medicaid benefits did not pay for it. It is a grave injustice that she had to have me, a stranger, interpreting for her during her abortion because her own doctor could not perform the procedure at her clinic. It was not a matter of choice for her to abort her pregnancy, but a matter of basic survival.

Kai Ling speaks no English. Kai Ling will probably never attend a march or a rally for choice. She will not sign any petitions. She might not even vote. But it is for her and the countless thousands of immigrant women like her that we need to continue to struggle for reproductive rights. Within the Asian-American communities, the immigrant women who are most affected by the lack of access to abortions have the least power. They do not speak English; they do not demand equal access to health care; their needs are easily overlooked.

Thus, it is up to those of us who are bilingual, who can speak English, and who can speak to these issues, to do so. We need to ensure that the issue of reproductive rights is an essential item on the Asian-American political agenda. It is not a women's issue; it is a community issue.

We must speak for the Kai Lings, for their children, for their right to survive as a family. We must, as activists, make the connections between the issues of oppression based upon gender, race, national origin, sexual orientation, class, or language. We can and must lead the Asian-American communities to recognize the importance of the essential issue of reproductive rights for the survival of these communities.

68

WHY THE PRECAUTIONARY PRINCIPLE? A Meditation on Polyvinyl Chloride (PVC) and the Breasts of Mothers*

SANDRA STEINGRABER

Those of you who know me know that when I talk on these topics I usually speak out of two identities: biologist and cancer activist. My diagnosis with bladder cancer at age 20 makes more urgent my scientific research. Conversely, my Ph.D. in ecology informs my understanding of how and why I became a cancer patient in the first place: bladder cancer is considered a quintessential environmental disease. Links between environment and public health became the topic of my third book, *Living Downstream,* but since I have been given the task of speaking about the effect of toxic materials on future generations, I'm going to speak out of another one of my identities—that of a mother.

I'm a very new mother. I gave birth in September 1998 to my daughter and first child. So, I'm going to speak very intimately and in the present tense. You know it's a very powerful thing for a person with a cancer history to have a child. It's a very long commitment for those of us unaccustomed to looking far into the future. My daughter's name is Faith.

I'm also learning what all parents must learn, which is a new kind of love. It's a love that's more than an emotion or a feeling. It's a deep physical craving like hunger or thirst. It's the realization that you would lay down your life for this eight-pound person without a second thought. You would pick up arms for them. You would empty your bank account. It's love without boundaries and were this kind of love directed at another adult, it would be considered totally inappropriate. A kind of fatal attraction. Maybe, when directed at babies, we should call this "natal attraction."

I say this to remind us all what is at stake. If we would die or kill for our children, wouldn't we do anything within our power to keep toxics out of their food supply? Especially if we knew, in fact, there were alternatives to these toxics?

---

*Remarks delivered at the Lowell Center for Sustainable Production's workshop, Building Materials into the Coming Millennium, Boston, November 1998.

Of all human food, breast milk is now the most contaminated. Because it is one rung up on the food chain higher than the foods we adults eat, the trace amounts of toxic residues carried into mothers' bodies become even more concentrated in the milk their breasts produce. To be specific, it's about 10 to 100 times more contaminated with dioxins than the next highest level of stuff on the human food chain, which are animal-derived fats in dairy, meat, eggs, and fish. This is why a breast-fed infant receives its so-called "safe" lifetime limit of dioxin in the first six months of drinking breast milk. Study after study also shows that the concentration of carcinogens in human breast milk declines steadily as nursing continues. Thus the protective effect of breast feeding on the mother appears to be a direct result of downloading a lifelong burden of carcinogens from her breasts into the tiny body of her infant.

When it comes to the production, use, and disposal of PVC, the breasts of breast-feeding mothers are the tailpipe. Representatives from the vinyl industry emphasize how common a material PVC is, and they are correct. It is found in medical products, toys, food packaging, and vinyl siding. What they don't say is that sooner or later all of these products are tossed into the trash, and here in New England, we tend to shovel our trash into incinerators. Incinerators are de facto laboratories for dioxin manufacturer, and PVC is the main ingredient in this process. The dioxin created by the burning of PVC drifts from the stacks of these incinerators, attaches to dust particles in the atmosphere, and eventually sifts down to Earth as either dry deposition or in rain drops. This deposition then coats crops and other plants, which are eaten by cows, chickens and hogs. Or, alternatively, it's rained into rivers and lakes and insinuates itself into the flesh of fish. As a breast-feeding mother, I take these molecules into my body and distill them in my breast tissue. This is done through a process through which fat globules from throughout my whole body are mobilized and carried into the breast lobes, where, under the direction of a pituitary hormone called prolactin, they are made into human milk. Then, under the direction of another pituitary hormone called oxytocin, this milk springs from the grape-like lobes and flows down long tubules into the nipple, which is a kind of sieve, and into the back of the throat of the breast-feeding infant. My daughter.

So, this, then, is the connection. This milk, my milk, contains dioxins from old vinyl siding, discarded window blinds, junked toys, and used I.V. bags. Plastic parts of buildings that were burned down accidentally are also housed in my breasts. These are indisputable facts. They are facts that we scientists are not arguing about. What we do spend a lot of time debating is what exactly are the health effects on the generation of children that my daughter belongs to. We don't know with certainty because these kids have not reached the age at which a lot of diseases possibly linked to dioxin exposure would manifest themselves. Unlike mice and rats, we have long generational times. We do know with certainty that childhood cancers are on the rise, and indeed they are rising faster than adult cancers. We don't have any official explanation for that yet.

Let me tell you something else I've learned about breast feeding. It's an ecstatic experience. The same hormone (oxytocin) that allows milk to flow from the back of the chest wall into the nipple also controls female orgasm. This so-called let-down reflex makes the breast feel very warm and full and fizzy, as if it were a shaken-up Coke bottle. That's not unpleasant. Moreover, the mouths of infants—their gums, tongues, and palates—are perfectly designed to receive this milk. A newborn's mouth and a woman's nipple are like partners in a tango. The most expensive breast pump—and I have a $500 one—can only extract about half of the volume that a newborn baby can because such machines cannot possibly imitate the intimate and exquisite tonguing, sucking, and gumming motion that infants use to extract milk from the nipple, which is not unpleasant either.

Through this ecstatic dance, the breast-fed infant receives not just calories, but antibodies. Indeed the immune system is developed through the process of breast feeding, which is why breast-fed infants have fewer bouts of infectious diseases than bottle-fed babies. In fact, the milk produced in the first few days after birth is almost all immunological in function. This early milk is not white at all but clear and sticky and is called colostrum. Then, from colostrum you move to what's called transitional milk, which is very fatty and looks like liquid butter. Presumably then, transitional milk is even more contaminated than mature milk, which comes in at about two weeks post-partum. Interestingly, breast milk is so completely digested that the feces of breast-fed babies doesn't even smell bad. It has the odor of warm yogurt and the color of French mustard. By contrast, the excretions of babies fed on formula are notoriously unpleasant.

What is the price for the many benefits of breast milk? We don't yet know. However, one recent Dutch study found that schoolchildren who were breast fed as babies had three times the level of PCBs in their blood as compared to children who had been exclusively formula fed. PCBs are probably carcinogens. Why should there be any price for breast feeding? It should be a zero-risk activity.

If there was ever a need to invoke the Precautionary Principle—the idea that we must protect human life from possible toxic danger well in advance of scientific proof about that danger—it is here, deep inside the chest walls of nursing mothers where capillaries carry fat globules into the milk-producing lobes of the mammary gland. Not only do we know little about the long-term health effects of dioxin and PCB exposure in newborns, we haven't even identified all the thousands of constituent elements in breast milk that these contaminants might act on. For example, in 1997 researchers described 130 different sugars unique to human milk. Called oligosaccharides, these sugars are not digested but function instead to protect the infant from infection by binding tightly to intestinal pathogens. Additionally, they appear to serve as a source of sialic acid, which is essential to brain development.

So, this is my conclusion. Breast feeding is a sacred act. It is a holy thing. To talk about breast feeding versus bottle feeding, to weigh the known risks of infectious diseases against the possible risks of childhood or adult cancers is an obscene argument. Those of us who are advocates for women and children and those of us who are parents of any kind need to become advocates for uncontaminated breast milk. A woman's body is the first environment. If there are toxic materials from PVC in the breasts of women, then it becomes our moral imperative to solve the problem. If alternatives to PVC exist, then it becomes morally imperative that we embrace the alternatives and make them a reality.

69

DOES SILENCIO = MUERTE? Notes on Translating the AIDS Epidemic

DR. RAFAEL CAMPO

Palomita chatters in one of my clinic exam rooms in Boston, her strongly accented voice filling the chilly institutional chrome-and-vinyl space with Puerto Rican warmth. She's off on another dramatic monologue, telling me about her new boyfriend.

"Edgar, he loves me, you know, he call me *mamacita.* He want me to be the mother of his children someday, OK? I ain't no slut. *Mira,* I don't need to use no condom with him."

Even the way she dresses is a form of urgent communication—the plunging neckline of her tropically patterned blouse, whose tails knotted above her waist also expose her flat stomach, the skin-tight denim jeans, the gold, four-inch hoop earrings, and the necklace with her name spelled out in cursive with tiny sparkling stones. Her black hair is pulled back tightly, except for a small squiggle greased flat against her forehead in the shape of an upside-down question mark.

"People think bad of him 'cause they say he dealing drugs. I tell them, 'No way, you shut your stupid mouths. He good to me and beside, he cleaner than you is.' Sure, he got his other girls now and then, but he pick them out *bien* carefully, you know what I mean. That his right as man of the house. No way he gonna give me *la SIDA.* We too smart for none of that shit. We trust each other. We communicate. We gonna buy us a house somewhere *bien bonita.* Someday we gonna make it."

Rafael Campo, "Does Silencio = Muerte? Notes on Translating the AIDS Epidemic" from *The Progressive* 63 (10). Reprinted with the permission of *The Progressive* magazine, 409 East Main Street, Madison, WI 53703.

She is seventeen years old, hasn't finished high school, and cannot read English. I have just diagnosed her with herpes, and I am trying to talk to her about AIDS and "safer sex." Her Edgar, who is also a patient of mine, tested HIV-positive last week. It's clear they have not discussed it.

Latinos are dying at an alarming rate from AIDS. And for all our glorious presence on the world's stage—in music, literature, art, from MacArthur grants to MTV to *Sports Illustrated*—this is one superlative no one can really boast about. Few Latinos dare even to mention the epidemic. The frenetic beat of salsa in our dance clubs seems to drown out the terrifying statistics, while the bright murals in our barrios cover up the ugly blood-red graffiti, and that "magical realism" of our fictions imagines a world where we can lose our accents and live in Vermont, where secret family recipes conjure up idealized heterosexual love in an ultimately just universe unblemished by plague.

Here, loud and clear, for once, are some of the more stark, sobering facts: In the U.S., Latinos accounted for one-fifth of all AIDS cases reported to the Centers for Disease Control last year, while making up only one-tenth of the U.S. population; AIDS has been the leading cause of death since 1991 for young Latino men in this country; in areas with especially high numbers of Latinos, such as Fort Lauderdale, Miami, Los Angeles, and New York, AIDS deaths among Latina women were four times the national average since 1995. While the infection rate among whites continues to decline, today, and every day, 100 people of color are newly diagnosed with HIV infection. Behold our isolated and desperate substance users, the most marginalized of the marginalized, our forsaken impoverished, and our irreplaceable young people.

I do not have to wonder at the reasons for the silence among Latinos about the burgeoning AIDS epidemic that is decimating us. Though I stare into its face every day in the clinic where I work, there are times when even I want to forget, to pretend it is not happening, to believe my people are invincible and can never be put down again. I want to believe Palomita is HIV-negative, that Edgar will stop shooting drugs and someday return to get on the right triple combination of anti-viral medications. I fervently hope that César, a twenty-year-old Colombian man who keeps missing his appointments, is taking his protease inhibitors so that his viral load remains undetectable. I do not really know who pays for his drugs, since he is uninsured, but my thoughts do not dwell on it. In the end, I want to go home and rest after a long day in the clinic, to make love to my partner of fourteen years and feel that I'll never have to confront another epidemic. I want to look into his dark, Puerto Rican eyes and never have to speak of AIDS again.

But I know better. I know we must speak out—about the ongoing disenfranchisement of Latinos despite our much-touted successes, about the vicious homophobia of a *machista.* Latino culture that especially fears and hates gay people whom it believes "deserve" AIDS, about the antipathy of the Catholic Church so many Latinos pray to for guidance they don't receive, about the unfulfilled dream of total and untainted assimilation for so many Mexicans, Dominicans, Cubans, and Puerto Ricans who came to America with nothing.

To break any of these silences is especially tempting, since together they allow me to blame most of the usual targets of my rage and frustration. Others are more difficult to penetrate, such as the persistent lack of access in Latino communities to lifesaving information about AIDS. Still others make almost no sense to me at all. Rosa, another patient of mine, tells me she knows she should not have sex without condoms, but continues to do so anyway because she is afraid her drug-dealing boyfriend would think she no longer loves him. Yet she hardly imagines that he might be using drugs, or wonders whether he has other sexual partners.

Our silence, in all its forms, is killing us. I wince at the familiar ring of this realization. I can't help but remember my patient Ernesto in his hospital bed with his partner Jesús sitting quietly at his side, a tiny statue of the Virgin of Guadalupe keeping its mute vigil, no other family or friends around. Ernesto died years ago of AIDS. It is not passé or trite or irrelevant to ask why we remain silent. It is absolutely imperative. We must understand the causes of our *silencio.*

Most of the Spanish-speaking patients who come to my clinic do not much resemble Ricky Martin or Daisy Fuentes or Antonio Sabato Jr. They are "the working poor," janitors or delivery boys or hotel laundry workers or high school dropouts or dishwashers—people with jobs that pay subsistence wages and provide no health benefits. Still, they consider themselves fortunate because so many have no jobs at all.

Many of them are illiterate, and many more speak no English. They have come to Boston mostly from Puerto Rico, but some are from Cuba, the Dominican Republic, Mexico, Colombia, Guatemala, El Salvador, and Nicaragua. Some sleep on park benches when the weather is warm enough and in shelters during the winter. Some live in crowded apartments. Some are undocumented immigrants. Some have lost their welfare benefits, some are trying to apply for temporary assistance, and almost none have enough to feed themselves and their families.

Older couples too often have lost children to drugs, street violence, and AIDS. Young people too often blame their parents and their teachers for their problems. Some know very little about AIDS and fault homosexuals, injection drug users, and prostitutes for poisoning the community. Some view *la SIDA* with resignation and see it as inevitable, part of the price some must pay for a chance at a better life.

But the vast majority of Latinos in the U.S. remain shortchanged, despite the glittering success of a few. For every Federico Peña, many more anonymous "illegals" are deported to Mexico each day, never given the chance to contribute to our society at all. For every Sammy Sosa, a makeshift boat full of Dominicans is lost at sea. And even more noxious than the large-scale efforts to dismantle affirmative action or to deny basic social services (including health care) to undocumented immigrants are the daily insults and obstacles that prevent Latinos from sharing fully in our nation's life. Lack of economic opportunities pushes Latinos toward criminal activities as a means to survive. Discrimination and rejection breed the kind of despair that drug use and unsafe sex only temporarily ameliorate. The despair and the apathy, heightened by what the very few who are successful have achieved, numb the soul.

It's a common litany, yet I can't help but see how this imposed demoralization is manifest in the behavior of so many of my patients. Why leave an abusive relationship, they say, when all that awaits is the cold streets? Why insist on a condom when it's so much easier not to and the reasons to go on living are not so clear anyway? It doesn't seem farfetched to me that this cumulative hopelessness is fueling the AIDS epidemic.

But these causes, the subject of so many lefty social work dissertations, do not get at the entire problem. We remain ourselves a culture in which men treat women as icons—or as powerless objects of our legendary sexual passions. Our wives must be as pure as we believe our own mothers to be, and yet we pursue our mistresses with the zeal of matadors about to make the kill. Brute force is excused as a necessary means by which Latino men must exert control over weak-willed women, and it is by no means secret that in the shadow of the AIDS epidemic lurks another senseless killer, the domestic violence that too often goes unreported.

Could Palomita and Rosa fear more then just losing the financial support of their boyfriends? For Yolanda, another patient of mine with HIV infection, it was the beatings from her husband that finally drove her onto the streets, where prostitution soon became her only means of making a living. Now she is dying.

Sexism's virulent *hermano* is homophobia. AIDS has long been considered a disease exclusively of homosexuals—especially in Spanish-speaking communities, where not only is HIV strongly associated with gayness, it is further stigmatized as having been imported from the decadent white world. Since we cannot speak calmly and rationally of homosexuality, we certainly cannot bring up AIDS, perhaps the only affliction that could be worse.

Latinos are allowed to be gay only outside the confines of their families and old neighborhoods. Indeed, many Latino men who have sex with men would never even consider themselves "gay" at all, a derogatory term that they would apply only to those whom they consider to be their "passive" partners. Even those who take pride in their homosexuality are not immune to this hatred. I have many gay Latino friends whose parents will not allow their partners to visit during holidays, friends who go to great lengths to (literally) "straighten out" their homes when family is coming to visit by creating fictitious separate bedrooms and removing anything suggestive of homosexuality (which can get difficult, when one gets down to the joint Andy Garcia fan club application, the Frida Kahlo shrine, or the autographed and framed Gigi Fernandez poster).

Hand in hand with both sexism and homophobia goes Catholicism. Latinos are overwhelmingly Catholic, and the Catholic hierarchy remains overwhelmingly not only anti-gay, but also opposed to the use of condoms as a means to prevent HIV transmission. (The only time I have ever heard AIDS mentioned in a Catholic church was at a wedding service, when it was invoked as a reminder of what punishments lay in store for the fornicators and homosexuals who scorned marriage.) While on the one hand preaching about the sanctity of life, our religious leaders have abetted the deaths of countless Latinos by refusing to endorse the use of condoms as a means to prevent AIDS transmission.

No one disagrees with the monotonous message that abstinence is the safest sex of all. Yet in today's ascendant moment, when young Latinos must party—we drink our Cuba libres followed by café con leche, dance the merengue provocatively with shiny crucifixes dangling around our necks, and later engage in sultry, unsafe sex, even if always (supposedly) with partners of the opposite sex—such teaching is utterly impractical.

Then there are the people like me, the Cuban doctors and Chicano lawyers, the Nuyorican politicians and the displaced Argentine activists—those who mean well but who have allowed the silence to engulf us, too. The thick warm blanket of our insularity and relative power comforts us. We are a small, tightly knit group; we work hard and hope to send our children to Harvard or Stanford or Yale, praying that they stay out of trouble. We increasingly vote Republican, elated that George W. Bush tosses out a few words in a halting Spanish, and fearing that a liberal government might take away too much of what we have struggled to make for ourselves—and might allow too many others in for a share of our pie. We would hardly acknowledge Palomita and Edgar if we passed them in the street, and we might even regret their very existence, the way they bring all of us down by their ignorance and poverty. Full of our quiet self-righteousness, gripping our briefcases just a bit more tightly, we might not even feel sorry for them if we knew they were being afflicted with AIDS.

Mario Cooper, a former deputy chief of staff for the Democratic National Committee, knows first-hand about a community's indifference to AIDS. Black, gay, and HIV-positive, he spearheaded an initiative sponsored by the Harvard AIDS Institute called Leading for Life. The summit brought together prominent members of the African American community to talk frankly about their own AIDS epidemic—just as uncontrolled, just as deadly, and until last year's summit, just as silent as the one ravaging Latinos.

"The key is to make people understand this is about all of us," Cooper says, as we brainstorm a list of possible invitees to another meeting, to be called *Unidos para la Vida.* Inspired by his past success in Boston, where the likes of Marian Wright Edelman, Henry Louis Gates Jr., and Dr. Alvin Poussaint eventually heeded his call to action, Cooper is now intent on tackling the same issue for Latinos.

"What came out of the Leading for Life meeting was incredible," he says. "Suddenly, everyone was paying attention, and things started happening for young African Americans. They started to learn more about AIDS."

He is beaming, and we add Oscar de la Renta, Cristina, and Edward James Olmos to the list. "We have the chance to do the same thing here."

But after a few weeks of working on the project with him and others at the Harvard AIDS Institute, it became clear to us that we might be facing even greater obstacles than those he encountered in the black community. We had hardly even gotten started when conflicts over terminology almost sank the entire effort. "Latino" competed with "Hispanic," while all of us felt that neither term fully articulated the rich diversity and numerous points of origin of those who undeniably formed some kind of a community. Some of us secretly questioned whether a shared vulnerability to AIDS was itself enough to try to unify us. Was a Puerto Rican injection drug user in Hartford, Connecticut, really facing the same issues as a Salvadoran undocumented immigrant selling sex in El Paso, Texas? Was loyalty to the Venezuelan community, or Nicaraguan community, imperiled by joining this larger group? At times, we saw evidence of the kind of pecking-order mentality (in which certain nationalities consider themselves superior to others) that has since the days of Bolívar interfered with efforts to unify Spain's colonies in the New World.

If these mostly suppressed internal divisions were not enough to surmount, we also battled the general lack of interest in AIDS—yesterday's news, no matter how loudly we shouted the latest statistics, no matter how emphatically we pointed out the lack of access for Latinos to the new treatments.

"Don't they have a cure for that now?" remarked one person I called, exemplifying precisely the sort of misinformation we were working to correct, her breathy laugh further revealing both the kind of distancing from—and absence of comfort with—the entire issue that surely reinforced her lack of knowledge.

Others were simply fatalistic. "You can't change the way these kids think and behave," said one person who declined the invitation to attend the summit, "so why bother?"

"Tell them to stop having sex," came one memorably blunt response, before the phone crashed down on the other end.

"I pray for them," said another pious woman. "I pray that they will renounce their wicked ways and find peace in Christ." She then regretted to inform me that she would be unable to attend the summit.

The special insight I thought I could bring to the effort, as a gay Latino poet doctor who writes both poems and prescriptions, seemed to be of less and less use, as more and more "no" answers, accompanied by their usually polite excuses, filtered back to us. Weeks later, when the situation grew bleakest, Cooper only urged us to redouble our efforts. "We're dealing with a situation that is almost unfathomable to most of these people," he said. "It's an epidemic no one wants to believe exists. Latinos are supposed to be the rising stars of the next millennium, not the carriers of a disease that could wipe out humanity." What was on one level a glaring public health crisis had to be understood more radically. "We have to ask ourselves why this message isn't getting out. We're kidding ourselves if we think we're the magic solution. In fact, we may be part of the problem."

The work of Walt Odets, the Berkeley psychologist who shook up the safer sex establishment, immediately came to mind. Odets observed young gay men at the height of the AIDS epidemic in San Francisco, noting a pervasive hopelessness in the face of a belief that infection with HIV was inevitable. Behind the apathy and denial, might not the same thing exist in this second-wave epidemic among inner-city Latinos? The stupidity of our early efforts at sloganeering, which tried to encapsulate a myriad of complex issues under a single bright banner, suddenly became utterly apparent to me. What faced us was not simply a matter of speaking out, of breaking a silence so many Latinos already living with HIV had already renounced. What we had to do was learn to speak their language, to incorporate in our every effort an entirely new mode of expression.

I knew right then that we had a lot more work to do.

Palomita's mood is decidedly less cheerful today. She is three-and-a-half-months pregnant, but that's not why she starts to cry. It's the end of January, and my office is just as cold as ever. A thin crust of ice is gradually forming on everything outside. Last week, while Palomita's HIV test was being run, a storm knocked out power to most of New England. My heart feels as empty and dark as one of the houses caught in the blackout now that I've read out her result.

"I don't believe you. You mean, I'm gonna die of AIDS?" A leaden moment passes before the inevitable next question. "And what about my baby?"

Looking at Palomita, I wonder again at how AIDS does not get prevented, how it seems to have a terrible life of its own. I want to answer her questions, explain to her that AZT lowers the risk of maternal fetal transmission, that the new triple combination anti-retroviral regimens, if she takes them exactly as prescribed, could buy her many years with her child. But I can't. Instead I keep thinking about her name, which means "little dove," and trying to imagine the innocence her parents must have seen in her tiny face when they named her, trying to feel that boundless joy at the earliest moment of a new life. I am looking at Palomita as she cries, framed by a window from which she cannot fly. I am imagining peace. In her beautiful brown face, mirror of a million souls, I try to envision us all in a world without AIDS.

PART XI
A World That Is Truly Human

We must create an environment, not only in the workplace but in our communities generally, in which harassment, abuse, and violence are no longer tolerated because men and women understand the damage such behavior does to all of us.

ROBERT L. ALLEN[1]

Significant numbers of the world's population are routinely subject to torture, starvation, terrorism, humiliation, mutilation, and even murder simply because they are female.

CHARLOTTE BUNCH[2]

In the introduction to this book, Gerda Lerner calls for " . . . a world free of dominance and hierarchy, a world that is truly human." A democratic society depends on equal access to the rights and benefits of the social order. It requires a system in which people born tied down by ropes of oppression are given the means to untie themselves and are offered equal opportunities once they are free. In a truly human world, the ropes would not exist. Our social, political, and economic systems do not provide such opportunities, so individuals, groups, and communities are left on their own to devise empowerment strategies.

As many authors in this book have said or implied, altering the gender system, entrenched as it is in many structural arrangements, requires change at many levels—in individuals, in relationships, in families, in communities, in all social institutions, in national alliances, through legal reform, and through global policy and action. Recall Elizabeth Janeway's conclusion, reported in the introduction to this book, that disempowered people can become empowered only after we question the truth of the ideas of those in power. Janeway argues that disbelief, the first stage of empowerment, needs to be followed by action, both individual and collective.

A current strategy used to address gender injustice is to call for the treatment of women's rights as human rights. This call harks back to an early women's movement definition of feminism: *feminism is the radical notion that women are human.* Human rights activist and scholar Charlotte Bunch, director of the Center for Women's Global Leadership at Rutgers University, argues that gender-related abuse "offers the greatest challenge to the field of human rights today."[3] She reports that women and girls are subjected to a wide range of abuse not perpetrated on men and boys, such as abortion of female fetuses, restricted nutrition, women's and girls' lack of control over their bodies (as reflected in high death rates from illegal abortions and female genital mutilation), and overt violence against them of the types described earlier in this book by Robert Jensen, Melanie Kaye/Kantrowitz, Jan Goodwin, and Helen

Zia. Bunch concludes, "Female subordination runs so deep that it is still viewed as inevitable or natural, rather than seen as a politically constructed reality maintained by patriarchal interests, ideology, and institutions."[4]

Bunch recommends four approaches to alleviating these injustices. Attention to *political and civil rights* would focus, for example, on the sexual abuse of female political prisoners and female refugees. Attention to *socio-economic rights* would address the right to food, shelter, health care, and employment. Attention to *legal rights* would protect women against sex discrimination. And finally, a *feminist transformation of human rights* designed to explicitly focus on violations in women's lives would address other ways in which women are oppressed such as battering, rape, forced marriage, lack of reproductive rights, compulsory heterosexuality, and genital mutiliation.[5] In her essay in this part, Bunch lays out a series of actions that would need to happen in order to move this agenda forward.

A new approach to peace—the "culture of peace" perspective—addresses gender in the context of violence. Analyzing the gendered nature of war and warriors, critics of world violence have dissected masculinity with the goal of changing how masculine identities and behaviors are developed and expressed, both at the microlevel in interpersonal relationships and at the international level as expressed in wars.[6] They have also examined women's roles and their potential for helping to create a more peaceful world.[7] Although many women have struggled to actively intervene in the interest of peace (see for example Svirsky, this part), political scientist Cynthia Enloe believes that we have a long way to go before women can make a serious impact on moving the world away from militarization and toward peace: "At the opening of the new century, militarization continues to rely on women located in different social, economic, ideological, and cultural locations remaining uninformed about, unconnected to, or even hostile toward one another. The experiences of fragmentation have provided an incentive for some current feminists to expend more intellectual and organizing energy in understanding those differences and reducing the hostilities they can foment."[8]

In the preceding readings, we have heard from many people working for change in specific areas. In this final section, we hear from several people working toward a more human world across various differences and at various levels, including organizational policies (National Organization for Men Against Sexism); community organizing (Robert Allen and Roberta Praeger); movement politics (Cherríe Moraga); national policy (Michelle Fine and Lois Weis); international peace activism (Gila Svirsky); and global human rights strategies (Charlotte Bunch).

Given the power of gender oppression and the other oppressions addressed in this book, there is no way to create a humane world unless many women and men are able to work within and across groups to fight for change that will benefit the largest number of people. Educators Rita Hardiman and Bailey Jackson have proposed a theory of stages of social identity development that helps me to think about this issue at both a personal and a collective level.[9] They argue that in order to struggle against oppression, people first need to have a critical analysis of oppressive aspects of the social order. Next, they need to gather with members of their own groups to solidify their indentities independent of the systems of oppression. For people with privilege—who Hardiman and Jackson call agents—this means identifying their privilege and understanding how it contributes to the oppression of others. For people without privilege—who Hardiman and Jackson call targets—this means understanding how oppression has affected them, both externally and internally as internalized subordination. Given that most people experience a mix of privilege and oppression, the development of one's identity is a complex process.

Ultimately, Hardiman and Jackson suggest that once people have gained enough confidence in their new identities, having embraced both the privileged and the oppressed aspects of themselves, they will be ready to work for social justice across the boundaries of identity and special interests. Instead of focusing only on the needs of their own group(s), they will be able to work in broad-based movements for social justice, understanding how others are oppressed, and building coalitions that have political clout. Oppression against anyone contributes to an unequal world. The writers in this book would ask us to use our sociological imaginations to understand the dimensions of oppression, work on our identities, become clear about our privileges, root out our internalized oppression, solidify our sense of pride and empowerment, and go about working creatively with other women and men to create peace in a world that is truly human.

NOTES

1. Robert L. Allen, "Stopping Sexual Harassment: A Challenge for Community Education," in Anita Fay Hill and Emma Coleman Jordan, eds., *Race, Gender, and Power in America: The Legacy of the Hill-Thomas Hearings* (New York: Oxford, 1995), p. 130.
2. Charlotte Bunch, "Women's Rights as Human Rights: Toward a Re-Vision of Human Rights," in Charlotte Bunch and Roxanna Carrillo, *Gender Violence: A Development and Human Rights Issue* (New Brunswick, NJ: Center for Women's Global Leadership, 1991), p. 3.
3. Bunch, "Women's Rights," p. 3.
4. Bunch, "Women's Rights," p. 7.
5. Bunch, "Women's Rights," pp. 10–13.
6. Ingeborg Breines, Robert Connell, & Ingrid Eide, eds., *Male Roles, Masculinities and Violence: A Culture of Peace Perspective* (Paris: UNESCO, 2000).
7. Ingeborg Breines, Dorota Gierycz and Betty Reardon, eds., *Towards a Women's Agenda for a Culture of Peace* (Paris: UNESCO Publishing, 1999).
8. Cynthia Enloe, *Maneuvers: The International Politics of Militarizing Women's Lives* (Berkeley, CA: University of California Press, 2000), p. 295.
9. Rita Hardiman and Bailey Jackson, "Conceptual Foundations for Social Justice Courses," in Maurianne Adams, Lee Ann Bell, and Pat Griffin, eds., *Teaching for Diversity and Social Justice: A Sourcebook* (New York: Routledge, 1997).

70

A WORLD WORTH LIVING IN

ROBERTA PRAEGER

As an impoverished woman I live with the exhaustion, the frustration, the deprivation of poverty. As a survivor of incest I struggle to overcome the emotional burden. One thing has led to another in my life as the causes of poverty, of incest, of so many issues have become increasingly clear. My need to personalize has given way to a realization of social injustice and a commitment to struggle for social change.

Living on Welfare

I live alone with my four-year-old child, Jamie. This state (Massachusetts) allocates $328 a month to a family of two living on Aid to Families with Dependent Children (AFDC). This sum places us, along with other social service recipients, at an income 40 percent below the federal poverty line. In today's economy, out of this sum of money, we are expected to pay for rent, utilities, clothing for two, child-care expenses, food not covered by food stamps, and any other expenses we may incur.

My food stamps have been cut to the point where they barely buy food for half the month. I have difficulty keeping up with the utility bills, and my furniture is falling apart. Furniture breaks, and there is no money to replace it. Things that others take for granted, such as sheets and towels, become irreplaceable luxuries.

Chaos exists around everything, even the most important issues, like keeping a roof over one's head. How are people expected to pay rent for their families on the shameful amount of income provided by the Welfare Department? The answer, in many cases, is reflected in the living conditions of welfare recipients. Some of us live in apartments that should be considered uninhabitable. We live with roaches, mice, sometimes rats, and floors about to cave in. I live in subsidized housing. It's that or the street. My rent without the subsidy is $400 a month, $72 more than my entire monthly income. It took over a year of red tape between the time of my first application to the time of final acceptance into the program, all the while watching the amount of my rent climb higher and higher. What becomes of the more than 80 percent of AFDC recipients who are not subsidized because there isn't enough of this housing available?

Emergencies are dealt with in the best way possible. One cold winter day, Jamie broke his ankle in the day-care center. It was the day my food stamps were due to arrive. With no food in the house, I had to take him, on public transportation, to the hospital emergency room and then walk to the supermarket with my shopping cart in a foot of snow. This was not an unusual event in my life. All AFDC mothers get caught up in situations like this, because we are alone, because we have few resources and little money.

Ronald Reagan's war on the poor has exacerbated an already intolerable situation. Human service programs have been slashed to the bone. Regulations governing the fuel assistance program have been changed in ways that now make many of the impoverished ineligible. Energy assistance no longer pays my utility bills. For some these changes have meant going without needed fuel, thereby forcing people to endure freezing temperatures.

The food stamp situation has gone from bad to worse. The amount of money allocated for the program has been drastically reduced. My situation reflects that of most welfare recipients. Last year, my food stamps were cut back from $108 to $76 a month, barely enough to buy food for two weeks. Reagan doesn't even allow us to work to supplement our meager income. His reforms resulted in a law, the Omnibus Budget Reconciliation Act, that, in one fell swoop, instituted a number of repressive work-related changes. Its main impact came when it considerably lowered the amount of money a recipient can earn before the termination of benefits. Under this new law even a low-paying, part-time job can make a person no longer eligible for assistance.

The complexity of our lives reaches beyond economic issues. Monday through Friday, I work as an undergraduate student at the University of Massachusetts. On weekends, when in two-parent families, one parent can sometimes shift the responsibility to the other, I provide the entertainment for my child. All the household chores are my responsibility, for I have no one to share them with. When Jamie is sick I spend nights awake with him. When I am sick, I have no one to help me. I can't do things others take for granted, such as spend an evening out at the movies, because I don't have enough money to pay both the admission fee and for child care. Even if I did, I would be too exhausted to get out the front door. Often I wind up caught in a circle of isolation.

What kind of recognition do I and other welfare mothers get for all this hard work? One popular image of welfare recipients pictures us as lazy, irresponsible women, sitting at home, having babies, and living off the government. Much of society treats us like lepers, degrading and humiliating us at every turn, treating us as if we were getting something for nothing. One day I walked into a small grocery store wearing a button that read "Stop

Reagan's War on the Poor." The proprietor of the store looked at my button and said to me, "You know, all those people on welfare are rich." Most welfare recipients would say anything rather than admit to being on welfare because of the image it creates. My brother-in-law had the audacity to say to me in conversation one day, "People are poor because they're lazy. They don't want to work."

And the Welfare Department shares this image of the recipient with the general public. From the first moment of contact with the department, the client is treated with rudeness, impatience, mistrust, and scorn. She is intimidated by constant redeterminations, reviews, and threats of being cut off. Her life is controlled by a system wracked with ineptness and callous indifference. Two years ago, unable to pay my electric bill, I applied for emergency assistance. It took the Welfare Department so long to pay the bill that the electric company turned the power off. We lived for two days without electricity before my constant badgering of the Welfare Department and the utility company produced results.

The department gives out information that is misleading and/or incomplete. The recipient is made to feel stupid, guilty, and worthless, a "problem" rather than a person. When I first applied I had to answer all sorts of questions about my personal life time and again. Many of my replies were met with disbelief. I sat there for hours at a time, nine months pregnant, waiting to be interviewed. And that was just the beginning of hours and hours of waiting, of filling in forms for the programs that keep us and our children alive.

The Personal Is Political

For most women in this situation, suffering is nothing new. Poverty is seldom an isolated issue. It's part of a whole picture. Other issues complicate our lives. For myself, as for many of us, suffering is complicated by memories, the results of trauma brought forward from childhood. Under frilly pink dresses and little blue sailor suits lay horror stories shared by many. The memories I bring with me from my childhood are not very pretty.

I was born in a Boston neighborhood in 1945. My father was a linoleum installer, my mother a homemaker. I want to say that my childhood was colored by the fact that I was an abused child. It's still difficult for me to talk about some things to this day.

My mother didn't give me a life of my own. When I was an infant she force-fed me. At age nine, she was still spoon-feeding me. Much of the time she didn't let me out of her sight. She must have seen school as a threat to her control, for she kept me home half the time. In me she saw not a separate person but an extension of herself. She felt free to do as she wished with my body. Her attempts to control my elimination process have had a lasting impact on my sexuality. The methods she used have been documented for their use in cases of mother-daughter incest. She had an obsessive-compulsive desire to control what went into me, to control elimination, to control everything about me. I had no control over anything. I couldn't get out from under what was happening to me psychologically. Powerlessness, frustration, and emotional insecurity breed a chain of abuse as men abuse women and children and women abuse children.

In the face of all the adverse, perverted attention received from my mother, I turned to my father for love and affection. We became close. In time, though, it became clear he knew as little about child rearing as my mother. His own deprived childhood had taught him only bitterness.

Throughout the years I knew him, he had gambled literally thousands of dollars away at the horse track. He left me alone outside the track gate at age five or six when the sign read "No children allowed." When I was twelve, he set fire to our house. He had run out of money for gambling purposes, and the house was insured against fire. When the insurance money arrived, my mother somehow managed to intercept it and bought new furniture. When my father found out what she had done, he went on a rampage. I had a knickknack shelf, charred from the fire. He threw it across the room, splinters of glass flying everywhere, and then he hit my mother. This was not an uncommon scene in my childhood.

By the time I reached eleven, my father was beginning to see me in a different light. At this point, the closeness that had developed between him and me still existed. And he proceeded to take advantage of it.

My mother belonged to a poker club, and once a week she would leave the house to go to these sessions. On these occasions my father would come over to me and remove both my clothes and his. He would then use my body to masturbate until he reached orgasm. He attempted to justify these actions by saying, "A man has to have sex and your mother won't." This occurred a number of times when I was between the ages of eleven and thirteen. I cried the last time he did this and he stopped molesting me sexually. In incestuous situations there doesn't have to be any threat; very often there isn't, because parents are in a position of trust, because parents are in a position of power, and because the child needs love. Children are in a developmental stage where they have no choice.

I went to public school and did very well. When I was sixteen, the school authorities told me that no matter how well I did, no matter how high my grades were, they could not keep me in school if I appeared only half the time. So I dropped out. I just spent the whole time sitting in front of the television until my mother died.

I didn't understand the extent of my mother's sickness in her treatment of me. Fear that if my mother knew what my father was doing she would kill him seemed realistic to me at the time. And so, I kept silent. I looked at my parents, as all children do, as authority figures. Longing for a way out of the situation, I felt trapped. In the face of all this I felt overwhelmed, afraid, and isolated. I retreated from reality into a world of fantasy. For only through my imagination could I find any peace of mind or semblance of happiness. The abuse I had taken all these years began to manifest itself in psychosomatic symptoms. Periodically, I started suffering intense abdominal pain. Once I fainted and fell on the bathroom floor. There were three visits to the hospital emergency room. My doctor had misdiagnosed the symptoms as appendicitis.

When I was seventeen, my father, after a major argument with my mother, moved out. Without money to pay the rent, with no job training or other resources, we rented out a room. Ann, the young woman renting the room, was appalled at the situation she discovered. She began to teach me some basic skills such as how to wash my own clothes. For the first time in my life I related positively to someone. My father moved back two months later. For two years this is how the situation remained, my mother, father, Ann, and I all living together.

In 1965 my mother was diagnosed as having lung cancer. Three months later she was dead. I felt nothing, no sorrow, no anger, no emotion. I had long ago learned how to bury my emotions deep down inside of me. I packed my belongings and moved out with Ann, in the midst of my father's ranting and raving.

Living in an apartment with Ann made things seem to improve on the surface. My life was quieter. I held a steady job for the first time. There was a little money to spend. I could come and go as I pleased. It felt good, and I guess, at that point I thought my life had really changed. It took me a long time to realize what an adult who has had this kind of childhood must still go through. I had nightmares constantly. There were times when I went into deep depressions. I didn't know what was going on, what was happening to me, or why.

After holding my first job for three years, I went through a series of jobs in different fields: sales, hairdressing, and, after a period of training, nursing. It seemed I was not functioning well in any area. I fell apart in any situation where demands were made of me. I had no tolerance for hierarchy. I discovered that I performed best when I was acting as charge nurse. Unfortunately, in my role as a Licensed Practical Nurse, I usually wound up low person on the totem pole, generally having to answer to someone else. In time, it became clear to me, that control was a major factor in a variety of situations that I encountered.

My self-confidence and self-esteem were abysmally low. Every time something went wrong my first thought was, "There must be something wrong with me." I didn't know then, what I know now. Children never blame their parents for the wrong that is done. They blame themselves. This feeling carries on into adulthood until it is difficult not to blame oneself for everything that does not go right.

I was depressed, suicidal, frightened out of my wits, and completely overwhelmed by life. After a series of failed relationships and a broken marriage, I wound up alone, with a small child, living on welfare. The emotional burden I carried became complicated by the misery and exhaustion of poverty.

Why have I survived? Why am I not dead? Because I'm a survivor. Because I have Jamie and I love him more than words can say. In him I see the future, not the past.

A Major Change

I survived because in the midst of all this something happened, something that was to turn out to be the major guiding force in my life. In 1972 the owner of my building sent out notices threatening eviction if the tenants did not pay a huge rent increase. Everyone in the building was aghast at the prospect and so formed a tenant union to discuss alternatives. Through my activities with the union, I learned of an organization that did community work throughout the city. Cambridge Tenants Organizing Committee (CTOC) was a multifaceted organization involved in work around issues such as tenants' rights, welfare advocacy, antiracist work, and education concerning sexism in society. I began working with a group of people unlike any that I had been exposed to in the past. They treated me as a person capable of assuming responsibility and doing any job well. My work with CTOC included organizing tenant unions throughout the city, counseling unemployed workers, and attending countless demonstrations, marches, picketings, and hearings. As a group we organized and/or supported eviction blocking, we helped defend people against physical racist attacks, and we demonstrated at the state house for continuation of rent control. I wasn't paid for my work. What I earned was far more important than money. I learned respect for myself as a woman. I learned the joys and pitfalls of working collectively and began assimilating more information than I had at any other time of my life.

And I flourished. I went to meeting after meeting until they consumed almost all of my nonwork time. Over the years I joined other groups. One of my major commitments was to a group that presented political films. My politics became the center of my life.

Through counseling and therapy groups with therapists who shared my political perspective, the guilt I had shouldered all these years began to lessen. Within a period of three years, through groups and conventions, I listened to and/or spoke with more than three hundred other survivors of incest. I heard stories that would make your hair stand on end. New learning led to making connections. Although the true extent of incest is not known, owing to the fact that sexual abuse within families usually goes unreported, various statistics estimate that 100,000 to 250,000 children are sexually molested each year in the United States. Other studies show that one out of every three to four women in this country is a victim of sexual abuse as a child. Incest Resources, my primary resource for group counseling, believes these statistics heavily underestimate the extent of actual abuse. So do I. Although the guilt for the abuse lies with the abuser, the context of the problem reaches far beyond, beyond me or my parents, into society itself as power and inequality surround us.

Connections with other people have become part and parcel of my life as my life situation has led me into work surrounding the issue of poverty. Although I had known for years of the existence of the Coalition for Basic Human Needs (CBHN)—a progressive group composed almost totally of welfare recipients—my political work, reflecting my life situation, had led me in other directions. Now I found myself alone with a toddler, living on AFDC. When Jamie was two, I returned to school to acquire additional skills. My academic work led me into issues concerning poverty as I became involved in months of activity, along with students and faculty and a variety of progressive women's groups, constructing a conference on the issue of women and poverty. Members of CBHN were involved in work on the conference, and we connected.

Social change through welfare-rights struggles became a major focus in my life as I began working with CBHN. Collectively, we sponsored legislative bills that would improve our lives financially while, at the same time, we taught others how we actually live. Public education became intertwined with legislative work as I spoke at hearings on the reality of living on AFDC. Political support became intertwined with public education as I spoke on the work of CBHN to progressive groups and their constituencies, indicting this country's political system for the impoverishment of its people.

CBHN is composed of chapters representing various cities and towns across Massachusetts. Grass-roots organizing of welfare recipients takes place within local chapters, while the organization as a whole works on statewide issues. We mail out newsletters, hold press conferences, and initiate campaigns. We are currently involved in our most ambitious effort. Whereas in the past our work has been directed toward winning small goals such as a clothing allowance or a small increase in benefits, this time we have set about to bring welfare benefits up to the poverty level, a massive effort involving all of our past strategies and more. We have filed a bill with the state legislature. Public education has become concentrated in the campaign as we plan actions involving the work of welfare-rights groups and individuals throughout the state.

The courage we share as impoverished women has been mirrored throughout this effort. At a press conference to announce the campaign a number of us gave truth to the statement that we and our children go without the basic necessities of life. One woman spoke of sending her child to school without lunch because there was no food in the house. Others had no money for winter jackets or shoes for their children. Sharing the reality of living at 40 percent below the poverty level brings mutual support as well as frustration and anger. In mid-April hundreds of welfare recipients—women carrying infants, the disabled, and the homeless—came from all over Massachusetts to rally in front of the state house along with our supporters and testify to the legislature in behalf of our "Up to the Poverty Level" bill. Courage and determination rang out in statements such as this:

> Take the cost of implementing this program and weigh it, if it must be weighed at all; then weigh it against the anguish suffered by the six-month-old twins who starved to death in a Springfield housing project.
>
> The day that the state legislature has to scrape the gilt off the dome of the state house and sell it for revenue is the day that this state can answer to us that there is not the means to do this.

The complexity of the situation comes home to me again and again as I sit in the CBHN office answering the telephone and doing welfare advocacy work. I've spoken with women on AFDC who have been battered to within an inch of their lives, some who are, like myself, survivors of child abuse, and others who are reeling from the effects of racism as well as poverty.

In this society so many of us internalize oppression. We internalize the guilt that belongs to the system that creates the conditions people live in. When we realize this and turn our anger outward in an effort to change society, then we begin to create a world worth living in.

The work isn't easy. Many of us become overwhelmed as well as overextended. It takes courage and fortitude to survive. For we live in a society laden with myths and an inequality that leads to human suffering. In order to alleviate the suffering and provide the equality each and every one of us deserves, we must effect social change. If we are to effect social change, then we must recognize social injustice and destroy the myths it creates. Little did I realize, years ago, when I first began this work how far it reached beyond my own survival. For those of us involved in creating a new society are doing the most important work that exists.

71

LA GÜERA

CHERRÍE MORAGA

It requires something more than personal experience to gain a philosophy or point of view from any specific event. It is the quality of our response to the event and our capacity to enter into the lives of others that help us to make their lives and experiences our own.

EMMA GOLDMAN[1]

I am the very well-educated daughter of a woman who, by the standards of this country, would be considered largely illiterate. My mother was born in Santa Paula, Southern California, at a time when much of the central valley there was still farm land. Nearly thirty-five years later, in 1948, she was the only daughter of six to marry an anglo, my father.

I remember all of my mother's stories, probably much better than she realizes. She is a fine story-teller, recalling every event of her life with the vividness of the present, noting each detail right down to the cut and color of her dress. I remember stories of her being pulled out of school at the ages of five, seven, nine, and eleven to work in the fields, along with her brothers and sisters; stories of her father drinking away whatever small profit she was able to make for the family; of her going the long way home to avoid meeting him on the street, staggering toward the same destination. I remember stories of my mother lying about her age in order to get a job as a hat-check girl at Agua Caliente Racetrack in Tijuana. At fourteen, she was the main support of the family. I can still see her walking home alone at 3 A.M., only to turn all of her salary and tips over to her mother, who was pregnant again.

The stories continue through the war years and on: walnut-cracking factories, the Voit Rubber factory, and then the computer boom. I remember my mother doing piecework for the electronics plant in our neighborhood. In the late evening, she would sit in front of the T.V. set, wrapping copper wires into the backs of circuit boards, talking about "keeping up with the younger girls." By that time, she was already in her mid-fifties.

Meanwhile, I was college-prep in school. After classes, I would go with my mother to fill out job applications for her, or write checks for her at the supermarket. We would have the scenario all worked out ahead of time. My mother

---

would sign the check before we'd get to the store. Then, as we'd approach the checkstand, she would say—within earshot of the cashier—"oh honey, you go 'head and make out the check," as if she couldn't be bothered with such an insignificant detail. No one asked any questions.

I was educated, and wore it with a keen sense of pride and satisfaction, my head propped up with the knowledge, from my mother, that my life would be easier than hers. I was educated; but more than this, I was "la güera": fair-skinned. Born with the features of my Chicana mother, but the skin of my anglo father, I had it made.

No one ever quite told me this (that light was right), but I knew that being light was something valued in my family (who were all Chicano, with the exception of my father). In fact, everything about my upbringing (at least what occurred on a conscious level) attempted to bleach me of what color I did have. Although my mother was fluent in it, I was never taught much Spanish at home. I picked up what I did learn from school and from overheard snatches of conversation among my relatives and mother. She often called other lower-income Mexicans "braceros," or "wet-backs," referring to herself and her family as "a different class of people." And yet, the real story was that my family, too, had been poor (some still are) and farmworkers. My mother can remember this in her blood as if it were yesterday. But this is something she would like to forget (and rightfully), for to her, on a basic economic level, being Chicana meant being "less." It was through my mother's desire to protect her children from poverty and illiteracy that we became "anglocized"; the more effectively we could pass in the white world, the better guaranteed our future.

From all of this, I experience, daily, a huge disparity between what I was born into and what I was to grow up to become. Because (as Goldman suggests) these stories my mother told me crept under my "güera" skin. I had no choice but to enter into the life of my mother. *I had no choice.* I took her life into my heart, but managed to keep a lid on it as long as I feigned being the happy, upwardly mobile heterosexual.

When I finally lifted the lid to my lesbianism, a profound connection with my mother reawakened in me. It wasn't until I acknowledged and confronted my own lesbianism in the flesh, that my heartfelt identification with and empathy for my mother's oppression—due to being poor, uneducated, and Chicana—was realized. My lesbianism is the avenue through which I have learned the most about silence and oppression, and it continues to be the most tactile reminder to me that we are not free human beings.

You see, one follows the other. I had known for years that I was a lesbian, had felt it in my bones, had ached with the knowledge, gone crazed with the knowledge, wallowed in the silence of it. Silence *is* like starvation. Don't be fooled. It's nothing short of that, and felt most sharply when one has had a full belly most of her life. When we are not physically starving, we have the luxury to realize psychic and emotional starvation. It is from this starvation that other starvations can be recognized—if one is willing to take the risk of making the connection—if one is willing to be responsible to the result of the connection. For me, the connection is an inevitable one.

What I am saying is that the joys of looking like a white girl ain't so great since I realized I could be beaten on the street for being a dyke. If my sister's being beaten because she's Black, it's pretty much the same principle. We're both getting beaten any way you look at it. The connection is blatant; and in the case of my own family, the difference in the privileges attached to looking white instead of brown are merely a generation apart.

In this country, lesbianism is a poverty—as is being brown, as is being a woman, as is being just plain poor. The danger lies in ranking the oppressions. *The danger lies in failing to acknowledge the specificity of the oppression.* The danger lies in attempting to deal with oppression purely from a theoretical base. Without an emotional, heartfelt grappling with the source of our own oppression, without naming the enemy within ourselves and outside of us, no authentic, non-hierarchical connection among oppressed groups can take place.

When the going gets rough, will we abandon our so-called comrades in a flurry of racist/heterosexist/what-have-you panic? To whose camp, then, should the lesbian of color retreat? Her very presence violates the ranking and abstraction of oppression. Do we merely live hand to mouth? Do we merely struggle with the "ism" that's sitting on top of our own heads?

The answer is: yes, I think first we do; and we must do so thoroughly and deeply. But to fail to move out from there will only isolate us in our own oppression—will only insulate, rather than radicalize us.

To illustrate: a gay male friend of mine once confided to me that he continued to feel that, on some level, I didn't trust him because he was male; that he felt, really, if it ever came down to a "battle of the sexes," I might kill him. I admitted that I might very well. He wanted to understand the source of my distrust. I responded, "You're not a woman. Be a woman for a day. Imagine being a woman." He confessed that the thought terrified him because, to him, being a woman meant being raped by men. He *had* felt raped by men; he wanted to forget what that meant. What grew from that discussion was the realization that in order for him to create an authentic alliance with me, he must deal with the primary source of his own sense of oppression. He must, first, emotionally come to terms with what it feels like to be a victim. If he—or anyone—were to truly do this, it would be impossible to discount the oppression of others, except by again forgetting how we have been hurt.

And yet, oppressed groups are forgetting all the time. There are instances of this in the rising Black middle class, and certainly an obvious trend of such "unconsciousness" among white gay men. Because to remember may mean giving up whatever privileges we have managed to squeeze out of this society by virtue of our gender, race, class, or sexuality.

Within the women's movement, the connections among women of different backgrounds and sexual orientations have been fragile, at best. I think this phenomenon is indicative of our failure to seriously address ourselves to some very frightening questions: How have I internalized my own oppression? How have I oppressed? Instead, we have let rhetoric do the job of poetry. Even the word "oppression" has lost its power. We need a new language, better words that can more closely describe women's fear of and resistance to one another; words that will not always come out sounding like dogma.

What prompted me in the first place to work on an anthology by radical women of color was a deep sense that I had a valuable insight to contribute, by virtue of my birthright and background. And yet, I don't really understand first-hand what it feels like being shitted on for being brown. I understand much more about the joys of it—being Chicana and having family are synonymous for me. What I know about loving, singing, crying, telling stories, speaking with my heart and hands, even having a sense of my own soul comes from the love of my mother, aunts, cousins. . . .

But at the age of twenty-seven, it is frightening to acknowledge that I have internalized a racism and classism, where the object of oppression is not only someone outside of my skin, but the someone inside my skin. In fact, to a large degree, the real battle with such oppression, for all of us, begins under the skin. I have had to confront the fact that much of what I value about being Chicana, about my family, has been subverted by anglo culture and my own cooperation with it. This realization did not occur to me overnight. For example, it wasn't until long after my graduation from the private college I'd attended in Los Angeles, that I realized the major reason for my total alienation from and fear of my classmates was rooted in class and culture. CLICK.

Three years after graduation, in an apple-orchard in Sonoma, a friend of mine (who comes from an Italian Irish working-class family) says to me, "Cherríe, no wonder you felt like such a nut in school. Most of the people there were white and rich." It was true. All along I had felt the difference, but not until I had put the words "class" and "color" to the experience, did my feelings make any sense. For years, I had berated myself for not being as "free" as my classmates. I completely bought that they simply had more guts than I did—to rebel against their parents and run around the country hitchhiking, reading books and studying "art." They had enough privilege to be atheists, for chrissake. There was no one around filling in the disparity for me between their parents, who were Hollywood filmmakers, and my parents, who wouldn't know the name of a filmmaker if their lives depended on it (and precisely because their lives didn't depend on it, they couldn't be bothered). But I knew nothing about "privilege" then. White was right. Period. I could pass. If I got educated enough, there would never be any telling.

Three years after that, another CLICK. In a letter to Barbara Smith, I wrote:

> I went to a concert where Ntosake Shange was reading. There, everything exploded for me. She was speaking a language that I knew—in the deepest parts of me—existed, and that I had ignored

> in my own feminist studies and even in my own writing. What Ntosake caught in me is the realization that in my development as a poet, I have, in many ways, denied the voice of my brown mother—the brown in me. I have acclimated to the sound of a white language which, as my father represents it, does not speak to the emotions in my poems—emotions which stem from the love of my mother.
>
> The reading was agitating. Made me uncomfortable. Threw me into a week-long terror of how deeply I was affected. I felt that I had to start all over again. That I turned only to the perceptions of white middle-class women to speak for me and all women. I am shocked by my own ignorance.

Sitting in that auditorium chair was the first time I had realized to the core of me that for years I had disowned the language I knew best—ignored the words and rhythms that were the closest to me. The sounds of my mother and aunts gossiping—half in English, half in Spanish—while drinking cerveza in the kitchen. And the hands—I had cut off the hands in my poems. But not in conversation; still the hands could not be kept down. Still they insisted on moving.

The reading had forced me to remember that I knew things from my roots. But to remember puts me up against what I don't know. Shange's reading agitated me because she spoke with power about a world that is both alien and common to me: "the capacity to enter into the lives of others." But you can't just take the goods and run. I knew that then, sitting in the Oakland auditorium (as I know in my poetry), that the only thing worth writing about is what seems to be unknown and, therefore, fearful.

The "unknown" is often depicted in racist literature as the "darkness" within a person. Similarly, sexist writers will refer to fear in the form of the vagina, calling it the "orifice of death." In contrast, it is a pleasure to read works such as Maxine Hong Kingston's *Woman Warrior,* where fear and alienation are described as "the white ghosts." And yet, the bulk of literature in this country reinforces the myth that what is dark and female is evil. Consequently, each of us—whether dark, female, or both—has in some way *internalized* this oppressive imagery. What the oppressor often succeeds in doing is simply *externalizing* his fears, projecting them into the bodies of women, Asians, gays, disabled folks, whoever seems most "other."

> call me
> roach and presumptuous
> nightmare on your white pillow
> your itch to destroy
> the indestructible
> part of yourself
>
> —AUDRE LORDE[2]

But it is not really difference the oppressor fears so much as similarity. He fears he will discover in himself the same aches, the same longings as those of the people he has shitted on. He fears the immobilization threatened by his own incipient guilt. He fears he will have to change his life once he has seen himself in the bodies of the people he has called different. He fears the hatred, anger, and vengeance of those he has hurt.

This is the oppressor's nightmare, but it is not exclusive to him. We women have a similar nightmare, for each of us in some way has been both oppressed and the oppressor. We are afraid to look at how we have failed each other. We are afraid to see how we have taken the values of our oppressor into our hearts and turned them against ourselves and one another. We are afraid to admit how deeply "the man's" words have been ingrained in us.

To assess the damage is a dangerous act. I think of how, even as a feminist lesbian, I have so wanted to ignore my own homophobia, my own hatred of myself for being queer. I have not wanted to admit that my deepest personal sense of myself has not quite "caught up" with my "woman-identified" politics. I have been afraid to criticize lesbian writers who choose to "skip over" these issues in the name of feminism. In 1979, we talk of "old gay" and "butch and femme" roles as if they were ancient history. We toss them aside as merely patriarchal notions. And yet, the truth of the matter is that I have sometimes taken society's fear and hatred of lesbians to bed with me. I have sometimes hated my lover for loving me. I have sometimes felt "not woman enough" for her. I have sometimes felt "not man enough." For a lesbian trying to survive in a heterosexist society, there is no easy way around these emotions. Similarly, in a white-dominated world, there is little getting around racism and our own internalization of it. It's always there, embodied in some one we least expect to rub up against.

When we do rub up against this person, *there* then is the challenge. *There* then is the opportunity to look at the nightmare within us. But we usually shrink from such a challenge.

Time and time again, I have observed that the usual response among white women's groups when the "racism issue" comes up is to deny the difference. I have heard comments like, "Well, we're open to *all* women; why don't they (women of color) come? You can only do so much. . . ." But there is seldom any analysis of how the very nature and structure of the group itself may be founded on racist or classist assumptions. More importantly, so often the women seem to feel no loss, no lack, no absence when women of color are not involved; therefore, there is little desire to change the situation. This has hurt me deeply. I have come to believe that the only reason women of a privileged class will dare to look at *how* it is that *they* oppress, is when they've come to know the meaning of their own oppression. And understand that the oppression of others hurts them personally.

The other side of the story is that women of color and working-class women often shrink from challenging white middle-class women. It is much easier to rank oppressions and set up a hierarchy, rather than take responsibility for changing our own lives. We have failed to demand that white women, particularly those who claim to be speaking for all women, be accountable for their racism.

The dialogue has simply not gone deep enough.

I have many times questioned my right to even work on an anthology which is to be written "exclusively by Third World women." I have had to look critically at my claim to color, at a time when, among white feminist ranks, it is a "politically correct" (and sometimes peripherally advantageous) assertion to make. I must acknowledge the fact that, physically, I have had a *choice* about making that claim, in contrast to women who have not had such a choice, and have been abused for their color. I must reckon with the fact that for most of my life, by virtue of the very fact that I am white-looking, I identified with and aspired toward white values, and that I rode the wave of that Southern Californian privilege as far as conscience would let me.

Well, now I feel both bleached and beached. I feel angry about this—the years when I refused to recognize privilege, both when it worked against me, and when I worked it, ignorantly, at the expense of others. These are not settled issues. That is why this work feels so risky to me. It continues to be discovery. It has brought me into contact with women who invariably know a hell of a lot more than I do about racism, as experienced in the flesh, as revealed in the flesh of their writing.

I think: what is my responsibility to my roots—both white and brown, Spanish-speaking and English? I am a woman with a foot in both worlds; and I refuse the split. I feel the necessity for dialogue. Sometimes I feel it urgently.

But one voice is not enough, nor two, although this is where dialogue begins. It is essential that radical feminists confront their fear of and resistance to each other, because without this, there *will* be no bread on the table. Simply, we will not survive. If we could make this connection in our heart of hearts, that if we are serious about a revolution—better—if we seriously believe there should be joy in our lives (real joy, not just "good times"), then we need one another. We women need each other. Because my/your solitary, self-asserting "go-for-the-throat-of-fear" power is not enough. The real power, as you and I well know, is collective. I can't afford to be afraid of you, nor you of me. If it takes head-on collisions, let's do it: this polite timidity is killing us.

As Lorde suggests in the passage I cited earlier, it is in looking to the nightmare that the dream is found. There, the survivor emerges to insist on a future, a vision, yes, born out of what is dark and female. The feminist movement must be a movement of such survivors, a movement with a future.

September, 1979

NOTES

1. Alix Kates Shulman, "Was My Life Worth Living?" *Red Emma Speaks.* (New York: Random House, 1972), p. 388.
2. From "The Brown Menace or Poem to the Survival of Roaches", *The New York Head Shop and Museum* (Detroit: Broadside, 1974), p. 48.

72

STOPPING SEXUAL HARASSMENT
A Challenge for Community Education

ROBERT L. ALLEN

There can be little doubt that an important outcome of the 1991 Senate Judiciary Committee hearings has been growing public recognition of sexual harassment as a major social problem. Virtually the entire nation has engaged in the public discourse around this issue, and this engagement is to be welcomed.

Like many men in the aftermath of Anita Hill's testimony, I found myself hearing harrowing reports of sexual harassment from women relatives and friends who had previously felt constrained to remain silent. They told me of awful things that had been said or done to them, on the job or in the streets, sometimes recently and sometimes years ago. They spoke of their anger and humiliation, of their shame and feelings of self-blame, of their fear of the consequences of speaking out or rebuking their harassers. They experienced sexual harassment—the imposition of unwanted sexual attention—as a violation of their human dignity.

I listened and shared their outrage—but I also found myself recalling things I had said or done to women in the recent or distant past, and the recollections were sometimes distinctly discomforting. I think an important value of these exchanges was the opportunity for men to learn from the personal testimony of women they love and respect how widespread sexual harassment is. At the same time, the self-reflection and discussions among men that were sometimes provoked by the women's stories offered an opportunity for men to recognize that harassing behavior is not simply an aberration, nor is it exclusively the province of macho males; on the contrary, harassing behavior is something that many of us men have engaged in at some point, if not on the job, then on the streets or on campus or even in our homes. We knew what we were doing, because we knew the women involved were made to feel uncomfortable or humiliated by our words or actions.

Why did we do it? Why do men harass women? Why, until recently, was such behavior generally acceptable in our culture—that is, acceptable to men? Aside from punishment, what can be done to stop harassing behavior?

In this essay I want to raise two points for consideration as part of the discourse on sexual harassment.

First, sexual harassment should not be dismissed as aberrant behavior, as the macho mentality gone wild, or as the result of male biology or uncontrollable sexual desire. Sexual harassment, like child abuse and domestic violence, is an outgrowth of socialization into male and female gender roles in a sexist society. It is learned behavior.

Second, if harassment, abuse, and violence are forms of learned behavior, they can also be unlearned. I therefore argue that in addition to legal or punitive approaches to sexual harassment, it is imperative to adopt a preventive approach through community education. We must create an environment, not only in the workplace but in our communities generally, in which harassment, abuse, and violence are no longer tolerated because men and women understand the damage such behavior does to all of us. That means adopting a social change perspective critical of the values of the dominant culture, a culture that is premised on inequality.

Gender roles are not foreordained by our biology or our genes. We learn gender roles as part of our socialization into the culture. When a child is born, the first question inevitably asked is "Boy or girl?" Our response to the child is then mediated by our knowledge of its genitals, and it is *our* actions that tell the child its gender identity and the behavior appropriate to that identity.

In California I work with an organization called the Oakland Men's Project (OMP). Formed in 1979, OMP is a nonprofit multiracial organization of men and women devoted to community education around issues of male violence, sexism, racism, and homophobia. Over the years we have worked with thousands of boys and men (and girls and women) in high schools, church groups, colleges, prisons, community groups, and rehabilitation programs. We conduct workshops that involve interactive role playing and discussions that allow men and women to examine gender roles and the social training we get in this culture.

In our workshops we ask young people what they think it means to be a man or a woman. It is remarkable how consistently they express the same set of expectations about appropriate male and female behavior. Men are expected to be in control, tough, aggressive, independent, competitive, and emotionally unexpressive (with the exception of anger and sexual desire, which are allowable emotions for men). Women, on the other hand, are expected to be polite, dependent, emotional, and sexy, to take care of others, and not to be too smart or pushy. In recent years we have noticed that sometimes girls will challenge these role expectations and occasionally even a boy will object, but for the most part they remain widely accepted. Paul Kivel, who has summed up the experience of the Oakland Men's Project in his *Men's Work: How to Stop the Violence That Tears Our Lives Apart,* refers to these as "core expectations" that we all have, especially men, regarding appropriate male and female behavior.

How do young men learn these expectations? At OMP, to illustrate the socialization process, we use what we call role plays that dramatize common situations most boys and men have experienced. One of these involves an interaction between a father and his ten-year-old son, both played by facilitators. The son is sitting at home watching television when the father comes in from work, orders the boy to turn off the TV, and berates him for the messiness of the room. When the boy tries to explain that he was going to clean up later, the father tells him to shut up and stop making excuses. Then he shoves the son's report card in his face and demands to know why he got a D in math. The boy says he did the best he could. The father shames the son, telling him that he is stupid and that D stands for "dummy." The boy says that's not fair and begins to stand up. The father shoves him down, saying, "Don't you dare get up in my face, I didn't say you could go anyplace!" The boy is visibly upset and begins to cry. The father gets even more angry: "Now what? You're crying? You little mama's boy! You sissy! You make me sick. When are you going to grow up and start acting like a man?" The father storms out of the room.

When we do this role play, it gets the undivided attention of everyone in the room, especially the boys. Almost every young person has had the experience of being scolded and shamed by an adult. Most boys have had the experience of being humiliated by an older male and being told that they are not acting like men.

When we stop the role play, we ask the boys how it made them feel to witness this scene between the father and son. There may be a moment of embarrassed silence, but then the boys speak up and say it made them mad, upset, sad, etc. Often this is the first time they have articulated the feelings brought up by such an encounter, which sadly often replicates their own experience. Indeed, the power of this role play is that it is so familiar.

We ask the boys what messages such encounters send. They say things like, "A man is tough. A man is in control. A man doesn't cry. It's okay for a man to yell at someone. A man can take it. A man is responsible. A man is competent. A man doesn't take crap from anyone else." As they speak, we write their comments on a blackboard. Then we draw a box around the comments and label it the "Act Like a Man" box. Most males in this culture are socialized to stay in the box. We learn this from our fathers, older brothers, guys on the street, television, sports, movies, and so on. We may also learn it from our mothers and grandmothers, or from the reactions of girls in school. The fact is that this notion of manhood is so pervasive in our culture that everyone knows the role and anyone can teach it to a boy.

We ask the boys what happens if you step out of the box, if you stop acting tough enough or man enough. They reply that you get called names: sissy, wimp, nerd, fag, queer, mama's boy, punk, girl, loser, fairy. And what is the point of the name calling? The boys say that it is a challenge and you're expected to fight to prove that you're not what they called you. In other words, if challenged, boys are expected to fight to prove that they're in the box—that they're tough and not gay or effeminate. Homophobia and fear of being identified with women in any way are strong messages boys receive from an early age.

We also ask about expectations of female behavior. The young people say things like, "A girl should be polite and clean, she shouldn't argue, she's pretty, she doesn't fight or act too smart, she helps others, she's emotional." We ask what happens when a girl refuses to be submissive and dependent, when she's assertive and smart and doesn't kowtow to the boys. Again the reply is that she will be called names: bitch, tomboy, dyke, whore, ball-breaker, cunt. And what is the point of the name calling? To tell the girl she'd better start "acting right." In other words, the name calling is like a slap in the face, reducing the girl to a despised sexual object, with the purpose of humiliating her and intimidating her into resuming "acceptable" behavior. If a girl fights when called names, she may emerge the victor, but her very success raises questions about her femininity.

Though our forays into junior highs and high schools hardly constitute systematic research, again and again we find the same core expectations of acceptable male and female behavior among young people. As I have said, there is a growing tendency to question these expectations, especially among young women, but the grip of traditional roles remains very strong.

Our work at OMP involves challenging role expectations by showing that male and female behaviors are neither biologically determined nor a function of "human nature" but are learned from our interactions with significant others and from the culture at large. Our workshops and role plays give boys and girls and men and women a way of analyzing social roles, not abstractly, but by drawing insights from their own experiences. Moreover, we show that social interactions involve making choices, and that we can break free of old roles by supporting each other in changing our choices.

An important component of our work is to look at structural relationships of power and inequality in our society. We ask workshop participants to think about their experiences with different social groups and to tell us which groups they think are more powerful and which are less powerful. Most often this elicits statements to the effect that men as a group are more powerful than women as a group, whites more powerful than people of color, parents more powerful than children, teachers more powerful than pupils, the rich more powerful than the poor, straights more powerful than gays, bosses more powerful than workers, and so on. If we ask how these inequalities are maintained, we are told that it is done through laws, through rules and regulations, through discrimination and stereotypes, and ultimately through force and violence. Thus, despite our country's rhetoric of equality, experience teaches us that people are not treated equally, that we all have assigned places in the social hierarchy, and that violence is used to keep less powerful groups "in their place."

This violence takes many forms and is often legitimized through the process of blaming the victim. Consider the Rodney King case, in which the jury was told that the police officers thought he was dangerous because he was high on drugs and "out of control," and at the same time was persuaded that he was actually "in control," deliberately taunting and manipulating the officers. Either way, the message of this incredible argument was that Rodney King "deserved" the brutal beating he received and the policemen could be acquitted. Blaming victims for their own victimization is a widely employed means of justifying abuse and violence of all kinds.

Sexual harassment plays a part in reinforcing the power differential between men and women in our society, and that distinguishes it from flirtation or a simple mistake in judgment. For example, a man may harass a woman when she steps out of the role he expects her to play. In the workplace, "uppity" women who hold jobs traditionally held by men, or who are regarded as "too" assertive, competent, competitive, or emotionally reserved, are likely targets of harassment. Men may also harass women who are not "uppity" as a kind of ritual that confirms male dominance and female submissiveness. Thus, the female secretary or domestic worker may be "teased" or pinched or subjected to sexual remarks that serve to remind her of her low status and her vulnerability to men. She is expected to acquiesce in this treatment by laughing or otherwise acting as if the harassment is okay, thereby reaffirming the male's superior status and power. A woman worker may also be harassed by a male worker who is angry at the boss but fearful of the boss's power, and seeks to regain a sense of his own power by humiliating her.

Whether in the workplace or on the street, the purpose of sexual harassment is to reduce women to objects sexually vulnerable to men, and to reestablish the traditional power relationship between men and women. Indeed, women's sexual vulnerability to men is a key locus of male power, something men learn to expect. As boys we learn it from stories of sexual "conquest" we hear from older males; we learn it from films, magazines, pornography, advertising. We live in a capitalist culture that promises women's sexual availability as a reward to the male consumer of everything from cars to cigarettes. It is not surprising, then, that men come to believe that every woman should be sexually available to any man. Sexual harassment is both a manifestation and a reinforcement of an exploitive system in which men are socialized collectively and individually to expect to have power over women collectively and individually.

Moreover, of the thousands of women who experience sexual harassment every day, a great many of them are women of color and poor women employed in the jobs that racist and sexist discrimination forces them to take—as domestics, clerical workers, farm workers, sweatshop and factory workers. Not only are these women especially vulnerable to sexual harassment, they also have less access to the levers of power needed to seek redress. Often they do not report harassment because they fear revenge from their employers or know their complaints will be dismissed. They are doubly oppressed: subjected to abuse and then constrained to remain silent about it.

The nature of sexual harassment is such that it is particularly easy to blame the victims. Often there is a suggestion that the woman somehow provoked or invited the objectionable behavior by something she said or did, or simply the way she was dressed. And if she did not protest the behavior immediately, it is insinuated that she must have enjoyed it, and any subsequent protests are suspect. In any case, the female victim's character is called into question and the male harasser is conveniently let off the hook, again reinforcing male dominance.

Of course, all men don't engage in sexual harassment, but we must ask why men who witness it often fail to intervene. One reason is obvious: male bonding to maintain male dominance. Men who would not engage in harassing behavior themselves may condone it in others because they agree that women must be "kept in their place." A second reason is more hidden: men's fear of being shamed or even attacked by other men.

As boys, most men learn that other men are dangerous. How many of us were called names or beaten up by other males when we were young? How many of us were ridiculed and humiliated by fathers or older brothers or coaches or teachers? How many were sexually assaulted by another male? We protected ourselves in various ways. Some of us withdrew into the private world of our fantasies. Some of us became bullies. Some of us became alcoholics and addicts so we wouldn't have to feel the pain and fear. Most of us learned to camouflage ourselves: we took on the coloration of the men we feared, and we hoped that no one would challenge us. We never talked about our fear because that in itself was dangerous and could mark us as targets of ridicule or violence from other men.

Instead we learned to keep our fear inside, a secret. In fact, we learned to keep most of our emotions bottled up inside because any sincere expression of emotion in front of other men was risky business that set you up to be put down. Only one emotion was considered manly: anger. Some of us learned to take other feelings—pain, grief, sadness, shame, loneliness, depression, jealousy, helplessness, fearfulness—and translate them into anger, and then pass them on to someone weaker in the form of physical or psychological violence. The humiliation we experienced at work, the fear we experienced when hassled by cops, the grief we felt when a relationship ended, the helplessness we felt when we lost a job—we learned to take these feelings, roll them into a heavy fist of rage, and slam it into our wives, our children, our lovers, women on the job or on the streets, less powerful men.

Thus, women and children often live in fear of men, and men frequently live in fear of each other. Most of us men won't admit this, but deep inside we recognize that harassment, abuse, rape, and violence are not simply "women's issues"—they're our issues as well. We know, but seldom admit, that if we didn't constantly protect ourselves, other men would do to us what we all too often do to women and children—as men who have been imprisoned can attest. So those of us who are not abusers or harassers sometimes wear the camouflage suits; we try to be "one of the boys." We present a front of manly power and control no matter what we may be feeling inside. We jostle and joke and push and shove, we make cracks about women and boast of our conquests, and we haze any guy who is different. We go along with harassers so as not to expose our own vulnerability, our fear of being shamed by other men—the weak point in our male armor.

Nevertheless, men have a stake in challenging sexual harassment, abuse, violence, and the sexist role training that underpins these behaviors. In the first place, men are not unconnected to women. We form a community of men and women—and children—together. A woman who suffers harassment might be my mother, my sister, my niece. She might be your daughter or your sister or your wife. A woman who is harassed, abused, or raped is part of a community that includes male relatives, lovers, and friends who are also hurt by the injury done to her. Men have a stake in stopping the abuse because it is directed against women we love and cherish.

I would argue that men have a further stake in challenging sexual abuse and the sexism on which it is based. Men are also damaged by sexism. A system that requires us to act as though we are always in control and to repress our emotions takes a heavy toll. It undermines our sense of authenticity. It results in a loss of intimacy with women and children. It conceals but does not change our fear of other men. It produces stress that is hazardous to our health and shortens our life spans. It makes us sick in our souls and bodies, and it turns us into enemies of those we love and of ourselves.

Historically, Black men and women in America have been victims of especially brutal and systematic violence. In the past our community has been terrorized by the lynching (and castration) of thousands of Black men by white men, and the rape (and lynching) of thousands of Black women by white men. Today white mob violence and police brutality continue unabated. African American men know intimately the violent capabilities of other men. It is a tragedy that many of us have internalized the violence of this oppressive system and brought it into our communities and our homes. The injuries done by racism to Black men's self-esteem are sometimes devastating, but the expectations of manhood we have learned block us from revealing or acknowledging our pain. Instead, we too often transform it into rage and violence against those we love. This must stop. African American men, as frequent victims of white male violence, have a particular stake in standing with women and children against all forms of violence.

How can men of all races be brought into the struggle against harassment, abuse, and violence? That is the question we have been seeking to answer through our work at the Oakland Men's Project. We have learned that it is extremely important for men to begin talking with each other about these issues. In our experience we have seen that there are growing numbers of men who are critical of sexism. All too often, however, these men as individuals are isolated and fearful of raising their concerns with other men. It is time for men who want to stop the violence to reach out to other men and break through the barrier of fear that has silenced us.

This is not an easy task, but as we have learned at OMP, it can be done. The male sex role, with its insistence on emotional "coolness" and reserve, makes open and honest communication from the heart difficult between men. We can begin to break through this isolation by sharing the often painful and humiliating ways we were socialized into the male role as young boys. At OMP we have found that workshops using interactive role plays, like the father-son encounter described earlier, are an effective method of opening up communication between men. Such techniques enable us to examine how the male sex role often sets men up to be dominating, controlling, and abusive. In another role play we watch a bully harassing the new boy at school. We discuss what the bully gains or fails to gain by bullying. For example, the bully may be seeking to compel respect from the victim, but what the victim often feels is contempt. At the same time, the bully models abusive behavior for the victim. He fails to get what he wants, but he may teach the victim how to bully someone else.

Through role plays like these, we look at how men are trained to take the hurt that has been done to them, translate it into anger, and direct the anger at a weaker person in the form of violence. This is the cycle of violence. We see it, for example, in the fact that the great majority of child abusers were themselves abused as children.

Another role play we use recreates a high school dating scene in which a boy and his girlfriend are sitting in his car in a secluded spot at night. We recruit two students from the audience to play the roles. We tell them that the boy wants to have sex that night but the girl, although she likes him, does not. Then we ask them to play out the scene. Sometimes the two actors work out a resolution acceptable to both. Sometimes the girl gets out of the car and walks away. But often the tension simply builds as the boy attempts to dominate and get his way while the girl tries to be responsive without giving in to his demands. We stop the role play and talk with the actors about the pressures they felt to behave as they did in the situation. We relate these pressures to the male and female role expectations discussed earlier. We also talk about the risk of the situation escalating into violence and rape, and the need to recognize danger signs to prevent this from happening. (For other examples of role plays and antiviolence exercises for teens, see *Helping Teens Stop Violence,* by Allan Creighton and Paul Kivel.)

Interrupting the cycle of violence requires that we unlearn sex roles that set us up to be perpetrators and victims of abuse. I am not talking only about men who are harassers or batterers, or women who have been abused. I believe that in this culture most of us are at risk for abusive behavior because most of us have been socialized into traditional sex roles. The cycle of abuse and violence can be broken at its root by challenging those roles and the institutions that support them—that is, through a process of community education and social change.

It is important for men of all races to become involved in this process. Men can take responsibility for stopping the cycle of violence and offering alternatives to violence. Men working with boys can model supportive ways of interacting and constructive methods of using anger to bring about change. All of us constantly make choices about how we relate to others, and in the power of choice is the power of change, for we are not simply passive victims of our socialization. For African American men there is a special urgency to this work. Our sons are dying in record numbers, often at each other's hands in angry acts of violence whose goal is to prove their manhood. We need to be clear that anger itself is not the problem. In a racist society Black people and other people of color have good reason to be angry. The problem lies in how the anger is expressed. Turning the anger against ourselves or others in acts of abuse and violence is self-destructive. Using righteous anger to challenge racist and oppressive institutions empowers individuals and communities, creates the possibility of real change, and builds self-esteem. Black men's organizations such as Simba, the Omega Boys' Club, and 100 Black Men of America are helping to develop new models of manhood among teenage Black males. We need organizations like these in every city.

Equally important, men working together can model a new version of power—*power with* others to make change, as opposed to *power over* others to perpetuate domination. In our society power generally means the ability to control others directly, with violence as the ultimate means of control. Men are socialized to exercise this form of power in all their relationships. Women sometimes learn to do the same. But this kind of power necessarily sets up conflicts with others—those we seek to control—and is alienating and isolating for the individual power holder. Power *with* others breaks down the isolation we feel and makes it possible to relate as allies rather than as competitors or opponents. It allows us to recognize that we are a community of people—men, women, and children—who are interdependent.

All of us have had the experience of powerlessness, for all of us have been children. As children we learned what it meant to be controlled by others, and often we learned what it meant to be humiliated and shamed by others. Such experiences are painful, and we may prefer to forget them, but ironically, by "owning" them, we create the possibility of empowerment through establishing our connection with others who have had similar experiences. In this way it becomes possible for men to become allies of women and children, not out of guilt, but through insight into their own lives.

Harassment, abuse, and violence arise from a system of sexual and racial inequality. To stop them we must challenge the gender roles, institutions, and power structures upon which sexism and racism stand. This is a big task, but it is one each of us can undertake in small ways—in our homes, in our schools, in our communities. We can educate ourselves and offer our children new models of male and female behavior. We can support each other in finding healing responses to the pain and hurt we have suffered. We can insist that the schools educate young people about empowering ways to counter sexism and racism. We can confront institutionalized oppression and violence. We can support movements and organizations that work for progressive social change. In sum, working together with others as allies, we can build community responses to the system of inequality and the cycle of violence that blight our lives.

REFERENCES

Beneke, Timothy. *Men on Rape: What They Have to Say about Sexual Violence.* New York: St. Martin's Press, 1982.

Bravo, Ellen, and Ellen Cassedy. *The 9 to 5 Guide to Combatting Sexual Harassment.* New York: John Wiley and Sons, 1992.

Chrisman, Robert, and Robert L. Allen, eds. *Court of Appeal: The Black Community Speaks Out on the Racial and Sexual Politics of Thomas vs. Hill.* New York: Ballantine Books, 1992.

Creighton, Allan, with Paul Kivel. *Helping Teens Stop Violence: A Practical Guide for Parents, Counselors, and Educators.* Alameda, Calif.: Hunter House, 1992.

Hagan, Kay Leigh, ed. *Women Respond to the Men's Movement.* San Francisco: HarperCollins, 1992.

Hemphill, Essex, ed. *Brother to Brother: New Writings by Black Gay Men.* Boston: Alyson Publications, 1991.

Jackson, Walter H. *Sporting the Right Attitude: Surviving Family Violence.* Los Angeles: Self Expansion, 1992.

Kaufman, Michael, ed. *Beyond Patriarchy: Essays by Men on Pleasure, Power, and Change.* New York: Oxford University Press, 1987.

Kimmel, Michael S., ed. *Men Confront Pornography.* New York: Meridian, 1990.

Kivel, Paul. *Men's Work: How to Stop the Violence That Tears Our Lives Apart.* Center City, Minn.: Hazelden, 1992.

Kunjufu, Jawanza. *Countering the Conspiracy to Destroy Black Boys.* Chicago: African American Images, 1985.

Lewis, Michael. *Shame: The Exposed Self.* New York: Free Press, 1992.

Madhubuti, Haki. *Black Men: Obsolete, Single, Dangerous?* Chicago: Third World Press, 1990.

Majors, Richard, and Janet Mancini Billson. *Cool Pose: The Dilemmas of Black Manhood in America.* New York: Lexington Books, 1992.

McGill, Michael E. *The McGill Report on Male Intimacy.* New York: Harper and Row, 1985.

Miedzian, Myriam. *Boys Will Be Boys: Breaking the Link between Masculinity and Violence.* New York: Doubleday, 1991.

Staples, Robert, ed. *The Black Family: Essays and Studies.* 4th ed. Belmont, Calif. Wadsworth, 1991.

Strauss, Susan, with Pamela Espeland. *Sexual Harassment and Teens: A Program for Positive Change.* Minneapolis: Free Spirit Publishing, 1992.

Wilkinson, Doris Y., and Ronald L. Taylor, eds. *The Black Male in America: Perspectives on His Status in Contemporary Society.* Chicago: Nelson-Hall, 1977.

73

STATEMENT OF PRINCIPLES

NATIONAL ORGANIZATION FOR MEN AGAINST SEXISM

The National Organization for Men Against Sexism is an activist organization of men and women supporting positive changes for men. NOMAS advocates a perspective that is pro-feminist, gay-affirmative, and committed to justice on a broad range of social issues including race, class, age, religion, and physical abilities. We affirm that working to make this nation's ideals of equality substantive is the finest expression of what it means to be men.

We believe that the new opportunities becoming available to women and men will be beneficial to both. Men can live as happier and more fulfilled human beings by challenging the old-fashioned rules of masculinity that embody the assumption of male superiority.

Traditional masculinity includes many positive characteristics in which we take pride and find strength, but it also contains qualities that have limited and harmed us. We are deeply supportive of men who are struggling with the issues of traditional masculinity. As an organization for changing men, we care about men and are especially concerned with men's problems, as well as the difficult issues in most men's lives.

As an organization for changing men, we strongly support the continuing struggle of women for full equality. We applaud and support the insights and positive social changes that feminism has stimulated for both women and men. We oppose such injustices to women as economic and legal discrimination, rape, domestic violence, sexual harassment, and many others. Women and men can and do work together as allies to change the injustices that have so often made them see one another as enemies.

One of the strongest and deepest anxieties of most American men is their fear of homosexuality. This homophobia contributes directly to the many injustices experienced by gay, lesbian, and bisexual persons, and is a debilitating restriction for heterosexual men. We call for an end to all forms of discrimination based on sexual–affectional orientation, and for the creation of a gay-affirmative society.

We also acknowledge that many people are oppressed today because of their race, class, age, religion, and physical condition. We believe that such

---

National Organization of Men Against Sexism, "Statement of Principles" (1991).

injustices are vitally connected to sexism, with its fundamental premise of unequal distribution of power.

Our goal is to change not just ourselves and other men, but also the institutions that create inequality. We welcome any person who agrees in substance with these principles to membership in the National Organization for Men Against Sexism.

74

DISAPPEARING ACTS
The State and Violence against Women in the Twentieth Century

MICHELLE FINE AND LOIS WEIS

As children we held our breath, our senses filled with the musty smells of elephants, the staccato flashes of twirling plastic flashlights, the terrors of trapeze. With mystery, moustache, and elegance, the magician waved a wand, invited a woman, usually White, seemingly working class, into a box. She disappeared or was cut in half. Applause. Our early introduction to the notion of the sponsored disappearing act.

So, too, at the end of the twentieth century, we witness poor and working-class women shoved into spaces too small for human form, no elegance, no wand. And they too disappear. Disappearing from welfare rolls, from universities, being swept off the streets. Dumped out of mental institutions and poured into prisons. We write to map the State-sponsored disappearing acts of the late twentieth century, the loss of welfare rights, higher education, and public spaces for women, as a conscience point for us to re-imagine what could be, what must be, for girls and women—poor and working class—in the twenty-first century.

A Tale of Research

In 1992, as we embarked on interviews for The Unknown City (Fine and Weis 1998), we thought we were collecting 150 oral histories of the economic, educational, and activist lives of poor and working-class men and women growing up in urban America during the 1980s and 1990s. From literacy programs, Headstart centers, church basements, and GED classes, we heard stories of physical and sexual abuse from these poor and working-class girls and women—White, African-American, and Latina, ages 23 to 35. Women reported painfully high levels of violence across groups, and yet they also narrated culturally distinct patterns of going public (or not) and seeking assistance from kin, neighbors, or the State (or not).

A full 92 percent of the White women we interviewed described experience with childhood and/or adult abuse. Almost without exception, these women reported that they had never told anyone, never sought refuge in a shelter, never sought an order of protection, never called the police. Sixty-eight percent of the African-American women we spoke with reported experiences of domestic violence, but these women were far more likely to have told others about the abuse, fled their homes for shelter, or thrown out their abusers. They were also more likely, despite their mistrust of the police, to secure orders of protection and called the police as needed (see Richie 1996 for important analysis of these issues). While 85 percent of the Latinas reported experiences of domestic abuse, many, if not most, chose to leave their men quietly late in the evening, trying to find a safe space for themselves and their children (see Hurtado 1996; Gordon 1997; Espin 1999).

No class or cultural group of women is exempt from domestic violence. Sixty percent of women killed in the United States were killed by a husband or boyfriend; 25 percent of female psychiatric patients who attempt suicide are victims of domestic violence, and between 40 percent (Del Tufo 1995) and 63 percent (Browne 1987) of New York's homeless families include women fleeing abuse at home. Over 70 percent of women entering the New York State prison system have had a history of physical and/or sexual abuse (New York State Department of Correctional Services 1996).

The "why doesn't she just leave?" question has finally been answered: Because she is as likely, if not more likely, to endure violence or homicide should she leave. Evidence from the U.S. Department of Justice suggests that a woman may be in even greater life-threatening jeopardy once she leaves or separates from an abusive man. Cecilia Castelano reports that "almost 25 percent of the women killed by male partners were separated and divorced from the men who killed them; another 29 percent were attempting to end the relationship when they were killed" (1996, 11), and Lenore Walker reports that "in one U.S. study, 70 percent of the reported injuries from domestic violence occurred after the separation of the couple" (1999, 24).

We exit this century and enter another with violence against women smarting, bound to another form of violence. That is, State-sponsored violence by which the public sphere, the State-sponsored safety net (always frayed and inadequate), has rapidly been dismantled, first by right-wing Republicans and soon thereafter by "moderate" Democrats, as poor and working-class women and their children fall through the huge holes in the webbing. And yet today, with no public accountability, working-class and poor women (and men) have been tossed from our collective moral community, in particular by severe curtailments in their access to welfare, shelter, and higher education. These very well traveled exit ramps from domestic abuse are under intensive and deliberate destruction. These are among the most devastating State-sponsored disappearing acts of the twentieth century.

Disappearing Act I: Access to Welfare and Higher Education

With the draconian disappearance of a social safety net for women—not that a very good one ever existed—we witness a twinning of State and domestic violence against women (see Gordon's [1997] analysis of women's complex relations to the State). Women's access to sustained welfare and public higher education have narrowed to a choke. These two social projects, as we (and many others) have learned, have been, quietly and profoundly, the primary strategies by which poor and working-class women have been able to interrupt what has been perversely called the "cycle of violence."

Synchronous with the dismantling of the welfare system has been the assault on public higher education, rendering it increasingly out of reach for many poor and working-class youth and adults. This has happened at precisely the time when poor and working-class women began to enroll in public higher education at unprecedented rates, in the 1980s and 1990s. The U.S. Department of Education has documented well a substantial gender discrepancy (many higher ed policy makers are worried—where are the men?), especially within public institutions among part-time students, older students, and African-American students (*New York Times* 1998a). (When there are too many men, how many policy makers worry about where the women are?) While the percentage of White male high school graduates enrolled in college dropped from 61 percent in 1970 to 55 percent in 1986, rates for females in the same period rose from 47 to 55 percent for White women and 39 to 50 percent for African-American women. Women across racial and ethnic groups are today pursuing formal education to a far greater extent than are men (see Fine and Weis 1998).[1] And today, public university tuition has risen, financial aid has dropped, and affirmative action has been struck down in the University of California and Texas systems (with Michigan in the wings), as remediation is threatened in the City University of New York system. Workfare demands that women work, not go to school.[2] Thus, cuts to public higher education, retreats from affirmative action, restrictions on using welfare benefits to pursue higher education, and the withdrawal of remediation services has disproportionately hit young and older women returning to college.

We are arguing that these cuts to welfare and public higher education produce, in effect, women's increased reliance on the family, compelling them to remain in violent homes, to exit or delay entry into college, and to move off welfare after only a short period of time. With a retreat in the public sphere comes not only the privatization of the economy, health care, and education but also an increasing privatization of the family.

What Poor and Working-Class Women Get Instead

Upon reflection, it is inaccurate to claim that the public sphere has been dismantled. It may be more appropriate to point to the fact that public commitments and expenditures have been realigned to support elite and White interests and, consequently, contain poor and working-class, and often racially oppressed, children and families in underfunded schools and neighborhoods, thereby locking most out of the academy and the "booming" economy. The swell in the public sector is in prison construction. And here, the poor and working class, men and women of color, are the primary "recipients."

If we use New York State as a case, we find troubling patterns of shifting state expenditures. From 1988 to 1998, New York State cut support for public higher education in the same proportion as it increased funding for prisons (Gangi, Schiraldi, and Ziedenberg 1999). Nationally, from 1977 to 1995, the average state increased correctional funding by two times more than funding for public colleges,[3] supporting "the prison-industrial complex" (Schlosser 1998). Since 1991, the nation's violent crime rate has decreased by 20 percent, but the number of people in prison or jail has risen by 50 percent. In New York State, from 1971 to 1995, the inmate population has increased almost fivefold.

In 1988 New York's public university funding was double that of the prison system. Over the past decade, New York reduced public higher education spending by 29 percent, while state corrections enjoyed a 76 percent increase. During this time period, the governor raised State University of New York (SUNY) and City University of New York (CUNY) tuition. The SUNY schools saw a drop of 10,000 in the number of enrolled students. Current SUNY annual tuition costs an average of 25 percent of White families' income and 42 percent for Black or Latino families (Gangi, Schiraldi, and Ziedenberg 1999).

As for the related growth in prison expenditures, while women constitute only a small fraction of the entire prison population, they are the fastest growing subpopulation. From 1982 to 1995, the number of women in prison in New York State increased more than 300 percent. In 1997, 65 percent of New York State's women inmates had been sentenced for possession or sale of drugs, compared to 40 percent in 1994 and 12.5 percent in 1968 ("The Mentality between Prisons and Schools" 1999; College Bound Programs 1997).

When we recognize that most of these women are undereducated, have been exposed to domestic violence, and are mothers whose children are often assigned to foster care, this public sector realignment seems profoundly mean-spirited, shortsighted, fiscally expensive, and morally bankrupt.

Disappearing Act II: Spaces to Support Poor and Working-Class Girls and Women

We hear from women, mostly mothers, about yet another disappearing act in poor and working-class communities that is deeply related to the retreat of the State from community life. Evaporating are the spaces—in communities and schools—for poor and working-class girls and women to come together, share stories, educate, and organize. Local library branches are shutting down; streets and parks seem increasingly unsafe or are locked; public gardens are being sold off; young women report fear about neighbors "getting into my business"; calling the cops is too risky. Even social services, child-care agencies, and local programs—once upon a time, places and people to whom a girl/woman could sometimes turn for help, assistance, guidance, advice—are now viewed by most as "untrustworthy." The women with whom we spoke explain that these agencies have been transformed from (sometimes) activist/contradictory sites into explicit (often contracted) arms of the State obliged to report abuse and neglect, requiring women to give the social security numbers of the fathers of their babies, provide documentation of citizenship, and cover up any evidence of child-rearing difficulties lest they be read as neglect (Fine and Weis 1998). With the realignment of the commitments of the State with the elite, in the name of accountability public sites of help have been appropriated into sites of surveillance.

As the State retreats in public policy and practice, we worry that social responsibilities and violence are being thrust on the bodies and souls of girls and women. As German social theorist Frigga Hang (1992) has argued, when the State withdraws from social projects of economy, community, education, and family, women are assumed to have, and often take on, responsibility for social and "personal" relations. And women live, consequently, with guilt and judgment. We witness, and have been taught by the women we interviewed, that in poor and working-class communities women have no choice but to accept responsibilities that are, at base, impossible to satisfy. They are often raising two or three generations, with little material support and much surveillance. To add to the burden, African-American and Latina women confront the daily razors of racism. All of these women live with the threat of loss of their children ever dangling, and more often than we were ready to hear, under the fist of violence at home. Stuffed into spaces of danger and threat, the women see few exits, except for spirituality.

We imagine, with great respect for and in the shadows of those women who have paid the greatest price, a restored feminist public sphere that recognizes the ravaged and intimate connections among the economy, public support for education, violence against women, and a restored welfare state. In addition to the obvious need for organizing around reproductive freedoms, health care, housing, and child care, those women remind us that a restructured economy, with strong engagement of labor, must be linked with struggles for adequate funding for urban education, reengagement of affirmative action, and remediation in public and higher education struggles. We see that economics and education cannot be separated from struggles against violence. While crime and violence are central concerns for poor and working-class women, building more and more prisons accelerates the undermining of poor and working-class communities, imprisons women, and disrupts the lives of children who are then exported through the foster care system. Finally, welfare rights must be central to a feminist project, so that resources are available for women to provide financial respite, time out, and a violence-free zone.

Domestic violence will accompany us in the twenty-first century, as will the violence done to and within communities and the violence perpetrated on working-class and poor girls and women by the State. Here and globally. Organizing for a restored public sphere—with accessible public education, available welfare and jobs, quality child care, and Affirmative Action—must be at the heart of our next generation of feminist work. Little girls are watching and waiting.

NOTES

1. And yet, as the *New York Times* reports, "The welfare law is too tilted toward short term work activity. . . . The current law . . . sets a cap on the percentage of the welfare population that can be enrolled in educational or vocational training at any one time. By 2000, all teen age parents pursuing high school diplomas would be counted under the educational cap, thus reducing the number of adults who can enroll in training and still receive benefits" (1998b, A18).
2. A recent survey by the U.S. General Accounting Office finds a sharp drop in the percentage of welfare recipients assigned to education and training programs. In Connecticut, for instance, while 85 percent of welfare-work participants were enrolled in education/training in 1994, this figure dropped to 31.7 percent in 1997; in Maryland the figures moved from 65.1 percent to 10.5 percent; and in Wisconsin from 60.4 percent to 12.5 percent. The "welfare reform" act "allows education or vocational training to count as a work activity for only 12 months, after which the student must work 20 hours a week to continue getting benefits. For many recipients" concludes the *New York Times,* "that requirement means dropping out of school" (1998b, A18).
3. In Texas the ratio is six to one.

REFERENCES

Browne, Angela. 1987. *When Battered Women Kill.* New York: Free Press.

Castelano, Cecilia. 1996. "Staying Put: Why, How and to What Effect Do Some Battered Women (Re)claim Their Homes." Ph.D. diss. proposal, Environmental Psychology Program, City University of New York Graduate Center.

College Bound Programs. 1997. Bedford Hills, Wyo: Center for Redirection through Education.

Del Tufo, Alisa. 1995. *Domestic Violence for Beginners.* New York: Writers and Readers.

Espin, Oliva M. 1999. *Women Crossing Boundaries: A Psychology of Immigration and Transformations of Sexuality.* New York: Routledge.

Fine, Michelle, and Lois Weis. 1998. *The Unknown City: Lives of Poor and Working Class Young Adults.* Boston: Beacon.

Gangi, Robert, Vincent Schiraldi, and Jason Ziedenberg. 1999. *New York State of Mind? Higher Education vs. Prison Funding in the Empire State, 1988–1998.* Washington, D.C.: Justice Policy Institute; New York: Correctional Association of New York.

Gordon, Linda. 1997. "Family Violence, Feminism and Social Control." In *Gender Violence,* ed. Laura L. O'Toole and Jessica R. Schiffman, 314–30. New York: New York University Press.

Haug, Frigga. 1992. *Beyond Female Masochism: Memory, Work, and Politics.* London: Verso.

Hurtado, Aida. 1996. "Strategic Suspensions: Feminists of Color Theorize the Production of Knowledge." In *Women's Ways of Knowing Revisited,* ed. N. Goldberg, M. Belenky, B. Clinchy, and J. Tarule. New York: Basic.

"The Mentality between Prisons and Schools." 1999. *Black Issues in Higher Education,* January 7, 12–14.

New York State Department of Correctional Services. 1996. "Women under Custody." April 1. Albany, N.Y.: Department of Corrections.

New York Times. 1998a. "American Colleges Begin to Ask: Where Have All the Men Gone?" *New York Times,* December 6, A1, A38.

———. 1998b. "Reforming Welfare with Education." *New York Times,* July 31, A18.

Richie, Beth. 1996. *Compelled to Crime: The Gender Entrapment of Battered Black Women.* New York: Routledge.

Schlosser, Eric. 1998. "The Prison-Industrial Complex" *Atlantic Monthly,* December, 51–77.

Walker, Leonore. 1999. "Psychology and Domestic Violence around the World." *American Psychologist* 54(1):21–29.

75

REPORT FROM JERUSALEM 'A Ray of Sunshine Within This Long Winter of Violence and Tragedy'

GILA SVIRSKY

The following is a report on a major peace demonstration in Jerusalem on December 28, 2001.

Today was a ray of sunshine in an otherwise bleak Middle East.

At 9:30 A.M., the organizers were still discussing whether the march should be held single file or two-by-two, as the police refused to grant us a permit to walk in the streets, wanting to contain us on the broad sidewalk. By 10:30 am, we saw there would be no hope of containing the vast crowd that had shown up.

An amazing 5,000 people, most dressed in black, turned up for today's events, beginning with the March of Mourning for all the victims—Palestinian and Israeli—of the Occupation. Responding to the call of the Coalition of Women for a Just Peace, people from all over the world found their way to the vigil plaza today. When the signal came to begin, we were all mixed up with each other—Israeli, Palestinian, European, American—and began a slow, solemn walk, in silence (mostly), with only a funereal cadence sounded by two women drummers at the center of this long procession. Although the extreme right wing staged a counter-demonstration at the beginning of our route, their small number (about 30) and angry shouts only served to dramatize the power of our own dignified presence.

Suddenly Feeling Hopeful

We led with a huge banner, "The Occupation Is Killing Us All," followed by hundreds of black hands with white lettering, "Stop the Occupation," and scores of signs calling for peace; a state of Palestine beside the state of Israel;

Gila Svirsky, "Report from Jerusalem: 'A Ray of Sunshine Within This Long Winter of Violence and Tragedy'" from *Sojourner: The Women's Forum* 27, no. 6 (February 2002).

and sharing this beautiful city of Jerusalem, loved so long by so many. It was an unseasonably warm and balmy winter morning, and we were suddenly feeling hopeful and powerful marching together this way. Although the police were trying to keep us all walking on the sidewalk, soon we burst our seams and spread out into the road, blocking traffic along the route. And Ezra, long-time supporter of Women in Black in Jerusalem, walked among us, handing out a thousand red roses to Women in Black until the roses ran out, though the women did not.

We made our way slowly toward the broad, new plaza just outside historic Jaffa Gate, one of the main entrances to the Old City of Jerusalem. By the time everyone arrived, we had filled up the plaza completely, with spillover inside the gate and along the roads leading up to it. Past the stage, participants could see as backdrop the beautiful Citadel, rising from the walls of the Old City, with the Valley of Gethsemane spread out beyond in a breathtaking view.

The entire program was moderated in Hebrew and Arabic by Dalit Baum and Camilia Bader-Araf, co-MCs. They acknowledged the Knesset members who had joined us for the events—Muhammed Barake, Naomi Chazan, Zehava Galon, Tamar Gozansky, Anat Maor, Issam Makhoul, and Mossi Raz—as well as the delegations from Belgium, Canada, England, France, Italy, Portugal, Spain, and the United States. Marcia Freedman, former Israeli Member of Knesset and long-standing Woman in Black, read the list of 118 locations around the world where solidarity events were planned for the same day (from Adelaide to Zaragoza—see our website, www.coalitionofwomen4peace.org, for the full list).

Success Called Inevitable

Speeches opened with Shulamit Aloni, first lady of human rights in Israel and former government minister, comparing our struggle to end the occupation with the struggles led by Nelson Mandela and Martin Luther King, reminding us that although the task is arduous, it will inevitably be crowned with success. She was followed by other powerful speakers—Nurit Peled Elhanan, winner of the Sakharov Peace Prize, awarded by the European Parliament, and mother of Smadar, 13 years old when she was killed by a terrorist bomb in Jerusalem; Zahira Kamal, courageous Palestinian activist for peace as well as the rights of women and workers, who found a way to outwit the closure in order to reach Jerusalem and address this rally; Luisa Morgantini, irrepressible Italian member of the European Parliament and devoted supporter of the women's peace movement in the Middle East; Khulood Badawi, chair of the Association of Arab Students in Israel; and Vera Lichtenfels, a 17-year-old Portuguese peace activist, representing youth all over the world who are working for peace.

These speeches were eloquent and inspiring, but I myself was especially moved by the ceremony of torch lighting by thirteen Israeli organizations that have shown extraordinary commitment to activism for peace and human rights. Each representative lit a torch about one aspect related to their work—the killed, the wounded, the homes demolished, the trees uprooted, the children whose lives were fractured, as well as the efforts of those who refuse to give in to the despair, but keep on struggling to transform this nightmare into a vision of peace and partnership [see end of reading for the names and descriptions of these organizations].

These are words that one simply doesn't hear in this region, so publicly, by Israelis and Palestinians together. And then we held a concert rarely heard in the Middle East—a "peace happening" of Palestinian and Israeli performers. It opened with the Elisheva Trio—three talented Black Jewish women from Dimona, singing peace songs in soul and rock arrangements. There were readings of poetry and plays, a performance piece, and an amazing duo of young Palestinian rappers from Lydda/Lod doing Arabic and Hebrew political lyrics. Ending it all was a hopeful reprise by the Elisheva Trio, with many in the crowd holding hands, swaying, and singing together.

Another Rally

When the concert was over, few wanted to leave and let go of the feeling that peace is really possible. Fortunately, we didn't really have to, because Peace Now was holding its own optimistic rally just inside Jaffa Gate, with Palestinians and Israelis signing a Peace Declaration and releasing doves into the sky over the city. Palestinians and Israelis wandered in and out of the streets of the Old City trying to hold tight to the beautiful warm thaw in the air, within this long winter of violence and tragedy.

This evening, I watched Israeli TV to see if anything was reported about the hope for peace that had swept through Jerusalem today. I saw nothing about either the Coalition of Women for Peace or the Peace Now events, though I did hear that the Coalition action made the radio news several times today. We are used to this by now, and it brought to mind the words of Shulamit Aloni earlier today: "Even though Israel's 'patriotic' media seek to ignore you, there is no doubt that your voice will be heard and that a great many others will join your cause. You will break through the silence because yours is a vision of freedom, justice, and peace."

May it come to pass. Today I feel more hopeful than I have for a long, long while.

Thank you to everyone all over the world who joined us in solidarity today, whether in vigils, through contributions, or in your hearts.

Shalom, salaam.

Supporters

Special thanks for their support, which made this event possible: Svinna till Svinna Foundation, the Moriah Fund, Sally Gottesman, the Steve Berman Social Action Award, and many individuals from all over the world.

The organizations represented at the torch lighting ceremony (in alphabetical order):

Bat Shalom: the Israeli side of The Jerusalem Link: A Women's Joint Venture for Peace, seeking peace through partnership with Palestinian women.

Gush Shalom: determined fighters to end the occupation, recent recipients of the "Alternative Nobel Peace Prize."

High School Seniors: a group of Israeli high school seniors who signed a letter asserting their refusal to serve in the army to support the occupation.

Israel Committee Against Home Demolitions: seeking to expose and end the crime of demolishing homes of Palestinians.

Machsom Watch: women monitoring military checkpoints to end the abuse of Palestinians at these locations.

Mothers and Women for Peace: formerly the 4 Mothers Movement, who were instrumental in getting Israel out of Lebanese occupation.

New Profile: seeking to end militarism in Israeli society and support conscientious objection to army service.

Peace Now: mobilizing to end the occupation, and focused on the illegality of the Israeli settlements in the territories.

Rabbis for Human Rights: bringing a religious Jewish perspective to the struggle to end the injustice of occupation.

Ta'ayush: a partnership of Jewish and Palestinian citizens of Israel, providing aid and resistance to the occupation throughout the territories.

TANDI: struggling for rights for Arab women, and coexistence between Jews and Arabs within Israel.

Women in Black: holding vigils throughout the world to stop violence and injustice, founded in Jerusalem in 1988 to end the occupation.

Yesh Gvul: encouraging soldiers to refuse service in the occupied territories.

76

ON BEHALF OF THE GLOBAL CAMPAIGN FOR WOMEN'S HUMAN RIGHTS

CHARLOTTE BUNCH

The Center for Women's Global Leadership welcomes this opportunity to contribute to the review of the Vienna Declaration and Programme of Action (VDPA) on behalf of hundreds of organizations from around the world who are participating in the 1998 Global Campaign for Women's Human Rights. We also speak as convertors of the "Working Group on Violence, Gender, and Bodily Integrity" at the Vienna Plus Five Global NGO Forum in Ottawa and commend those recommendations for implementation of the VDPA to you.

The 1993 World Conference on Human Rights in Vienna took a giant step forward with its strong affirmation of the universality and indivisibility of women's rights as human rights and its explicit recognition that violence against women and girls, in public and private, constitutes a serious human rights violation requiring urgent international attention and more effective governmental responses. Indeed this was seen by many as one of the conference's major breakthroughs.

Following Vienna, the International Conference on Population and Development in Cairo and the Fourth World Conference on Women in Beijing reaffirmed the Vienna commitment to women's human rights and spelled out in greater detail the critical actions necessary to realize the rights of women and girls in a wide array of areas ranging from health and education to the economy and situations of armed conflict. These platforms, along with all human rights instruments, and in particular the Convention on the Elimination of All Forms of Discrimination Against Women, provide a significant outline of steps that governments and the UN need to take to protect and promote the human rights of women.

The task now as the Global Campaign has emphasized is to "Take Action to Make It Happen" or in the apt words of the High Commissioner for Human Rights yesterday, "it is time to put up or shut up." Obviously we do not want the world to shut up about women's human

---

Charlotte Bunch, "On Behalf of the Global Campaign for Woman's Human Rights" (New Brunswick, New Jersey: Rutgers University Center for Women's Global Leadership). Reprinted with the permission of the author.

rights, so let's look at what needs to be done to advance the promotion and protection of these fundamental human rights.

But first let me be clear that important advances in the international community's commitment to the human rights of women have been made since Vienna. The appointment of the Special Rapporteur on Violence Against Women, the establishment of an Advisor on Gender Issues to the Secretary General, and the creation of the UNIFEM Trust Fund in Support of Actions to Eliminate Violence Against Women are examples of vital steps taken by the U.N. Some progress toward universal ratification and strengthening of the Women's Convention has taken place, but it still falls far short of the goals set in Vienna and Beijing. The recent recognition by the Rwanda Tribunal of rape in war as an act of genocide and the inclusion of a gender perspective in crucial parts of the Statute for the International Criminal Court are encouraging moves toward gender integration into human rights theory and practice.

Nevertheless, the broad mandate of gender integration throughout the UN human rights machinery has, with a few such notable exceptions, moved quite slowly. At the rate that the recommendations in these documents are being implemented and funded, it will be more like the 23rd century rather than the 21st before we see substantial progress.

Indeed, for the human rights of women today, it is not simply a question of how fast will we advance but also of how far back are we falling? Globalization for many women has so far meant that their rights are being narrowed by economic transitions, crisis, and cutbacks; growing numbers of women and girls are falling prey to international trafficking for purposes of economic and sexual exploitation. The past five years has brought an erosion of many women's right to health, education, freedom of movement and expression, and for some, even subordination to gender apartheid.

While the VDPA affirms that the human rights of women and girls are inalienable, integral, and indivisible, the protection of these rights is constantly undermined by profoundly discriminatory and extremist interpretations of culture, religion and tradition that encourage, excuse or condone the subordination of women. The violence that results from these positions in all regions of the world constitutes one of the greatest threats to the human rights of all today.

Recommendations

We urge the General Assembly — the UN and governments here — to take bolder and more decisive action and to commit significant resources to addressing the human rights commitments made to women in Vienna and Beijing. The one million people concerned with the advancement of women's human rights globally who signed the petition of the Global Campaign for Women's Human Rights are working to put those words into action and are ready to develop partnerships with the UN and governments in implementing world conference platforms.

1. *Allocate more resources to addressing women's human rights.* If there are no new resources to meet this need, then governments should reallocate existing resources—for example, take 20% of the war making/defense budgets and use that to feed and house women and children who are the poorest of the poor and to give them peace at home and in public. Women want to see what muscle governments and the UN will put behind their promises.
2. *Outlaw all forms of discrimination against women.* The pace of universal ratification and removal of reservations to the Women's Convention must be accelerated. National laws and policies need to be brought into compliance with the convention, and work toward adopting a strong optional protocol establishing a right of petition needs to be a higher priority if the commitments of Vienna are to be realized in law.
3. *Take high level action to ensure women's right to live free from violence.* While the recognition of violence against women as a human rights abuse was a central tenet of Vienna, such violence continues unabated. Therefore, women are calling upon all UN officials and Heads of State/mayors/governors/chiefs/parliamentarians to take leadership on this issue by speaking out against violence against women and presenting concrete plans for how to make such violence in daily life unacceptable in their communities and nations. Ending violence against women is a community responsibility and it is time for men, and especially male leaders, to assume this responsibility along with women.
4. *Take steps to secure women's economic, social and cultural rights including their rights to health, reproductive and sexual rights.* One of Vienna's other commitments was to expand UN attention to the right to development and socio-economic rights. Women suffer disproportionally in their lack of access to education, health, and economic resources. Therefore the integration of gender sensitive perspectives and women's concerns as new procedures and mechanisms are developed to advance these rights is urgent.
5. *Ensure gender integration and training throughout all human rights activities nationally and internationally.* Full integration of women's human rights and gender perspectives requires gender sensitive training and specific guidelines for all UN and governmental human rights activities. We want to note particularly the opportunity to advance this in technical assistance, in the new field operations of the office of the High Commissioner and throughout the newly reformed UN structures. (Recommendations outlining this in more detail prepared by the

1998 Global Campaign for Women's Human Rights at the last session of the Commission on Human Rights are available.)

6. *Ratify the Declaration on the Rights of Human Rights Defenders and include the protection of women's human rights advocates in it.* Women and men who support women's human rights are being threatened, often violently, throughout the world—whether by killings of reproductive health care providers in the USA or attacks in the streets of Afghanistan. Therefore this body must call upon the UN and governments to protect women's human rights advocates and all human rights defenders in their exercise of internationally recognized rights to freedom of expression, association and security of the person.

The Global Campaign for Women's Human Rights emphasizes not only that women's rights are human rights but also that human rights depend on women's rights. If one half of the world's population can be systematically denied their human rights, it is impossible to build a world that respects the universal human rights called for in Vienna and in the Universal Declaration of Human Rights.

NAME INDEX

SUBJECT INDEX